OXFORD MONOGRAPHS IN INTERNATIONAL LAW

International Law Obligations on Climate Change Mitigation

OXFORD MONOGRAPHS IN INTERNATIONAL LAW

The aim of this series is to publish important and original pieces of research on all aspects of international law. Topics that are given particular prominence are those which, while of interest to the academic lawyer, also have important bearing on issues which touch the actual conduct of international relations. Nonetheless the series is wide in scope and includes monographs on the history and philosophical foundations of international law.

RECENT TITLES IN THE SERIES

International Human Rights and Islamic Law
Second Edition
Mashood Baderin

Coastal State Jurisdiction over Living Resources in the Exclusive Economic Zone
Camille Goodman

International Law and Corporate Actors in Deep Seabed Mining
Joanna Dingwall

The Concept of an International Organization in International Law
Lorenzo Gasbarri

Necessity and Proportionality and the Right of Self-Defence in International Law
Chris O'Meara

Neutrality in Contemporary International Law
James Upcher

Geographical Change and the Law of the Sea
Kate Purcell

Statehood and the State-Like in International Law
Rowan Nicholson

Confronting the Shadow State
Henri Decoeur

Irresolvable Norm Conflicts in International Law
The Concept of a Legal Dilemma
Valentin Jeutner

Institutionalizing State Responsibility *Global Security and UN Organs*
Vincent-Joël Proulx

International Law Obligations on Climate Change Mitigation

BENOIT MAYER

OXFORD
UNIVERSITY PRESS

OXFORD
UNIVERSITY PRESS

Great Clarendon Street, Oxford, OX2 6DP,
United Kingdom

Oxford University Press is a department of the University of Oxford. It furthers the University's objective of excellence in research, scholarship, and education by publishing worldwide. Oxford is a registered trade mark of Oxford University Press in the UK and in certain other countries

First Edition published in 2022

Published in the United States of America by Oxford University Press
198 Madison Avenue, New York, NY 10016, United States of America

British Library Cataloguing in Publication Data

Data available

Library of Congress Control Number: 2022933568

ISBN 978–0–19–284366–1

DOI: 10.1093/oso/9780192843661.001.0001

Preface

This book presents a doctrinal analysis of the international law on climate change mitigation: it seeks to determine the content of the law as, for instance, a court would interpret it. This involves identifying and interpreting various obligations on climate change mitigation which arise from specific instruments such as climate treaties, from other instruments such as human rights treaties, or from general principles of customary international law. The book shows that, while the content of mitigation obligations is difficult to ascertain with precision, there are nevertheless some reasonably practical ways for a court to test a state's compliance with its obligations.

The analysis can be summarized through five main propositions.

- States have general obligations on climate change mitigation which arise from the UN Framework Convention on Climate Change and customary international law. These general mitigation obligations, as obligations of conduct, require them to exercise due diligence and to take appropriate measures to mitigate climate change. These are the most important among the various categories of mitigation obligations, in particular from a litigation perspective.
- States have also made more specific commitments. For instance, they have committed to taking the necessary measures to implement their nationally determined contributions under the Paris Agreement. Most academic attention in climate law has focused on these specific commitments rather than on general obligations. Yet, in states' own understanding, these specific commitments lack ambition. States' general mitigation obligations often require more than compliance with these specific commitments.
- Human rights treaties may sometimes imply obligations on climate change mitigation but only if and insofar as the state's mitigation action can effectively advance the protection of the rights within the scope of the treaty. Most of the impacts of climate change cannot be described in terms of human rights (but rather in terms of global utility) or else they fall beyond the geographical scope of a state's treaty obligation to protect human rights. Therefore, human rights treaties open only narrow windows onto the applicability of general mitigation obligations.
- A state's general mitigation obligation, as an obligation of conduct, requires the making of a certain level of effort. In practice, however, an assessment of a state's requisite level of mitigation action faces considerable difficulty. States have agreed on vague collective objectives (eg the 1.5/2°C targets of the Paris

Agreement) but not on an obligation for each of them to act consistently with these objectives. Nor have they agreed on a comprehensive burden-sharing formula. A judicial determination of a state's requisite level of mitigation action implies an extraordinary degree of judicial discretion, which courts would often try to avoid exercising, especially on matters of major consequences to states' interests.

- The more likely way of testing a state's compliance with its general mitigation obligations relies on the identification of the necessary or otherwise appropriate measures that a state would be expected to take when exercising due diligence. Three main corollary duties can be identified (the duties of cooperation, vigilance, and consistency), each of which can be broken down into more concrete implications. For instance, the duty of consistency implies that a state should act consistently with its own interpretation of collective objectives and burden-sharing criteria—that is, that the state applies what the state itself considers to be its 'fair share'. Non-compliance with a corollary duty is at least an indicium of a breach of general mitigation obligations.

Acknowledgements

This book builds on eight years of research on the international legal obligations relating to climate change mitigation. I am grateful to the institutions that provided me with the environment and resources to conduct this research: the National University of Singapore as I was finishing a doctoral thesis on the concept of climate migration; the University of Wuhan, which offered me a first teaching position; and the Chinese University of Hong Kong since 2016.

Critical aspects of the analysis benefited immensely from years-long discussions with Alexander Zahar and John Knox. I also received valuable comments on drafts from Anatole Boute, Jutta Brunnée, Christopher Campbell-Duruflé, Stephen Humphreys, Md Saiful Karim, Massimo Lando, Gerry Liston, Frédéric Mégret, Lavanya Rajamani, Christina Voigt, and many unidentified reviewers. The development of my analysis has benefited from discussions and comments received at various occasions from Antony Anghie, Eyal Benvenisti, Ben Boer, Agnes Chong, Christel Cournil, James Crawford, François Crépeau, Sandrine Maljean-Dubois, Calum Nicholson, James Penner, M Sornarajah, Jaap Spier, Alan Tan, and Harro van Asselt—to name but a few. I received valuable comments and suggestions from four anonymous reviewers and the book series editors, Roger O'Keefe and Catherine Redgwell. All errors are my own.

I am also grateful to all librarians who went out of their way to help me access documents, in particular Agnes Cheung and her colleagues at the Chinese University of Hong Kong. Thanks are also due to Amanda Anstee, for copy-editing some of the manuscript, and to all the OUP team, for helping to turn an idea into a book—in particular Jack McNichol as commissioning editor, Jordan Burke as project editor, Ashirvad Moses as project manager, and Fiona Barry as copy-editor.

* * *

Some parts of the book draw on arguments that I have tested in previous publications. The permission of publishers is gratefully acknowledged.

- Chapter II, section A, draws in part on 'Article 4: Migration', in Leonie Reins and Geert van Calster (eds), *The Paris Agreement on Climate Change: A Commentary* (Edward Elgar 2021).
- Chapter II, section B, builds on 'International Law Obligations Arising in Relation to Nationally Determined Contributions' (2018) 7 Transnational Environmental Law 251.

- Chapter IV as a whole is adapted from 'Climate Change Mitigation as an Obligation Under Human Rights Treaties?' (2021) 115 American Journal of International Law 3.
- Chapter V, section A, develops arguments that I first presented in 'Obligations of Conduct in the International Law on Climate Change: A Defence' (2018) 27 Review of European, Comparative, and International Environmental Law 130.
- Chapter VI, section A, develops a line of analysis that I first attempted in 'Interpreting States' General Obligations on Climate Change Mitigation: A Methodological Review' (2019) 28 Review of European, Comparative, and International Environmental Law 10.
- Chapter VI, section B, builds on a thesis that I developed in 'Temperature Targets and State Obligations on the Mitigation of Climate Change' (2021) 33 Journal of Environmental Law 585.
- Chapter VII, section B.3, summarizes my findings in 'Climate Assessment as an Emerging Obligation under Customary International Law' (2019) 68 International and Comparative Law Quarterly 271.

***

The manuscript was finalized in late December 2021, with minor changes made on proofs in May 2022. All weblinks were last accessed in December 2021.

Contents

Table of Cases

INTERNATIONAL ADJUDICATIVE BODIES

Goodwin v UK, App No 28957/95, 2002-VI ECHR 1 . . . . 163, 256
Greenpeace Nordic v Norway, Communicated Case No 34068/21 (ECtHR, 16 December 2021) <https://hudoc.echr.coe.int/eng?i=001-214943> 131, 176
Hassan v UK, App 29750/09, 2014-VI ECHR 161–62, 163
Hatton v UK, App No 36022/97, 2003-VIII ECHR 189 . . . . 144–45, 303
Hirsi Jamaa v Italy, App No 27765/09, 2012-II ECHR 97 163
Ireland v UK, Application No 5310/71, Series A No 25, (1978) 2 EHRR 25 222–23
Loizidou v Turkey, App No 15318/89, 1996-VI ECHR 163
López Ostra v Spain, App No 16798/90, (1994) 303-C ECHR Series A 144–45, 308
Marckx v Belgium, App No 6833/74, 31 ECHR (Ser A) 163, 256
Mazurek v France, App No 34406/97, 2000-II ECHR 1 . . . . 163, 256
McCann v UK (ECtHR, 13 May 2008) 47 EHHR 40 . . . . 172–73, 209–10, 222–23
MN v Belgium, App No 3599/18 (ECtHR, 5 May 2020) <http://hudoc.echr.coe.int/eng?i=001-202468> 150–51
Nachova v Bulgaria, App No 43577/98, 2005-VII ECHR 1 . . . . 209–10, 222–23
Öneryildiz v Turkey, App No 48939/99, 2004-XII ECHR 1 144–45
Osman v UK, App No 23452/94, 1998-VIII ECHR 142, 222–23
Sabeh El Leil v France, App No 34869/05 (ECtHR, 29 June 2011) <http://hudoc.echr.coe.int/eng?i=001-105378> 163
Sbârnea v Romania, App No 2040/06 (ECtHR, 21 June 2011) <http://hudoc.echr.coe.int/eng?i=001-105047> 194
Soering v UK (ECtHR, 7 July 1989) 11 EHHR 439 163
Sørensen v Denmark, App No 52562/99, 2006-I ECHR 1 . . . . 163, 256
Stoicescu v Romania, App No 9718/03 (ECtHR, 26 July 2011) <http://hudoc.echr.coe.int/eng?i=001-105820> 137, 194
Stübing v Germany, App No 43547/08 (ECtHR, 12 April 2012) <http://hudoc.echr.coe.int/eng?i=001-110314> 223–24
Taşkın v Turkey, App No 46117/99, 2004-X ECHR 179 . . . . 144–45, 163, 303
Verein gegen Tierfabriken v Switzerland (No 2), App No 32772/02, 2009-IV ECHR 1 159
Verein Klimaseniorinnen Schweiz v Switzerland, Communicated Case No 53600/20 (ECtHR, 17 March 2021) <http://hudoc.echr.coe.int/eng?i=001-209313> 131, 144–45, 250

UN Human Rights Treaty Bodies

CEDAW, Concluding Observations on national reports
Norway (ninth report) 131, 319
UK (eighth report) 139
Korea (eighth report) 318–19
CEDAW, General Recommendation No 37 on the Gender-Related Dimensions of Disaster Risk Reduction in the Context of Climate Change, CEDAW/C/GC/37 (2018) 131
CEDAW and others, Joint Statement on 'Human Rights and Climate Change' (16 September 2019) <https:// perma.cc/ 6VXT- LAD4> 131, 150–51, 165–66
CESCR, Concluding Observations on national reports
Australia (fifth report) 9–10
Russia (sixth report) 9–10, 131
Argentina (fourth report) 131, 165–66, 319
Germany (sixth report) 131, 139
Ecuador (fourth report) 131, 139, 165–66, 319
Norway (sixth report) 131, 139, 165–66
Belgium (fifth report) 131, 139, 165–66

Inter-American Court of Human Rights

International Court of Justice

International Tribunal for the Law of the Sea

Permanent Court of International Justice

World Trade Organization

Other International Courts and Tribunals

NATIONAL COURTS

Australia

Austria

Belgium

Canada

Colombia

France

Germany

Ireland

Kenya

Nepal

Netherlands

Table of International and Domestic Instruments

TREATIES

DECISIONS OF THE PARTIES TO CLIMATE TREATIES

Conference of the Parties to the UNFCCC

Meeting of the Parties to the Kyoto Protocol

Meeting of the Parties to the Paris Agreement

EUROPEAN UNION INSTRUMENTS

NATIONAL INSTRUMENTS

Canada

China

Denmark

Abbreviations

For abbreviated titles of journals and law reports that are not included in the list, the reader should refer to the Cardiff Index to Legal Abbreviations (http://www.legalabbrevs.cardiff.ac.uk/).

AJIL	American Journal of International Law
All ER	All England Law Reports
All SA	All South African Law Reports
APEC	Asia-Pacific Economic Cooperation
AR4	IPCC Fourth Assessment Report (published 2007)
AR5	IPCC Fifth Assessment Report (published 2013–14)
ASEAN	Association of Southeast Asian Nations
BYBIL	British Yearbook of International Law
CBDRRC	common but differentiated responsibilities and respective capabilities (UNFCCC)
CBDRRC +	common but differentiated responsibilities and respective capabilities, interpreted in light of different national circumstances (Paris Agreement)
CCLR	Carbon and Climate Law Review
CEDAW	Committee on the Elimination of Discrimination against Women
CESCR	Committee on Economic, Social and Cultural Rights
CFCs	chlorofluorocarbons
CJEU	Court of Justice of the European Union
CMA	Conference of the Parties serving as the Meeting of the Parties to the Paris Agreement
CMP	Conference of the Parties serving as the Meeting of the Parties to the Kyoto Protocol
CO_2	carbon dioxide
CO_2 eq	carbon-dioxide equivalent
COP	Conference of the Parties to the UN Framework Convention on Climate Change
COP/CBD	Conference of the Parties to the Convention on Biological Diversity
CORSIA	carbon offsetting and reduction scheme for international aviation
CRC	Committee on the Rights of the Child
CUP	Cambridge University Press
DC	District Court
DRC	Democratic Republic of the Congo
DTU	Technical University of Denmark
ECHR	Convention for the Protection of Human Rights and Fundamental Freedoms ('European Convention on Human Rights')
ECLI	European Case Law Identifier

ECtHR	European Court of Human Rights
EE	Edward Elgar
EEA	European Economic Area
EIA	environmental impact assessment
EJIL	European Journal of International Law
EJIR	European Journal of International Relations
ESIL	European Society of International Law
EWCA	England and Wales Court of Appeal
FC	Federal Court (Canada)
FCA	Federal Court of Australia
GHG	greenhouse gas emissions
Gt	gigatonne (a billion metric tons)
HCFC	hydrochlorofluorocarbon
HFC	hydrofluorocarbon
HRC	Human Rights Committee (ICCPR)
IACtHR	Inter-American Court of Human Rights
ICAO	International Civil Aviation Organization
ICCPR	International Covenant on Civil and Political Rights
ICESCR	International Covenant on Economic, Social and Cultural Rights
ICJ	International Court of Justice
ICLQ	International and Comparative Law Quarterly
IESC	Supreme Court of Ireland
ILA	International Law Association
ILC	International Law Commission (UN)
ILDC	International Law in Domestic Courts (database)
ILM	International Legal Materials
ILR	International Law Reports
IMO	International Maritime Organization
INDC	intended nationally determined contributions
IPCC	Intergovernmental Panel on Climate Change
ITLOS	International Tribunal for the Law of the Sea
JEL	Journal of Environmental Law
LULUCF	land use, land-use change, and forestry
MARPOL 73/78	International Convention for the Prevention of Pollution from Ships of 1973 as modified by its Protocol of 1978
MEPC	Marine Environment Protection Committee (IMO)
MPGs	modalities, procedures, and guidelines (Paris Agreement)
Mt	megatonne (a million metric tons)
NAMA	nationally appropriate mitigation action (Copenhagen Accord and Cancun Agreements)
NDC	nationally determined contributions
NET	National Environmental Tribunal (Kenya)
NGO	non-governmental organization
NSWLEC	New South Wales Land and Environment Court
NZHC	New Zealand High Court

OAS	Organization of American States
ODS	ozone-depleting substances
OECD	Organization for Economic Co-operation and Development
OHCHR	Office of the United Nations High Commissioner for Human Rights
OP	Optional Protocol
OUP	Oxford University Press
ppm	parts per million
PCIJ	Permanent Court of International Justice
PLD	Pakistan Legal Decisions
QCCS	Superior Court of Quebec
QEET	quantified economy-wide emissions target for 2020 (Copenhagen Accord and Cancun Agreements)
QELRC	quantified emission limitation or reduction commitment (Kyoto Protocol)
RdC	Recueil des Cours, Collected Courses of The Hague Academy of International Law
RECIEL	Review of European, Comparative, and International Environmental Law
RIAA	Reports of International Arbitral Awards (UN)
SARPs	international standards and recommended practices ('Chicago' Convention on International Civil Aviation)
SBI	Subsidiary Body for Implementation (UNFCCC)
SBSTA	Subsidiary Body for Scientific and Technological Advice (UNFCCC)
SC	Supreme Court
SEA	strategic environmental assessment
SIDS	small island developing states
SR1.5	IPCC Special Report on Global Warming of 1.5°C (published 2019)
TEL	Transnational Environmental Law
TIAS	Treaties and Other International Acts Series (US)
UNCLOS	UN Convention on the Law of the Sea
UNECE	UN Economic Commission for Europe
UNEP	UN Environment Programme
UNFCCC	UN Framework Convention on Climate Change
UNGA	UN General Assembly
UNSC	UN Security Council
UNTS	UN Treaty Series
VCLT	Vienna Convention on the Law of Treaties
WHC	World Heritage Committee
WMO	World Meteorological Organization
WRI	World Resources Institute
YBILC	Yearbook of the International Law Commission
ZAGPPHC	South Africa North Gauteng High Court, Pretoria

I
Introduction

A. Climate Change

Since the Industrial Revolution, societies have emitted increasingly large quantities of greenhouse gases (GHGs) into the atmosphere. These anthropogenic GHG emissions consist mainly in carbon dioxide, methane, nitrous oxide, and various halogen compounds.[1] They result from the combustion of fossil fuels for energy production and various other industrial and agricultural processes as well as land-use change (eg deforestation) and the degradation of organic waste.[2]

GHGs naturally present in the atmosphere reflect infrared radiation emitted by the Earth's surface, thus, in effect, 'trapping' heat within the Earth's atmosphere—a phenomenon often dubbed as the 'greenhouse effect'.[3] Over time, anthropogenic emissions have caused a significant increase in GHG concentrations in the atmosphere, thus enhancing the greenhouse effect and warming the climate system.[4] The Intergovernmental Panel on Climate Change (IPCC)—a UN body in charge of assessing the science related to climate change[5]—ascertained that '[i]t is unequivocal that human influence has warmed the atmosphere, ocean and land'.[6] The IPCC further noted that '[g]lobal surface temperature will continue to increase until at least the mid-century under all emissions scenarios considered'.[7] These scientific observations are beyond reasonable argument and they have long been acknowledged by states.[8]

[1] Marc Fleurbaey and others, 'Sustainable Development and Equity' in Ottmar Edenhofer and others (eds), *Climate Change 2014: Mitigation of Climate Change: Working Group III Contribution to the Fifth Assessment Report of the Intergovernmental Panel on Climate Change* (CUP 2014) 354. Relevant halogen compounds include chlorofluorocarbons (CFCs), hydrochlorofluorocarbons (HCFCs), hydrofluorocarbons (HFCs), halons, methyl chloride, methyl bromide, and nitrogen trifluoride. For a complete list, see Chris Smith and others, 'The Earth's Energy Budget, Climate Feedbacks, and Climate Sensitivity' in Valérie Masson-Delmotte and others (eds), *Climate Change 2021: The Physical Science Basis. Contribution of the Working Group I to the Sixth Assessment Report of the Intergovernmental Panel on Climate Change* (accepted version subject to final editing, IPCC 2021) table 7.SM.7.

[2] Gabriel Blanco and others, 'Drivers, Trends and Mitigation' in Edenhofer and others (eds) (n 1) 360.

[3] JB Robin Matthews and others, 'Glossary' in Masson-Delmotte and others (eds), *Climate Change 2021* (n 1) Annex VII, defining 'Greenhouse effect'.

[4] Richard P Allan and others, 'Summary for Policymakers' in Masson-Delmotte and others (eds), *Climate Change 2021* (n 1) §A.1.1.

[5] See UNGA Res 43/53 (6 December 1988) ¶5.

[6] Allan and others (n 4) §A.1.

[7] Ibid §B.1.

[8] See eg United Nations Framework Convention on Climate Change (9 May 1992, in force 21 March 1994) 1771 UNTS 107, Preamble ¶3.

International Law Obligations on Climate Change Mitigation. Benoit Mayer, Oxford University Press. © Benoit Mayer 2022.
DOI: 10.1093/oso/9780192843661.003.0001

Climate change has disastrous environmental and social consequences, some of which will not fully unfold for centuries or millennia.[9] The IPCC concluded that climate change is already causing 'impacts on natural and human systems on all continents and across the oceans',[10] and it further highlighted that continued GHG emissions would 'increas[e] the likelihood of severe, pervasive and irreversible impacts'.[11] Climate change affects various physical systems, resulting in particular in sea-level rise (caused by the thermal expansion of seawater and increasingly by the melting of land-borne icesheets and glaciers), the acidification of seawater (from absorption of carbon dioxide), changes in precipitation patterns, and more extreme weather events.[12] These physical effects are taking a heavy toll on species and ecosystems[13] and, in turn, on societies, affecting sources of livelihoods, food security, and human health, while also exacerbating conflicts and forced migration.[14] Risks are particularly acute for communities living in low-lying coastal areas, small islands, or arid and flood-prone regions, especially in developing countries that have a limited ability to cope with climate impacts.[15] States have long acknowledged these scientific findings about the adverse impacts of climate change; they characterized climate change as 'a common concern of humankind',[16] 'an urgent and potentially irreversible threat to human societies and the planet',[17] and 'one of the greatest challenges of our time'.[18]

There are two main types of human intervention aimed at addressing climate change. First, climate change *mitigation* aims to address the cause of climate change by limiting and reducing GHG emissions by sources (eg the combustion of fossil fuel) and by enhancing the removal of GHGs by sinks (eg reforestation) and their storage by reservoirs.[19] Second, *adaptation* to climate change seeks to facilitate adjustments to climate change in order to manage, as far as possible, its

[9] See Stefan Dullinger and others, 'Extinction Debt of High-Mountain Plants under Twenty-First-Century Climate Change' (2012) 2 Nature Climate Change 619; Peter U Clark and others, 'Consequences of Twenty-First-Century Policy for Multi-Millennial Climate and Sea-Level Change' (2016) 6 Nature Climate Change 360.

[10] Christopher B Field and others, 'Summary for Policymakers' in Christopher B Field and others (eds), *Climate Change 2014: Impacts, Adaptation, and Vulnerability: Part A: Global and Sectoral Aspects: Working Group II Contribution to the Fifth Assessment Report of the Intergovernmental Panel on Climate Change* (CUP 2014) 4.

[11] Ibid 14.

[12] Ibid 11.

[13] Ibid 13 et passim.

[14] Ibid 17–20 et passim.

[15] Ibid 21–25 et passim.

[16] UNFCCC (n 8) Preamble ¶2; Paris Agreement (12 December 2015, in force 4 November 2016) (2016) 55 ILM 740, Preamble ¶8.

[17] Paris Agreement (n 16) Preamble ¶6.

[18] Transforming Our World: The 2030 Agenda for Sustainable Development, UNGA Res 70/1 (25 September 2015) ¶14. See also Political Declaration of the High-Level Political Forum on Sustainable Development Convened under the Auspices of the General Assembly, UNGA Resolutions 74/4 (15 October 2019) ¶11; 75/217 (21 December 2020) ¶1.

[19] For convenience, this book considers sinks as 'negative emissions' and uses the word 'emissions' to refer to emissions net of removals.

social and ecological consequences[20]—for instance, through disaster risk management, investments in freshwater or flood-prevention infrastructure, or even population migration and resettlement programmes. Mitigation and adaptation are not alternative but complementary objectives: even the most drastic mitigation action will not immediately stop the adverse impacts of climate change,[21] while adaptation alone will become increasingly challenging if GHG emissions continue unabated.[22] The focus of this book is on the mitigation of climate change and, more specifically, on international law obligations in this regard.

B. The International Law on Climate Change Mitigation

Law can help mitigate climate change in various ways. On the one hand, pre-existing rules of a general ambit may be applied so as to require climate action. Thus, on the domestic plane, the US Supreme Court interpreted the Environmental Protection Agency's statutory obligation to regulate 'air pollution' as extending to GHG emissions.[23] On the other hand, new rules can also be adopted specifically to foster climate action.[24] With regard to climate change mitigation, states, subnational governments, and regional organizations have introduced cap-and-trade mechanisms[25] and taxes,[26] along with technical regulations[27] and decision-making procedures,[28] aimed at limiting and reducing GHG emissions.

Yet, domestic law alone is unlikely to prompt effective action on climate change mitigation. Climate change is a global phenomenon: the sources of GHG emissions are scattered across countries[29] and, as GHGs rapidly mix in the atmosphere,

[20] See generally Core Writing Team and others (eds), *Climate Change 2014: Synthesis Report: Contribution of Working Groups I, II and III to the Fifth Assessment Report of the Intergovernmental Panel on Climate Change* (IPCC 2015) 118, 125.

[21] Field and others (n 10) 14.

[22] Richard JT Klein and others, 'Adaptation Opportunities, Constraints, and Limits' in Field and others (eds) (n 10) 902–03. See generally UNFCCC (n 8) art 4(1)(b).

[23] *Massachusetts v Environmental Protection Agency* (2007) 549 US 497.

[24] See generally the database 'Climate Change Law of the World', developed by the Grantham Research Institute on Climate Change and the Environment and the Sabin Center for Climate Change Law <https://climate-laws.org/>.

[25] See in particular Directive 2003/87/EC of the European Parliament and of the Council of 13 October 2003 establishing a scheme for greenhouse gas emission allowance trading within the Community and amending Council Directive 96/61/EC [2003] OJ L275/32.

[26] See eg Council Directive 2003/96/EC of 27 October 2003 restructuring the Community framework for the taxation of energy products and electricity [2003] OJ L283/51, amended; Greenhouse Gas Pollution Pricing Act, SC 2018 (Canada), c12; Singapore, Carbon Pricing Act, 2018 No 26.

[27] See eg Regulation (EC) No 443/2009 of the European Parliament and of the Council of 23 April 2009 setting emission performance standards for new passenger cars as part of the Community's integrated approach to reduce CO_2 emissions from light-duty vehicles [2009] OJ L140/1; Executive Order 14037 of 5 August 2021, Strengthening American Leadership in Clean Cars and Trucks, 86 FR 43583.

[28] See generally Benoit Mayer, 'Climate Assessment as an Emerging Obligation under Customary International Law' (2019) 68 ICLQ 271.

[29] China, currently the largest country per GHG emissions, was only responsible for about one-quarter of global GHG emissions in 2018 (24 per cent of emissions including LULUCF, 26 per cent

any country is affected by any other country's GHG emissions.[30] Mitigating climate change thus requires coordinated efforts by every significant emitter to regulate the emissions that take place within its jurisdiction. This cooperation is unlikely to take place spontaneously as long as each state, prioritizing national interests, discounts the global benefits of reducing GHG emissions within its territory. While cooperation on climate change mitigation is in states' common interest, it is in each state's individual interest to try to free-ride on the efforts of others.[31]

In principle, this collective action problem could be solved with the adoption of international rules requiring states to cooperate in their common interest. Yet, defining the modalities of international mitigation action has revealed one of the most daunting tasks of international governance to date. A patent difficulty is the sheer cost of what is required[32]—nothing short of 'deep emissions reductions in all sectors'[33] and 'a transformation of the global economy'.[34] Another difficulty relates to the absence of any simple, objective way of splitting this cost between states and assessing each state's 'fair share' of mitigation action.[35] This moral indeterminacy makes it more challenging for observers to assess whether any given state is co-operating in good faith and consequently easier for any state to evade its responsibilities.[36] Beside the challenges of international cooperation, mitigation is further hindered by an intergenerational issue: current governments may be inclined to ignore the impacts of climate change that will unfold decades or centuries later, thus in effect 'passing the buck' of climate change to future generations, despite the greater risks associated with delaying mitigation action.[37]

Some of the most intense and complex international negotiations have been taking place for more than three decades in an attempt to develop international legal rules to spur action on climate change mitigation.[38] The 1992 UN Framework

excluding it), according to data from the Climate Analysis Indicators Tool. See ClimateWatch, 'Historical GHG Emissions' (no date) <https://www.climatewatchdata.org/> (CAIT database).

[30] Ottmar Edenhofer and others, 'Summary for Policymakers' in Edenhofer and others (eds) (n 1) 5.

[31] See Garrett Hardin, 'The Tragedy of the Commons' (1968) 162 Science 1243; Stephen M Gardiner, 'A Perfect Moral Storm: Climate Change, Intergenerational Ethics and the Problem of Moral Corruption' (2006) 15 Environmental Values 397; Eric A Posner and David Weisbach, *Climate Change Justice* (Princeton UP 2010) 181.

[32] See Edenhofer and others (n 30) 15–16.

[33] Myles Allen and others, 'Summary for Policymakers' in Valérie Masson-Delmotte and others (eds), *Global Warming of 1.5°C: An IPCC Special Report* (IPCC 2019) 15.

[34] Joeri Rogelj and others, 'Scenarios towards Limiting Global Mean Temperature Increase below 1.5°C' (2018) 8 Nature Climate Change 325, 327.

[35] Factors that may be relevant include levels of historical and present emissions, populations, levels of development, financial and technological capacities, geographical resources, and adjustment costs. See Aaditya Mattoo and Arvind Subramanian, 'Equity in Climate Change: An Analytical Review' (2012) 40 World Development 1083.

[36] See Robert Stavins and others, 'International Cooperation: Agreements & Instruments' in Edenhofer and others (eds) (n 1) 1007.

[37] See Stephen M Gardiner, *A Perfect Moral Storm: The Ethical Tragedy of Climate Change* (OUP 2011) 143–84; Charles Kolstad and others, 'Social, Economic, and Ethical Concepts and Methods' in Edenhofer and others (eds) (n 1) 216.

[38] See eg UNGA Resolutions 43/53 (n 5) ¶10(e); 44/207 (22 December 1989) ¶10; 75/217 (n 18) ¶1.

Convention on Climate Change (UNFCCC) outlined general objectives, principles, and commitments; it also created processes and institutions to carry out and support further negotiations, including the Conference of the Parties (COP).[39] The Kyoto Protocol was adopted five years later to define quantified emission limitation and reduction commitments applicable to developed country parties for a first commitment period from 2008 to 2012.[40] The Doha Amendment extended the Kyoto Protocol to a second commitment period from 2013 to 2020,[41] while the COP had also invited the communication of informal national targets for the same period.[42] In 2015, the parties to the UNFCCC adopted another treaty, the Paris Agreement, which requires each party to communicate regularly its 'nationally determined contribution' (NDC) to the global response to climate change and to take the measures necessary to achieve this contribution.[43]

States have also adopted relevant legal norms under the Vienna Convention for the Protection of the Ozone Layer (with regard to halogen compounds)[44] and under treaties on international aviation[45] and on the prevention of marine pollution.[46] They have discussed climate change mitigation at the UN General Assembly,[47] the Security Council,[48] the Human Rights Council,[49] and conferences of the parties to various multilateral environmental agreements.[50] Other initiatives have taken

[39] UNFCCC (n 8).

[40] Kyoto Protocol to the United Nations Framework Convention on Climate Change (11 December 1997, in force 16 February 2005) 2303 UNTS 162.

[41] Doha Amendment to the Kyoto Protocol (8 December 2012, in force 31 December 2020) C.N.718.2012.TREATIES-XXVII.7.c.

[42] Decision 1/CP.16, 'The Cancun Agreements: Outcome of the work of the Ad Hoc Working Group on Long-Term Cooperative Action under the Convention' (10–11 December 2010) FCCC/CP/2010/7/Add.1, 2, ¶¶37, 50. See also Copenhagen Accord of 18 December 2009, appended to Decision 2/CP.15, 'Copenhagen Accord' (18–19 December 2009) FCCC/CP/2009/11/Add.1, ¶¶4–5.

[43] Paris Agreement (n 16) art 4(2).

[44] See Vienna Convention for the Protection of the Ozone Layer (22 March 1985, in force 22 September 1988) 1513 UNTS 293; Montreal Protocol on Substances that Deplete the Ozone Layer (16 September 1987, in force 1 January 1989) 1522 UNTS 3; Amendment to the Montreal Protocol on Substances that Deplete the Ozone Layer (15 October 2016, in force 1 January 2019) (2017) 56 ILM 193 ('Kigali Amendment').

[45] Convention on International Civil Aviation (7 December 1944, in force 4 April 1947) 15 UNTS 295 ('Chicago Convention') Annex 16 vol III 'Aeroplane CO_2 Emissions' (2017), vol IV 'Carbon Offsetting and Reduction Scheme for International Aviation (CORSIA)' (2018).

[46] International Convention for the Prevention of Pollution from Ships (2 November 1973), as modified by Protocol of 1978 relating thereto (17 February 1978, in force 2 October 1983) 1340 UNTS 61 ('MARPOL 73/78'); Protocol of 1997 to amend the International Convention for the Prevention of Pollution from Ships of 2 November 1973, as modified by the Protocol of 17 February 1978 (26 September 1997, in force 19 May 2005) TIAS No 9–108; Res MEPC.203(62), 'Amendments to the Annex of the Protocol of 1997 to Amend the International Convention for the Prevention of Pollution from Ships, 1973, as Modified by the Protocol of 1978 Relating Thereto' (15 July 2011, amendment entered into force 1 January 2013).

[47] See eg UNGA Resolutions 43/53 (n 5); 75/217 (n 18).

[48] See generally Security Council Report, 'The UN Security Council and Climate Change' (Research Report 2021 No 2).

[49] See eg Human Rights Council Resolutions 10/4 (25 March 2009) A/HRC/RES/10/4; 47/24 (14 July 2021) A/HRC/RES/47/24.

[50] See eg COP/CBD decision 14/5, 'Biodiversity and Climate Change' (Sharm El-Sheikh, 17–29 November 2018). See also references below at 132.

place under the aegis of the Asia-Pacific Economic Cooperation,[51] the G7,[52] the G20,[53] the World Bank,[54] or through regional or bilateral negotiations.[55] Beyond states, multilateral initiatives have involved autonomous territories, subnational governments, and even private actors.[56]

Despite such intense effort, negotiations have not prompted sufficient international action on climate change mitigation. Echoing the warnings of the scientific community and the concerns of civil societies, states have repeatedly expressed 'profound alarm that emissions of greenhouse gases continue to rise globally'.[57] The specific commitments that states have made, for instance through their NDCs, fall short of what would be needed to achieve the collective objectives that they have agreed upon.[58] These shortcomings of international negotiations have led civil society organizations to explore the potential of holding governments (or possibly other stakeholders) to account on the basis of general legal norms, including under international law, which can be applied as requiring more mitigation action than states have expressly committed to. In particular, some recent and ongoing judicial cases contemplate the possibility of inferring general mitigation obligations from customary international law or from human rights treaties,[59] and small island developing states have been actively contemplating the possibility of initiating advisory proceedings before the International Court of Justice (ICJ) and the International Tribunal for the Law of the Sea.[60]

[51] See eg APEC (Sydney Summit), 'Leaders' Declaration on Climate Change, Energy Security and Clean Development' (2007); APEC (Lima Summit), Leaders' Declaration (2016).

[52] G7 Climate and Environment Ministers' Communiqué (21 May 2021).

[53] See eg G20 (Pittsburgh Summit), 'Leaders' Statement' (2009) ¶29.

[54] See eg Coalition of Finance Ministers for Climate Action, *Helsinki Principles* (February 2019), principles 3, 4; World Bank, 'Zero Routine Flaring by 2030' (no date) <https://perma.cc/V34J-29HZ>.

[55] See eg US–China Joint Announcement on Climate Change (12 November 2014); EU–China Leaders' Statement on Climate Change and Clean Energy (16 July 2018); ASEAN, 'Joint Statement on Climate Change to the 25th Session of the Conference of the Parties to the United Nations Framework Convention on Climate Change' (2 November 2019).

[56] See Jolene Lin, *Governing Climate Change: Global Cities and Transnational Lawmaking* (CUP 2018); David Miller, *Solved: How the World's Great Cities Are Fixing the Climate Crisis* (Buffalo 2020).

[57] The Future We Want, UNGA Resolutions 66/288 (27 July 2012) ¶190; 75/217 (n 18) ¶1; Political Declaration of the High-Level Political Forum on Sustainable Development (n 18) ¶11.

[58] See eg Decisions 1/CP.21, 'Adoption of the Paris Agreement' (12 December 2015) FCCC/CP/2015/10/Add.1, 2, ¶17; UNEP DTU Partnership, 'Emissions Gap Report 2021' (UNEP 2021); Decision –1/CP.26, 'Glasgow Climate Pact' (13 November 2021) FCCC/CP/2021/12/Add.1 (advance version), 2, ¶¶4, 18.

[59] See eg *Urgenda v Netherlands*, ECLI:NL:HR:2019:2007 (SC, 20 December 2019), English translation in (2020) 59 ILM 811; *Grande-Synthe v France* (Conseil d'Etat, 19 November 2020), ECLI:FR:CECHR:2020:427301.20201119; *R (Friends of the Earth) v Heathrow* [2020] UKSC 52, [2021] 2 All ER 967; *Natur og Ungdom v Norway*, Case No 20–051052SIV-HRET (SC, 22 December 2020), English translation <https://perma.cc/5PCS-A8YH>; *Klimaatzaak v Belgium*, Case No 2015/4585/A (French-Speaking Tribunal of First Instance of Brussels, 17 June 2021), English translation <https://perma.cc/68ZJ-2F96>.

[60] See Agreement for the Establishment of the Commission of Small Island States on Climate Change and International Law (31 October 2021) <https://perma.cc/D688-7R93> art 2(2); Bernadette Carreon, 'Vanuatu to Seek International Court Opinion on Climate Change Rights', *The Guardian* (26 September

Various norms of general international law could possibly be interpreted as requiring action on change mitigation. The principle of sovereign equality—one of the foundations of the contemporary world order[61]—implies that each state has a due diligence obligation to respect and protect the rights of other states,[62] including by preventing transboundary environmental harm.[63] States also have a general obligation to cooperate in solving international problems, including those of a global environmental nature such as climate change.[64] Treaty provisions relating to the protection and preservation of environmental and cultural resources may require states to mitigate climate change insofar as this is essential to preventing the foreseeable impacts of climate change on these resources.[65] Similarly, given the impact of climate change on the enjoyment of various human rights, there is at least a plausible argument that human rights treaties may imply an obligation for states to mitigate climate change.[66]

C. Doctrinal Analysis

This book is a doctrinal study of the international law on climate change mitigation. This section justifies the need for, and the possibility of, this doctrinal analysis.

2021). On a previous attempt, see 'Palau Seeks UN World Court Opinion on Damage Caused by Greenhouse Gases' UN News (22 September 2011). See also Benoit Mayer, 'International Advisory Proceedings on Climate Change' 44 Mich J Intl L (forthcoming).

[61] Charter of the United Nations (26 June 1945, in force 24 October 1945) art 2(1).

[62] See eg Declaration on Principles of International Law Concerning Friendly Relations and Cooperation among States in Accordance with the Charter of the United Nations, UNGA Res 625 (XXV) (24 October 1970).

[63] See Declaration of the United Nations Conference on the Human Environment (16 June 1972) A/Conf.48/14/Rev.1 (1972) 11 ILM 1416 ('Stockholm Declaration'), principle 21; Rio Declaration on Environment and Development (14 June 1992) A/CONF.151/26 (vol I) (1992) 31 ILM 874, principle 2; *Legality of the Threat or Use of Nuclear Weapons*, Advisory Opinion (8 July 1996), [1996] ICJ Rep 226, ¶29. See generally Philippe Sands and Jacqueline Peel, *Principles of International Environmental Law* (4th edn, CUP 2018) 201, characterizing the no-harm principle as 'the cornerstone of international environmental law'; ILC, 'Draft Guidelines on the Protection of the Atmosphere' in ILC Report, 72nd session, A/76/10 (2021) 13, guideline 3, inferring an 'obligation to protect the atmosphere'.

[64] See UN Charter (n 61) art 56 (read alongside arts 1(3), 55); United Nations Convention on the Law of the Sea (10 December 1982, in force 16 November 1994) 1833 UNTS 3, art 197; Rio Declaration (n 63) principle 7; ILC, 'Atmosphere' (n 63) guideline 3.

[65] See eg Convention for the Protection of the World Cultural and Natural Heritage (16 November 1972, in force 17 December 1975) 1037 UNTS 551, art 4; UNCLOS (n 64) art 192; Convention on Biological Diversity (5 June 1992, in force 29 December 1993) 1760 UNTS 79, art 6.

[66] See eg International Covenant on Economic, Social and Cultural Rights (16 December 1966, in force 3 January 1976) 993 UNTS 3, art 2(1); Convention on the Rights of the Child (20 November 1989, in force 2 September 1990) 1577 UNTS 3, art 2(1).

1. The Need for Doctrinal Analysis

The expansion of climate law as a field of practice has been accompanied by an increasing amount of research on climate law. A growing number of monographs and edited volumes have been published in recent years, including two textbooks,[67] along with numerous articles in two specialized peer-reviewed journals[68] and in mainstream environmental and international law journals. Most of this burgeoning literature describes, comments on, or analyses recent developments that are taking place on the international or domestic plane, involving at times comparative, critical, or empirical legal methodologies as well as policy, economic, and normative analyses of the law.[69] The literature often seeks to assess the significance of developments in climate law, whether in terms of effectiveness or of justice, and to suggest possible or desirable ways forward.

By contrast, the emphasis of the literature has not generally been on doctrinal research aimed at determining what the law is, and thus predicting how courts would decide future cases,[70] especially not beyond the scope of climate treaties.[71] The prevailing view in the field puts legal force in broader perspective. Thus, as Daniel Bodansky pointed out, the legal force of the Paris Agreement is, after all, 'only one factor in assessing the significance of the Paris outcome'[72]—non-binding documents could be highly effective in prompting international cooperation, while legally binding ones may be ineffective if the rules that they contain are unhelpful. That does not mean, however, that the legal force of the Paris Agreement is irrelevant. While doctrine is obviously not the only thing worth researching, it does, however, matter for at least three reasons.

[67] Daniel Bodansky, Jutta Brunnée, and Lavanya Rajamani, *International Climate Change Law* (OUP 2017); Benoit Mayer, *The International Law on Climate Change* (CUP 2018).

[68] 'Carbon and Climate Law Review' (Lexxion) was founded by Michael Mehling in 2007, while 'Climate Law' (Brill) was founded by Alexander Zahar in 2010.

[69] See Ronald B Mitchell, 'Climate Law: Accomplishments and Areas for Growth' (2018) 8 Climate Law 135, 137, noting the prevalence of articles 'describing and analysing international, national, and subnational legal developments' in the articles published in two specialized journals.

[70] See Emerson H Tiller and Frank B Cross, 'What Is Legal Doctrine?' (2006) 100 Northwestern UL Rev 517, 517; Mike McConville and Wing Hong Chui, 'Introduction and Overview', *Research Methods for Law* (Edin UP 2007) 3–4.

[71] On climate treaties, see Sebastian Oberthür and Hermann E Ott, *The Kyoto Protocol: International Climate Policy for the 21st Century* (Springer 1999); Farhana Yamin and Joanna Depledge, *The International Climate Change Regime: A Guide to Rules, Institutions and Procedures* (CUP 2004); Daniel Klein and others (eds), *The Paris Agreement on Climate Change: Analysis and Commentary* (OUP 2017); Geert van Calster and Leonie Reins (eds), *The Paris Agreement on Climate Change: A Commentary* (EE 2021).

[72] Daniel Bodansky, 'The Legal Character of the Paris Agreement' (2016) 25 RECIEL 142, 142. See also Jutta Brunnée, 'COPing with Consent: Law-Making under Multilateral Environmental Agreements' (2002) 15 LJIL 1, 32, suggesting that bindingness does not always render a norm enforceable or otherwise able to influence state conduct; Lavanya Rajamani, 'Innovation and Experimentation in the International Climate Change Regime' (2020) 404 RdC 9, 104; David B Hunter, 'The Hard Choice for Soft Commitments in the Climate Change Regime' in Daniel Bradlow and David Hunter (eds), *Advocating Social Change through International Law* (Brill 2020).

First, legal norms have a distinct influence on the conduct of various actors, including states, that non-binding instruments do not have.[73] With the identification of legal norms comes an understanding that 'certain kinds of human conduct are no longer optional, but in *some* sense obligatory'.[74] The strenuous efforts that states make to justify their conduct in light of international law says something about the importance their governments attach to complying with international law—or, at least, appearing to do so. To name but a few prominent illustrations, intense scholarly and political debates took place regarding the legality of the US invasion of Iraq,[75] China's assertion of sovereignty in the South China Sea,[76] and Russia's 2014 annexation of Crimea,[77] possibly because of the implications that claims of illegality could have for the internal and international legitimacy of even the most powerful governments.[78] Likewise, the content of states' mitigation obligations can be expected to matter to governments and their constituencies.

Second, the existence of legal norms matters to processes aimed at interpreting or applying the law. Admittedly, climate treaties do not create compulsory dispute settlement mechanisms, and the compliance mechanisms they establish are relatively weak.[79] Yet, nothing precludes the use of non-specific dispute settlement mechanisms. As such, it is not inconceivable that, sooner or later, an international court or tribunal may be asked to interpret states' obligations on climate change mitigation, whether in contentious or (perhaps more appropriately) advisory proceedings.[80] In any case, such questions can be brought to domestic courts, either

[73] Robert Howse and Ruti Teitel, 'Beyond Compliance: Rethinking Why International Law Really Matters' (2010) 1 Global Policy 127; Jana von Stein, 'The Engines of Compliance' in Jeffrey L Dunoff and Mark A Pollack (eds), *Interdisciplinary Perspectives on International Law and International Relations: The State of the Art* (CUP 2013).

[74] HLA Hart, *The Concept of Law* (3rd edn, OUP 2012) 6 (emphasis in the original).

[75] See Sean D Murphy, 'Assessing the Legality of Invading Iraq' (2003) 92 Georgetown LJ 173; Ronli Sifris, 'Operation Iraqi Freedom: United States v Iraq: The Legality of the War' (2003) 4 Melbourne JIL 521; Philippe Sands, 'Lawless World: The Bush Administration and Iraq: Issues of International Legality and Criminality' (2005) 29 Hastings Intl & Comp LR 295.

[76] See Robert Beckman, 'The UN Convention on the Law of the Sea and the Maritime Disputes in the South China Sea' (2013) 107 AJIL 142; S Jayakumar, Tommy Koh, and Robert Beckman (eds), *The South China Sea Disputes and Law of the Sea* (EE 2014); special issue on 'South China Sea Arbitration' (2016) 110 AJIL Unbound 263–95; Chinese Society of International Law, 'The South China Sea Arbitration Awards: A Critical Study' (2018) 17 Chinese JIL 207.

[77] See Christian Marxsen, 'The Crimea Crisis: An International Law Perspective' (2014) 74 ZaoRV 367; Thomas D Grant, 'Annexation of Crimea' (2015) 109 AJIL 68; Alisa Gdalina, 'Crimea and the Right to Self-Determination: Questioning the Legality of Crimea's Secession from Ukraine Note' (2015) 24 Cardozo J Intl & Comp L 531.

[78] See Andrew T Guzman, 'A Compliance-Based Theory of International Law' (2002) 90 Cal L Rev 1823; Shirley V Scott and Olivia Ambler, 'Does Legality Really Matter? Accounting for the Decline in US Foreign Policy Legitimacy Following the 2003 Invasion of Iraq' (2007) 13 EJIR 67, explaining how illegality affected the perceived legitimacy of the US's invasion of Iraq.

[79] See UNFCCC (n 8) art 14; Kyoto Protocol (n 40) art 19; Paris Agreement (n 16) art 24.

[80] See note 60. See also Philippe Sands, 'Climate Change and the Rule of Law: Adjudicating the Future in International Law' (2016) 28 JEL 19; Margaretha Wewerinke-Singh, *State Responsibility, Climate Change and Human Rights under International Law* (Hart 2019); Margaretha Wewerinke-Singh and Diana Hinge Salili, 'Between Negotiations and Litigation: Vanuatu's Perspective on Loss and Damage from Climate Change' (2019) 20 Climate Policy 681; Tim Stephens, 'See You in Court? A Rising Tide of International Climate Litigation' *The Interpreter* (30 October 2019).

directly (in monistic states) or as background to interpreting national law. Already, the Supreme Court of the Netherlands in *Urgenda* has interpreted the European Convention on Human Rights (ECHR) as requiring the state to achieve a 25 per cent emission reduction by 2020 compared with 1990.[81] Courts in several other countries have discussed international climate law in the context of the interpretation of domestic law,[82] and several human rights treaty bodies have discussed the obligations on climate change mitigation that can be inferred from human rights treaties.[83] Several relevant cases and individual communications have been filed before the European Court of Human Rights (ECtHR) and human rights treaty bodies.[84]

Third, an accurate understanding of legal norms matters as a prerequisite for other types of research. Scholars in climate law have recognized the importance of making use of innovative methodologies in further research, including empirical, comparative, interdisciplinary, and critical research,[85] but each of these methodologies requires a preliminary understanding of what the law is. It is only when informed by a thorough understanding of the law that legal scholars can make a distinct contribution to academic and political debates on the responses to climate change.

Existing scholarship does not fulfil this need for a coherent doctrinal analysis of the international law on climate change mitigation. A government adviser, a judge, or a researcher, reading the current literature on climate law to try to find out what states or other entities are required to do regarding climate change mitigation, would find few clear answers, even with regard to some of the most essential questions.

A case in point is the question of the legal force of NDCs—the documents that contain parties' main targets on climate change mitigation under the Paris Agreement. An admittedly rather convoluted provision of the Agreement requires its parties to 'pursue domestic mitigation measures, with the aim of achieving the objectives of' these NDCs.[86] The literature on the Paris Agreement provides no definitive interpretation of this key legal provision.[87] Bodansky suggests that this

[81] See *Urgenda* (SC) (n 59).

[82] See eg *Thomson v Minister for Climate Change Issues* [2017] NZHC 733, [2018] 2 NZLR 160, ¶38; *Grande-Synthe* (n 59) ¶9–13; *Friends of the Earth* (n 59) ¶70; *Natur og Ungdom* (n 59) ¶¶56–58.

[83] See eg Concluding Observations of the CESCR on the Fifth Periodic Report of Australia, E/C.12/AUS/CO/5 (2017) ¶12; on the Sixth Periodic Report of Russia, E/C.12/RUS/CO/6 (2017) ¶¶42–43.

[84] See below at 131.

[85] See Michael Mehling, 'The Comparative Law of Climate Change: A Research Agenda' (2015) 24 RECIEL 341; Sébastien Jodoin, *Forest Preservation in a Changing Climate: REDD + and Indigenous and Community Rights in Indonesia and Tanzania* (CUP 2017); Mitchell (n 69) 143; Benoit Mayer, 'The Critical Functions of Scholarship in Climate Law' (2018) 8 Climate Law 151; Sarah Mason-Case, 'On Being Companions and Strangers: Lawyers and the Production of International Climate Law' (2019) 32 LJIL 625.

[86] Paris Agreement (n 16) art 4(2), second sentence.

[87] See Harro van Asselt, 'Review of Daniel Klein and others (eds), *The Paris Agreement on Climate Change: Analysis and Commentary*' (2019) 8 TEL 379, 381.

provision 'was formulated as an "aim" rather than as a legal obligation'.[88] Likewise, Jutta Brunnée asserts that NDCs 'are not internationally binding'.[89] By contrast, Lavanya Rajamani views this provision as the expression of 'binding obligations of conduct coupled with a good faith expectation of results'.[90] Yet, Rajamani does not further elaborate on the definitions or implications of a 'good faith expectation', a concept largely unknown in international law scholarship,[91] therefore with little explanatory value.

Other concepts are widely used in the literature on climate law in spite of their uncertain meaning and implications. For instance, much of the legal literature on the Paris Agreement orbits around what is presented as a dichotomy between 'procedural' and 'substantive' obligations.[92] In the broader context of international environmental law, the distinction is known to be rather confusing—the ICJ characterized the requirement to conduct an environmental impact assessment (EIA) as a substantive obligation in its 2010 judgment in *Pulp Mills*,[93] yet, in its 2015 judgment in *Certain Activities*, this same obligation was presented as a procedural obligation.[94] Similarly, there is no obvious ground to consider that the obligation to 'pursue domestic mitigation measures' is distinctively procedural rather than substantive,[95] or the other way

[88] Daniel Bodansky, 'The Paris Climate Change Agreement: A New Hope?' (2016) 110 AJIL 288, 295.

[89] Jutta Brunnée, 'Procedure and Substance in International Environmental Law' (2019) 450 RdC 9, 89.

[90] Lavanya Rajamani, 'The 2015 Paris Agreement: Interplay between Hard, Soft and Non-Obligations' (2016) 28 JEL 337, 354. See also Lavanya Rajamani and Jutta Brunnée, 'The Legality of Downgrading Nationally Determined Contributions under the Paris Agreement: Lessons from the US Disengagement' (2017) 29 JEL 537, 541–542.

[91] No occurrence of the phrase 'good faith expectation' could be found in either the *Recueil des Cours of the Hague Academy of International Law* or the *Max Planck Encyclopedias of Public International Law*. Nonetheless, a dozen subsequent publications reaffirm that the Paris Agreement creates a 'good faith expectation of results' without explaining what this means. See eg Sharaban Tahura Zaman, 'Exploring the Legal Nature of Nationally Determined Contributions (NDCs) under International Law' (2015) 26 YB Intl Envtl L 98, 117, 125; Mario Gervasi, 'On the United States' Decision to Withdraw from and Cease Implementation of the Paris Agreement on Climate Change' (2019) 18 Chinese JIL 98, 117; Myele Rouxel, 'The Paris Rulebook's Rules on Transparency: A Compliance Pull?' (2020) 14 CCLR 18, 20, 31.

[92] See James Crawford, 'The Current Political Discourse Concerning International Law' (2018) 81 MLR 1, 21; Brunnée, 'Procedure and Substance' (n 89); Sebastian Oberthür and Lisanne Groen, 'Hardening and Softening of Multilateral Climate Governance towards the Paris Agreement' (2020) 22 J Envtl Policy & Planning 801, 803, 305; Rajamani, 'Innovation and Experimentation' (n 72) 114–15; Brian J Preston, 'The Influence of the Paris Agreement on Climate Litigation: Legal Obligations and Norms (Part I)' (2021) 33 JEL 1, 6.

[93] *Pulp Mills on the River Uruguay (Argentina v Uruguay)*, Judgment (20 April 2010), [2010] ICJ Rep 14, ¶204.

[94] *Certain Activities Carried Out by Nicaragua in the Border Area (Costa Rica v Nicaragua) and Construction of a Road in Costa Rica along the San Juan River (Nicaragua v Costa Rica)*, Judgment on Merit (16 December 2015), [2015] ICJ Rep 665, ¶104.

[95] Paris Agreement (n 16) art 4(2), second sentence. See Lavanya Rajamani and Jacob Werksman, 'The Legal Character and Operational Relevance of the Paris Agreement's Temperature Goal' (2018) 376 Philos Trans R Soc A 2016.0458, 3; Crawford, 'The Current Political Discourse' (n 92) 21; Lavanya Rajamani, 'Integrating Human Rights in the Paris Climate Architecture: Contest, Context, and Consequence' (2019) 9 Climate Law 180, 181–2, each suggesting that the Paris Agreement only creates procedural obligations.

round.[96] As far as a doctrinal analysis is concerned, it appears that the characterization of an obligation as either substantive or procedural is unhelpful because it has no direct implications for the interpretation of the obligation.[97] In the literature on the Paris Agreement, this distinction seems mainly intended to reflect judgments about the effectiveness of a rule, based on the assumption that 'substantive' obligations are generally more effective than 'procedural' ones.

'Collective obligation' is another concept whose use has burgeoned in the literature on climate law (in particular on the Paris Agreement)[98] even though it is unheard of in the broader international law literature.[99] If the concept is understood as an obligation held by a collective, it is a contradiction in terms: only an (individual) legal person has the legal capacity necessary for possessing an international obligation and being held responsible for its breach.[100] Conversely, if a 'collective obligation' were to bind a group that has a legal personality (like a state or an international organization), then the obligation would not genuinely be collective: it would be an obligation applicable to an individual legal person. Yet, nothing in the Paris Agreement suggests that the parties were given legal personality to act as a group. Rather, the use of the concept seems to reflect a confusion between obligations (the breach of which entails responsibility) and objectives (the non-achievement of which does not automatically entail any legal consequences).[101]

Further adding to the confusion, commentators have depicted legal bindingness as a matter of degree, suggesting the existence of a continuum between obligations and 'non-obligations' in climate law.[102] An obligation, by definition, is

[96] Alan Boyle and Catherine Redgwell, *International Law and the Environment* (4th edn, OUP 2021), 393.

[97] See below at 210.

[98] See Rajamani, 'The 2015 Paris Agreement' (n 90) 343; Christina Voigt, 'The Paris Agreement: What Is the Standard of Conduct for Parties?' (2016) 18 QIL 17, 17; Bodansky, 'Legal Character' (n 72) 145; Anna Huggins, 'The Evolution of Differential Treatment in International Climate Law: Innovation, Experimentation, and "Hot" Law' (2018) 8 Climate Law 195, 204; Alexander Zahar, 'Collective Obligation and Individual Ambition in the Paris Agreement' (2020) 9 TEL 165.

[99] The phrase 'collective obligation' could be found only once in the entire *Recueil des Cours of the Hague Academy of International Law* and once in the entire *Max Planck Encyclopedias of Public International Law*, each time in different senses. See Malgosia A Fitzmaurice, 'International Protection of the Environment' (2019) 293 RdC 9 219, where the concept is used to refer to obligations owed to the international community as a whole (erga omnes); Said Mahmoudi, 'Islamic Approach to International Law' in *Max Planck Encyclopedia of Public International Law* (online edn, OUP 2019) ¶39, referring to an obligation borne by each member of a group.

[100] See *Reparation for Injuries Suffered in the Service of the United Nations*, Advisory Opinion (11 April 1949), [1949] ICJ Rep 174, 178–79; Hugh Thirlway, 'The Law and Procedure of the International Court of Justice 1960–1989: Part Seven' (1996) 66 BYBIL 1, 49 (defining an obligation as 'something owed by one or more subjects of international law to one or more subjects of international law'); Robert Jennings and Arthur Watts (eds), *Oppenheim's International Law: Volume 1 Peace* (9th edn, OUP 2008) §33 (Oppenheim's); Roland Portmann, *Legal Personality in International Law* (CUP 2010) 8.

[101] See eg Zahar, 'Collective Obligation' (n 98) 15, 24, referring interchangeably to 'collective obligation' and 'collective aim'.

[102] See Antto Vihma, 'Analyzing Soft Law and Hard Law in Climate Change' in Erkki J Hollo, Kati Kulovesi, and Michael Mehling (eds), *Climate Change and the Law* (Springer 2013); Rajamani, 'The 2015 Paris Agreement' (n 90); Peter Lawrence and Daryl Wong, 'Soft Law in the Paris Climate Agreement: Strength or Weakness?' (2017) 26 RECIEL 276. See also Stavins and others (n 36) 1019–20,

'binding':[103] it is therefore difficult to make sense of Judge James Crawford's assertion of the need 'to distinguish between binding and non-binding obligations within the Paris Agreement'.[104] Rajamani suggested the existence of a 'spectrum of legal character from hard obligations to non-obligations' with an intermediary category of 'soft obligations'.[105] Yet, unlike other characteristics of a norm (such as its significance, clarity, or effectiveness), bindingness is a question that requires a binary treatment:[106] non-performance either entails state responsibility or it does not.[107] Thus, the concept of 'soft law'[108] does not allow a better grasp of what the law is:[109] there is no room in a doctrinal analysis for conceptualizing 'soft', 'quasi', or 'half' obligations,[110] any more than a court could find a state 'half-responsible' for a 'half-wrongful' act. There is often a confusion between the legal force of a provision, on the one hand, and its content or nature, on the other hand: an obligation remains binding even if its content is vague[111] and even if the obligation only requires an endeavour rather than a result.[112] Determining that a provision is non-binding, naturally, does not necessarily exclude the relevance of this provision to the emergence, interpretation, or application of legal obligations.[113]

noting that 'international agreements … may be more or less "legally binding"' and that 'commitments may be more or less legally binding'.

[103] 'Obligation' in *Oxford English Dictionary* (online edn, OUP 2021).

[104] Crawford, 'The Current Political Discourse' (n 92) 21. See also Sandrine Maljean-Dubois, Thomas Spencer, and Matthieu Wemaere, 'The Legal Form of the Paris Climate Agreement: A Comprehensive Assessment of Options' (2015) 9 CCLR 68, 83 ('Non-Mandatory Substantive Obligations'); Lawrence and Wong (n 102) ('"soft" non-binding obligations').

[105] Rajamani, 'The 2015 Paris Agreement' (n 90) 352.

[106] Jan Klabbers, 'The Redundancy of Soft Law' (1996) 65 Nordic J Intl L 167, 181; Kal Raustiala, 'Form and Substance in International Agreements' (2005) 99 AJIL 581, 586.

[107] Cf Jonathan Pickering and others, 'Global Climate Governance between Hard and Soft Law: Can the Paris Agreement's "Crème Brûlée" Approach Enhance Ecological Reflexivity?' (2019) 31 JEL 1, 14, discussing the 'relatively low degree of obligation' in the Copenhagen Accord and the Cancun Agreements.

[108] See RR Baxter, 'International Law in "Her Infinite Variety"' (1980) 29 ICLQ 549, 554, 556.

[109] See Prosper Weil, 'Towards Relative Normativity in International Law?' (1983) 77 AJIL 413; Jan Klabbers, 'The Undesirability of Soft Law' (1998) 67 Nordic J Intl L 381; Raustiala (n 106) 588.

[110] See David Hume, *A Treatise of Human Nature* (Clarendon Press 1896), book III, pt II, §VI, qualifying 'half rights and obligations' as 'perfect absurdities'.

[111] See Tullio Scovazzi, 'Some Remarks on International Responsibility in the Field of Environmental Protection', in Maurizio Ragazzi (ed), *International Responsibility Today: Essays in Memory of Oscar Schachter* (Brill 2005) 201; Rosa M Fernández Egea, 'State Responsibility for Environmental Harm, "Revisited" within the Climate Change Regime' in Sandrine Maljean-Dubois and Lavanya Rajamani (eds), *La mise en œuvre du droit international de l'environnement, Implementation of International Environmental Law* (Martinus Nijhoff 2011) 338, arguing that '[t]he vagueness of rules does not mean that States are not bound to the obligations they might entail'.

[112] See *Indus Waters Kishenganga (Pakistan/India)*, Partial Award (18 February 2013), 31 RIAA 55, ¶372. Cf Brunnée, 'Procedure and Substance' (n 89) 89.

[113] See Vienna Convention on the Law of Treaties (23 May 1969, in force 27 January 1980) 1155 UNTS 331, art 31; Pierre-Marie Dupuy, 'Soft Law and the International Law of the Environment' (1990) 12 Mich J Intl L 420, 433; Dinah Shelton, 'Introduction: Law, Non-Law and the Problem of "Soft Law"' in Dinah Shelton (ed), *Commitment and Compliance: The Role of Non-Binding Norms in the International Legal System* (OUP 2003) 1; Hollin Dickerson, 'Best Practices' in *Max Planck Encyclopedia of Public International Law* (online edn, OUP 2010) ¶¶21–22.

While scholarship on climate law has largely focused on negotiated instruments, far less scholarly research has explored the potential relevance of customary international law and treaties of a general ambit such as human rights treaties. For instance, the leading textbook on international climate law devotes only ten pages to these questions.[114] And when the complex questions relating to the identification and interpretation of relevant customary obligations have been addressed at all, it has often been in brief preliminary sections in studies focused on the responsibility of states for alleged breaches of these obligations.[115]

Both the International Law Association and the International Law Commission (ILC) have sought to clarify the general international law on climate change, but their conclusions remain overly general. The ILC's Draft Guidelines on the Protection of the Atmosphere adopted in second reading in 2021, for instance, note that states have 'the obligation to protect the atmosphere by exercising due diligence in taking appropriate measures', but they do not define the requirement of due diligence or the 'appropriate measures' that must be taken—except that they must be 'in accordance with applicable rules of international law'.[116] This limited collective understanding of mitigation obligations is increasingly problematic as courts and other institutions are called upon to interpret and apply these obligations.

2. The Possibility of Doctrinal Analysis

While agreeing to the need for doctrinal analysis of the international law on climate change mitigation, one could question the possibility of conducting this analysis. In particular, one could question the existence of a complete and consistent set of international legal norms on climate change mitigation that doctrinal analysis could discover.

At the most fundamental level, this objection goes against influential theories that describe international law—or, in fact, any legal system—as necessarily a complete and consistent normative system. Hersch Lauterpacht's seminal book,

[114] Bodansky, Brunnée, and Rajamani (n 67) 40–44, 304–08. See also Yamin and Depledge (n 71) 13, briefly acknowledging that customary law may apply to climate change.

[115] See Roda Verheyen, *Climate Change Damage and International Law: Prevention Duties and State Responsibility* (Brill 2005) 145–92; René Lefeber, 'Climate Change and State Responsibility' in Rosemary Rayfuse and Shirley V Scott (eds), *International Law in the Era of Climate Change* (EE 2012) 321; Elena Kosolopova, *Interstate Liability for Climate Change-Related Damage* (Eleven 2013) 145–61; Wewerinke-Singh (n 80) 55–59; Agnes Chong, 'The Positive Obligation to Prevent Climate Harm under the Law of Responsibility', Georgetown Envtl L Rev (forthcoming).

[116] ILC, 'Atmosphere' (n 63) guideline 3. See discussion in Benoit Mayer, 'A Review of the International Law Commission's Guidelines on the Protection of the Atmosphere' (2019) 20 Melbourne JIL 453, 476–77. See also International Law Association, 'Resolution 2/2014: Declaration of Legal Principles Relating to Climate Change' (2014) 76 ILA Rep Conferences 21, in particular draft arts 7A (obligation of Prevention), 7B (precautionary principle), 8 (obligation of cooperation).

The Function of Law in the International Community, has already argued that 'the completeness of the rule of law ... is an *a priori* assumption of every system of law'.[117] Likewise, Hans Kelsen submitted that the absence of any applicable norm in a concrete case 'is logically not possible'.[118] From a more pragmatic perspective, *Oppenheim's International Law* suggests that international law has developed into a 'complete system' whereby 'every international situation is capable of being determined as a matter of law, either by the application of specific legal rules where they already exist, or by the application of legal rules derived, by the use of known legal techniques, from other legal rules or principles'.[119]

The completeness and consistency of the law is a necessary condition for the requirement of judges to adjudicate disputes before them. Legal systems require judges to apply the law notwithstanding the difficulty of the task,[120] and international law is no exception. Thus, international courts and tribunals have never refused to decide a contentious case on the basis that the law was unclear (*non liquet*).[121] The closest there is to an exception has been the ICJ's Advisory Opinion on *Legality of the Threat or Use of Nuclear Weapons*, where an equally divided bench declared, by the president's casting vote, that it could not 'conclude definitively whether the threat or use of nuclear weapons would be lawful or unlawful in an extreme circumstance of self-defence, in which the very survival of a state would be at stake'.[122] This, however, does not indicate that the Court would ever be unable to apply the law in an actual dispute where the Court could assess, in light of concrete facts, the proportionality and necessity of the use or threat of use of such weapons.[123] Unlike contentious cases, the exercise of jurisdiction in advisory proceedings is left to the Court's appreciation,[124] and it may not always be practically possible for a court to explore all remote aspects of broad, abstract questions.[125]

[117] Hersch Lauterpacht, *Function of Law in the International Community* (Clarendon 1933) 64.

[118] Hans Kelsen, *Principles of International Law* (Rinehart 1952) 305. See also Lucien Siorat, *Le problème des lacunes en droit international* (LGDJ 1959).

[119] *Oppenheim's* (n 100) §3 (12–13) (emphasis removed).

[120] Alfredo Mordechai Rabello, 'Non Liquet: From Modern Law to Roman Law' (1974) 9 Israel L Rev 63, 63. In civil law traditions, see Code Civil (Civil Code, France) art 4; Codice Civile Italiano (Civil Code, Italy) art 12(2); Schweizerisches Zivilgesetzbuch (Civil Code) art 1(2); Louisiana Civil Code, art 4. In common law traditions, see *Vaughan v Menlove* (1837) 132 ER 490.

[121] See eg Hersch Lauterpacht, 'Some Observations on the Prohibition of "Non Liquet" and the Completeness of the Law' in *Symbolae Verzijl: présentées au professeur J.H.W. Verzijl à l'occasion de son LXXème anniversaire* (Martinus Nijhoff 1958) 200; Ian Brownlie, 'Politics and Law in International Adjudication' (2003) 97 ASIL Proc 282, 285; *Oppenheim's* (n 100) §3(13).

[122] *Nuclear Weapons* (n 63) ¶¶97, 105(E). See generally Daniel Bodansky, 'Non Liquet' in *Max Planck Encyclopedia of Public International Law* (online edn, OUP 2006); Hugh Thirlway, *The Sources of International Law* (2nd edn, OUP 2019) 125–30.

[123] See Susan Breau, 'Low-Yield Tactical Nuclear Weapons and the Rule of Distinction' (2013) 15 Flinders LJ 219.

[124] Statute of the International Court of Justice (26 June 1945, in force 24 October 1945) [1946] UKTS 67, art 65(1); *Western Sahara*, Advisory Opinion (16 October 1975), [1975] ICJ Rep 12, ¶23.

[125] Prosper Weil, 'The Court Cannot Conclude Definitively ... Non Liquet Revisited' (1998) 36 Colum J Transnatl L 109, 117.

Admittedly, the prohibition of findings of *non liquet* does not mean that the content of the law is always clear. Complex cases arise in particular with regard to the application of ill-defined customary norms. Like any other legal system, international law involves some techniques to decide hard cases.[126] For instance, the recognition of general principles as a source of law was intended to ensure that judges would always find a legal basis to decide a case.[127] For lack of a better solution, a court may seek to decide a dispute on the basis of 'the principle which it considers ... most in conformity with the fundamental principles of international law'.[128] One way or another, 'a decision must be made',[129] and this decision may not be entirely unpredictable.

These observations apply also, of course, in relation to states' obligations on climate change mitigation. Some specific treaty commitments are relatively clear, but they are undemanding and therefore unlikely to be the main focus of legal disputes. By contrast, courts face greater challenges when applying general mitigation obligations that arise from the UNFCCC and customary international law or mitigation obligations that are implied from human rights treaties or multilateral environmental agreements. For instance, to apply the law, a court may have to balance antithetical interpretations of sovereign rights either as allowing economic development and the exploitation of natural resources at the expense of GHG emissions or as prohibiting interference with multiple rights of other states through the emissions of GHGs. In such circumstances, a judge will find no simple and objective method to determine what precisely a state is required to do, but a careful review of judicial practice provides significant insights on the conclusions the judge is most likely to arrive at.

There is no denial that judges exercise, in ordinary practice, a certain degree of appreciation, or discretion, when applying general mitigation obligations.[130] Discretion, however, is not arbitrariness: judicial decisions are constrained and guided by legal norms, and these legal norms can be the object of doctrinal analysis. Although legal doctrine will not provide a comprehensive formula to interpret and apply general mitigation obligations, it may nonetheless help to achieve more consistent judicial decisions, for instance by narrowing down the scope of permissible legal arguments and by clarifying probable applications of these obligations. As such, a doctrinal analysis of the international law on climate change, albeit uneasy, is not completely impossible.

[126] See ibid 118; Vaughan Lowe, 'The Role of Equity in International Law' (1992) 12 Aust YBIL 54.

[127] Lauterpacht, 'Non Liquet' (n 121) 205. See also *Pulp Mills* (n 93) Separate Opinion of Judge Cançado Trindade, ¶¶8–15.

[128] *Mavrommatis Palestine Concessions (Greece v UK)*, Jurisdiction (30 August 1924), PCIJ Rep Series A/B No 2, 16. See also *Boundaries of British and American Northeastern Territories*, Award (10 January 1831), 28 RIAA 33, 42.

[129] *Indus Waters Kishenganga*, Partial Award (n 112) ¶437.

[130] Hart (n 74) 272; Joseph Raz, 'Dworkin: A New Link in the Chain Review' (1986) 74 Cal L Rev 1103.

D. The Objective of this Book

This book presents a doctrinal analysis of the international law on climate change mitigation: it seeks to determine the content of this law as, for instance, courts would apply it. Its focus is on obligations—requirements that are binding under international law. This focus on obligations is not to suggest that the law only creates obligations;[131] it merely reflects the fact that the law on climate change mitigation, as evidenced in the context of litigation, is mainly concerned with (or more naturally framed in terms of) obligations. These obligations apply to legal persons, typically states but also some non-state actors such as international organizations and self-governed territories. Obligations are contrasted with other requirements such as provisions that define objectives or expectations, or express recommendations or encouragements. The breach of an obligation entails international responsibility, and thus involves legal consequences,[132] whereas the non-achievement of other requirements does not have such consequences. Among obligations relating to climate change mitigation, this book focuses on those that retain a general and abstract character (comparable to statutory law in a domestic context), to the exclusion of more transactional obligations typically negotiated between two or a few states (which could be compared with contractual commitments).[133]

Some of the central questions addressed in this book are the following:

- What is the legal nature of the various agreements, decisions, and other instruments intended to promote climate change mitigation? What obligations do they entail, if any, with regard to climate change mitigation?
- What mitigation obligations, if any, arise from customary international law, human rights treaties, and multilateral environmental agreements?
- How do mitigation obligations arising from different sources relate to one another? For instance, do climate treaties preclude the application of obligations arising from general international law? Can one rightly assume that obligations arising from human rights treaties require compliance with other mitigation obligations?

[131] See Oscar Schachter, 'International Law in Theory and Practice' (1982) 178 RdC 9, 25, describing law as 'in essence a system based on a set of rules and obligations'; A Pellet, 'The Normative Dilemma: Will and Consent in International Law-Making' (1988) 12 Aust YBIL 22, 26, noting that the law also defines 'permissions'.

[132] ILC, 'Draft Articles on the Responsibility of States for Internationally Wrongful Acts' [2001] II(2) YBILC 26, arts 1, 28.

[133] For examples of the latter, see Memorandum of Understanding between the Government of the Kingdom of Denmark and the Government of Romania on Co-operation for the Implementation of the Kyoto Protocol to the UN Framework Convention on Climate Change (adopted 28 January 2003, in force 8 December 2004) 2448 UNTS 71; Exchange of notes constituting an arrangement between the Government of the Federal Republic of Germany and the Government of the Republic of Ecuador concerning additional measures for the preservation of forests/biodiversity under the special energy and climate fund (adopted and in force 14 November 2014) 3029 UNTS I-52619.

- What are the nature and content of mitigation obligations, in particular the general mitigation obligations arising from the UNFCCC and customary international law?
- When these obligations appear exceedingly abstract, how can they be applied meaningfully in actual cases? Can a judge assess a state's requisite level of mitigation action implied from its general mitigation obligations? Or else, how can one determine a state's compliance with its general mitigation obligations?

The analysis in this book proceeds in two steps. The first Part of the book identifies international law obligations related to climate change mitigation—obligations arising from specific instruments (such as climate treaties), general international law, and human rights treaties. The second Part analyses the nature of general mitigation obligations and determines specifically what they entail. In particular, it discusses the possibility of assessing a requisite level of mitigation action or assessing implementation of corollary duties of cooperation, vigilance, and consistency.

Three preliminary caveats are in order. First, this book is limited to climate change mitigation (to the exclusion, in particular, of adaptation). It does not discuss international law obligations that constrain the ways states decide and implement mitigation action (eg on public participation and unintended consequences). Its focus is on primary obligations, thus leaving aside any questions relating to the content of state responsibility for any breach of mitigation obligations. Second, this book does not directly address the prospects of litigation as it focuses on the substance of the law rather than on procedures to apply it. The book is informed by a belief that mitigation obligations can be implemented through diplomatic and political processes, domestic litigation, and possibly international adjudication. Yet, the ineffectiveness of these implementation mechanisms would not affect the substance of the analysis, just its relevance.[134] Third, to state the obvious, this book is an academic endeavour, not a work of political advocacy. Its aim is not to promote any cause other than a better collective understanding of international law. The aim is not to determine what the law should be but what it is.

E. Framework of Analysis

This section presents some of the foundations of the analysis developed in the following chapters. More specifically, it outlines the doctrine of sources, introduces

[134] See *Application of the Convention on the Prevention and Punishment of the Crime of Genocide (Bosnia v Serbia)*, Judgment (26 February 2007), [2007] ICJ Rep 43, ¶148, recalling 'the fundamental distinction between the existence and binding force of obligations arising under international law and the existence of a court or tribunal with jurisdiction to resolve disputes about compliance with those obligations', and adding: 'The fact that there is not such a court or tribunal does not mean that the obligations do not exist'; Hart (n 74) 83.

the difference between ascending and descending reasoning, and highlights the need for, and challenges to, a systemic interpretation of the law.

1. A Standard Doctrinal Methodology

A tension exists between more or less normative conceptions of doctrinal analysis. At one extreme, seeking to determine what a court *would* likely decide could involve sociological, anthropological, or psychological methodologies rather than the type of inquiries generally associated with doctrinal analysis. At the other extreme, trying to determine what a court *should* decide could lead one to discard many, perhaps most, judicial decisions as wrongly decided, leading to conclusions fundamentally at odds with—hence of limited relevance to—actual judicial practice. Standard doctrinal research seeks to find a balance somewhere between these two extremes. The focus in this book is generally on international law as international courts (in particular the ICJ) claim to interpret it—that is, in line with the prevailing doctrine as reflected in particular by the ILC.

Thus, the book largely embraces the general tenets of positivism, which, as defined by Wolfgang Friedmann, 'accepts posited legal authority, *i.e.*, the commands issued by the supreme authority of the state, as absolutely compelling, and rejects the inquiry into higher moral norms, into the law as it ought to be, as improper for the lawyer'.[135] As such, the book relies on the identification and interpretation of norms of international law on the basis of the formal sources of international law that emanate from the will of states. The analysis builds on a rich corpus of judicial decisions and doctrinal studies on various relevant aspects of international law, and yet it is also hindered by the lack of agreed solutions to some fundamental problems, perhaps most obviously regarding the identification and interpretation of customary international law. It may be useful to highlight here some of the key assumptions that inform the analysis, although these assumptions are arguably based on a standard understanding of the doctrine of sources. Some more specific questions are discussed in other parts of the book.

At the most basic level, states are assumed to be equal sovereigns, which implies that no state or entity can impose its will on other states. Therefore, as the Permanent Court of International Justice (PCIJ) observed in the *Lotus* case, the international law binding upon states must—at least at some level of abstraction—'emanate from their own free will'.[136] On the other hand, states are not free to act as they wish: once they have agreed to a rule, they are bound to comply with it. The

[135] Wolfgang Friedmann, *The Changing Structure of International Law* (Colum UP 1964) 76.

[136] *SS Lotus (France/Turkey)*, Judgment (7 September 1927), PCIJ Rep Series A No 10, 18. See also *Oppenheim's* (n 100) §9, emphasizing that 'the will of individual states does not play an unrestricted role', as illustrated, for instance, in relation to custom or to peremptory norms; James Crawford, *Brownlie's Principles of Public International Law* (8th edn, OUP 2012) 20 (*Brownlie's*).

will of a state to be bound by international norms can be expressed in various ways, ranging from the expressed declaration of consent by an individual state through the ratification of a treaty or the communication of a unilateral declaration, to more diffuse acceptance of customary norms and general principles by states as a group.[137] By contrast, as judicial decisions and legal doctrine do not necessarily reflect the will of states to be bound, they are not sources of international law, even though they provide 'subsidiary means for the determination of rules of law'.[138] Despite the absence of binding precedent in international law, courts frequently rely on previous judicial decisions as persuasive authorities.[139]

With regard to treaties, the analysis will primarily be guided by the customary international law codified in provisions of the Vienna Convention on the Law of Treaties[140] and by the doctrine on the subject.[141] As such, references will primarily be made to the 'ordinary meaning to be given to the terms of the treaty in their context and in light of its object and purpose'.[142] In general, the word 'shall', within a treaty, will be interpreted as indicating an obligation, unless other elements indicate otherwise (eg when 'shall' does not apply to a legal person),[143] whereas 'should' is taken to indicate a requirement that is not legally binding. The analysis will also build, at times, on subsequent practice and agreements between the parties[144] and on multiple authentic versions in different languages.[145]

In line with the prevailing doctrine of sources, the analysis in this book will not generally involve a detailed review of the political negotiations that led to the adoption of relevant instruments (eg *travaux préparatoires*). The main reason for this is that 'the text of the treaty must be presumed to be the authentic expression of the intentions of the parties'.[146] The statements that parties make in the course

[137] ICJ Statute (n 124) art 38(1). See also VCLT (n 113) art 11; League of Nations Advisory Committee of Jurists, *Procès-verbaux of the proceedings of the Committee, 16 June to 24 July 1920* (van Langenhuysen 1920) 335 (Lord Phillimore), describing general principles as 'those which were accepted by all nations *in foro domestico*'; ILC, 'Draft Conclusions on Identification of Customary International Law' in ILC Report, 70th session, A/73/10 (2018) 119, conclusion 2.

[138] ICJ Statute (n 124) art 38(1)(d). See also *Paquete Habana* (1900) 175 US 677, 700; *Brownlie's* 37.

[139] ICJ Statute (n 124) art 59; Mohamed Shahabuddeen, *Precedent in the World Court* (CUP 1996). As such, there is no fundamental difference in the nature of the authority of judgments and individual pronouncements, or between *ratio decidendi* and *obiter dictum*, or contentious decisions and advisory opinions except for what concerns the rights and obligations of the parties to contentious proceedings.

[140] VCLT (n 113) arts 31–33. See also *Immunities and Criminal Proceedings (Equatorial Guinea v France)*, Judgment on Preliminary Objections (6 June 2018), [2018] ICJ Rep 292, ¶91, assessing the customary nature of the rules in arts 31, 32.

[141] See in particular Mark E Villiger, *Commentary on the 1969 Vienna Convention on the Law of Treaties* (Martinus Nijhoff 2008); Olivier Corten and Pierre Klein, *The Vienna Conventions on the Law of Treaties: A Commentary* (OUP 2011); Richard K Gardiner, *Treaty Interpretation* (2nd edn, OUP 2015); Oliver Dörr and Kirsten Schmalenbach (eds), *Vienna Convention on the Law of Treaties: A Commentary* (2nd edn, Springer 2018).

[142] VCLT (n 113) art 31(1).

[143] See Paris Agreement (n 16) art 4(5), affirming that '[s]upport shall be provided', without specifying who will provide it.

[144] VCLT (n 113) art 31(3).

[145] Ibid art 33.

[146] ILC, 'Draft Articles on the Law of Treaties' [1966] II YBILC 219, 223.

of negotiations do not necessarily qualify their understanding of the final text. As such, the law of treaties limits the recourse to supplementary means of interpretation to situations where authentic means would '[l]eave . . . the meaning ambiguous or obscure' or '[l]ead . . . to a result which is manifestly absurd or unreasonable'.[147] As far as climate treaties are concerned, such ambivalence can frequently be resolved by comparing the equally authentic version in their six languages. At any rate, the cogency of *travaux préparatoires* 'depends on the extent to which they furnish proof of the *common* understanding of the parties as to the meaning attached to the terms of the treaties'.[148] Identifying the common understanding of the parties is a challenging task in relation to any multilateral negotiations, but it is made virtually impossible, with regard to climate treaties, as a result of the absence of any systematic records (eg summary or verbatim) of climate negotiations, the constraints imposed on reporting by civil society organizations, and the fact that much of the negotiations take place in informal settings, not infrequently behind closed doors,[149] whereas statements made beyond the scope of treaty negotiations will not generally be considered as preparatory works.[150]

The application of customary international law faces more daunting challenges. Custom has long been described as a particularly uncertain source of law, sometimes derided as merely a 'matter of taste'[151] which is 'asserted'[152] rather than demonstrated, and remains 'indeterminate and manipulable'.[153] Fernando Tesón, for instance, denounces 'the practice of claiming customary status for rules notwithstanding the fact that these rules cannot be traced back to any plausible rule of recognition'[154]—a phenomenon he considers 'widespread' in academic publications, which he views as really, in effect, 'pieces of advocacy'.[155] These criticisms do not

[147] VCLT (n 113) art 32. See also eg *Conditions of Admission of a State to Membership in the United Nations (Article 4 of the Charter)*, Advisory Opinion (28 May 1948), [1948] ICJ Rep 57, 63, noting the consistent judicial practice 'according to which there is no occasion to resort to preparatory work if the text of a convention is sufficiently clear in itself'. See also *Fisheries Jurisdiction (UK v Iceland)*, Judgment on Merits (25 July 1974), [1974] ICJ Rep 3, ¶12; *Iron Rhine Railway (Belgium v Netherlands)*, Award (24 May 2005), 27 RIAA 35, ¶48.

[148] Humphrey Waldock, Third Report on the Law of Treaties, A/CN.4/167 (1964) 58 (para 21) (emphasis in the original).

[149] See generally Joanna Depledge, *The Organization of Global Negotiations: Constructing the Climate Change Regime* (Earthscan 2005); Naghmeh Nasiritousi and Björn-Ola Linnér, 'Open or Closed Meetings? Explaining Nonstate Actor Involvement in the International Climate Change Negotiations' (2016) 16 Intl Envtl Agreements: Politics, Law and Economics 127.

[150] See Oliver Dörr, 'Article 32' in Dörr and Schmalenbach (eds) (n 141) ¶¶15, 19.

[151] J Patrick Kelly, 'The Twilight of Customary International Law' (1999) 40 Va JIL 449, 451.

[152] Stefan Talmon, 'Determining Customary International Law: The ICJ's Methodology between Induction, Deduction and Assertion' (2015) 26 EJIL 417.

[153] Kelly (n 151) 451. See also Michael Akehurst, 'Custom as a Source of International Law' (1976) 47 BYBIL 1; László Blutman, 'Conceptual Confusion and Methodological Deficiencies: Some Ways That Theories on Customary International Law Fail' (2014) 25 EJIL 529.

[154] Fernando R Tesón, 'Fake Custom' in Brian D Lepard (ed), *Reexamining Customary International Law* (CUP 2017) 86.

[155] Ibid 87.

generally question the fact that custom is a source of international law, but they call for greater methodological caution.

This book builds on a large body of judicial decisions, scholarship, and the work of the ILC, which together outline, if not a complete theory, at least a working method to identify and interpret international custom in a way that is generally consistent with the practice of international courts and tribunals.[156] Accordingly, customary international law can be identified based on evidence of a general practice of states and its acceptance as law (*opinio juris*).[157] However, it is not always practical to conduct a comprehensive survey of state practice and acceptance as law.[158] Courts,[159] scholars,[160] and the ILC[161] recognize the possibility of deducing potential customary norms from broadly accepted premises of the international legal order (eg state sovereignty), at least when such deduction is confirmed by some (albeit incomplete) evidence of state practice and acceptance as law. Judicial decisions, in particular those of international courts and tribunals, are another indication of what courts would likely continue to consider as customary international law.

A question of particular relevance, when international law is applied to climate change mitigation, relates to the legal regime applicable in the absence of clear and specific rules. The PCIJ in the *Lotus* case affirmed that '[r]estrictions upon the independence of States cannot . . . be presumed'.[162] This sentence has often been misconstrued as suggesting that 'whatever is not *explicitly* prohibited by international law is permitted'.[163] This would, in effect, excludes any prohibition from the scope of customary law, whose norms are never 'explicit'. In fact, the *Lotus* judgment clearly

[156] See in particular Anthea Elizabeth Roberts, 'Traditional and Modern Approaches to Customary International Law: A Reconciliation' (2001) 95 AJIL 757; ILC, 'Customary International Law' (n 137); Orfeas Chasapis-Tassinis, 'Customary International Law: Interpretation from Beginning to End' (2020) 31 EJIL 235.

[157] See *North Sea Continental Shelf (Germany/Denmark, Germany/Netherlands)*, Judgment (20 February 1969), [1969] ICJ Rep 3, ¶77; *Military and Paramilitary Activities in and against Nicaragua (Nicaragua v US)*, Judgment on Merits (27 June 1986), [1986] ICJ Rep 132, ¶207; ILC, 'Customary International Law' (n 137), conclusion 2.

[158] See eg Tesón (n 154) 96.

[159] See eg *Corfu Channel (UK v Albania)*, Judgment on Merits (9 April 1949), [1949] ICJ Rep 4, 35 (identifying 'respect for territorial sovereignty' as 'an essential foundation of international relations . . . [b]etween independent States'); *Delimitation of the Maritime Boundary in the Gulf of Maine Area (Canada/US)*, Judgment (12 October 1984), [1984] ICJ Rep 246, ¶111, noting the existence of 'a limited set of norms for ensuring the co-existence and vital co-operation of the members of the international community' and implying that these norms are to be identified by deduction; *Pulp Mills* (n 93) ¶204.

[160] C Wilfred Jenks, *The Prospects of International Adjudication* (Stevens & Sons 1964) 9; Christian Tomuschat, 'Obligations Arising for States without or against Their Will' (1993) 241 RdC 195, 294.

[161] ILC, 'Customary International Law' (n 137) commentary on conclusion 2, ¶5.

[162] *Lotus* (n 136) 18.

[163] Weil, 'The Court Cannot Conclude Definitively' (n 125) 112 (emphasis in original). See also discussion in Helen Quane, 'Silence in International Law' (2014) 84 BYIL 241, 253–60; Alain Pellet, 'Le droit international à la lumière de la pratique: L'introuvable théorie de la réalité' (2021) 414 RdC 9, 130–32.

recognizes the existence of 'implicit' international law obligations.[164] A principle of freedom would have relied on an untenable logic: equal states can have no implicit right to freedom unless they also have a corollary implicit obligation to safeguard the rights of others.[165] As Martti Koskenniemi pointedly observed, '[t]o say that "freedom" should be given preference fails singularly to indicate which State's freedom is meant'[166]—for protecting a state's freedom would often come at the expense of the rights of another state. At any rate, international courts and tribunals have regularly identified state obligations based on general principles despite the absence of clear and specific rules.[167] Therefore, one cannot simply assume that the absence of explicit rules on climate change mitigation implies an unrestrictive freedom to emit GHGs any more than a sovereign right to a stable climate system.

2. Ascending and Descending Reasoning

Another transversal issue relates to the difference between what Koskenniemi calls ascending and descending reasoning in the process of legal interpretation, which corresponds broadly to a distinction between chiefly deductive arguments and chiefly inductive ones. Descending arguments seek to identify legal norms based on 'justice, common interests, progress, nature of the world community or other similar ideas to which it is common that they are anterior, or superior, to State behaviour, will or interest'.[168] By contrast, ascending arguments rely on empirical evidence of state consent or state practice. Koskenniemi's thesis is that these two types of reasoning are not fully reconcilable and that this unsolvable conflict 'provides the dynamics of international legal argument'.[169]

The tension between ascending and descending reasoning raises major issues in the doctrinal analysis of the international law on climate change mitigation. A descending reasoning may suggest that a state must do whatever is necessary to prevent climate change. This could be interpreted in light of states' agreement on collective objectives such as the objective of the Paris Agreement of holding global

[164] See *Lotus* (n 136) 18, recognizing 'usages generally accepted as expressing principles of law' as an (implicit) source of law, and noting 'the first and foremost restriction imposed by international law upon a State ... that—failing the existence of a permissive rule to the contrary—it may not exercise its power in any form in the territory of another State'. See also An Hertogen, 'Letting Lotus Bloom' (2015) 26 EJIL 901.

[165] See *Nuclear Weapons* (n 63) Dissenting Opinion of Judge Shahabuddeen, 393; Lauterpacht, *Function of Law* (n 117) 94–96; Alain Pellet, 'Lotus que de sottises on profère en ton nom! Remarques sur le concept de souveraineté dans la jurisprudence de la Cour mondiale' in *L'État Souverain dans le Monde d'Aujourd'hui: Mélanges en l'Honneur de Jean-Pierre Puissochet* (Pedone 2008) 221; Evan J Criddle and Evan Fox-Decent, 'Mandatory Multilateralism' (2019) 113 AJIL 272, 291.

[166] Martti Koskenniemi, *From Apology to Utopia: The Structure of International Legal Argument* (CUP 2006) 45.

[167] See eg *Corfu Channel* (n 159) 22; *Nuclear Weapons* (n 63) ¶29.

[168] Koskenniemi (n 166) 59.

[169] Ibid 60.

warming 'well below' 2°C, or close to 1.5°C, above pre-industrial temperatures.[170] Yet, from an ascending perspective, it appears that states have neither consented to acting consistently with these temperature targets, nor is their general practice in line with these targets. To the contrary, states have recognized that their current NDCs, in aggregate, are not consistent with what they consider to be a necessary level of global efforts.[171] There is therefore a wide gap, in the international law on climate change mitigation, between what Koskenniemi calls apology and utopia—between what states do and what, in their own recognition, ought to be done.

This book seeks to predict how a court (in particular, an international court or tribunal) would interpret and apply the law in light of the standard doctrine of sources. As evidenced above, the positivist tenets of this doctrine point mainly to ascending reasoning—on empirical evidence of state consent.[172] Yet, scholars and judges are not entirely dismissive of the possibility of relying on rigorous deductive reasoning based on well-established legal principles, at least to define presumptions that are then to be tested against empirical evidence.[173] For instance, courts have inferred, from general principles of international law (presumably the principle of sovereign equality), states' obligations to exercise due diligence to protect the rights of other states,[174] to maintain vigilance in environmental matters,[175] to cooperate,[176] to prevent transboundary environmental harm,[177] to conduct EIAs before approving projects liable to cause such harm,[178] and to notify and consult in good faith with state that may be affected by such harm.[179] Such inferences were frequently presented with little, if any, discussion (or even assertion) of state practice,[180] but none of these findings went clearly against settled state practice. Descending reasoning appeared to be used to fill the gap left when state practice was incomplete or inconsistent, but never to impose norms that were clearly incompatible with consistent state practice.[181]

[170] Paris Agreement (n 16) art 2(1)(a). See *Urgenda* (SC) (n 59) ¶7.2.1. But see Benoit Mayer, 'Temperature Targets and State Obligations on the Mitigation of Climate Change' (2021) 33 JEL 585.

[171] See n 58.

[172] See n 135.

[173] See Georg Schwarzenberger, 'The Inductive Approach to International Law' (1947) 60 Harv LR 539, 566–67; Jenks (n 160) 627; Tomuschat (n 160) 303–05; ILC, 'Customary International Law' (n 137) commentary on conclusion 2, ¶5.

[174] *Corfu Channel* (n 159) 22.

[175] *Gabčíkovo-Nagymaros Project (Hungary/Slovakia)*, Judgment (25 September 1997), [1997] ICJ Rep 7, ¶140.

[176] *MOX Plant (Ireland v UK)*, Order on Provisional Measures (3 December 2001), [2001] ITLOS Rep 95, ¶82.

[177] *Pulp Mills* (n 93) ¶101.

[178] Ibid ¶204.

[179] *Certain Activities* (n 94) ¶104.

[180] See Rudolf H Geiger, 'Customary International Law in the Jurisprudence of the International Court of Justice: A Critical Appraisal' in Ulrich Fastenrath and others (eds), *From Bilateralism to Community Interest: Essays in Honour of Bruno Simma* (OUP 2011) 673; Talmon (n 152).

[181] *Certain Activities* (n 94) Separate Opinion of Judge Donoghue ¶¶3, 13. On the lack of practice on prevention and environmental assessment, see John H Knox, 'The Myth and Reality of Transboundary Environmental Impact Assessment' (2002) 96 AJIL 291; Brunnée, 'Procedure and Substance' (n 89) 151.

Following these general observations, the following chapters rely mostly on ascending reasoning, with the difficulties this implies to ascertain general state practice. The analysis refers at times to descending reasoning, in line with judicial practice, but only for simple deductions from unquestionable premises of the international legal order (mainly the principle of sovereign equality) and only as a complement to ascending reasoning. On the other hand, this book does not rely on descending reasoning that is directly contradicted by state practice.

3. Relationships between Obligations

Multiple obligations on climate change mitigation arise from treaties and custom as part of what Nico Krisch elegantly called a 'dazzlingly multifaceted regime complex'.[182] To make sense of these obligations, one needs to situate them as part of a system of norms and, more specifically, to acknowledge the meaningful relationships between them: norms applicable to the same subject matter (eg climate change mitigation) do not merely coexist; inevitably, they also interact.[183] Understanding these interactions—in particular those between specific instruments (eg climate treaties) and general norms (eg customary international law)—is essential to a comprehensive and consistent understanding of international law as it applies to climate change mitigation.

This book's analysis is informed, in particular, by the principle of harmonization, identified by the ILC Study Group on the fragmentation of international law, according to which, 'when several norms bear on a single issue, they should, to the extent possible, be interpreted so as to give rise to a single set of compatible obligations'.[184] Accordingly, one norm on climate change mitigation (eg a treaty commitment) cannot simply be assumed to exclude the application of any other norm (eg a customary norm). Such could not be the case unless one norm either expressed or implied the will of states to exclude the application of the other norm on the same subject matter.[185] However, climate treaties neither contain any provision nor reflect any intention of their parties with the effect of excluding the application of customary international law.[186] To the contrary, the Preamble to the UNFCCC reaffirms principles of customary international law,[187] while several states have expressly stated their understanding that climate treaties do not derogate from

[182] Nico Krisch, 'The Decay of Consent: International Law in an Age of Global Public Goods' (2014) 108 AJIL 1, 18.

[183] ILC, 'Conclusions of the Work of the Study Group on the Fragmentation of International Law: Difficulties Arising from the Diversification and Expansion of International Law' [2006] II(2) YBILC 179, ¶1.

[184] Ibid ¶4.

[185] ILC, 'Draft Articles on the Responsibility of States' (n 132) commentary on art 55, ¶4.

[186] See below at 115.

[187] UNFCCC (n 8) Preamble ¶¶8–9.

general principles of customary international law.[188] Therefore, to use the terminology of the ILC's Study Group, there is no 'relationship of conflict' *stricto sensu* (ie incompatibility) between climate treaties and customary international law but rather a 'relationship of interpretation' whereby 'one norm assists in the interpretation of another'.[189]

This relationship of interpretation implies neither identity nor complete independence. On the one hand, international courts and tribunals have interpreted norms applicable to the same subject matter as creating separate obligations, which may differ, for instance, in nature and scope.[190] In relation to climate change mitigation, an ascending reasoning does not exclude the relevance of customary international law, nor does it suggest that customary norms are less stringent than treaty rules. In fact, the general agreement among states necessary for the emergence of customary law is in some respects an easier condition than the consensus required for the adoption of substantive decisions under the UNFCCC regime,[191] and it is more immediately reflective of states' evolving understanding of their obligations than climate treaties—as such, it would not be particularly surprising if customary law, even when identified through purely ascending reasoning, imposed more demanding obligations than climate treaties.

On the other hand, norms may be relevant to identify or interpret one another, whether it is as part of the context in light of which a norm is to be interpreted[192] or as constituting some of the state practice and acceptance from which customary norms arise.[193] Thus, the following chapters suggest that NDCs can be viewed as a minimal benchmark to determine the content of states' general mitigation obligations under the UNFCCC and customary international law, even though the implementation or achievement of NDCs, by itself, does not demonstrate a state's compliance with its general mitigation obligations.[194] On the other hand, the mitigation obligations implied by human rights treaties or multilateral environmental

[188] See the declarations made by Fiji, Kiribati, Papua New Guinea, and Tuvalu in connection with the UNFCCC, by the Cook Island, Kirabati, Nauru, and Niue in connection with the Kyoto Protocol, and by the Cook Islands, the Marshall Islands, Micronesia, Nauru, the Solomon Islands, Tuvalu, and Vanuatu in connection with the Paris Agreement.

[189] ILC, 'Conclusions on Fragmentation' (n 183) ¶2. See also Yamin and Depledge (n 71) 13. See also below at 119.

[190] See *Paramilitary Activities* (n 157) ¶178; *MOX Plant* (n 176) ¶50; *Proceedings Pursuant to the OSPAR Convention (Ireland/UK)*, Final Award (2 July 2003), 23 RIAA 59, ¶141. See also Institut de Droit International, 'Resolution: Problems Arising from a Succession of Codification Conventions on a Particular Subject' (1995) 66 Ann Inst Droit Intl 245, conclusion 10.

[191] On the inability of the COP to agree to a departure from the default rule of consensus, see UNFCCC, Draft Rules of Procedure of the Conference of the Parties and its Subsidiary Bodies, FCCC/CP/1996/2 (22 May 1996), rule 42; UNFCCC, Report of the Conference of the Parties on its Twenty-Fifth Session, FCCC/CP/2019/13, ¶¶4–5.

[192] See VCLT (n 113) art 31(3); Campbell McLachlan, 'The Principle of Systemic Integration and Article 31(3)(C) of the Vienna Convention' (2005) 54 ICLQ 279.

[193] See RR Baxter, 'Multilateral Treaties as Evidence of Customary International Law' (1965) 41 BYBIL 275; ILC, 'Customary International Law' (n 137) conclusion 11.

[194] See below at 121 and 312.

agreements are distinct from the general mitigation obligations under the UNFCCC and customary international law—the former can only require compliance with the latter if, and inasmuch as, in the circumstances of the case at issue, mitigation action effectively promotes the protection of the human rights or environmental resources at issue.[195]

4. Concepts and Terminology

The analysis in this book involves distinctions between various types of international law obligations on climate change mitigation. Two alternative typologies are used to reflect how obligations differ in terms of source, on the one hand, and of nature and content, on the other.

With regard to sources, a distinction is drawn between customary obligations arising from general acceptance and obligations arising from express consent. Among the latter, a further distinction is made between commitments on climate change mitigation and obligations implied from other (eg human rights) treaties.

- *Customary obligations.* Customary international law includes obligations of particular relevance to climate change such as the obligation of a state to protect the rights of other states,[196] to prevent transboundary environmental harm,[197] and to cooperate in protecting global environmental resources.[198] More specifically, there is an increasing amount of evidence of state practice and acceptance as law of a general obligation to mitigate climate change.[199] These obligations must be interpreted with caution: a standard cannot be found to be customary if more than a few states systematically ignore it or deny its existence. Customary obligations do not require a state to do more than others usually do; they merely prevent a state from breaking ranks.[200]
- *Commitments.* A mitigation commitment is an obligation, originating directly from a state's consent, which aims more or less directly at fostering mitigation action. Climate treaties are the main source of commitments, although some can be created through unilateral declarations or by relevant developments under other treaty regimes (eg the ozone regime). Commitments can be obligations of result[201] or obligations of conduct;[202] they can be broad or

[195] See below at 161.
[196] See eg *Corfu Channel* (n 159) 22.
[197] See eg *Trail Smelter (US/Canada)*, Award of 11 March 1941, 3 RIAA 1938, 1965; *Nuclear Weapons* (n 63) ¶29; *Pulp Mills* (n 93) ¶101; *Certain Activities* (n 94) ¶104; *South China Sea (Philippines v China)*, Award (12 July 2016), 31 RIAA 153, ¶941.
[198] See eg UN Charter (n 61) art 56; Rio Declaration (n 63) principle 7; *MOX Plant* (n 176) ¶82.
[199] See below at 110.
[200] But see *Urgenda* (SC) (n 59).
[201] See eg Kyoto Protocol (n 40) art 3(1).
[202] See eg Paris Agreement (n 16) art 4(2), second sentence.

specific. For instance, they range from the general commitments of the parties to the UNFCCC, to implement unspecified measures to mitigate climate change,[203] to far more procedural commitments to communicate NDCs[204] and national inventories.[205] Commitments are distinguished from pledges in that the former are legally binding while the latter are not.[206]

- *Implied obligations*. Some mitigation obligations may be derived from instruments that were not negotiated specifically to promote climate change mitigation. A case in point is treaties on human rights and environmental protection, which impose on states an obligation to protect individuals or resources. When these individuals and resources are liable to be affected by the impacts of climate change, these treaties may imply an obligation to make efforts to mitigate climate change. Yet, these implied obligations do not necessarily require full compliance with commitments or customary obligations on climate change mitigation; in fact, they only open a narrow window on the applicability of general mitigation obligations.[207]

Two other concepts are used to distinguish between obligations according to their nature and content: general mitigation obligations and their corollary duties.

- *General mitigation obligations*. A general obligation on climate change mitigation is an obligation of conduct (or due diligence), requiring the implementation of appropriate measures and, more generally, an appropriate level of effort, in order to mitigate climate change.[208] Albeit highly abstract, the concept is central to the international law on climate change mitigation. General mitigation obligations arise from customary international law and from the general substantive provisions of the UNFCCC.[209] Obligations implied from human rights and environmental treaties are of a similar nature (as obligations of conduct), but their content differs as they involve lower standards of due diligence for what concerns climate change mitigation. In principle, general mitigation obligations imply a requisite level of mitigation action, but a judicial determination of this requisite level of mitigation action faces major practical challenges.[210] An alternative way of applying general mitigation obligations relies on the identification of corollary duties.[211]

203 UNFCCC (n 8) art 4(1)(b), 4(2)(a).
204 Paris Agreement (n 16) art 4(2), first sentence.
205 UNFCCC (n 8) art 12(1)(a).
206 See eg Bodansky, 'New Hope?' (n 88) 297.
207 See below at 128–179.
208 See below at 90.
209 UNFCCC (n 8) arts 4(1)(b), 4(2)(a). See below at 38.
210 See below at 227–280.
211 See below at 213.

- *Corollary duties*. General mitigation obligations, as obligations of conduct, involve the implementation of necessary and other appropriate measures. Corollary duties are the requirements to implement such measures so that the breach of a corollary duty demonstrates (when the duty relates to a necessary measure) or at least suggests (when the duty relates to another appropriate measure) that the state is not complying with its general mitigation obligations. This book identifies three main corollary duties—the duties of cooperation, vigilance, and consistency—and some of their more concrete applications.[212] The word 'duty' is used to distinguish these requirements from discrete obligations originating directly from sources of international law.[213] By contrast with what applies to a discrete obligation, the breach of a corollary duty does not directly entail international responsibility, although it suggests a possible violation of the general obligation from which the duty is inferred, which can result in more extensive remedial obligations than the breach of a discrete obligation.

F. Structure of the Book

The book is organized into two Parts that explore first the identification then the application of obligations on climate change mitigation.

1. Identification of Mitigation Obligations

The three chapters that constitute the first Part of this book identify three types of mitigation obligations: commitments, customary obligations, and obligations implied from human rights treaties.

Chapter II identifies mitigation commitments—the obligations to which states consent directly and specifically with the aim of fostering mitigation action. The main commitments are created by climate treaties, namely, the UNFCCC, the Kyoto Protocol, and the Paris Agreement. In particular, the UNFCCC creates general commitments to implement mitigation action, whereas the Paris Agreement requires states to take the necessary measures to achieve their NDCs. Other commitments arise from unilateral declarations, including possibly some NDCs. Finally, some other treaty regimes define specific commitments in the context of international efforts to protect the ozone layer or to regulate pollution from international aviation and shipping.

212 See 281–320.

213 The content of corollary duties may coincide with that of discrete obligations, for instance, the obligation to cooperate under the UN Charter or the discrete customary obligation to conduct EIAs.

Chapter III turns to customary international law. Whilst acknowledging important methodological difficulties, this chapter shows that customary law includes general obligations relevant to climate change mitigation (eg an obligation of prevention and an obligation of cooperation) as well as a discrete obligation on climate change mitigation. This chapter then demonstrates the existence of a relationship of interpretation, rather than a relationship of conflict, between customary obligations and commitments, highlighting what this implies for the interpretation of both customary law and climate treaties. It suggests that similar interpretations should be given to the customary obligation to mitigate climate change and to the general commitments under the UNFCCC—which, throughout the book, are collectively referred to as general mitigation obligations.

Chapter IV identifies obligations that may be derived from treaties requiring states to protect human rights. While a broadly similar analysis could be made with regard to environmental treaties, the chapter focuses on human rights treaties due to their particular practical relevance: the notion that human rights treaties imply a state obligation to mitigate climate change has been instrumental to the development of climate litigation. Yet, the identification of implied obligations faces important challenges in light of the territorial nature of the relevant treaty obligations and the relatively indirect link between a state's mitigation action and the effective enjoyment of human rights within its jurisdiction. The chapter argues that human rights treaties require a state to cooperate on climate change only if, and insofar as, this really helps with the protection of the rights within the scope of the treaty. As such, implied obligations allow the interpreter of human rights treaties to open only, at most, a narrow window onto the applicability of general mitigation obligations.

2. Applications of General Mitigation Obligations

The second Part of the book considers the application of general mitigation obligations. It starts by characterizing the nature of these obligations. This forms the background to two following chapters that envisage two alternative ways of assessing compliance with general mitigation obligations: the determination of a state's requisite level of mitigation action and the identification of corollary duties.

Chapter V explores the nature of general mitigation obligations. It shows that these obligations are obligations of conduct, by contrast with some specific mitigation obligations (including some treaty commitments) that are obligations of result. Obligations of conduct are fully fledged obligations, but there are practical challenges to assessing compliance with them. A practical way to overcome these challenges is to identify the concrete implications of these obligations—that is, the steps that a state would normally take when it is exercising its due diligence. In this regard, the chapter disputes the relevance of the distinction between procedure and substance, noting that it is not only ill defined but also deprived of any automatic consequences. A review of judicial interpretations of obligations of conduct, in particular in international environmental law, reveals that the distinction between substance and procedure has concealed the more useful differentiation between discrete obligations and corollary duties. Non-compliance with a duty that is the corollary of an obligation of conduct suggests the breach of this obligation of conduct, with potentially far-reaching consequences for remedial obligations under the law of state responsibility.

Chapter VI assesses the possibility of determining a state's requisite level of mitigation action—that is to say, the stringency of the mitigation outcomes, expressed for instance as a rate of emission reduction, that a state would have to achieve in order to comply with its general mitigation obligations. The chapter reveals that this determination faces major obstacles. While states have outlined some collective objectives, they have neither accepted an obligation to act consistently with these objectives nor defined what these objectives mean for either collective or individual action on climate change mitigation. Various arguments that have been advanced in the context of domestic litigation rely on illusory legal or scientific benchmarks (eg an emission budget). Until states agree on more specific objectives and burden-sharing criteria, a judicial determination of a state's requisite level of mitigation action may not be entirely impossible, but it would inevitably involve an extraordinary degree of judicial discretion.

Chapter VII turns back to the more likely way of assessing compliance with general mitigation obligations, outlined in Chapter V, which involves the identification of appropriate measures that a state would be expected to implement when complying with its general mitigation obligations. Non-performance of a duty corollary to a general mitigation obligation would create a presumption that the state has breached its general mitigation obligations. The chapter identifies three main corollary duties and it emphasizes some of their applications in light of state practice. First, the duty of cooperation implies that a state can be expected to take part in negotiations, to participate in climate treaties, and not to deliberately free-ride on the efforts of others. Second, the duty of vigilance entails investment in research, the creation of a mechanism to monitor emissions, and the assessment of relevant activities, with a view to understanding sources of GHG emissions and ways of limiting them. Third, and overall, the duty of consistency reflects the expectation that a state, when exercising due diligence, would seek to define a national mitigation strategy consistent with the collective objectives it has agreed upon; that it would then implement mitigation action in line with this strategy; and that it would generally follow at least some of the good practices on climate change mitigation that states are generally accepting.

All in all, this book's analysis shows that it is possible to identify mitigation obligations arising from various sources of international law, to interpret these obligations as a single set of consistent obligations, and—up to a point—to apply them in predictable and meaningful manners. There is no formal legal gap in international law with regard to climate change mitigation, even though the relevant norms arguably lack both clarity and ambition. Doctrinal analysis and litigation can help to address the issue of clarity (ie provide a better understanding of what states must do) but they cannot address the lack of ambition reflected in both climate treaties and state practice.

G. Responses to Some Objections

The legal analysis presented in this book will certainly appear too conservative to some readers, too liberal to others. This is almost unavoidable given the political sensitivity of the topic and the extreme preconceptions circulated in various circles. The analysis aims to achieve a better understanding of the law, not to defend any pre-existing policy considerations, and no effort has been spared in presenting, as far as possible, an impartial treatment of the topic.

As it should be clear at this point, the methodology in this book is not confined to taking note of treaty provisions and other rules that states have expressly consented to or that international courts and tribunals have specifically recognized, assuming that, absent express treaty provisions or relevant judicial decisions, states enjoy an unbridled freedom to do whatever their power allows.[214] This approach would be conservative in any field of law, but even more so in the international law on climate change as national mitigation action under the Paris Agreement is nationally determined, while any international court or tribunal is yet to hear a relevant case. As the ILC noted in an early reflection on its function, '[c]odification which constitutes a record of the past rather than a creative use of the existing materials ... for the purpose of regulating the life of the community is a brake upon progress'.[215] Like any doctrinal analysis of existing law, the analysis presented in this book is necessarily 'progressive', even admittedly somewhat 'creative', in the sense that it anticipates how international courts and tribunals would construe existing law in difficult cases that are yet to be brought to them.

Some might find that custom occupies too much space in this book. Some scholars disrelish customary international law on the ground that it is more difficult to apply it than treaty law.[216] Others have advocated for the development of

214 See Alexander Zahar, 'The Contested Core of Climate Law' (2018) 8 Climate Law 244, presenting the lack of clear evidence of the application of the obligation of prevention to climate change (ie the absence of international judicial decision to this effect) as evidence of an unbridled freedom of states to emit GHGs.

215 See UN Secretary-General, Survey of International Law in Relation to the Work of the ILC, A/CN.4/Rev.1 (1949) ¶13.

216 See Daniel H Joyner, 'Why I Stopped Believing in Customary International Law' (2019) 9 Asian JIL 31; Laurence R Helfer and Ingrid B Wuerth, 'Customary International Law: An Instrument Choice Perspective' (2015) 37 Mich J Intl L 563.

customary law as a fair and effective source of international law, in particular in relation to global collective action problems such as climate change.[217] There is something to be said for Judge Cançado Trindade's concern that (some) '[p]ositivists only have eyes for treaty law'[218] and for Judge Christopher Weeramantry's prediction that treaties will find themselves 'hopelessly inadequate to handle such matters as the urgent environmental problems we already have on our hands'.[219] As state practice on climate change mitigation is rapidly evolving, one could question whether the text of treaties adopted years or decades earlier really reflects states' contemporary understanding of their obligations. As the consensus needed for the widespread ratification of a treaty is in some respects a more restrictive condition than general acceptance from which customary law emerges, treaty law is likely to remain several steps behind customary law. The uncertainty associated with the identification of customary law—even its relative indeterminacy—is perhaps a price worth paying for international law not to be entirely at the mercy of the political forces of the time but rather to rely on the accretion of principles of justice recognized by nations over time.

Yet, these arguments about the respective advantages and drawbacks of treaties and custom, albeit important in a policy context, do not inform the scope of this book's analysis. A norm remains a norm when it is unclear;[220] the difficulty of applying customary international law makes the work of scholars and judges more challenging (and perhaps more interesting) whether they like it or not. Despite genuine methodological difficulties, customary international law is largely recognized as a source of international law,[221] which is routinely applied by international courts and tribunals as well as domestic courts.[222] As Omri Sender and Michael Wood noted, 'the theoretical torment that accompanies custom in the books simply does not impede it in action'.[223] The frequency of unfounded claims about the existence of customary rules calls for analytical rigour, not for eluding analysis of one of the main sources of international law. The analysis in this book shows that customary international law is particularly relevant to climate change mitigation because states have not been able to adopt treaties containing commitments which they generally view as defining an appropriate response to climate change.

[217] Such arguments can be found, for instance, in Tomuschat (n 160) 290–91; Andrew T Guzman, 'Against Consent' (2011) 52 Va JIL 747; Krisch (n 182).

[218] *Obligations Concerning Negotiations Relating to Cessation of the Nuclear Arms Race and to Nuclear Disarmament (Marshall Islands v India)*, Judgment on Jurisdiction and Admissibility (5 October 2016), [2016] ICJ Rep 255, Dissenting Opinion of Judge Cançado Trindade, ¶77.

[219] CG Weeramantry, *Universalising International Law* (Brill 2004) 223.

[220] Raustiala (n 106) 589.

[221] ICJ Statute (n 124) art 38(1)(b).

[222] See Brian D Lepard, 'Introduction: Why Does Customary International Law Need Reexamining?' in Lepard, *Reexamining* (n 154) 3–8.

[223] Omri Sender and Michael Wood, 'Custom's Bright Future: The Continuing Importance of Customary International Law' in Curtis A Bradley (ed), *Custom's Future: International Law in a Changing World* (CUP 2016) 365.

Consistently, litigation on climate change mitigation often focuses on general mitigation obligations rather than on specific treaty commitments. As such, a book that seeks to determine how courts would identify and apply international law obligations on climate change mitigation simply cannot avoid substantial discussion of customary international law.

On the other hand, some readers will probably think that this book provides an exceedingly narrow conception of mitigation obligations, specifically with regard to several somewhat 'heretical' arguments. In particular, they may object to the argument in Chapter IV which denounces the idea that a state's obligation to protect a human right automatically requires its full compliance with general mitigation obligations. They may also raise eyebrows when reading Chapter VI, which presents sceptical views on the possibility of a judicial determination of a state's requisite level of mitigation action. In particular, they may question the conclusion that states may not currently have any direct obligation to implement mitigation action consistent with the temperature targets they have agreed upon as collective objectives. These chapters include responses to many potential objections. The goal of this book, once again, is not to promote any particular vision of what the law ought to be but to develop a consistent understanding of what the law is.

PART 1

IDENTIFICATION OF MITIGATION OBLIGATIONS

II
Commitments

Introduction

The first Part of this book identifies the international law obligations applicable to climate change mitigation. It starts, in this chapter, with a survey of the obligations on climate change mitigation that are directly based on express state consent. Such commitments arise from climate treaties, from treaties addressing related subject matters, and from unilateral declarations. These commitments have a common origin in the specific consent of the state, which can be expressed through ratification or other acts manifesting its will to be bound. Commitments can thus be distinguished from customary obligations, which arise from a more diffuse and collective acceptance (see Chapter III), and from implied obligations, deriving from obligations that were not intended specifically for climate change mitigation (see Chapter IV).

Negotiations on the protection of the global climate system, initiated at the turn of the 1990s,[1] have led to the adoption of three main treaties—the UN Framework Convention on Climate Change (UNFCCC),[2] its Kyoto Protocol,[3] and the Paris Agreement[4]—which define commitments on the mitigation of climate change. Other treaty regimes have imposed commitments relevant only to certain aspects of climate change mitigation, whether in the context of the adoption of measures to protect the ozone layer or with regard to the sectoral regulation of international aviation and shipping. Commitments may also be created by unilateral declarations that manifest the will of a state to be bound—as could be the case, among other things, with some nationally determined contributions (NDCs) communicated under the Paris Agreement.

Commitments on climate change mitigation vary in scope, nature, and content. They may be highly specific or overly general; apply to a specified period of time or without time limitation; and relate to all or most of the state's greenhouse gas (GHG) emissions, or only to some gases, or to the emissions of some sectors. While the emphasis here is on commitments to implement or achieve mitigation action,

[1] See UNGA Res 45/212 (21 December 1990) ¶1.

[2] United Nations Framework Convention on Climate Change (9 May 1992, in force 21 March 1994) 1771 UNTS 107.

[3] Kyoto Protocol to the United Nations Framework Convention on Climate Change (11 December 1997, in force 16 February 2005) 2303 UNTS 162.

[4] Paris Agreement (12 December 2015, in force 4 November 2016) (2016) 55 ILM 740.

International Law Obligations on Climate Change Mitigation. Benoit Mayer, Oxford University Press.
DOI: 10.1093/oso/9780192843661.003.0002

mention will also be made of commitments on some related aspects of climate action, in particular those requiring a state to assist other states in mitigating climate change or to carry out procedural steps that help build confidence among states. Out of all the commitments identified in this chapter, Articles 4(1)(b) and 4(2)(a) of the UNFCCC stand out as creating general, open-ended obligations, prone to an evolutive interpretation in light of subsequent state practice, which have perhaps more in common with customary obligations than with other commitments.

Section A of the chapter identifies commitments arising from of the UNFCCC regime, section B focuses on commitments created by unilateral declarations, and section C reviews obligations arising under other treaty regimes.

A. The UNFCCC Regime

Climate treaties are the natural starting point for a recension of commitments on climate change mitigation. The following identifies the most relevant commitments made under the three main climate treaties. For the purpose of exposition, a distinction can be drawn, within each treaty, between three types of commitments: (1) substantive commitments, which require a state to implement mitigation action or to achieve specified outcomes; (2) commitments that require states to support mitigation action in other states by providing financial assistance, developing and transferring technologies, or assisting in capacity-building; and (3) commitments that relate to the communication of information on implementation, in particular on emission data and on the implementation of national mitigation action. This distinction does not suggest a rigid typology or present a comprehensive account of climate treaties—it only aims to structure a preliminary account of the commitments most relevant to climate change mitigation.

1. The UNFCCC

The UNFCCC was adopted on 9 May 1992; it opened for signature at the Earth Summit in Rio de Janeiro on 4 June 1992 and entered into force on 21 March 1994. Participation is open to states and regional economic integration organizations.[5] The UNFCCC has achieved virtually universal ratification (as of late 2021, by 196 states and the EU).[6]

As a framework convention, the UNFCCC lays ground for further negotiations towards the adoption of protocols that would progressively impose more specific commitments. Thus, the UNFCCC seeks to emulate the architecture of previous

[5] UNFCCC (n 2) art 22(1).
[6] By contrast, the UN has 193 member states.

multilateral environmental agreements, in particular the 1979 Convention on Long-Range Transboundary Air Pollution[7] and the 1985 Vienna Convention for the Protection of the Ozone Layer.[8] The UNFCCC outlines a comprehensive regime by defining an ultimate objective, some principles and institutional processes, and some general commitments, but it also refers to further negotiations to define more specific commitments.

Many provisions of the UNFCCC do not create obligations but merely provide the basis for the adoption of further instruments. Article 2 of the UNFCCC defines the regime's 'ultimate objective': to 'achieve … stabilization of greenhouse gas concentrations in the atmosphere at a level that would prevent dangerous anthropogenic interference with the climate system'.[9] This provision assists in the identification of the object and purpose of the treaty, thus contributing to the interpretation of commitments, and forms part of the context relevant to the interpretation of other sources of international law.[10]

Article 3 lays out some principles, the most important being that parties should act 'on the basis of equity and in accordance with their common but differentiated responsibilities and respective capabilities' (CBDRRC), with developed country parties '[a]ccordingly tak[ing] the lead in combating climate change'.[11] The UNFCCC contains two lists of developed country parties, which have additional obligations. Annex II is the narrower list: it includes the members of the Organization for Economic Co-operation and Development as of 1992. The broader list of developed country parties, in Annex I, includes all Annex II parties as well as 'countries that are undergoing the process of transition to a market economy' (ie states of Eastern Europe and the former Soviet Union).

Article 7 establishes the Conference of the Parties (COP), as the Convention's 'supreme body', to 'keep under regular review the implementation of the Convention' and to 'make, within its mandate, the decisions necessary to promote [its] effective implementation'.[12] COP decisions are not legally binding by themselves,[13] although they may be relevant to the interpretation of the treaty,[14] most

[7] See Convention on Long-Range Transboundary Air Pollution (13 November 1979, in force 16 March 1983) 1302 UNTS 217. Eight protocols were adopted between 1984 and 1999.

[8] See Vienna Convention for the Protection of the Ozone Layer (22 March 1985, in force 22 September 1988) 1513 UNTS 293; Montreal Protocol on Substances that Deplete the Ozone Layer (16 September 1987, in force 1 January 1989) 1522 UNTS 3.

[9] UNFCCC (n 2) art 2.

[10] See Matthew Happold, 'The Relationship between the United Nations Framework Convention on Climate Change and Other Rules of Public International Law, in Particular on States' Responsibility for the Adverse Effects of Climate Change' (Legal Response Initiative, 2013) 3–4.

[11] UNFCCC (n 2) art 3(1). See also Rio Declaration on Environment and Development (14 June 1992) A/CONF.151/26 (vol I) (1992) 31 ILM 874, principle 7.

[12] UNFCCC (n 2) art 7(2).

[13] On the authority of the COP to take non-binding decisions, see eg UNFCCC (n 2) art 7(2)(g). A COP decision is not binding, even if it uses the word 'shall', when it addresses matters to which climate treaties do not authorize the COP to make binding decisions. See eg Decision 2/CP.17 (n 78) Annex I ¶4.

[14] See by analogy *Whaling in the Antarctic (Australia v Japan; NZ intervening)*, Judgment (31 March 2014), [2014] ICJ Rep 226, ¶46.

obviously when a treaty provision requires parties to comply with COP decisions on particular subject matters.[15] Other institutions established by the UNFCCC include a Secretariat,[16] subsidiary bodies for scientific and technological advise[17] and for implementation,[18] and a financial mechanism.[19]

Overall, Article 4 defines a number of 'commitments'.[20] The text of the UNFCCC leaves no room for doubt about the legal force of these provisions: by contrast to the word 'should' in most of Article 3,[21] the recurrent use of the word 'shall' in Article 4 confirms that what the UNFCCC designates as 'commitments' are legal obligations. Incidentally, this interpretation is confirmed by other provisions of the UNFCCC, which mention 'obligations . . . under the Convention' when referring to the commitments defined in Article 4.[22]

While some commitments defined in Article 4 apply to all parties, others are limited to developed country parties listed in Annex I or in Annex II. More specifically, the first paragraph defines general substantive and other commitments applicable to all parties, the second paragraph imposes slightly more specific substantive commitments to Annex I parties, and the third to fifth paragraphs create additional commitments for Annex II parties with regard to the provision of support for developing country parties.

These commitments were envisaged merely as a starting point for further negotiations. Thus, the COP is required to '[p]eriodically examine the obligation of the Parties . . . in the light of the objective of the Convention, the experience gained in its implementation and the evolution of scientific and technological knowledge'.[23] These reviews can lead to recommendations[24] or to the adoption of amendments[25] and protocols[26] to the Convention. The expectation was that the commitments contained in the UNFCCC would be specified by successive protocols.[27]

[15] See eg n 75.

[16] UNFCCC (n 2) art 8.

[17] Ibid art 9.

[18] Ibid art 10.

[19] Ibid art 11.

[20] Compared with previous framework treaties (nn 7, 8), the commitments contained in the UNFCCC appear more detailed and specific. See discussion in Daniel Bodansky, 'The United Nations Framework Convention on Climate Change: A Commentary' (1993) 18 Yale J Intl L 451, 495.

[21] The word 'shall' is used in the chapeau of art 3, but 'should' is systematically used in each of the following paragraphs.

[22] UNFCCC (n 2) arts 7(2)(a), 12(8).

[23] Ibid art 7(2)(a).

[24] Ibid art 7(2)(e).

[25] Ibid art 15(2). See also art 4(2)(d).

[26] Ibid art 17(1).

[27] Thus, it is telling that the first decision of the COP was to establish a process for the 'strengthening of the commitments' of Annex I parties through the adoption of 'a protocol or another legal instrument'. See Decision 1/CP.1, 'The Berlin Mandate: Review of the Adequacy of Article 4, paragraph 2 (a) and (b), of the Convention, Including Proposals Related to a Protocol and Decisions on Follow-Up' (7 April 1995) FCCC/CP/1995/7/Add.1, 4, Preamble ¶1.

a) Mitigation action

The UNFCCC defines two general commitments on mitigation action—one applicable to all parties, the other only to Annex I parties. Thus, Article 4(1)(b) requires all parties to

> [f]ormulate, implement, publish and regularly update national ... programmes containing measures to mitigate climate change by addressing anthropogenic emissions by sources and removals by sinks of all greenhouse gases not controlled by the Montreal Protocol.

Under Article 4(2)(a), each Annex I party must

> adopt national policies and take corresponding measures on the mitigation of climate change, by limiting its anthropogenic emissions of greenhouse gases and protecting and enhancing its greenhouse gas sinks and reservoirs.

The text of these two provisions clearly indicates that they create legal obligations,[28] even though neither of them expressly requires the achievement of a specified mitigation outcome.[29] These commitments were rightly described as the central substantive obligations contained in the UNFCCC.[30] Yet, they could be subject to widely diverging interpretations. René Lefeber suggested that the obligation to communicate programmes under Article 4(1)(b) 'is not accompanied by a binding obligation to implement these programmes'.[31] Yet, the text of the provision seems rather to indicate that, once a party has communicated a programme, it must implement *this* programme.[32] Article 4(2)(a) leaves no room for interpretation: parties are expressly required to take measures 'corresponding' to their policies.

Another question regards the content of the policies or programmes. A purely textual interpretation could suggest that a party will comply with these provisions if it regularly adopts, implements, and publicizes any programmes or policies on climate change mitigation, notwithstanding their content.[33] Nonetheless, one could question whether a state would really be fulfilling its commitment in good faith by merely implementing a programme or a policy, however insignificant it

[28] See *Greenpeace Australia Ltd v Redbank Power Co* [1994] NSWLEC 178, ILDC 985, ¶¶24–25.

[29] See Jutta Brunnée, 'Procedure and Substance in International Environmental Law' (2019) 450 RdC 9, 194.

[30] See Bodansky, 'Framework Convention' (n 20) 467 (fn 102); Philippe Sands, 'The United Nations Framework Convention on Climate Change' (1992) 1 RECIEL 270, 273; Farhana Yamin and Joanna Depledge, *The International Climate Change Regime: A Guide to Rules, Institutions and Procedures* (CUP 2004) 95.

[31] René Lefeber, 'Climate Change and State Responsibility' in Rosemary Rayfuse and Shirley V Scott (eds), *International Law in the Era of Climate Change* (EE 2012) 330 (emphasis added).

[32] See Roda Verheyen, *Climate Change Damage and International Law: Prevention Duties and State Responsibility* (Brill 2005) 85; Yamin and Depledge (n 30) 95.

[33] Lefeber (n 31) 331.

may be (say, installing a few solar panels on the roof of the presidential palace). Indeed, this narrow textual interpretation fails to take into account the context, and in particular subsequent agreements and practice, in light of which a treaty is to be interpreted.[34] This general commitment is to be interpreted as requiring the parties to comply with an evolving standard of due diligence.[35]

These provisions hold Annex I parties to a higher standard than other parties, in application of the CBDRRC principle: in addition to mere 'programmes containing measures',[36] Annex I parties must implement more comprehensive 'policies'.[37] Article 4(2)(a) further suggests that the policies and measures to be implemented by Annex I parties 'will demonstrate' that they 'are taking the lead in modifying longer-term trends in anthropogenic emissions consistent with the objective of the Convention'. It further recognizes that by the end of the 1990s a return to earlier levels of GHG emissions 'would contribute to such a modification'.[38] Moreover, Article 4(2)(b) announces that Annex I parties aim for 'returning individually or jointly to their 1990 levels' of GHG emissions by the end of the 1990s.[39] Yet, this aspirational language does not directly qualify the commitment of any individual Annex I party. As such, the UNFCCC did not create an obligation for any Annex I party to ensure the achievement of this aim.[40]

Other subparagraphs of Article 4 highlight some implications of the general commitments under Articles 4(1)(b) and 4(2)(a). Thus, Article 4(1)(d) requires all parties to promote the sustainable management of sinks and reservoirs of GHGs and to cooperate in their conservation and enhancement.[41] Under Article 4(1)(f), all parties must '[t]ake climate change considerations into account, to the extent feasible, in their relevant social, economic and environmental policies and action'[42]—a vague allusion to national environmental impact assessment procedures. In addition, each Annex I parties is required, under Article 4(2)(e), to coordinate with others for the implementation of 'relevant economic and administrative instruments' on climate change mitigation and to 'identify and periodically review its own policies and practices which encourage activities that lead to greater levels' of GHG emissions.[43] Even though these provisions are written in broad and heavily qualified terms, they highlight some possible implications of general mitigation commitments.[44]

[34] Vienna Convention on the Law of Treaties (23 May 1969, in force 27 January 1980) 1155 UNTS 331, art 31(1), (3).
[35] See below at 126.
[36] UNFCCC (n 2) art 4(1)(b).
[37] Ibid art 4(2)(a).
[38] Ibid.
[39] Ibid art 4(2)(b).
[40] See eg Sands (n 30) 174; Bodansky, 'Framework Convention' (n 20) 516; Brunnée (n 29) 194.
[41] UNFCCC (n 2) art 4(1)(d).
[42] Ibid art 4(1)(f).
[43] Ibid art 4(2)(e).
[44] See generally below at 281–320.

While the UNFCCC's objective and principles refer to all GHG emissions, its commitments only apply to those GHGs that are not controlled by the Montreal Protocol on Substances that Deplete the Ozone Layer.[45] This aims to avoid an overlap between two treaty regimes with regard to GHGs that are also ozone-depleting substances.[46] This exclusion concerns various halogens whose production and consumption is regulated by the Montreal Protocol, including its subsequent amendments. As an exception, the UNFCCC does apply to hydrofluorocarbons (HFCs, a class of GHGs), despite their being regulated by the Kigali Amendment to the Montreal Protocol, in application of an express provision of the Amendment.[47]

The UNFCC does not define the territorial scope of these substantive commitments. While the UNFCCC's reporting commitments apply to the emissions that take place within the state's territory,[48] there is no reason to assume that substantive commitments have the same territorial scope.[49] The general presumption that 'a treaty is binding upon each party in respect of its entire territory'[50] implies that the state must take measures within its territory but not necessarily that these measures must only be concerned with the emissions that take place within its territory. Thus, parties have occasionally implemented territorial measures aimed at regulating the production of fossil fuels for export,[51] at limiting international aviation as a source of extraterritorial GHG emissions,[52] or at controlling the operations of a multinational corporation headquartered in its territory.[53]

b) Support

The UNFCCC imposes some commitments on Annex II parties with the aim of assisting developing country parties in adopting and implementing mitigation action and in monitoring and reporting national information. Under Article 4(3), Annex II parties must provide financial resources to developing country parties. These financial resources must be 'new and additional':[54] they must not substitute

[45] UNFCCC (n 2) arts 4(1)–(2). See also Kyoto Protocol (n 3) arts 2, 5, 7, 10.

[46] See below at 78.

[47] Amendment to the Montreal Protocol on Substances that Deplete the Ozone Layer (15 October 2016, in force 1 January 2019) (2017) 56 ILM 193 ('Kigali Amendment') art III. While the Kigali Amendment cannot directly modify the UNFCCC, it may constitute a 'relevant rule . . . of international law applicable in the relations between the parties'. See VCLT (n 34) art 31(3)(c). See also Kyoto Protocol (n 3) Annex A.

[48] See below at 49.

[49] But see *Greenpeace v Netherlands*, ECLI:NL:RBDHA:2020:12440 (DC The Hague, 9 December 2020) ¶4.4; *Natur og Ungdom v Norway*, Case No 20-051052SIV-HRET (SC, 22 December 2020), English translation <https://perma.cc/5PCS-A8YH> ¶159, each asserting that the UNFCCC only requires a party to regulate emissions that take place within its territory.

[50] VCLT (n 34) art 29.

[51] See *Montana Environmental Information Center v US Office of Surface Mining* (DC Montana, 2017) 274 FSupp3d 1074, 1092, 1099; *Gloucester Resources v Minister for Planning* [2019] NSWLEC 7.

[52] See EU, First NDC, Updated (2020) 9; Switzerland, Long-Term Mitigation Strategy (2021) 31, 37.

[53] See *Milieudefensie v Royal Dutch Shell*, ECLI:NL:RBDHA:2021:5337 (DC The Hague, 26 May 2021), English translation <https://perma.cc/VKG6-TZ4A>.

[54] UNFCCC (n 2) art 4(3), first sentence.

to pre-existing or foreseeable transfers of financial resources, in particular on development aid.[55]

Financial assistance under Article 4(3) must cover two types of expenses as agreed with the UNFCCC's financial mechanism.[56] First, this provision covers the 'incremental costs' of mitigation action implemented by developing country parties. The concept of 'incremental costs' was subsequently interpreted as referring to 'additional ... costs on countries beyond the costs that are strictly necessary for achieving their own development goals'[57]—for instance, the higher cost of generating power from renewable energy rather than from (presumably) more affordable energy from fossil fuels.[58] Second, financial resources provided by Annex II parties must also cover the 'full costs' that developing country parties incur to comply with their commitment to communicate national information.[59]

The UNFCCC aims also to facilitate the transfer of technologies. Article 4(1)(c) commits all parties to 'promote and cooperate in the development, application and diffusion, including transfer, of technologies, practices and processes'.[60] More specifically, Article 4(5) commits Annex II parties to 'take all practicable steps to promote, facilitate and finance, as appropriate, the transfer of, or access to, environmentally sound technologies and know-how to other Parties, particularly developing country Parties, to enable them to implement the provisions of the Convention'.[61]

Article 4(7) presents the 'effective implementation' by developed country parties of their commitments on support as a factor defining '[t]he extent to which developing country Parties will effectively implement' their own commitments.[62] This implies that the mitigation commitments of developing country parties, in particular their general commitment under Article 4(1)(b), are conditional—at least in part—to the provision of support by developed country parties. On the other hand, the UNFCCC does not define the concept of 'developing country Parties'.[63] While it is often assumed that any party not listed in Annex I is a developing country,[64] this understanding is not explicitly anchored in the UNFCCC. The use of the expression 'developing country Parties' in Article 4(3), (5), and (7) contrasts

[55] See Yamin and Depledge (n 30) 276–78; Alexander Zahar, *Climate Change Finance and International Law* (Routledge 2016) 25.

[56] UNFCCC (n 2) art 4(3), second sentence. On the financial mechanism, see also ibid art 11.

[57] Global Environment Facility, 'Incremental Costs' (1996) GEF/C.7/Inf.5, ¶2.

[58] As such, measuring incremental costs requires the calculation of a hypothetical baseline. In practice, this can be a challenging exercise.

[59] UNFCCC (n 2) art 4(3), first sentence.

[60] Ibid art 4(1)(c).

[61] Ibid art 4(5).

[62] Ibid art 4(7).

[63] Yamin and Depledge (n 30) 272–75. Nothing in the treaty affirms or necessarily implies that Annex I includes all 'developed' country parties or even that a country party is necessarily either a developed country or a developing country.

[64] See eg Bodansky, 'Framework Convention' (n 20) 506–07; Zahar, *Climate Change Finance* (n 55) 31.

with the more specific notion of parties 'not included in Annex I' in other provisions.[65] As such, what constitutes a 'developing country Party' for the purpose of the UNFCCC provisions on support could be the object of an evolving interpretation in light of subsequent agreements and practice,[66] and the qualification of a state may change depending on its evolving circumstances.

Not unlike the commitments on mitigation action, the commitments on support remain overly general. The main provision, Article 4(3), suggests a goal for Annex II parties—as a group—to provide sufficient financial resources to cover the full agreed costs of reporting and the full agreed incremental costs of implementing mitigation action. Yet, Article 4(3) does not determine the contribution of each Annex II party to the realization of this goal; it merely highlights 'the importance of appropriate burden sharing among the developed country Parties'.[67] This provision is perhaps best understood as creating an obligation for Annex II parties to cooperate in good faith in the determination of agreed costs and their allocation among themselves. This provision is to be interpreted in light of subsequent practice, which indicates how far, and in what ways, each Annex II party may be expected to support mitigation action in developing country parties.

c) Communication of information

Other provisions of the UNFCCC define commitments on the communication of two types of information. First, to facilitate a better understanding of GHG emissions and their evolution, each party must '[d]evelop, periodically update, publish and make available to the [COP] ... national inventories of anthropogenic [GHG emissions], using comparable methodologies to be agreed by the [COP]'.[68] Second, to promote transparency on the implementation of the Convention, each party must communicate '[a] general description of steps taken or envisaged by the Party to implement the Convention'.[69] In addition to the latter, each Annex I party must provide 'detailed information on its policies and measures' on climate change mitigation as well as an estimate of the effects of such policies and measures on the party's GHG emissions and removals.[70] Each Annex II party must also communicate information on the measures it has taken in accordance with its commitments relating to the provision of support to developing country parties.[71]

The UNFCCC defines some of the modalities of these national communications and GHG inventories (eg the timing of initial communications)[72] and

[65] UNFCCC (n 2) art 4(2)(g). See also art 12(5).
[66] VCLT (n 34) art 31(3)(a)–(b). See also n 195.
[67] UNFCCC (n 2) art 4(3), third sentence. See also Decision 7/CP.7, 'Funding under the Convention' (10 November 2001) FCCC/CP/2001/13/Add.1, 43, ¶1(d).
[68] UNFCCC (n 2) art 4(1)(a). See also art 12(1)(a).
[69] Ibid art 12(1)(b). See also art 4(1)(j).
[70] Ibid art 4(2)(b). See also arts 4(2)(c), 12(2).
[71] Ibid art 12(3).
[72] Ibid arts 4(2)(b), 12(5).

refers to future COP decisions to define additional modalities such as their frequency[73] and methodology.[74] Thus, the parties have a treaty obligation to comply with the provisions of COP decisions on this topic.[75] On methodological issues, the relevant COP decisions refer to successive inventory guidelines adopted by the Intergovernmental Panel on Climate Change (IPCC).[76] These guidelines build on the assumption that a party should generally report the emissions that take place within its territory or, when this is impractical (eg for transportation), emissions resulting from the combustion of fuel sold within its territory.[77] As an exception, however, the IPCC guidelines provide that the emissions of international aviation and international shipping 'are to be excluded ... from national totals' and 'should be reported separately'.[78]

Some related commitments concern the production, sharing, and circulation of more general information about climate change. In particular, under Article 4(1)(g), every party commits to promote and cooperate on research, the circulation of information, and education.[79] These obligations are intended to enhance understanding and raise awareness of climate change, thus facilitating long-term cooperation.

2. The Kyoto Protocol

The COP, at its first session (COP1), adopted its first decision to define a mandate for further negotiations aimed at strengthening the commitments of Annex I parties without introducing any new commitments for non-Annex I parties.[80] The outcome of this process, the Kyoto Protocol, was adopted on 11 December 1997

[73] Ibid art 12(5).

[74] Ibid arts 4(1)(a), 12(1)(a).

[75] See above at 39. For instance, with regard to the frequency of national communications, see Decision 1/CP.16, 'The Cancun Agreements: Outcome of the work of the Ad Hoc Working Group on Long-Term Cooperative Action under the Convention' (10–11 December 2010) FCCC/CP/2010/7/Add.1, 2, ¶60(b).

[76] See eg Decision 4/CP.1, 'Methodological Issues' (7 April 1995) FCCC/CP/1995/7/Add.1, 15, ¶¶1(a)–(b).

[77] See IPCC, *Revised Guidelines for National Greenhouse Gas Inventories* vol 1 (IPCC 1996), 'Overview', 5; Kristin Rypdal and others, 'Introduction to the 2006 Guidelines' in Simon Eggleston and others (eds), *Guidelines for National Greenhouse Gas Inventories* (IPCC 2006) 4; Justin Goodwin and others, 'Introduction to National GHG Inventories' in Calvo Buendia and others (eds), *2019 Refinement to the 2006 IPCC Guidelines for National Greenhouse Gas Inventories* vol 1 (IPCC 2019) 6.

[78] IPCC, *Revised Guidelines* (n 77), 'Understanding the Common Reporting Framework', 4; Christina Davies Waldron and others, 'Mobile Combustion' in Eggleston and others (eds) (n 77) 57; Goodwin and others (n 77) 7. See also Decisions 2/CP.17, 'Outcome of the Work of the Ad Hoc Working Group on Long-Term Cooperative Action under the Convention' (11 December 2011) FCCC/CP/2011/9/Add.1, 4, Annex I ¶34; 24/CP.19, 'Revision of the UNFCCC Reporting Guidelines on Annual Inventories for Parties Included in Annex I to the Convention' (22 November 2013) FCCC/CP/2013/10/Add.3, 2, Annex ¶53. See generally below at 82 (aviation) and 85 (ships).

[79] UNFCCC (n 2) art 4(1)(g), 4(1)(i). See also arts 5–6.

[80] Decision 1/CP.1 (n 27).

at COP3 and opened for signature on 16 March 1998; it entered into force on 16 February 2005. Almost all parties to the UNFCCC are parties to the Kyoto Protocol with two notable exceptions: the United States (which signed the Kyoto Protocol but did not ratify it) and Canada (which ratified the Protocol in 2002 but withdrew in 2012).

The Kyoto Protocol aims to enhance the mitigation action of Annex I parties by imposing on them quantified emission limitation and reduction commitments (QELRCs) 'with a view to reducing their overall emissions of such gases by at least 5 percent below 1990 levels in the commitment period 2008 to 2012'.[81] The parties are expected to achieve their QELRCs mainly by implementing policies and measures within their own jurisdiction, but the Kyoto Protocol also sets up three mechanisms that provide some flexibility for parties to trade mitigation outcomes in order to achieve their commitments in more cost-effective ways.[82] Moreover, the Protocol defines commitments regarding the monitoring, reporting, and verification of GHG emissions in order to document implementation.[83] Finally, it establishes a compliance mechanism.[84]

The Kyoto Protocol was designed to allow amendments that would define additional commitment periods.[85] The Doha Amendment created a second commitment period from 2013 to 2020, in which some Annex I parties agreed to additional QELRCs.[86] The Amendment was adopted on 8 December 2012 and it entered into force on 31 December 2020[87]—thus allowing, formally, only a single day for the parties to ensure the achievement of their QELRC over the entire eight-year commitment period.[88] The Kyoto Protocol and its Doha Amendment remain in force following the end of the second commitment period but, when the post-commitment reporting and reviewing processes are completed, the Protocol will become almost entirely irrelevant and will likely either be terminated by decision of the parties or fall progressively into desuetude.

[81] Kyoto Protocol (n 3) art 3(1).

[82] Ibid arts 6, 12, 17.

[83] Ibid art 5.

[84] Ibid art 18.

[85] Ibid arts 20, 21.

[86] Doha Amendment to the Kyoto Protocol (8 December 2012, in force 31 December 2020) C.N.718.2012.TREATIES-XXVII.7.c, art 1A. Japan, New Zealand, and Russia remained party to the Kyoto Protocol but did not agree to an additional QELRC.

[87] See ibid art 2; Kyoto Protocol (n 3) art 20(4), requiring the acceptance of three-quarters of the parties to the Kyoto Protocol for an Amendment to enter into force with regard to these parties.

[88] See Decision 1/CMP.8, 'Amendment to the Kyoto Protocol Pursuant to its Article 3, Paragraph 9 (the Doha Amendment)' (8 December 2012) FCCC/KP/CMP/2012/13/Add.1, 2, ¶6, suggesting that parties 'will implement their commitment' before the entry into force of the Protocol. Yet, this decision is not a source of international law. See discussion in Benoit Mayer, 'The Curious Fate of the Doha Amendment' *EJIL:Talk!* (4 May 2020) <https://perma.cc/D4M5-SP4R>.

a) Mitigation action

The main innovation of the Kyoto Protocol consists in the imposition of quantified mitigation commitments. Under Article 3(1), Annex I parties must

> ensure that their aggregate anthropogenic carbon dioxide equivalent emissions of the greenhouse gases listed in Annex A do not exceed their assigned amounts, calculated pursuant to their quantified emission limitation and reduction commitments inscribed in Annex B and in accordance with the provisions of this Article, with a view to reducing their overall emissions of such gases by at least 5 per cent below 1990 levels in the commitment period 2008 to 2012.[89]

Annex B originally contains two columns: the list of Annex I parties and their respective QELRCs for the first commitment period. QELRCs are expressed as a percentage of the base-year or period applicable to that party (generally its 1990 emissions).[90] The 'assigned amount' of GHG emissions for an Annex I party, under Article 3(1), is calculated by multiplying the party's base-year or period by the percentage inscribed for that party in Annex B and further multiplying this product by five (as the assigned amount applies for a five-year commitment period).[91] The values included in the second column of Annex B vary significantly as a reflection of differences in national circumstances among Annex I parties: these values range from 92 (indicating a commitment to a reduction by 8 per cent) to 108 (a commitment to limit the increase of emissions to 8 per cent).

The Doha Amendment adds Article 3(1 bis), which defines additional QELRCs for Annex I parties, 'with a view to reducing their overall emissions of [GHGs] by at least 18 percent below 1990 levels in the commitment period 2013 to 2020'.[92] These commitments are calculated in a way similar to those applicable in the first commitment period but using the value added in a third column to Annex B (ranging from 76 to 99.5).[93] The Doha Amendment inserts other columns in Annex B to allow parties to mention informal pledges that they have made in application of the Cancun decision.[94] A footnote clarifies that the content of these additional columns 'is not internationally binding under the Kyoto Protocol', by contrast to the QELRCs for the first and second commitment periods, 'which are internationally legally binding'.[95]

[89] Kyoto Protocol (n 3) art 3(1).

[90] Ibid. See also art 3(5), (8); UNFCCC (n 2) art 4(6); Decision 9/CP.2, 'Communications from Parties Included in Annex I to the Convention: Guidelines, Schedule and Process for Consideration' (19 July 1996) FCCC/CP/1996/15/Add.1, 15, ¶5.

[91] Kyoto Protocol (n 3) art 3(7).

[92] Doha Amendment (n 86) art 1C (inserting art 3(1*bis*) in the Kyoto Protocol).

[93] Ibid art 1A.

[94] Decision 1/CP.16 (n 75) ¶¶36, 49.

[95] Doha Amendment (n 86) (fn 1).

The Kyoto Protocol originally applied to the six GHGs (or groups of GHGs) that account for most anthropogenic emissions, and a seventh GHG was added by the Doha Amendment for the second commitment period.[96] The GHGs covered during both commitment periods include carbon dioxide, methane, and nitrous oxide, as well as HFCs. As the UNFCCC regime does not normally apply to GHGs that are regulated under the Montreal Protocol,[97] an exception had to be made when the Kigali Amendment to the Montreal Protocol extended the application of the Montreal Protocol to HFCs.[98] Thus, the Kigali Amendment contains an express provision according to which it is not 'intended to have the effect of excepting hydrofluorocarbons from the scope of' the UNFCCC or the Kyoto Protocol.[99] The relevant emissions covered by the Kyoto Protocol are those that the party reports[100]—that is, generally, those taking place within its territory.[101]

By all accounts, the Kyoto Protocol and the Doha Amendment define 'clear and precise'[102] commitments: parties are required to achieve the emission limitation or reduction indicated in Annex B. On the other hand, parties are let free to decide on the means of implementation. As QELRCs apply to multi-year commitment periods and allow the international transfer of mitigation outcomes, compliance is not disproportionately vulnerable to a sudden increase in GHG emissions at a given time, although it may be affected by more structural economic changes (eg unforeseen rapid economic growth in the global economy over several years). The thirty-six Annex I parties bound by the Kyoto Protocol for the entirety of the first commitment period were all in compliance (often with a comfortable margin), but this was at least in part by luck rather than design. On the one hand, GHG emissions in countries with an economy in transition fell far lower than had generally been expected, allowing plenty of emission allowances to circulate among Annex I parties through the flexibility mechanisms.[103] On the other hand, the 2008 global economic crisis further reduced GHG emissions in Annex I parties during the commitment period.[104]

The Kyoto Protocol creates some other commitments on climate change mitigation. Article 3(2) requires each Annex I party to 'have made demonstrable progress in achieving its commitments' under the Protocol by 2005.[105] In contrast

[96] Ibid art 1(B), adding nitrogen trifluoride (NF3).

[97] See n 45.

[98] Kigali Amendment (n 47) art I.

[99] Ibid art III.

[100] See Kyoto Protocol (n 3) art 5(2).

[101] See n 77.

[102] Daniel Bodansky, Jutta Brunnée, and Lavanya Rajamani, *International Climate Change Law* (OUP 2017) 172.

[103] See eg Yamin and Depledge (n 30) 140; Quirin Schiermeier, 'The Kyoto Protocol: Hot Air' (2012) 491 Nature 656. Annex I parties were allowed, among other things, to exchange Assigned Amount Units under the emissions trading mechanism established under art 17.

[104] See detailed analysis in Igor Shishlov, Romain Morel, and Valentin Bellassen, 'Compliance of the Parties to the Kyoto Protocol in the First Commitment Period' (2016) 16 Climate Policy 768.

[105] Kyoto Protocol (n 3) art 3(2).

with QELRCs, this commitment is vague: the Kyoto Protocol does not define what would constitute 'demonstrable progress' or how such progress should be assessed.[106] In any case, the effectiveness of this obligation was hindered by the late entry into force of the Kyoto Protocol on 16 February 2005. Moreover, Article 2(1)(a) reaffirms the commitment of each Annex I party to implement policies and measures on climate change mitigation and further provides eight illustrations of such policies and measures. Article 2(1)(b) commits Annex I parties to cooperate by taking steps to share experience and exchange information. Article 2(2) commits Annex I parties to pursue limitation or reduction of GHG emissions from aviation and marine bunker fuels working through, respectively, the International Civil Aviation Organization (ICAO) and the International Maritime Organization (IMO). Finally, Article 10 reaffirms existing commitments applicable to all parties under Article 4(1) of the UNFCCC.[107]

b) Communication of information

Article 7 of the Kyoto Protocol expands the reporting obligations of Annex I parties under the UNFCCC in order to facilitate the assessment of compliance with QELRCs. In particular, each of these parties must establish a national registry and provide the 'necessary supplementary information for the purposes of ensuring compliance with Article 3'.[108] Each Annex I party must also provide, as part of its national communications under the UNFCCC, 'the supplementary information necessary to demonstrate compliance with its commitments under this Protocol'.[109] The parties must fulfil these commitments in accordance with the relevant decisions adopted by the COP and by the Meeting of the Parties to the Protocol.[110]

3. The Paris Agreement

The text of the Paris Agreement was adopted by decision 1/CP.21 on 12 December 2015; it was opened for signature on 22 April 2016, and it entered into force on 4 November 2016. The Paris Agreement has been ratified by almost every party to the UNFCCC.[111] The United States accepted the treaty on 3 September 2016 under the Obama administration, withdrew from it with effect on 4 November 2020

[106] For a general assessment of compliance in fact limited to a description of the steps taken by parties, see generally UNFCCC SBI, 'Synthesis of Reports Demonstrating Progress in Accordance with Article 3, Paragraph 2, of the Kyoto Protocol', FCCC/SBI/2006/INF.2 (9 May 2006); Decision 7/CMP.3, 'Demonstration of Progress in Achieving Commitments under the Kyoto Protocol by Parties Included in Annex I to the Convention' (14–15 December 2007) FCCC/KP/CMP/2007/9/Add.1, 23.

[107] Kyoto Protocol (n 3) art 10(b)(i).

[108] Ibid art 7(1).

[109] Ibid art 7(2).

[110] Ibid arts 7(1), 7(3).

[111] The only exceptions, as of May 2022, are Eritrea, Iran, Libya, and Yemen.

under the Trump administration, and eventually accepted it again on 20 January 2021 under the Biden administration.[112]

There is no reason to doubt that the Paris Agreement is a treaty within the meaning of the Vienna Convention on the Law of Treaties, that is, 'an international agreement concluded between States in written form and governed by international law'.[113] That the Paris Agreement is governed by international law is evidenced by its provisions on its entry into force, its registration with a Depository (the UN Secretary-General), and its procedure for dispute settlement, among other things.[114] As a treaty, the Paris Agreement is a source of international law: the obligations it defines are binding upon its parties under international law.[115]

The Paris Agreement is not expressly characterized as a 'protocol' to the UNFCCC, but this does not seem to affect its status in any way.[116] Like a Protocol, the Paris Agreement was adopted by the COP and situated 'under the [UNFCCC]';[117] it aims for the 'pursuit of the objective of the Convention' and it is 'guided by its principles'.[118] Like the Kyoto Protocol, the Paris Agreement builds on institutions and processes established by the UNFCCC,[119] and participation is limited to the parties to the UNFCCC.[120]

Article 2(1) of the Paris Agreement recognizes the need to 'strengthen the global response to the threat of climate change'. More specifically, Article 2(1)(a) defines the objective of the Paris Agreement on climate change mitigation as follows:

> Holding the increase in the global average temperature to well below 2°C above pre-industrial levels and pursuing efforts to limit the temperature increase to 1.5°C above pre-industrial levels.[121]

[112] See respectively the Depositary Notifications C.N.612.2016.TREATIES-XXVII.7.d (3 September 2016), C.N.575.2019.TREATIES-XXVII.7.d (4 November 2019), C.N.10.2021.TREATIES-XXVII.7.d (20 January 2021).

[113] VCLT (n 34) art 2(1)(a). See also Daniel Bodansky, 'The Paris Climate Change Agreement: A New Hope?' (2016) 110 AJIL 288, 296; Jacob Werksman, 'Remarks on the International Legal Character of the Paris Agreement' (2019) 34 Maryland JIL 343, 354. Some domestic legal systems admit a difference between a treaty (subject to ratification) and other types of international agreements (subject to simplified procedures of acceptance or approval), but the distinction does not exist at the international level.

[114] See UNFCCC (n 2) arts 20, 29, 24, respectively. See also *Maritime Delimitation in the Indian Ocean (Somalia v Kenya)*, Judgment on Preliminary Objections (2 February 2017), [2017] ICJ Rep 3, ¶42.

[115] VCLT (n 34) art 26. For a clear example of an obligation, see Paris Agreement (n 4) art 4(2), first sentence.

[116] Werksman (n 113) 354.

[117] Decision 1/CP.21, 'Adoption of the Paris Agreement' (12 December 2015) FCCC/CP/2015/10/Add.1, 2, ¶1.

[118] Paris Agreement (n 4) Preamble ¶4.

[119] See ibid arts 16–19.

[120] Ibid arts 20(1), 28(3).

[121] Ibid art 2(1)(a).

Article 4(1) further flags some milestones that appear as the logical implications of this objective:

> Parties aim to reach global peaking of greenhouse gas emissions as soon as possible ... and to undertake rapid reductions thereafter in accordance with best available science, so as to achieve a balance between anthropogenic [GHG] emissions by sources and removals by sinks of greenhouse gases in the second half of this century.[122]

These provisions define the treaty's objectives, but they do not create commitments. As the International Court of Justice (ICJ) held in *Oil Platforms*, provisions defining a treaty's objective may 'throw light on the interpretation of [its other] provisions', and they are 'thus not without legal significance'[123]—but they do not create any obligations by themselves. Thus, as the UK Supreme Court pointed out, 'the Paris Agreement did not impose an obligation on any state to adopt a binding domestic target to ensure that those objectives were met'.[124]

Article 3 introduces the tool on which the Paris Agreement relies to pursue its objectives, namely, 'nationally determined contributions to the global response to climate change' (NDCs). The Article suggests that, as their NDCs, 'all Parties are to undertake and communicate ambitious efforts ... with the view to achieving the purpose of this Agreement'.[125] The phase 'are to', by contrast to 'shall', indicates that this provision is declaratory of existing obligations rather than constitutive of new commitments.[126] In other words, Article 3 does not create any new obligation; it merely reflects the fact that parties already have obligations to communicate and implement ambitious efforts. The sources of this obligation include the general mitigation obligations arising under Article 4(1)(b) and 4(2)(a) of the UNFCCC and under customary international law. This general obligation is specified by the commitments defined by other provisions of the Paris Agreement.

As far as these commitments on climate change mitigation are concerned, the key provision of the Paris Agreement is Article 4(2), whose two sentences create two distinct obligations, discussed at greater length below. The first sentence requires all parties to communicate NDCs—this could be qualified as a procedural

[122] Ibid art 4(1).

[123] *Oil Platforms (Iran v US)*, Judgment on Preliminary Objections (12 December 1996), [1996] ICJ Rep 803, ¶31.

[124] *R (Friends of the Earth) v Heathrow* [2020] UKSC 52, [2021] 2 All ER 967, ¶71. See generally Lavanya Rajamani and Jacob Werksman, 'The Legal Character and Operational Relevance of the Paris Agreement's Temperature Goal' (2018) 376 Philos Trans R Soc A 2016.0458; Benoit Mayer, 'Temperature Targets and State Obligations on the Mitigation of Climate Change' (2021) 33 JEL 585.

[125] Paris Agreement (n 4) art 3.

[126] Cf Alexander Zahar, 'Collective Obligation and Individual Ambition in the Paris Agreement' (2020) 9 TEL 165, 169. Neither the French version ('il incombe') nor the Chinese version ('将') supports an interpretation of art 3 as creating an obligation.

commitment. The second sentence obligates all parties to take the measures necessary to achieve their NDCs—a more substantive commitment.

The Paris Agreement does not specifically refer to any GHGs (by contrast to the Kyoto Protocol), nor does it expressly exclude from its scope the GHGs regulated under the Montreal Protocol (by contrast to the UNFCCC). As such, it belongs in principle to each party to decide which GHGs are included within the scope of its NDC.[127] Yet, to the extent that NDCs are expected to include 'economy-wide' targets (eg for developed country parties),[128] they should cover at least the GHGs that contribute the most to the party's aggregate emissions. Likewise, the Paris Agreement is silent on the territorial scope of NDCs.

Some other provisions create commitments for developed country parties relating to the provision of support to developing country parties.[129] The Paris Agreement also imposes new obligations on the gathering, communication, and circulation of information relating to climate change mitigation as part of an 'enhanced transparency framework'.[130]

On the institutional and procedural side, the Paris Agreement defines two mechanisms for the international transfer of mitigation outcomes, which provide some flexibility for states to implement their NDCs.[131] Another mechanism is created 'to facilitate implementation of and promote compliance with the provisions of this Agreement'.[132] Finally, the Agreement establishes a process for the Conference of the Parties serving as the Meeting of the Parties to the Paris Agreement (CMA) to 'take stock of the implementation of this Agreement and its long-term goals (referred to as the "global stocktake")'.[133] This global stocktake 'shall inform Parties in updating and enhancing' their NDCs.[134]

a) Mitigation action

NDCs have often been described as 'voluntary' in nature, a statement which can cause some confusion.[135] Parties indeed determine the content of their NDC by themselves, but they do have an obligation to adopt an NDC. Overall, once a party has communicated its NDC, it is bound to implement the necessary measures to

[127] Paris Agreement (n 4) art 4(8); Decision 4/CMA.1, 'Further Guidance in Relation to the Mitigation Section of Decision 1/CP.21' (15 December 2018) FCCC/PA/CMA/2018/3/Add.1, 6, Annex ¶3(b). See also, by implication, Decision 18/CMA.1, 'Modalities, Procedures and Guidelines for the Transparency Framework for Action and Support Referred to in Article 13 of the Paris Agreement' (15 December 2018) FCCC/PA/CMA/2018/3/Add.2, 18, Annex ¶48.

[128] See below at 55.

[129] See in particular Paris Agreement (n 4) art 9(1).

[130] Ibid art 13.

[131] Ibid art 6(2), 6(4).

[132] Ibid art 15(1).

[133] Ibid art 14(1).

[134] Ibid art 14(3).

[135] See Richard Falk, '"Voluntary" International Law and the Paris Agreement', *Global Justice in the 21st Century* (16 January 2016) https://perma.cc/XK8H-623Q; Tess Bridgeman, 'Paris Is a Binding Agreement: Here's Why That Matters' *Just Security* (4 June 2017) <https://perma.cc/3J9C-7EMH>.

ensure the realization of its mitigation objectives: in that sense, the frequent description of NDCs as 'non-binding' is a mischaracterization. The following distinguishes, for the purpose of exposition, between a procedural commitment to communicate NDCs and a substantive commitment to implement appropriate measures.

(i) Procedural commitment

The Paris Agreement relies on an explicit 'bottom-up' architecture, whereby each party determines its own contribution to global efforts on climate change mitigation.[136] As such, an essential element of the Paris Agreement is its emphasis on the commitment of each party to adopt national mitigation objectives. Article 3 notes that 'Parties are to undertake and communicate ambitious efforts' on climate change mitigation, adaptation, support, and transparency '[a]s nationally determined contributions to the global response to climate change'.[137] In addition to the general commitments under the UNFCCC,[138] the first sentence of Article 4(2) of the Paris Agreement requires each party to 'prepare, communicate and maintain successive nationally determined contributions that it intends to achieve'.[139]

Further modalities of this procedural commitment are defined under several provisions of Article 4, often referring to COP and CMA decisions, sometimes requiring the parties to comply with these decisions. According to Article 4(9), NDCs must be communicated every five years.[140] This provision refers to decision 1/CP.21 and subsequent CMA decisions to specify the time at which NDCs must be communicated.[141] Article 4(10) calls on the CMA to 'consider common time frames' (ie the time to which the NDC applies), but parties are not expressly required to comply with CMA decisions on this topic.[142]

Overall, Article 4(8) commits (using 'shall') all parties to 'provide the information necessary for clarity, transparency and understanding' in accordance with decision 1/CP.21 and any relevant CMA decisions.[143] Decision 1/CP.21, however, only lists elements that NDCs '*may* include', thus not imposing any requirement on parties.[144] By contrast, decision 4/CMA.1 creates secondary law when stating

[136] This is often opposed to the would-be 'top down' approach to the Kyoto Protocol. In reality, the QELRCs were often defined by the parties to which they would apply, in particular in the negotiations leading to the adoption of the Doha Amendment. See discussion in Michael Grubb, 'Full Legal Compliance with the Kyoto Protocol's First Commitment Period: Some Lessons' (2016) 16 Climate Policy 673, 675.

[137] Paris Agreement (n 4) art 3.

[138] UNFCCC (n 2) arts 4(1)(b), 4(2)(a).

[139] Paris Agreement (n 4) art 4(2), first sentence.

[140] Ibid art 4(9).

[141] Ibid. See also Decision 1/CP.21 (n 117) ¶¶23–25.

[142] Paris Agreement (n 4) art 4(10). See also Decision 6/CMA.3, 'Common Time Frames for Nationally Determined Contributions Referred to in Article 4, paragraph 10, of the Paris Agreement' (13 November 2021) FCCC/PA/CMA/2021/10/Add.3 (advanced version), 3.

[143] Paris Agreement (n 4) art 4(8).

[144] Decision 1/CP.21 (n 117) ¶27 (emphasis added).

that each party 'shall provide' certain information in its second and subsequent NDCs[145]—including information on the reference point, time frames, scope and coverage, planning process, assumptions, and methodological approaches and on how the party considers that its NDC is fair and ambitious and contributes towards achieving the collective objectives of climate treaties.[146]

The Paris Agreement does not oblige a party to communicate an NDC when it ratifies the treaty. Decision 1/CP.21 merely invites parties to communicate their first NDC when submitting their instrument of ratification.[147] In reality, most UNFCCC parties had communicated their intended NDCs (INDCs) prior to COP21[148] and, according to Decision 1/CP.21, a party's INDCs would be considered as that party's first NDC when that party joins the Paris Agreement, 'unless that Party decides otherwise'.[149] Nevertheless, a few parties without INDCs ratified the Paris Agreement without submitting an NDC, thus finding themselves in an odd situation, albeit presumably a transitory one given their commitment to communicate an NDC every five years.[150]

The Paris Agreement contains several provisions relating to the ambition of NDCs, but none of these provisions creates any particularly constraining obligation. Article 4(9) commits parties, when communicating new NDCs, to 'be informed by the outcomes of the global stocktake'.[151] Other provisions express mere recommendations or expectations without legal force. Thus, Article 4(4) suggests that developed country parties '*should* continue taking the lead by undertaking economy-wide absolute emission reduction targets', while developing country parties '*are encouraged to* move over time towards economy-wide emission reduction or limitation targets'.[152] Likewise, no commitment arises under Article 4(3), according to which each party's successive NDC 'will ... reflect its highest possible ambition'.[153] The word 'will' points to an expectation; it does not suggest that the parties consented to a legal commitment. Nonetheless, this provision could be relevant to the interpretation of a state's due diligence obligation.[154] English judges suggested that 'the assessment of [a Party's] appropriate contribution will be complex

[145] Decision 4/CMA.1 (n 127) ¶7.

[146] Ibid Annex I ¶¶6–7. See generally Meinhard Doelle, 'The Heart of the Paris Rulebook: Communicating NDCs and Accounting for Their Implementation' (2019) 9 Climate Law 3, 6.

[147] Decision 1/CP.21 (n 117) ¶22.

[148] UNFCCC Secretariat, 'Synthesis Report on the Aggregate Effect of the Intended Nationally Determined Contributions', FCCC/CP/2015/7 (2015) ¶8.

[149] Decision 1/CP.21 (n 117) ¶22.

[150] See n 140. For instance, the Philippines ratified the Paris Agreement in March 2017 but did not communicate its first NDC until April 2021.

[151] See n 134.

[152] Ibid art 4(4) (emphasis added).

[153] Ibid art 4(3). See also art 3.

[154] See eg Christina Voigt, 'The Paris Agreement: What Is the Standard of Conduct for Parties?' (2016) 18 QIL 17, 21, suggesting that this provision indicates a high standard of due diligence.

and a matter of high level policy for the national government'.[155] The availability of judicial remedies, whether before domestic or international courts, will depend on the willingness of a court to mingle with such complex policy assessments.[156]

It has frequently been suggested that the Paris Agreement affirms a 'principle of progression'.[157] Yet, no provision of the Paris Agreement defines any clear legal commitment to progression.[158] Article 3 expresses merely an expectation that '[t]he efforts of all Parties will represent a progression over time'.[159] Likewise, Article 4(3) notes that each party's successive NDC 'will represent a progression beyond the Party's then current [NDC]'.[160] Neither of these provisions is expressed in terms that indicate the intention of the parties to enter into a legal obligation. These provisions are at most indications of a standard of due diligence. In practical terms, assessing progression could reveal a challenging task when, for instance, a state communicates a new target for a different period, applicable to different sectors, using different methodologies, or relying to a different extent on the international transfer of mitigation outcomes. At any rate, it is unclear whether progression would be assessed based on the overall amount of GHG emissions, on per capita emissions, on GDP intensity, or on the intensity of the party's effort to limit or reduce these emissions, among other alternative ways of accounting for a party's ambition. If referring to the absolute level of emissions, a strict requirement of progression could lead to unjust or untenable conclusions, for instance when a country is facing substantial changes in national circumstances (eg mass immigration or rapid economic growth) that make it increasingly difficult to maintain its level of emission.

Different rules apply to adjustments to existing NDCs (ie within the five-year period between the submission of two successive NDCs). Article 4(11) expressly allows a party to adjust its NDC 'at any time ... with a view to enhancing its level of ambition'.[161] This provision is to be interpreted following the principle of effectiveness (*effet utile*)—that is, 'in such a way that a reason and a meaning can be attributed to every part of the text'[162] and following the presumption that 'the treaty terms were intended to mean something, rather than nothing'.[163] Article 4(11)

[155] *R (Plan B Earth) v Secretary of State for Transport*, [2020] EWCA Civ 214, [2019] All ER (D) 11 (May) ¶607. While the judgment was reversed in appeal, the Supreme Court appeared to agree with this particular point. See *Friends of the Earth* (n 124) ¶71.

[156] See below at 227–280.

[157] See eg UN Secretary-General, 'Gaps in International Environmental Law and Environment-Related Instruments: Towards a Global Pact for the Environment', A/73/419 (30 November 2018) ¶22.

[158] On progression as part of a duty of consistency, see below at 312.

[159] Paris Agreement (n 4) art 3.

[160] Ibid art 4(3).

[161] Ibid art 4(11).

[162] Gerald Fitzmaurice, 'The Law and Procedure of the International Court of Justice 1951-4: Treaty Interpretation and Other Treaty Points' (1957) 33 BYBIL 203, 211.

[163] Mark E Villiger, *Commentary on the 1969 Vienna Convention on the Law of Treaties* (Martinus Nijhoff 2008) 425. See also *Corfu Channel (UK v Albania)*, Judgment on Merits (9 April 1949), [1949] ICJ Rep 4, 24; *Reparation for Injuries Suffered in the Service of the United Nations*, Advisory Opinion (11 April 1949), [1949] ICJ Rep 174, 179; *Fisheries Jurisdiction (Spain v Canada)*, Judgment

would be meaningless if any adjustment, whether upward or downward, was allowed at any time from any party anyway. A related tenet of treaty interpretation is that the express mention of one thing suggests the exclusion of others: *expressio unius est exclusio alterius*.[164] Accordingly, the mention of the possibility of upward adjustments suggests that downward adjustments are not generally permitted. Therefore, while the Paris Agreement does not require parties to maintain or enhance their level of ambition in successive NDCs, it does not normally allow them to reduce the ambition of an existing NDC at any time.[165] However, this interpretation of Article 4(11) may permit some exceptions where downward adjustment would be permitted—such would arguably be the case when a party faces extraneous unforeseen circumstances that make the achievement of the NDC significantly more difficult that initially envisaged.[166]

(ii) Substantive commitment

The second sentence of Article 4(2) provides that 'Parties shall pursue domestic mitigation measures, with the aim of achieving the objectives of' their successive NDCs. This provision, succinct but somewhat cryptic, is the main anchor of NDCs in the Paris Agreement.

The word 'shall' is generally used, in a treaty, to create an obligation. Nevertheless, Bodansky argues that this provision 'does not create an individual obligation on each Party' because its subject is in the plural form ('Parties', rather than 'each Party').[167] By contrast, Rajamani suggests that this provision applies to each individual party because 'it is framed by the first sentence' of the same paragraph (which applies to '[e]ach Party') and 'flows from it'.[168] Yet, there is no reason to assume that what applies to the first sentence of Article 4(2) also applies to the second sentence; one could argue just as well, siding with Bodansky, that the contrast between the singular in the first sentence and the plural in the second sentence indicates that a distinction was intended to be made between these two provisions.

on Jurisdiction and Admissibility (4 December 1998), [1998] ICJ Rep 432, ¶52; *Application of the International Convention on the Elimination of All Forms of Racial Discrimination (Georgia v Russia)*, Judgment on Preliminary Objections (11 April 2011), [2011] ICJ Rep 70, ¶¶133–34; Robert Jennings and Arthur Watts (eds), *Oppenheim's International Law: Volume 1 Peace* (9th edn, OUP 2008) §633(9) (*Oppenheim's*).

164 See *Oppenheim's* (n 163) §633(5); Anthony Aust, *Modern Treaty Law and Practice* (3rd edn, CUP 2014) 221.

165 See Lavanya Rajamani and Jutta Brunnée, 'The Legality of Downgrading Nationally Determined Contributions under the Paris Agreement: Lessons from the US Disengagement' (2017) 29 JEL 537; Benoit Mayer, 'Article 4', in Geert van Calster and Leonie Reins (eds), *The Paris Agreement on Climate Change: A Commentary* (EE 2021) 117.

166 There is no reason to assume that these circumstances would necessarily meet the high threshold to qualify as circumstances precluding wrongfulness. Cf Rajamani and Brunnée (n 165) 548.

167 Daniel Bodansky, 'The Legal Character of the Paris Agreement' (2016) 25 RECIEL 142, 146.

168 Lavanya Rajamani, 'The 2015 Paris Agreement: Interplay between Hard, Soft and Non-Obligations' (2016) 28 JEL 337, 354 (fn 69).

If Bodansky's argument is unconvincing, it is for another reason. As noted, the word 'shall' is a strong suggestion that the sentence creates an obligation. By contrast, Bodansky's argument relies merely on the ambivalence of the plural in the English version of the treaty. It is noteworthy that the equally authentic Chinese version of the treaty makes no distinction between singular and plural when referring to 'Parties' in Article 4(2) and, thus, does not support the contrasting interpretation between the two sentences of this paragraph that Bodansky suggests.[169] At any rate, it is quite common for a treaty provision to be phrased in the plural to indicate an obligation applicable to each individual component of a group—prominent examples include the obligations that the UN Charter imposes on the UN 'Members'[170] and those that the UN Convention on the Law of the Sea applies to 'States'.[171] Likewise (as Bodansky concedes), the Paris Agreement contains several provisions applicable to 'Parties' and using the word 'shall' that can only be understood, given their context, as denoting an obligation applicable to each party.[172] Therefore, altogether, the phrase 'Parties shall' is more consistently interpreted as 'each Party shall' than as 'Parties should'.

Two provisions of the Paris Agreement confirm the existence of a substantive mitigation obligation. First, as noted above, Article 3 notes that parties 'are to undertake and communicate ambitious efforts' contained in their NDCs.[173] While the phrase 'are to' is declaratory rather than constitutive, it does confirm the interpretation of the second sentence of Article 4(2) as requiring states to implement measures devised to achieve the objective of their NDCs. Second, the first sentence of Article 4(2) requires each party to prepare, communicate, and maintain successive NDCs 'that it intends to achieve'.[174] The mention of this intent to achieve does not create any obligations to achieve; rather, it merely reflects an expectation that each party will take the requisite measures to achieve its NDC.[175] This phrase broadly supports the interpretation of the second sentence of Article 4(2) as creating a substantive obligation to implement NDCs rather than an alternative interpretation of the treaty as creating no substantive mitigation obligation.[176]

169 See Paris Agreement (n 4) art 29. See also VCLT (n 34) art 33(4).

170 Charter of the United Nations (26 June 1945, in force 24 October 1945) arts 25, 56.

171 United Nations Convention on the Law of the Sea (10 December 1982, in force 16 November 1994) 1833 UNTS 3, arts 192, 194.

172 See Paris Agreement (n 4) arts 4(13), 6(2), 9(5), 13(9). See also Sandrine Maljean-Dubois and Lavanya Rajamani, 'L'Accord de Paris sur les changements climatiques du 12 décembre 2015' (2015) 61 AFDI 615; Harald Winkler, 'Mitigation (Article 4)' in Daniel Klein and others (eds), *The Paris Agreement on Climate Change: Analysis and Commentary* (OUP 2017) 147.

173 See n 126.

174 Paris Agreement (n 4) art 4(2), first sentence.

175 See Rajamani, 'Interplay' (n 168) 354.

176 See also Canada Net-Zero Emissions Accountability Act, SC, 2021, c22, Preamble ¶3, interpreting the Paris Agreement as creating a commitment to 'undertake ambitious national measures for climate change mitigation'.

Contemplating that Article 4(2), second sentence, could create a legal obligation, Bodansky suggested that it should be read as containing two unrelated clauses, severed by a comma: the pursuance of 'domestic mitigation measures' would be the object of the obligation, whereas the 'aim of achieving the objectives' of NDCs would be purely contextual or explanatory.[177] Bodansky thus suggests that this sentence merely reaffirms parties' general commitment under Article 4(1)(b) of the UNFCCC.[178] However, it is far from clear that a comma could have the effect of entirely isolating the obligation in the first clause from the mention of NDCs in the second clause of the same sentence. Here again, this interpretation appears inconsistent with two of the six equally authentic versions of the treaty:[179] the Arabic and French texts, which do not use any comma within the second sentence of Article 4(2). As such, even if the English version could be considered ambivalent, the meaning 'which best reconciles the texts'[180] is one that reads the second sentence of Article 4(2) as requiring each party to pursue domestic mitigation measures that aim to achieve the objectives of NDCs.

Thus, the mitigation objectives of successive NDCs are to be read as a qualifier of the obligation of states to pursue mitigation measures. This means that each party must implement measures which, the party has reasonable grounds to believe, will achieve the objective of its NDC—in plain English, the necessary measures to achieve its NDC.[181] This interpretation is consistent with Articles 4(1)(b) of the UNFCCC, which requires a party, once it has communicated a programme on climate change mitigation, to implement it, and with Article 4(2)(a), which requires an Annex I party, once it has communicated a policy on climate change mitigation, to 'take corresponding measures'.[182] On the other hand, the obligation under the Paris Agreement relates only to the main objective on climate change mitigation contained in the party's NDC and not to the additional sectorial targets that a party may also have communicated when describing the measures it intends to implement. When the party's NDC contains several mitigation goals which are not (or not entirely) redundant (for instance, goals covering different sectors or gases), it should be assumed that the mitigation 'objective', for the purpose of Article 4(2), includes all these goals.[183]

As Christina Voigt suggested, this provision implies that the parties to the Paris Agreement must take 'the reasonable measures which a well-administered government could be expected to adopt under similar circumstances'.[184] Chapter V will

177 Bodansky, 'Legal Character' (n 167) 150.

178 Ibid.

179 Paris Agreement (n 4) art 29.

180 VCLT (n 34) art 33(4).

181 Benoit Mayer, 'International Law Obligations Arising in Relation to Nationally Determined Contributions' (2018) 7 TEL 251, 261.

182 See above at 41.

183 See eg China, First NDC (2016) 5, defining four independent goals.

184 Voigt (n 154) 19, citing Alwyn V Freeman, 'Responsibility of States for Unlawful Acts of their Armed Forces' (1955) 88 RdC 263, 277–78.

show that this language creates an obligation of conduct—a commitment to strive towards a result without guaranteeing its achievement.[185] An obligation of conduct is not necessarily weaker than an obligation of result (ie an obligation to achieve the result), as often assumed.[186] While an obligation of conduct is less demanding in the sense that the party does not need to achieve the result, it is also more demanding in the sense that the mere achievement of the result (eg by luck or external intervention) may not be sufficient to demonstrate compliance.

The difference between obligations of conduct and obligations of result depends on the ability of the duty-holder to take effective measures to achieve the outcome. A doctor's obligation of due diligence is certainly no guarantee of prompt recovery for their patients for there are medical conditions that a doctor's best endeavours cannot cure. By contrast, there may only be few circumstances where a state, having made its best endeavours, would really be unable to achieve the mitigation objective contained in its NDC. While the state may face difficulties in reducing emissions within its own territory, it could in principle rely on mechanisms for the international transfer of mitigation outcomes to make up for any shortfalls.[187] Thus, if economic growth results in an unforeseen increase in GHG emissions, the party should also be able to set aside the necessary funding to enhance domestic mitigation action or, on the shorter term, purchase mitigation outcomes from other countries. A conceivable exception would be a situation of warfare, where the party increases significantly its economic production and yet is unable to set aside the necessary financial resources to enhance its mitigation action or purchase mitigation outcomes from overseas.[188] In most circumstances, however, the UK Supreme Court's interpretation of the Paris Agreement as creating an obligation 'to meet any NDC applicable to the state' is a close enough approximation.[189]

b) Support

The Paris Agreement defines commitments relating to support to mitigation action in developing countries. Article 4(5) declares that '[s]upport shall be provided to developing country Parties' for the implementation of other provisions of this article.[190] As it uses the passive voice without specifying the agent, however, this provision does not impose onto any party an obligation to provide such support. It does nonetheless refer to Articles 9, 10, and 11, which contain more

[185] See Voigt (n 154); Annalisa Savaresi, 'The Paris Agreement: A New Beginning?' (2016) 34 JERL 16; Winkler (n 172) 146; Charlotte Streck, Paul Keenlyside, and Moritz von Unger, 'The Paris Agreement: A New Beginning' (2016) 13 JEEPL 3, 13; Benoit Mayer, 'Obligations of Conduct in the International Law on Climate Change: A Defence' (2018) 27 RECIEL 130.

[186] See Bodansky, 'A New Hope?' (n 113) 304; Peter Lawrence and Daryl Wong, 'Soft Law in the Paris Climate Agreement: Strength or Weakness?' (2017) 26 RECIEL 276, 280.

[187] See n 131.

[188] Such circumstances would often, albeit not necessarily, fall within the scope of circumstances precluding wrongfulness, such as force majeure or necessity.

[189] *Friends of the Earth* (n 124) ¶71. See also ibid ¶122.

[190] Paris Agreement (n 4) art 4(5).

specific provisions, respectively, on financial assistance, the transfer of technologies, and capacity-building. Article 9(1) states that '[d]eveloped country Parties shall provide financial resources to assist developing country Parties ... in continuation of their existing obligations under the Convention'.[191] This provision creates an obligation on each developed country party, even though it does not specify the amount or the form of financial assistance that must be provided by each party. Likewise, Article 10(2) imposes a vague obligation for parties to 'strengthen co-operative action on technology development and transfer',[192] while noting that '[s]upport, including financial support, shall be provided to developing country Parties for the implementation' of this article.[193] Article 11(5) declares that '[c]apacity-building activities shall be enhanced through appropriate institutional arrangements',[194] but here again, the passive voice avoids imposing a commitment for any party to engage in such activities.

These provisions are to be read in the context of the UNFCCC provisions on support, in particular Articles 4(3) and 4(5).[195] An important difference between Article 4(3) of the UNFCCC and Article 9(1) of the Paris Agreement is the personal scope: the UNFCCC commitment applies to Annex II parties, while the commitment under the Paris Agreement applies more vaguely to 'developed country Parties', a term that the treaty leaves undefined. As there is no reason to assume that Article 9(1) of the Paris Agreement only reaffirms Article 4(3) of the UNFCCC, 'developed country Parties' in Article 9(1) should in principle be given its ordinary meaning in the context of climate negotiations—thus, potentially including some non-Annex II parties.[196] Yet, several parties with an economy in transition made interpretative declarations on the Paris Agreement, suggesting that, in light of Article 4(3) of the UNFCCC, Article 9(1) of the Paris Agreement should be construed as applying only to Annex II parties.[197] Such interpretative declarations cannot modify the treaty (to which reservations are not permitted),[198] but they 'may be taken into account' when interpreting it.[199] As such, there remains significant uncertainty as to the personal scope of the commitment under Article 9(1) of the Paris Agreement beyond the parties listed in Annex II of the UNFCCC.

[191] Ibid art 9(1).
[192] Ibid art 10(2).
[193] Ibid art 10(6).
[194] Ibid art 11(5).
[195] See n 66.
[196] See eg VCLT (n 34) art 9(1); *Oppenheim's* (n 163) §632(2)–(3).
[197] See the declaration by the declarations made by Bulgaria, Poland, and Russia in connection to the Paris Agreement.
[198] See Paris Agreement (n 4) art 27.
[199] See generally *Belilos v Switzerland*, Application No 10328/83, Report of the European Commission of Human Rights (7 May 1986), ECLI:CE:ECHR:1986:0507REP001032883, ¶102; DM McRae, 'The Legal Effect of Interpretative Declarations' (1979) 49 BYBIL 155, 160; ILC, 'Guide to Practice on Reservations to Treaties' [2011] II(3) YBILC 35, guideline 4.7.1 and its commentary.

c) Communication of information

The Paris Agreement imposes commitments relating to the communication of information relevant to mitigation action and support. Under Article 4(13), parties must account for their NDCs.[200] In doing so, they must 'promote environmental integrity, transparency, accuracy, completeness, comparability and consistency, and ensure the avoidance of double counting, in accordance with guidance adopted by the [CMA]'.[201] This provision delegates power to the CMA to adopt the rule on accounting for NDCs that parties must follow. The word 'guidance', however, suggests that these rules should not be overly specific, or else that parties should be given some flexibility when implementing them.[202]

Moreover, developed country parties commit, under Article 9, to provide information *ex ante* and *ex post* in relation on the provision of financial assistance to developing country parties. Thus, under Article 9(5), developed country parties must 'communicate indicative quantitative and qualitative information'[203] related to the provision and mobilization of financial assistance. There is no formal treaty requirement for parties to comply with subsequent CMA decisions that identify the information to be provided in accordance with Article 9(5).[204] On the other hand, Article 9(7) binds developed country parties to provide 'transparent and consistent information on support for developing country Parties provided and mobilized through public interventions' in accordance with the rules included in subsequent CMA decisions.[205] Moreover, Article 11 requires '[a]ll Parties enhancing the capacity of developing country Parties to implement this Agreement' to 'regularly communicate on these actions or measures on capacity-building'.[206]

Overall, Article 13 of the Paris Agreement establishes an 'enhanced transparency framework for action and support'[207] which should 'build on and enhance the transparency arrangements under the Convention'.[208] According to Article 13(7), 'each Party' must 'regularly provide' a national GHG inventory and information necessary to track progress made in implementing and achieving its NDC under Article 4.[209] In addition, Article 13(9) reaffirms the commitment of developed country parties to communicate information on the support provided to developing country parties.[210] Following a technical expert review for their biennial

[200] Paris Agreement (n 4) art 4(13).

[201] Ibid. See Decision 4/CMA.1 (n 127) ¶¶11–15, Annex II.

[202] Bodansky, Brunnée, and Rajamani (n 102) 232–33.

[203] Paris Agreement (n 4) art 9(5).

[204] See Decision 12/CMA.1, 'Identification of the Information to Be Provided by Parties in Accordance with Article 9, Paragraph 5, of the Paris Agreement' (15 December 2018) FCCC/PA/CMA/2018/3/Add.1, 35. See also Decision 1/CP.21 (n 117) ¶55; Hao Zhang, 'Implementing Provisions on Climate Finance under the Paris Agreement' (2019) 9 Climate Law 21.

[205] Paris Agreement (n 4) art 9(7). See also Decision 18/CMA.1 (n 127) Annex pt V.C.

[206] Paris Agreement (n 4) art 11(4).

[207] Ibid art 13(1).

[208] Ibid art 13(3).

[209] Ibid art 13(7).

[210] Ibid art 13(9).

transparency reports, each party is to 'participate in a facilitative, multilateral consideration of progress' focusing on 'its ... implementation and achievement of its [NDC]'.[211]

The Paris Agreement calls on the CMA to adopt 'common modalities, procedures and guidelines' (MPGs),[212] but it does not impose a general obligation for parties to comply with these MPGs. Parties are bound by these MPGs only in two circumstances. First, when developing their national GHG inventories, parties must use 'good practice methodologies accepted by the [IPCC] and agreed upon by the [CMA]'.[213] Second, in application of Article 9(7), developed country parties must follow the MPGs when reporting on the provision of financial support.[214] On the other hand, the Paris Agreement does not expressly require parties to follow the MPGs when providing information necessary to track progress made in implementing NDCs. Nevertheless, the technical expert review is tasked with flagging any issue relating to the transparency and completeness of the information provided by the parties in light of the MPGs.[215]

Other provisions of the Paris Agreement reaffirm the parties' commitments to creating, sharing, and circulating knowledge about climate change. In particular, Article 12 commits parties to 'cooperate in taking measures, as appropriate, to enhance climate change education, training, public awareness, public participation and public access to information'.[216] This Article, however, does not go significantly beyond the relevant provisions of the UNFCCC.[217]

B. Unilateral Declarations

States have repeatedly declared their intention to implement action on climate change mitigation. Some of these declarations relate closely to the UNFCCC regime, most obviously when climate treaties require parties to make such declarations (eg NDCs). Other declarations took place within other processes, or they were entirely spontaneous. A party's multiple declarations often reaffirm similar objectives, policies, and measures. This section shows that these declarations, or series of declarations, can sometimes create legal obligations independently from, and in addition to, treaty commitments. The section starts with a brief overview of the doctrine of unilateral declarations as a source of international law before

[211] Ibid art 13(11).
[212] Ibid art 13(13). See Decision 18/CMA.1 (n 127). See generally Benoit Mayer, "Transparency under the Paris Rulebook: An Enhanced Transparency Framework?" (2019) 9 Climate Law 40.
[213] Paris Agreement (n 4) art 13(7)(a). See also UNFCCC (n 2) art 12(1)(a).
[214] Paris Agreement (n 4) art 9(7).
[215] Ibid art 13(12).
[216] Ibid art 12. See also art 11(1).
[217] See n 79.

applying this doctrine to a discussion of the most relevant declarations made under the UNFCCC and beyond.

For the purpose of presentation, the discussion of unilateral declarations in this section is separated from the discussion of other sources of international law, such as climate treaties (in section A) and customary international law (in Chapter III). This separation is somewhat artificial, however, because the context in which a declaration is made is instrumental to its interpretation. In particular, a declaration is more likely to be considered as manifesting a will to be bound when it merely applies or specifies the content of pre-existing obligations than when it suggests an entirely new obligation. Most of the declarations discussed in this section can actually be viewed as specifying the content of general mitigation obligations already applicable to states under the UNFCCC[218] and customary international law.[219] In other words, the context in which the declarations discussed in the following are made is conducive to the creation of legal obligations.

1. The Recognition of Unilateral Declarations as a Source of Legal Obligations

Unilateral declarations are not specifically included among the sources of international law listed in Article 38(1) of the ICJ Statute,[220] but judicial practice and doctrine have recognized that such declarations can create legal obligations.[221] In particular, the ICJ in the *Nuclear Tests* cases stated that it is 'well recognized that declarations made by way of unilateral acts ... may have the effect of creating legal obligations'.[222] Relying on a 'principle of good faith', the ICJ noted that 'interested States may take cognizance of unilateral declarations and place confidence in them, and are entitled to require that the obligations thus created be respected'.[223] The ICJ insisted, however, that 'to have legal effect, there was no need for [unilateral declarations] to be addressed to a particular State, nor was acceptance by any other State required'.[224] In the case at issue, the ICJ found that a series of statements made by the French government constituted such a unilateral declaration, which had created an obligation for France to stop atmospheric nuclear tests.[225] The capacity of

[218] See above at 38.
[219] See below at 110.
[220] On the hypothesis that unilateral declarations are inchoate treaties, and thus fall within the scope of art 38(1)(a), see eg Hugh Thirlway, *The Sources of International Law* (2nd edn, OUP 2019) 51–59.
[221] See generally, eg Eric Suy, *Les actes juridiques unilatéraux en droit international public* (LGDJ 1962); Przemyslaw Saganek, *Unilateral Acts of States in Public International Law* (Brill 2015)chs 10–11.
[222] *Nuclear Tests (Australia v France)*, Judgment (20 December 1974), [1974] ICJ Rep 253, ¶43.
[223] Ibid ¶46.
[224] Ibid ¶50.
[225] Ibid ¶51.

unilateral declarations to create legal obligations was reaffirmed in several subsequent judicial decisions.[226]

The International Law Commission (ILC) studied the topic from 1996 to 2006, when it adopted the Guiding Principles Applicable to Unilateral Declarations Capable of Creating Legal Obligations. In the ILC's analysis, a declaration capable of creating legal obligations must be made publicly[227] by a competent state agent,[228] and it must 'manifest ... the will to be bound',[229] as evidenced by the content of the declaration and its context.[230] On the other hand, such declaration 'may be formulated orally or in writing',[231] as long as it is 'stated in clear and specific terms'.[232] In case of doubt as to their scope, 'obligations must be interpreted in a restrictive manner'.[233] Finally, the ILC confirmed that declarations capable of creating legal obligations are not limited to bilateral settings: they may 'be addressed to the international community as a whole, to one or several States or to other entities'.[234]

2. Relevance to Climate Change Mitigation

Despite their frequent oversight in climate law scholarship,[235] unilateral declarations are arguably of particular relevance with regard to climate change

[226] See *Military and Paramilitary Activities in and against Nicaragua (Nicaragua v US)*, Judgment on Merits (27 June 1986), [1986] ICJ Rep 132, ¶¶59–60; Panel Report, *US—Sections 301–310 of the Trade Act of 1974*, WT/DS152/R (27 January 2000) ¶7.118; *Proceedings Pursuant to the OSPAR Convention (Ireland/UK)*, Final Award (2 July 2003), 23 RIAA 59, ¶90; *Chagos Marine Protected Area Arbitration (Mauritius/UK)*, Award (18 March 2015) (2018) 31 RIAA 359, ¶446; *Obligation to Negotiate Access to the Pacific Ocean (Bolivia v Chile)*, Judgment on Merits (1 October 2018), [2018] ICJ Rep 507, ¶¶146–48. See also *M/T San Padre Pio (Switzerland v Nigeria)*, Order on Provisional Measures (6 July 2019), [2019] ITLOS Rep 375, Dissenting Opinion of Judge Kateka, ¶11.

[227] ILC, 'Guiding Principles Applicable to Unilateral Declarations of States Capable of Creating Legal Obligations' [2006] II(2) YBILC 161, principle 1.

[228] Ibid principle 4.

[229] Ibid principle 1.

[230] Ibid principle 3. See generally *Nuclear Tests* (n 222) ¶43; *Frontier Dispute (Burkina Faso/Mali)*, Judgment (22 December 1986), [1986] ICJ Rep 573, ¶39; *Armed Activities on the Territory of the Congo (DRC v Uganda)*, Judgment (19 December 2005), [2005] ICJ Rep 168, ¶53.

[231] ILC, 'Unilateral Declarations' (n 227) principle 5. See generally *Temple of Preah Vihear (Cambodia v Thailand)*, Judgment on Preliminary Objections (26 May 1961), [1961] ICJ Rep 17, 31; *Nuclear Tests* (n 222) ¶45.

[232] ILC, 'Unilateral Declarations' (n 227) principle 7. See also *Nuclear Tests* (n 222) ¶43; *Armed Activities on the Territory of the Congo (New Application: 2002) (DRC v Rwanda)*, Judgment on Jurisdiction and Admissibility (3 February 2006), [2006] ICJ Rep 6, ¶¶50, 52.

[233] ILC, 'Unilateral Declarations' (n 227) principle 7. See also *US—Sections 301–210* (n 226) ¶7.118.

[234] ILC, 'Unilateral Declarations' (n 227) principle 6. See also *Nuclear Tests* (n 222) ¶50.

[235] For notable exceptions, see Chester Brown, 'International, Mixed, and Private Disputes Arising Under the Kyoto Protocol' (2010) 1 JIDS 447, 468 (fn 124); Lavanya Rajamani, 'The Making and Unmaking of the Copenhagen Accord' (2010) 59 ICLQ 824, 836–37; Jorge Viñuales, 'The Paris Climate Agreement: An Initial Examination (Part II of III)' *EJIL:Talk!* (8 February 2016) <https://perma.cc/8SDU-35VX>; Annalisa Savaresi, 'The Paris Agreement: A Rejoinder' *EJIL:Talk!* (16 February 2016) <https://perma.cc/L8Z2-GE5F>; Mayer, 'Nationally Determined Contributions' (n 181); Lawrence and Wong (n 186) 285; Lavanya Rajamani, 'Innovation and Experimentation in the International Climate Change Regime' (2020) 404 RdC 9, 135–37.

mitigation. As the ICJ noted in *Nuclear Tests*, unilateral declarations may be the instrument of choice for states willing to enter into an obligation addressed not just towards one or several states (in which case, a treaty would generally appear more suitable) but also towards the international community as a whole.[236] There is not necessarily any reason for a state willing to commit to climate change mitigation to enter into a treaty with other states rather than simply making a unilateral declaration addressed to all; this state does not seek to acquire any particular right from other parties to a treaty, or to commit to any obligations towards any state in particular, but only to bind itself to act in the global good, hoping that the rest of the world would follow.

The UNFCCC regime invites or requires parties to communicate certain documents in which they announce the mitigation action they intend to implement. These documents include the NDCs that parties to the Paris Agreement must communicate every five years, the long-term mitigation strategies that they were invited to produce by 2020, and the pledges that most UNFCCC parties made in the early 2010s under the Copenhagen Accord and the Cancun Agreements. Relevant documents include also the national communications, the biennial reports and the biennial update reports under the UNFCCC, and the Biennial Transparency Reports under the Paris Agreement insofar as they declare the parties' commitment to mitigation action. Besides, parties and other entities have made multiple public statements of their intention to implement specified mitigation action, for instance through high-profile political speeches or the publication of press releases or action plans.

Whether these declarations are made within the context of international negotiations or not does not affect their legal force. Neither the ICJ nor the ILC suggested that any distinction had to be made between declarations made in the context of international negotiations, under a treaty framework, or independently from any multilateral process.[237]

These declarations display at least some of the characteristics of unilateral declarations capable of creating legal obligations. Most obviously, they are all made publicly, often through the UNFCCC Secretariat, which then ensures their availability to parties and the general public.[238] Many of the communications made

[236] *Nuclear Tests* (n 222) ¶51. See also *Frontier Dispute* (n 230) ¶40; Suy (n 221) 111.

[237] *Nuclear Tests* (n 222) ¶43. See also *Land and Maritime Boundary between Cameroon and Nigeria (Cameroon v Nigeria, Equatorial Guinea intervening)*, Judgment on Preliminary Objections (11 June 1998), [1998] ICJ Rep 293, ¶30; *Fisheries Jurisdiction (Spain v Canada)* (n 163) ¶46.

[238] On national communications, see UNFCCC (n 2) art 12(1). On pledges, see Copenhagen Accord of 18 December 2009, appended to Decision 2/CP.15, 'Copenhagen Accord' (18–19 December 2009) FCCC/CP/2009/11/Add.1, ¶¶4, 5; Decision 1/CP.16 (n 75) ¶¶36, 49–50. On NDCs, see Decisions 1/CP.19, 'Further Advancing the Durban Platform' (23 November 2013) FCCC/CP/2013/10/Add.1, 3, ¶2(b); 1/CP.20, 'Lima Call for Climate Action' (14 December 2014) FCCC/CP/2014/10/Add.1, 2, ¶¶9, 16(a); 1/CP.21 (n 117) ¶¶13–14; Paris Agreement (n 4) art 4(12); Decision 5/CMA.1, 'Modalities and Procedures for the Operation and Use of a Public Registry Referred to in Article 4, paragraph 12, of the Paris Agreement' (15 December 2018) FCCC/PA/CMA/2018/3/Add.1, 14.

under the UNFCCC are either required or expected to follow detailed guidance on forms and methodologies that seek to ensure that these communications are clear and specific. Each relevant communication is intended to inform other states and entities, or perhaps the international community as a whole, about that state's intentions and to create an expectation that the party will at least seek to implement the measures it announced. More generally, a party's declaration of its intention is aimed at incentivizing similar action by other parties. As such, the principle of good faith lends some support to the existence of legal obligations arising from party declarations.[239]

Beyond these general observations, the critical question to assess whether legal obligations may arise from a declaration is whether this declaration manifests a will of the party to bind itself to an obligation.[240] This question will necessarily depend on the context and content of each declaration, but some general remarks can be made. As shown in the following, national reports are unlikely to create legal commitments on their own, and the context in which pledges were communicated under the Copenhagen Accord and the Cancun Agreements creates a strong (though not irrebuttable) presumption against the creation of such commitments. By contrast, NDCs and long-term strategies are more likely to constitute declarations capable of creating legal obligations. Altogether, the will of a state to be bound may more convincingly be demonstrated by reference not to a single document but to a consistent pattern of declarations.

3. National Reports

As noted above, all parties to the UNFCCC have committed to report on, among other things, the 'steps taken or envisaged ... to implement the Convention'.[241] COP decisions provide guidelines on 'national communications' as well as 'biennial reports' (Annex I parties) and 'biennial update reports' (non-Annex I parties).[242] Moreover, the Paris Agreement requires its parties to communicate biennial transparency reports, which will replace the biennial reports and biennial update reports but will coexist with national communications.[243] It is worth considering

[239] See, by analogy, *Nuclear Tests* (n 222) ¶46.

[240] See nn 229–30.

[241] UNFCCC (n 2) art 12(1)(b). See above at 38.

[242] See Decisions 17/CP.8, 'Guidelines for the Preparation of National Communications from Parties not Included in Annex I to the Convention' (1 November 2002) FCCC/CP/2002/7/Add.2, 2; 2/CP.17 (n 78) Annex I (biennial reports) and III (biennial update reports); 6/CP.25, 'Revision of the UNFCCC Reporting Guidelines on National Communications for Parties included in Annex I to the Convention' (12 December 2019) FCCC/CP/2019/13/Add.1, 28, Annex (national communications by Annex I parties).

[243] See Paris Agreement (n 4) art 13(7); Decision 1/CP.24, 'Preparations for the Implementation of the Paris Agreement and the First Session of the Conference of the Parties Serving as the Meeting of the Parties to the Paris Agreement' (15 December 2018) FCCC/CP/2018/10/Add.1, 2, ¶39.

that these various national reports may constitute unilateral declarations capable of creating legal obligations insofar as they announce the intention of a party to pursue objectives, policies, or measures on climate change mitigation.

The COP's initial guidelines on national communications by Annex I parties only observed that parties may 'briefly describe … policies and measures under consideration'.[244] Over time, revisions of these guidelines put more emphasis on the announcement of measures at the planning stage or under consideration for both Annex I and non-Annex I parties.[245] Parties were also asked to report on the 'progress of implementation' of steps they had announced[246] or, as the case may be, to explain why steps that they had mentioned in prior communications were no longer in place.[247] This evolution thus shows an increasing accountability of states for the implementation of the steps they had announced, but this accountability does not necessarily amount to legal responsibility.

National reports do not ordinarily create legal obligations because they do not manifest a will of the party to be bound: a mere 'description' of steps 'envisaged' does not create an obligation to implement these steps. On the other hand, at least theoretically, nothing prevents a party from using national reports as a platform to proclaim its will to be bound to the implementation of certain measures or the achievement of specific outcomes. This, however, would have to be clearly manifested in the terms of the report or in its context, for instance in light of other declarations made by the same party.

Some developed country parties have communicated relatively clear objectives, policies, and measures, in their national reports,[248] but they have not generally indicated a will to be bound to pursuing them. A party willing to commit to implement mitigation action would likely look for a more prominent platform but could use national reports to confirm their commitment or to clarify some of the modalities of this commitment. For instance, the EU biennial reports have provided important clarifications on the EU's targets in its Cancun Pledge[249] and NDC.[250]

[244] Decision 9/CP.2 (n 90) Annex ¶26. See also Decision 10/CP.2, 'Communications from Parties not Included in Annex I to the Convention: Guidelines, Facilitation and Process for Consideration' (19 July 1996) FCCC/CP/1996/15/Add.1, 42, Annex ¶15; UNFCCC COP5, 'Guidelines for the Preparation of National Communications by Parties Included in Annex I to the Convention, Part II: UNFCCC Reporting Guidelines on National Communications', FCCC/CP/999/7 (16 February 2000) ¶15.

[245] See UNFCCC COP5 (n 244) ¶14; Decisions 17/CP.8 (n 242) Annex ¶40; 2/CP.17 (n 242) Annex I ¶6; 18/CMA.1 (n 127) Annex ¶82(e); 6/CP.25 (n 242) Annex ¶10.

[246] Decision 2/CP.17 (n 242) Annex III ¶12(c)–(d).

[247] See UNFCCC COP5 (n 244) ¶26; Decisions 18/CMA.1 (n 127) Annex ¶87; 6/CP.25 (n 242) Annex ¶23.

[248] See European Communities, Fourth National Communication under the UNFCCC (2006) 4.

[249] EU, Second Biennial Report under the UNFCCC (2015) 7–8.

[250] EU, Fourth Biennial Report under the UNFCCC (2020) 41–44.

4. Copenhagen and Cancun Pledges

The parties to the UNFCCC have pledged to implement specified mitigation actions during the 2010s through unilateral declarations invited by the Copenhagen Accord and the Cancun Agreements. The Copenhagen Accord is a document drafted on 18 December 2009, in a last-ditch effort at salvaging negotiations at COP15;[251] in the following weeks, it was informally endorsed by 151 parties.[252] The Accord calls upon Annex I parties to communicate 'quantified economy-wide emissions targets for 2020' (QEETs)[253] and upon non-Annex I parties to communicate 'nationally appropriate mitigation actions' (NAMAs).[254] The pledges were to be communicated to the Secretariat by 31 January 2010, although it was agreed that non-Annex I parties could also communicate mitigation actions subsequently through national reports.[255] This arrangement was formalized the following year with the adoption of a comprehensive COP decision, the Cancun Agreements, which took note of the QEETs and NAMAs submitted so far[256] and called for parties to make additional pledges or to enhance the pledges they had already made.[257] Parties were also requested to report on the implementation of their pledges through biennial reports (for Annex I parties) and biennial update reports (for non-Annex I parties).[258]

Some QEETs and NAMAs contained language suggestive of a will to be bound. In particular, most European parties expressed their QEETs as 'commitments',[259] a word which, in both its ordinary meaning and its prevailing use in the context of climate negotiations, suggests a legal obligation. By contrast, few NAMAs included language suggestive of a will to be bound and, more generally, carefully avoided any legal qualification. Some non-Annex I parties presented their NAMAs as voluntary, although it was not always clear whether they were referring to the communication of the NAMA or also to its implementation.[260] India, for one, avoided any

[251] For an account of the political context, see Daniel Bodansky, 'The Copenhagen Climate Change Conference: A Post-Mortem' (2010) 104 AJIL 230; Rajamani, 'The Making and Unmaking' (n 235).

[252] See UNFCCC Secretariat, Communications received from Parties in relation to the listing in the chapeau of the Copenhagen Accord (no date) <http://unfccc.int/meetings/items/5276.php>.

[253] Copenhagen Accord (n 238) ¶4.

[254] Ibid ¶5.

[255] Ibid.

[256] Decision 1/CP.16 (n 75) ¶¶36, 49.

[257] Ibid ¶¶37, 50.

[258] Ibid ¶¶40(1), 60(c).

[259] See Letter by Cristóbal González-Aller Jurado and Karl Falkenberg to Yvo de Boer, 'Expression of Willingness to Be Associated with the Copenhagen Accord and Submission of the Quantified Economy-Wide Emissions Reduction Targets for 2020' (28 January 2010) 2 (on behalf of the EU and its Member States; Letter by Magnús Jóhannesson and Hugi Ólafsson to the UNFCCC, 'Iceland's Target in the Copenhagen Accord' (8 February 2010) 1; Letter by Helmut Kindle to Mr De Boer, 'Copenhagen Accord' (27 January 2010) 1 (on behalf of Liechtenstein); Letter by Gilles Tonelli and Franck Bianceri, 'Letter to Mr De Boer' (5 February 2010) 1 (on behalf of Monaco).

[260] See eg the NAMAs of Brazil, Chad, China, Ethiopia, India, Indonesia, the Maldives, Thailand, in UNFCCC AWG–LCA, 'Compilation of Information on Nationally Appropriate Mitigation Actions to

doubt by declaring that 'the proposed domestic actions are voluntary in nature and will not have a legally binding character'.[261]

When the wording of QEETs or NAMAs leaves open the question of their legal force, the context in which they were communicated needs to be considered more closely. The Copenhagen Accord presents QEETs as objectives that Annex I parties 'commit to implement'.[262] This provision is not constitutive of an obligation (the Copenhagen Accord, in any case, is not a source of international law), but it could be construed as declaratory of an obligation arising from QEETs as unilateral declarations. More ambiguously, the Copenhagen Accord merely states that NAMAs 'will' be implemented by non-Annex I parties,[263] and the Cancun Agreements mention that QEETs and NAMAs are 'to be implemented' by parties.[264] This language permits but does not demonstrate an interpretation of QEETs and NAMAs as creating legal obligations. The word 'pledge' suggests that the documents are not legally binding, but it is noteworthy that this word was not used in either the Copenhagen Accord or the Cancun Agreements, and its use in subsequent decisions[265] does not necessarily help to understand the contemporary intention of the states when communicating their QEETs and NAMAs. And while the Doha Amendment notes that QEETs 'are not internationally binding under the Kyoto Protocol',[266] this does not rule out their possible bindingness as unilateral declarations.

Rajamani argued that a state's association with the Copenhagen Accord could not constitute unilateral declarations, citing a letter of the UNFCCC Secretariat to the parties which clarified that the Copenhagen Accord had 'no legal standing within the UNFCCC process'[267] and statements by some parties which characterized the Copenhagen Accord as a 'political agreement' with no binding force.[268] This characterization of the Copenhagen Accord, however, does not clarify the legal force of QEETs and NAMAs, which are separate instruments. The Secretariat letter and the party statements that Rajamani mentions suggest the absence of legal

Be Implemented by Parties not Included in Annex I to the Convention', FCCC/AWGLCA/2011/INF.1 (2011).

[261] Rajani Ranjan Rashmi, 'Letter to Mr Yvo de Boer' (30 January 2010) (on behalf of India).

[262] Copenhagen Accord (n 238) ¶¶4.

[263] Ibid ¶5 (emphasis added).

[264] Decision 1/CP.16 (n 75) ¶¶36, 49.

[265] See eg Decisions 1/CP.17, 'Establishment of an Ad Hoc Working Group on the Durban Platform for Enhanced Action' (11 December 2011) FCCC/CP/2011/9/Add.1, 2, Preamble ¶2; 1/CP.21 (n 117) ¶105(b).

[266] Doha Amendment (n 86) art 1A (fn 1).

[267] Rajamani, 'The Making and Unmaking' (n 235) 837, citing UNFCCC Secretariat, 'Clarification Relating to the Notification of 18 January 2010' (25 January 2010).

[268] Rajamani, 'The Making and Unmaking' (n 235) 837; UNFCCC Secretariat, 'Communications received' (n 252). See also Embassy of Brazil in Germany, Communication (10 January 2010) <https://perma.cc/YQ9B-97SS> 1.

force of the Copenhagen Accord, but they are not helpful in determining the potential legal force of QEETs and NAMAs as unilateral declarations.

Thus, it is possible that some Copenhagen and Cancun pledges—most likely QEETs—may create legal commitments for the parties that communicate them. QEETs communicated by some European parties appear to be the likeliest candidates.[269] Whether this is the case depends on the wording of the declaration and its context, including the terms of contemporary or subsequent communications that reaffirm or clarify the nature of the pledge.

5. NDCs and Long-Term Strategies

The parties to the Paris Agreement have made two types of declarations that indicate their intended objectives, policies, and measures on climate change mitigation. First, almost all of them adopted NDCs, at first often building on the prior communication of INDCs in the run-up to the adoption and entry into force of the Paris Agreement.[270] Second, some parties have also communicated what the Paris Agreement refers to as 'long-term low greenhouse gas emission development strategies',[271] typically in the form of mid-century objectives accompanied by the description of a set of policies intended to achieve them.

These declarations have sometimes been discounted as 'voluntary',[272] but this conflates several questions. While long-term strategies were merely invited,[273] a party to the Paris Agreement assumes an obligation to communicate NDCs every five years;[274] on the other hand, the level of ambition embedded in NDCs and long-term strategies is largely left to the party's discretion, at least initially.[275] Yet, the right of a state to decide whether to communicate a document and, if so, what to include in it, does not in any way determine the legal force of this document.[276] This legal force could stem from the Paris Agreement and the UNFCCC but also from the declarations themselves.[277] On the one hand, the Paris Agreement requires its parties to adopt the necessary measures to achieve its NDC,[278] although it does

[269] See n 259.

[270] See UNFCCC Secretariat, 'INDCs as communicated by Parties' (no date) <https://www4.unfccc.int/sites/submissions/INDC/Submission%20Pages/submissions.aspx>; UNFCCC Secretariat, 'NDC Registry (interim)' (no date) <https://www4.unfccc.int/sites/NDCStaging/>.

[271] Paris Agreement (n 4) art 4(19). See UNFCCC Secretariat, 'Communication of long-term strategies' (no date) <https://unfccc.int/process/the-paris-agreement/long-term-strategies>.

[272] See n 135.

[273] See Paris Agreement (n 4) art 4(19); Decisions 1/CP.21 (n 117) ¶35; 1/CMA.2, 'Chile Madrid Time for Action' (15 December 2019) FCCC/PA/CMA/2019/6/Add.1, 2, ¶11; 1/CMA.3, 'Glasgow Climate Pact' (13 November 2021) FCCC/PA/CMA/2021/10/Add.1 (advance version), 2, ¶32.

[274] See n 140.

[275] But see, with regard to NDCs, Paris Agreement (n 4) art 4(3), (8), (9).

[276] By analogy, treaties and contracts are sources of obligations even though they are voluntarily consented to.

[277] See Mayer, 'Nationally Determined Contributions' (n 181).

[278] See above at 59.

not create any similar obligation with regard to long-term strategies. Likewise, the UNFCCC requires its parties to 'formulate [and] implement ... programmes containing measures to mitigate climate change',[279] a provision that normally requires a state to implement the programmes—including, arguably, NDCs and long-term strategies—that it has formulated.[280] On the other hand, it is worth considering whether the parties may also have obligations arising directly from NDCs and long-term strategies as unilateral declarations. While the obligation to implement NDCs under the Paris Agreement is an obligation of conduct limited to the main mitigation objective, the NDC itself may create obligations of a different nature and scope.

Whether obligations arise from NDCs and long-term strategies depends first on whether these declarations are phrased in clear and specific terms. These declarations, in particular those made by developed countries, frequently contain clear and specific objectives, such as quantified, economy-wide absolute emission reduction targets, and they are frequently accompanied by necessary supplementary information (eg scope and coverage, base-year, period, and information on reliance on international transfer of mitigation outcomes).[281] NDCs can be expected to show increasing clarity and specificity as the parties commit to provide the information identified by the CMA.[282] By contrast, the format and content of long-term strategies is almost entirely left to the party's discretion, and the contents of the declarations made so far vary significantly.

Likewise, some NDCs suggest or manifest a will to be bound. A clear example is the EU's first NDC, which clearly expresses that the EU is 'committed to a binding target'.[283] The US's first NDC (before its withdrawal) expressed that it 'intend[ed] to achieve' a specified target[284]—by contrast, the US's new first NDC (after re-accepting the treaty) carefully avoids any such language.[285] Argentina emphasized that it is 'committed to' the objective contained in its NDC.[286] Likewise, Ghana referred to 'a formal emission reduction obligation',[287] while Pakistan noted that its objective 'should not be considered as an international obligation of the country, unless the resource provisioning is ensured'[288]—thus, implying the existence of an obligation conditional to support. By contrast, Liberia has clearly provided that its NDC 'does not constitute an international obligation'.[289]

[279] UNFCCC (n 2) art 4(1)(b).
[280] The same argument can be made with regard to ibid art 4(2)(a).
[281] See EU, First NDC, Updated (2020) 7–19. But see India, INDC (2015) 29.
[282] See n 143.
[283] EU, First NDC (2016) ¶3; EU, First NDC, Updated (2020) ¶27. These documents appear to situate bindingness on the international plane rather than merely under EU law. Cf Rajamani, 'Innovation and Experimentation' (n 235) 137, suggesting that the EU NDC is binding only under EU law.
[284] US, First NDC (2016) 4.
[285] See US, First NDC (2021).
[286] Argentina, Second NDC (2020) 9.
[287] Ghana, First NDC (2016) 9.
[288] Pakistan, First NDC (2016) 6.
[289] Liberia, First NDC (2018) 1. See also Turkmenistan, First NDC (2016) 1.

As for long-term strategies, they were, at the outset, mainly presented as mere aspirations or objectives, without legal force,[290] although there has been a trend towards the inclusion of a more robust language. Some long-term strategies were expressed as 'legally binding targets',[291] or otherwise as a 'commitment'.[292] Yet, it is admittedly not always clear whether these commitments take place within domestic or international law.[293]

The context in which NDCs were communicated lends some support to their potentially binding nature. The word 'contribution' was used as a neutral alternative to 'pledge' (presumably non-binding) and 'commitment' (impliedly binding),[294] and INDCs were invited 'without prejudice to the legal nature of the contributions'.[295] Yet, Article 3 of the Paris Agreement suggested that NDCs were to be undertaken,[296] while Article 4(2) noted the expectation that each party would 'intend ... to achieve' the NDCs that it would communicate.[297] The mention of a mere intention to achieve an NDC does not create an obligation to do so,[298] but it provides part of the context which makes it more likely that the terms of an NDC could be viewed as manifesting the will of the party to be bound.

The ICJ in the *Nuclear Tests* cases concluded that the public communication of an intention to do something could imply a will to be bound when this communication was made with full knowledge that other states were interested in the outcome and would likely rely on this declaration to determine their own conduct. In that case, the French government had 'made public its intention to cease the conduct of atmospheric nuclear tests'[299] as Australia and New Zealand were disputing the legality of these tests. At no time had the French government explicitly declared its will to be bound by its declaration of intent. Nevertheless, the ICJ held that, as a result of a statement expressing 'its intention effectively to terminate these tests', France 'was bound to assume that other States might take note of these statements and rely on their being effective'.[300] The Court concluded that, through a series of unilateral declarations of its 'intent', France had undertaken an obligation to cease its nuclear tests.[301] By analogy, NDCs and conceivably long-term strategies

[290] See eg EU, Long-Term Mitigation Strategy (2020) 1; Singapore, Long-Term Mitigation Strategy (2020) 9.

[291] See eg UK, Long-Term Mitigation Strategy (2018), 'Cover Note', 1; Denmark, Long-Term Mitigation Strategy (2020) 2; Norway, Long-Term Mitigation Strategy (2020) 16.

[292] See eg Canada, First NDC, Updated (2021) 10 ('Canada is committed to reaching net-zero GHG emissions by 2050'); Canada Net-Zero Emissions Accountability Act (n 176) Preamble ¶8, ss 4, 6, 16. As of May 2022, Canada was yet to communicated an update of its 2016 Long-Term Mitigation Strategy that would reflect this target.

[293] See n 283.

[294] Bodansky, 'A New Hope?' (n 113) 297.

[295] Decision 1/CP.19 (n 238) ¶8.

[296] Paris Agreement (n 4) art 3. See above at 52.

[297] Paris Agreement (n 4) art 4(2), first sentence.

[298] Rajamani, 'Interplay' (n 168) 354.

[299] *Nuclear Tests* (n 222) ¶41.

[300] Ibid ¶51.

[301] Ibid.

expressing the intention of a party to implement or achieve well-defined objectives, policies, or measures, presumably with the view to informing the decisions of other parties as to their own mitigation action, could be considered as suggestive of a will of this party to be bound.

6. Other Unilateral Declarations

In addition to communications under the UNFCCC and the Paris Agreement, obligations could also be created by unilateral declarations made by states or other entities outside of the UNFCCC regime.[302] States regularly make declarations that announce, confirm, or specify the content of the NDC or other commitments under the UNFCCC regime.[303]

Besides states, unilateral declarations are an attractive instrument for entities that do not participate in climate treaties for legal or political reasons but are nevertheless able and willing to make commitments on climate change mitigation. Such entities include international organizations, which can bear obligations within the scope of their functions,[304] but which, with the exception of regional economic integration organizations, are not authorized to participate in climate treaties.[305] Some other organizations have pledged to implement mitigation action within the operations they implement or support. Thus, the World Bank has adopted five-year 'Climate Change Action Plans' that outline its goal to increase climate finance,[306] whereas the European Investment Bank announced in 2019 that it would stop funding fossil-fuels projects.[307]

Another type of entity that may be particularly attracted by unilateral declarations is the de facto territorial government (eg Taiwan, North Cyprus, Kosovo, Abkhazia, and South Ossetia), where governments may not meet the conditions for participating in climate treaties as states[308] but may nevertheless be willing to

[302] See n 237.

[303] See Address by Xi Jinping (22 September 2020) in UN General Assembly Official Records, A/75/PV.4, 29; The White House Briefing Room, 'Leaders Summit on Climate: Summary of Proceedings' (23 April 2021) <https://www.whitehouse.gov/briefing-room/statements-releases/2021/04/23/leaders-summit-on-climate-summary-of-proceedings/>.

[304] *Reparation for Injuries* (n 163) 9.

[305] See UNFCCC (n 2) arts 1(6), 20. The EU is the only organization that has made use of this provision.

[306] See World Bank, 'World Bank Group climate change action plan' (2016); World Bank, 'Climate Change Action Plan 2021–25: Supporting Green, Resilient, and Inclusive Development' (2021).

[307] European Investment Bank, 'EU Bank launches ambitious new climate strategy and Energy Lending Policy' (14 November 2019) <https://perma.cc/44XH-NLZT>.

[308] Signature of climate treaties is only permitted for states that are members of the UN or any of its specialized agency or parties to the Statute of the International Court of Justice, but it is unclear whether the same condition applies to accession. In practical terms, the decision on the validity of an instrument of accession would have to be made by the UN Secretary-General as the treaty Depositary. See UNFCCC (n 2) arts 19–20.

make commitments on climate change mitigation. Taiwan, for instance, has publicly communicated its 'Intended Nationally Determined Contribution' in the run-up to COP21.[309] As it is generally accepted that de facto territorial governments can hold some rights and bear some obligations,[310] it is not unconceivable that they may seek to bind themselves to commitments on climate change mitigation through unilateral declarations. A comparable circumstance is that of autonomous or semi-autonomous regions (eg Hong Kong and Macau, the Faeroe Islands and Greenland, or New Caledonia), which, whether for constitutional or political reasons, are not generally included in national mitigation strategies[311] but could—and, arguably, should—make their own commitments.

Subnational governments have also declared a number of pledges to mitigation action. The Global Covenant of Mayors for Climate and Energy brings together commitments made by over 10,000 subnational governments.[312] The effectiveness of commitments by subnational governments depends in part on their capacity to adopt and implement effective mitigation action, in light of their competence in national law and of the resources they command. States often tolerate that their federated states, autonomous territories, or other subnational governments take part in some international transactions,[313] and the legality of the initiatives of local governments on climate change mitigation has been questioned only in exceptional cases.[314] As subnational governments are not permitted to participate in climate treaties, they may find that unilateral declarations are the most natural instrument to create binding commitments on climate change mitigation.

A number of private actors have also made various declarations of their intention to implement mitigation action—a phenomenon which has achieved some

[309] Taiwan, 'Intended Nationally Determined Contribution' (2015). See also Bonnie S Glaser, *Taiwan's Quest for Greater Participation in the International Community* (Center for Strategic & International Studies 2013) 23–25; Chi-Jen Yang and Hui-Chen Chien, 'Could Taiwan Be Included in UNFCCC Negotiations?' (2010) 10 Climate Policy 317.

[310] See Jochen A Frowein, 'De Facto Regime' in *Max Planck Encyclopedia of Public International Law* (online edn, OUP 2013) ¶¶4–9.

[311] See Lov om klima (Climate Act) No 865 (26 June 2020) <https://perma.cc/RKM7-76MT> (Denmark) s 14 (noting that the 'Act is not applicable in the Faeroe Islands and Greenland'). See also Benoit Mayer, 'Climate Change Mitigation in the Hong Kong Special Administrative Region' (2017) 7 Climate Law 65.

[312] Global Covenant of Mayors for Climate and Energy (no date) <https://www.globalcovenantofmayors.org/>.

[313] See Christian Tomuschat, 'Component Territorial Units of States under International Law' in Enrico Carloni and Fulvio Cortese (eds), *Regioni ed autonomie territoriali nel diritto internazionale ed europeo* (Editoriale Scientifica 2006); Anne Peters, 'Treaty Making Power' in *Max Planck Encyclopedia of Public International Law* (online edn, OUP 2009) ¶¶19–34; Walter Rudolf, 'Federal States' in *Max Planck Encyclopedia of Public International Law* (online edn, OUP 2011) ¶12. On Hong Kong, see Roda Mushkat, *One Country, Two International Legal Personalities: The Case of Hong Kong* (Hong Kong UP 1997) 99; Zhichao Sun, 'International Legal Personality of the Hong Kong Special Administrative Region' (2008) 7 Chinese JIL 339.

[314] See *US v California* (DC ED California, 2020) 444 FSupp3d 1181, dismissing a challenge of the Federal government to the constitutionality of the agreement between California and Quebec on a joint cap-and-grade programme.

degree of recognition under the UNFCCC regime.[315] Notwithstanding whether these declarations are made in clear and specific terms and manifest the will to be bound, an obvious obstacle to the creation of legal obligations is that private actors are not generally viewed as capable of having a legal personality under international law[316] and that international courts do not have jurisdiction to settle disputes brought against such actors. As such, it does not appear that these declarations can be binding under international law in its current state. However, these declarations may be relevant in a domestic legal context, if not as source of law, at least as the recognition of a standard of care applicable in construing general obligations, for instance under tort law.[317]

7. The Cumulative Effect of Series of Declarations

Rather than from a single declaration, clear evidence of a will to be bound may arise—as in *Nuclear Tests*—from a consistent series of declarations, which may amount to more than the sum of its parts.[318] For instance, a state's NDC may define its mitigation objective, its biennial report may clarify the scope and modalities of this objective, and statements by prominent government officers may confirm the will of the state to be bound by this objective.

Parties that have communicated an (I)NDC had frequently made prior announcements of their intention to do so, and they have subsequently reaffirmed their contribution in terms that shed some light on their intentions. For instance, the EU has repeatedly affirmed that its NDC objective for 2030 is 'binding'.[319] China first announced the content of its INDC as something it 'intend[ed] to achieve'[320] and, while its INDC and national reports avoided the use of language suggestive of a will to be bound,[321] President Xi Jinping's speech at COP21 presented China's INDC as its 'commitments'.[322] The US Department of State, by contrast, responded to a Senator's question that the INDC was 'not intended to constitute an obligation the United States must fulfill under international law'.[323]

[315] See Decision 1/CP.21 (n 117) ¶117.

[316] See discussion in Peters (n 313) ¶¶72–76.

[317] See *Milieudefensie* (n 53), interpreting the duty of care of a company.

[318] See *Nuclear Tests* (n 222) ¶¶34–41, identifying a series of statements as constituting, collectively, a 'unilateral declaration'.

[319] See eg European Council, Conclusions (11 December 2020) EUCO22/20, ¶12.

[320] US–China Joint Announcement on Climate Change (12 November 2014) ¶2.

[321] China, INDC (2015) 5. See also China, Third National Communication under the UNFCCC (2019) 98.

[322] Xi Jinping, 'Work Together to Build a Win–Win, Equitable and Balanced Governance Mechanism on Climate Change', speech delivered at the opening of the Paris Conference on Climate Change (30 November 2015) <https://perma.cc/M5ZJ-FRLN>.

[323] Letter by Julia Frifield to Bob Corker (19 October 2015) <https://perma.cc/6ZXE-CE6R>.

To determine whether a state manifested the will to be bound to a mitigation target, it may thus be useful to consider its various relevant declarations as a whole. For instance, Norway communicated its QEET as a 'pledge',[324] thus implying that it had no legal force. To confirm this, the state secured the inclusion of a footnote in the Doha Amendment affirming that its QEET, despite its mention in the Amendment, 'retain[ed] the status of the pledge made under the Cancun Agreements'.[325] Likewise, Norway's biennial reports distinguished its commitment under the Doha Amendment with its QEET[326] (even though its third biennial report contained a more ambivalent reference to a 'commitment' stemming from its QEET which had been made 'operational' by the Doha Amendment).[327] By contrast to its QEET, Norway seems to have presented its NDC as an obligation.[328] Both its biennial reports to the UNFCCC and its reports to the European Economic Area consistently presented its NDC as a 'commitment',[329] and its Supreme Court characterized this document as creating an obligation ('plikt') of Norway.[330] When communicating its long-term strategy, Norway contrasted its 'binding' NDC with this strategy which 'does not ... entail any new international commitments for Norway'.[331] As such, viewed in context, there is a strong argument that Norway is bound by its NDC as unilateral declaration.

Bhutan provides another simple illustration of the relevance of a holistic interpretation of series of declarations. At COP15, Bhutan announced its intention to ensure GHG neutrality in its territory 'for all times'.[332] This objective was reaffirmed in Bhutan's NAMA.[333] In a foreword to Bhutan's second national communication, this objective was presented as a 'commitment'.[334] The same 'commitment' was affirmed in other communications of Bhutan under the UNFCCC and other multilateral processes.[335] Again, Bhutan's INDC stated its 'resolve and efforts to

[324] UNFCCC SBSTA, 'Compilation of Economy-Wide Emission Reduction Targets to Be Implemented by Parties Included in Annex I to the Convention', FCCC/SBSTA/2014/INF.6 (2014) ¶27.

[325] Doha Amendment (n 86) art IA (fn 10).

[326] Norway, First Biennial Report under the UNFCCC (2014) 8, 258, 272; Norway, Second Biennial Report under the UNFCCC (2016) 9, 35; Norway, Third Biennial Report under the UNFCCC (2018) 63; Norway, Fourth Biennial Report under the UNFCCC (2020) 12.

[327] Norway, Third Biennial Report (n 326) 315.

[328] Norway, First NDC (2016) 1; Norway, First NDC, Updated (2020) 3.

[329] Norway, Second Biennial Report (n 326) 8, 63; Norway, Third Biennial Report (n 326) 65–66; Norway, Fourth Biennial Report (n 326) 12–13; Norwegian Ministry of Climate and Environment, 'Norway's National Plan related to the Decision of the EEA Joint Committee No 269/2019 of 25 October 2019' (2019) 5.

[330] *Natur og Ungdom* (n 49) ¶59.

[331] Norway, Long-Term Mitigation Strategy (2020) 3. See also Norway, Fourth Biennial Report (n 326) 13–14.

[332] See Bhutan National Human Development Report, 'Sustaining Progress: Rising to the Climate Challenge' (2011) 3–4.

[333] See Lyonpa Ugyen Tshering, Letter to UNFCCC Executive Secretary (5 February 2010).

[334] Bhutan, Second National Communication under the UNFCCC (2011) Foreword, 6, 37. See also Bhutan, Third National Communication under the UNFCCC (2021) x, 23, 58.

[335] See Bhutan, Second National Communication (n 334) iv; Bhutan, National Report for the UN Conference on Sustainable Development, 'Bhutan: In Pursuit of Sustainable Development' (2012) 5;

fulfil this commitment'[336] before describing measures to achieve it.[337] Such clear and consistent statement of a 'commitment' is strongly suggestive of Bhutan's will to be bound by this target.

C. Commitments under Other Treaty Regimes

Some treaty commitments on climate change mitigation are created incidentally under treaty regimes focusing on other subject matters. The following surveys the obligations arising from treaties relating to the protection of the ozone layer, the development of international civil aviation, and the prevention of pollution from ships.

1. Commitments Incidental to the Protection of the Ozone Layer

The regime on the protection of the ozone layer was established by the 1985 Vienna Convention for the Protection of the Ozone Layer, soon complemented by its 1987 Montreal Protocol on Substances that Deplete the Ozone Layer, both of which are widely ratified.[338] These treaties aim to protect the stratospheric ozone layer by regulating the production and consumption of ozone-depleting substances (ODSs). ODSs include various halogen compounds mainly used as refrigerants, fire extinguishers, solvents, aerosol propellants, foam-blowing agents, and fumigants. Once released in the atmosphere, under particular weather conditions occurring mainly over the poles, these substances react with stratospheric ozone, thus thinning the ozone layer.[339] The ozone layer plays an essential role in protecting the Earth's surface from harmful solar ultraviolet radiations; its depletion raises ecological and public health concerns.

Each party to the Montreal Protocol must implement certain 'control measures' relating to the phasing out of both the production and consumption of control substances. These control measures are expressed as a rate of reduction from the party's 1986 level of consumption and production of controlled substances (weighed according to their ozone-depleting potential).[340] Developing country parties whose annual level of consumption of the controlled substances is below

Bhutan National Environment Commission, 'Technology Needs Assessment and Technology Action Plans for Climate Change Mitigation' (2013) Preface, 4.

[336] Bhutan, INDC (2015) 1.
[337] Ibid 2.
[338] Vienna Convention for the Protection of the Ozone Layer (n 8); Montreal Protocol (n 8).
[339] See Donald Wuebbles, 'Ozone Depletion' in Britannica Academic (Encyclopædia Britannica 2021).
[340] Montreal Protocol (n 8) art 2.

0.3 kilograms per capita were entitled to delay their compliance with these control measures by ten years, provided that their consumption always remained below this threshold.[341]

In addition, each party to the Montreal Protocol commits to banning the import and export of controlled substances and products containing such substances from and to any states not party to the Protocol, unless these states comply with the control measures of the Protocol.[342] Parties must also 'undertake to the fullest practicable extent to discourage' the export of technology for producing or utilizing controlled substances to such non-parties[343] and refrain from providing support to non-parties for the production of controlled substances.[344] The Protocol empowers the Meeting of the Parties to ban or restrict the import of 'products produced with, but not containing, controlled substances' from non-parties.[345] The Meeting of the Parties has not acted upon this provision, presumably because of the difficulty of determining whether controlled substances were used in production processes abroad. In any case, the practical relevance of provisions on international trade was limited by the widespread ratification of the Protocol.[346]

The Montreal Protocol has proven highly effective in protecting the ozone layer. Its scope, initially limited to some chlorofluorocarbons (CFC) and halons, has been extended to other ODSs by four subsequent amendments in the 1990s.[347] In addition, the Meeting of the Parties has adopted a dozen adjustments to enhance control measures when technological progress allowed. The Montreal Protocol has achieved considerable reduction in the emissions of ODSs. The stratospheric ozone layer started to recover around the year 2000 and full recovery is expected by the end of the twenty-first century.[348]

The ozone regime did not only offer a template for the architecture of the UNFCCC regime,[349] but its own outcomes also contributed significantly to the mitigation of climate change because most ODSs are also highly potent GHGs. For

[341] Ibid art 5(1).

[342] Ibid art 4(1)–(3), (8); Decision III/15, 'Annex to the Montreal Protocol', UNEP/OzL.Pro.3/11, 20 (21 June 1991) (extending the application of the Protocol to a list of products containing controlled substances).

[343] Montreal Protocol (n 8) consolidated version, art 4(5).

[344] Ibid art 4(6).

[345] Ibid art 4(4).

[346] See Decision V/17, 'Feasibility of Banning or Restricting from States not Party to the Montreal Protocol the Import of Products Produced with, but not Containing, Controlled Substances in Annex A, in Accordance with Paragraph 4 of Article 4 of the Protocol', UNEP/OzL.Pro.5/12 (19 November 1993) ¶2; Report of the Ninth Meeting of the Open-Ended Working Group of the Parties to the Montreal Protocol (30 August–1 September 1993), UNEW/OzL.Pro/WG.1/9/7, ¶60.

[347] Amendments to the Montreal Protocol on Substances that Deplete the Ozone Layer adopted in London on 29 June 1990, 1598 UNTS 469; in Copenhagen on 25 November 1992, 1785 UNTS 517; in Montreal on 17 September 1997, 2054 UNTS 522; in Beijing on 3 December 1999, 2173 UNTS 183.

[348] See generally WMO, Scientific Assessment of Ozone Depletion (WMO 2018). See also MP Chipperfield and others, 'Quantifying the Ozone and Ultraviolet Benefits Already Achieved by the Montreal Protocol' (2015) 6 Nature Communications 7233.

[349] See above at 38.

instance, a tonne of CFC-13 is estimated to have the same global warming potential on 100 years as 16,200 tonnes of carbon dioxide.[350] While the ozone treaties were only aimed at protecting the ozone layer,[351] they took note of the impact of ODSs on the climate system.[352] Reduction in the production and consumption of controlled substances contributed massively to climate change mitigation—in one estimate, their climate benefit was 'far larger' than the expected outcome of the Kyoto Protocol.[353]

However, some controlled substances were replaced by other halogen compounds, including hydrofluorocarbons (HFCs) and some hydrochlorofluorocarbons (HCFCs). These ODS substitutes generally do not affect the ozone layer,[354] but, like ODSs, they are potent GHGs. With the rapid increase in demand for refrigerants in emerging economies, there was a risk that large quantities of such ODS substitutes would be produced, consumed, and eventually released into the atmosphere, thus accelerating climate change.[355] Even though ODS substitutes fall within the scope of the UNFCCC regime, many observers argued that gas-specific obligations, based on the structure of control measures under the ozone regime, would be more effective.[356] Thus, on 15 October 2016, the parties to the Montreal Protocol adopted the Kigali Amendment to regulate the consumption and production of ODS substitutes as another group of controlled substances.[357] The Kigali Amendment stretches the Montreal Protocol beyond its original scope by addressing the production and consumption of an ODS substitute with the exclusive aim of mitigating climate change. The Amendment entered into force on 1 January 2019 between the parties that accepted it.[358] China accepted this treaty in 2021 and the United States may be heading in the same direction.[359]

[350] See Chris Smith and others, 'The Earth's Energy Budget, Climate Feedbacks, and Climate Sensitivity' in Valérie Masson-Delmotte and others (eds), *Climate Change 2021: The Physical Science Basis. Contribution of the Working Group I to the Sixth Assessment Report of the Intergovernmental Panel on Climate Change* (accepted version subject to final editing, IPCC 2021) table 7.SM.7.

[351] Vienna Convention for the Protection of the Ozone Layer (n 8) art 2(1).

[352] See ibid arts 1(2), 3(1)(c); Montreal Protocol (n 8) Preamble ¶5.

[353] Guus JM Velders and others, 'The Importance of the Montreal Protocol in Protecting Climate' (2007) 104 PNAS 4814. See also Rishav Goyal and others, 'Reduction in Surface Climate Change Achieved by the 1987 Montreal Protocol' (2019) 14 Environmental Research Letters 124041. Any such estimates rely on questionable counterfactual scenarios to estimate how ODSs and GHGs emissions would have evolved without treaties.

[354] HCFCs have a mild ozone-depleting potential, whereas HFCs have no such potential. See Francis A Carey, 'Chlorofluorocarbon (CFC)', *Britannica Academic* (Encyclopædia Britannica 2009).

[355] Guus JM Velders and others, 'The Large Contribution of Projected HFC Emissions to Future Climate Forcing' (2009) 106 PNAS 10949.

[356] See Twenty-Second Meeting of the Parties to the Montreal Protocol, 'Declaration on the Global Transition Away from Hydrochlorofluorocarbons (HCFCs) and Chlorofluorocarbons (CFCs)', UNEP/OzL.Pro.22/9, 53 (26 November 2010); Guus JM Velders and others, 'Preserving Montreal Protocol Climate Benefits by Limiting HFCs' (2012) 335 Science 922.

[357] Kigali Amendment (n 47).

[358] See Vienna Convention for the Protection of the Ozone Layer (n 8) art 9(5).

[359] See Executive Order 14008 of 27 January 2021, 'Tackling the Climate Crisis at Home and Abroad', 86 Fed Reg 7619 (US), s 102(h); US–China Joint Statement Addressing the Climate Crisis (17 April 2021) ¶4(c); <https://perma.cc/DYJ4-CPC2>; US Senate (117th Congress), 'Amendment to Montreal

Each party to the Kigali Amendment commits to a gradual reduction of its levels of production and consumption of ODS substitutes.[360] The baseline for this rate of reduction is the party's own average level of consumption and production rates of ODS substitutes from 2011 to 2013. Each party must achieve an 85 per cent reduction on production and consumption by 2036,[361] except for developing countries with a low consumption level, which must generally achieve an 80 per cent reduction by 2045.[362] The Meeting of the Parties can authorize additional delays and exemptions for specific uses.[363]

A more specific provision of the Kigali Amendment relates to a particular ODS substitute, HFC-23, which is mainly generated as a by-product of the synthesis of other controlled substances and has no large-scale industrial application. For a long time, factories had simply vented out waste HFC-23 in the atmosphere, despite its high global warming potential.[364] Under the flexibility mechanisms of the Kyoto Protocol,[365] projects were implemented to provide financial incentives for the incineration of HFC-23. However, these projects had to be abruptly discontinued when it emerged that the subsidy was inadvertently promoting an increase in the production of other controlled substances by making the whole production process far more profitable.[366] Following a more traditional regulatory approach, the Kigali Amendment requires its parties to ensure, 'to the extent practicable', that any HFC-23 generated during the production of some other controlled substances is destroyed using technologies approved by decisions of the Meeting of the Parties.[367]

Finally, the Kigali Amendment extends the application of the provisions of the Montreal Protocol on the control of trade with non-parties to ODS-substitutes. In particular, the parties to the Kigali Amendment committed to ban the import and export of ODS substitutes to any state not party to the Montreal Protocol from 2033.[368] This provision will be of little practical use given the near universal ratification of the Montreal Protocol.

Protocol ("Kigali Amendment")' Senate Consideration of Treaty Document 117-1, received on 16 November 2021.

360 Montreal Protocol (n 8) consolidated version, art 2J.

361 Ibid art 2(J)(1), (3).

362 Ibid art 5(8qua)(a).

363 See eg ibid arts 2J(2), (4)–(5), 5(8qua)(b)–(g).

364 One tonne of HFC-23 has the same global warming potential on 100 years as 14,600 tonnes of carbon dioxide. See Smith (n 350).

365 See n 82.

366 See Environmental Investigation Agency, 'Two Billion Tonne Climate Bomb: How to Defuse the HFC-23 Problem' (2013); Lambert Schneider and Anja Kollmuss, 'Perverse Effects of Carbon Markets on HFC-23 and SF6 Abatement Projects in Russia' (2015) 5 Nature Climate Change 1061.

367 Montreal Protocol (n 8) consolidated version, art 2J(6)–(7). See also Decision XXX/6, 'Destruction Technologies for Controlled Substances', UNEP/OzL.Pro.30/11 (15 November 2018).

368 Montreal Protocol (n 8) consolidated version, art 4(1)sept, (2)sept. On the delayed entry into force of this provision, see Kigali Amendment (n 47) art IV(2).

2. Commitments Incidental to the Regulation of International Civil Aviation

Aviation contributes significantly to causing climate change through both GHG emissions (in particular carbon dioxide)[369] and the formation of contrails.[370] While domestic aviation squarely falls within the jurisdiction of a single state, there is no consensus on the way to allocate responsibility for the climate impacts of international civil aviation.[371] As noted above, the UNFCCC is silent, hence ambivalent, on the geographical scope of its substantive obligations.[372] The Kyoto Protocol committed Annex I parties to 'pursue' limitation or reduction of GHG emissions from aviation by 'working through' ICAO.[373] By contrast, the Paris Agreement did not mention international civil aviation, thus neither precluding a potential role of ICAO nor excluding the potential application of NDCs to international aviation.[374]

ICAO is an international organization and a UN specialized agency established by the Convention on International Civil Aviation of 1944 ('Chicago Convention'),[375] which has achieved almost universal ratification. The main objective of ICAO, as defined by the Chicago Convention, is to ensure 'the safe and orderly growth of international civil aviation throughout the world'.[376] Although the Convention does not mention environmental protection or climate change, the ICAO Assembly (a plenary body) has sought to 'maintain the initiative in developing policy guidance' on environmental matters, if only in order 'not [to] leave such initiative to other organizations'.[377]

[369] See OECD, 'Air Transport CO2 Emissions' OECD.Stat (2020), estimating that airplanes emitted 883 Mt CO_2 in 2018, including 543 Mt from international civil aviation.

[370] See Lisa Bock and Ulrike Burkhardt, 'Contrail Cirrus Radiative Forcing for Future Air Traffic' (2019) 19 Atmospheric Chemistry & Physics 8163; EASA, 'Updated Analysis of the Non-CO_2 Climate Impacts of Aviation and Potential Policy Measures pursuant to the EU Emissions Trading System Directive Article 30(4)' (2020) 7; David S Lee and others, 'The Contribution of Global Aviation to Anthropogenic Climate Forcing for 2000 to 2018' (2021) 244 Atmospheric Environment 117834.

[371] UNFCCC SBSTA, 'Detailed Information on Electricity Trade and International Bunker Fuels', FCCC/SBSTA/1996/9/Add.2 (26 June 1996); Uwe M Erling 'How to Reconcile the European Union Emissions Trading System (EU ETS) for Aviation with the Carbon Offsetting and Reduction Scheme for International Aviation (CORSIA)?' (2018) 43 Air & Space L 371, 374.

[372] See n 49.

[373] Kyoto Protocol (n 3) art 2(2).

[374] The EU extended the application of its emission trading scheme to international aviation before suspending this measure in light of the progress of international negotiations towards a multilateral market-based mechanism, but its position remains that it has the right to regulate emissions from international aviation. See Directive 2008/101/EC of the European Parliament and of the Council of 19 November 2008 amending Directive 2003/87/EC so as to include aviation activities in the scheme for greenhouse gas emission allowance trading within the Community [2009] OJ L8/3; Thomas Leclerc, 'Aviation et secteur maritime face aux enjeux climatiques' in Christel Cournil (ed), *La fabrique d'un droit climatique* (Pedone 2021) 181, 196–98.

[375] Convention on International Civil Aviation (7 December 1944, in force 4 April 1947) 15 UNTS 295 ('Chicago Convention') art 43; Protocol Concerning the Entry into Force of the Agreement between the United Nations and the International Civil Aviation Organization (1 October 1947) 8 UNTS 315.

[376] Chicago Convention (n 375) art 44(a).

[377] ICAO Assembly Res A22-12 (1977) Doc 9215, Res A22-51, ¶2. See also Brian F Havel and Gabriel S Sanchez, *The Principles and Practice of International Aviation Law* (CUP 2014) 228–29; Ruwantissa

The Convention recognizes each contracting state's 'complete and exclusive sovereignty over the airspace above its territory'.[378] On the other hand, each party 'undertakes to collaborate in securing the highest practicable degree of uniformity in regulations, standards, procedures, and organization' in relation to various aspects of international civil aviation.[379] The ICAO Council (composed of thirty-six elected contracting states)[380] is to 'adopt ... international standards and recommended practices' (SARPs), which, 'for convenience', are designated as Annexes to the Chicago Convention.[381] SARPs become 'effective' three months after their communication to the parties unless a majority of the parties register their disapproval.[382]

The legal status of SARPs remains a debated question.[383] The most likely interpretation is that, in general, SARPs are not directly legally binding, although states have an obligation to notify ICAO if they do not comply with a standard. Article 38 of the Chicago Convention requires a state 'which finds it impracticable to comply' to 'give immediate notification to the [ICAO] of the differences between its own practice and that established by the international standard'.[384] As such, a state would be acting in breach of this procedural obligation if it was not complying with a standard without having notified ICAO that it found it impracticable to comply. However, the consequences of a breach of this obligation of notification may be different from the consequences that would follow from the breach of an obligation to implement SARPs, if there was such an obligation.

Nevertheless, some support can be found for a more extensive interpretation of the Chicago Convention as implying an obligation to implement SARPs. For instance, the Convention's provision on dispute settlement refers to disputes 'relating to the interpretation or application of this Convention and its Annexes'.[385] Moreover, the ICAO Assembly introduced a distinction between 'standards' to which states 'will conform in accordance with the Convention' and 'recommended practices' with which parties 'will endeavor to conform in accordance with the Convention'.[386] This distinction could suggest that standards are legally binding,

Abeyratne, 'Carbon Offsetting as a Trade Related Market Based Measure for Aircraft Engine Emissions' (2017) 51 JWT 425; Baine P Kerr, 'Clear Skies or Turbulence Ahead? The International Civil Aviation Organization's Obligation to Mitigate Climate Change' (2020) 16 Utrecht LR 101.

[378] Chicago Convention (n 375) art 1.

[379] Ibid art 37. See also art 12.

[380] Ibid (consolidated version) art 50(a).

[381] Ibid art 54(l). See also arts 37, 90.

[382] Ibid art 90.

[383] See RIR Abeyratne, 'The Legal Status of the Chicago Convention and its Annexes' (1994) 19 Air & Space L 113, 120–23; Michael Milde, *International Air Law and ICAO* (Eleven 2008) 46; Havel and Sanchez (n 377) 60–64.

[384] Chicago Convention (n 375) art 38. Unfortunately, ICAO does not make these notifications publicly available.

[385] Chicago Convention (n 375) art 84.

[386] ICAO Assembly Res A1-31 (1947) A1-P/45, Doc 4411, 27, ¶3.

whereas recommended practices are not.[387] It remains, however, that nothing in the Chicago Convention expressly requires states to comply with SARPs, which, themselves, are rarely, if ever, drafted in a mandatory language. In particular, a treaty provision on the condition for ICAO Annexes to 'become effective'[388] does not necessarily imply that they have any legal force.[389]

Since the early 1980s, the ICAO Council has adopted SARPs to regulate the environmental impacts of international aviation, which have been designated as Annex 16 to the Chicago Convention. Volumes I and II relate to noise and engine emissions of air pollutants, respectively. In 2017 and 2018, the Council adopted volumes III and IV, which are concerned with climate change mitigation. Volume III establishes consideration for fuel efficiency standards as part of the process through which a state recognizes the airworthiness of a new aircraft or aircraft type.[390] In application of Article 39 of the Chicago Convention, if a contracting state issues an airworthiness certificate to an aeroplane that does not comply with the standards defined in Volume III, this certificate must contain appropriate annotations,[391] and other contracting states may decide not to authorize the use of this aeroplane in their airspace.[392] This standard does not apply to pre-existing aircraft or aircraft types which have already been recognized as airworthy. In practical terms, however, Volume III appears ineffective because the standards it defines are merely following the current technology and do not require any additional efforts.[393]

Volume IV establishes a carbon offsetting and reduction scheme for international civil aviation (CORSIA). This mechanism seeks to make up for any increase of international aviation emissions from 2020 onwards by requiring airlines to acquire and cancel emission units from eligible emission reduction projects. CORSIA's 'pilot phase' (2021–23) and 'first phase' (2024–26) apply only to the states that decide to opt in, whereas a 'second phase' (2027–35) will be applicable to all contracting states other than the least-developed countries, small

[387] See generally Havel and Sanchez (n 377) 62.

[388] See n 382.

[389] Cf Marek Jaśkowski, 'External Aspects of the EU ETS in Aviation in Light of CORSIA' (2021) 23 ICLR 271, 276.

[390] Chicago Convention (n 375) Annex 16 vol III, 'Aeroplane CO_2 Emissions' (2017), in particular §II.1, ¶1.1–1.3.

[391] Ibid art 39(1).

[392] Ibid art 40.

[393] See eg Regulatory Impact Analysis Statement to the Regulation Amending the Canadian Aviation Regulation (CO_2 Emissions), SOR/2020-251, [2020] Canada Gazette II.154(25) 3348; Control of Air Pollution from Aircraft and Aircraft Engines: GHG Emissions Standards and Test Procedures (proposed 11 January 2021), 86 Fed Reg 2136, 2164 (supplementary information) (US), both finding that the standard would impose no genuine constraint on the industry. See generally Benoit Mayer and Zhuoqi Ding, 'Climate Change Mitigation in the Aviation Sector: A Critical Overview of National and International Initiatives' (2022) 11 TEL (forthcoming).

island developing states, and landlocked developing countries.[394] In each phase, offsetting requirements apply only to international flights between participating states.[395] Given the legal nature of SARPs, the applicability of CORSIA to a flight does not imply a legal obligation for the contracting party (let alone the aeroplane operator) to implement CORSIA, but a participating state would be in violation of its obligation under Article 38 of the Chicago Convention if it failed to comply with CORSIA without notifying ICAO.[396] Moreover, when the state has made a declaration of its will to participate in CORSIA's pilot phase or first phase, this unilateral declaration could conceivably create legal obligations by itself, depending on its wording and context.[397]

3. Commitments Incidental to the Regulation of Pollution from Ships

Like international civil aviation, international shipping contributes significantly to global GHG emissions,[398] but the responsibility for these emissions does not fall squarely onto any state, and the Kyoto Protocol commits Annex I parties to 'pursue' limitation or reduction of GHG emissions from marine bunker fuels by 'working through' the IMO.[399] The IMO is a UN Specialized Agency aiming to facilitate co-operation on 'technical matters of all kinds affecting shipping engaged in international trade'.[400] While the IMO supervises the application of multiple treaties, the negotiations on climate change mitigation were situated under the International Convention for the Prevention of Pollution from Ships of 1973 as modified by its Protocol of 1978 ('MARPOL 73/78').[401] As for international aviation,[402] the IMO competence is not exclusive, and nothing precludes national initiatives aimed at limiting emissions from international shipping.[403]

394 ICAO Assembly Res A39-3 (2016) Doc 10075, I-80, ¶9; Chicago Convention (n 375) Annex 16 vol IV 'Carbon Offsetting and Reduction Scheme for International Aviation (CORSIA)' (2018) §II.3, ¶1.3(b).

395 ICAO Assembly Res A39-3 (n 394) ¶10.

396 See n 384.

397 See above at 63.

398 See IEA, International Shipping: Tracking Report (2020); IMO, Fourth IMO Greenhouse Gas Study (2020), both estimating that international shipping was responsible for about 2 per cent of global carbon dioxide emissions in 2018.

399 Kyoto Protocol (n 3) art 2(2).

400 International Maritime Organization Convention (6 March 1948, in force 17 March 1958) 289 UNTS 3, art 1(a).

401 International Convention for the Prevention of Pollution from Ships (2 November 1973), as modified by Protocol of 1978 relating thereto (17 February 1978, in force 2 October 1983) 1340 UNTS 61.

402 See above at 82.

403 See eg EU Commission, Communication, '"Fit for 55": Delivering the EU's 2030 Climate Target on the Way to Climate Neutrality' COM(2021)550 final (14 July 2021) §2.2.2.

MARPOL 73/78 was originally focused on preventing discharge of oil and other noxious liquids at sea, but its broad provisions provided a flexible framework to address air pollutants as one of the 'harmful substances' discharged by ships.[404] Thus, Annex VI on the prevention of air pollution from ships was adopted by a Protocol of 1997, which entered into force in 2005 with regard to the states that had accepted it.[405] Annex VI regulates emissions of nitrogen oxide, sulphur oxides, volatile organic compounds, and ODSs from ships engaged on international or domestic voyages.[406] The states that have accepted the Annex are to issue international air pollution prevention certificates and conduct enforcement measures.[407]

Several amendments have been made to extend the provisions of Annex VI.[408] Each of these amendments is applicable to every state party to the Annex, unless it objects to it.[409] A 2011 amendment added regulations relating to energy efficiency with the view of regulating GHG emissions more effectively.[410] It requires every new ship engaged in international voyages to achieve a specified level of energy efficiency, which is set to increase gradually between 2013 and 2025.[411] Pre-existing ships are not required to comply with this standard, but every ship engaging in international voyages must adopt an energy efficiency management plan compliant with technical guidelines developed by the IMO.[412] Further negotiations are ongoing,[413] and a new amendment, adopted in 2021, will establish an energy efficiency rating for existing ships and require carbon intensity reductions from each vessel over time.[414]

MARPOL 73/78 commits its parties to 'undertake to give effects' to the provisions contained in its Annexes.[415] More specifically, every party must exercise its

[404] MARPOL 73/78 (n 401) Preamble ¶5, art 2(2).

[405] Protocol of 1997 to amend the International Convention for the Prevention of Pollution from Ships of 2 November 1973, as modified by the Protocol of 17 February 1978 (26 September 1997, in force 19 May 2005) TIAS No 9–108.

[406] MARPOL 73/78 (n 401) consolidated, Annex VI regulations 12–15.

[407] Ibid consolidated, Annex VI regulations 5–6.

[408] See generally Md Saiful Karim, *Prevention of Pollution of the Marine Environment from Vessels: The Potential and Limits of the International Maritime Organisation* (Springer 2015); Dorota Pyć, 'Ship Energy Efficiency Measures and Climate Protection' (2021) 23 Int C L Rev 241.

[409] MARPOL 73/78 (n 401) art 16(2)(f)–(g).

[410] Res MEPC.203(62), 'Amendments to the Annex of the Protocol of 1997 to Amend the International Convention for the Prevention of Pollution from Ships, 1973, as Modified by the Protocol of 1978 Relating Thereto' (15 July 2011, amendment entered into force 1 January 2013). While there is no mention of GHG emissions in the amendment and only a fleeting reference to the UNFCCC in its Preamble, the IMO has highlighted that this amendment aims to reduce GHG emissions. See eg IMO, 'Mandatory Energy Efficiency Measures for International Shipping Adopted at IMO Environment Meeting' (15 July 2011).

[411] See also MARPOL 73/78 (n 401) consolidated, Annex VI ch 4 regs 20–21, on a 'Attained Energy Efficiency Design Index'.

[412] Ibid reg 22, on a 'Ship Energy Efficiency Management Plan'.

[413] See Resolution MEPC.304(72), 'Initial IMO Strategy on Reduction of GHG Emissions from Ships' (13 April 2017).

[414] Res MEPC.328(76) amending MARPOL Annex VI concerning mandatory goal-based technical and operational measures to reduce carbon intensity of international shipping (EEXI and CII) (June 2021, expected to enter into force 1 November 2022).

[415] MARPOL 73/78 (n 401) art 1(1).

flag, coastal, and port jurisdiction to prohibit and sanction any violations of the regulations contained in the Annexes that the party has accepted.[416] This simultaneous enforcement by the flag, coastal, and port states makes it difficult for ships to evade the scope of applicability of MARPOL 73/78 once a critical mass of parties has accepted an Annex,[417] as is unquestionably the case with Annex VI.[418]

Conclusion

This chapter has shown that commitments related to climate change mitigation arise from climate treaties, unilateral declarations, and several treaties on related subject matters. These obligations vary in many respects, for instance in content, nature, and scope. The complex web they form, however, is built from a unique thread: the consent of states to bind themselves, while expecting that other states would do the same, in order to mitigate climate change.

Unfortunately, these commitments have failed, so far, to achieve the objectives that states collectively set for themselves. For instance, the NDCs communicated to date are not consistent with the most likely pathways towards the mitigation objectives agreed upon in the Paris Agreement.[419] Explaining this failure of climate negotiations is the project of other books.[420] For our purpose, suffice it to note that the international law on climate change mitigation is not limited to the obligations to which states have expressly consented. Chapter III shows that relevant obligations arise from states' acceptance of certain customary norms.

[416] Ibid arts 4–6. See generally Doris König, 'Marine Environment, International Protection' in *Max Planck Encyclopedia of Public International Law* (online edn, OUP 2013) ¶29.

[417] Karim (n 412) 115.

[418] As of May 2022, the 102 parties to the Protocol represented more than 97 per cent of the gross tonnage of the world's merchant fleet. See IMO, 'Status of Conventions' (27 October 2021) <https://www.imo.org/en/About/Conventions/Pages/StatusOfConventions.aspx>.

[419] See Decisions 1/CP.21 (n 117) ¶17; 1/CMA.3 'Glasgow Climate Pact' (n 273) ¶23; UNEP DTU Partnership, 'Emissions Gap Report 2021' (UNEP 2021).

[420] See eg Stephen M Gardiner, *A Perfect Moral Storm: The Ethical Tragedy of Climate Change* (OUP 2011); David G Victor, *Global Warming Gridlock: Creating More Effective Strategies for Protecting the Planet* (CUP 2011); Dale Jamieson, *Reason in a Dark Time: Why the Struggle against Climate Change Failed—and What It Means for Our Future* (OUP 2014).

III
Customary Obligations

Introduction

Chapter II explored commitments arising from state consent to be bound to mitigate climate change. The present chapter turns to another source of international law obligations on climate change mitigation: customary international law. It shows that, in addition to any commitments it may have consented to, every state also has a mitigation obligation arising from international custom.

Custom has attracted relatively little attention in academic research and debates on climate law. Rather, the prevailing emphasis has been on normative and institutional developments taking place under the UN Framework Convention on Climate Change (UNFCCC).[1] Yet, as this chapter shows, there is no reason to think that climate treaties prevent the application of customary international law to climate change. In fact, the relevance of climate treaties is limited by the shortcomings of the political processes through which they are adopted. Consensus-based negotiations[2] tend to achieve little more than the lowest common denominator. Moreover, a state is free not to consent to treaties and not to express a will to be bound by unilateral declarations. Customary international law makes up for some of these shortcomings. While there is no denying the difficulty of identifying and interpreting customary norms, it remains that these norms apply more broadly and are possibly more stringent than commitments.

At the very least, customary international law acts as a 'safety net', creating obligations applicable to any state notwithstanding its consent to climate treaties or its will to be bound by unilateral declaration. A potential exception, under the doctrine of the persistent objector, is unlikely to apply in relation to climate change mitigation because virtually every state has seemingly recognized a general

[1] This emphasis is perhaps most obvious in the short overviews of climate law provided in textbooks on public international law and international environmental law. See eg James Crawford, *Brownlie's Principles of Public International Law* (8th edn, OUP 2012) 347–48 (*Brownlie's*); Philippe Sands and Jacqueline Peel, *Principles of International Environmental Law* (4th edn, CUP 2018) 297–334; Alan Boyle and Catherine Redgwell, *International Law and the Environment* (4th edn, OUP 2021) 378–403.

[2] Unlike other negotiation forums, the COP has never been able to agree to rules of procedures allowing votes on substantive decisions. See UNFCCC, 'Draft Rules of Procedure of the Conference of the Parties and its Subsidiary Bodies', FCCC/CP/1996/2 (1996), draft rule 42 (containing two alternatives); UNFCCC COP25, Report of the Conference, FCCC/CP/2019/13 (2020) ¶¶4–5; Antto Vihma, 'Climate of Consensus: Managing Decision Making in the UN Climate Change Negotiations' (2015) 24 RECIEL 58, 62.

International Law Obligations on Climate Change Mitigation. Benoit Mayer, Oxford University Press. © Benoit Mayer 2022.
DOI: 10.1093/oso/9780192843661.003.0003

obligation on climate change mitigation by ratifying the UNFCCC.[3] As such, the hypothetical decision of a state to withdraw from all climate treaties would not allow that state to cause unlimited amounts of greenhouse gas (GHG) emissions. Rather, that state would continue to be bound, under customary international law, by substantive obligations similar to the general mitigation commitments affirmed in the UNFCCC.[4]

Customary international law also has a broader role to play in defining the obligations of every state, notwithstanding its treaty participation. The content of customary obligations may differ from that of commitments. The condition for the formation of a custom—relying on the practice and views of most, or almost all, states—may be satisfied in circumstances where states are not able to achieve the consensus necessary for the adoption of a treaty under the UNFCCC regime: the opposition of a single state could, in principle, prevent the adoption of a decision by consensus but not the emergence of general state practice accepted as law.[5] In addition to specific norms on climate change mitigation, customary law includes broad principles that states have gradually accepted as law because they reflected their common conception of justice. Compared with climate treaties, these customary principles are one degree removed from political negotiations; they may impose on powerful states the idea of justice that those states had agreed on in different circumstances but, in light of their vested interests, may be reluctant to recognize in the context of climate change. As such, it is unsurprising that litigation on states' mitigation obligations tends to focus on customary obligations rather than on more specific commitments.[6]

On the other hand, applying customary international law to climate change mitigation raises difficult questions. Despite the recent work of the International Law Commission (ILC) on the topic,[7] the law on the identification of customary international law is far from settled.[8] Even less is known about how a norm of customary international law, once identified, is to be interpreted and applied to a set

[3] See *Asylum (Columbia/Peru)*, Judgment (20 November 1950), [1950] ICJ Rep 266, 277–78; *Fisheries (UK v Norway)*, Judgment (18 December 1951), [1951] ICJ Rep 116, 131; ILC, 'Draft Conclusions on Identification of Customary International Law' in ILC Report, 70th session, A/73/10 (2018) 119, conclusion 15. A potential counter-objection is that acceptance of an obligation under the UNFCCC does not necessarily reflect acceptance of this obligation as customary law; but see discussion above at 113. One could, in any case, question the continuing applicability of the doctrine, especially in relation to communitarian norms on the protection of global commons that are (nearly) universally accepted. See Niels Petersen, 'The Role of Consent and Uncertainty in the Formation of Customary International Law' in Brian D Lepard (ed), *Reexamining Customary International Law* (CUP 2017) 120.

[4] See Evan J Criddle and Evan Fox-Decent, 'Mandatory Multilateralism' (2019) 113 AJIL 272, 320–21.

[5] See n 2. See generally Jonathan I Charney, 'The Persistent Objector Rule and the Development of Customary International Law' (1986) 56 BYBIL 1, 19, noting that customary law develops on the basis of a 'weighted majority'.

[6] See eg *Urgenda v Netherlands*, ECLI:NL:HR:2019:2007 (SC, 20 December 2019), English translation in (2020) 59 ILM 811.

[7] ILC, 'Customary International Law' (n 3).

[8] See eg BS Chimni, 'Customary International Law: A Third World Perspective' (2018) 112 AJIL 1.

of facts.[9] As such, this chapter inevitably builds on weak foundations—but so do the courts, which have to apply the law, despite all these difficulties, in the cases brought before them. While this chapter identifies the most relevant questions and proposes conclusions that a judge would likely arrive at, there is no denial that reasonable disagreement is possible on some important aspects of the argument.

Acknowledging these difficulties front and centre, section A explores two preliminary methodological issues that are instrumental in the following analysis: first, the relation between ascending and descending reasoning in the process of identifying customary international law; then, the individuation of customary law obligations. Section B identifies two broad customary obligations relevant to climate change mitigation: the obligations of prevention and cooperation. Section C identifies a discrete customary obligation on climate change mitigation. It shows that this obligation can be identified both by deduction from the general obligations identified in section B and by induction from empirical evidence. Section D demonstrates that the application of treaties does not exclude the application of customary obligations on climate change mitigation. Finally, section E explores further how climate treaties assist in the interpretation of customary obligations and vice versa.

A. Preliminary Methodological Issues

The identification of customary international law in relation to climate change mitigation faces two major methodological issues. The first issue regards the respective roles for descending and ascending reasoning in the identification of customary international law.[10] An obligation to mitigate climate change may be induced from evidence of a general practice of states accepted as law (ascending reasoning) or it could be deduced from the existence of broader norms of customary international law or from the premises of the international legal order (descending reasoning). The two types of reasoning, however, may lead to different interpretations of customary law.

The second issue relates to the process of distinguishing individual norms within the body of customary law (individuation). An obligation to mitigate climate change could be viewed as part of broad obligations to prevent environmental harm and to cooperate in addressing international problems, but it could also be construed as a distinct obligation to mitigate climate change whose existence and content are to be assessed separately.

[9] See Benoit Mayer, 'Climate Change Mitigation as an Obligation under Customary International Law' 48 Yale J Int'l L (forthcoming). See generally Orfeas Chasapis-Tassinis, 'Customary International Law: Interpretation from Beginning to End' (2020) 31 EJIL 235.

[10] See above at 23.

These two methodological issues extend far beyond the reach of this book, and yet they must be explored, if only briefly, as they inevitably play an important role in an analysis of the customary international law on climate change mitigation. A descending reasoning could suggest that states are required to do whatever is considered as necessary to mitigate climate change, whereas an ascending reasoning would not suggest an obligation for a state to do anything more than the standard inferred from general state practice. In turn, an ascending reasoning could lead to markedly different conclusions, depending on how one approaches the question of individuation of customary law—that is, on whether the empirical evidence of state practice and acceptance as law that one relies on to ascertain states' mitigation obligations relates to a discrete obligation of mitigation or to broader obligations of prevention and cooperation.

1. Ascending and Descending Approaches to the Identification of Customary Law

Legal scholars have repeatedly highlighted the difficulty of identifying customary international law. They have suggested that this source of law is both 'indeterminate and manipulable',[11] that academic works that claim to identify customary norms are often merely 'pieces of advocacy',[12] and that judges tend to 'assert' rather than demonstrate the existence of such norms.[13] These critiques do not affect the relevance of customary international law (judges do, frequently, rely on customary norms to make their judgments), but they call for caution and methodological rigour. The recent work of the ILC on the topic, albeit helpful, leaves many important questions unanswered.

In particular, a distinction can be drawn between ascending and descending approaches to the identification of customary international law.[14] The ascending approach, following the definition of customary international law, induces a norm of customary international law from empirical evidence of a 'general practice' of states that they generally accept as law.[15] This approach has been central to the ILC's work on the identification of customary international law,[16] but it faces obvious

[11] J Patrick Kelly, 'The Twilight of Customary International Law' (1999) 40 Va JIL 449, 451.

[12] Fernando R Tesón, 'Fake Custom' in Lepard (n 3) 87.

[13] Stefan Talmon, 'Determining Customary International Law: The ICJ's Methodology between Induction, Deduction and Assertion' (2015) 26 EJIL 417.

[14] The distinction often drawn between 'traditional' and 'modern' approaches is actually two-fold. At times, what scholars distinguish is not induction and deduction but induction based on general practice and induction based on acceptance as law. See eg Anthea Elizabeth Roberts, 'Traditional and Modern Approaches to Customary International Law: A Reconciliation' (2001) 95 AJIL 757; William Thomas Worster, 'The Inductive and Deductive Methods in Customary International Law Analysis: Traditional and Modern Approaches' (2013) 45 Georgetown JIL 445.

[15] See Statute of the International Court of Justice (26 June 1945, in force 24 October 1945) 3 Bevans 1153, art 38(1)(b).

[16] ILC, 'Customary International Law' (n 3) conclusions 2, 3.

practical and conceptual limitations. Assessing a general practice of states on any topic would require a comprehensive survey, which courts cannot or, at least, do not generally conduct in any rigorous manner—instead, courts tend to rely on anecdotal evidence on the practice of just a few (mostly Western) states.[17] Acceptance as law is even more difficult to establish, given the multiplicity of individuals and institutions involved in the determination of the conduct of a state and the distinct possibility that these individuals may hold different views about the existence of a legal obligation.

By contrast, the descending approach to the identification of customary international law infers (eg by deduction) the existence of a norm from that of other norms (which, themselves, may have been identified based on an ascending reasoning). While it is undeniable that 'customary law is empirical',[18] it nevertheless remains that deduction is an essential part of any form of legal reasoning,[19] and the identification of norms of customary international law (or, at least, of norms implied by customary international law) is no exception. As a valid deduction from true premises conclusively demonstrates the truth of its conclusion,[20] there does not appear to be any limitation to the use of deductive argument in legal reasoning other than the truth of the premises. Yet, when the descending arguments are based on norms whose scope and nature are often ill understood, there is a risk that such 'abstract' reasoning elides the many contradictions and lacunae that plague the law as it is, conveying instead a somewhat utopian vision of an entirely consistent and effective legal system—that is, the law as (the interpreter believes) it *should* be.[21]

Ascending reasoning may at times appear sufficient to identify a norm of customary law but, in most cases, descending reasoning plays an indispensable complementary role—if only to frame the hypothetical norm whose existence can then be confirmed by empirical evidence. Thus, the ILC's conclusions mostly describe an ascending approach, but they do not 'preclude a measure of deduction as an aid, to be employed with caution'.[22] As Stefan Talmon noted, even Georg Schwarzenberger, 'the main proponent of the inductive approach to international law, was not advocating a complete renunciation of the deductive method'.[23] On

[17] Chimni (n 8) 20–27.

[18] Kelly (n 11) 453.

[19] One could not apply a general norm to a particular case without using a deductive reasoning.

[20] Patrick J Hurley and Lori Watson, *A Concise Introduction to Logic* (13th edn, Cengage 2018) 34.

[21] See eg Christian Tomuschat, 'Obligations Arising for States Without or Against Their Will' (1993) 241 RdC 195, 293–94, observing that the prohibition of the use of force could be viewed as a logical implication of sovereign equality, but that it had not always been recognized as a positive legal norm.

[22] ILC, 'Customary International Law' (n 3) commentary on conclusion 2, ¶5.

[23] Talmon (n 13) 423, citing Georg Schwarzenberger, *Inductive Approach to International Law* (Stevens & Sons 1965) 38. See also Georg Schwarzenberger, 'The Inductive Approach to International Law' (1947) 60 Harv LR 539, 566 noting that '[e]ven the most experimental of sciences use the deductive method', while being 'usually aware of the fact that, unless and until verified, such deductions are but provisional'.

the other hand, the proponents of deductive reasoning certainly recognize its limitation to a complementary role. Christian Tomuschat, for instance, highlighted the importance of deductive reasoning in the process of identifying customary law, but he also acknowledged that 'care must be taken to avoid abstract reasoning that does not take into account the overall political context'.[24]

Judicial practice frequently relies on descending reasoning to identify customary norms, in particular on the basis of the general premises of the international legal order such as the principle of sovereign equality.[25] Thus, the International Court of Justice (ICJ) in *Gulf of Maine* recognized that customary international law contains not only norms that 'can be tested by induction' but also 'a limited set of norms for ensuring the co-existence and vital co-operation of the members of the international community'.[26] It is noteworthy that descending reasoning has played a particularly prominent role in the identification of customary law on environmental protection. International courts and tribunals have identified the obligation of states to prevent transboundary environmental harm without conducting any systematic survey of state practice or its acceptance as law but essentially by relying on deduction from the principle of sovereign equality and the due diligence obligation that it implies.[27] As a step further, the ICJ in *Pulp Mills* interpreted this obligation of prevention as entailing a state obligation to require the conduct of an environmental impact assessment (EIA) before authorizing an activity likely to cause transboundary environmental harm—here again, without a systematic survey of empirical evidence.[28]

This reliance on descending reasoning can be explained and justified as a way of overcoming the inherent limitation of a purely ascending reasoning: its inability to ascertain the applicable law in the absence of clearly defined general state practice accepted as law. Ascending reasoning cannot determine the law applicable when there is no (or very little) relevant state practice or when the relevant state practice is evenly divided in support of two or several hypothetical norms.[29] It has been suggested (often by reference to a misreading of the *Lotus* decision) that, if the

[24] Tomuschat (n 21) 294.

[25] See ibid 303.

[26] *Delimitation of the Maritime Boundary in the Gulf of Maine Area (Canada/US)*, Judgment (12 October 1984), [1984] ICJ Rep 246, ¶111. See also *Corfu Channel (UK v Albania)*, Judgment on Merits (9 April 1949), [1949] ICJ Rep 4, 35; *North Sea Continental Shelf (Germany/Denmark, Germany/Netherlands)*, Judgment (20 February 1969), [1969] ICJ Rep 3, ¶¶39–56; *Military and Paramilitary Activities in and against Nicaragua (Nicaragua v US)*, Judgment on Merits (27 June 1986), [1986] ICJ Rep 132, ¶202.

[27] See *Trail Smelter (US/Canada)*, Award of 11 March 1941, 3 RIAA 1938, 1965; *Legality of the Threat or Use of Nuclear Weapons*, Advisory Opinion (8 July 1996), [1996] ICJ Rep 226, ¶29; *Pulp Mills on the River Uruguay (Argentina v Uruguay)*, Judgment (20 April 2010), [2010] ICJ Rep 14, ¶101; *Certain Activities Carried Out by Nicaragua in the Border Area (Costa Rica v Nicaragua) and Construction of a Road in Costa Rica along the San Juan River (Nicaragua v Costa Rica)*, Judgment on Merit (16 December 2015), [2015] ICJ Rep 665, ¶104.

[28] *Pulp Mills* (n 27) ¶204. See also *Certain Activities* (n 27) ¶104.

[29] Talmon (n 13) 422–23.

existence of an obligation cannot be conclusively demonstrated, one ought to conclude that there is no such obligation, hence that the state has an unrestricted right to act as it wishes.[30] Yet, this argument is unconvincing in situations where this unrestricted right of a state would inevitably come at the expense of the rights of other states. For instance, considering *arguendo* that there was no conclusive evidence of state practice accepted as law either confirming or ruling out the existence of an obligation to prevent transboundary environmental harm, it is unclear why one would presume that a state has the right to cause such harm rather than presuming that other states have the right not to be harmed (inferred, for instance, from their right to development). In such circumstances, ascending reasoning by itself is inconclusive,[31] and a judge must rely on a descending reasoning to identify the norm that, being relatively consistent with state practice, appears most consistent with the broader normative system.

The strongest arguments for the identification of customary international law combine descending and ascending reasoning; whenever ascending reasoning is not fully conclusive these arguments rely on a sound deductive argument and test its validity against any available (albeit fragmentary) empirical evidence of state practice and acceptance as law.[32] This book uses such a syncretic method aimed at reflecting the eclectic practice of international courts and tribunals. Thus, as ascending reasoning in isolation may not provide a very clear understanding of relevant customary law, this book relies in part on descending reasoning, but it recognizes that all except the most obvious inferences from the most strongly recognized norms of general international law, once tentatively identified by a descending reasoning, must be confirmed by at least some evidence of state practice and acceptance as law. Descending reasoning will sometimes be presented first, not to suggest that it assumes a higher importance but simply because it helps to identify the hypothetical norms whose existence can then be tested in light of empirical evidence. For instance, the analysis that follows will suggest that a state's obligation to mitigate climate change can be inferred from the general premises of the international legal order (eg the principle of sovereign equality) and more specifically from general principles of customary international law (eg the principle of prevention), but the conclusions of this descending reasoning will then be tested against (and confirmed by) evidence of general state practice and acceptance as law.

[30] See discussion in Prosper Weil, 'The Court Cannot Conclude Definitively... Non Liquet Revisited' (1998) 36 Colum J Transnatl L 109, 112. See also above at 22.

[31] Talmon (n 13) 423.

[32] See C Wilfred Jenks, *The Prospects of International Adjudication* (Stevens & Sons 1964) 9, noting that '[a]s a practical matter, induction and deduction are complementary to each other at every stage in the development of the law'.

2. The Problem of Individuation

The analysis in this chapter raises another issue—the problem of individuation—that the doctrine on customary international law is really just starting to explore. As James Harris noted, 'rules are to systems, not as members are to a club, but as slices are to a cake':[33] they do not initially exist in any divided units. Individuation refers to the process of slicing the law into individual norms—or, as Joseph Raz put it, of 'carving small and manageable units out of the total legal material in a way which will promote our understanding of the law'.[34] There is a nearly infinite number of ways a cake can be sliced and legal norms can be individuated. Individuation has implications not only for the way the law is explained (eg the number of chapters of a textbook) but also possibly for the way it is interpreted and applied. The problem of individuation is precisely that, sometimes, individuation may affect the interpretation of the law.

This problem appears in relation to the identification of customary international law, as Orfeas Chasapis-Tassinis showed, when one seeks to determine 'which rules are the right candidates for the identification and application of customary law in a given instance'.[35] For example, one could alternatively suggest that states have a very specific (ie narrowly individuated) obligation to mitigate climate change or that they only have broader (ie loosely individuated) obligations of prevention of transboundary environmental harm and cooperation on the prevention of such harm, implying that they must mitigate climate change. The choice is of no obvious consequence if one follows a purely descending reasoning, except for the terminological difference between presenting climate change mitigation as either an 'implied obligation' or 'the implication of obligations'. Yet, when relying on an ascending reasoning, individuation has important implications for the scope of empirical evidence that is to be assessed. To ascertain the existence of a discrete norm on climate change mitigation, one would need evidence of state practice accepted as law regarding climate change mitigation. By contrast, to ascertain the existence of more general norms on prevention and cooperation, one would need to refer to a broader set of evidence. The two methods could suggest different conclusions. It could be, for instance, that a general state practice accepted as law could be identified with regard to prevention and cooperation in general but not with regard to climate change mitigation in particular. Beyond the identification of an obligation, individuation may also have implications about the interpretation of any obligation that has been identified, for instance with regard to the content, nature, or

[33] James Harris, *Law and Legal Science: An Inquiry into the Concepts: Legal Rule and Legal System* (Clarendon Press 1979) 84. See also Ronald Dworkin, *Taking Rights Seriously* (Bloomsbury 2013) 88; James Penner, *The Idea of Property in Law* (OUP 2000) 39.

[34] Joseph Raz, *The Concept of a Legal System: An Introduction to the Theory of Legal System* (Clarendon Press 1980) 115.

[35] Chasapis-Tassinis (n 9) 238.

scope of the obligation. For instance, one may observe a different standard of care when framing the obligation more or less broadly.

Regrettably, this problem has rarely been identified in relation to customary international law and it has never been addressed in any systematic way. This book follows, here again, a syncretic approach. Thus, some empirical evidence will be discussed to verify the existence of both a specific obligation of mitigation and general obligations of prevention and cooperation. As will be shown, state practice and acceptance as law suggest the existence of general obligations of states to exercise due diligence and, when necessary, to cooperate, in order to prevent harm to other states; and similar evidence confirms the implication that states must cooperate on the mitigation of climate change.

B. General Customary Obligations Relevant to Climate Change Mitigation

At least two principles of customary international law are relevant to climate change mitigation. First, states must exercise due diligence in order to prevent activities contrary to the rights of other states, in particular activities that result in transboundary environmental harm. Second, states must cooperate when necessary to address issues of international concern. The following subsections identify the general customary obligations of prevention and cooperation. Section C explores further the possibility of identifying a discrete obligation on climate change mitigation, including by inference from the general obligations of prevention and cooperation. To avoid repetition, the applicability of these general obligations of prevention and cooperation to climate change mitigation is mainly discussed in section C, as part of the identification of discrete mitigation obligations from a deductive reasoning.

1. Obligation of Prevention

Under customary international law, states have an obligation to exercise due diligence to prevent activities contrary to the rights of other states. In particular, they must prevent activities likely to cause transboundary environmental harm. This obligation of prevention has been characterized as the 'cornerstone' of international environmental law,[36] and its existence has been said to be 'beyond reasonable argument'.[37] Far more could be written about this obligation than could conceivably be

[36] Sands and Peel (n 1) 191 (in relation to the no-harm principle).
[37] Boyle and Redgwell (n 1) 159.

discussed here.[38] For the present purpose of assessing whether and how this obligation applies to climate change mitigation, one only needs to briefly retrace how it can be identified from both a descending and an ascending approach.

a) Descending approach

A state's general due diligence obligation is a logical implication of some of the most fundamental premises of the international legal order. Under the principle of sovereign equality, states 'have equal rights and duties and are equal members of the international community'.[39] These sovereign rights include, among other things, the rights of every state to territorial integrity,[40] to permanent sovereignty over its natural resources,[41] and to the protection of its citizens.[42] These rights imply corresponding obligations,[43] which are imposed on states, as the main subjects of international law, and apply on all of them normally in an equal manner.[44]

This reasoning is captured by the Latin maxim *Sic utere tuo ut alienum non laedas* ('Use your own property in such a way that you do not injure other people's').[45] This maxim is not a positive legal norm, but it reflects a logical way of understanding the law—if every person in a legal system is equal, the rights of this person must be protected by corresponding obligations imposed on all. For instance, as every state has the right to territorial integrity and to permanent sovereignty over its natural

[38] See Leslie-Anne Duvic-Paoli, *The Prevention Principle in International Environmental Law* (CUP 2018).

[39] Declaration on Principles of International Law Concerning Friendly Relations and Cooperation among States in Accordance with the Charter of the United Nations, UNGA Res 625 (XXV) (24 October 1970). See also Charter of the United Nations (26 June 1945, in force 24 October 1945) art 2(1); Juliane Kokott, 'States, Sovereign Equality' in *Max Planck Encyclopedia of Public International Law* (online edn, OUP 2011) ¶1.

[40] See UN Charter (n 39) art 2(4); *Corfu Channel* (n 26) 35; *Accordance with International Law of the Unilateral Declaration of Independence in Respect of Kosovo*, Advisory Opinion (22 July 2010), [2010] ICJ Rep 403, ¶80.

[41] See International Covenant on Economic, Social and Cultural Rights (16 December 1966, in force 3 January 1976) 993 UNTS 3 art 1(2); International Covenant on Civil and Political Rights (16 December 1966, in force 23 March 1976) 999 UNTS 171, art 1(2); Declaration on Permanent Sovereignty over Natural Resources, UNGA Res 1803 (XVII) (14 December 1962); Declaration on the Establishment of the New International Economic Order, UNGA Res 3201(S-VI) (1 May 1974) ¶4(e); Charter of Economic Rights and Duties of States, UNGA Res 3281 (XXIX) (12 December 1974) art 2(1); Rio Declaration on Environment and Development (14 June 1992) A/CONF.151/26 (vol I) (1992) 31 ILM 874, principle 21; Declaration of the United Nations Conference on the Human Environment (16 June 1972) A/Conf.48/14/Rev.1 (1972) 11 ILM 1416 ('Stockholm Declaration'), principle 2; *Texaco Overseas Petroleum Company v Libya*, Award (19 January 1977) (1978) 17 ILM 1, ¶87; *Armed Activities on the Territory of the Congo (DRC v Uganda)*, Judgment (19 December 2005), [2005] ICJ Rep 168, ¶244; Nico J Schrijver, 'Natural Resources, Permanent Sovereignty Over' in *Max Planck Encyclopedia of Public International Law* (online edn, OUP 2008).

[42] See *Mavrommatis Palestine Concessions (Greece v UK)*, Jurisdiction (30 August 1924), PCIJ Rep Series A/B No 2, 12; ILC, 'Draft Articles on Diplomatic Protection' [2006] II(2) YBILC 24, art 2.

[43] See Wesley Newcomb Hohfeld, 'Some Fundamental Legal Conceptions as Applied in Judicial Reasoning' (1913) 23 Yale LJ 16, 30–32.

[44] These equal obligations can unfold differently when states are in relevantly different circumstances.

[45] Jonathan Law and Elizabeth A Martin, 'Sic Utere Tuo Ut Alienum Non Laedas' in Jonathan Law and Elizabeth A Martin, *A Dictionary of Law* (7th edn, OUP 2014).

resources, it also has an obligation to respect the same rights of other states.[46] This reasoning relates broadly to the concept of abuse of rights: a state must not exercise its sovereign rights 'in a way which impedes the enjoyment by other States of their own rights'.[47]

Various authorities have long followed this reasoning when interpreting international law. Judge Max Huber, in his award in *Island of Palmas*, noted that '[t]erritorial sovereignty ... has as corollary a duty: the obligation to protect within the territory the rights of other States'.[48] The ICJ's 1949 judgment in *Corfu Channel* identified 'every State's obligation not to allow knowingly its territory to be used for acts contrary to the rights of other states'.[49] The same year, an initial survey of international law by the ILC identified 'the rule that a State must not permit the use of its territory for purposes injurious to the interests of other States in a manner contrary to international law'.[50] The maxim continues to be commonly mentioned in authoritative international law scholarship.[51]

This reasoning can be applied to a wide range of circumstances such as the laying of mines (as in *Corfu Channel*), the fomentation of terrorist activities,[52] attacks against state agents,[53] or possibly the organization of cyberattacks.[54] An important application for our purpose regards transboundary environmental harm.[55] The 1941 *Trail Smelter* award recognized that, '[u]nder the principles of international law ... no state has the right to use or permit the use of its territory in such a manner as to cause injury by fumes in or to the territory of another'.[56] Although the tribunal provided minimal explanation for its reasoning, the 'principles of international

[46] See ILC, 'Draft Articles on Prevention of Transboundary Harm from Hazardous Activities' [2001] II(2) YBILC 146, commentary on art 3, ¶1; Jutta Brunnée, 'Sic Utere Tuo Ut Alienum Non Laedas' in *Max Planck Encyclopedia of Public International Law* (online edn, OUP 2010) ¶4.

[47] Alexander Kiss, 'Abuse of Rights' in *Max Planck Encyclopedia of Public International Law* (online edn, OUP 2006) ¶1. See also Dinah Shelton, 'Equitable Utilization of the Atmosphere: A Rights-Based Approach to Climate Change?' in Stephen Humphreys (ed), *Human Rights and Climate Change* (CUP 2009) 94.

[48] *Island of Palmas (Netherlands v US)*, Award (4 April 1928), 2 RIAA 829, 839.

[49] *Corfu Channel* (n 26) 22. See also *Paramilitary Activities* (n 26) ¶115; UNSC Res 1373 (28 September 2001) S/RES/1373.

[50] UN Secretary-General, Survey of International Law in Relation to the Work of the ILC, A/CN.4/Rev.1 (1949) ¶57.

[51] See eg Robert Jennings and Arthur Watts (eds), *Oppenheim's International Law: Volume 1 Peace* (9th edn, OUP 2008) §124 (428) (*Oppenheim's*); *Brownlie's* (n 1) 359; Samantha Besson, 'La *due diligence* en droit international' (2020) 409 RdC 153, 179–205.

[52] International Convention for the Suppression of Terrorist Bombings (15 December 1997, in force 23 May 2001) 2149 UNTS 256; International Convention for the Suppression of the Financing of Terrorism (9 December 1999, in force 10 April 2002) 2178 UNTS 197; Res 1373 (n 49) ¶1.

[53] *United States Diplomatic and Consular Staff in Tehran (US v Iran)*, Judgment (24 May 1980), [1980] ICJ Rep 3, ¶63.

[54] Michael N Schmitt (ed), *Tallinn Manual 2.0 on the International Law Applicable to Cyber Operations* (CUP 2017).

[55] UN Secretary-General (n 50) ¶58.

[56] *Trail Smelter* (n 27) 1965. See also, between 'quasi-sovereign' states, *Georgia v Tennessee Copper* (1907) 206 US 230, 238.

law' to which the award refers seem to include the principle of sovereign equality and its interpretation following the *Sic utere tuo* maxim.[57]

More recent judicial decisions have confirmed this understanding of customary international law. They have also highlighted that every state has not only a negative obligation to refrain from acting in ways that would violate the rights of other states but also a positive obligation to take appropriate measures to prevent such activities conducted by others, whether they are agents of foreign states, corporations, or citizens under its control. Thus, the ICJ's 1996 Advisory Opinion on *Nuclear Weapons* recognized as part of customary international law 'the general obligation of States to ensure that activities within their jurisdiction and control respect the environment of other States or of areas beyond national control'.[58] In 2010, the Court's judgment in *Pulp Mills* confirmed that 'the principle of prevention, as a customary rule, has its origin in the due diligence that is required of a State in its territory',[59] referring to its dictum in *Corfu Channel*.[60] The obligation of states 'to exercise due diligence in preventing significant transboundary environmental harm' was applied once again in the ICJ's 2015 judgment in *Certain Activities*.[61]

The obligation of prevention is not an obligation of result but an obligation of conduct. Thus, as Crawford noted, what is required of a state is not necessarily to succeed in preventing harm but to 'take all reasonable or necessary measures to ensure that the event does not occur'.[62] Arbitral tribunals in *Iron Rhine* and *Indus Waters Kishenganga* pointed out that the obligation of prevention may apply even when a state cannot avoid the harm entirely, but can only hope to mitigate it.[63] In fact, as Brunnée underscored, 'harm is not actually an element of the primary rule': the obligation of prevention 'is triggered not by harm, but by the risk of causing … harm'.[64] The precautionary approach embodies the idea that, in the absence of full scientific certainty, a state must take all cost-effective measures to minimize threats of serious or irreversible damage as part of its obligation of

[57] See eg Brunnée 'Sic Utere' (n 46) ¶10; Shinya Murase, Second Report on the Protection of the Atmosphere, A/CN.4/681 (2015) ¶52.

[58] *Nuclear Weapons* (n 27) ¶29.

[59] *Pulp Mills* (n 27) ¶101.

[60] See n 49.

[61] *Certain Activities* (n 27) ¶104. See also Separate Opinion of Judge Donoghue, ¶8.

[62] James Crawford, *State Responsibility: The General Part* (CUP 2013) 227. Crawford distinguishes an 'obligation of prevention' (an obligation of result) from an 'obligation of due diligence' (an obligation of conduct). In this book, 'obligation of prevention' refers to the obligation of due diligence. There does not appear to be a general obligation of result, at customary international law, with regard to the prevention of environmental harm.

[63] *Indus Waters Kishenganga (Pakistan/India)*, Partial Award (18 February 2013), 31 RIAA 55, ¶451. See also *Iron Rhine Railway (Belgium v Netherlands)*, Award (24 May 2005), 27 RIAA 35, ¶59.

[64] Jutta Brunnée, 'International Environmental Law and Climate Change: Reflections on Structural Challenges in a "Kaleidoscopic" World' (2020) 33 Georgetown Envtl L Rev 113, 120. See also ILC, 'Prevention of Transboundary Harm' (n 46) art 3. But see René Lefeber, 'Climate Change and State Responsibility' in Rosemary Rayfuse and Shirley V Scott (eds), *International Law in the Era of Climate Change* (EE 2012) 338.

prevention.[65] In turn, the obligation of prevention has been interpreted as implying various substantive and procedural obligations, including the conduct of EIAs, notification, and consultation with potentially affected states, as well as negotiation and cooperation in good faith.[66]

Some of the international environmental law literature suggests a distinction between 'no harm' and 'prevention', but it is unclear what this distinction refers to, and it does not seem to be helpful, at least for the present purposes. The authorities used to justify the existence of no harm and prevention are generally the same[67] and, from a purely terminological perspective, there is no obvious difference between the 'prevention' of environmental harm and the attempt to ensure that, as far as possible, 'no harm' occurs. Leslie-Anne Duvic-Paoli and Jorge Viñuales suggest that 'preventing harm' requires more than the 'horizontal tort-like duty on States' that the 'no-harm rule' entails.[68] However, a tort-like obligation, in international law, would precisely take the form of a primary rule on the prevention of harm (similar to the duty of care under tort law), the breach of which would entail secondary obligations of state responsibility. Another hypothesis is that prevention could focus more on environmental resources per se, rather than merely on sovereign rights. Thus, Duvic-Paoli argues that, while no harm aims at 'the avoidance of a tortious act in a world of sovereign States', 'prevention' focuses on 'resource management'.[69] Yet, resource management can very well be understood in terms of sovereign rights, whether in relation to a state's exclusive right to permanent sovereignty over its natural resources or to its non-exclusive rights to the protection of the global commons.[70] In fact, in the world of sovereign states that Duvic-Paoli justly describes, these values can hardly be understood otherwise than through the prism of sovereign rights. A last hypothesis is that a no-harm obligation could be understood literally as an obligation of result requiring states to guarantee that no harm occurs, or at least that no harm directly results from the state's own actions (rather than omissions), by contrast to the obligation of prevention, which is an obligation of conduct. Yet, there is no obvious ground to suggest that a state must comply, in its own conduct, with a stricter obligation than what it imposes on its

[65] See Rio Declaration (n 41) principle 15; *Southern Bluefin Tuna (NZ v Japan, Australia v Japan)*, Order on Provisional Measures (27 August 1999), [1999] ITLOS Rep 280, ¶¶77–80; *Responsibilities and Obligations of States Sponsoring Persons and Entities with Respect to Activities in the Area*, Advisory Opinion (1 February 2011), [2011] ITLOS Rep 10, ¶¶125–35. On the legal status of this concept (or principle), see generally the discussion in Boyle and Redgwell (n 1) 177–83.

[66] See below at 216.

[67] See Leslie-Anne Duvic-Paoli and Jorge E Viñuales, 'Principle 2' in Jorge E Viñuales (ed), *The Rio Declaration on Environment and Development: A Commentary* (OUP 2015) 113; Jutta Brunnée, 'Procedure and Substance in International Environmental Law' (2019) 450 RdC 9, 115–62.

[68] See Duvic-Paoli and Viñuales (n 67) 113.

[69] Duvic-Paoli (n 38) 21; Sands and Peel (n 1) 212.

[70] On the distinction between exclusive and non-exclusive rights, see below at 107. There is no evidence to date of a customary obligation requiring states to protect their own environment, but this obligation could be justified as an *erga omnes* obligation to protect every part of the global environment.

subjects; and, from an ascending perspective, there is no support in state practice for the existence of a general obligation to guarantee that no transboundary environmental harm occurs.[71]

b) Ascending approach

There is relatively strong evidence that, at least in the most general terms, states seek to avoid infringing the rights of one another and that they recognize this as their legal obligation. The most obvious body of evidence of both state practice and its acceptance as law is to be found in a series of declarations, resolutions, and treaty provisions which explicitly recognize this obligation and, to a large extent, endorse the descending reasoning presented above.[72]

Over the past half a century, states have repeatedly affirmed their understanding that their equal sovereign rights imply an obligation for each of them to prevent transboundary environmental harm. In particular, Principle 21 of the 1972 Stockholm Declaration and Principle 2 of the 1992 Rio Declaration note that 'States have, in accordance with the Charter of the United Nations and the principles of international law, the sovereign right to exploit their own resources', and the corresponding obligation ('responsibility') 'to ensure that activities within their jurisdiction or control do not cause damage to the environment of other States'.[73]

States have reaffirmed this principle in several UN General Assembly resolutions[74] and in the Preambles of several major multilateral environmental agreements,[75] including the UNFCCC.[76] Multiple other treaties have sought to implement specific aspects of this obligation.[77] Among them, the general provisions of the UN Convention on the Law of the Sea (UNCLOS) on the protection and preservation of the marine environment are generally viewed as the codification of customary international law.[78] Article 3 of the Convention on Biological Diversity

[71] See eg Boyle and Redgwell (n 1) 153. See also below at 185.

[72] On the relevance of declarations, resolutions, and treaty declarations to the identification of general state practice and acceptance as law, see ILC, 'Customary International Law' (n 3) conclusions 6(2), 10(2), 11(1)(c). See also the references in *Indus Waters Kishenganga*, Partial Award (n 63) ¶449. On the relevance of widely ratified treaties and the 'Baxter paradox', see RR Baxter, 'Treaties and Customs' (1970) 129 RdC 25, 64; James Crawford, 'Chance, Order, Change: The Course of International Law' (2013) 365 RdC 9, 90–112.

[73] See Stockholm Declaration (n 41) principle 21; Rio Declaration (n 41) principle 2.

[74] See Charter of Economic Rights and Duties (n 41) art 30; UNGA Resolutions 48/192 (21 December 1993) Preamble ¶3; Agenda for Development, 51/240 (20 June 1997) ¶142; 73/234 (20 December 2018) Preamble ¶15; World Charter for Nature, 37/7 (28 October 1982) ¶21(d).

[75] See Convention on Long-Range Transboundary Air Pollution (13 November 1979, in force 16 March 1983) 1302 UNTS 217, Preamble ¶6; Vienna Convention for the Protection of the Ozone Layer (22 March 1985, in force 22 September 1988) 1513 UNTS 293, Preamble ¶3; United Nations Convention to Combat Desertification in those Countries Experiencing Serious Drought and/or Desertification, Particularly in Africa 1994 (14 October 1994, in force 26 December 1996) 1954 UNTS 3, Preamble ¶16.

[76] United Nations Framework Convention on Climate Change (9 May 1992, in force 21 March 1994) 1771 UNTS 107, Preamble ¶9.

[77] For a comprehensive survey of relevant treaties, see Sands and Peel (n 1) 214–15.

[78] United Nations Convention on the Law of the Sea (10 December 1982, in force 16 November 1994) 1833 UNTS 3, arts 192, 194. See Detlef Czybulka, 'Article 192: General Obligation' in Alexander

directly reiterates the content of Principle 21,[79] while the Convention on the Law of Non-Navigational Uses of International Watercourses notes that 'States shall, in utilizing an international watercourse in their territories, take all appropriate measures to prevent the causing of significant harm to other watercourse States'.[80] The phrasing of these provisions suggests that they are not intended to constitute a new obligation applicable to the parties but rather that they aim to recognize a pre-existing obligation applicable to all states concerned notwithstanding their participation in the treaty.[81]

Most states have ratified various multilateral environmental agreements through which they commit to take measures aimed at preventing the most common types of transboundary environmental harm, and it can generally be assumed that states comply with their treaty obligations. Indeed, most states appear to be taking measures to limit their environmental impact on other states, for instance by establishing a mandatory environmental assessment procedure that must be completed before a project likely to have an environmental impact can be carried out.[82] Of course, one could question whether consent to, and compliance with, these conventions reflect state practice and acceptance as law relevant to the assessment of a distinct customary obligation rather than more transactional obligations. Arguably, however, these various conventional measures aimed at preventing transboundary environmental harm are not merely following 'considerations of convenience or simple political expediency';[83] rather, they indicate the effort of states to comply with what they seem therefore to assume to accept as an independent legal obligation.

Beside the statements that states have made and the conduct that they have adopted in application of the treaties they have ratified, additional evidence of acceptance as law is the nearly complete absence of contrary statements. As Alan Boyle and Catherine Redgwell note, even in response to judicial claims against them, states have generally not 'sought to argue that general international law does not require them to control transboundary pollution'.[84] Rather, 'the focus of most of the litigation has been on the adequacy … of the measures states have

Proelss (ed), *United Nations Convention on the Law of the Sea: A Commentary* (Beck 2017) 1284–1285 (paras 21–2).

[79] Convention on Biological Diversity (5 June 1992, in force 29 December 1993) 1760 UNTS 79, art 3.

[80] Convention on the Law of the Non-Navigational Uses of International Watercourses (21 May 1997, in force 17 August 2014) (1997) 36 ILM 700, art 7(1).

[81] See ILC, 'Customary International Law' (n 3) commentary on conclusion 11, ¶5.

[82] UNEP, *Assessing Environmental Impacts: A Global Review of Legislation* (2018).

[83] *Asylum* (n 3) 277, 286, noting that such considerations would suggest no acceptance as law. See also *SS Lotus (France/Turkey)*, Judgment (7 September 1927), PCIJ Rep Series A No 10, 28; *Paramilitary Activities* (n 26) ¶¶206–09. See generally ILC, 'Customary International Law' (n 3) commentary on conclusion 9, ¶3.

[84] Boyle and Redgwell (n 1) 159.

taken'[85]—that is, either on the specific contents of the obligation or merely on matters of facts.

The main objection to this ascending argument has been raised separately by three US scholars, Bodansky, John Knox, and Oscar Schachter, in the 1990s and early 2000s. Their objection is that the frequency of transboundary environmental harm in today's world excludes the existence of a general practice of states consistent with the obligation to prevent such harm: as Bodansky puts it, in reality, 'transboundary pollution seems much more the rule than the exception'.[86] However, transboundary pollution is no evidence of the breach of the obligation of prevention when the latter is conceived as an obligation of conduct. States may well be taking 'all reasonable or necessary measures'[87] to prevent transboundary environmental harm without being able to prevent such harm in all circumstances. At most, the frequency of transboundary harm suggests that states have not agreed on a particularly high standard of due diligence, a remark which is relevant at the stage of interpreting this obligation rather than when identifying it.

2. Obligation of Cooperation

Another general customary obligation relevant to climate change is the obligation of states to cooperate—that is to say, to act in a coordinated way towards common objectives[88]—in addressing issues of common concern. This obligation can be identified rather straightforwardly following an ascending reasoning. As Pierre-Marie Dupuy noted, the existence of this obligation is evidenced by 'the very considerable mass of bilateral, regional or universal treaties concluded at least since 1945 with the avowed aim of specifically establishing and reinforcing cooperation among the states concerned', which is itself 'underpinned by an even more voluminous quantity of non-treaty legal instruments asserting the same obligation of cooperation'.[89] Cooperation has been a defining feature of international law for more than half a century,[90] even though its achievements remain limited. States now routinely seek to cooperate to address international problems of an economic, social, cultural, humanitarian, or environmental character.

[85] Ibid. See eg Chinese Society of International Law, 'The South China Sea Arbitration Awards: A Critical Study' (2018) 17 Chinese JIL 207, ¶¶782–820.

[86] Daniel Bodansky, 'Customary (and Not So Customary) International Environmental Law' (1995) 3 Indiana J Global Legal Studies 105, 110–11. See also Oscar Schachter, 'The Emergence of International Environmental Law' (1991) 44 J Intl Affairs 457, 463; John H Knox, 'The Myth and Reality of Transboundary Environmental Impact Assessment' (2002) 96 AJIL 29.

[87] See n 62.

[88] See Rüdiger Wolfrum, 'Cooperation, International Law of' in *Max Planck Encyclopedia of Public International Law* (online edn, OUP 2010) ¶2.

[89] Pierre-Marie Dupuy, 'The Place and Role of Unilateralism in Contemporary International Law' (2000) 11 EJIL 19, 22–23.

[90] Wolfgang Friedmann, *The Changing Structure of International Law* (Colum UP 1964).

There is little doubt that states have accepted this general practice as a legal obligation. The UN Charter, in particular, recognizes 'international co-operation in solving international problems of an economic, social, cultural, or humanitarian character' not just as one of the purposes of the UN Organization,[91] but also as a positive obligation requiring every member to 'take joint and separate action in co-operation with the Organization'.[92] The UN General Assembly interpreted this provision as creating a 'duty of states to co-operate with one another'.[93] With the adoption of the 2005 World Summit Outcome, the General Assembly further acknowledged the reality of 'an interdependent and global world' in which many 'threats ... must be tackled at the global, regional and national levels in accordance with the Charter and international law'.[94]

The UN Charter did not single out environmental issues among those requiring cooperation but, over time, states have largely accepted that cooperation should extend to such issues.[95] The 1972 Stockholm Declaration had already affirmed that 'international matters concerning the protection and improvement of the environment should be handled in a cooperative spirit by all countries'.[96] The Charter on Economic Rights and Duties of states, likewise, highlighted the obligation of all states to adjust their policies in conformity with their responsibility for '[t]he protection, preservation and enhancement of the environment for the present and future generations'.[97] Twenty years later, the Rio Declaration went beyond this recommendation, noting that 'States *shall* co-operate in a spirit of global partnership to conserve, protect and restore the health and integrity of the Earth's ecosystem'.[98]

Multilateral environmental agreements confirm and apply this obligation in various contexts, for instance regarding the protection and preservation of the marine environment,[99] the conservation and sustainable use of biological diversity,[100] and the optimal utilization and adequate protection of international watercourses.[101] These treaties also highlight particular forms of cooperation such as financial assistance, the transfer of technology, and capacity-building,[102] or the

[91] UN Charter (n 39) art 1(3).

[92] Ibid art 56. See also art 55.

[93] Friendly Relations Declaration (n 39) 123. See also Charter of Economic Rights and Duties (n 41); New International Economic Order (n 41) ¶3; World Charter for Nature (n 74) ¶21(a).

[94] World Summit Outcome, UNGA Res 60/1 (16 September 2005) ¶71.

[95] See ILC, 'Prevention of Transboundary Harm' (n 46) art 4; Boyle and Redgwell (n 1) 200, noting that '[i]f due diligence is the first rule of transboundary environmental risk management, cooperation is the second'.

[96] Stockholm Declaration (n 41) principle 24.

[97] Charter of Economic Rights and Duties (n 41) art 30.

[98] Rio Declaration (n 41) principle 7 (emphasis added).

[99] UNCLOS (n 78) art 197.

[100] Convention on Biological Diversity (n 79) art 5.

[101] International Watercourses Convention (n 80) art 9(1).

[102] See Montreal Protocol on Substances that Deplete the Ozone Layer (16 September 1987, in force 1 January 1989) 1522 UNTS 3, art 10(1); Convention against Desertification (n 75) art 12; Minamata Convention on Mercury (10 October 2013, in force 16 August 2017) (2016) 55 ILM 582, art 14(1).

conduct of further negotiations.[103] Consistently, the International Tribunal for the Law of the Sea (ITLOS) recognized 'the duty to cooperate' as 'a fundamental principle in the prevention of pollution of the marine environment', not only in the application of specific provisions of UNCLOS but also 'under general international law'.[104] More specifically, states have repeatedly and emphatically affirmed the importance of cooperation in addressing climate change.[105]

Judicial decisions help to outline the nature and content of this general obligation of cooperation in environmental matters. In bilateral settings, as the arbitral award in *Lake Lanoux* illustrates, the obligation of cooperation implies an obligation to consult with any affected state and to negotiate an agreement.[106] Even though the affected state has no veto right, this obligation of negotiations is more than a formality: states are obligated to negotiate *in good faith* with a view of arriving at a mutually acceptable agreement.[107] By analogy, the Permanent Court of International Justice in *Railway Traffic between Lithuania and Poland* interpreted a state's obligation to negotiate as requiring it 'not only to enter into negotiations but also to pursue them as far as possible with a view to concluding agreements'.[108] The ICJ in *North Sea Continental Shelf* pointed out that the negotiating states must seek to conclude agreements 'arrived at in accordance with equitable principles'.[109]

When applied to global environmental concerns, the obligation of cooperation requires states to negotiate in good faith in view of reaching a mutually acceptable and equitable agreement and to implement this agreement. In effect, this obligation of cooperation in relation to global environmental issues largely overlaps with the obligation of prevention. On the one hand, cooperation is certainly among the appropriate or necessary measures that a state must take to comply with its obligation of prevention.[110] On the other hand, the obligation of cooperation against global environmental harm implies a good faith attempt at taking and implementing concrete measures to prevent or minimize transboundary environmental harm.

[103] See International Watercourses Convention (n 80) art 3(5); UNCLOS (n 78) art 197. For a comprehensive review, see Sands and Peel (n 1) 214–15.

[104] *MOX Plant (Ireland v UK)*, Order on Provisional Measures (3 December 2001), [2001] ITLOS Rep 95, ¶82.

[105] See nn 161–63.

[106] *Lac Lanoux*, Award (16 November 1957), 12 RIAA 281, ¶1.

[107] Ibid ¶¶13, 16, 20, 22, 24. See also *Nuclear Tests (Australia v France)*, Judgment (20 December 1974), [1974] ICJ Rep 253, ¶46; *Gabčíkovo-Nagymaros Project (Hungary/Slovakia)*, Judgment (25 September 1997), [1997] ICJ Rep 7, ¶¶141–42; *Pulp Mills* (n 27) ¶145; *Request for Advisory Opinion by the Sub-Regional Fisheries Commission*, Advisory Opinion (2 April 2015), [2015] ITLOS Rep 4, ¶210; Rio Declaration (n 41) principle 27; ILC, 'Prevention of Transboundary Harm' (n 46) art 4.

[108] *Railway Traffic between Lithuania and Poland*, Advisory Opinion (15 October 1931), PCIJ Rep Series A/B No 42, 116.

[109] *North Sea Continental Shelf* (n 26) ¶85.

[110] See also below at 284.

C. A Discrete Customary Obligation on Climate Change Mitigation

This section demonstrates that states have a discrete customary obligation to mitigate climate change. It does so in two complementary ways. From a descending perspective, it shows that states' general mitigation obligations of prevention and cooperation appear to imply a discrete obligation on climate change mitigation. From an ascending perspective, this section then highlights relevant empirical evidence of a general practice accepted as law as evidenced, in particular, by treaty practice.

1. Deduction from General Obligations

The obligation of prevention has generally been implemented in simple scenarios where an activity within a state's territory caused a direct and localized harm within another state's territory.[111] As noted in section B, this obligation is to be understood as part of a broader obligation of a state 'to protect within [its] territory the rights of other States',[112] which requires a state to prevent harm to foreign warships[113] or diplomats,[114] among other things. In typical circumstances, a relatively direct and proximate causal link could be drawn between an activity under a state's jurisdiction or control, on the one hand, and harm affecting another state, on the other. Yet, it may rarely be possible to establish such a proximate causal link between a state's GHG emissions and any concrete damage suffered by another state.[115] A state's GHG emissions are perhaps more convincingly understood as impacting the global environment (through an interference with the climate system) rather than directly affecting any particular state. As such, one may question whether the obligation of prevention implies an obligation to mitigate global environmental harm that affects the international community as a whole rather than any state in particular.

International courts and tribunals have not yet had the opportunity to discuss the applicability of the obligation of prevention in relation to cumulative global environmental harm. In *Nuclear Tests*, New Zealand argued that France's

[111] See *Trail Smelter* (n 27); *Pulp Mills* (n 27); *Certain Activities* (n 27).

[112] *Island of Palmas* (n 48) 839. See also *Corfu Channel* (n 26) 22; *Paramilitary Activities* (n 26) ¶115.

[113] *Corfu Channel* (n 26) 22.

[114] *Diplomatic Staff in Tehran* (n 53) ¶63.

[115] See Alexander Zahar, 'Mediated versus Cumulative Environmental Damage and the International Law Association's Legal Principles on Climate Change' (2014) 4 Climate Law 217; Alexander Zahar, 'The Contested Core of Climate Law' (2018) 8 Climate Law 244. On the limited usefulness of the science on weather events attribution, see Greg Lusk, 'The Social Utility of Event Attribution: Liability, Adaptation, and Justice-Based Loss and Damage' (2017) 143 Climatic Change 201; Benoit Mayer, 'Climate Change Adaptation and the Law' (2021) 39 Virginia Envtl LJ 141.

atmospheric testing of nuclear bombs was violating 'the rights of all members of the international community' to the protection of the global environment from radioactive fallout and contamination,[116] but the Court did not have occasion to discuss this claim as it found that France, through its unilateral declarations, had committed to stopping such activities.[117] The ICJ in *Nuclear Weapons* noted that the consequences of the use of nuclear weapons 'would be widespread and would have transboundary effects',[118] but the Court did not seek to distinguish between localized and global environmental harm when affirming the obligation of prevention.

On the other hand, it is now well established that the obligation of prevention applies notwithstanding whether the potential harm would unfold within the territory of a neighbouring state, a non-neighbouring state,[119] or even in areas beyond national jurisdiction. Thus, the Stockholm and Rio Declarations affirm the obligation of states to prevent environmental harm 'to the environment of other States or of areas beyond the limits of national jurisdiction'.[120] Likewise, the ICJ in *Nuclear Weapons* refers to an obligation to 'respect the environment of other States or of areas beyond national control'.[121] The Advisory Opinion of ITLOS in *Activities in the Area* confirmed the applicability of the obligation of prevention to 'the Area',[122] which UNCLOS defines as 'the seabed and ocean floor and subsoil thereof, beyond the limits of national jurisdiction'.[123]

ITLOS further highlighted the *erga omnes* character of states' treaty and customary obligations relating to the preservation of the environment of the high seas and in the Area.[124] The Tribunal interpreted the obligation of prevention as requiring states to prevent harm to areas beyond national jurisdiction on the ground that such harm would affect the non-exclusive right of every other state to the preservation of these 'shared resources'.[125] When identifying a state's non-exclusive

[116] Application Instituting Proceedings Submitted by the Government of New Zealand (9 May 1973), in (1978) ICJ Pleadings, Nuclear Tests, vol II, 3, ¶28(a)–(b); Request for the Indication of Interim Measures of Protection Submitted by the Government of New Zealand (14 May 1973), in (1978) ICJ Pleadings, Nuclear Tests, vol II, 49, ¶¶2(i)–(ii), 30, 31; Memorial on Jurisdiction and Admissibility Submitted by the Government of New Zealand (29 October 1973), in (1978) ICJ Pleadings, Nuclear Tests, vol II, 145, ¶190(a)–(b).

[117] *Nuclear Tests (NZ v France)*, Judgment (20 December 1974), [1974] ICJ Rep 457, ¶¶53, 58.

[118] *Nuclear Weapons* (n 27) ¶27.

[119] See ILC, 'Prevention of Transboundary Harm' (n 46) art 2(c); Roda Verheyen, *Climate Change Damage and International Law: Prevention Duties and State Responsibility* (Brill 2005) 166–68.

[120] Stockholm Declaration (n 41) principle 21; Rio Declaration (n 41) principle 21 (emphasis added).

[121] *Nuclear Weapons* (n 27) ¶29.

[122] *Activities in the Area* (n 65) ¶¶147–48.

[123] UNCLOS (n 78) art 1(1)(1).

[124] *Activities in the Area* (n 65) ¶142.

[125] Ibid ¶148, citing *Pulp Mills* (n 27) ¶204 and alluding to UNCLOS (n 78) art 136, which qualifies the Area and its resources as 'the common heritage of mankind'. See also *Whaling in the Antarctic (Australia v Japan; NZ intervening)*, Judgment (31 March 2014), [2014] ICJ Rep 226, where the right of Australia to invoke Japan's obligation to preserve natural resources in the high sea remains unchallenged; Christian J Tams, 'Roads Not Taken, Opportunities Missed: Procedural and Jurisdictional Questions Sidestepped in the *Whaling* Judgment' in Malgosia Fitzmaurice and Dai Tamada (eds), *Whaling in the Antarctic: Significance and Implications of the ICJ Judgment* (Brill Nijhoff 2016) 201–211.

right to the protection of shared resources, there does not appear to be any good reason to distinguish between those shared resources that are situated within a defined 'area' (eg the high seas) and those that are global in scope (eg the atmosphere).[126] Accordingly, the obligation of prevention can reasonably be interpreted as implying an obligation for every state to regulate its GHG emissions in order to prevent both a direct infringement of states' non-exclusive rights to the protection of the atmosphere and an indirect infringement of their exclusive rights.

Climate change affects states' non-exclusive rights as well as (albeit less directly) their exclusive rights. On the one hand, states have non-exclusive rights to the protection of the atmosphere and the global climate system (as a necessary implication of various sovereign states)[127] in much the same way as they have non-exclusive rights to the protection of areas beyond national jurisdiction such as the high seas and the Area. The climate system, in particular, is a shared resource, on which every state depends—in fact in far more essential ways than the Area or the high seas.[128] Even if that was not the case, climate change has significant impacts on many other shared resources, the protection of which is also largely recognized as a right of every state (eg biological diversity,[129] the world heritage,[130] or the high seas and the Area).[131] On the other hand, GHG emissions also infringe states' exclusive rights to territorial integrity, permanent sovereignty over natural resources, and the protection of their citizens.[132] Even though these impacts are indirect, they are certainly no less serious or foreseeable.[133]

A potential objection is that *a state*'s efforts to mitigate climate change would not really 'prevent' harm to the climate system—it would only reduce it, often in very limited ways.[134] This objection is based on a misconception of the obligation of prevention. As noted above, the obligation of prevention is an obligation to minimize the risk of harm, not necessarily to avoid it entirely.[135] The existence of an injury is not a general condition for the existence of an internationally wrongful act,[136] nor is it a condition for a breach of the obligation of prevention as long as it is

[126] Cf Zahar, 'The Contested Core' (n 115) 247–48; Zahar, 'Mediated versus Cumulative' (n 115) 226–27, 229.

[127] For instance, a state could not assert effective rights to the protection of its territory, to natural resources, or to protection of its citizens if it could not ensure a stable climate system.

[128] On the recognition of climate change as a 'common concern', see UNFCCC (n 76) Preamble ¶2; Paris Agreement (12 December 2015, in force 4 November 2016) (2016) 55 ILM 740, Preamble ¶12.

[129] Convention on Biological Diversity (n 79) Preamble ¶4.

[130] Convention for the Protection of the World Cultural and Natural Heritage (16 November 1972, in force 17 December 1975) 1037 UNTS 551, Preamble ¶3.

[131] UNCLOS (n 78) arts 87, 136, 137(2).

[132] See nn 40–42.

[133] See above at 2.

[134] See Zahar, 'The Contested Core' (n 115) 249.

[135] See nn 63–64.

[136] It is only when considering the secondary obligation of the responsible state to make reparation that one may need to identify the injury, including any 'damage … caused by the internationally wrongful act of a State'. ILC, 'Draft Articles on the Responsibility of States for Internationally Wrongful Acts' [2001] II(2) YBILC 26, commentary on arts 2, ¶9 and 31, ¶6.

understood as an obligation of conduct.[137] In other words, a state may be found to have violated its obligation of prevention even if no distinct damage can be attributed to its failure to exercise due diligence.[138]

A reasoning based exclusively on the obligation of prevention could face another, stronger objection: many states contribute only a tiny fraction to global GHG emissions; as such, the mitigation outcomes they could achieve would only be a 'drop in the ocean'. It needs to be highlighted that this objection clearly does not apply to large states, which contribute significantly to a massive global issue, resulting in harm (albeit diffuse) of great consequences. The objection would only concern smaller developed countries or developing countries without an industrial economy.

There are at least two ways to counter this objection. One is purely factual. The impacts of climate change are several orders of magnitude larger than the typical transboundary environmental harm in relation to which the obligation of prevention has typically been applied. Moreover, one can assume an approximately linear relation between GHG concentrations in the atmosphere and global warming.[139] As such, the reduction in a state's GHG emissions, even if it represents a very small proportion of global GHG emissions, may nevertheless achieve a significant global benefit, albeit a diffuse one. A tiny contribution to a very large objective is not necessarily insignificant. In other words, it may be that a state's action is neither necessary nor sufficient to guarantee that climate change does not exceed an arbitrary threshold (eg a 2°C target) but this action contributes nevertheless in incremental but significant ways to the prevention of greater environmental harm (or to mitigating the risk of such harm).

An alternative response to the objection would rely on the obligation of cooperation, which applies to every state notwithstanding its size. There is no denial that, as a common concern of humankind, climate change requires international cooperation: states have affirmed as much innumerable times.[140] Climate change is a collective action problem par excellence—a paradigmatic tragedy of the commons.[141] As such, one cannot take the obligation of cooperation seriously without recognizing its applicability to climate change. To cooperate 'in a spirit of global partnership', as prompted by the Rio Declaration,[142] states must seek not to

[137] See Ilias Plakokefalos, 'Prevention Obligations in International Environmental Law' (2012) 23 YB Intl Envtl L 3, 37. See also n 71.

[138] ILC, 'State Responsibility' (n 136) art 31(1).

[139] See Josep G Canadell and others, 'Global Carbon and Other Biogeochemical Cycles and Feedback' in Valérie Masson-Delmotte and others (eds), *Climate Change 2021: The Physical Science Basis. Contribution of the Working Group I to the Sixth Assessment Report of the Intergovernmental Panel on Climate Change* (accepted version subject to final editing, IPCC 2021) §5.5. There may be tipping points triggered by a certain level of GHG emissions, but the level of GHG emissions triggering these tipping points is not known with precision. See Timothy M Lenton and others, 'Climate Tipping Points—Too Risky to Bet Against' (2019) 575 Nature 592.

[140] See nn 161–63.

[141] See above at 3.

[142] Rio Declaration (n 41) principle 7.

free-ride on the efforts of others but to do their fair share in global efforts to address climate change. As such, every state—notwithstanding its size—must seek to regulate global GHG emissions, as far as it can, in order to protect the rights of other states.

2. Induction from the General Practice of States Accepted as Law

States have adopted numerous multilateral agreements aimed at protecting shared resources, in particular 'global commons' such as biological diversity,[143] the intangible natural and cultural heritage of humankind,[144] and areas beyond national jurisdiction (eg the high seas, the Area,[145] and the Antarctic).[146] They have also adopted treaties for the protection of the atmosphere, for instance to reduce regional haze[147] and long-range air pollution,[148] to protect the ozone layer,[149] to minimize the long-range atmospheric transport of mercury[150]—and, of course, to mitigate climate change. As a whole, these treaties either reflect or contribute to the development of a norm of customary international law requiring states to take measures for the protection of the global environment, and in particular the atmosphere. Thus, the ILC Guidelines on the Protection of the Atmosphere, as adopted in second reading in 2021, reflects that 'States have the obligation to protect the atmosphere by exercising due diligence in taking appropriate measures ... to prevent, reduce or control atmospheric pollution and atmospheric degradation.'[151]

As evidence of anthropogenic climate change emerged, states recognized the link with their obligations of prevention and cooperation. Thus, a 1989 UN General Assembly resolution on the 'protection of the global climate' already paraphrased Principle 21 of the Stockholm Declaration on prevention, adding that states had more specifically a 'responsibility ... to play their due role in preserving and protecting the global and regional environment in accordance with their capacities and specific responsibilities.'[152] As in the Vienna Convention for the Protection of the Ozone Layer a few years earlier,[153] negotiators included in the Preamble to

[143] Convention on Biological Diversity (n 79) Preamble ¶4.
[144] See World Heritage Convention (n 130) art 4.
[145] See eg UNCLOS (n 78) arts 117–20, 145, 192.
[146] Protocol on Environmental Protection to the Antarctic Treaty (4 October 1991, in force 14 January 1998) 2941 UNTS 3 ('Madrid Protocol').
[147] ASEAN Agreement on Transboundary Haze Pollution (10 June 2002, in force 25 November 2003) <www.ecolex.org/> (TRE-001344).
[148] Convention on Long-Range Transboundary Air Pollution (n 75).
[149] Vienna Convention for the Protection of the Ozone Layer (n 75); Montreal Protocol (n 102).
[150] Minamata Convention (n 102).
[151] ILC, 'Draft Guidelines on the Protection of the Atmosphere' in ILC Report, 72nd session, A/76/10 (2021) 13, guideline 3. See also International Law Association, 'Resolution 2/2014: Declaration of Legal Principles Relating to Climate Change' (2014) 76 ILA Rep Conferences 21, art 7B.
[152] UNGA Resolutions 43/53 (6 December 1988) ¶10(e); 44/207 (22 December 1989) ¶4.
[153] Vienna Convention for the Protection of the Ozone Layer (n 75) Preamble ¶3.

the UNFCCC a provision recalling the relevance of 'pertinent provisions' of the Stockholm Declaration,[154] along with a reaffirmation of the obligation of prevention as defined in Principle 2 of the Rio Declaration.[155] This preambular provision, as Matthew Happold noted, 'at least suggests' that the obligation of prevention is relevant in the context of climate change.[156]

States have also acknowledged their obligation to cooperate on climate change mitigation. The General Assembly highlighted as early as 1988 that 'climate change is a common concern of mankind'[157]—a characterization, reaffirmed by the UNFCCC[158] and the Paris Agreement,[159] which clearly presents climate change as an issue requiring international cooperation.[160] Thus, the UNFCCC acknowledges as a mere statement of fact that 'the global nature of climate change calls for the widest possible cooperation by all countries and their participation in an effective and appropriate international response'[161]—and a similar language has been repeated *ad nauseam* in COP decisions[162] and General Assembly resolutions.[163] States, thus, have unambiguously recognized, within the UNFCCC

[154] UNFCCC (n 76) Preamble ¶8.

[155] Ibid Preamble ¶9.

[156] Matthew Happold, 'The Relationship between the United Nations Framework Convention on Climate Change and Other Rules of Public International Law, in Particular on States' Responsibility for the Adverse Effects of Climate Change' (Legal Response Initiative 2013) 3.

[157] Res 43/53 (n 152) ¶1. See also Res 44/207 (n 152) Preamble ¶2; Ministerial Declaration of the Second World Climate Conference, A/45/696/Add.1, 16 (8 November 1990) ¶4; UNGA Resolutions 45/212 (21 December 1990) Preamble ¶2; 46/169 (19 December 1991) Preamble ¶2; 47/195 (22 December 1992) Preamble ¶2, ¶2; 57/258 (23 December 2016) Preamble ¶2.

[158] UNFCCC (n 76) Preamble ¶2.

[159] Paris Agreement (n 128) Preamble ¶12. See also Decision 1/CP.21, 'Adoption of the Paris Agreement' (12 December 2015) FCCC/CP/2015/10/Add.1, 2, Preamble ¶8; ILC, 'Atmosphere' (n 151) Preamble ¶3.

[160] See Jutta Brunnée, 'Common Areas, Common Heritage, and Common Concern' in Daniel Bodansky, Jutta Brunnée and Ellen Hey (eds), *The Oxford Handbook of International Environmental Law* (OUP 2008) 566.

[161] UNFCCC (n 76) Preamble ¶7.

[162] See Decisions 1/CP.1, 'The Berlin Mandate: Review of the Adequacy of Article 4, paragraph 2 (a) and (b), of the Convention, Including Proposals Related to a Protocol and Decisions on Follow-Up' (7 April 1995) FCCC/CP/1995/7/Add.1, 4, ¶1(e); 5/CP.1, 'Activities Implemented Jointly under the Pilot Phase' (7 April 1995) FCCC/CP/7/Add.1, 18, Preamble ¶4; 1/CP.11, 'Dialogue on Long-Term Cooperative Action to Address Climate Change by Enhancing Implementation of the Convention' (9–10 December 2005) FCCC/CP/2005/5/Add.1, 3, Preamble ¶8; 2/CP.12, 'Review of the Financial Mechanism' (17 November 2006) FCCC/CP/2006/5/Add.1, 6, Preamble ¶10; 1/CP.17, 'Establishment of an Ad Hoc Working Group on the Durban Platform for Enhanced Action' (11 December 2011) FCCC/CP/2011/9/Add.1, 2, Preamble ¶2; 2/CP.18, 'Advancing the Durban Platform' (8 December 2012) FCCC/CP/2012/8/Add.1, 19, Preamble ¶3; 1/CP.21 (n 159) Preamble ¶6.

[163] See UNGA Resolutions 57/257 (20 December 2002) Preamble ¶4; 57/258 (n 157) Preamble ¶3; 58/243 (23 December 2003) Preamble ¶3; 59/234 (22 December 2004) Preamble ¶3; 60/197 (22 December 2005) Preamble ¶3; World Summit Outcome (n 94) ¶53; 61/201 (20 December 2006) Preamble ¶3; 62/86 (10 December 2007) Preamble ¶3; 63/1 (22 September 2008) ¶24; 63/32 (26 November 2008) Preamble ¶3; 63/281 (3 June 2009) Preamble ¶7; 64/73 (7 December 2009) Preamble ¶3; 65/159 (20 December 2010) Preamble ¶3; The Future We Want, 66/288 (27 July 2012) ¶191; 67/210 (21 December 2012) Preamble ¶3; 68/212 (20 December 2013) ¶15; SIDS Accelerated Modalities of Action (SAMOA) Pathway, 69/15 (14 November 2014) ¶35; 69/220 (19 December 2014) ¶4; 70/205 (22 December 2015) Preamble ¶5; 71/228 (21 December 2016) Preamble ¶3; 72/219 (20 December

regime and beyond, that climate change is an issue that commands international cooperation[164]—and, by implication, action on climate change mitigation.

While the UNFCCC regime can now be viewed as confirming the existence of a customary obligation on climate change mitigation, it clearly is not a codification treaty. For one, climate treaties were drafted entirely through political processes rather than on the basis of substantive inputs by legal experts.[165] In fact, at the turn of the 1990s, as the text of the UNFCCC was being drafted, there was scant evidence of any state practice—few states, if any, were taking measures to mitigate climate change. However, climate treaties did contribute to the development of customary international law by spurring state practice.[166]

Every state that ratified the UNFCCC committed to taking measures on the mitigation of climate change,[167] and most, if not all, honoured this commitment: they monitored their emissions, adopted and implemented statutes and policies aimed at limiting or reducing these emissions, and reported on it all.[168] Likewise, almost every party has communicated a nationally determined contribution (NDC) under the Paris Agreement,[169] and states have generally appeared to be taking measures that seek to achieve the targets described in their NDCs. Global GHG emissions may have continued to increase but at a slower pace than they would have had states not taken such measures.[170] Domestic courts have also contributed to the development of state practice and its acceptance as law[171] by requiring national governments to step up their mitigation action[172] and by reviewing administrative approvals to projects likely to increase GHG emissions.[173]

2017) Preamble ¶3; 73/232 (20 December 2018) Preamble ¶3; 74/219 (19 December 2019) Preamble ¶3; 75/217 (21 December 2020) Preamble ¶3.

[164] See also ILC, 'Atmosphere' (n 151) guideline 8.

[165] Res 45/212 (n 157) ¶¶1–2.

[166] On the capacity of treaties to contribute to the emergence of state practice relevant to the identification of customary law, see generally ILC, 'Customary International Law' (n 3) conclusion 11.1(c).

[167] UNFCCC (n 76) art 4(1)(b).

[168] See UNFCCC SBI, Compilation and synthesis of fourth biennial reports of parties included in Annex I to the Convention, FCCC/SBI/2020/INF.10 (12 November 2020).

[169] See UNFCCC Secretariat, 'NDC Registry (interim)' (no date) <https://www4.unfccc.int/sites/NDCStaging/>.

[170] See Robert Stavings and others, 'International Cooperation: Agreements & Instruments' in Ottmar Edenhofer and others (eds), *Climate Change 2014: Mitigation of Climate Change: Working Group III Contribution to the Fifth Assessment Report of the Intergovernmental Panel on Climate Change* (CUP 2014) 1041–51.

[171] See *Arrest Warrant of 11 April 2000 (DRC v Belgium)*, Judgment (14 February 2002), [2002] ICJ Rep 3, ¶58; *Jurisdictional Immunities of the State (Germany v Italy, Greece intervening)*, Judgment (3 February 2012), [2012] ICJ Rep 99, ¶55; ILC, 'Customary International Law' (n 3) conclusions 6(2), 10(2).

[172] See *Urgenda* (SC) (n 6); *Neubauer v Germany*, 1 BvR 2656/18 (Federal Constitutional Court, 24 March 2021) <https://perma.cc/UJM6-QCCY>; *Klimaatzaak v Belgium*, case 2015/4585/A (French-Speaking Tribunal of First Instance of Brussels, 17 June 2021), English translation <https://perma.cc/68ZJ-2F96>; *Grande-Synthe v France* (Conseil d'Etat, 1 July 2021), ECLI:FR:CECHR:2021:427301.20210701.

[173] See *Mid States Coalition for Progress v Surface Transportation Board* (8th Cir, 2003) 345 F3d 520; *Gloucester Resources v Minister for Planning* [2019] NSWLEC 7; *Earthlife Africa Johannesburg v Minister*

One could question the significance of climate treaties as evidence of customary law. RR Baxter has famously shown the difficulty of using multilateral agreements as evidence of customary law.[174] Yet, international courts and the ILC did recognize the possibility for treaties to play 'an important role in ... developing' customary law.[175] This scenario is particularly relevant to climate treaties for two reasons. First, the general commitments contained in climate treaties—in particular Articles 4(1)(b) and 4(2)(a) of the UNFCCC, requiring states to take measures on climate change mitigation—are more akin to statutory norms than to contractual provisions: they are what the ICJ in *North Sea Continental Shelf* called provisions 'of a fundamentally norm-creating character such as could be regarded as forming the basis of a general rule of law'.[176] Second, these commitments do not appear in isolation; rather, they confirm a pre-existing understanding of customary law consistent with the principles of general international law, repeatedly acknowledged by states, as requiring every state to take some measures to mitigate climate change rather than granting states complete freedom to emit GHGs. Rather than a transactional arrangement, these treaties should be understood as the expression of a general norm on climate change mitigation that states believe to be applicable to all.[177]

D. The Relation between Commitments and Customary Obligations

This section addresses an objection to the applicability of customary international law to climate change mitigation. Chapter II has shown that virtually every state has committed to taking specific steps to mitigate climate change by participating in relevant treaties and sometimes also by communicating unilateral declarations manifesting the will to be bound. In light of this, some scholars have objected that these commitments (in particular those made under climate treaties) may preclude the application of customary international law. Alexander Zahar, for instance, asserts that the Paris Agreement simply 'displaces everything that was

of Environmental Affairs, [2017] ZAGPPHC 58, [2017] 2 All SA 519; *Center for Biological Diversity v Bernhardt* (9th Cir, 2020) 982 F3d 723, 740; *Natur og Ungdom v Norway*, Case No 20-051052SIV-HRET (SC, 22 December 2020), English translation <https://perma.cc/5PCS-A8YH>; *R (Friends of the Earth) v Heathrow* [2020] UKSC 52, [2021] 2 All ER 967.

174 RR Baxter, 'Multilateral Treaties as Evidence of Customary International Law' (1965) 41 BYBIL 275, 300. See also *Ahmadou Sadio Diallo (Guinea v DRC)*, Judgment on Compensation (19 June 2012), [2012] ICJ Rep 324, ¶90.

175 *Continental Shelf (Libya/Malta)*, Judgment (3 June 1985), [1985] ICJ Rep 13, ¶27. See also Eritrea–Ethiopia Claims Commission, *Partial Award: Prisoners of War, Ethiopia's Claim 4* (1 July 2003), 26 RIAA 73, ¶31; ILC, 'Customary International Law' (n 3) conclusion 11(1)(c).

176 *North Sea Continental Shelf* (n 26) ¶72.

177 See eg Criddle and Fox-Decent (n 4) 320–21.

there before'.[178] Likewise, a Rapporteur at France's State Council assumes that two obligations from different sources could not be concurrently applicable to climate change mitigation.[179] With more nuance, Bodansky claims that '[t]he growing importance of treaties suggests a diminished role for customary international law'.[180]

It is worth observing that, even if this objection was valid, it would not entirely exclude the relevance of customary international law to the mitigation of climate change. Customary law would apply at least with regard to any state that is not participating in climate treaties. One could perhaps also discuss whether customary law applies to some non-state actors (eg de facto territorial governments or international organizations) which cannot participate in climate treaties.[181] Presumably, it could also apply to states that are participating in climate treaties with regard to matters that do not fall within the scope of their treaty commitments.[182] Commitments on climate change mitigation are generally limited in time and space, and they only apply in relation to certain emissions and activities. The Kyoto Protocol, for instance, imposed commitments on some developed country parties with regard to emissions of specified GHGs from certain activities taking place within the parties' territory during two commitment periods.[183] The Paris Agreement extends commitments to developing country parties, but the scope of these commitments remains limited—most obviously so for the many developing states that have not communicated an unconditional economy-wide target but also for any other state as NDCs have a limited temporal and geographical application. If one agrees with Bodansky that the Paris Agreement 'does not create an individual obligation on each Party' to implement its NDC,[184] there is little terrain that the Paris Agreement can take away from customary law.

At any rate, this section demonstrates the invalidity of the argument that commitments preclude the applicability of customary law. The following shows that, as there is no conflict between customary and treaty obligations, one of these sources does not exclude the application of the other. Rather, customary and

[178] Zahar, 'The Contested Core' (n 115) 255–56. For an argument of a similar nature, see Opinion of Mr Stéphane Hoynck, Advocate General of the Conseil d'Etat, on *Grande-Synthe v France* (19 November 2020), ECLI:FR:CECHR:2020:427301.20201119, No 427301, English translation <https://perma.cc/9Y88-VY5T> 6, considering that a putative obligation to enhance national ambition on climate change mitigation would be in conflict with the state's obligation to reduce its emissions under EU law.

[179] See Stéphane Hoynck, Advocate General of the Conseil d'Etat, Opinion on Grande-Synthe, 19 November 2020, English translation <https://perma.cc/9Y88-VY5T> 5.

[180] Bodansky, 'Customary (and Not So Customary)' (n 86) 106.

[181] See eg Kristina Daugirdas, 'How and Why International Law Binds International Organizations' (2016) 57 Harv Intl LJ 325.

[182] See Rosa M Fernández Egea, 'State Responsibility for Environmental Harm, "Revisited" within the Climate Change Regime' in Sandrine Maljean-Dubois and Lavanya Rajamani (eds), *La mise en œuvre du droit international de l'environnement, Implementation of International Environmental Law* (Martinus Nijhoff 2011) 391.

[183] Kyoto Protocol to the United Nations Framework Convention on Climate Change (11 December 1997, in force 16 February 2005) 2303 UNTS 162, art 3(1), Annex A.

[184] Daniel Bodansky, 'The Legal Character of the Paris Agreement' (2016) 25 RECIEL 142, 146.

treaty obligations are in a relationship of interpretation: while they are separate and distinct, each provides part of the context in light of which the other is to be interpreted.

1. The Absence of Normative Conflict

The ILC's Study Group on the fragmentation of international law observed that the relationship between two norms applicable to the same situation can be characterized as either a 'relationship of interpretation' or a 'relationship of conflict'.[185] When two norms are in a relationship of interpretation, 'one norm assists in the interpretation of another' so that 'both norms are applied in conjunction'.[186] By contrast, a relationship of conflict is one where the two norms 'point to incompatible decisions so that a choice must be made between them'.[187] The ILC thus endorsed Wilfred Jenks's narrow definition of 'conflict' of norms, which Jenks distinguished from a mere 'divergence' between two norms that are not incompatible even though their contents differ.[188] Divergence, in the ILC's analysis, entails a relationship of interpretation rather than a relationship of conflict.

Thus, the ILC recognized a 'principle of harmonization' according to which, 'when several norms bear on a single issue, they should, to the extent possible, be interpreted so as to give rise to a single set of compatible obligations'.[189] Both judicial decisions[190] and the writings of publicists[191] confirm that, when a norm can reasonably be interpreted in two alternative ways, one should prefer the interpretation that avoids a conflict with another norm. In other words, there is 'a strong presumption'[192] that any two norms relevant to the same situation are in a relationship of interpretation rather than in a relationship of conflict. In the Commentary

[185] ILC, 'Conclusions of the Work of the Study Group on the Fragmentation of International Law: Difficulties Arising from the Diversification and Expansion of International Law' [2006] II(2) YBILC 179, ¶2.

[186] Ibid.

[187] Ibid.

[188] C Wilfred Jenks, 'The Conflict of Law-Making Treaties' (1953) 30 BYBIL 401, 426. See also ILC, Report of the Study Group on the Fragmentation of International Law, A/CN.4/L.682 (13 April 2006) ¶24.

[189] ILC, 'Conclusions on Fragmentation' (n 185) ¶4. See also *Right of Passage over Indian Territory (Portugal v India)*, Judgment on Preliminary Objections (26 November 1957), [1957] ICJ Rep 125, 142.

[190] See eg *Right of Passage* (n 189) 142; *Nuclear Weapons* (n 27) ¶¶25–64; Panel Report, *Turkey–Restrictions on Imports of Textile and Clothing Products*, WT/DS34/R (19 November 1999) ¶9.92; *Lawfulness of the Recall of the Privately Held Shares on 8 January 2001 and the Applicable Standards for Valuation of those Shares*, Partial Award (22 November 2002), 23 RIAA 183, ¶170; *Indus Waters Kishenganga*, Partial Award (n 63) ¶452.

[191] See eg Quincy Wright, 'Conflicts between International Law and Treaties' (1917) 11 AJIL 566, 575; Charles Rousseau, 'De la compatibilité des normes juridiques contradictoires dans l'ordre international' (1932) 39 RGDIP 153, 153; Jenks 'The Conflict of Law-Making Treaties' (n 188) 427–28; Joost Pauwelyn, *Conflict of Norms in Public International Law: How WTO Law Relates to Other Rules of International Law* (CUP 2003) 240–44; *Oppenheim's* (n 51) §632 (1275).

[192] ILC, Report on Fragmentation (n 188) ¶37.

on its Articles on State Responsibility, the ILC had already suggested that this presumption could only be overcome when there is 'some actual inconsistency between [the two norms], or at least a discernible intention that one provision is to exclude the other'.[193]

The relationship between customary and treaty obligations cannot be understood as a relationship of conflict because there is neither any inconsistency between these norms nor any discernible intention that climate treaties are to exclude the application of customary law. On the one hand, nothing in any climate treaties suggests that the application of climate treaties was intended to exclude the application of customary international law. To the contrary: as noted, the UNFCCC's Preamble 'recall[s] the pertinent provisions' of the Stockholm Declaration,[194] in particular the obligation of prevention.[195] Furthermore, both the UNFCCC and the Paris Agreement characterize climate change as a 'common concern'[196] of humankind and highlight the need for cooperation.[197] Thus, climate treaties situate the commitments they define within the context of states' customary obligations of prevention and cooperation. Any remaining doubt about the intention of the parties is dispelled by the declarations that several states made when signing and ratifying climate treaties to the effect that nothing in these treaties could 'be interpreted as derogating from the principles of general international law'.[198] No party appears to have recorded any objections to these declarations.

On the other hand, there is no inconsistency between customary and treaty obligations on climate change mitigation. A treaty would be incompatible with states' customary obligation on climate change mitigation only if this treaty created an obligation not to regulate GHG emissions—as it is only in this hypothesis that a choice would have to be made between its treaty commitment and its customary obligation.[199] By contrast, two obligations applicable to the same subject matter are not in a relationship of conflict merely because they set different thresholds.[200] By analogy, domestic law frequently imposes two types of speed limitations to road vehicles: one is applicable to certain roads (eg in town), the other to certain kinds of vehicles (eg trucks). There is no conflict between such rules when their scope overlaps: a truck driving through town must simply comply with both limitations; for practical purposes, the driver simply needs to respect the lower speed limitation,

[193] ILC, 'State Responsibility' (n 136) commentary on art 55, ¶4. See also Hans Kelsen, 'Derogation' in Ralph A Newman (ed), *Essays in Jurisprudence in Honor of Roscoe Pound* (Bobbs-Merrill 1962) 349.

[194] UNFCCC (n 76) Preamble ¶8.

[195] Ibid Preamble ¶9.

[196] See n 128.

[197] UNFCCC (n 76) Preamble ¶7; Paris Agreement (n 128) Preamble ¶5.

[198] Declaration made by Fiji in connection to the UNFCC. See also the declarations made by Kiribati, Papua New Guinea, and Tuvalu in connection to the UNFCCC, by the Cook Islands, Kirabati, Nauru, and Niue in connection to the Kyoto Protocol, and by the Cook Islands, the Marshall Islands, Micronesia, Nauru, the Solomon Islands, Tuvalu, and Vanuatu in connection to the Paris Agreement.

[199] See n 187.

[200] See n 188.

but the two rules coexist, possibly with different penalties. Thus, the ICJ in *Certain Activities* observed that a bilateral treaty creating procedural obligations aimed at preventing transboundary harm 'does not exclude any other procedural obligations with regard to transboundary harm which may exist in treaty or customary international law'.[201]

It has been suggested that there could be a relationship of conflict between climate treaties and customary international law on the ground that the former could be interpreted as asserting a *right* to emit GHGs.[202] This objection is unconvincing because no climate treaty creates any self-standing entitlement to GHG emissions that is applicable beyond the scope of the treaty. In particular, the 'assigned amounts' of GHG emissions mentioned in the Kyoto Protocol[203] are not intended to create a right to emit. Interpreted in light of the object and purpose of the treaty, which has to do with the mitigation of climate change, 'assigned amounts' refer merely to a benchmark used to assess a party's compliance with its quantified mitigation commitment. Decisions of the COP and of the Meeting of the Parties to the Kyoto Protocol confirm that the Protocol 'has not created or bestowed any right, title or entitlement to emissions of any kind' on Annex I parties.[204] And, as noted above, no state appears to have protested to declarations according to which the Kyoto Protocol or other climate treaties do not derogate from general international law.[205] Consistently, states have not systematically accepted the possibility of carrying over any 'assigned amount' beyond the scope of the Protocol.[206] The idea that climate treaties entitle states to emit GHGs is even less convincing in relation to the Paris Agreement—under which each party determines its own 'contribution' to global mitigation action but certainly not, in light of the treaty's object and purpose, its right to emit GHGs. And unilateral declaration, by nature, cannot create legal rights for the declaring state as this would impose obligations on third

[201] *Certain Activities* (n 27) ¶108.

[202] See Stephen Humphreys, 'Introduction: Human Rights and Climate Change' in Humphreys (ed) (n 47) 15; Zahar, 'The Contested Core' (n 115) 256–57.

[203] Kyoto Protocol (n 183) art 3(1).

[204] Decisions 15/CP.7, 'Principles, Nature and Scope of the Mechanisms Pursuant to Articles 6, 12 and 17 of the Kyoto Protocol' (10 November 2001) FCCC/CP/2001/13/Add.2, 2, Preamble ¶6; 2/CMP.1, 'Principles, Nature and Scope of the Mechanisms Pursuant to Articles 6, 12 and 17 of the Kyoto Protocol' (30 November 2005) FCCC/KP/CMP/2005/8/Add.1, 4, Preamble ¶6.

[205] See n 198.

[206] See Decisions 3/CMP.11, 'Implications of the Implementation of Decision 2/CMP.7' (10 December 2015) FCCC/KP/CMP/2015/8/Add.1, 5, Annex ¶14 (replacing ¶36 of Decision 13/CMP.1); 3/CMA.3, 'Rules, Modalities and Procedures for the Mechanism Established by Article 6, Paragraph 4, of the Paris Agreement' (13 November 2021) FCCC/PA/CMA/2021/10/Add.1 (advanced version), 25, Annex ¶75. See also Matthieu Wemaere, Charlotte Streck, and Thiago Chagas, 'Legal Ownership and Nature of Kyoto Units and EU Allowances' in David Freestone and Charlotte Streck (eds), *Legal Aspects of Carbon Trading: Kyoto, Copenhagen, and Beyond* (OUP 2009) 45; San Jose Principles for High Ambition and Integrity in International Carbon Markets (2019) <https://cambioclimatico.go.cr/sanjoseprinciples/> (backed by thirty-two states), third principle; Letter by Tim Stephens and others to Prime Minister Scott Morrison (3 March 2020) 1.

states without their consent.[207] As the Procurator General suggested in *Urgenda*, commitments on climate change mitigation, from whichever source they arise, establish only 'minimum standards': they 'do not relieve states of their general obligations under international law, such as obligations under ... the no harm rule'.[208]

But even if one was to maintain that climate treaties create a right to GHG emissions, a relationship of conflict does not necessarily arise between the norm allowing a thing and the other limiting it.[209] Rights are generally not absolute;[210] they only act as 'trumps' against certain forms of interference,[211] and their enjoyment is commonly curtailed by law. Thus, it is far from exceptional for the enjoyment of the right created by a legal norm to be limited by other legal norms. Some scholars have suggested that any right and obligation on the same subject matter necessarily create a 'conflict',[212] but this is only because these scholars use the word 'conflict' in a broader meaning—as including what Jenks calls 'divergence' and what the ILC Study Group considered to fall within a 'relationship of interpretation'.[213] In light of the principle of harmonization and the presumption it creates against the identification of a relationship of conflict, a right to emit GHGs would only exclude an obligation to mitigate climate change if the norm protecting the right was such as to render the performance of the obligation impossible. Such is clearly not the case of the relationship between climate treaties and customary law on climate change mitigation.

Alternatively, scholars have sometimes invoked the concept of '*lex specialis*' to suggest that climate treaties preclude the application of customary law to climate change mitigation.[214] There is no denial that the obligations arising from climate treaties are often more specific than those arising from customary law; in that sense, the UNFCCC regime can be characterized as 'special law'—or, in Latin, '*lex specialis*'. Yet, as the ILC Study Group pointed out, '[t]he application of the special law does not normally extinguish the relevant general law'.[215] The maxim '*Lex specialis derogat lege generali*' ('Special law repeals general law') applies only when

[207] ILC, 'Guiding Principles Applicable to Unilateral Declarations of States Capable of Creating Legal Obligations' [2006] II(2) YBILC 161, principle 9.

[208] Conclusions of the Procurator General of the Supreme Court on *Urgenda* (SC) (n 6), ECLI:NL:HR:2019:290 (6 February 2019) ¶2.77.

[209] See Jenks, 'The Conflict of Law-Making Treaties' (n 188) 426–27, addressing this hypothesis as a 'divergence'.

[210] See eg Frédéric Mégret, 'Nature of Obligations' in Daniel Moeckli, Sangeeta Shah, and Sandesh Sivakumaran (eds), *International Human Rights Law* (OUP 2018) 99–104.

[211] See Ronald Dworkin, 'Rights as Trumps' in Aileen Kavanagh (ed), *Arguing about Law* (Routledge 2013).

[212] See in particular Erich Vranes, *Trade and the Environment: Fundamental Issues in International Law, WTO Law, and Legal Theory* (OUP 2009) 23–27; Pauwelyn (n 191) 173–75.

[213] See nn 185, 188.

[214] See eg Teresa Thorp, 'Climate Justice: A Constitutional Approach to Unify the Lex Specialis Principles of International Climate Law' (2012) 8 Utrecht LR 7; Zahar, 'Mediated versus Cumulative' (n 115) 230; Stephen Riley, 'Architectures of Intergenerational Justice: Human Dignity, International Law, and Duties to Future Generations' (2016) 15 J Hum R 272, 287.

[215] ILC, 'Conclusions on Fragmentation' (n 185) ¶9.

the special law is in a relationship of conflict with the general law.[216] And, as far as customary and treaty obligations on climate change mitigation are concerned, there is no such relationship of conflict.

2. A Relationship of Interpretation

It is far from exceptional for two or more norms of international law to apply to the same situation.[217] Such norms are in a relationship of interpretation: each norm remains in principle 'separate and distinct',[218] even though each norm forms part of the context in light of which the other is to be interpreted.[219] As these obligations are distinct, there is no reason to presume that they have the same nature, content, or scope. As such, a state's compliance with its commitments under climate treaties (or unilateral declarations) does not necessarily demonstrate compliance with its customary obligation on climate change mitigation and vice versa.

With these observations in mind, one could question why states are adopting commitments on climate change mitigation at all since they are bound by customary international law anyway. An obvious but partial explanation is historical: some commitments were defined before the emergence of customary obligations. This certainly is the case of the UNFCCC, whose adoption contributed to the emergence of a general state practice on climate change mitigation.[220] But commitments may also fulfil any of three other functions that make them continuously relevant as a complement to customary law. First, commitments may clarify and specify the content of general norms of customary law.[221] Second, treaty commitments may bring the content of customary norms (or some of it) within the ambit of procedures and mechanisms that the treaty establishes, for instance on transparency, compliance, and dispute settlement.[222] Third, even if they only reaffirm existing norms, treaty commitments may alert states (and their constituencies) on common issues of compliance.[223]

[216] Ibid ¶5. See also Hugo Grotius, *The Rights of War and Peace* Bk II (1625, Liberty Fund 2012) 881 (ch XVI, §XXIX); ILC, 'State Responsibility' (n 136) commentary on art 55, ¶4; ILC, Report on Fragmentation (n 188) ¶¶56–57, 88.

[217] See *Southern Bluefin Tuna (Australia and NZ v Japan)*, Award on Jurisdiction and Admissibility (4 August 2000), 23 RIAA 1, ¶52.

[218] *Application of the Convention on the Prevention and Punishment of the Crime of Genocide (Croatia v Serbia)*, Judgment on Merits (3 February 2015), [2015] ICJ Rep 3, ¶88. See also *Paramilitary Activities* (n 26) ¶179; *Amoco International Finance v Iran*, Partial Award (24 July 1987) (1988) 27 ILM 1314, ¶112; *MOX Plant* (n 104) ¶50; *Proceedings Pursuant to the OSPAR Convention (Ireland/UK)*, Final Award (2 July 2003), 23 RIAA 59, ¶141.

[219] See Vienna Convention on the Law of Treaties (23 May 1969, in force 27 January 1980) 1155 UNTS 331, art 31(3)(c).

[220] See also below at 112.

[221] See ILC, Report on Fragmentation (n 188) ¶¶56, 88.

[222] See by analogy *Southern Bluefin Tuna* (Award on Jurisdiction and Admissibility) (n 217) ¶52.

[223] See by analogy discussion in Frédéric Mégret, 'The Disabilities Convention: Human Rights of Persons with Disabilities or Disability Rights?' (2008) 30 Hum Rts Q 494, 496; Paul de Guchteneire

Each substantive treaty commitment performs one or several of these functions. For instance, the general commitment in Article 4(1)(b) of the UNFCCC spells out a general obligation on climate change mitigation which, in 1992, may still have been an emerging norm but is now firmly anchored in customary international law. Today, this commitment is of little help in interpreting the scope or content of the customary obligation as it lacks specificity. Yet, it inserts this obligation within the scope of a reporting and review mechanism[224] and of an optional dispute settlement procedure.[225] Overall, this treaty provision makes it more difficult for states to deny the existence of their general mitigation obligation.

By contrast, subsequent commitments under the Kyoto Protocol and the Paris Agreement aim mainly at specifying some of the content of states' general mitigation obligations. In particular, the Paris Agreement requires its parties to take the necessary measures to achieve their NDCs,[226] and NDCs must be communicated with 'the information necessary for clarity, transparency and understanding'.[227] On the other hand, there is no reason to presume that the NDC communicated by a state will necessarily be in line with its customary obligation on climate change mitigation and with its general commitments under the UNFCCC. States have acknowledged that the aggregate effect of their NDCs does not achieve a level of ambition consistent with their collective objectives on climate change mitigation.[228] This could be taken to suggest that, to comply with their general mitigation obligations under the UNFCCC and customary international law, states generally have to do more than what their current NDCs suggest.

As a whole, the UNFCCC regime is to be construed as an ongoing attempt to define states' customary obligation on climate change mitigation, to facilitate the implementation of this obligation, and to raise states' and civil society's awareness on this obligation—thus promoting compliance with customary international law.[229] Negotiations on individual commitments have been ongoing for three decades, and the UNFCCC regime will remain a work in progress until states can agree on individual commitments that they are satisfied with.

and Antoine Pécoud, 'Introduction: The UN Convention on Migrant Workers' Rights' in Paul de Guchteneire, Antoine Pécoud, and Ryszard Cholewinski (eds), *Migration and Human Rights: The United Nations Convention on Migrant Workers' Rights* (CUP 2009) 1.

[224] UNFCCC (n 76) art 12(1)–(2).

[225] Ibid art 14.

[226] Paris Agreement (n 128) art 4(2), second sentence.

[227] Ibid art 4(8). See also Decision 4/CMA.1, 'Further Guidance in Relation to the Mitigation Section of Decision 1/CP.21' (15 December 2018) FCCC/PA/CMA/2018/3/Add.1, 6.

[228] See Decision 1/CP.21 (n 159) ¶17.

[229] Benoit Mayer, 'Construing International Climate Change Law as a Compliance Regime' (2018) 7 TEL 115.

E. Interpretative Interactions between Commitments and Customary Obligations

Section D has demonstrated that the relationship between customary obligations and commitments is a relationship of interpretation rather than a relationship of conflict. The present section explores what this implies for the interpretation of these two types of mitigation obligations. It first assesses how climate treaties may help make sense of customary international law before questioning how customary international law may contribute to the interpretation of commitments.

1. Interpreting Customary Law in Light of Negotiated Instruments

Climate treaties are likely to exercise a certain influence on the interpretation of customary international law. Baxter, in his classical study on multilateral treaties as evidence of customary international law, observed that '[t]he convenience of reliance on the multilateral treaty is such that it may have a centripetal force' simply because the treaty—unlike customary international law—'speaks loudly and clearly'.[230] For better or for worse, there is plenty of evidence of this centripetal force, not only for codification treaties such as the Vienna Convention on Diplomatic Relations[231] but also for other treaties, including regional ones, for instance the Espoo Convention on Environmental Impact Assessment in a Transboundary Context.[232] Likewise, climate treaties, NDCs, and other party communications are likely to be on top of the reading list of a judge seeking to interpret a state's mitigation obligation under customary international law. The following assesses whether a state's customary obligation on climate change mitigation requires it at least to fulfil its commitments and pledges on climate change mitigation and to act consistently with the collective objectives defined in climate treaties.

a) Compliance with commitments and pledges

A state's customary obligation on climate change mitigation can certainly be interpreted in light of the state's general commitment under Article 4(1)(b) (and, for an Annex I party, 4(2)(a)) of the UNFCCC. This, however, may appear rather unhelpful as these general commitments do not provide much clarity on what states

[230] Baxter, 'Multilateral Treaties' (n 174) 300. See also Alexandre Hermet, *La convergence des dispositions conventionnelles et la determination du droit international coutumier* (Pedone 2021).

[231] See Fernando Lusa Bordin, 'Reflections of Customary International Law: The Authority of Codification Conventions and ILC Draft Articles in International Law' (2014) 63 ICLQ 535.

[232] See Convention on Environmental Impact Assessment in a Transboundary Context (25 February 1991, in force 10 September 1997) 1989 UNTS 309 ('Espoo Convention'); *Pulp Mills* (n 27) ¶¶203–05, 210; Alan Boyle, 'Developments in the International Law of Environmental Impact Assessments and their Relation to the Espoo Convention' (2011) 20 RECIEL 227, 229, 231.

are required to do. By contrast, some specific commitments may provide clearer insights on a state's customary mitigation obligation. These specific commitments include, for instance, the commitment of a party to the Paris Agreement to take the necessary measures to achieve its NDC[233] and the commitment that a state may have made through unilateral declaration manifesting the will to be bound.[234] There is a strong presumption that a state does not comply in good faith with its general customary obligations of prevention and cooperation, and with the discrete customary obligation on climate change mitigation that they entail, if this state does not honour the specific commitments it has made. States do not commit to climate change mitigation out of self-interest, convenience, or political expediency[235] but rather because they have a general obligation to do so: therefore, it can safely be assumed that such commitments generally reflect the state's own interpretation of its pre-existing obligations. This presumption could conceivably be set aside if the commitment had been made based on an error, but, in such a case, the commitment itself would probably be invalid.[236]

A slightly more difficult question is whether this reasoning could also be based on (non-binding) pledges. On the one hand, like a commitment, a pledge expresses the state's own view about what it ought to achieve with regard to climate change mitigation, even though this view is expressed as a fact—as a mere description of the state's assessment of what it can and should do—rather than as a legal commitment. A state's obligation to cooperate in good faith is breached when a state blows hot and cold[237]—when it arbitrarily discards its own assessment of its requisite level of mitigation action. Thus, the Supreme Court of the Netherlands in *Urgenda* seemed to assume that the state had at the very least to comply with the level of ambition suggested by its Cancun pledge[238]—perhaps not because of the legal force of this document but rather by using it as a relevant benchmark to interpret the state's customary obligation on climate change mitigation.

On the other hand, one cannot deny the relevance of the state's decision to make a pledge rather than a binding commitment. As states are likely to weigh their commitments more carefully than their pledges, commitments have greater value as evidence of a state's interpretation of its general mitigation obligations. The context of some pledges may be relevant in determining the weight that ought to be attached to them. For instance, when a party communicates a pledge and a commitment with regard to the same period, and when the pledge includes more ambitious targets than the commitments, the distinction between the pledge and the

233 See Paris Agreement (n 128) art 4(2), second sentence. See above at 57.

234 See above at 63.

235 See n 83.

236 See VCLT (n 219) art 48.

237 See Arnold D McNair, 'The Legality of the Occupation of the Ruhr' (1924) 5 BYBIL 17, 35 (discussing the theory of estoppel).

238 *Urgenda* (SC) (n 6).

commitment reveals the merely aspirational value of the former.[239] By contrast, if a party communicates a pledge but no commitment, a judge is more likely to use the pledge as a benchmark to assess the state's requisite level of mitigation action under its general mitigation obligations. However, the presumption that the state must fulfil its pledge in order to comply with its general mitigation obligation could be overturned by indication to the contrary.

Another question is whether customary law may require more than what a state has specifically consented or pledged to do. In 2013, Boyle suggested that a court would most likely 'be reluctant to require more of States than they have agreed to' through their commitments under the Kyoto Protocol.[240] By contrast, several states formally recorded their view that the commitments contained in the Protocol were 'inadequate to prevent dangerous anthropogenic interference with the climate system', thus suggesting that these commitments were not sufficient to ensure compliance with 'principles of general international law'.[241] At any rate, Boyle's position would be far more difficult to defend in relation to the bottom-up approach of the Paris Agreement than with regard to the commitments included in (and thus, in a sense, 'endorsed' by the parties to) the Kyoto Protocol. When a state's pledge or commitment is its own decision, rather than part of a negotiated agreement, there is no reason to assume that this pledge or commitment reflects the state's due diligence. In this regard, the Supreme Court of the Netherlands in *Urgenda* justly understood that a state's compliance with its specific commitments or pledges does not necessarily demonstrate its compliance with customary international law.[242]

b) Consistency with collective objectives

What states commit or pledge to do has repeatedly fallen short of what they collectively acknowledge needs to be done on climate change mitigation. The parties to the UNFCCC agreed to the 'ultimate objective' of preventing 'dangerous' climate change.[243] The Cancun Agreements interpreted this as implying the need to achieve emission reductions 'so as to hold the increase in global average temperature below 2°C above pre-industrial levels', and it was noted that 'Parties should take urgent action to meet this long-term goal'.[244] Yet, the following COP expressed

[239] See Doha Amendment to the Kyoto Protocol (8 December 2012, in force 31 December 2020) C.N.718.2012.TREATIES-XXVII.7.c, art 1A (fn 1).

[240] Alan Boyle, 'Law of the Sea Perspectives on Climate Change' in David Freestone (ed), *The 1982 Law of the Sea Convention at 30: Successes, Challenges and New Agenda* (Martinus Nijhoff 2013) 162. See also Boyle and Redgwell (n 1) 166, making a similar remark in the broader context of the obligation of prevention.

[241] Declarations made by the Cook Islands and Niue upon signature of the Kyoto Protocol. See also the similar declaration made by Nauru at the same occasion.

[242] *Urgenda* (SC) (n 6).

[243] UNFCCC (n 76) art 2.

[244] Decision 1/CP.16, 'The Cancun Agreements: Outcome of the work of the Ad Hoc Working Group on Long-Term Cooperative Action under the Convention' (10–11 December 2010) FCCC/CP/2010/7/Add.1, 2, ¶4. See also Copenhagen Accord of 18 December 2009, appended to Decision 2/CP.15, 'Copenhagen Accord' (18–19 December 2009) FCCC/CP/2009/11/Add.1.

'great concern' about the gap between the aggregate effect of their individual pledges and the global level of ambition required to achieve this temperature target.[245] The parties to the Paris Agreement decided to 'enhanc[e] the implementation of the Convention, including its objectives' with the adoption of a more ambitious goal—holding global warming '*well* below 2°C' while also 'pursuing efforts to limit the temperature increase to 1.5°C'.[246] In turn, it is largely understood that, in aggregate, current NDCs are not consistent with the most likely global emission reduction pathways consistent with these objectives.[247]

Thus, if a state's customary obligation on climate change mitigation is interpreted as requiring mitigation action consistent with the collective objectives that states have agreed upon, this customary obligation will likely require more from most states than merely honouring their commitments and pledges.[248] This was the approach followed by the Supreme Court of the Netherlands in *Urgenda*, which relied on the Cancun Agreements' 'below 2°C' target to determine the state's requisite level of mitigation action in 2020.[249] Plaintiffs have sought to transplant *Urgenda*'s reasoning in ongoing litigation before various other courts on the basis of the temperature targets of the Paris Agreement.[250]

This reasoning faces considerable difficulties. From a practical perspective, temperature targets do not easily translate into national mitigation objectives—not without a clear agreement on what these temperature targets mean and, overall, how efforts are to be shared among states.[251] At any rate, the mere definition of an objective does not directly create legal obligations.[252] In fact, the UNFCCC and the Paris Agreement, as well as relevant decisions on their implementation, all present collective objectives as, precisely, objectives, rather than obligations.[253] Thus, as the UK Supreme Court pointed out, '[n]otwithstanding the common objectives set out in articles 2 and 4(1), the Paris Agreement did not impose an obligation on any state to adopt a binding domestic target to ensure that those objectives were met'.[254]

[245] Decision 1/CP.17 (n 162) Preamble ¶3. See also Decisions 1/CP.18, 'Agreed Outcome Pursuant to the Bali Action Plan' (8 December 2012) FCCC/CP2012/8/Add.1, 3, second recital before ¶4, third recital before ¶14; 2/CP.18 (n 162) Preamble ¶4; 1/CP.20, 'Lima Call for Climate Action' (14 December 2014) FCCC/CP/2014/10/Add.1, 2, Preamble ¶7; 1/CP.21 (n 159) Preamble ¶10; 1/CP.25, 'Chile Madrid Time for Action' (25 December 2019) FCCC/CP/2019/13/Add.1, 2, ¶8; Decision 1/CMA.2, 'Chile Madrid Time for Action' (15 December 2019) FCCC/PA/CMA/2019/6/Add.1, 2, ¶5.

[246] Paris Agreement (n 128) art 2(1)(a) (emphasis added).

[247] See Decision 1/CP.21 (n 159) ¶17; UNEP DTU Partnership, 'Emissions Gap Report 2021' (UNEP 2021); UNFCCC Secretariat, 'Nationally Determined Contributions under the Paris Agreement: Synthesis Report', FCCC/PA/CMA/2021/2 (2021) ¶13.

[248] See Alan Boyle, 'Climate Change, the Paris Agreement and Human Rights' (2018) 67 ICLQ 759, 774.

[249] *Urgenda* (SC) (n 6) ¶4.5.

[250] See below at 131.

[251] See below at 243.

[252] See below at 250.

[253] See Benoit Mayer, 'Temperature Targets and State Obligations on the Mitigation of Climate Change' (2021) 33 JEL 585, 595–97.

[254] *Friends of the Earth* (n 173) ¶71.

To assess the relevance of temperature targets to the interpretation of customary international law, one needs to turn back to one of the methodological issues discussed at the beginning of this chapter: the difference between descending and ascending reasoning.[255] From a descending approach, it would appear reasonable to interpret states' general mitigation obligations as requiring them to avoid contributing to dangerous climate change, given the inevitable impact that such harm would cause on sovereign rights. This analysis, in turn, can be informed by the proclamation of temperature targets as an indication of subsequent agreement on what constitutes dangerous climate change. In other words, the descending approach suggests that states must cooperate towards the achievement of collective objectives, presumably by taking and implementing measures consistent with these objectives, even though states have not expressly consented to any such commitment or defined how consistency is to be assessed.

The ascending approach, however, points to a different direction. Here, the focus is on empirical evidence of state practice accepted as law. In practice, states are not generally acting consistently with the temperature targets that they have agreed upon. In line with various economic assessments, states themselves have acknowledged that, in aggregate, their pledges and commitments do not announce mitigation action consistent with the least-cost way of achieving either of the temperature targets adopted in the Paris Agreement.[256] As a result of this ambition gap, an ascending reasoning does not currently support the notion that states have a customary obligation to act consistently with the collective objectives that they have agreed upon. As such, in light of the working methodology described in the beginning of this chapter, one cannot identify a customary obligation requiring states to implement mitigation action consistent with either temperature target.

Yet, closer scrutiny reveals a possible way of reconciling ascending and descending reasoning. State practice surely does not suggest that collective objectives are entirely irrelevant to states' mitigation obligations. In fact, parties routinely refer to collective objectives when they review or communicate their mitigation commitments and, as part of the information to facilitate clarity, transparency, and understanding of their NDCs, they agreed to specify how their objective 'contributes towards achieving' the collective mitigation obligations.[257] Likewise, some domestic judicial decisions have suggested that public authorities must take collective objectives into account when reviewing their mitigation strategy or assessing development projects.[258] The ambition gap is not due to a lack of willingness of states

[255] See above at 91.

[256] See nn 245, 247. This inconsistency in the aggregate effect of pledges and commitments suggests the inconsistency of many (or all) individual pledges and commitments.

[257] Decision 4/CMA.1 (n 227) Annex ¶7.

[258] See eg *Urgenda* (SC) (n 6); *Friends of the Earth* (n 173) ¶¶141–43, suggesting that the SEA report should include a reference to the objective of the Paris Agreement, even though failure to do so was not considered a ground to invalidate the decision.

to achieve the collective mitigation objective of the Paris Agreement: although states, in aggregate, are not acting consistently with their collective objectives, they do, at least, appear to be trying. Rather, the ambition gap results from differences in states' interpretations of their collective objectives, in particular concerning burden-sharing criteria. Thus, several separate studies of NDCs suggest that each of these documents is generally consistent with at least one plausible interpretation of the collective objective of the Paris Agreement.[259]

Therefore, ascending and descending reasoning converge to suggest that, in order to comply with their customary obligation on climate change mitigation, states must follow consistently a reasonable interpretation of the collective objectives that they have agreed upon. Admittedly, this is not a highly demanding obligation: selecting the least demanding interpretation of the temperature targets and the most accommodating effort-sharing criteria allows states to comply with this obligation with limited effort. Over time, however, this obligation can act like a noose around the neck of GHG-intensive economies: the room for manoeuvre that states can use to evade stringent obligations will continue to shrink as states agree on clearer objectives and on more specific burden-sharing criteria.

2. Interpreting Commitments in Light of Customary Law

While customary norms on climate change mitigation must be interpreted in light of negotiated instruments on the topic, commitments must also be interpreted in light of relevant customary norms.[260] Customary law may form part of the context of a treaty for the purpose of the Vienna Convention on the Law of Treaties, whether as subsequent practice or, more generally, as 'relevant rules ... applicable in the relations between the parties'.[261] The Preamble to the UNFCCC suggests that these relevant rules include 'pertinent provisions' of the Stockholm Declaration

[259] See Yann Robiou du Pont and others, 'Equitable Mitigation to Achieve the Paris Agreement Goals' (2017) 7 Nature Climate Change 38; Yann Robiou du Pont and Malte Meinshausen, 'Warming Assessment of the Bottom-Up Paris Agreement Emissions Pledges' (2018) 9 Nature Communications 4810; Xunzhang Pan and others, 'Exploring Fair and Ambitious Mitigation Contributions under the Paris Agreement Goals' (2017) 74 Environmental Science & Policy 49.

[260] See VCLT (n 219) art 31(1); ILC, 'Unilateral Declarations' (n 207) conclusion 7. See also *Nuclear Tests (Australia v France)* (n 107) ¶51; *Frontier Dispute (Burkina Faso/Mali)*, Judgment (22 December 1986), [1986] ICJ Rep 573, ¶40; *Armed Activities on the Territory of the Congo (New Application: 2002) (DRC v Rwanda)*, Judgment on Jurisdiction and Admissibility (3 February 2006), [2006] ICJ Rep 6, ¶53.

[261] VCLT (n 219) art 31(3). On the customary nature of this rule, see *Territorial Dispute (Libya / Chad)*, Judgment (3 February 1994), [1994] ICJ Rep 6, ¶41; *Kasikilil Sedudu Island (Botswana/Namibia)*, Judgment (13 December 1999), [1999] ICJ Rep 1045, ¶18; *Pulp Mills* (n 27) ¶65; *Maritime Delimitation in the Indian Ocean (Somalia v Kenya)*, Judgment on Preliminary Objections (2 February 2017), [2017] ICJ Rep 3, ¶63; Mark E Villiger, *Commentary on the 1969 Vienna Convention on the Law of Treaties* (Martinus Nijhoff 2008) 439–40.

such as the obligation of prevention.[262] The ILC Study Group on the fragmentation of international law pointed out that customary international law can be 'of particular relevance to the interpretation of a treaty ... especially where ... the treaty rule is unclear or open-textured'.[263] Even though customary norms themselves are often unclear and open-textured, they could help to clarify the meaning of treaty provisions and other commitments in at least two ways.

First, and at the most general level, customary international law helps to identify the object and purpose of relevant treaties[264] or to determine whether unilateral declarations manifest the will to be bound. As noted above, climate treaties are neither codification treaties[265] nor attempts to depart from customary international law;[266] rather, they are best construed as a gradual attempt to develop and implement norms of general international law on climate change mitigation.[267] Customary international law informs the interpreter of climate treaties or unilateral declarations that those documents are not purely transactional in nature and that the commitments they create are parts of a broader obligation of states to mitigate climate change.

Second, customary international law can also assist more concretely in the interpretation of commitments. In particular, the existence of customary obligations on climate change mitigation confirms that Article 4(1)(b) and 4(2)(a) of the UNFCCC are not merely aspirational provisions but that they impose a substantive commitment. This general commitment, being open-textured, must be interpreted in the context of subsequent agreements and practice,[268] including states' participation in, and implementation of, subsequent climate treaties containing more specific commitments. Subsequent practice has gradually raised the standard of due diligence applicable in relation to states' customary obligation on climate change mitigation and to their general commitment under the UNFCCC.[269]

Commitments made through subsequent instruments adopted under the UNFCCC must be interpreted in light of the general commitments under the UNFCCC as well as the general customary obligation on climate change mitigation.

[262] UNFCCC (n 76) Preamble ¶¶8–9. See, by analogy, *Maritime Delimitation in the Indian Ocean* (n 261) ¶89, considering UNCLOS relevant to the interpretation of a memorandum of understanding on the ground that the latter expressly mentioned the former.

[263] ILC, 'Conclusions on Fragmentation' (n 185) ¶20. See also *Oil Platforms (Iran v US)*, Judgment on Preliminary Objections (12 December 1996), [1996] ICJ Rep 803, ¶41.

[264] See by analogy *Pulp Mills* (n 27) ¶177.

[265] See above at 112.

[266] See above at 114–115.

[267] See above at 120.

[268] See VCLT (n 219) art 31(3)(a)–(b). See also *Legal Consequences for States of the Continued Presence of South Africa in Namibia (South West Africa) Notwithstanding Security Council Resolution 276 (1970)*, Advisory Opinion (21 June 1971), [1971] ICJ Rep 16, 31; *Gabčíkovo-Nagymaros* (n 107) ¶140; *Indus Waters Kishenganga*, Partial Award (n 63) ¶452; *Oppenheim's* (n 51) §633 (1282).

[269] On the debate about intertemporal law, see generally ILC, 'Draft conclusions on subsequent agreements and subsequent practice in relation to the interpretation of treaties' in ILC Report, 70th session, A/73/10 (2018) 16, conclusion 8 and its commentary.

This context suggests that states may intend to define their pre-existing general mitigation obligations through the adoption of treaties and the communication of declarations. This makes it more likely that a treaty provision and overall a unilateral declaration could be interpreted as imposing commitments when there could otherwise be doubts about the state's consent.[270] As such, if one were to concede to Bodansky that the text of Article 4(2) of the Paris Agreement permits different interpretations,[271] it remains that the context of this provision lends support to its interpretation as creating a substantive obligation for each state to take all necessary measures to achieve its NDC. In fact, NDCs are certainly among the 'programmes containing measures to mitigate climate change' that states committed to 'implement' under the UNFCCC[272] and which they must implement under customary international law.

Conclusion

This chapter has identified and laid the bases for the interpretation of customary international law obligations on climate change mitigation. The argument has built on both descending and ascending reasoning. It has shown that customary international law can alternatively be approached as the application of general obligations of prevention and cooperation to climate change mitigation or as a discrete obligation on climate change mitigation. Either way, states appear to have an obligation of conduct with regard to the mitigation of climate change: they must exercise due diligence and take appropriate steps.

The chapter has also shown that the relationship between customary and treaty obligations is not one of conflict but one of interpretation: climate treaties can help to interpret customary international law and vice versa. The empirical grounding of customary international law precludes its interpretation as requiring states to do more than they generally do (eg as acting consistently with temperature targets), but it does not exclude the possibility that compliance with customary law may require more than the fulfilment of specific commitments. In particular, there appears to be a general practice accepted as law, hence a norm of customary international law, requiring each state to act consistently with a consistent and reasonable interpretation of collective mitigation objectives.

[270] This consideration may have played a role, although this was not expressly acknowledged by the Court, in *Nuclear Tests (Australia v France)* (n 107) ¶51.

[271] See Bodansky, 'The Legal Character' (n 184) 146. But see above at 50.

[272] UNFCCC (n 76) art 4(1)(b).

IV
Obligations Implied from Human Rights Treaties

Introduction

In addition to commitments and customary obligations, mitigation obligations can also be inferred from treaties that require states to protect resources or individuals that are vulnerable to the impacts of climate change. In particular, as climate change adversely affects human rights, states' obligations to protect these rights could be interpreted as requiring them to mitigate climate change. Unlike the treaties discussed in Chapter II, the treaties from which these obligations are inferred were neither designed nor amended with a view to responding to climate change—in fact, some of them were adopted long before the scientific discovery of climate change.

At the most basic level, the identification of implied obligations relies on a simple reasoning. The argument starts from a treaty provision requiring a state to take measures to prevent or reduce a certain type of harm. These provisions can be found not only in human rights treaties[1] but also in various treaties that protect environmental resources[2] or treaties that protect certain groups (eg Indigenous peoples).[3] The argument then builds on scientific evidence that climate change threatens to cause such illicit harm. On these bases, the argument concludes that the treaty must be interpreted as requiring the state to take measures to mitigate climate change in order to reduce or avoid the illicit harm.

[1] See International Covenant on Civil and Political Rights (16 December 1966, in force 23 March 1976) 999 UNTS 171, art 2(1); International Covenant on Economic, Social and Cultural Rights (16 December 1966, in force 3 January 1976) 993 UNTS 3, art 2(1); Convention for the Protection of Human Rights and Fundamental Freedoms (4 November 1950, in force 3 September 1953) 213 UNTS 221, as amended ('ECHR'), art 1.

[2] See Convention for the Protection of the World Cultural and Natural Heritage (16 November 1972, in force 17 December 1975) 1037 UNTS 551, art 4; Convention on Biological Diversity (5 June 1992, in force 29 December 1993) 1760 UNTS 79, art 5 et passim; United Nations Convention on the Law of the Sea (10 December 1982, in force 16 November 1994) 1833 UNTS 3, arts 192ff.

[3] See Noelia Gravotta, 'A Great Nation Keeping Its Word: The Role of Tribal Treaty Rights in Climate Change Litigation Note' (2021) 29 NYU Envtl LJ 118; Statement of Claim (30 May 2016) in *Re Mataatua District Māori Council v NZ*, Wai 2607 (Waitangi Tribunal, pending) <https://perma.cc/VE94-KPQU> ¶52.

International Law Obligations on Climate Change Mitigation. Benoit Mayer, Oxford University Press.
DOI: 10.1093/oso/9780192843661.003.0004

This reasoning points, most obviously, to the need for the state to promote adaptation to climate change, that is, to seek to manage the impacts of climate change.[4] However, it is well known that adaptation, on its own, has a limited capacity to reduce adverse climate impacts; climate change mitigation is often necessary to prevent far-reaching climate impacts on societies and ecosystems. Thus, to comply with these treaty obligations, a state may also be required to mitigate climate change if mitigation action could significantly reduce the illicit harm.

As a matter of substantive law, these implied mitigation obligations add little, if anything, that commitments and customary obligations do not already impose on states. Implied obligations are neither as specific as some commitments arising from climate treaties or unilateral declarations (eg nationally determined contributions (NDCs)) nor as demanding as the general mitigation obligations under customary international law and the UN Framework Convention on Climate Change (UNFCCC). Their scope of application does not extend beyond that of customary law (which applies to every state) or the UNFCCC (to which virtually every state is a party). Nor is there any reason to think that implied mitigation obligations are more demanding than general mitigation obligations—rather to the contrary, as the chapter will show. If implied obligations are nonetheless relevant, it is for a practical reason: these obligations can often be enforced or applied through more effective procedures and mechanisms than climate treaties or customary law. The judicial enforcement of commitments and customary obligations is limited, at the international level, by conditions of jurisdiction[5] and generally, at the domestic level, by the lack of standing of individual claimants to invoke state-to-state obligations. Relying on other treaties can allow access to international dispute settlement procedures to which states have consented, thus overcoming the issue of jurisdiction.[6] Overall, framing climate change mitigation as a matter of compliance with human rights treaties may allow standing to individuals or non-state entities before domestic courts, regional human rights courts, and international quasi-judicial institutions.

[4] See eg *Leghari v Pakistan*, WP No 25501/2015, Order of 4 September 2015 (Lahore High Court) <https://elaw.org/pk_Leghari>; Jacqueline Peel and Hari M Osofsky, 'A Rights Turn in Climate Change Litigation?' (2018) 7 TEL 37, 62–63.

[5] The UNFCCC establishes an optional dispute settlement mechanism, but only two states (Cuba and the Netherlands) have opted in. See United Nations Framework Convention on Climate Change (9 May 1992, in force 21 March 1994) 1771 UNTS 107, art 14(2); Kyoto Protocol to the United Nations Framework Convention on Climate Change (11 December 1997, in force 16 February 2005) 2303 UNTS 162, art 19; Paris Agreement (12 December 2015, in force 4 November 2016) (2016) 55 ILM 740, art 24. Many of the largest GHG emitters have not recognized the compulsory jurisdiction of the ICJ: Statute of the International Court of Justice (26 June 1945, in force 24 October 1945) 3 Bevans 1153, art 36(2).

[6] On human rights treaties, see below at 143. On the law of the sea, see UNCLOS (n 2) art 288(1)–(2). More specifically on the possibility of advisory proceedings, see ITLOS, Rules of the Tribunal, ITLOS/8 (28 October 1997, last amended 25 March 2021) art 138(1); *Request for Advisory Opinion by the Sub-Regional Fisheries Commission*, Advisory Opinion (2 April 2015), [2015] ITLOS Rep 4, ¶60.

Thus, human rights treaties have been central to a rapid expansion of climate litigation in recent years.[7] Yet, a considerable amount of uncertainty remains about their relevance. On the one hand, the Supreme Court of the Netherlands, in *Urgenda*, held that the state's obligation to protect the right to life and the right to private and family life under the European Convention on Human Rights (ECHR) implied an obligation to reduce its greenhouse gas (GHG) emissions by at least 25 per cent by the end of 2020 compared with 1990 levels.[8] On the other hand, the Supreme Court of Norway, in *Natur og Ungdom*, found that the issuance of ten petroleum production licences on the continental shelf did not involve a 'real and immediate' threat on the rights to life or to private and family life under the ECHR.[9] Other claims based on mitigation obligations implied from human rights treaties are currently pending before other national courts,[10] the European Court of Human Rights (ECtHR),[11] and UN treaty bodies.[12] Five human rights treaty bodies have stated their understanding that, to comply with human rights treaties, states 'must adopt and implement policies aimed at reducing emissions ... which reflect the highest possible ambition';[13] some of these institutions have included recommendations on climate change mitigation in their concluding observations on national periodic reports.[14]

[7] See Peel and Osofsky (n 4); Jacqueline Peel and Jolene Lin, 'Transnational Climate Litigation: The Contribution of the Global South' (2019) 113 AJIL 679, 684–85; Joana Setzer and Catherine Higham, 'Global Trends in Climate Litigation' (Grantham Research Institute on Climate Change and the Environment 2021) 6.

[8] *Urgenda v Netherlands*, ECLI:NL:HR:2019:2007 (SC, 20 December 2019), English translation in (2020) 59 ILM 811. See also *Klimaatzaak v Belgium*, case 2015/4585/A (French-Speaking Tribunal of First Instance of Brussels, 17 June 2021), English translation <https://perma.cc/68ZJ-2F96>.

[9] *Natur og Ungdom v Norway*, Case No 20-051052SIV-HRET (SC, 22 December 2020), English translation <https://perma.cc/5PCS-A8YH>.

[10] See generally the Climate Change Litigation Databases developed by the Sabin Center for Climate Change Law, <http://climatecasechart.com/>; Climate in the Courts <https://www.climateinthecourts.com/>.

[11] See *Duarte Agostinho v Portugal*, Communicated Case No 39371/20 (ECtHR, 13 November 2020) <http://hudoc.echr.coe.int/eng?i=001-206535>; *Verein Klimaseniorinnen Schweiz v Switzerland*, Communicated Case No 53600/20 (ECtHR, 17 March 2021) <http://hudoc.echr.coe.int/eng?i=001-209313>; Complaint in 'Mex M against Austria' (ECtHR, 25 March 2021) <https://perma.cc/MRR6-KK4W>; *Greenpeace Nordic v Norway*, Communicated Case No 34068/21 (ECtHR, 16 December 2021) <https://hudoc.echr.coe.int/eng?i=001-214943>.

[12] See 'Torres Strait Islanders/Australia' (no date) <http://climatecasechart.com/non-us-case/petition-of-torres-strait-islanders-to-the-united-nations-human-rights-committee-alleging-violations-stemming-from-australias-inaction-on-climate-change> mentioning a petition filed on 13 May 2019. See also CRC, Views, Sacchi/Argentina, Communication No 104/2019, CRC/C/88/D/104/2019 (22 September 2021) (rejecting standing for failure to exhaust national remedies). By contrast, see HRC, Views, Teitiota/NZ, Communication No 2728/2016, CCPR/C/127/D/2728/2016 (24 October 2019), which was only interested (at most) in consequences of climate change.

[13] CEDAW and others, Joint Statement on 'Human Rights and Climate Change' (16 September 2019) <https://perma.cc/6VXT-LAD4>. See also CESCR, Statement: 'Climate Change and the International Covenant on Economic, Social and Cultural Rights', E/C.12/2018/1 (31 October 2018) ¶6; CEDAW, General Recommendation No 37 on the Gender-Related Dimensions of Disaster Risk Reduction in the Context of Climate Change, CEDAW/C/GC/37 (2018) ¶14.

[14] See the Concluding Observations of CEDAW on the Ninth Periodic Report of Norway, CEDAW/C/NOR/CO/9 (2017) ¶¶14–15; of the CESCR on the Sixth Periodic Report of Russia, E/C.12/RUS/CO/6 (2017) ¶¶42–43; on the Fourth Periodic Report of Argentina, E/C.12/ARG/CO/4 (2018) ¶¶13–15;

Similarly, there has also been some discussion about the possibility of interpreting state obligations under environmental treaties as requiring them to mitigate climate change.[15] Thus, scholars have highlighted the broad obligations on environmental protection in Part XII of the UN Convention on the Law of the Sea (UNCLOS),[16] including from land-based sources of pollution,[17] and the expansive definition of pollution of the marine environment could capture major impacts of climate change such as ocean acidification[18] and sea-level rise.[19] In late 2021, Antigua and Barbuda and Tuvalu created the Commission of Small Island States on Climate Change and International Law with the express goal of initiating advisory proceedings before the International Tribunal for the Law of the Sea.[20] The parties to the Convention on Biological Diversity have acknowledged climate change as 'a major and growing driver of biodiversity loss'.[21] They have called for a 'transformational change ... in order to address climate change'.[22] In light of climate impacts on some world heritage sites, the World Heritage Committee has called upon parties to the World Heritage Convention to participate in climate negotiations 'with a view to ... mobilize global climate action'[23] and to take measures 'that

on the Sixth Periodic Report of Germany, E/C.12/DEU/CO/6 (2018) ¶¶18–19; on the Fourth Periodic Report of Ecuador, E/C.12/ECU/CO/4 (2019) ¶¶11–12; on the Sixth Periodic Report of Norway, E/C.12/NOR/CO/6 (2020) ¶¶10–11; on the Fifth Periodic Report of Belgium, E/C.12/BEL/CO/5 (2020) ¶¶9–10; on the second periodic report of Latvia, E/C.12/LVA/CO/2 (2021) ¶¶10–11; of the CRC on the Combined Fifth and Sixth Periodic Reports of Australia, CRC/C/AUS/CO/5-6 (2019) ¶¶40–41; on the Combined Fourth and Fifth Periodic Reports of Japan, CRC/C/JPN/CO/4-5 (2019) ¶37; on the Combined Fifth and Sixth Periodic Reports of Austria, CRC/C/AUT/CO/5-6 (2020) ¶35; of the HRC on the Fourth Periodic Report of Kenya, CCPR/C/KEN/CO/4 (2021) ¶¶26–27.

[15] See Roda Verheyen, *Climate Change Damage and International Law: Prevention Duties and State Responsibility* (Brill 2005) 192–224.

[16] UNCLOS (n 2) arts 192ff.

[17] Ibid arts 194(3)(a), 207, 213.

[18] Ibid art 1(1)(4). See discussion in Alan Boyle, 'Law of the Sea Perspectives on Climate Change' in David Freestone (ed), *The 1982 Law of the Sea Convention at 30: Successes, Challenges and New Agenda* (Martinus Nijhoff 2013) 158; Tim Stephens, 'Warming Waters and Souring Seas: Climate Change and Ocean Acidification' in Donald Rothwell and others (eds), *The Oxford Handbook of the Law of the Sea* (OUP 2015) 783; James Harrison, *Saving the Oceans through Law: The International Legal Framework for the Protection of the Marine Environment* (OUP 2017) 256; Yoshifumi Tanaka, *The International Law of the Sea* (CUP 2019) 396.

[19] Meinhard Doelle, 'Climate Change and the Use of the Dispute Settlement Regime of the Law of the Sea Convention' (2006) 37 Ocean Development & Intl Law 319, 322–24; Natalie Klein, 'Adapting UNCLOS Dispute Settlement to Address Climate Change' in Jan McDonald, Jeffrey McGee, and Richard Barnes (eds), *Research Handbook on Climate Change, Oceans and Coasts* (EE 2020) 97.

[20] Agreement for the Establishment of the Commission of Small Island States on Climate Change and International Law (31 October 2021) <https://perma.cc/D688-7R93> art 2(2).

[21] COP/CBD decision 14/5, 'Biodiversity and Climate Change' (Sharm El-Sheikh, 17–29 November 2018) Preamble ¶6. See also COP/CBD decision X/33, 'Biodiversity and Climate Change' (Nagoya, 18–29 October 2010) ¶2.

[22] COP/CBD decision XII/20, 'Biodiversity and Climate Change and Disaster Risk Reduction' (Pyeongchang, 6–17 October 2014) Preamble, ¶6. See also COP/CBD decision 14/5, 'Biodiversity and Climate Change' (Sharm El-Sheikh, 17–29 November 2018) ¶7.

[23] WHC Decision 39 COM 7, 'State of Conservation of World Heritage Properties' (2015) WHC-15/39.COM/19, 9, ¶12.

are fully consistent with their obligations within the World Heritage Convention'.[24] Relevant discussions have also taken place under the Ramsar Convention on Wetlands.[25]

Whether a treaty implies a mitigation obligation is fundamentally a matter of treaty interpretation: it depends on the terms of the treaty, its context, and its object and purpose.[26] Notwithstanding the context and object and purpose of a treaty, however, a provision that requires the prevention of an illicit harm cannot be interpreted as requiring a state to mitigate climate change unless such measures could realistically prevent or reduce the illicit harm (or the risk of illicit harm). Moreover, no implied mitigation obligation can be identified when the link between climate change and the illicit harm is exceedingly tenuous.[27] For instance, while some studies suggest that climate change could increase the risk of genocide,[28] one could question whether this link, tenuous and uncertain, is sufficient to infer an obligation to mitigate climate change from states' obligation to prevent genocide.[29] But even in the presence of a clearer link between climate change and the illicit harm, one must also ascertain whether the implementation of appropriate measures by the state could really make a difference. A likely objection in this regard is that, by regulating GHG emissions under its control, a given state can only achieve marginal reductions in global GHG emissions and even more tenuous reductions in GHG concentrations in the atmosphere. However, this objection can conceivably be overcome by pointing at the far-reaching implications of climate change: like a tiny slice of a very large cake, even a small reduction in global GHG emissions can achieve a significant (albeit diffuse) reduction in the illicit harm.

Another question relates to the standard of due diligence—that is, the appropriate measures that the state would be required to take under the treaty at issue.

[24] WHC Decision 41 COM 7, 'State of Conservation of the Properties Inscribed on the World Heritage List' (2017) WHC/17/41.COM/18, 8, ¶22. See also Draft Policy Document on Climate Change Action for World Heritage, WHC/21/44.COM/7C, 13 (2021); WHC Decision 44 COM 7C, 'Draft Updated Policy Document on the Impacts of Climate Change on World Heritage Properties' (2021) WHC/21/44.COM/7c, 300, ¶8.

[25] See Convention on Wetlands of International Importance Especially as Waterfowl Habitat (2 February 1971, in force 21 December 1975) 996 UNTS 245 ('Ramsar Convention'); Conference of the Contracting Parties to the Ramsar Convention on Wetlands Res XIII.13, 'Restoration of Degraded Peatlands to Mitigate and Adapt to Climate Change and Enhance Biodiversity and Disaster Risk Reduction' (21–29 October 2018) ¶12.

[26] Vienna Convention on the Law of Treaties (23 May 1969, in force 27 January 1980) 1155 UNTS 331, art 31(1).

[27] See generally HLA Hart and Tony Honoré, *Causation in the Law* (OUP 1985) 86. See also, by analogy, ILC, 'Draft Articles on the Responsibility of States for Internationally Wrongful Acts' [2001] II(2) YBILC 26, commentary on art 31, ¶10.

[28] See eg Jürgen Scheffran, Tobias Ide, and Janpeter Schilling, 'Violent Climate or Climate of Violence? Concepts and Relations with Focus on Kenya and Sudan' (2014) 18 IJHR 369; Alex Alvarez, *Unstable Ground: Climate Change, Conflict, and Genocide* (Rowman & Littlefield 2017).

[29] See Convention on the Prevention and Punishment of the Crime of Genocide (9 December 1948, in force 12 January 1951) 78 UNTS 277 art I, as interpreted in *Application of the Convention on the Prevention and Punishment of the Crime of Genocide (Bosnia v Serbia)*, Judgment (26 February 2007), [2007] ICJ Rep 43, ¶165. See also World Summit Outcome, UNGA Res 60/1 (16 September 2005) ¶138.

As the Study Group of the International Law Association on Due Diligence observed, the standard of due diligence applicable under a treaty 'varies according to the importance of the interest requiring protection'.[30] At one extreme, this can be illustrated with the hypothetical example of a bilateral treaty requiring two neighbouring states to ensure the preservation of a few boundary markers. Consider that the boundary markers are threatened by foreseeable impacts of climate change (eg flooding from a melting glacier). Consider also that it would be within the capabilities of each party to avoid, or at least to delay, this illicit harm by implementing expansive mitigation action—and that there is no other way for the parties to protect the markers. Implementing mitigation action, however, would likely involve measures out of all proportion to the applicable standard of due diligence, given the rather trivial nature of the harm at issue: it would be absurd to suggest that this bilateral treaty on the protection of a few boundary markers requires the parties to transform their entire economic system when states could simply replace the boundary markers whenever necessary. The states may have an obligation to implement such expansive mitigation action, but this obligation is not part of their bilateral treaty, which only requires them to take measures that are reasonable in light of the importance that the parties attach to the protection of the boundary markers.

The standard of due diligence applicable under an implied obligation thus depends on the importance given to the prevention of the illicit harm under the treaty from which the obligation is inferred. Any implied mitigation obligation reflects some of the impacts of climate change (ie some of the benefits of climate change mitigation) but ignores others. For instance, an environmental treaty on biological diversity would be sensitive to the impacts of climate change on species and ecosystems, but it would generally ignore impacts on human societies. Likewise, human rights treaties shed light on climate change solely as a human rights issue—they do not perceive the broader impacts of climate change on ecosystems, future generations, or human welfare beyond individuals' rights. In other words, the mitigation obligation implied from any such treaty involves a cost–benefit analysis that ignores many of the benefits of mitigation action and, thus, provides an incomplete justification for mitigation action.

In line with these preliminary remarks, this chapter presents a critical yet constructive perspective on the possibility of interpreting human rights treaties as the source of mitigation obligations. The chapter makes the argument that, to comply with its treaty obligation to protect a human right, a state must cooperate on the

[30] Study Group on Due Diligence in International Law, 'Second Report on Due Diligence' (2016) 77 ILA Rep Conferences 1062, 1081–82. On the variation of due diligence depending on the degree of risk of harm, see *Alabama Claims (US/UK)*, Award (14 September 1872), 29 RIAA 125, 129; Jorge E Viñuales, 'Due Diligence in International Environmental Law: A Fine-Grained Cartography' in Heike Krieger, Anne Peters, and Leonhard Kreuzer (eds), *Due Diligence in the International Legal Order* (OUP 2020) 112.

mitigation of climate change only *if* and *inasmuch as* climate change cooperation may effectively protect the enjoyment of the right at issue by individuals within its territory or under its jurisdiction. While human rights treaties may have a role to play in the mitigation of climate change under certain circumstances, this role is far more limited than has often been suggested.[31]

Section A outlines the relevant conceptual background on the relationship between climate change mitigation and human rights treaties. By contrast with the general obligations on climate change mitigation that arise from international environmental agreements or customary law, human rights treaties provide a bizarre, frequently ill-fitting legal ground to envision states' obligations to mitigate climate change—one that tends to emphasize the direct, local, short-term costs of mitigation action within the state's territory rather than its more diffuse, global, long-term benefits. Nevertheless, and despite the absence of identifiable victims of climate change, human rights treaties could enable the use of some implementation mechanisms not otherwise available in relation to general mitigation obligations.

Section B demonstrates the possibility of identifying mitigation obligations on the basis of human rights treaties. The key problem it addresses is that human rights treaties require states to protect human rights chiefly within their own territory, thus remaining insensitive to most of the global benefits of mitigation action. Contrary to prevailing theories, this problem cannot be overcome by extending the extraterritorial application of human rights treaties, by invoking 'collective obligations', or by reference to states' general international law obligation to cooperate on matters of international concern (an other-regarding obligation of cooperation). The problem, however, can partly be addressed based on the understanding that a state's obligation to protect human rights implies an inward-looking obligation of cooperation: a state must cooperate on climate change mitigation in good faith if—assuming other states follow the same precept—this can be anticipated to help protect the rights of individuals within its territory.

Finally, section C discusses how the mitigation obligations derived from human rights treaties are to be interpreted. Under the principle of systemic integration, the interpretation of implied mitigation obligations should take into account other relevant norms, including general mitigation obligations arising under climate treaties and customary international law. Scholarship and judicial practice have frequently misconstrued this principle when assuming that, for a state to comply

[31] Cf John H Knox, 'Climate Change and Human Rights Law' (2009) 50 Va JIL 163; Stephen Humphreys (ed), *Human Rights and Climate Change* (CUP 2009); Michael Burger and Jessica Wentz, 'Climate Change and Human Rights' in Michael Faure (ed), *Elgar Encyclopedia of Environmental Law* vol 7 (EE 2015) 205; Sumudu Atapattu, *Human Rights Approaches to Climate Change* (Routledge 2016); John Knox, Report of the Special Rapporteur on the issue of human rights obligations relating to the enjoyment of a safe, clean, healthy and sustainable environment, A/HRC/31/52 (2016); Margaretha Wewerinke-Singh, *State Responsibility, Climate Change and Human Rights under International Law* (Hart 2019); UN OHCHR, 'Frequently Asked Questions on Human Rights and Climate Change', Fact Sheet No 38 (2021) 31. See also most of the concluding observations cited in n 14.

with its mitigation obligation implied from a human rights treaty, it must fully comply with all its general mitigation obligations. Rather, the chapter suggests that human rights treaties open only a certain window onto the applicability of general mitigation obligations. The size of this window of applicability varies according to the treaty, the right, and the national circumstances at issue—in particular, the potential benefits of mitigation action for the enjoyment of the right within the state's territory and under its jurisdiction. As no human rights treaty fully comprehends the benefits of climate change mitigation for human welfare, future generations, and ecological resources, implied mitigation obligations can only open a narrow window on the applicability of general mitigation obligations.

The chapter focuses on human rights treaties because of their greater practical relevance, in particular in light of ongoing litigation. This, however, is not to deny the possibility of applying a similar analysis to other treaties, including environmental agreements—perhaps most convincingly UNCLOS. In fact, it is arguably easier to infer mitigation obligations from environmental treaties than from human rights treaties because, while human rights treaties define obligations that are chiefly territorial in scope, environmental agreements have a broader geographical scope: the provisions of UNCLOS on the protection of the marine environment, for instance, have been interpreted as applying 'with respect to the marine environment in all maritime areas, both inside the national jurisdiction of States and beyond it'.[32] Thus, environmental agreements avoid the difficulties with inferring implied mitigation obligations from human rights treaties that are discussed in section B. On the other hand, the argument on narrow windows of applicability in section C is entirely applicable, *mutatis mutandis*, to environmental agreements as (like human rights treaties) they consider only some of the benefits of mitigation action. Overall, environmental agreements do not provide for the same practical opportunities, for instance for domestic litigation, as human rights treaties, even though some environmental agreements may provide for jurisdiction for classical contentious or advisory proceedings.

A. The Relevance of Human Rights Treaties

This section makes some introductory observations about the relevance of human rights to climate change mitigation. First, it explores the ambivalent relationship between climate change and the enjoyment of human rights: while climate change hinders the enjoyment of human rights, this is also true of action taken to mitigate climate change, the 'cost' of which for the enjoyment of human rights tends to be more local and immediate than its 'benefit'. Second, this section discusses the

[32] *South China Sea (Philippines v China)*, Award (12 July 2016), 31 RIAA 153, ¶940. See also *Sub-Regional Fisheries Commission* (n 6) ¶120.

strategic procedural advantages of human rights law from the viewpoint of potential plaintiffs, noting that the difficulty of attributing any 'victim' to a state's failure to mitigate climate change may hinder access to some (but not all) of the judicial and quasi-judicial procedures generally available under human rights treaties.

1. The Ambivalent Relation between Climate Change Mitigation and Human Rights

a) The human rights impact of climate change

Human rights treaties create two types of obligations: negative obligations to 'respect' (ie to refrain from violating) human rights and positive obligations to 'protect' and 'fulfil' these rights.[33] With regard to the latter, some human rights treaties specifically point to the obligation of states 'to take the necessary steps ... to adopt such legislative or other measures as may be necessary to give effect to' human rights[34] or simply to 'take all appropriate measures to ensure' that individuals can enjoy their rights.[35] More generally, a state must take appropriate measures to address any threat to the enjoyment of human rights, whether this threat is of human origin (eg crime) or triggered by a natural event (eg a natural disaster).[36] Positive human rights obligations are obligations of conduct: a state can be held responsible for a wrongful act only if it fails to exercise due diligence, notwithstanding the consequences.[37]

The fifth assessment report of the Intergovernmental Panel on Climate Change (IPCC) reflects the global scientific consensus that climate change has 'caused impacts on natural and human systems'[38] by increasing the frequency or severity of some extreme weather events, reducing the availability of freshwater resources,

[33] See eg Walter Kälin and Jörg Künzli, *The Law of International Human Rights Protection* (2nd edn, OUP 2019) 87.

[34] ICCPR (n 1) art 2(2). See also ICESCR (n 1) art 2(1).

[35] Convention on the Rights of the Child (20 November 1989, in force 2 September 1990) 1577 UNTS 3, art 2(2).

[36] See *Budayeva v Russia*, App No 15339/02, 2008-II ECHR 269, ¶¶128–29; HRC, General Comment No 36, 'Article 6: Right to Life', CCPR/C/GC/36 (3 September 2019); HRC, Views, Portillo Cáceres/Paraguay, Communication No 2751/2016, CCPR/C/126/D/2751/2016 (20 September 2019) ¶7.3; John H Knox, Report of the Independent Expert on the issue of human rights obligations relating to the enjoyment of a safe, clean, healthy and sustainable environment, 'Mapping Report', A/HRC/25/53 (2013) ¶¶47–61.

[37] See *Velásquez-Rodríguez v Honduras*, Judgment (29 July 1988) IACtHR Series C No 4, ¶172; HRC, General Comment No 31, 'The Nature of the General Obligation Imposed on States Parties to the Covenant', CCPR/C/21/Rev.1/Add.13 (26 May 2004) 8; *Stoicescu v Romania*, App No 9718/03 (ECtHR, 26 July 2011) <http://hudoc.echr.coe.int/eng?i=001-105820> ¶59. On the concept of obligation of conduct, see Pierre-Marie Dupuy, 'Reviewing the Difficulties of Codification: On Ago's Classification of Obligations of Means and Obligations of Result in Relation to State Responsibility' (1999) 10 EJIL 371.

[38] Christopher B Field and others, 'Technical Summary' in Christopher B Field and others (eds), *Climate Change 2014: Impacts, Adaptation, and Vulnerability: Part A: Global and Sectoral Aspects: Working Group II Contribution to the Fifth Assessment Report of the Intergovernmental Panel on Climate Change* (CUP 2014) 40.

and affecting ecosystems, food production, human health, livelihood, and poverty, among other things.[39] Many of the effects of climate change affect the enjoyment of human rights. A vast range of human rights can be concerned, including civil and political rights (eg rights to life and to property),[40] economic, social, and cultural rights (eg rights to an adequate standard of living and to the highest attainable standard of health),[41] and third-generation rights (eg the right to a healthy environment).[42] Climate change could well be, as Mary Robinson famously suggested, 'the greatest threat to human rights in the twenty-first century'.[43]

States' obligation to protect human rights must be informed by scientific knowledge about the current and predictable impacts of climate change. The first and most obvious implication is that states must implement measures to promote *adaptation* to climate change.[44] Some of the impacts of climate change can be avoided or reduced, for instance by preventing urban development in coastal regions that will be affected by sea-level rise or through early-warning systems aimed at reducing the vulnerability of populations to extreme weather events.[45] A state can generally implement such measures on its own, although some states may need international financial or technical assistance. As many of the impacts of climate change affect the enjoyment of human rights, states' obligation to protect human rights can be interpreted as an obligation to take adaptation measures to avoid or reduce these impacts. Accordingly, the High Court of Lahore pointed out that a state's 'delay and lethargy' in implementing adaptation action could constitute a breach of its human rights obligations.[46] However, adaptation is insufficient to prevent the increasingly harmful consequences of ongoing GHG emissions. As the IPCC noted, the existence of 'biophysical limits to adaptation' and constraints of

[39] Ibid 40–51.

[40] See eg Protocol to the Convention for the Protection of Human Rights and Fundamental Freedoms (20 March 1952, in force 18 May 1954) 213 UNTS 262 ('First Protocol'), art 1; ICCPR (n 1) art 6.

[41] See eg ICESCR (n 1) arts 11–12.

[42] See eg African Charter on Human and Peoples' Rights (27 June 1981, in force 21 October 1986) 1520 UNTS 217, art 24; Additional Protocol to the American Convention on Human Rights in the Area of Economic, Social and Cultural Rights (17 November 1988, in force 16 November 1999), OAS Treaty Series No 69 ('Protocol of San Salvador'), art 11.

[43] Mary Robinson, 'Social and Legal Aspects of Climate Change' (2014) 5 JHRE 15, 15.

[44] See Human Rights Council Res 41/21 (12 July 2019) A/HRC/RES/41/21 ¶2; Knox, 2016 Report (n 31) ¶68; *Neubauer v Germany*, 1 BvR 2656/18 (Federal Constitutional Court, 24 March 2021) <https://perma.cc/UJM6-QCCY> ¶157; CESCR, 'Climate Change and the International Covenant on Economic, Social and Cultural Rights', E/C.12/2018/1 (31 October 2018) ¶7; Alan Boyle, 'Climate Change, the Paris Agreement and Human Rights' (2018) 67 ICLQ 759 771. On the distinction between mitigation and adaptation, see above at 2.

[45] See Field and others (eds) (n 38) 85–92.

[46] *Leghari* (2015) (n 4) ¶8. See also *Leghari v Pakistan*, WP No 25501/2015, Judgment of 25 January 2018, PLD 2018 Lahore 364. The Court referred to a policy framework which also contains some measures on climate change mitigation, but it is with regard to adaptation that the Court found that the state was at fault. For a similar reasoning, see eg the Concluding Observations of the CESCR on the Sixth Periodic Report of Finland, E/C.12/FIN/CO/6 (2014) ¶9; on the Sixth Periodic Report of Canada, E/C.12/CAN/CO/6 (2016) ¶¶53–54; of the CRC on the Combined Second to Fifth Periodic Reports of Tuvalu, CRC/C/TUV/CO/2-5 (2020) ¶¶42–43.

costs and resources mean that 'adaptation cannot generally overcome all climate change effects'.[47] Adaptation needs to be complemented by mitigation.

A second implication of climate change could be that, in order to protect the enjoyment of human rights, states should promote the *mitigation* of climate change by taking measures to reduce GHG emissions. The Human Rights Council's special procedure mandate-holders have suggested that human rights treaties require states 'to adopt the mitigation measures necessary to reduce global emissions so as to hold the increase in global temperature below levels that would cause widespread harm to the enjoyment of human rights'.[48] A similar reasoning led the Supreme Court of the Netherlands, in *Urgenda*, to interpret the obligation of states to protect the right to life and to private and family life under the ECHR as implying an obligation to mitigate climate change.[49] Human Rights Treaty Bodies have recommended that parties take measures to achieve their Cancun Agreements,[50] NDCs,[51] or long-term mitigation targets,[52] or even enhance their NDCs,[53] and take more specific measures such as reducing fossil-fuel production,[54] investing in renewable energies,[55] or phasing out adverse subsidies.[56]

However, the benefits of a state's mitigation action for the enjoyment of human rights are not as direct, immediate, and predictable as those of adaptation action. With adaptation action, a state may achieve some effective human rights benefits for its population, for instance by establishing early-warning systems that help reduce casualties in the event of a natural disaster[57] or by implementing various policies to support food production when it is threatened as a consequence of climate change.[58] By contrast, a national mitigation policy aimed at reducing the state's

[47] Field and others (eds) (n 38) 62. See Ottmar Edenhofer and others, 'Technical Summary' in Ottmar Edenhofer and others (eds), *Climate Change 2014: Mitigation of Climate Change: Working Group III Contribution to the Fifth Assessment Report of the Intergovernmental Panel on Climate Change* (CUP 2014) 50.

[48] UN Special Procedures Mandate-Holders, 'A New Climate Change Agreement Must Include Human Rights Protection for All' (2014) 3.

[49] *Urgenda* (SC) (n 8).

[50] CESCR, Observations on Report of Germany (n 14) ¶19.

[51] CESCR, Observations on Report of Latvia (n 14) ¶11.

[52] Ibid.

[53] CESCR, Observations on Report of Belgium (n 14) ¶10.

[54] Observations of CESCR on Report of Norway (n 14) ¶11; of CEDAW on report of the UK, CEDAW/C/GBR/CO/8 (2019) ¶54.

[55] CESCR, Observations on Report of Ecuador (n 14) ¶12.

[56] CRC, Observations on Report of Austria (n 14) ¶35(b).

[57] See Marilyn Aparicio-Effen and others, 'A Successful Early Warning System for Hydroclimatic Extreme Events: The Case of La Paz City Mega Landslide' in Walter Leal Filho and Leonardo Esteves de Freitas (eds), *Climate Change Adaptation in Latin America* (Springer 2018); Renan Braga Ribeiro and others, 'First Approach of a Storm Surge Early Warning System for Santos Region' in Lucí Hidalgo Nunes, Roberto Greco, and José A Marengo (eds), *Climate Change in Santos Brazil: Projections, Impacts and Adaptation Options* (Springer 2019).

[58] See Bonizella Biagini and others, 'A Typology of Adaptation Actions: A Global Look at Climate Adaptation Actions Financed through the Global Environment Facility' (2014) 25 Global Envtl Change 97; Gina Ziervogel and Polly Ericksen, 'Adapting to Climate Change to Sustain Food Security' (2010) 1 WIREs Climate Change 525. See generally UNFCCC SBI, 'Progress in the Process to Formulate and Implement National Adaptation Plans', FCCC/SBI/2020/INF.13 (2020) 12–14.

GHG emissions can only have a minor influence on the global rate of GHG emissions ('flow'), and this will only gradually reflect on the atmospheric concentrations in GHGs ('stock') that cause climate change so that such policy will achieve very little, if any, tangible human rights benefits for the state's population.[59] Thus, while a state may adapt to climate change by implementing national policies on its own, effective mitigation action requires international cooperation in order to achieve significant cuts in GHG emissions at the global scale. And while adaptation action may achieve tangible outcomes in the short-to-medium term, the full benefits of mitigation action unfold only in the long term, when years-long emission reductions efforts start reflecting in lower-than-expected GHG concentrations in the atmosphere.

b) The human rights impacts of mitigation action

Climate change mitigation could possibly have three types of impacts on the enjoyment of human rights. First, the implementation of mitigation action can involve human rights violations, for instance the forcible relocation of populations to give room to a hydroelectric project[60] or to the production of biofuel.[61] However, states have an obligation to comply with their human rights obligations when implementing mitigation action, and there is no inevitable conflict between the protection of human rights and the mitigation of climate change.[62] Human rights violations in the process of implementing mitigation action can, and must, be prevented.

Second, climate change mitigation may sometimes be presented as one of the objectives of general interest which human rights treaties recognize as justifying limitations to the protection of rights—along with national security, public order, and economic development. For instance, climate change mitigation has been invoked to justify measures that limited the enjoyment of the right to equality of treatment or to property.[63] This objective could also be taken to justify (under conditions of necessity, proportionality, and legality) hydroelectric projects involving land expropriation or even population displacements, which would otherwise be

[59] See also below at 148.

[60] See Atapattu, *Human Rights Approaches* (n 31) 135; Philip Martin Fearnside, 'Belo Monte: Actors and Arguments in the Struggle Over Brazil's Most Controversial Amazonian Dam' (2017) 148 Die Erde 14.

[61] See Elizabeth Cushion, Adrian Whiteman, and Gerhard Dieterle, *Bioenergy Development: Issues and Impacts for Poverty and Natural Resource Management* (World Bank 2010); UNEP, Climate Change and Human Rights (2015) viii.

[62] See Paris Agreement (n 5) Preamble ¶12; Decision 1/CP.16, 'The Cancun Agreements: Outcome of the Work of the Ad Hoc Working Group on Long-Term Cooperative Action under the Convention' (10–11 December 2010) FCCC/CP/2010/7/Add.1, 2 ¶8; Res 41/21 (n 44) Preamble ¶¶7–8.

[63] See Cour d'Arbitrage, Decision 92/2006, Décret de la Région wallonne du 10 novembre 2004 instaurant un système d'échange de quotas d'émissions de gaz à effet de serre (7 June 2006) (Belgium) §B.15, in relation to the regulation of emissions from certain industries; *JRBS v Fiscal General del Estado*, Judgment 1935/2017, ILDC 2884 (PY 2017) (SC, 29 December 2017) (Paraguay), in relation to the banning of land clearance and deforestation.

incompatible with the state's human rights obligation.[64] Besides, the recognition of a 'climate emergency' by various national institutions in recent years[65] suggests the need for exceptional measures that could conceivably include derogations from human rights.[66] In fact, climate change mitigation is perhaps more naturally framed as an objective justifying limitations of and possibly derogations from human rights, rather than as a way to protect the enjoyment of individual rights—although one does not necessarily exclude the other.[67]

Third, and overall, climate change mitigation involves a massive redeployment of resources, which will inevitably compete with other priorities relevant to the protection of human rights, even when this does not translate directly into any violations or limitations of human rights.[68] At times, mitigation action may compete with other policies for the use of natural resources: for instance, mitigation strategies relying heavily on biofuel or on negative emission technologies would increase demand for land and water, with potential impacts for the rights to food and water.[69] Other mitigation strategies may increase the price of energy,[70] with potential adverse effects on poverty.[71]

In more general terms, mitigation action is expensive:[72] it will require financial investments at a pace and scale that imply substantial costs of opportunities

[64] Report of the Representative of the Secretary-General Francis M Deng, 'Guiding Principles on Internal Displacement', E/CN.4/1998/53/Add.2 (1998) Princ. 6(2)(c); Kälin and Künzli (n 33) 540. By analogy, see C-346/14, *European Commission v Austria*, ECLI:EU:C:2016:322 (CJEU, 4 May 2016) ¶73, recognizing climate change mitigation and the promotion of renewable energy as an overriding public interest justifying the environmental impacts caused by a hydroelectric power plant.

[65] See eg Parl Deb HC, 6th Series, vol 659, columns 317–18 (2019) (declaring an environment and climate emergency) (UK); House of Commons, Journals 42:1, No 435, Vote No 1366 (17 June 2019) (Canada); Parliament Resolution on the Climate and Environment Emergency, 2019/2930(RSP) (28 November 2019) (EU); Motion to Declare a Climate Change Emergency, 749 NZPD 233–50 (2 December 2020) (NZ).

[66] See ECHR (n 1) art 15; ICCPR (n 1) art 4. See also Knox, 'Climate Change' (n 31) 200; Stephen Humphreys, 'Introduction: Human Rights and Climate Change' in Humphreys (ed) (n 31) 6.

[67] Thus, a common justification for human rights limitation is the protection of the rights of others. See eg ICCPR (n 1) arts 12(3), 18(3), 19(3)(a), 21, 22(2).

[68] See eg Humphreys, 'Introduction' (n 66) 2, 22. See also *Neubauer* (n 44) ¶245, noting that delayed mitigation action may cause unreasonable impairment of human rights.

[69] Pete Smith and others, 'Agriculture, Forestry and Other Land Use (AFOLU)' in Edenhofer and others (eds) (n 47) 835 (box 11.5). See generally Benoit Mayer, 'Bioenergy with Carbon Capture and Storage: Existing and Emerging Legal Principles' (2019) 13 CCLR 113.

[70] Edenhofer and others, 'Technical Summary' (n 47) 63.

[71] See Shoibal Chakravarty and Massimo Tavoni, 'Energy Poverty Alleviation and Climate Change Mitigation' (2013) 40 Energy Economics S67; Abidah B Setyowati, 'Mitigating Energy Poverty: Mobilizing Climate Finance to Manage the Energy Trilemma in Indonesia' (2020) 12 Sustainability 1603.

[72] Emission reduction measures may at times (but not always) be justified by their direct economic benefits (eg producing renewable energy may be cheaper than producing energy from fossil fuels) and co-benefits (eg shutting down coal plants may be justified by public health considerations; investing in clean energy can create jobs). See Gabriel Blanco and others, 'Drivers, Trends and Mitigation' in Edenhofer and others (eds) (n 47) 392; Diana Ürge-Vorsatz and others, 'Measuring the Co-Benefits of Climate Change Mitigation' (2014) 39 Annual Rev Envt & Resources 549.

for the pursuance of other policies.[73] Developed states, for instance, have pledged to mobilize jointly USD 100 billion per year by 2020 to support climate action (a goal which, by 2022, was yet to be achieved),[74] and they have agreed to set a higher goal applicable from 2025.[75] Compliance with the judgment in *Urgenda* cost the Netherlands an estimated €3 billion.[76] The IPCC estimated that, under the most cost-effective scenarios, mitigation action could entail global consumption loss of 1.7 per cent by 2030 and 4.8 per cent by 2100.[77]

The ability of a state to effectively protect human rights is resource-dependent,[78] and some of the resources that states invest in reducing GHG emissions are inevitably taken away from other priorities, including priorities that advance the protection of human rights. As an immediate budgetary constraint, mitigation action hinders perhaps more obviously the efforts to protect social and economic rights such as the rights to an adequate standard of living, to the highest attainable standard of health, or to education; but it also impedes the effective protection of civil and political rights as states may not, for instance, be able to invest as much in road safety, crime prevention, or the justice system, when they are massively investing in mitigation action.[79]

None of these remarks are disputing that, from a global utilitarian perspective, the costs of mitigation action are justified by its benefits: humankind is certainly better off investing in stringent measures to reduce GHG emissions than enduring the increasingly severe impacts of climate change on individuals, societies, and ecosystems for centuries to come.[80] States have acknowledged that it is in their

[73] States have long recognized the conundrum of reconciling climate change mitigation with economic development and poverty eradication, in particular in the context of developing countries. See UNFCCC (n 5) art 3(1); Paris Agreement (n 5) Preamble ¶9, arts 2(1), 4(1).

[74] Decision 1/CP.16 (n 62) ¶98; Decision 1/CMA.3, 'Glasgow Climate Pact' (13 November 2021) FCCC/PA/CMA/2021/10/Add.1 (advance version), 2, ¶¶44, 46.

[75] Decisions 1/CP.21, 'Adoption of the Paris Agreement' (12 December 2015) FCCC/CP/2015/10/Add.1, 2, ¶53; 14/CMA.1, 'Setting a New Collective Quantified Goal on Finance in Accordance with Decision 1/CP.21, Paragraph 53' (15 December 2018) FCCC/PA/CMA/2018/3/Add.2, 3, ¶1; 9/CMA.3, 'New Collective Quantified Goal on Climate Finance' (13 November 2021) FCCC/PA/CMA/2021/10/Add.3 (advanced version), 8.

[76] Jonathan Watts, 'Dutch Officials Reveal Measures to Cut Emissions After Court Ruling', *The Guardian* (24 April 2020).

[77] Edenhofer and others, 'Technical Summary' (n 47) 57.

[78] See ICESCR (n 1) art 2(1); *Osman v UK*, App No 23452/94, 1998-VIII ECHR, ¶116; Kälin and Künzli (n 33) 102–03.

[79] For instance, there can be no fair trial without a budget to hire and train judges and lawyers. See Sigrun Skogly, 'The Requirement of Using the "Maximum of Available Resources" for Human Rights Realisation: A Question of Quality as Well as Quantity?' (2012) 12 HRL Rev 393, 394, 397. On positive human rights obligations as obligations of conduct, see n 37.

[80] Marshall Burke, Solomon M Hsiang, and Edward Miguel, 'Global Non-Linear Effect of Temperature on Economic Production' (2015) 527 Nature 235, suggesting that climate inaction would cost humankind about 23 per cent of global income by 2100. How stringent these measures ought to be, however, is debated. See William D Nordhaus, *The Climate Casino: Risk, Uncertainty and Economics for a Warming World* (Yale UP 2013) 205–19. For a rare sceptical view on the need for onerous mitigation policies and measures, see Bjorn Lomborg, *False Alarm: How Climate Change Panic Costs Us Trillions, Hurts the Poor, and Fails to Fix the Planet* (Basic Books 2020).

common interest to implement 'an effective and progressive response to the urgent threat of climate change'.[81] Justifications for climate change mitigation, however, are expressed in terms of global utility, for instance by reference to economic development, food production, or human security.[82] By contrast, human rights treaties require each state not to maximize global utility but to protect the rights of individuals within its territory and under its jurisdiction. The lenses that human rights treaties offer tend to magnify the immediate, proximate costs of a state's mitigation action, which are borne primarily by the individuals within the state's territory, while being unable to fully appreciate the utility of such action: the global, diffuse, long-term benefits for individuals, societies, and ecosystems that justify mitigation action from a broader policy perspective. When it comes to justifying mitigation action, human rights treaties thus miss most of the picture.[83]

2. The Strategic Advantages of Human Rights Law

Human rights treaties provide neither the only nor the most compelling legal basis for claiming that states ought to mitigate climate change. As previous chapters have shown, states have general obligations to mitigate climate change arising from customary international law and the UNFCCC. These obligations provide a legal basis to challenge a state's lack of ambition on climate change mitigation.

As such, the interest for human rights treaties in relation to climate change mitigation stems not from their added value in defining substantive mitigation obligations but rather from the access they provide to litigation and other complaint mechanisms.[84] Neither the UNFCCC nor the Paris Agreement has an effective mechanism to review compliance,[85] while the prospects for international litigation on general mitigation obligations are limited by the voluntary nature of international dispute settlement and (to a lesser extent) by the limited incentive for a state to initiate contentious proceedings against another with respect to an *erga omnes* obligation.[86] By contrast, human rights treaties provide potential plaintiffs

[81] Paris Agreement (n 5) Preamble ¶5.

[82] UNFCCC (n 5) arts 1(1), 2; Paris Agreement (n 5) arts 2(1), 4(1), 7(1); Field and others (eds) (n 38) 61; Edenhofer and others, 'Technical Summary' (n 47) 40. On the other hand, states have rejected a proposal of framing the objective of the Paris Agreement as the protection of human rights. See Benoit Mayer, 'Human Rights in the Paris Agreement' (2016) 6 Climate Law 109, 114–15.

[83] On the implications of this remark, see below at 171.

[84] See Lavanya Rajamani, 'The Increasing Currency and Relevance of Rights-Based Perspectives in the International Negotiations on Climate Change' (2010) 22 JEL 391, 417.

[85] On the limits of the facilitation and compliance mechanism established under the Paris Agreement, see Paris Agreement (n 5) art 15(2); Sylvia I Karlsson-Vinkhuyzen and others, 'Entry into Force and Then? The Paris Agreement and State Accountability' (2018) 18 Climate Policy 593, 594.

[86] Admissibility, on the other hand, should not be an obstacle as mitigation obligations are inevitably *erga omnes* obligations. See *Barcelona Traction, Light and Power Company, Limited (Belgium v Spain)*, Judgment on Second Phase (5 February 1970), [1970] ICJ Rep 3, ¶33; *Responsibilities and Obligations of States Sponsoring Persons and Entities with Respect to Activities in the Area*, Advisory Opinion (1 February 2011), [2011] ITLOS Rep 10, ¶180; *Questions relating to the Obligation to Prosecute*

with various institutional and procedural advantages. In addition to establishing state-to-state dispute settlement and complaint mechanisms,[87] human rights treaties often allow individuals, and sometimes groups, to file complaints before international bodies or cases before regional human rights courts,[88] while treaty bodies periodically review and make concluding observations on national reports.[89] Overall, human rights treaties or their instrument of incorporation allow individuals or groups to claim standing regarding the performance of a state's obligation before domestic courts, whereas these individuals or groups would typically have no standing to directly invoke climate treaties or customary law.[90]

A major procedural caveat, however, is that applicants claiming the implementation of a state's obligation under a human rights treaty are often required to prove that they are, or would imminently become, the 'victims' of a human rights violation.[91] This condition has already been a hurdle in simpler cases concerning local environmental harm,[92] where admissibility was limited to applicants who were 'directly and seriously affected'[93] or otherwise could prove 'a reasonably foreseeable threat to' their rights.[94] The relevant cases admitted by the ECtHR, for instance, typically concern individuals affected by a disaster[95] or directly exposed to

or Extradite (Belgium v Senegal), Judgment (20 July 2012), [2012] ICJ Rep 422, ¶¶68–69; *Application of the Convention on the Prevention and Punishment of the Crime of Genocide (Gambia v Myanmar)*, Order on Provisional Measures (23 January 2020), [2020] ICJ Rep 3, ¶41; ILC, 'State Responsibility' (n 27) art 48; Benoit Mayer, 'A Review of the International Law Commission's Guidelines on the Protection of the Atmosphere' (2019) 20 Melbourne JIL 453, 490–92. See also *Whaling in the Antarctic (Australia v Japan; NZ intervening)*, Judgment (31 March 2014), [2014] ICJ Rep 226, where the right of Australia to claim the implementation of Japan's obligation to protect the environment in the high seas remained unchallenged. But see ILC, 'Draft Guidelines on the Protection of the Atmosphere' in ILC Report, 72nd session, A/76/10 (2021) 13, commentary on guideline 3, ¶5, suggesting that 'there are different views' on the question of the existence of an *erga omnes* obligation to protect the atmosphere.

87 See eg ICCPR (n 1) arts 41–42; ECHR (n 1) art 33.

88 See eg ECHR (n 1) art 34; Optional Protocol to the International Covenant on Civil and Political Rights (16 December 1966, in force 23 March 1976) 999 UNTS 302, arts 1–2; Optional Protocol to the International Covenant on Economic, Social and Cultural Rights (10 December 2008, in force 5 May 2013) (2009) 48 ILM 256, arts 1–2.

89 See eg ICCPR (n 1) art 40(4).

90 See Eric A Posner, 'Climate Change and International Human Rights Litigation' (2006) 155 U Pa L Rev 1925, 1927; André Nollkaemper and others, *International Law in Domestic Courts* (OUP 2019) 7.

91 See ECHR (n 1) art 34; ICCPR-OP (n 88) art 2; ICESCR-OP (n 88) art 2; *López Ostra v Spain*, App No 16798/90 (1994) 303-C ECHR Series A, ¶51.

92 See HRC, Views, Vaihere Bordes/France, Communication No 645/1995, CCPR/C/57/D/645/1995 (22 July 1996) ¶¶5.5–5.7; Richard Desgagné, 'Integrating Environmental Values into the European Convention on Human Rights' (1995) 89 AJIL 263, 284–85; Loukis Loucaides, 'Environmental Protection through the Jurisprudence of the European Convention on Human Rights' (2004) 75 BYBIL 249, 250–52.

93 *Hatton v UK*, App No 36022/97, 2003-VIII ECHR 189, ¶96. See also *Cordella v Italy*, App No 54414/13 (ECtHR, 24 January 2019) <http://hudoc.echr.coe.int/eng?i=001-189421> ¶¶100–09; *Dmitriyev v Russia*, App No 17840/06 (ECtHR, 1 December 2020) <http://hudoc.echr.coe.int/eng?i=001-206265> ¶32.

94 Portillo Cáceres/Paraguay (n 36) ¶7. See also *Caron v France*, App No 48629/08 (ECtHR, 29 June 2010) <http://hudoc.echr.coe.int/eng?i=001-99981>.

95 See *Öneryildiz v Turkey*, App No 48939/99, 2004-XII ECHR 1; *Budayeva* (n 36).

a major local source of pollution[96] rather than those exposed to more diffuse environmental harms. The condition of victimhood is particularly problematic in climate litigation. Climate change hinders the enjoyment of human rights in a diffuse fashion; it may rarely, if ever, be possible to consider someone a 'victim' (whether actual or potential) of climate change—and, a fortiori, of *the failure of a state* to implement the requisite mitigation action.[97]

Arguments aimed at overcoming this challenge have sometimes relied on scientific studies regarding probabilistic event attribution to suggest the possibility of identifying 'victims' of climate change.[98] However, scientists are divided about the soundness of such studies and, even more, about their relevance to litigation.[99] At any rate, attributing a weather event to climate change is only one of the links in the causal chain that must be established to prove that an individual is a victim of the failure of a state to take appropriate measures to protect their human rights. A weather event only affects an individual when, as the result of successive individual and collective decisions, this individual is exposed and vulnerable to the event. Thus, migration studies deny the possibility of identifying a discrete population of 'climate migrants' on the ground that the influence of climate change on migration, albeit real, is diffuse and indirect.[100] At the other end of the causal chain, attributing any 'climate victim' to a state's conduct would require evidence that events affecting the individual were caused by the failure of that state to mitigate climate

[96] See *López Ostra* (n 91); *Taşkın v Turkey*, App No 46117/99, 2004-X ECHR 179; *Fadeyeva v Russia*, App No 55723/00, 2005-IV ECHR 255; *Cordella* (n 93).

[97] See *Verein KlimaSeniorinnen Schweizet v Eidgenössisches Departement für Umwelt*, case 1C_37/2019 (SC, Switzerland, 5 May 2020) ¶¶5.4–5.5; *Natur og Ungdom* (n 9) ¶¶167–68, 171, both dismissing claims based on the ECHR because of the absence of actual and imminent risk. The applicants in both cases have since filed complaints before the ECtHR (see n 11). See also Mex M against Austria (n 11), trying to present an applicant suffering from a rare medical condition exacerbated by heat as a direct 'victim'—but presumably a victim of climate change, not to the allegedly insufficient action of Austria. But see Sacchi/Argentina (n 12) ¶10.14, asserting that the authors of the complaint had 'established prima facie that they ha[d] personally experienced real and significant harm', though the Committee did not establish whether this harm was caused by the fault of the respondent state rather than by the emissions that had occurred throughout the world and which may not involve any wrongful conduct by any state.

[98] See Knox, 2016 Report (n 31) ¶36; Sophie Marjanac and Lindene Patton, 'Extreme Weather Event Attribution Science and Climate Change Litigation: An Essential Step in the Causal Chain?' (2018) 36 J Energy & Natural Resources L 265; Petra Minnerop and Friederike Otto, 'Climate Change and Causation: Joining Law and Climate Science on the Basis of Formal Logic' (2020) 27 Buff Envtl LJ 49.

[99] Field and others (eds) (n 38) 40. See also Kevin E Trenberth, 'Attribution of Climate Variations and Trends to Human Influences and Natural Variability' (2011) 2 WIREs Climate Change 925; Mike Hulme, 'Attributing Weather Extremes to 'Climate Change': A Review' (2014) 38 Progress in Physical Geography 499; Greg Lusk, 'The Social Utility of Event Attribution: Liability, Adaptation, and Justice-Based Loss and Damage' (2017) 143 Climatic Change 201.

[100] See Foresight, 'Migration and Global Environmental Change: Final Project Report' (2011); W Neil Adger and others, 'Human Security' in Field and others (eds) (n 38) 770; Calum TM Nicholson, 'Climate Change and the Politics of Causal Reasoning: The Case of Climate Change and Migration' (2014) 180 Geographical J 151; Benoit Mayer, *The Concept of Climate Migration* (EE 2016) 10–12. But see Jane McAdam, 'Protecting People Displaced by the Impacts of Climate Change: The UN Human Rights Committee and the Principle of Non-refoulement' (2020) 114 AJIL 708, assuming (in the very title) the existence of a discrete population of 'people displaced by the impacts of climate change'.

change rather than by historical GHG emissions that took place before the scientific discovery of climate change, emissions of other states, or emissions taking place within the state but which even the state's most stringent mitigation action would not have been able to prevent.

The absence of identifiable 'victims' could strike a fatal blow to individual or group applications before regional human rights courts and to individual communications to treaty bodies. On the other hand, this caveat does not necessarily affect the other strategic advantages of human rights treaties, in particular the periodic adoption of concluding observations by treaty bodies or even the possibility of interstate complaint and dispute settlement procedures based on human rights treaties. Overall, domestic legal systems define their own conditions for standing,[101] which are sometimes more favourable to the implementation of human rights treaties in the absence of identifiable victims, for instance when they permit public interest litigation.

Thus, the Supreme Court of the Netherlands allowed Urgenda to invoke the ECHR in defence of a public interest even while noting that the association would lack standing before the ECtHR as 'it is not itself a potential victim'.[102] Similarly, standing remained unchallenged in *Natur og Ungdom*[103] as Norwegian law expressly allows public interest litigation by interested NGOs.[104] By contrast, the European Court of Justice dismissed as inadmissible a case challenging the compatibility of the EU's 2030 mitigation target in light of the Charter of Fundamental Rights, in application of the limited conditions for standing under EU law,[105] on the ground that the applicants had not established that the legislation they sought to challenge could infringe *their* rights.[106] The Administrative Court of Berlin also denied standing, on comparable grounds, to individual farmers and an NGO that claimed that additional mitigation action was essential to protect fundamental rights.[107] Meanwhile, the French State Council allowed standing to townships and associations representing public interests to challenge the legality of the state's

[101] See Opinion of Mr Stéphane Hoynck, Advocate General of the Conseil d'Etat, on *Grande-Synthe v France* (19 November 2020), ECLI:FR:CECHR:2020:427301.20201119, No 427301, English translation <https://perma.cc/9Y88-VY5T> 2–3; *Klimaatzaak* (n 8) 51.

[102] *Urgenda* (SC) (n 8) ¶5.9.3. See also *Friends of the Irish Environment v Ireland* [2020] IESC 49, [2020] 2 ILRM 233, ¶¶7.6, 7.24, seemingly accepting that a distinction has to be made between standing before the European Court and before a domestic court but nonetheless finding that the NGO did not have standing before domestic courts.

[103] *Natur og Ungdom* (n 9).

[104] Lov om mekling og rettergang i sivile tvister (Act Relating to Mediation and Procedure in Civil Disputes), LOV-2017-06-16-63, ss 15–18.

[105] Consolidated version of the Treaty on the Functioning of the European Union [2016] OJ C202/47, art 263(4).

[106] C-565/19 P, *Carvalho v Parliament*, ECLI:EU:C:2021:252 (CJEU, 25 March 2021).

[107] *Backsen v Germany*, VG10K412.18 (Administrative Court, Berlin, 31 October 2019), English translation <https://perma.cc/7P8H-N6PS>.

mitigation action but not to individuals pursuing their own interests.[108] Few courts have recognized standing to claimants on the basis of a personal interest.[109]

This procedural difficulty reveals a more fundamental questions about the limitations of human rights law and adjudication with regard to climate change mitigation. When no victim can be identified, human rights no longer act as a 'trump' over objectives of general interest;[110] rather, what is framed as 'human rights protection'—the mitigation of climate change—itself becomes, in effect, an objective of general interest, which competes with other such objectives and with the protection of individual rights. One may question whether human rights law permits a judicial cost–benefit analysis of these various objectives of general interest[111] and, more specifically, whether human rights law can be interpreted as requiring states to pursue one such objective (with indirect human rights benefits) even if it comes at the expense of direct impacts on human rights. If so, how can it be ensured that the judicial process of interpreting and applying human rights law does not take over the political process of defining and balancing objectives of general interest? This question goes far beyond the scope of this chapter, but it necessarily informs what, ultimately, one considers as the potential for human rights treaties to be interpreted *at all* as the source of an obligation to mitigate climate change.

B. The Identification of Implied Mitigation Obligations

This section assesses whether human rights treaties imply an obligation to mitigate climate change. First, it identifies the difficulty of approaching the need for mitigation action in terms of human rights obligations: a state, acting on its own, is unable to achieve sufficient mitigation outcomes to effectively protect the human rights of individuals within its territory or under its jurisdiction. Second, it refutes three common arguments for the identification of implied mitigation obligations which rely, respectively, on (1) the extraterritorial application of human rights treaties; (2) the interpretation of human rights obligations as 'collective obligations'; and (3) the existence of other-regarding obligations of cooperation as part of human rights treaties. Third, as an alternative theory, this section submits that a state's obligation to protect a human right should be interpreted as implying

[108] *Grande-Synthe v France* (Conseil d'Etat, 19 November 2020), ECLI:FR:CECHR:2020:427301.20201119, ¶¶3–7. See also *Oxfam v France*, Application 1904967, Decision 44-008.60-01-02-02.R (Administrative Tribunal, Paris, 2 February 2021), in which the standing of environmental NGOs was not challenged.

[109] See *Klimaatzaak* (n 8) 48–56.

[110] Ronald Dworkin, Taking Rights Seriously (Bloomsbury 2013).

[111] See Daniel Bodansky, 'Introduction: Climate Change and Human Rights: Unpacking the Issues' (2010) 38 Georgia J Intl & Comp L 511, 514. See also *Misdzi Yikh v Canada* [2020] FC 1059, ¶¶19, 72; William J Aceves, 'Cost–Benefit Analysis and Human Rights' (2018) 95 St John's L Rev 431; Sacchi/Argentina (n 12) ¶3.6.

a narrower, inward-looking obligation of cooperation, according to which a state must cooperate on the mitigation of climate change only to the extent that this may effectively benefit the enjoyment of that right by individuals within the state's territory or under its jurisdiction.

1. The Problem

Acting on its own, a state is not generally capable of achieving mitigation outcomes that will make any real difference for the protection of the human rights of individuals within its territory or under its jurisdiction.[112] For instance, in *Urgenda*, the Netherlands was ordered to enhance its mitigation action in such a way as to achieve a 9 per cent reduction in its projected level of emissions for 2020.[113] This represented about a 0.03 per cent reduction in global GHG emissions that year.[114] Even if the same increase of ambition had been imposed on China, the largest GHG emitter, it would have translated into only about a 2 per cent reduction in global emissions.[115] Such incremental changes in global GHG emissions (a flow) would translate, after many years, into only very small differences in GHG concentration in the atmosphere (a stock), hence in very little concrete and tangible outcomes.

Incremental mitigation outcomes may nevertheless be worth achieving if one considers their diffuse, global, long-term benefits—even a very small contribution to addressing 'the greatest threat to human rights in the twenty-first century'[116] should be welcomed as addressing a tiny part of an enormous problem. Yet, most of these benefits do not fall within the scope of what human rights treaties require states to do. In particular, a key obstacle to interpreting human rights treaties as the source of an obligation to mitigate climate change is that a state's human rights obligations are generally limited to its territory or jurisdiction,[117] whereas the impacts

[112] See Alan Boyle, 'Human Rights and the Environment: Where Next?' (2012) 23 EJIL 613, 640–41.

[113] See Netherlands, Second Biennial Report under the UNFCCC (2015) 54, predicting that existing measures would result in emissions around 181 Mt CO_2 eq by 2020. The courts ordered the state to achieve 25 per cent emission reduction compared with 1990 levels. Assuming, as suggested by the same report, 1990 levels at 219 Mt CO_2 eq, 25 per cent emission reduction would require the state to reduce its emissions to 164 Mt CO_2 eq by 2020.

[114] Calculated based on data for 2017 GHG emissions including LULUCF, retrieved from ClimateWatch, 'Historical GHG Emissions' (no date) <https://www.climatewatchdata.org/> (CAIT database).

[115] Outcome of a 9 per cent reduction in China's 2017 emissions, calculated based on data from ibid.

[116] See Robinson (n 43).

[117] See ICCPR (n 1) art 2(1); ECHR (n 1) art 1; Marko Milanović, *Extraterritorial Application of Human Rights Treaties* (OUP 2011) 263. This problem applies often a fortiori in relation to constitutional rights, which states are not typically trying to apply to non-nationals outside their territory. See *Agency for International Development v Alliance for Open Society International* (2020)140 S Ct 2082, 2086 (US); *Natur og Ungdom* (n 9) ¶149, concluding that the constitutional right to a healthy environment 'does not generally protect against acts and effects outside the Kingdom of Norway'; *Neubauer* (n 44) ¶¶173–81, noting that constitutional rights could apply extraterritorially but would not impose expansive positive obligations such as mitigation action.

of climate change are global in nature.[118] When one only takes into account the benefits of a state's mitigation action within the state's own territory, these mitigation outcomes appear not just tiny but vanishingly small.

It is therefore likely that, within a state's territory or under its jurisdiction, the costs of any ambitious mitigation action will outweigh its benefits. For instance, all other things being equal, the inhabitants of the Netherlands would surely be better off if additional mitigation action had *not* been imposed on the state (hence, ultimately, on them): *Urgenda* imposed significant public expenditure, and presumably higher energy prices, on the state's residents for vanishingly small benefits for their human rights.[119] A state (especially a small one), taken in isolation, would often do a better job at protecting the rights of individuals within its territory or under its jurisdiction by deciding not to burden them with mitigation action, investing instead in adaptation action or in various other policies that could achieve more tangible human rights benefits within the state's jurisdiction (eg police training, public education, or road safety). Thus, embedded in human rights treaties is precisely the issue that has constantly plagued the UNFCCC negotiations: each state is expected to protect its own population—and, human rights treaties seem to suggest, is bound to do so—rather than pursuing their common interest in mitigating climate change.[120]

This problem is exacerbated by other limitations of human rights treaties: as these treaties focus on the rights of humans, they do not fully comprehend the utility of climate change mitigation for human welfare,[121] future generations,[122] or ecological resources.[123] Yet, addressing these exacerbating factors would not solve the key problem of territorial limitation. Nor is the recognition of new rights (eg to a healthy environment)[124] sufficient to address the problem described here. As long as human rights treaties remain treaties on the protection of *human rights*

[118] See Knox, 'Climate Change' (n 31) 197; Boyle, 'Climate Change' (n 44) 771. See also *Duarte Agostinho* (n 11) first question to the parties.

[119] See n 76.

[120] Eric A Posner and David Weisbach, *Climate Change Justice* (Princeton UP 2010) 181; Robert Stavins and others, 'International Cooperation: Agreements & Instruments' in Edenhofer and others (eds) (n 47) 1007.

[121] See Eric A Posner, 'Human Welfare, Not Human Rights' (2008) 108 Colum L Rev 1758.

[122] See *Natur og Ungdom* (n 9) ¶¶163, 168, discounting the importance of climate impacts that 'will not appear until far into the future'. But see *Neubauer* (n 44) ¶182, finding that the German lawmaker breached its obligation to protect the right to life by failing to adopt adequate mitigation action applicable in the 2020s as this would result in a need for more drastic mitigation action post-2030 with a disproportionate impact on future generations. See generally Anthony D'Amato, 'Do We Owe a Duty to Future Generations to Preserve the Global Environment?' (1990) 84 AJIL 190; Edith Brown Weiss, 'Our Rights and Obligations to Future Generations for the Environment' (1990) 84 AJIL 198.

[123] See Conor Gearty, 'Do Human Rights Help or Hinder Environmental Protection? (2010) 1 JHRE 7. See also *Klimaatzaak* (n 8) 56, refusing standing to eighty-two trees on the ground that they do not have legal personality; Maria Hook and others, 'Tort to the Environment: A Stretch Too Far or a Simple Step Forward?' (2021) 33 JEL 195, noting that environmental torts could 'open ... up the possibility of successfully suing corporations for harm to the climate'.

[124] See Ademola Oluborode Jegede, 'Arguing the Right to a Safe Climate under the UN Human Rights System' (2020) 9 Intl HRL Rev 184.

in a world of *sovereign states*, these treaties will maintain generally an individualistic approach to human welfare,[125] an anthropocentric approach to ecological resources,[126] and, overall, a territorial approach to state obligations,[127] thus remaining indifferent to the many important benefits of mitigation action beyond the scope of treaty rights. Likewise, even if human rights treaties were to be interpreted as granting rights to 'future generations',[128] the cost that a state incurs when implementing mitigation action would often exceed the long-term benefits for present and future generations within its territory—most of the benefits that justify ambitious mitigation action in any one country are those that would be enjoyed by the future population living in other countries.

2. Invalid Solutions

Three main arguments have been made in attempts to overcome the problem described above and to justify the interpretation of human rights treaties as the source of an obligation to cooperate on the mitigation of climate change. The first argument is that human rights treaties create extraterritorial obligations relevant to climate change mitigation. The second argument is that states have 'collective obligations' to protect human rights that require them to act in concert on climate change mitigation. The third argument is that human rights treaties include an extensive obligation for states to cooperate on the international protection of human rights, hence also on the mitigation of climate change. The following refutes these three arguments.

a) Extraterritorial obligations

Scholars have continuously highlighted innovative legal developments regarding the extraterritorial application of human rights treaties to suggest that these treaties could extend to the impacts of a state's failure to mitigate climate change.[129] But while some aspects of the extraterritorial application of human rights treaties

[125] Desgagné (n 92) 283–84, 294.

[126] See Boyle, 'Climate Change' (n 44) 768.

[127] Atapattu, *Human Rights Approaches* (n 31) 63; Sumudu Atapattu, 'The Right to a Healthy Environment and Climate Change: Mismatch or Harmony?' in John H Knox and Ramin Pejan (eds), *The Human Right to a Healthy Environment* (CUP 2018) 265.

[128] See Bridget Lewis, 'The Rights of Future Generations within the Post-Paris Climate Regime' (2018) 7 TEL 69; Peter Lawrence, *Justice for Future Generations: Climate Change and International Law* (EE 2014).

[129] See Humphreys, 'Introduction' (n 66) 5; Boyle, 'Where Next?' (n 112) 617; John H Knox, 'Human Rights Principles and Climate Change' in Cinnamon P Carlarnet, Kevin R Gray, and Richard Tarasofksy (eds), *The Oxford Handbook of International Climate Change Law* (OUP 2016) 226–32. See also CEDAW and others (n 13) ¶¶1, 3; Helen Duffy and Lucy Maxwell, 'People v Arctic Oil Before Supreme Court of Norway: What's at Stake for Human Rights Protection in the Climate Crisis?' EJIL:Talk! (13 November 2020) <https://perma.cc/88YT-2PSD>.

have long been unsettled, it is well understood that states' human rights obligations apply extraterritorially only in limited circumstances—mainly where the state exercises 'effective control' over an area or a person,[130] for instance in cases relating to '[b]elligerent occupation and physical custody over detained individuals'.[131] The capacity of a state to achieve incremental emission reduction does not imply any 'effective control', for instance, on the human rights impact of a heatwave occurring decades later in a different part of the world.[132] A few authorities continue to suggest an extension of the geographical scope of some treaty obligations, in particular with regard to the right to life, to situations where a state merely exercises 'power' (not necessarily amounting to 'effective control') upon an individual's right in such a way as to affect that individual 'in a direct and reasonably foreseeable manner'.[133] Yet, it is difficult to see how a state's capacity to achieve nominal reductions in global GHG emissions could constitute such power or affect individuals' rights in any 'direct' manner.

A 2017 advisory opinion of the Inter-American Court of Human Rights, on human rights and the environment, pointed out that individuals whose rights are affected by transboundary environmental harm could be found to be under the effective control of the state of origin.[134] The Court, however, insisted that such extraterritorial application of human rights obligations is limited to 'exceptional situations'[135] and occurs only where 'there is a causal link between the act that originated in its territory and the infringement of the human rights of persons outside its territory'.[136] In other words, a state's failure to prevent transboundary environmental harm may—but does not necessarily—imply a breach of its obligation to protect human rights. For the human rights impact to be within the state's effective control, the causal link between the state's conduct and the human rights impacts must at the very least be significant, probably even relatively proximate, rather than

[130] See *Legal Consequences of the Construction of a Wall in the Occupied Palestinian Territory*, Advisory Opinion (9 July 2004), [2004] ICJ Rep 136, ¶109; *Armed Activities on the Territory of the Congo (DRC v Uganda)*, Judgment (19 December 2005), [2005] ICJ Rep 168, ¶216; *Al-Skeini v UK*, App No 55721/07, 2011-IV ECHR 99, ¶131; *Environment and Human Rights*, Advisory Opinion OC-23/17 (15 November 2017) IACtHR Series A No 2, ¶81; *MN v Belgium*, App No 3599/18 (ECtHR, 5 May 2020) <http://hudoc.echr.coe.int/eng?i=001-202468> ¶¶96–126; Olivier de Schutter and others, 'Commentary to the Maastricht Principles on Extraterritorial Obligations of States in the Area of Economic, Social and Cultural Rights' (2012) 34 Hum Rts Q 1084, 1104–05.

[131] Yuval Shany, 'The Extraterritorial Application of International Human Rights Law' (2019) 409 RdC 9, 28.

[132] See Stephen Humphreys, 'Competing Claims: Human Rights and Climate Harms' in Humphreys (ed) (n 31) 55. See also above at 145.

[133] HRC, General Comment No 36 (n 36) ¶63. See also African Commission on Human and Peoples Rights, General Comment No 3, 'The Right to Life (Article 4)' (18 November 2015) <https://www.refworld.org/docid/5e67c9cb4.html> ¶14 ('conduct which could reasonably be foreseen to result in an unlawful deprivation of life'); *Andreou v Turkey*, App No 45653/99 (ECtHR, 27 October 2009) <http://hudoc.echr.coe.int/eng?i=001-95295> ¶25 ('direct and immediate cause of . . . injuries').

[134] Advisory Opinion OC-23/17 (n 130) ¶104.

[135] Ibid ¶104(d). See also Sacchi/Argentina (n 12) ¶10.3 ('extraterritorial jurisdiction should be interpreted restrictively').

[136] Advisory Opinion OC-23/17 (n 130) ¶¶101, 103, 104(h), 120, 238.

remote and tenuous.[137] Having accepted this test, it is unclear how the Committee on the Rights of the Child (CRC) in *Sacchi* then came to the conclusion that, 'for the purposes of establishing jurisdiction', the impacts of a state's failure to take sufficient mitigation action had 'reasonably foreseeable' adverse consequences on the enjoyment of the rights of a few individuals.[138] Rather than the remote and diffuse impacts of a state's failure to mitigate climate change on individuals' rights, Walter Kälin and Jörg Künzli compare the advisory opinion with a case where a bullet had been shot at someone across an international border.[139] By contrast to what may happen in certain cases of direct transboundary environmental harm, there is no 'smoking gun' (or factory) to blame for the impacts of climate change on human rights. As such, it is implausible that the impacts of climate change could ever fall within the effective control of a state—or that they could be considered the direct and reasonably foreseeable consequence of a state's conduct—on the sole ground of the state's ability to achieve marginal reductions in global GHG emissions.[140]

There is no obvious possibility for the judicial interpretation of human rights treaties to evolve in ways that would apply human rights obligations to the global impacts of a state's GHG emissions. In many cases, a broad extraterritorial application would be irreconcilable with the text of human rights treaties whose geographical scope is explicitly limited to the state's 'territory' or 'jurisdiction'.[141] These treaty provisions would be devoid of any effectiveness ('*effet utile*')[142]if every individual affected by the state's conduct, however remotely, was considered ipso facto within that state's 'jurisdiction'—that is, if a state was bound to prevent transboundary human rights infringements, as the CRC suggested, every time it 'is in a position to prevent them'.[143] Even with regard to treaties without explicit jurisdictional limitation, such as the International Covenant on Economic, Social and Cultural Rights (ICESCR),[144] an extensive extraterritorial application of positive human rights obligations would be inconsistent with a contextual and teleological interpretation of

[137] See de Schutter and others (n 130) 1109.

[138] Sacchi/Argentina (n 12) ¶10.14.

[139] Kälin and Künzli (n 33) 133–34, referring to *Andreou* (n 133).

[140] But see Monica Feria-Tinta and Simon C Milnes, 'The Rise of Environmental Law in International Dispute Resolution: The Inter-American Court of Human Rights Issues a Landmark Advisory Opinion on the Environment and Human Rights' (2016) 27 YB Intl Envtl L 64, 78–79; Christopher Campbell-Duruflé and Sumudu Anopama Atapattu, 'The Inter-American Court's Environment and Human Rights Advisory Opinion: Implications for International Climate Law' (2018) 8 Climate Law 321; Jutta Brunnée, 'Procedure and Substance in International Environmental Law' (2019) 450 RdC 9, 180–81 (2019); Annalisa Savaresi and Juan Auz, 'Climate Change Litigation and Human Rights: Pushing the Boundaries' (2019) 9 Climate Law 244, 255.

[141] See eg Kälin and Künzli (n 33) 134.

[142] On the doctrine of effectiveness (*effet utile*) in treaty interpretation, see *Free Zones of Upper Savoy and the District of Gex (France v Switzerland)*, Order (19 August 1929), PCIJ Rep Series A No 22, 13; *Territorial Dispute (Libya /Chad)*, Judgment (3 February 1994), [1994] ICJ Rep 6, ¶51; *Application of the International Convention on the Elimination of All Forms of Racial Discrimination (Georgia v Russia)*, Judgment on Preliminary Objections (11 April 2011), [2011] ICJ Rep 70, ¶133.

[143] Sacchi/Argentina (n 12) ¶10.5.

[144] ICESCR (n 1) art 2(1).

the treaty. The object of purpose of such treaties situates the protection of human rights chiefly as part of the political community of a state. Moreover, subsequent state practice precludes an extensive interpretation of the extraterritorial application of such treaties:[145] for instance, states do not generally take the same measures to protect the right to health beyond their territory as they do within it.[146] Thus, the authors calling for an extensive interpretation of extraterritorial jurisdiction generally 'accept that States cannot be legitimately expected to be held accountable for all acts or omissions that somehow adversely affect the enjoyment of human rights by all individuals, anywhere in the world'.[147]

b) 'Collective obligations'

Another line of argument suggests that, when approaching climate change mitigation as a human rights obligation, states must set their national interests aside and discharge their obligations as a group (ie the international community or the group of the parties to a treaty). Such a 'collective obligation',[148] if it is understood as an obligation held by a collective, is probably a contradiction in terms: only an (individual) legal person can incur an obligation and be held responsible for its breach.[149] No source or authority demonstrates the existence of a 'collective obligation' held by the international community as a whole or the parties to a treaty, as a single legal person, to protect human rights or to mitigate climate change.[150] Rather, as the CRC noted, states carry 'individual responsibility for their own acts or omissions'.[151]

[145] VCLT (n 26) art 31(3)(b). See generally *Wall* (n 130) ¶112, noting that the ICESCR 'guarantees rights which are essentially territorial'; Kälin and Künzli (n 33) 126. But see CESCR, General Comment No 14, 'Right to Health (Art 12)', E/C.12/2000/4 (11 August 2000) ¶39; CESCR, General Comment No 24, 'State Obligations under the International Covenant on Economic, Social and Cultural Rights in the Context of Business Activities', E/C.12/GC/24 (10 August 2017) ¶30.

[146] For instance, in addressing the Covid-19 pandemic, states have generally not made as much effort to make vaccines available to the populations of foreign countries as they have done for the benefit of their own population. See OHCHR Press Release, 'Statement by UN Human Rights Experts: Universal Access to Vaccines Is Essential for Prevention and Containment of COVID-19 around the World' (9 November 2020), acknowledging widespread 'supply and vaccine nationalism'.

[147] Shany (n 131) 29. See also, by analogy, *Neubauer* (n 44) ¶¶173–81. While the Court does not exclude the possibility of extraterritorial obligations to protect constitutional rights of individuals abroad from the impacts of climate change, it highlights that these obligations would differ substantially from those applicable territorially.

[148] Daniel Bodansky, 'The Legal Character of the Paris Agreement' (2016) 25 RECIEL 142, 145–47; Christina Voigt, 'The Paris Agreement: What Is the Standard of Conduct for Parties?' (2016) 18 QIL 17, 17; Lavanya Rajamani, 'Ambition and Differentiation in the 2015 Paris Agreement: Interpretative Possibilities and Underlying Politics' (2016) 65 ICLQ 493, 503; Jacqueline Peel, 'Climate Change' in André Nollkaemper and Ilias Plakokefalos (eds), *The Practice of Shared Responsibility in International Law* (CUP 2017) 1024; Anna Huggins, 'The Evolution of Differential Treatment in International Climate Law: Innovation, Experimentation, and "Hot" Law' (2018) 8 Climate Law 195, 204.

[149] See *Reparation for Injuries Suffered in the Service of the United Nations*, Advisory Opinion (11 April 1949), [1949] ICJ Rep 174, 179.

[150] See below at 252. See also Birgit Peters, 'Zur Anwendbarkeit der Europäischen Menschenrechtskonvention in Umwelt- und Klimaschutzfragen' (2021) 59 AdV 164, 169, suggesting that the ECtHR would not have jurisdiction to address claims based on collective obligations.

[151] Sacchi/Argentina (n 12) ¶10.8.

John Knox appeared to envisage a sort of 'collective obligation' nested under human rights treaties to justify, in effect, their extraterritorial application. He suggested that 'the states contributing most to the warming' could be considered to have effective control over 'particularly extreme impacts [of climate change], such as the effect of climate change on small island states'.[152] For the reasons exposed above,[153] it is unlikely that an individual state would exercise 'effective control' over the impacts of climate change. Knox, however, appears to be suggesting that a different conclusion could be reached if one considered the largest GHG emitters as a group, collectively holding an obligation to protect human rights. However, there is no evidence that human rights treaties create any such 'collective obligation'.

Such arguments are often based on a misreading of the law of state responsibility. The applicants in *Duarte Agostinho*, a case currently pending before the ECtHR, refer to the Guiding Principles on Shared Responsibility to support their claim that states have a 'shared responsibility' for the impacts of climate change on human rights.[154] Similarly, Margaretha Wewerinke-Singh relies on the concept of joint and several responsibility to invoke the obligation of a state to contribute to climate change mitigation.[155] Yet, neither the Guiding Principles on Shared Responsibility nor the concept of joint and several responsibility support the purported conclusions. The Guiding Principles seek to define the content of a state's responsibility when one or several other states are concurrently responsible for an internationally wrongful act; these Principles do not define primary obligations or any other of the conditions under which one or several states may initially be considered to be in breach of a primary obligation.[156] Likewise, the doctrine of joint and several responsibility (if applicable in international law at all) determines the consequences of a state's responsibility, not its existence.[157]

These arguments often converge towards Article 47 of the Articles on State Responsibility, which envisages the situation where several states are responsible for the same internationally wrongful act.[158] However, the International Law Commission made it clear that Article 47 is only interested in the situation 'where

[152] Knox, 'Climate Change' (n 31) 204.

[153] See above at 148.

[154] Application Form in *Duarte Agostinho* (n 11) (2 September 2020) <https://perma.cc/8DW2-LTCB> Annex ¶¶11–13. See Paul Clark, Gerry Liston, and Ioannis Kalpouzos, 'Climate Change and the European Court of Human Rights: The Portuguese Youth Case', *EJIL:Talk!* (6 October 2020) <https://perma.cc/NW8R-EKQ9>>; Gerry Liston, 'Enhancing the Efficacy of Climate Change Litigation: How to Resolve the "Fair Share Question" in the Context of International Human Rights Law' (2020) 9 Cambridge Intl LJ 241, 250–54.

[155] Wewerinke-Singh (n 31) 93–96. See *Urgenda* (SC) (n 8) ¶5.7.6, referring to ILC, 'State Responsibility' (n 27) art 47.

[156] See André Nollkaemper and others, 'Guiding Principles on Shared Responsibility in International Law' (2020) 31 EJIL 15, 24 (commentary on principle 2, ¶2).

[157] See *Oil Platforms (Iran v US)*, Judgment on Merits (6 November 2003), [2003] ICJ Rep 161, Separate Opinion of Judge Simma, ¶¶73–74; ILC, 'State Responsibility' (n 27) commentary on art 47, ¶3.

[158] See eg *Urgenda* (SC) (n 8) ¶5.7.6; Wewerinke-Singh (n 31) 92; Liston (n 154) 251–54.

a single course of conduct is at the same time attributable to several states and is *internationally wrongful to each of them*',[159] and that Article 47 does not constitute an exception to the principle of independent responsibility.[160] The Commentary thus notes that Article 47 does not apply ipso facto to situations 'where several States by separate internationally wrongful conduct have contributed to causing the same damage', for instance where 'several States ... contribute to polluting a river by separate discharge of pollutants'.[161] In such situations, the Commission adds, 'the responsibility of each participating State is determined individually, on the basis of its own conduct and by reference to its own international obligations'.[162] Thus, nothing in the law of state responsibility extends to a group of states, as if it were a separate legal entity, the primary obligations applicable individually to each of them.

c) Other-regarding obligations of cooperation

It is only through international cooperation that global GHG emissions can be reduced in ways that benefit all. This observation led Knox, in an influential report to the Human Rights Council, to point out that all states have an obligation to cooperate in addressing issues of international concern, as spelled out in particular under Article 55 of the UN Charter and the preamble to the UNFCCC.[163] This general international law obligation of cooperation, Knox suggests, 'provides a framework for considering the application' of positive obligations on the protection of human rights in relation to climate change.[164] If a state must take the interests of other states into account through such an 'other-regarding'[165] obligation of cooperation, then, arguably, it must seek to mitigate climate change.[166] Crucially, Knox considers this other-regarding obligation of cooperation as one of 'the human rights obligations of States in relation to climate change'.[167] On this basis, Knox suggests that, under human rights law, states have 'not only to implement [their] current intended contributions, but also to strengthen those contributions to meet the [temperature] targets set out in article 2 of the Paris Agreement'.[168]

159 ILC, 'State Responsibility' (n 27) commentary on art 47, ¶3 (emphasis added).

160 Ibid.

161 Ibid ¶8. See *Corfu Channel (UK v Albania)*, Judgment on Merits (9 April 1949), [1949] ICJ Rep 4, 22–22.

162 ILC, 'State Responsibility' (n 27) commentary on art 47, ¶8.

163 Knox, 2016 Report (n 31) ¶¶43–44, citing Charter of the United Nations (26 June 1945, in force 24 October 1945) arts 55–56; UNFCCC (n 5) Preamble ¶7. See also de Schutter and others (n 130) 1091, 1095–96. This obligation is identified above at 103.

164 Knox, 2016 Report (n 31) ¶45.

165 This phrase is borrowed from Eyal Benvenisti, 'Sovereigns as Trustees of Humanity: On the Accountability of States to Foreign Stakeholders' (2013) 107 AJIL 295.

166 See above at 109, and below at 284.

167 Knox, 2016 Report (n 31) ¶48.

168 Ibid ¶77.

Yet, while states certainly have an obligation to cooperate on climate change mitigation under general international law, this obligation cannot readily be characterized as a 'human rights obligation'. Article 55 of the UN Charter mentions '*respect* for, and *observance* of, human rights'[169] as one of the fields in which states must cooperate, but it does not—at least not expressly—create a positive obligation to cooperate on the protection of human rights.[170] If climate change mitigation falls within the ambit of the obligation of cooperation under the UN Charter, it is more convincingly under the first two paragraphs of Article 55: as either an issue affecting 'standards of living ... and conditions of economic and social progress and development' or as the source of 'international economic, social, health, and related problems'.[171]

Overall, human rights treaties do not typically include any obligation of international cooperation. The few human rights treaties that mention 'international assistance and cooperation' at all, like the ICESCR,[172] have often been construed as requiring states to consider receiving the international assistance and cooperation that they need—it is not clear whether these treaties create an obligation for states to provide assistance and cooperation when they can.[173] Even if they do, this obligation—which must be interpreted within the confines of subsequent state practice[174]—surely does not amount to a fully fledged obligation for a state to protect economic, social, and cultural rights abroad in just the same way as it does within its own territory.[175]

Knox suggests that a similarly broad obligation of cooperation may be inferred from any human rights treaty, notwithstanding the absence of express provision. Recalling the obligation to perform treaties in good faith and its implication that every state must act 'so as not to undermine the ability of other States to meet their own obligation', he contends that the failure of states to cooperate on the mitigation

[169] Ibid art 55(c) (emphasis added). See eg Declaration on the Right to Development, UNGA Res 41/128 (4 December 1986) art 6(1).

[170] But see de Schutter and others (n 130) 1103–04.

[171] UN Charter (n 163) art 55(a)–(b). See generally Tobias Stoll, 'International Economic and Social Co-operation, Article 55 (a) and (b)' in Bruno Simma and others (eds), *The Charter of the United Nations* vol 2 (OUP 212) ¶70.

[172] See ICESCR (n 1) art 2(1); Convention on the Rights of the Child (n 35) art 4; Convention on the Rights of Persons with Disabilities (20 November 1989, in force 3 May 2008) 2515 UNTS 3, art 4(2).

[173] See CESCR, General Comment No 3, 'The Nature of States Parties' Obligations', E/1991/23 (14 December 1990) ¶13; Philip Alston and Gerard Quinn, 'The Nature and Scope of States Parties' Obligations Under the International Covenant on Economic, Social and Cultural Rights' (1987) 9 H Rts Q 156, 191; Ben Saul, David Kinley, and Jacqueline Mowbray, *The International Covenant on Economic, Social and Cultural Rights* (OUP 2014) 139. On the Convention on the Rights of the Child, see John Tobin, 'Art 4: A State's General Obligation of Implementation' in John Tobin (ed), *The UN Convention on the Rights of the Child: A Commentary* (OUP 2019) 146–47. On the Convention of Persons with Disabilities, see Andrea Broderick, 'Article 4: General Obligations' in Ilias Bantekas, Michael Ashley Stein, and Dimitrias Anastasiou (eds), *The UN Convention on the Rights of Persons with Disabilities: A Commentary* (OUP 2018) 133.

[174] VCLT (n 26) art 31(3)(b).

[175] See n 146. But see Paul Hunt and Rajat Khosla, 'Climate Change and the Right to the Highest Attainable Standard of Health' in Humphreys (ed) (n 31) 252.

of climate change would 'prevent individual States from meeting their duties under human rights law'.[176] Knox's observation relies on the doctrine of abuse of rights, which suggests that states must 'abstain from acts calculated to frustrate the object and purpose and thus impede the proper execution of the treaty'.[177] This doctrine has generally been envisaged as the source of an obligation not to act in a way that would defeat the object and purpose of the treaty; it is unclear whether it can also create a positive obligation to act in such a way as to enable the realization of the object and purpose of the treaty, especially one as open-ended and possibly as demanding as the obligation to cooperate could be.[178] Besides, although a state's failure to cooperate on the mitigation of climate change hinders the enjoyment of human rights, it does not impede other states from fulfilling their own treaty obligation to take appropriate measures to protect human rights.[179] In any case, a state's failure to cooperate on the mitigation of climate change is not 'calculated' to prevent other states from complying with their human rights obligations.

States have a broad, other-regarding obligation of cooperation under general international law but not under human rights treaties. This broad obligation of cooperation cannot be invoked by applicants under the same advantageous conditions as the obligation to protect human rights—in particular, it cannot be applied by treaty bodies or regional human rights courts. Subsection 3 shows, however, that a narrower, inward-looking obligation of cooperation could be inferred from a state's obligation to protect the human rights of individuals within its territory or under its jurisdiction.

3. An Alternative Solution: An Inward-Looking Obligation of Cooperation

The obligation to protect human rights requires a state to take the 'necessary steps' or, more broadly, to implement 'appropriate measures',[180] to protect the rights of individuals within its territory or under its jurisdiction. As already shown, a state's action on climate change mitigation, in itself, cannot be considered as a necessary or appropriate measure because it would result in virtually no benefit to the rights of individuals within that state's territory or under its jurisdiction;[181] in fact, such measure would rather undermine the rights of the individuals under the state's

[176] Knox, 2016 Report (n 31) ¶44 (fn 27). See VCLT (n 26) art 26.

[177] Mark E Villiger, *Commentary on the 1969 Vienna Convention on the Law of Treaties* (Martinus Nijhoff 2008) 367, cited in Knox, 2016 Report (n 31) ¶44 (fn 27).

[178] See Appellate Body Report, *US—Import Prohibition of Certain Shrimp and Shrimp Products*, WT/DS58/AB/R (6 November 1998) ¶158; Humphrey Waldock, Third Report on the Law of Treaties, A/CN.4/167 (1964) 7 (Art 55(2)).

[179] See above at 137.

[180] See above at 137.

[181] See above at 148.

jurisdiction by placing a burden on them and on public resources.[182] By contrast, international cooperation could be an effective strategy—and therefore an 'appropriate measure', or even arguably a 'necessary step'—for a state to protect the human rights of individuals within its territory or under its jurisdiction. By engaging in international cooperation, or at least by 'try[ing] to influence the international community', a state can contribute to the realization of global mitigation outcomes which, over time, could bring in some real benefit for the enjoyment of human rights by individuals under its jurisdiction.[183]

Human rights treaty bodies have sometimes construed the obligation to protect human rights as implying an inward-looking obligation of cooperation. For instance, the Human Rights Committee interpreted the obligation to protect the human rights of the child as implying that states must cooperate to ensure that every child has a nationality[184] and to facilitate family unity or reunification.[185] The application of a similar reasoning in relation to climate change mitigation is supported by the context in light of which human rights treaties are to be interpreted—states have repeatedly and emphatically recognized that mitigating climate change 'calls for the widest possible cooperation by all countries'.[186] Having recognized that climate change affects the enjoyment of human rights[187] and that cooperation is essential to the mitigation of climate change, states have accepted that cooperation on climate change mitigation could be an appropriate measure to protect human rights. In contrast to other-regarding obligations of cooperation under general international law, this obligation derives from human rights treaties and, as such, it can be applied as part of these treaties. By analogy, the Federal Constitutional Court of Germany interpreted a constitutional provision on the right to life as requiring the state to seek a solution to climate change on the international plane.[188]

A potential objection to the identification of this inward-looking obligation of cooperation is that a state's attempt to cooperate on climate change mitigation does not ensure that others will follow suit and, thus, that any tangible mitigation outcome will be achieved. In fact, cooperation by a given state is neither strictly necessary nor sufficient to ensure the realization of any mitigation outcome: the actions or omissions of other states can always fill the gap or cancel the state's mitigation outcomes. Instead of 'wasting' scarce national resources in an attempt to trigger international cooperation, the objection goes, a state should rather pursue national priorities that are more directly effective for the protection of human rights, leaving it for other states to devise and implement mitigation action from which

[182] See above at 149.
[183] See Knox, 'Climate Change' (n 31) 198.
[184] HRC, General Comment No 17, 'Article 24 (Rights of the Child)', HRI/GEN/1/Rev.1 (7 April 1989) ¶8.
[185] HRC, General Comment No 19, 'Article 23 (The Family)', HRI/GEN/1/Rev.1 (27 July 1990) ¶5.
[186] See eg UNFCCC (n 5) Preamble ¶7; Res 41/21 (n 44) Preamble ¶11.
[187] See eg Res 41/21 (n 44) ¶1.
[188] See *Neubauer* (n 44) ¶149.

that state would benefit. This objection points out that free-riding on other states' mitigation action is a state's best possible strategy to protect the human rights of the individuals under its jurisdiction[189]—unless, that is, other states follow the same reasoning.[190]

This objection must be discarded because it relies on an impermissible premise: the notion that a state could (or should) attempt to deceive other states. The obligation to interpret and perform treaties in good faith[191] requires states to act in a 'spirit of honesty'[192] and 'to refrain from taking unfair advantage'[193] of others. This obligation precludes a state from seeking to free-ride on mitigation action implemented by other states—to benefit from their action while avoiding their fair contribution to the costs.[194] This reasoning is confirmed by states' call for cooperation[195] and for equity[196] in responses to climate change. To comply in good faith with a treaty obligation to protect a human right, any given state must act in a way it considers fair and which would ensure, if other states followed the same precept, an optimal level of protection to the rights of everyone under that state's jurisdiction.

This implied obligation of cooperation does not require as much from states as the other-regarding obligation of cooperation that arises from general international law. The latter requires states essentially to set their national interests aside and to address international concerns in a spirit of global partnership by implementing their fair share of mitigation action.[197] Thus, when the general international law obligation of cooperation is applied to climate change, as Knox points out, it suggests that every state must contribute to climate change mitigation, notwithstanding its own interest in mitigation outcomes.[198] By contrast, the obligation of cooperation derived from human rights treaties requires a state to cooperate only if and inasmuch as international action contributes to the protection of the human rights of

[189] On each state's incentive to free-ride on the mitigation action of others, see n 120.

[190] This objection could perhaps be countered on the basis of game theory: a state's true interest is to act in a way that will persuade others to implement mitigation action, even if this may imply that the state needs to implement at least some level of mitigation action. See generally Stavins and others (n 120) 1012, noting that the literature on game theory with regard to cooperation on climate change mitigation has grown substantially but remains largely inconclusive.

[191] VCLT (n 26) arts 26, 31(1). See *Nuclear Tests (Australia v France)*, Judgment (20 December 1974), [1974] ICJ Rep 253, ¶46.

[192] *Interpretation of the Algerian Declarations of 19 January 1981 (Claims against US Nationals)* (1982) 62 ILR 595, 605.

[193] Villiger (n 177) 425. On the applicability of good faith to the interpretation of human rights treaties, see *Verein gegen Tierfabriken v Switzerland (No 2)*, App No 32772/02, 2009-IV ECHR 1, ¶87; HRC, General Comment No 33, 'Obligations of States Parties under the Optional Protocol', CCPR/C/GC/33 (25 June 2009) ¶15.

[194] See Evan J Criddle and Evan Fox-Decent, 'Mandatory Multilateralism' (2019) 113 AJIL 272, 320; Posner and Weisbach (n 120) 181–83.

[195] See n 186.

[196] See eg UNFCCC (n 5) art 3(1); Paris Agreement (n 5) art 2(2).

[197] *Urgenda* (SC) (n 8) ¶¶5.7.1, 6.3, 6.5. See Rio Declaration on Environment and Development (14 June 1992) A/CONF.151/26 (vol I) (1992) 31 ILM 874, principle 7.

[198] Knox, 2016 Report (n 31) ¶46.

individuals within that state's territory or under its jurisdiction. Considering—if only for argument's sake[199]—that a state may be entirely immune from any impact of climate change or otherwise able to manage all impacts affecting it through cost-effective adaptation measures, this state would not be bound to mitigate climate change under an inward-looking obligation of cooperation under human rights treaties, even though it would be bound to do so by other-regarding obligations of cooperation under general international law. As states are diversely exposed and vulnerable to the impacts of climate change,[200] their inward-looking obligation of cooperation varies in intensity. The content of this inward-looking obligation depends on the right in relation to which it is invoked (eg rights to life, health, property, or livelihood) and on the foreseeable benefits of climate change mitigation for the protection of that right for individuals under the state's jurisdiction.

To comply with this inward-looking obligation of cooperation, any state would presumably be expected at least to play a constructive role in international negotiations on climate change mitigation, facilitating rather than hindering the adoption of ambitious agreements. The inward-looking obligation of cooperation may also be interpreted as requiring that a state seek to limit or reduce GHG emissions within its territory, not for the sake of achieving nominal reduction in global GHG emissions but as an integral part of global efforts on climate change mitigation. But a state with few GHG emissions within its territory or few realistic ways of reducing them could cooperate in other ways, for instance by providing financial or technical support to emission reduction activities conducted overseas. Regulating the importation or consumption of GHG-intensive goods and services, or even imposing sanctions on non-complying states, could also be appropriate measures to promote cooperation as long as these measures are compatible with other international law obligations.[201]

The implementation of this inward-looking obligation of cooperation on climate change mitigation is facilitated by the various procedures associated with human rights treaties. When applicants have standing to invoke a state's obligation to protect human rights before a national court,[202] they would presumably also be allowed to invoke the implications of this obligation with regard to international cooperation. Likewise, treaty bodies could discuss compliance with these implied obligations in their concluding observations on national reports[203] and general

[199] But see Norway, Seventh National Communication under the UNFCCC (2018) 19, suggesting that '[t]he Norwegian society is in a good position to adapt to the effects of climate change'; Kian Mintz-Woo and Justin Leroux, 'What Do Climate Change Winners Owe, and to Whom?' (2021) 37 Econ & Phil 462, suggesting the existence of 'net winners'—states that benefit from the positive consequences of climate change more than they are affected by its adverse impacts.

[200] See Field and others (eds) (n 38) 75.

[201] See eg Michael A Mehling and others, 'Designing Border Carbon Adjustments for Enhanced Climate Action' (2019) 113 AJIL 433 .

[202] See nn 102–07.

[203] See n 14.

comments.[204] Interstate dispute settlement mechanisms and advisory proceedings before regional human rights courts or human rights treaty bodies should also be able to implement these implied obligations.

C. The Interpretation of Implied Mitigation Obligations

Section B demonstrated that, under human rights treaties, states have an inward-looking obligation of cooperation on the mitigation of climate change. The present section explores how this implied mitigation obligation can be interpreted. In light of the principle of systemic integration, an analysis of this implied mitigation obligation must *take into account* other relevant rules of international law, which could include general mitigation obligations arising from climate treaties and customary international law. This, however, does not necessarily mean that compliance with an implied mitigation obligation requires compliance with general mitigation obligations. This section identifies and refutes a common assumption according to which human-rights-based mitigation obligations *incorporate* general mitigation obligations in their entirety. It then advances an alternative theory according to which human rights treaties open only some 'windows' onto general mitigation obligations. A human rights treaty requires a state to comply with general mitigation obligations, it is argued, only if and inasmuch as justified by the protection of the treaty rights of individuals within its territory or under its jurisdiction.

1. Systemic Integration

The interpretation of human rights treaties generally follows the tenets of treaty interpretation, at least as a starting point.[205] Among these tenets is the principle of systemic integration, which reflects the idea that a rule of international law must be interpreted within the context provided by other rules of international law.[206]

[204] See eg CRC, General Comment No 15, 'The Right of the Child to the Enjoyment of the Highest Attainable Standard of Health (Art 24)', CRC/C/GC/15 (17 April 2013); HRC, General Comment No 36 (n 36) ¶62.

[205] See *Golder v UK*, App No 4451/70 (1975) 18 ECHR, ¶29; *Hassan v UK*, App 29750/09, 2014-VI ECHR, ¶100; *'Mapiripán Massacre' v Colombia*, Judgment (15 September 2005) IACtHR Series C No 134, ¶106; Malgosia Fitzmaurice, 'Interpretation of Human Rights Treaties' in Dinah Shelton (ed), *The Oxford Handbook of International Human Rights Law* (OUP 2013) 741–42; Richard Gardiner, *Treaty Interpretation* (2nd edn, OUP 2015) 478; David Harris and others, *Law of the European Convention on Human Rights* (4th edn, OUP 2018) 6.

[206] See Campbell McLachlan, 'The Principle of Systemic Integration and Article 31(3)(c) of the Vienna Convention' (2005) 54 ICLQ 279; ILC, Report of the Study Group on the Fragmentation of International Law, A/CN.4/L.682 (13 April 2006) ¶¶410–80; ILC, 'Conclusions of the Work of the Study Group on the Fragmentation of International Law: Difficulties Arising from the Diversification and Expansion of International Law' [2006] II(2) YBILC 179, ¶4.

Article 31(3)(c) of the Vienna Convention on the Law of Treaties suggests that a rule must be 'taken into account' in the interpretation of a treaty if this rule is (1) 'relevant' and (2) 'applicable in the relations between the parties'.[207]

The condition of relevance is understood broadly: the referential rule 'need have no particular relationship with the treaty other than assisting in the interpretation of its terms';[208] it may have been adopted before or after the rule that is being interpreted.[209] For instance, the International Court of Justice (ICJ) in *Gabčíkovo-Nagymaros* held that a treaty on the implementation of a development project had to be applied in light of subsequent norms on the evaluation of environmental risks.[210] Thus, general mitigation obligations arising from climate treaties or customary international law are certainly relevant to the interpretation of the mitigation obligations derived from human rights treaties.

The second condition—the applicability of the referential rule 'in the relations between the parties'—has also, oftentimes, been construed broadly, permitting reference to rules applicable to *most*, or even just to *some* of the parties to the treaty at issue, notwithstanding whether the referential rule was applicable to the parties to the dispute in relation to which the interpretation was taking place.[211] This broad approach to systemic integration suggests that any general mitigation obligation arising from climate treaties or customary international law should be taken into account when interpreting a human rights treaty as the source of an implied obligation on climate change mitigation. Some scholars, however, suggest a stricter approach to systemic integration, limiting reference to rules applicable to *all* parties to the treaty at issue.[212] This stricter approach could occasionally prevent the interpreter of some human rights treaties from taking climate treaties into account,[213] but it would not preclude references to customary international law. Either way,

[207] VCLT (n 26) art 31(3)(c).

[208] Villiger (n 177) 432. See also *Certain Questions of Mutual Assistance in Criminal Matters (Djibouti v France)*, Judgment (4 June 2008), [2008] ICJ Rep 177, ¶113; Ulf Linderfalk, *On the Interpretation of Treaties: The Modern International Law as Expressed in the 1969 Vienna Convention on the Law of Treaties* (Springer 2007) 178; Gardiner (n 205) 305.

[209] See *Legal Consequences for States of the Continued Presence of South Africa in Namibia (South West Africa) Notwithstanding Security Council Resolution 276 (1970)*, Advisory Opinion (21 June 1971), [1971] ICJ Rep 6, ¶53; *Navigational and Related Rights (Costa Rica v Nicaragua)*, Judgment (13 July 2009), [2009] ICJ Rep 213, ¶70.

[210] *Gabčíkovo-Nagymaros Project (Hungary/Slovakia)*, Judgment (25 September 1997), [1997] ICJ Rep 7, ¶140.

[211] See *Proceedings Pursuant to the OSPAR Convention (Ireland/UK)*, Final Award (2 July 2003), 23 RIAA 59, Dissenting Opinion of Gavan Griffith, ¶¶9–10; McLachlan (n 206) 315; Gardiner (n 205) 310–17.

[212] See Linderfalk (n 208) 178; Villiger (n 177) 433; Oliver Dörr, 'Article 31' in Olivier Dörr and Kirsten Schmalenbach (eds), *Vienna Convention on the Law of Treaties: A Commentary* (2nd edn, Springer 2018) 611 (para 103).

[213] For instance, this would exclude references to the UNFCCC when interpreting the Convention on the Rights of the Child because the Holy Sea has ratified the latter but not the former, and the brief US withdrawal from the Paris Agreement would have implied that, for a few months, this treaty could not be used as a referential rule for the interpretation of any human rights treaties to which the United States is a party.

some general obligations on climate change mitigation, from climate treaties or at least from customary international law, are among the applicable rules that a court could take into account when interpreting a human rights treaty as the source of an obligation on climate change mitigation.

Human rights treaty bodies and regional courts have embraced the principle of systemic integration and, generally, they have followed a broad approach to it.[214] For instance, the ECtHR in *Loizidou* highlighted that the ECHR 'cannot be interpreted and applied in a vacuum'; rather, the interpreter must 'take into account any relevant rules of international law'.[215] The Court found evidence of 'common ground in modern societies' on the basis of poorly ratified treaties[216] and non-binding documents.[217] Human rights treaties have been interpreted in light of other human rights treaties,[218] treaties in other fields of international law[219] (including environmental law treaties),[220] and customary international law.[221] The interest for systemic integration generally stems from the fact that it facilitates the adaptation of human rights treaties (as 'living instruments')[222] to changing circumstances[223] and provides judges with convenient benchmarks to interpret treaty rules that are otherwise 'unclear or open-textured'.[224] On the other hand, as Birgit Schlütter pointed out, this method creates a risk that human rights bodies could 'go cherry-picking when determining the international rules that are held to govern a particular interpretation' of the treaty.[225]

It is perfectly natural for the interpreter of an implied mitigation obligation to turn to the doctrine of systemic integration to determine the nature, scope, and content of these obligations. Accordingly, the Human Rights Committee suggested

[214] See eg Birgit Schlütter, 'Aspects of Human Rights Interpretation by the UN Treaty Bodies' in Geir Ulfstein and Helen Keller (eds), *UN Human Rights Treaty Bodies: Law and Legitimacy* (CUP 2012) 295; Adamantia Rachovitsa, 'The Principle of Systemic Integration in Human Rights Law' (2017) 66 ICLQ 557.

[215] *Loizidou v Turkey*, App No 15318/89, 1996-VI ECHR, ¶43. See *Al-Adsani v UK*, App No 35763/97, 2001-XI ECHR 79, ¶55; *Demír v Turkey*, App No 34503/97, 2008-V ECHR 333, ¶85.

[216] *Marckx v Belgium*, App No 6833/74, 31 ECHR (Ser A) ¶41; *Mazurek v France*, App No 34406/97, 2000-II ECHR 1, ¶49; *Demír* (n 215) ¶86.

[217] *Sørensen v Denmark*, App No 52562/99, 2006-I ECHR 1, ¶74; *Goodwin v UK*, App No 28957/95, 2002-VI ECHR 1, ¶100.

[218] *Soering v UK* (ECtHR, 7 July 1989) 11 EHHR 439, ¶88; *González ('Cotton Field') v Mexico*, Judgment (16 November 2009) IACtHR Series C No 205, ¶43; *Hassan* (n 205) ¶¶102–11.

[219] *Sabeh El Leil v France*, App No 34869/05 (ECtHR, 29 June 2011) <http://hudoc.echr.coe.int/eng?i=001-105378> ¶48; *Hirsi Jamaa v Italy*, App No 27765/09, 2012-II ECHR 97, ¶170.

[220] *Taşkın* (n 96) ¶¶98–99; *Demír* (n 215) ¶¶85–86.

[221] *Sabeh El Leil* (n 219) ¶58.

[222] *Soering* (n 218) ¶102. See also *Right to Information on Consular Assistance in the Framework of Guarantees of the Due Process of Law*, Advisory Opinion OC-16/99 (1 October 1999) IACtHR Series A No 16, ¶¶114–15; HRC, Views, Judge/Canada, Communication No 829/1998, CCPR/C/78/D/829/1998 (13 August 2003) ¶10.3.

[223] Philip Alston and Ryan Goodman, *International Human Rights* (2nd edn, OUP 2012) 117–18. See also George Letsas, 'The ECHR as a Living Instrument: Its Meaning and Legitimacy' in Andreas Føllesdal, Birgit Peters, and Geir Ulfstein (eds), *Constituting Europe* (OUP 2013) 106.

[224] ILC, Conclusions on Fragmentation (n 206) ¶20(a).

[225] Schlütter (n 214) 302.

that the obligations of states 'under international environmental law should ... inform' the content of Article 6 of the International Covenant on Civil and Political Rights (ICCPR) on the right to life.[226] However, a line needs to be drawn between an interpretation of human rights treaties that is *informed by*—that is, takes into account—general mitigation obligations and one that *defers entirely to* these general mitigation obligations. As the following shows, scholarship and judicial practice have failed to draw this line when interpreting implied mitigation obligations.

2. Refutation of the incorporation theory

The principle of systemic integration has generally been understood to suggest that, for a state to comply with a mitigation obligation implied from a human rights treaty, it must fully comply with all its general mitigation obligations. This incorporation theory has been tacitly accepted rather than carefully demonstrated. Closer scrutiny shows that it is inconsistent with the tenets of treaty interpretation.

a) The theory

The incorporation theory suggests that, if a human rights treaty implies a state's obligation to mitigate climate change, this obligation requires the state to fully comply with any obligation it has, under any source of international law, with regard to the mitigation of climate change. This theory has generally materialized in judicial practice and academic literature as a tacit assumption rather than an explicit argument. Nonetheless, it has been instrumental, in particular in national court decisions interpreting states' human rights obligations as the source of an obligation to mitigate climate change.

Thus, the judgment of the Supreme Court of the Netherlands in *Urgenda* relied on the Vienna rule on systemic integration and the 'common ground' method in European human rights law, according to which the interpretation of the ECHR must take 'generally accepted standards into account'.[227] On this basis, the Court asserted that, in order to comply with its obligation to protect the rights to life and to private and family life, the Netherlands had to comply with its customary law and climate treaty obligations[228]—which, in the Court's analysis, implied that the state had to reduce its emissions by 25 per cent by 2020, compared with 1990.[229] The Court thus largely followed the opinion of the procurator general, which called for the Court to 'base' its decision on customary international law.[230]

[226] HRC, General Comment No 36 (n 36) ¶62.
[227] *Urgenda* (SC) (n 8) ¶5.4.3.
[228] Ibid ¶5.7.5.
[229] Ibid ¶7.3.6.
[230] Conclusions of the Procurator General of the Supreme Court on *Urgenda* (SC) (n 8), ECLI:NL:HR:2019:290 (6 February 2019) ¶2.74.

Similarly, the Supreme Court of Colombia ordered the state to comply with its international commitment to stop deforestation in order to fulfil its constitutional obligation to protect the rights to life, food, and a healthy environment by mitigating climate change.[231] In doing so, the Court assumed that compliance with the former was a necessary condition for compliance with the latter.

The practice of treaty bodies reflects the same assumption. For instance, the CRC recommended that Austria and Japan reduce their GHG emissions 'in line with [their] international commitments',[232] while the Committee on Economic, Social and Cultural Rights (CESCR) called on Norway to 'intensify its efforts to achieve its [NDC] under the Paris Agreement'.[233] These recommendations are admittedly of an ambivalent nature (treaty bodies do not generally distinguish between observations that interpret the state's legal obligations from those that are mere policy recommendations),[234] but they do reflect the prevailing understanding, on the part of these quasi-judicial bodies, that protecting human rights means complying with any and all norms on climate change mitigation and that reviewing a state's compliance with its human rights obligations therefore justifies a review of its compliance with general mitigation obligations. Consistently, the CRC in *Sacchi* appeared to interpret the obligation of a state to protect the right of each child within its jurisdiction as requiring compliance with its 'obligation to prevent transboundary environmental damage or harm [under] international environmental law'.[235]

In fact, quasi-judicial bodies have often implemented the incorporation theory along with an extensive interpretation of referential 'rules'—including non-binding objectives. For instance, the CESCR suggested that the approval of fossil-fuel extraction projects ran against Ecuador's 'commitments under the Paris Agreement',[236] even though Ecuador had made no commitment relating to fossil-fuel extraction.[237] In other instances, the CESCR recommended that Belgium and Norway take on more ambitious pledges or commitments on climate change mitigation than they already had within the climate regime without explaining how the pledges or commitments of these states were insufficient.[238] A joint statement by five treaty bodies asserted that states '*must* adopt and implement policies' aimed at realizing 'the objectives of the Paris Agreement',[239] even though the treaty creates

[231] *Barragán v Presidencia*, STC-4360-2018, Radicación No 11001-22-03-000-2018-00319-01 (SC, 5 April 2018) <https://www.elaw.org/CO_Amazon> ¶¶6, 14.

[232] CRC, Observations on Reports of Austria (n 14) ¶35(a); of Japan (n 14) ¶37(d).

[233] CESCR, Observations on Report of Norway (n 14) ¶11.

[234] See Geir Ulfstein, 'Law-Making by Human Rights Treaty Bodies' in Rain Liivoja and Jarna Petman (eds), *International Law-Making: Essays in Honour of Jan Klabbers* (Routledge 2014) 249.

[235] Sacchi/Argentina (n 12) ¶10.5.

[236] CESCR, Observations on Report of Ecuador (n 14) ¶12. See CESCR, Observations on Report of Argentina (n 14) ¶¶13–14.

[237] See Ecuador, First NDC (2019). On the absence of general commitments relating to the extraction of fossil fuels, see generally *Natur og Ungdom* (n 9) ¶174; Michael Lazarus and Harro van Asselt, 'Fossil Fuel Supply and Climate Policy: Exploring the Road Less Taken' (2018) 150 Climatic Change 1.

[238] See CESCR, Observations on Report of Belgium (n 14) ¶10; of Norway (n 14) ¶11.

[239] CEDAW and others (n 13) ¶2 (emphasis added), referring to art 2(1) of the Paris Agreement.

no obligation for states to realize these treaty objectives, while state practice does not generally reflect acceptance of an obligation to adopt and implement mitigation action consistent with these objectives.[240]

Legal scholarship, likewise, has often assumed that, whenever a human rights treaty implies an obligation to mitigate climate change, it requires states, at least, to comply with any other treaty or customary obligation they have on climate change mitigation. For instance, Wewerinke-Singh suggests that the interpreter of human rights treaties should 'consider international climate change law as providing minimum standards of protection' and hold 'States to account for non-compliance with the standards they have set for themselves in domestic and international legal frameworks related to climate change'.[241] She and Ashleigh McCoach welcomed the Court's application of the common ground approach in *Urgenda* as an 'elegant way' of interpreting a specific benchmark that can be associated with open-textured human rights obligations.[242] Similarly, Petra Minnerop and Ida Røstgaard assume that, if a mitigation obligation can be implied from Norway's constitutional obligation to protect the right to a healthy environment, and if this obligation can be interpreted in light of international law, then this obligation should be understood as requiring compliance with the state's general mitigation obligations under the UNFCCC.[243] In the same line, David Boyd asserts that '[a] failure to fulfil international climate change commitments is a prima facie violation of the State's obligations to protect the human rights of its citizens'.[244]

Like treaty bodies, scholars have often contended that human rights treaties should actually be interpreted as requiring more mitigation action than what states had accepted under climate treaties or customary international law. Paul Hunt and Rajat Khosla suggest that, to comply with their obligation to protect the right to health, in light of the impact of climate change on the enjoyment of this right, 'states have a core obligation to take reasonable steps to stabilize [GHG] concentrations in the atmosphere at a level that prevents dangerous anthropogenic interference with the climate system'[245]—thus alluding to the 'ultimate objective' of the UNFCCC[246] rather than to any particular 'commitments' to which the parties had consented.[247] Similarly, Knox asserts that the 1.5 and 2°C targets

[240] See above at 123, and below, 251.

[241] Wewerinke-Singh (n 31) 132.

[242] Margaretha Wewerinke-Singh and Ashleigh McCoach, 'The State of the Netherlands v. Urgenda Foundation: Distilling Best Practice and Lessons Learnt for Future Rights-Based Climate Litigation' (2021) 30 RECIEL 275, 279.

[243] Petra Minnerop and Ida Røstgaard, 'In Search of a Fair Share: Article 112 Norwegian Constitution, International Law and an Emerging Inter-jurisdictional Discourse in Climate Litigation' (2021) 44 Fordham Intl LJ 847.

[244] David R Boyd, Report of the Special Rapporteur on the Issue of Human Rights Obligations Relating to the Enjoyment of a Safe, Clean, Healthy and Sustainable Environment, A/74/161 (2019) ¶74.

[245] Hunt and Khosla (n 175) 249.

[246] UNFCCC (n 5) art 2.

[247] Ibid arts 4(1)(b), (2)(a).

are 'consistent with the obligations of States ... to protect human rights from the dangerous effects of climate change',[248] adding that each party to a human rights treaty must immediately strengthen its NDC in accordance with these temperature targets.[249] Commenting on Knox's report, Boyle suggests that '[t]he UN special rapporteur is right in principle to argue that human rights law as a whole requires States to comply with expectations set out' by the mitigation objectives of the Paris Agreement.[250] Boyle asserts that 'human rights commitments could and should require States to implement Paris', and that 'their record in doing so can and should be monitored and assessed by UN human rights bodies'.[251]

Yet, as Boyle himself concedes just a few pages earlier, 'the argument that a policy which complies with the UN climate regime nevertheless violates the existing human rights obligation of States is not easy to make'.[252] Boyle then turns to Knox's 'more insightful approach',[253] but he does not explain how Knox, in his view, managed to make this uneasy argument. In a similar line, André Nollkaemper and Laura Burgers are sceptical of the analysis of the Supreme Court in *Urgenda* in that it blurs the 'distinction between law and non-law'[254]—the 25 per cent emission reduction target, after all, had only been mentioned (or rather alluded to) in non-binding party decisions.[255] But while Nollkaemper and Burgers question the way the incorporation theory was implemented in *Urgenda*, they do not interrogate the theory itself. Neither Boyle nor Nollkaemper and Burgers object to the possibility of a court, when interpreting a human rights treaty as implying a mitigation obligation, requiring the state, at least, to comply fully with all its obligations on climate change mitigation arising from any source.

b) The refutation

The problem with the incorporation theory is that it denatures the process of legal interpretation. Instead of merely taking general mitigation obligations into account to make sense of a human rights treaty, this theory overlooks the text as well as the object and purpose of the treaty at issue, focusing exclusively on general mitigation obligations.[256] Human rights treaties are thus reduced to a Trojan horse allowing extraneous rules and objectives to take hold of human rights institutions.

[248] Knox, 2016 Report (n 31) ¶73.
[249] Ibid ¶¶77, 80.
[250] Boyle, 'Climate Change' (n 44) 777. See also Res 41/21 (n 44) Preamble ¶15.
[251] Boyle, 'Climate Change' (n 44) 775.
[252] Ibid 773. See also Alan Boyle and Catherine Redgwell, *International Law and the Environment* (4th edn, OUP 2021) 166, making the same assessment with regard to customary law.
[253] Boyle, 'Climate Change' (n 44) 773.
[254] André Nollkaemper and Laura Burgers, 'A New Classic in Climate Change Litigation: The Dutch Supreme Court Decision in the Urgenda Case' *EJIL:Talk!* (6 January 2020) <https://perma.cc/Z8GT-LNMY>>.
[255] See Benoit Mayer, 'The State of the Netherlands v. Urgenda Foundation' (2019) 8 TEL 167, 186–87.
[256] On the risk of the principle of systemic integration leading to a denaturation of legal interpretation, see generally Rachovitsa (n 214) 561, 564, 588.

When the incorporation theory is at work, human rights treaties no longer pursue the objective of protecting the enjoyment of human rights, being instead entirely aimed at the mitigation of climate change.

The interpretation of a treaty should depend, among other things, on its text; its application, in turn, should take relevant, case-specific circumstances into account. Thus, Knox points out that 'the content of the obligations of States to protect against environmental harm depends on the content of their duties with respect to the particular rights threatened by the harm'.[257] Yet, similar conclusions will inevitably be reached, when applying obligations arising from various treaties recognizing different rights in diverse national circumstances, if one assumes—as Knox does—that, '[i]n applying their duty to protect against environmental harm that interferes with the enjoyment of human rights, ... States must implement and comply with the standards that they have adopted'.[258]

This reasoning is incongruous. The obligation to protect the right to life, for instance, probably does not imply exactly the same mitigation obligation as the obligation to protect the right to private and family life; and these obligations should apply differently in states where the enjoyment of these rights is more or less exposed to climate impacts that mitigation action could avoid. To take an extreme example, the obligation of a state to protect the right of coalminers to an adequate standard of living may not necessarily imply the state's obligation to mitigate climate change at all as closing coalmines—a measure that the state would likely take to mitigate climate change—would deprive the coalminers of their livelihood.[259]

This incongruity can be observed, for instance, in *Urgenda*, by comparing the judgment of the District Court of the Hague with that of the Supreme Court. The District Court thought that it could not apply the ECHR in a public interest litigation;[260] its judgment, instead, relies on the duty of care of the state under Dutch tort law. By contrast, the Supreme Court held that it could apply the ECHR in public interest litigation, and it relied exclusively on this substantive ground. Nevertheless, the two courts arrived at exactly the same conclusion. Furthermore, the Supreme Court made no difference between the impacts of climate change on the right to life, on the one hand, and on the right to private and family life, on the other hand, asserting that the state was expected to 'take the same measures'[261] pursuant to

[257] Knox, 2016 Report (n 31) ¶65.

[258] Ibid ¶67.

[259] On another, somewhat extreme example—an association of senior women claiming that Switzerland's obligation to protect their right to life and to private and family life requires full compliance with general mitigation obligations and more—see *Verein Klimaseniorinnen Schweiz* (ECtHR) (n 11). The case was dismissed for lack of standing.

[260] *Urgenda v Netherlands*, ECLI:NL:RBDHA:2015:7145 (DC The Hague, 24 June 2015), ILDC 2456 (NL 2015) ¶4.45.

[261] *Urgenda* (SC) (n 8) ¶5.2.4. The Court cites *Brincat v Malta*, App No 60908/11 (ECtHR, 24 July 2014) <http://hudoc.echr.coe.int/eng?i=001-145790> ¶102, stating that the scopes of obligations relating to these two rights 'may overlap'—but this does not justify the Supreme Court's assertion that, in the case at issue, the scopes of these obligation did 'largely overlap', and that their implications for mitigation were identical. See generally Petra Minnerop, 'Integrating the "Duty of Care" under the

both rights. From whichever ground or angle they looked at the issue, the Dutch courts found that the state had to comply with its customary obligation on climate change mitigation, which they interpreted as requiring at least 25 per cent emission reduction by 2020 compared with 1990 levels.

However, there is no reason to assume that the mitigation obligation derived from the protection of the right to life involves exactly the same standard of care as the mitigation obligation derived from the right to private and family life does[262] or that these two obligations, in turn, are identical to the obligation that arises under the duty of care of the state under tort law. Rather, one would expect that the standard of due diligence applicable in relation to these different obligations would vary, in particular 'according to the importance of the interest requiring protection'.[263] A risk of interference with the right to life is arguably a more pressing consideration than a risk of interference with the right to private and family life; and the duty of care arguably allows broader consideration for the need for mitigation action as it relates not only to the enjoyment of human rights but also to the enjoyment of human welfare in general. The two courts in *Urgenda* arrived at the same conclusion because, while claiming alternatively to apply tort law or European human rights law *in light of* customary international law,[264] they were in fact applying customary international law.

The incorporation theory is problematic because it leads judges to ignore rules on jurisdiction and admissibility. The applicants in *Urgenda* had standing to invoke the duty of care of the state and its obligation to protect human rights but not its customary international law obligations.[265] Likewise, treaty bodies and regional human rights courts have jurisdiction to interpret human rights treaties but not to apply general mitigation obligations arising from climate treaties or customary international law. Systemic integration provides no justification for overlooking the absence of state consent to jurisdiction with regard to the application of the referential rule.[266]

Questions about the implications of the principle of systemic integration for a court's jurisdiction are not entirely new or specific to the context of climate litigation. Judge Thomas Buergenthal accused the ICJ in *Oil Platforms* of using this principle 'to apply international law on the use of force simply because that law may

European Convention on Human Rights and the Science and Law of Climate Change: The Decision of The Hague Court of Appeal in the Urgenda Case' (2019) 37 J Energy & Natural Resources L 149, 161. See also *Klimaatzaak* (n 8) 61–62, which seems to assume that the obligation under arts 2 and 8 ECHR is identical to the duty of care of the state under the Belgian Civil Code.

262 See Ingrid Leijten, 'The Dutch Climate Case Judgment: Human Rights Potential and Constitutional Unease', *Leidenlawblog* (22 October 2018) <https://perma.cc/6PS7-R4S7>.

263 Study Group on Due Diligence (n 30) 1082.

264 *Urgenda* (DC) (n 260) ¶4.43; *Urgenda* (SC) (n 8) ¶5.7.1.

265 *Urgenda* (DC) (n 260) ¶4.42; *Urgenda* (SC) (n 8) ¶1.1.6. See also André Nollkaemper and Laura Burgers, 'The State of the Netherlands v. Urgenda' (2020) 59 ILM 811, 812.

266 See *Status of the Eastern Carelia*, Advisory Opinion (23 July 1923), PCIJ Rep Series B No 5, 27.

also be in dispute between the parties before it and bears some factual relationship to the dispute of which the Court is seised'.[267] The Court forcefully denied doing so.[268] Subsequently, in *Pulp Mills*, the Court stated in the clearest possible terms that systemic integration had 'no bearing on the scope of the jurisdiction conferred on the Court'[269] and, accordingly, that Argentina could not claim the application of general international law under the pretence of interpreting the treaty under which the Court had jurisdiction. Consistently, the Court held in *Jadhav* that its jurisdiction to interpret and apply the Vienna Convention on Consular Relations allowed it to take the ICCPR into account but not to apply it by entertaining claims of human rights violations per se.[270]

Thus, the principle of systemic integration does not justify a monolithic application of international law where a court, having jurisdiction to interpret a treaty, could apply, by the same token, any related rule of international law. Richard Gardiner's guide to treaty interpretation highlights the distinction to be drawn under Article 31(3)(c) of the Vienna Convention on the Law of Treaties 'between using rules of international law as part of the apparatus of treaty interpretation and applying the rules of international law directly to the facts in the context of which the treaty is being considered'. As Gardiner points out, '[t]he former is within the scope of the Vienna rules, the latter is not'.[271] Alexander Orakhelashvili, likewise, notes that 'the purpose of interpreting by reference to "relevant rules" is ... not to defer the provisions being interpreted to the scope and effect of those "relevant rules", but to clarify the content of the former by referring to the latter'.[272] International courts and tribunals have consistently recognized that every rule has a 'separate existence' even when several rules point to the same direction or are expressed in similar terms.[273] Thus, taking general mitigation obligations into account to interpret human rights treaties does not justify the incorporation of the former into the latter.

267 *Oil Platforms* (Merits) (n 157) Separate Opinion of Judge Buergenthal, ¶29. See also McLachlan (n 206); Rosalyn Higgins, 'A Babel of Judicial Voices: Ruminations from the Bench' (2006) 55 ICLQ 791, 802–03.

268 *Oil Platforms* (Merits) (n 157) ¶¶41–42.

269 *Pulp Mills on the River Uruguay (Argentina v Uruguay)*, Judgment (20 April 2010), [2010] ICJ Rep 14, ¶66.

270 *Jadhav (India v Pakistan)*, Judgment (17 July 2019) [2019] ICJ Rep 418, ¶¶36–37, 135.

271 Gardiner (n 205) 320.

272 Alexander Orakhelashvili, 'Restrictive Interpretation of Human Rights Treaties in the Recent Jurisprudence of the European Court of Human Rights' (2003) 14 EJIL 529, 537.

273 See *Military and Paramilitary Activities in and against Nicaragua (Nicaragua v US)*, Judgment on Merits (27 June 1986), [1986] ICJ Rep 132, ¶178; *MOX Plant (Ireland v UK)*, Order on Provisional Measures (3 December 2001), [2001] ITLOS Rep 95, ¶50; *Proceedings Pursuant to the OSPAR Convention* (n 211) ¶141; Institut de Droit International, 'Resolution: Problems Arising from a Succession of Codification Conventions on a Particular Subject' (1995) 66 Ann Inst Droit Intl 245, conclusion 10.

3. An Alternative Theory: Windows of Applicability

a) The theory

An obligation on the mitigation of climate change that derives from a human rights treaty is to be interpreted based on the terms of the treaty from which it is implied, its context, and its object and purpose.[274] Its interpreter is to take general mitigation obligations into account together with the context of the treaty, in light of the principle of systemic integration,[275] but without deferring to these general mitigation obligations.

The terms of human rights treaties and their objects and purposes generally allow consideration for the benefits of international cooperation on climate change mitigation with regard to the enjoyment of human rights, but these treaties are not interested in the broader benefits of climate change mitigation for human welfare, the interests of future generations, and the protection of nature per se.[276] By contrast, general mitigation obligations arising from climate treaties or customary law take at least some of these broader benefits into account. States' general obligations arising under climate treaties pursue the ultimate objective of preventing 'dangerous anthropogenic interference with the climate system',[277] a phrase which invites consideration for an open-ended list of benefits of mitigation action, where climate treaties highlight sustainable development,[278] food security,[279] ecological integrity,[280] and intergenerational equity,[281] among other things.[282] On the other hand, customary international law requires states to exercise due diligence to protect the various rights of other states (eg the right to exploit natural resources)[283]—including (but not limited to) their right to claim the protection of the human rights of their citizens.[284] As human rights treaties only take into account some of the benefits of climate change mitigation that inform general mitigation obligations, human rights treaties only require a part of the mitigation action that states must implement under their general mitigation obligations.[285]

One can use the metaphor of a window to suggest that a state's obligation to protect a human right of individuals within its territory or under its jurisdiction

[274] VCLT (n 26) art 31(1).

[275] Ibid art 31(3)(c).

[276] See nn 121–23.

[277] UNFCCC (n 5) art 2.

[278] Ibid arts 2, 3(4); Paris Agreement (n 5) art 2(1).

[279] UNFCCC (n 5) art 2; Paris Agreement (n 5) Preamble ¶10.

[280] UNFCCC (n 5) art 2; Paris Agreement (n 5) Preamble ¶14.

[281] UNFCCC (n 5) Preamble ¶24, art 3(1).

[282] Ibid Preamble ¶8, referring to 'the pertinent provisions' of the Stockholm Declaration on the Human Environment.

[283] See eg Rio Declaration (n 197) Principle 2.

[284] *Mavrommatis Palestine Concessions (Greece v UK)*, Jurisdiction (30 August 1924), PCIJ Rep Series A/B No 2, 12; ILC, 'Draft Articles on Diplomatic Protection' [2006] II(2) YBILC 24.

[285] On the variability of due diligence obligations (including under human rights treaties), see Samantha Besson, 'La *due diligence* en droit international' (2020) 409 RdC 153, 269–79.

provides only, at most, a limited opportunity to take the benefits of climate change mitigation into account, hence, to apply general mitigation obligations. For a state to comply with an implied mitigation obligation, it only needs to comply with the part of its general mitigation obligations that can be sighted through the window that the human rights treaty opens onto these general mitigation obligations. The size of this window of applicability—that is to say, the content of implied mitigation obligations, for instance in terms of a standard of due diligence[286]—is contingent on the treaty, the right, and the national circumstances.[287] More specifically, windows of applicability depend on the following four variables.

(i) Variable 1: The personal scope of the treaty

Some human rights treaties protect the rights of everyone within the state's territory or under its jurisdiction; other treaties protect only a specific category of population.[288] All other things being equal, general human rights treaties justify more ambition on climate change mitigation than specific human rights treaties because the former perceive the benefits of climate change mitigation for a larger population than the latter do.[289] For instance, the obligation to protect the right to life under the ICCPR (where it applies to the entire population within the state's territory and under its jurisdiction) requires more ambitious mitigation action than the obligation to protect the same right under the Convention on the Rights of the Migrant Workers (where it applies only to a subcategory of the same population).[290]

(ii) Variable 2: The relative importance of the right

Despite the absence of formal hierarchy among rights, more weight is generally attached to the protection of certain rights, in particular the rights that cannot be derogated from even in case of emergency (eg the right to life), as these rights often constitute a necessary condition for the effective enjoyment of other rights.[291]

[286] The emphasis here is on substantive obligations, but the analysis could be replicated *mutatis mutandis* to procedural obligations. The size of a window of applicability could determine the scope of a state's procedural obligations on climate change mitigation compliance with which is required under a human rights treaty—for instance, whether and how diligently it needs to envisage climate change mitigation in environmental assessments.

[287] See generally Riccardo Pisillo-Mazzeschi, 'The Due Diligence Rule and the Nature of the International Responsibility of States' (1992) 35 GYIL 9, 44, noting that 'the degree of diligence that the state must observe depends, largely, on the particular circumstances of each specific case'.

[288] See eg Convention on the Rights of the Child (n 35).

[289] See Paul de Guchteneire and Antoine Pécoud, 'Introduction: The UN Convention on Migrant Workers' Rights' in Paul de Guchteneire, Antoine Pécoud, and Ryszard Cholewinski (eds), *Migration and Human Rights: The United Nations Convention on Migrant Workers' Rights* (CUP 2009) 8.

[290] An exception to this could arise—in application of variables 2 and 3—in circumstances where a specific human rights treaty imposes more stringent obligations or broader rights than general treaties. See eg Convention on the Rights of the Child (n 35) art 3(1), requiring 'the best interests of the child' to be taken as 'a primary consideration'; Frédéric Mégret, 'The Disabilities Convention: Human Rights of Persons with Disabilities or Disability Rights?' (2008) 30 Hum Rts Q 494, 496.

[291] See *R v Home Secretary* [1987] AC 514, [1987] 1 All ER 940, 952; *McCann v UK* (ECtHR, 13 May 2008) 47 EHHR 40, ¶147; HRC, General Comment No 36 (n 36) ¶¶2, 20. See also Teraya Koji, 'Emerging

States are held to a higher standard when protecting objectives to which a higher value is attached:[292] they are expected to invest more resources to prevent a potential interference with the right to life, for instance, than they are to prevent an interference with the right to health, if only because the enjoyment of the former is a necessary condition for the enjoyment of the latter. Thus, all other things being equal, a state's obligation to protect the right to life commands greater ambition on climate change mitigation than its obligation to protect the right to health.

(iii) Variable 3: The potential benefits of climate change mitigation for the protection of the right within the state's territory and under its jurisdiction

Human rights treaties require states to mitigate climate change only as a way to protect the enjoyment of treaty rights. The benefits of climate change mitigation for the enjoyment of a right depend on national circumstances: the population's exposure and vulnerability to the impacts of climate change[293] and the likelihood that climate change mitigation may alleviate these impacts. For instance, the content of the mitigation obligation that can be inferred from a state's obligation to protect the right to food depends on whether climate change would likely affect food security within the state and on whether successful mitigation action remains capable of reducing this impact. In general, the rights to life and health would likely be severely affected in developing countries,[294] whereas developed countries are more exposed to economic loss,[295] which could be framed as an interference with the right to property. Where it is recognized, the right to a healthy environment could also justify relatively broad mitigation obligations, although—like other rights—it is unable to account for all the impacts of climate change on human welfare, future generations, and ecological resources.[296]

(iv) Variable 4: The potential unintended consequences of mitigation action for the enjoyment of treaty rights within the state's territory and under its jurisdiction

A state's obligation under a human rights treaty can justify mitigation action only to the extent that the benefits of mitigation action for the enjoyment of treaty rights

Hierarchy in International Human Rights and Beyond: From the Perspective of Non-Derogable Rights' (2001) 12 EJIL 917; Tom Farer, 'The Hierarchy of Human Rights' (1992) 8 Am U J Intl L & Policy 115.

[292] See n 263.

[293] On the heterogeneity of risks associated with climate change, see generally Field and others (eds) (n 38) 75–84.

[294] See Core Writing Team and others (eds), *Climate Change 2014: Synthesis Report: Contribution of Working Groups I, II and III to the Fifth Assessment Report of the Intergovernmental Panel on Climate Change* (2015). See generally nn 38–39.

[295] See Francisco Estrada, WJ Wouter Botzen, and Richard SJ Tol, 'Economic Losses from US Hurricanes Consistent with an Influence from Climate Change' (2015) 8 Nature Geoscience 880; Solomon Hsiang and others, 'Estimating Economic Damage from Climate Change in the United States' (2017) 356 Science 1362.

[296] See *Natur og Ungdom* (n 9) ¶¶78–145; Atapattu, *Human Rights Approaches* (n 31) 265.

prevail over its unintended consequences. In particular, this observation calls for considering the state's capacity to mitigate climate change without hindering other priorities instrumental to the protection of the rights of individuals within its territory and under its jurisdiction (eg economic development, poverty eradication, or climate change adaptation).[297] As such, developing countries may generally be held to a lower standard on climate change mitigation under their human rights treaty obligations, to the extent that, for lack of financial and other resources, they may not be able to invest in ambitious mitigation action without hindering the pursuance of these other priorities.[298]

On the basis of these four variables, the windows-of-applicability theory provides for an interpretation of implied mitigation obligations in line with the tenets of treaty interpretation. This theory reflects the terms as well as the object and purpose of human rights treaties by requiring a state to mitigate climate change only if and insofar as this contributes to the effective protection of the treaty rights. The theory also takes the context of application into account, acknowledging that not every right has the same implications for climate change mitigation in every country.

b) Applications

A few illustrations can reveal the ramification of the windows-of-applicability theory when compared with the incorporation theory. Applied to *Urgenda*, for instance, the windows-of-applicability theory would have attached great weight to the fact that the Netherlands is particularly exposed to some of climate change's life-threatening impacts[299] and to its large financial capacity, in light of variables 3 and 4.[300] Yet, if the Supreme Court of the Netherlands had followed the windows-of-applicability theory, it would also have distinguished the implications of the right to life from those of the right to private and family life as variables 2 and 3 apply differently in relation to these two rights. The Court's interpretation of the right to life as implying a far-reaching mitigation obligation is not entirely implausible given the fundamental importance that states attach to this right and the benefits that international cooperation on climate change mitigation could bring to its enjoyment within the territory of the Netherlands; the Court's identical interpretation of the right to private and family life is far less convincing.[301]

[297] See David Schlosberg, 'Further Uses for the Luxury/Subsistence Distinction' (2019) 21 British J Politics & Intl Rel 295 (2019); Henry Shue, 'Subsistence Emissions and Luxury Emissions' (1993) 15 L & Policy 39.

[298] See generally Study Group on Due Diligence (n 30) 1074–79.

[299] This is in particular because a large part of the state's territory is situated below sea-level. See Netherlands, Seventh National Communication under the UNFCCC (2018) 125, noting life-threatening implications of heat waves and flooding.

[300] The Dutch courts took these elements into account but not expressly as essential conditions to reaching their conclusions. See in particular *Urgenda* (SC) (n 8) ¶¶5.6.2, 7.3.4. See also discussion below at 248.

[301] The right to private and family life may admit a broad range of limitations and it can be derogated from in time of emergency. See ECHR (n 1) arts 8(2), 15. Moreover, the causal link with climate change

Overall, if the Supreme Court of the Netherlands had followed the windows-of-applicability theory, it would not have assumed that the state's obligation to protect either of these rights requires full compliance with its general mitigation obligation (eg under customary international law).[302] An obligation to protect the right to life, or a fortiori the right to private and family life, does not justify as much mitigation action as the general mitigation obligations that the state accepted in light of a broader consideration of the impacts of climate change. An unusual degree of judicial discretion would then, unavoidably, have been involved in assessing the precise level of mitigation action implied by the obligation of the Netherlands to take appropriate measures to protect each of these two rights. The judges could, of course, have concluded that, while the human rights treaty implies a far-reaching mitigation obligation, the state was already acting consistently with this obligation.[303] In fact, if the 'common ground' method is taken seriously, it should be expected that most states would, most of the time, be found to be acting in compliance with their obligation. Thus, the Court in *Urgenda* would likely, but not necessarily, have found that the Netherland's pre-existing policies and actions on climate change mitigation were sufficiently ambitious to be consistent with its obligation to protect the right to life. By contrast, as far as the right to private and family life is concerned, a finding of compliance would have been virtually unescapable.

As the windows-of-applicability theory recognizes the relevance of national circumstances, it is suspicious of any attempt to transplant *Urgenda* to other countries. In one of the first attempts to do so, the applicants in *Natur og Ungdom* failed to provide any evidence that climate change would significantly affect either the right to life or that of private and family life within Norway's territory or under its jurisdiction.[304] As such, the Supreme Court of Norway justly—at least on the basis of the parties' submissions—dismissed the applicants' submission that a

is arguably less obvious than it is under the right to life, even considering the ECtHR's admittedly broad interpretation of the right to private and family life as implying a right to a healthy home environment. See also Leijten (n 262).

[302] See *Urgenda* (SC) (n 8) ¶5.7.1.

[303] As of 2015, the Netherlands expected to reduce its GHG emissions from 196 Mt CO_2 eq in 2013 to 181 Mt CO_2 eq in 2020. See Netherlands, Second Biennial Report (n 113) 54. The Netherlands was also participating in efforts to achieve the EU's objective of a 20 per cent emission reduction in the EU's aggregate emission reduction by 2020 compared with 1990 levels. See Doha Amendment to the Kyoto Protocol (8 December 2012, in force 31 December 2020) C.N.718.2012.TREATIES-XXVII.7.c, art 1(A); UNFCCC SBSTA, 'Compilation of Economy-Wide Emission Reduction Targets to Be Implemented by Parties Included in Annex I to the Convention', FCCC/SBSTA/2014/INF.6 (2014) ¶¶11–13. The EU projected that it would overachieve this objective and achieve approximately 24 per cent emission reduction by 2020. See EU, Second Biennial Report under the UNFCCC (2015) 38.

[304] The plaintiffs mentioned physical impacts of climate change on the state's territory (eg warming), but they did not demonstrate any impact on the enjoyment of the rights at issue. See Writ of Summons in *Natur og Ungdom* (n 9) (18 October 2016) <https://perma.cc/6PS3-YK2Q> ss 6–7. See also n 199 on Norway's assertion that it is 'in a good position to adapt to the effects of climate change'.

far-reaching mitigation obligation could be implied from Norway's obligation to protect these rights.[305]

Likewise, the windows-of-applicability theory provides a sceptical outlook on the applicants' contention, in *Duarte Agostinho*, that all thirty-three high-income member states of the Council of Europe must enhance their ambition on climate change mitigation in order to comply with their obligation to protect the rights to life and to private and family life.[306] The interpretation of the ECHR proposed by the applicants is certainly not supported by state practice, and it does not constitute a common ground among the member states of the Council of Europe, if—as the applicants contend—none of the thirty-three respondent states complies with it.

Overall, the windows-of-applicability theory suggests that human rights and treaty bodies do not *all* have a role to play in promoting mitigation action. On the one hand, there is no denial that the Human Rights Committee and the CESCR may be able to interpret the obligation of some states to protect some rights under, respectively, the ICCPR and ICESCR, as implying substantive mitigation obligations, given in particular the broad personal scope of these treaties and the potential benefits of climate change mitigation for the enjoyment of these rights in many countries. On the other hand, the Convention on the Elimination of All Forms of Discrimination against Women, the Convention on the Rights of Persons with Disabilities, and the Migrant Workers Convention do not easily lend themselves to such interpretations: their personal scope is more limited and (by contrast to the Convention on the Rights of the Child) the rights that these treaties protect are not uniquely affected by the impacts of climate change. For instance, even though climate change may have different impacts on men and women,[307] climate change mitigation is unlikely to be a particularly effective way to fight against discrimination against women. Also, contrary to claims currently pending before the ECtHR, it is unlikely that a state's ambitious mitigation action could be justified solely as a way to protect the rights of a class of individuals suffering from a rare medical condition made worse by exposure to hot weather.[308]

c) Discussion

The windows-of-applicability theory results in a complex but nuanced interpretation of human rights treaties as the source of an obligation on climate change mitigation. On the one hand, this theory does not categorically exclude the possibility of interpreting human rights obligations as implying an obligation to mitigate climate change. Compliance with human rights treaties requires a state to implement mitigation action to the extent that this may effectively promote the enjoyment

[305] *Natur og Ungdom* (n 9) ¶¶168, 171.

[306] *Duarte Agostinho* (n 11). See also *Greenpeace Nordic* (n 11), making similar claims by reference to the 'common ground' method.

[307] See Field and others (eds) (n 38) 50.

[308] Mex M against Austria (n 11).

of the treaty's rights within the state's territory or under its jurisdiction. This interpretation would most likely be arrived at in relation to general human rights treaties, rights of a fundamental importance (such as the right to life), and states whose population is particularly likely to benefit from mitigation action without being adversely affected by its unintended consequences. In this sense, given the particular vulnerability of the Netherlands to climate impacts, *Urgenda* provided a relatively strong case for the recognition of a mitigation obligation under a human rights treaty in relation to the right to life.

On the other hand, this theory opposes the use of human rights treaties as a Trojan horse at the service of climate change mitigation. Human rights treaties are not a back door for judges to impose on states the obligations on climate change mitigation that states have never accepted;[309] nor can human rights institutions be transformed into substitutes for the fully fledged compliance mechanism that states decided not to create under the Paris Agreement.[310] This theory thus challenges any suggestion that human rights law 'may secure higher standards' on climate change mitigation than general mitigation obligations do.[311] Windows of applicability are always relatively narrow because many of the impacts of climate change that general mitigation obligations seek to avoid cannot be framed as human rights impacts. It remains nonetheless that the impacts of climate change are arguably so severe that even a narrow window of applicability could conceivably allow a judge to raise serious concerns for the protection of human rights and to infer relatively far-reaching mitigation obligations—but the argument is neither obvious nor easy to make, and it can unfold successfully only in very specific cases.

There is no denial that the windows-of-applicability theory is particularly difficult to implement. A judge can certainly not fully rely on any objective method to assess and weigh the four variables relevant to determining the size of a window of applicability. In particular, there is no generally accepted or objective way of measuring or comparing states' vulnerability to climate change,[312] let alone the benefits of climate change mitigation for the protection of a right. Surely, the difficulty of interpreting the law does not normally release a judge from their duty to adjudicate.[313] Nor should this difficulty necessarily lead to an extension of the deference

309 Cf Hunt and Khosla (n 175) 249; Knox, 2016 Report (n 31) ¶77; Wewerinke-Singh (n 31) 132.

310 See n 85. But see eg Boyle, 'Climate Change' (n 44) 775; Wewerinke-Singh (n 31) 133.

311 Boyle, 'Where Next?' (n 112) 613. See nn 245–50. There may be circumstances where an implied mitigation obligation is more demanding than a specific commitment (eg the obligation to pursue the implementation of an NDC in relation to an NDC that lacks ambition). However, an implied mitigation obligation cannot be as far-reaching as the general commitment under art 4(1)(b) of the UNFCCC and the general obligation of due diligence under customary international law as these general obligations reflect a broader rationale for climate change mitigation.

312 See James D Ford and others, 'How to Track Adaptation to Climate Change: A Typology of Approaches for National- level Application' (2013) 18 Ecology & Society 40.

313 See *Misdzi Yikh* (n 111) ¶56; Hersch Lauterpacht, *Function of Law in the International Community* (Clarendon 1933) 3.

that judges show to policy decisions[314]—on the contrary, one could argue that the risk of widespread impacts on fundamental rights justifies closer judicial scrutiny. Precisely what a state must do to comply with its implied obligation to cooperate on climate change mitigation under a specific human rights treaty and in relation to a particular right or precisely what it must do in order to comply with its general mitigation obligations under the UNFCCC and under customary international law are not questions that can be answered with mathematical accuracy, but they may nevertheless be judicial questions.

Conclusion

Human rights treaties may be interpreted as requiring a state to cooperate on climate change mitigation in good faith to the extent that this helps to protect the rights of individuals within its territory or under its jurisdiction. This implied mitigation obligation allows the interpreter of human rights treaties—or, through a similar reasoning, of environmental treaties—to open a window onto general mitigation obligations arising from climate treaties and customary law. Yet, this window is narrow: as human rights treaties do not fully take into account the broad benefits of climate change mitigation on human welfare, the interests of future generations, and the protection of nature per se, they do not require full compliance with general mitigation obligations. The size of a window of applicability—that is to say, how far a human rights treaty requires a state to comply with its general mitigation obligations—depends on the personal scope of the treaty and the importance of the right at issue as well as the potential benefits of climate change mitigation and unintended consequences for the enjoyment of rights, within the state's territory or under its jurisdiction.

This analysis suggests that human rights treaties may, after all, have a rather limited role to play with regard to climate change mitigation. In fact, the interpretation of human rights treaties as the source of mitigation obligations faces some of the major hurdles that have hindered international cooperation on climate change mitigation over the past three decades. For one thing, human rights treaties view nature mostly in instrumental terms and largely ignore the interests of future generations. Overall, international human rights law encourages each state to protect the rights of individuals within its territory—that is, to pursue national interests—rather than to cooperate on the global common good. This inherent tension between national interests and international cooperation will not be solved through an incremental extension of international human rights law, be it through the

[314] Cf *Neubauer* (n 44) ¶152, suggesting that the Court would find a violation of the state's obligation to protect human rights only if the state has taken no measure at all, if the measures it has taken are obviously unsuitable or if these measures fall significantly short of the requisite level of mitigation action.

recognition of new rights (eg to a healthy environment or a sustainable climate),[315] the identification of fictitious rights-holders (eg 'future generations' or 'Mother Earth'),[316] or the introduction of new theories on the extraterritorial application of human rights treaties—not, that is, without betraying the text, and the object and purpose, of human rights treaties and using them as a Trojan horse at the service of extraneous objectives.

[315] Cf David R Boyd, 'Catalyst for Change: Evaluating Forty Years of Experience in Implementing the Right to a Healthy Environment' in Knox and Pejan (n 127) 41.

[316] See UNFCCC (n 5) Preamble ¶24; Paris Agreement (n 5) Preamble ¶14.

PART 2

APPLICATIONS OF GENERAL MITIGATION OBLIGATIONS

V

The Nature of Mitigation Obligations

Introduction

The first Part of this book has identified three types of obligations on climate change mitigation: commitments, customary obligations, and obligations implied from human rights treaties. Among these obligations, a distinction has been introduced between general and specific obligations. On the one hand, general obligations on climate change mitigation require states to achieve unspecified mitigation outcomes. These obligations arise from customary international law[1] and the UN Framework Convention on Climate Change (UNFCCC);[2] their content may also be partly reflected under human rights and environmental treaties.[3] On the other hand, states have more specific obligations relating to climate change mitigation—for instance, under the Paris Agreement, the commitments to communicate nationally determined contributions (NDCs),[4] to implement the necessary measures to achieve them,[5] and to report on their implementation.[6]

This chapter aims to provide a better understanding of the nature of general mitigation obligations, including their relations with more specific mitigation obligations, and to devise possible ways to identify breaches of these general obligations. It does so by examining the relevance of three conceptual frameworks: the dichotomy between obligations of conduct and obligations of result, the distinction between substance and procedure, and the difference between a discrete obligation and a duty that is the corollary of another obligation. The thesis of the chapter is that the general mitigation obligations are obligations of conduct, the application of which implies the performance of a series of corollary duties. These corollary duties are often, but not necessarily, procedural in nature. To make this argument, the chapter engages, in particular, with judicial decisions and scholarship in general international law and international environmental

[1] See above at 88–128.

[2] See United Nations Framework Convention on Climate Change (9 May 1992, in force 21 March 1994) 1771 UNTS 107, art 4(1)(b), 4(2)(a).

[3] See above at 129–179.

[4] Paris Agreement (12 December 2015, in force 4 November 2016) (2016) 55 ILM 740, art 4(2), first sentence.

[5] Ibid second sentence.

[6] Ibid art 13(7).

International Law Obligations on Climate Change Mitigation. Benoit Mayer, Oxford University Press. © Benoit Mayer 2022.
DOI: 10.1093/oso/9780192843661.003.0005

law on the interpretation of obligations of conduct and on the distinction between substance and procedure.

Section A analyses mitigation obligations in light of the dichotomy between obligations of conduct and obligations of result, which it traces back to civil law traditions. It shows that the general obligations on climate change mitigation are obligations of conduct, whereas some specific mitigation obligations are obligations of result. Assessing compliance with an obligation of conduct is more difficult than with an obligation of result, as this involves a somewhat subjective appraisal of the efforts that the state is carrying out, rather than merely the verification of the realization of a result. A convenient way to demonstrate the breach of an obligation of conduct is to identify the appropriate measures that a state would be expected to take, or would need to take, when adopting the requisite conduct. The rest of the chapter seeks to determine how these appropriate measures can be identified.

Section B turns to a distinction that scholars and judges have often assumed to exist between substantive and procedural obligations. It questions whether this distinction can be helpful, in particular, to identify the appropriate measures that a state must take in accordance with its obligations of conduct on climate change mitigation. The response is negative: the section shows that this distinction between procedure and substance provides no obvious analytical insights, at least with regard to mitigation obligations. For one thing, the distinction is sometimes difficult to implement, as it requires an assessment of the purpose of the rule, a question on which there can often be reasonable disagreements. Overall, this distinction is not an effective tool for legal interpretation: no consequences result directly from the characterization of an obligation as either procedural or substantive in nature.

Finally, section C suggests an alternative conceptual framework to identify the appropriate measures that a state must take to comply with its general mitigation obligations. This section submits that non-compliance with a specific mitigation obligation demonstrates the breach of a general mitigation obligation if, and only if, the specific obligation can be construed as a corollary of the general obligation. Based on a critical review of judicial decisions in international environmental law, it suggests that the concept of a distinction between procedure and substance has hindered the recognition of this differentiation between what could be called 'discrete obligations' and 'corollary duties'. Whether a specific obligation is the corollary of a general obligation depends mainly on the logical relation between the two obligations, and not on their substantive or procedural nature—procedural obligations are not necessarily corollary duties, and corollary duties are not necessarily procedural in nature. The concept of corollary duties, it is argued, could play an important practical role in a judicial assessment of compliance with general mitigation obligations. This latter argument provides the foundation for further analysis in Chapter VII.

A. Conduct and Result

This section explores a concept essential to understanding the nature of mitigation obligations: the dichotomy between obligations of conduct and obligations of result. After explaining this dichotomy in greater detail, the section shows that general mitigation obligations are obligations of conduct, whereas more specific obligations relating to climate change mitigation include some obligations of result. This prevalence of obligations of conduct is justified by the fact that mitigation outcomes depend not only on state action, but also on extraneous factors that are relatively unpredictable at the relevant timescale—including economic, technological, and demographic circumstances. This section then refutes any notion that obligations of conduct are in any way 'less binding', or systematically less demanding or less effective, than obligations of result. Finally, the section acknowledges the difficulty of assessing compliance with an obligation of conduct—as this involves a subjective appraisal of the efforts that the state is carrying out rather than merely the achievement of the expected outcome—and it outlines a way to surmount this difficulty.

1. The Dichotomy between Conduct and Result

a) Origins

The dichotomy between conduct and result, which can be traced back to Roman law, remains commonly used in some legal systems of civil law tradition.[7] The 1804 French Civil Code establishes that the debtor of an obligation could generally be held responsible 'by reason of the non-performance of the obligation',[8] while other provisions characterize certain obligations—for instance, the obligation to watch over the preservation of a thing—as requiring the debtor 'to give it all the care of a prudent administrator'.[9] Courts[10] and the doctrine[11] interpret these provisions as defining two distinct types of obligations: 'obligation de résultat' (obligation of result) and 'obligation de moyens' (alternatively translated as obligation of means or obligation of conduct).

On the one hand, an obligation of result requires the realization of the object of the obligation.[12] When a judge identifies an obligation of result, their role is

[7] See eg René Demogue, *Traité des obligations en général* vol 5 (Rousseau 1925) 538; Jean Limpens, Robert M Kruithof, and Anne Meinertzhagen-Limpens, 'The Notion of Tort' in Konrad Zweigert and Ulrich Drobnig (eds), *International Encyclopedia of Comparative Law* vol XI (Springer 1983) §2–24; Jean Bellissent, *Contribution à l'analyse de la distinction des obligations de moyens et des obligations de résultat* (LGDJ 2001).

[8] Code Civil des Français (Civil Code) (France) art 1231-1 (originally art 1147).

[9] Ibid original version (1804) art 1137 (official translation). This article was revoked in 2016 as part of a general overhaul of this part of the Civil Code.

[10] See Court of Paris, 16 November 1927 (1928) Semaine Juridique 53.

[11] See Claude Thomas, 'La distinction des obligations de moyens et des obligations de résultat' (1937) 57 Revue Critique de Législation et de Jurisprudence 636, 640; Bellissent (n 7).

[12] The obligation to 'conduct' particular measures is an obligation of result as the obligation relates to the realization of an outcome (the implementation of the measure) rather to an endeavour. See

often limited to assessing whether the result has realized: the fault of the debtor is presumed whenever the result has not been achieved. This presumption could sometimes be rebutted but only if the debtor can demonstrate the existence of circumstances precluding wrongfulness such as force majeure.

On the other hand, an obligation of conduct requires an endeavour towards the object of the obligation. In relation to an obligation of conduct, the judge is to assess compliance not on the basis of what has been achieved but on the basis of what the debtor has done. The responsibility of the debtor is engaged by a failure to carry out the requisite efforts, notwithstanding the end result. A classic example of an obligation of conduct is the obligation of a medical doctor towards their patient. It would be unreasonable to impose an obligation of result on a medical doctor, and yet the doctor clearly has an obligation—one of trying to treat their patient to the best of their abilities. The breach of this obligation of conduct may engage their professional, civil, or even criminal liability.

An obligation of conduct can require an endeavour directed at a specific goal (eg curing a patient of a disease), whose realization can be assessed objectively, in binary terms of success or failure, and which could conceivably have been the object of an obligation of result. Alternatively, it can require an endeavour towards an open-ended objective, the achievement of which could not be determined on such a simple binary basis, but is rather a matter of degree (eg promoting a patient's well-being).[13] Notwithstanding whether an obligation of conduct defines an intended outcome or merely a general goal, the object of the obligation is the endeavour, not the result.

An obligation of conduct implies a standard of conduct, which defines the level of effort expected from the debtor. French law typically refers to the care expected from 'a reasonable person'[14]—a phrase that replaced the dated mention of a 'bon père de famille', a good family patriarch.[15] What this implies depends on the circumstances. For instance, a reasonable person would exercise greater care when they know of an imminent risk, and the efforts they implement may depend on the resources available to them.[16] Like other concepts codified in the civil code, this dichotomy was construed, taught, and applied not just as part of contract and tort law but as a general distinction relevant to any substantive legal obligations. For instance, the French Constitutional Council applied these concepts to analyse

Pierre-Marie Dupuy, 'Reviewing the Difficulties of Codification: On Ago's Classification of Obligations of Means and Obligations of Result in Relation to State Responsibility' (1999) 10 EJIL 371.

[13] Cf Rüdiger Wolfrum, 'General International Law (Principles, Rules, and Standards)' in *Max Planck Encyclopedia of Public International Law* (online edn, OUP 2010), suggesting that a category of 'goal-oriented obligations' could be distinguished from other 'obligations of conduct'.

[14] Code Civil (n 8) arts 1188(2), 1197, 1301-1(1).

[15] Ibid original version (1804) arts 450(2), 601, 1137(1), 1374, 1728, 1766, 1806, 1880, 1962(1).

[16] See Jean Carbonnier, *Droit Civil* (PUF 1955) 2190–91.

statutory obligations of educational institutions,[17] employers,[18] and territorial authorities.[19]

b) Reception in international law

The reception of this concept in international law has been plagued by misunderstanding and confusion.[20] The difficulties appear to have originated with the work of the International Law Commission (ILC) on the responsibility of states and, more specifically, with the mischaracterization of an 'obligation of conduct', in the English translation of Special Rapporteur Roberto Ago's report, as the obligation 'specifically calling for [a State] to adopt a particular course of conduct'.[21] In the original civil law typology, the obligation to adopt a 'particular course of conduct' (eg to take specified measures) would be considered an obligation of result because the debtor is required to achieve a result—namely, the implementation of the 'particular course of conduct'.[22] An obligation of conduct imposes a standard of conduct, not the implementation of a 'particular course of conduct', as it leaves it to the debtor to select the appropriate means of implementation. The ILC progressively departed from the conceptual framework suggested by Ago.[23]

Despite this unfortunate confusion, obligations of conduct (following the civil law definition) occupy a prominent role in international law. In some respects, obligations of conduct are the dark matter of the international law universe: they often go unnoticed and yet, in some accounts, they are 'far more common than

[17] Constitutional Council, Decision 2005-512 DC, Loi d'orientation et de programme pour l'avenir de l'école (21 April 2005) ¶19.

[18] Constitutional Council, Decision 2001-455 DC, Loi de modernisation sociale (12 January 2002) ¶40.

[19] Constitutional Council, Decision 2000-436 DC, Loi relative à la solidarité et au renouvellement urbains (7 December 2000) ¶13.

[20] See *Legality of the Threat or Use of Nuclear Weapons*, Advisory Opinion (8 July 1996), [1996] ICJ Rep 226, ¶99, interpreting a treaty obligation 'to pursue negotiations in good faith' not as an 'obligation of conduct' but as 'an obligation to achieve a precise result—nuclear disarmament in all its aspects'; *Gabčíkovo-Nagymaros Project (Hungary/Slovakia)*, Judgment (25 September 1997), [1997] ICJ Rep 7, ¶135; *Pulp Mills on the River Uruguay (Argentina v Uruguay)*, Judgment (20 April 2010), [2010] ICJ Rep 14, ¶187.

[21] Roberto Ago, Sixth Report on State Responsibility, A/CN.4/302 (1977) 8 (art 20), 20 (art 21). The issue may have been one of translation. The original version of the report, in French, used the concept of 'obligation de comportement' rather than 'obligation de moyens', thus seemingly referring to something other than the dichotomy between conduct and result.

[22] See discussion in Jean Combacau, 'Obligations de résultat et obligations de comportement: Quelques questions et pas de réponse' in *Mélanges offerts à Paul Reuter: Le droit international: Unité et diversité* (Pedone 1981) 194; Dupuy (n 12); Jean Salmon (ed), *Dictionnaire de droit international public* (Bruylant 2001) 767; Philippe Gautier, 'On the Classification of Obligations in International Law' in HP Hestermeyer and others (eds), *Coexistence, Cooperation and Solidarity: Liber Amoricum Rüdiger Wolfrum* vol 1 (Brill 2011) 853.

[23] See ILC, 'Draft Articles on the Responsibility of States for Internationally Wrongful Acts' in [2001] II(2) YBILC 26, commentary on art 12, ¶11, referring to the civil law definition, while trying to assimilate a different understanding of the same concepts in fn 209.

obligations of result'.[24] By all accounts, these obligations play an instrumental role in at least some fields of international law, such as international human rights law[25] and international environmental law,[26] where states are chiefly required to work towards certain goals rather than to achieve predetermined outcomes. More generally, the obligation of a state to respect the rights of other states is an obligation of conduct: it requires states to exercise due diligence, not to achieve a result.[27]

Various judicial decisions have relied, more or less explicitly, on the civil law concepts of obligations of conduct and result. It was implicit but central in the judgment of the International Court of Justice (ICJ) in *LaGrand*. The Court necessarily implied that the obligation of the United States to 'take all measures at its disposal to ensure that Walter LaGrand is not executed'[28] was an obligation of conduct when it found that the United States had violated this obligation, not because Mr LaGrand had been executed, but because state agents had failed to take any of the steps that could have prevented his execution.[29] A more explicit reasoning can be found in the ICJ judgment on the *Bosnian Genocide* case. There, the Court agreed with Serbia that the obligation to prevent genocide is 'one of conduct ... in the sense that a State cannot be under an obligation to succeed, whatever the circumstances, in preventing the commission of genocide', but can only commit 'to employ all means reasonably available to [it], so as to prevent genocide so far as possible'.[30] Consequently, the Court noted, '[a] State does not incur responsibility simply because the desired result is not achieved'.[31] The Court found Serbia responsible for a breach of its obligation of conduct because Serbia had not 'made the best efforts within [its] power to try and prevent' a genocide.[32] Finally, in a maritime delimitation dispute between Ghana and Côte d'Ivoire, the International Tribunal for the Law of the Sea (ITLOS) characterized a treaty obligation to reach an agreement

[24] Study Group on Due Diligence in International Law, 'Second Report on Due Diligence' (2016) 77 ILA Rep Conferences 1062, 1063. See also Heike Krieger, Anne Peters, and Leonhard Kreuzer (eds), *Due Diligence in the International Legal Order* (OUP 2020).

[25] See International Covenant on Economic, Social and Cultural Rights (16 December 1966, in force 3 January 1976) 993 UNTS 3, art 2(1); Philip Alston and Gerard Quinn, 'The Nature and Scope of States Parties' Obligations under the International Covenant on Economic, Social and Cultural Rights' (1987) 9 H Rts Q 156.

[26] See *South China Sea (Philippines v China)*, Award (12 July 2016), 31 RIAA 153, ¶¶972–75; Jorge E Viñuales, 'Due Diligence in International Environmental Law: A Fine-grained Cartography' in Krieger, Peters, and Kreuzer (eds) (n 24) 124; Lavanya Rajamani, 'Due Diligence in International Climate Change Law' in Krieger, Peters, and Kreuzer (eds) (n 24) 163.

[27] See *Alabama Claims (US/UK)*, Award (14 September 1872), 29 RIAA 125, 129; *Corfu Channel (UK v Albania)*, Judgment on Merits (9 April 1949), [1949] ICJ Rep 4, 22; *Pulp Mills* (n 20) ¶101.

[28] *LaGrand (Germany v US)*, Judgment (27 June 2001), [2001] ICJ Rep 466, ¶111.

[29] Ibid ¶¶111–15. See also *Difference Relating to Immunity from Legal Process of a Special Rapporteur of the Commission on Human Rights*, Advisory Opinion (29 April 1999), [1999] ICJ Rep 62, ¶59.

[30] *Application of the Convention on the Prevention and Punishment of the Crime of Genocide (Bosnia v Serbia)*, Judgment (26 February 2007), [2007] ICJ Rep 43, ¶430.

[31] Ibid.

[32] Ibid ¶438.

as an obligation of conduct, the violation of which 'cannot be assessed only upon the result expected by one side not being achieved'.[33]

2. Application to Mitigation Obligations

This subsection shows that many obligations on climate change mitigation are obligations of conduct. These include the general mitigation obligations under customary international law and the UNFCCC, the obligation of the parties to the Paris Agreement to take the necessary measures to achieve their NDCs, and the mitigation obligations that may be implied from human rights treaties. The main exception—leaving purely procedural obligations aside—is the quantified emission limitation and reduction commitments (QELRCs) applicable under the Kyoto Protocol, which were defined as an obligation of result.

a) Customary obligations

The customary obligation of states to mitigate climate change can be viewed as an aspect of a broader obligation to prevent transboundary environmental harm.[34] This obligation of prevention is often described as an obligation 'to ensure' the prevention of harm.[35] Yet, this expression is ambivalent: obligations 'to ensure' have, in various contexts, been interpreted alternatively as creating obligations of result[36] or obligations of conduct.[37] State practice, however, suggests that the obligation of prevention is an obligation of conduct. The observation of widespread transboundary environmental harm indicates that state practice does not support the existence of an obligation of result with regard to the prevention of such harm.[38] On the other hand, it appears that states are generally making significant efforts with a view to avoiding or reducing transboundary environmental harm,[39] including by taking measures to mitigate climate change.[40] While the scale

[33] *Delimitation of the Maritime Boundary in the Atlantic Ocean (Ghana/Côte d'Ivoire)*, Judgment (23 September 2017), [2017] ITLOS Rep 4, ¶604.

[34] See generally above at 96.

[35] *Nuclear Weapons* (n 20) ¶29; Declaration of the United Nations Conference on the Human Environment (16 June 1972) A/Conf.48/14/Rev.1 (1972) 11 ILM 1416 ('Stockholm Declaration'), Principle 21; Rio Declaration on Environment and Development (14 June 1992) A/CONF.151/26 (vol I) (1992) 31 ILM 874, Principle 2.

[36] *Proceedings Pursuant to the OSPAR Convention (Ireland/UK)*, Final Award (2 July 2003), 23 RIAA 59, ¶¶132–37.

[37] *Responsibilities and Obligations of States Sponsoring Persons and Entities with Respect to Activities in the Area*, Advisory Opinion (1 February 2011), [2011] ITLOS Rep 10, ¶¶110ff.

[38] See Oscar Schachter, 'The Emergence of International Environmental Law' (1991) 44 J Intl Affairs 457, 463; Daniel Bodansky, 'Customary (and Not So Customary) International Environmental Law' (1995) 3 Indiana J Global Legal Studies 105, 110–11; John H Knox, 'The Myth and Reality of Transboundary Environmental Impact Assessment' (2002) 96 AJIL 291, 293. See also UN Environment Programme, Global Environment Outlook (6th edn, CUP 2019).

[39] See above at 96.

[40] See above at 110.

of contemporary environmental harm excludes the existence of a customary obligation of result on the prevention of such harm, it does not preclude the identification of a customary obligation of conduct.

The obligation of prevention, indeed, has generally been interpreted as an obligation of conduct or with concepts of a similar effect, such as 'due diligence' and 'best efforts'.[41] Thus, the ILC's Draft Articles on State Responsibility observed that 'obligations of prevention are usually construed as best efforts obligations'.[42] Boyle and Redgwell highlighted that neither the obligation of prevention nor the obligation of cooperation 'prohibits all transboundary harm', further pointing out that 'it is erroneous (and deeply confusing) to refer to a "no-harm" rule in this context'.[43] Likewise, Ilias Plakokefalos noted that 'there is no requirement for damage to have occurred' for a breach of prevention obligations to be assessed.[44] The rationale for prevention to be an obligation of conduct is that, as the Commission on Sustainable Development pointed out, '[c]ertainly not all instances of transboundary damage resulting from activities within a State's territory can be prevented'.[45]

The ICJ confirmed this understanding of the obligation of prevention in two judgments. In *Pulp Mills*, it interpreted a state's prevention obligation as an obligation 'to take all means at its disposal in order to avoid activities ... causing significant damage to the environment of another State'.[46] In *Certain Activities*, the Court found Costa Rica in breach of a procedural obligation derived from its general obligation of due diligence—its obligation to conduct an environmental impact assessment (EIA) before authorizing a project likely to cause transboundary environmental harm[47]—even though, in the Court's own finding, no such harm had occurred.[48] As Judge Joan Donoghue emphasized in her separate opinion, '[t]he requirement to exercise due diligence ... is an obligation of conduct that applies to all phases of a project'.[49] Consequently, Judge Donoghue noted, 'a failure to exercise due diligence to prevent significant transboundary environmental harm can engage the responsibility of the State of origin even in the absence of material damage to potentially affected States'.[50] ITLOS and an arbitral tribunal have also noted that

[41] Leslie-Anne Duvic-Paoli and Jorge E Viñuales, 'Principle 2' in Jorge E Viñuales (ed), *The Rio Declaration on Environment and Development: A Commentary* (OUP 2015) 118–120.

[42] ILC, 'State Responsibility' (n 23) commentary on art 14, ¶14.

[43] Alan Boyle and Catherine Redgwell, *International Law and the Environment* (4th edn, OUP 2021) 153.

[44] Ilias Plakokefalos, 'Prevention Obligations in International Environmental Law' (2012) 23 YB Intl Envtl L 3, 37.

[45] UN Secretary-General, 'Rio Declaration on Environment and Development: Application and Implementation', E/CN.17/1997/8 (1997) ¶23.

[46] *Pulp Mills* (n 20) ¶101.

[47] *Certain Activities Carried Out by Nicaragua in the Border Area (Costa Rica v Nicaragua) and Construction of a Road in Costa Rica along the San Juan River (Nicaragua v Costa Rica)*, Judgment on Merit (16 December 2015), [2015] ICJ Rep 665, ¶162.

[48] Ibid ¶217. Yet, bizarrely, the Court did not find Costa Rica in breach of its substantive obligation. See discussion below at 216.

[49] *Certain Activities* (n 47) Separate Opinion of Judge Donoghue, ¶9.

[50] Ibid.

various provisions of the UN Convention on the Law of the Sea (UNCLOS) that codify the obligation of prevention are obligations of conduct.[51]

Like the obligation of prevention, the customary obligation on climate change mitigation has been recognized as an obligation of conduct. The International Law Association, for instance, found that states must 'exercise due diligence to avoid, minimize and reduce environmental and other damage through climate change'.[52] Likewise, the ILC's Draft Guidelines on the Protection of the Atmosphere conclude that 'States have the obligation to protect the atmosphere by exercising due diligence in taking appropriate measures'.[53] Accordingly, a state's general customary obligation on climate change mitigation is to make their best effort but not necessarily to achieve any predetermined outcome.[54]

b) Commitments

Consistently with customary law, the main substantive commitments on climate change mitigation are obligations of conduct. Such is the case, in particular, of the general commitment of the parties to the UNFCCC to 'formulate [and] implement ... programmes containing measures to mitigate climate change'.[55] This provision does not define a result that must be achieved; rather, it describes an obligation of conduct. In particular, it highlights that an obligation of conduct can imply more specific obligations of result: the general commitment of states to mitigate climate change implies that the state must formulate a programme and, once this has been done, that it must normally implement this programme. The failure to achieve either of these two steps would suggest a breach of the state's international obligation. In other words, as the state starts implementing its obligation of conduct, it takes steps (eg the formulation of programmes) which help to specify what precisely the obligation implies (eg the implementation of these programmes).

Likewise, an obligation of conduct lies at the core of the Paris Agreement. Under the second sentence of Article 4(2), the parties must 'pursue domestic mitigation measures, with the aim of achieving the objectives of [their successive nationally determined] contributions'. The obligation to pursue unspecified measures relates to the adoption of a conduct rather than to the achievement of a result. The French, equally authentic version of Article 4(2) ('*prennent des mesures internes ... en vue de réaliser les objectifs*') indicates more clearly than the convoluted English version that the measures must be such that they can reasonably be viewed as capable

[51] *Activities in the Area* (n 37) ¶¶110–11; *Request for Advisory Opinion by the Sub-Regional Fisheries Commission*, Advisory Opinion (2 April 2015), [2015] ITLOS Rep 4, ¶129; *South China Sea* (n 26) ¶¶744, 944.

[52] International Law Association, 'Resolution 2/2014: Declaration of Legal Principles Relating to Climate Change' (2014) 76 ILA Rep Conferences 21, art 7A(2).

[53] ILC, 'Draft Guidelines on the Protection of the Atmosphere' in ILC Report, 72nd session, A/76/10 (2021) 13, guideline 3.

[54] Ibid commentary on guideline 3, ¶6.

[55] UNFCCC (n 2) art 4(1)(b). See also art 4(2)(a).

of realizing the objective: the phrase '*measures en vue de*' (literally: 'measures in the view of') is an idiom[56] that has rightly been translated, in other contexts, as 'measures to'[57] or 'measures for',[58] thus implying that the measures must be fit for purpose. Thus, whereas the obligation of conduct under the UNFCCC relates to climate change mitigation as an open-ended objective, the obligation of conduct under the Paris Agreement refers to a specific goal—the achievement of the mitigation objective contained in the party's NDC.

Yet, not all substantive mitigation commitments define obligations of conduct. The most prominent exception—albeit of historical relevance—is to be found in Article 3(1) of the Kyoto Protocol, which required Annex I parties to 'ensure' that their aggregate greenhouse gas (GHG) emissions do not exceed their assigned amount calculated pursuant to their QELRCs.[59] As noted above, international courts and tribunals have alternatively interpreted an obligation 'to ensure' as imposing a conduct or a result.[60] Here, however, the context clearly indicates an obligation of result. For instance, the Protocol also requires its parties to make 'demonstrable progress in *achieving* its commitments' by 2005,[61] implying that the parties need to achieve their targets during the commitment period. The Protocol established a complex mechanism to account for the GHG emissions of each party[62] (and not just for the efforts implemented by states), ostensibly 'for the purposes of ensuring compliance with Article 3'.[63] The enforcement branch of the Compliance Mechanism established under the Protocol must declare that a party 'is not in compliance with its commitments under Article 3, paragraph 1, of the Protocol' when it determines that the party's emissions 'have exceeded its assigned amount',[64] notwithstanding the efforts that the state may have made.

Climate treaties also create a range of more procedural obligations, for instance to collect and report information[65] and to communicate NDCs.[66] These obligations require states not to make an endeavour but to achieve a result (the collection and reporting of information and the communication of NDCs). As such, these obligations are obligations of result.

[56] See 'vue' in *Dictionnaire de Français* (online edn, Larousse 2021), defining 'en vue de' as 'de façon à render cette chose possible, réalisable' ('so as to make something possible, realizable').

[57] *Gabčíkovo-Nagymaros* (n 20) ¶25.

[58] *Sovereignty over Pedra Branca/Pulau Batu Puteh, Middle Rocks and South Ledge (Malaysia/Singapore)*, Judgment (23 May 2008), [2008] ICJ Rep 12, ¶147.

[59] Kyoto Protocol to the United Nations Framework Convention on Climate Change (11 December 1997, in force 16 February 2005) 2303 UNTS 162, art 3(1). See also Doha Amendment to the Kyoto Protocol (8 December 2012, in force 31 December 2020) C.N.718.2012.TREATIES-XXVII.7.c.

[60] See nn 36–37.

[61] Kyoto Protocol (n 59) art 3(2) (emphasis added).

[62] Ibid arts 5–8.

[63] Ibid art 7(1).

[64] Decision 27/CMP.1, 'Procedures and Mechanisms Relating to Compliance under the Kyoto Protocol' (9–10 December 2005) FCCC/KP/2005/8/Add.3, 92, Annex ¶XV.5.

[65] See UNFCCC (n 2) art 12; Paris Agreement (n 4) art 13.

[66] Paris Agreement (n 4) art 4(2), first sentence.

Mitigation commitments arising from treaties outside the UNFCCC regime, even when substantive in nature, tend to be obligations of result, but their material scope is far narrower. For instance, the Montreal Protocol and its Kigali Amendment impose an obligation for each party to 'ensure' that its level of consumption and production of regulated substances does not exceed a specified level.[67] The context, here again, indicates an obligation of result. The non-compliance procedure provides expressly for the possibility that a party, 'despite having made its best, bona fide efforts', may be 'unable to comply fully with its obligations under the Protocol'.[68] If this had been an obligation of conduct, the best bona fide efforts would constitute full compliance.

Finally, whether unilateral declarations create obligations and, if so, whether those are obligations of conduct or result depends on the terms and context of the declarations. Leaving aside the question of their legal force, NDCs are often phrased in terms that suggest a result rather than merely a conduct. Thus, the EU indicated that what it communicated was a 'binding target'.[69] According to Canada's NDC, the state 'must reduce' (not just 'try' to reduce) its total economy-wide emissions.[70] Israel announced its intention 'to *achieve* an economy-wide unconditional target' by 2030, which it contrasted with an 'interim target . . . expected by 2025'.[71] Developing states' targets that are conditional to international support were likewise presented as the achievement, rather than the pursuance, of a mitigation outcome.[72]

On the other hand, some NDCs contain two objectives that seem to differentiate between conduct and result.[73] For instance, China announced an intent to 'achieve the peaking of carbon dioxide emissions around 2030' while 'making best efforts to peak early'.[74] Likewise, the United States' original NDC indicated its intention 'to achieve' a 26 per cent emission reduction below its 2005 level in 2025 'and to make best efforts to reduce its emissions by 28%'.[75] The NDC that the United States communicated after rejoining the Paris Agreement refers to a range of emission reduction ('50–52 per cent below 2005 levels in 2030'),[76] thus suggesting a strong

[67] Montreal Protocol on Substances that Deplete the Ozone Layer (16 September 1987, in force 1 January 1989) 1522 UNTS 3, art 2; Amendment to the Montreal Protocol on Substances that Deplete the Ozone Layer (15 October 2016, in force 1 January 2019) (2017) 56 ILM 193 ('Kigali Amendment').

[68] Non-compliance procedure (1998) in Ozone Secretariat, *Handbook for the Montreal Protocol on Substances That Deplete the Ozone Layer* (13th edn, 2019) 782. If the obligation had been an obligation of conduct, the 'best, bona fide efforts' would have constituted compliance.

[69] EU, First NDC, Updated (2020) ¶27.

[70] Canada, First NDC (2017) 4.

[71] Israel, First NDC (2016) 1 (emphasis added).

[72] Nigeria, First NDC (2017) 9; Vietnam, First NDC (2016) 4.

[73] Discussion in this paragraph is without prejudice to the capacity of any particular NDC to create legal obligations, a question that would require more extensive treatment. The conduct/result dichotomy can, in principle, be applied to any normative system, including (non-binding) pledges as well as (binding) obligations.

[74] China, First NDC (2016) 5.

[75] United States, First NDC (2016) 3.

[76] United States, First NDC (2021) 1.

intention to achieve the less demanding target and an endeavour towards the more ambitious target.

c) Obligations implied from human rights treaties

The mitigation obligations that may be implied from human rights treaties are also primarily obligations of conduct. Human rights treaties do not require states to protect human rights at all costs but rather to make their best endeavour.

Thus, the obligation of each party to the International Covenant on Economic, Social and Cultural Rights to 'take steps … to the maximum of its available resources, with a view to achieving progressively the full realization of'[77] economic, social, and cultural rights is an archetypical obligation of conduct.[78] Likewise, the Human Rights Committee interpreted the positive obligation to protect the rights recognized under the International Covenant on Civil and Political Rights (ICCPR) as an obligation to 'take appropriate measures or to exercise due diligence to prevent, punish, investigate or redress' harm caused by third parties.[79] The European Court of Human Rights (ECtHR) characterized as obligations of conduct[80] the obligations of national authorities to promote public health and safety,[81] to investigate unlawful killings,[82] and to take measures to facilitate the contact of a divorced parent with their child,[83] among other applications of the general obligation to protect the enjoyment of human rights. The Inter-American Court of Human Rights has long held that states must exercise 'due diligence to prevent the violation [of a human right] or to respond to it',[84] and it considers that a state's positive obligation is a 'best efforts obligation, rather than an obligation to ensure results'.[85]

Consistently, when an obligation to protect the environment can be inferred from human rights treaties, it is also an obligation of conduct. As Knox notes, 'it may not always be possible to prevent all environmental harm that interferes with

[77] ICESCR (n 25) art 2(1).

[78] See CESCR, General Comment No 3, 'The Nature of States Parties' Obligations', E/1991/23 (14 December 1990) ¶¶1–2; Alston and Quinn (n 25).

[79] HRC, General Comment No 31, 'The Nature of the General Obligation Imposed on States Parties to the Covenant', CCPR/C/21/Rev.1/Add.13 (26 May 2004) ¶8. See also HRC, General Comment No 3, 'Article 2 (Implementation at the National Level)', HRI/GEN/1/Rev.6 (29 July 1981) ¶1.

[80] The ECtHR uses the concept of 'obligation of means' in English, a more literal translation from the French '*obligation de moyens*' (which the Court uses in French).

[81] *Stoicescu v Romania*, App No 9718/03 (ECtHR, 26 July 2011) <http://hudoc.echr.coe.int/eng?i=001-105820> ¶59.

[82] *Da Silva v UK*, App No 5878/08 (ECtHR, 30 March 2016) <http://hudoc.echr.coe.int/fre?i=001-111334> ¶233.

[83] *Sbârnea v Romania*, App No 2040/06 (ECtHR, 21 June 2011) <http://hudoc.echr.coe.int/eng?i=001-105047> ¶127.

[84] *Velásquez-Rodríguez v Honduras*, Judgment on Merits (29 July 1988) IACtHR Series C No 4, ¶172.

[85] *Baldeon Garcia v Peru*, Judgment (6 April 2006) IACtHR Series C No 147, ¶93.

the full enjoyment of human rights', but states must 'undertake due diligence to prevent such harm and reduce it to the extent possible'.[86]

3. Understanding the Prevalence of Obligations of Conduct on Climate Change Mitigation

The rationale for distinguishing between obligations of conduct and obligations of result relates to the capacity of the debtor to secure an outcome. An obligation of result can only be imposed when the debtor is able to secure the outcome (except, possibly, for circumstances precluding wrongfulness, for which burden of proof falls on the debtor).[87] By contrast, an obligation of conduct is normally imposed when the realization of the objective depends partly on circumstances external to the debtor—whether it is the action of other persons or pure luck. For instance, a medical doctor cannot always secure the prompt improvement of their patient; they can only be held responsible for administering the best care available in the circumstances. When the realization of the outcome is not fully within the control of the debtor, all the debtor can reasonably promise is to make its best endeavour.[88]

Accordingly, international courts and tribunals have characterized obligations as obligations of conduct (whether they used this terminology or not) when the efforts of a state could favour an outcome but not guarantee its realization. For instance, in *Corfu Channel*, the ICJ identified 'every State's obligation not to allow knowingly its territory to be used for acts contrary to the rights of other states'.[89] The ICJ thus focused not on the result (ie whether the state's territory is used for acts contrary to the rights of other states), but on the efforts made by the state—something it later referred to as an obligation of the state to exercise 'due diligence ... in its territory'.[90] Although it would be nearly impossible for a state to prevent every (eg illegal) use of its territory for activities that would be harmful to third states, a state can reasonably be expected to take 'appropriate steps'[91] to prevent such activities.

Likewise, obligations on climate change mitigation are generally obligations of conduct because a state cannot guarantee the achievement of any mitigation outcome—at least, not through licit means. All a state can promise is to make its

[86] John Knox, Report of the Special Rapporteur on the issue of human rights obligations relating to the enjoyment of a safe, clean, healthy and sustainable environment, A/HRC/37/59 (2018) ¶5.

[87] See ILC, 'State Responsibility' (n 23) arts 20–25.

[88] Combacau (n 22) 196. See also Plakokefalos (n 44) 32.

[89] *Corfu Channel* (n 27) 22.

[90] *Pulp Mills* (n 20) ¶101. While the obligation 'not to allow' is strictly speaking an obligation of result (the negative obligation not to perform an act), the ICJ was in fact pointing to a broader obligation of conduct that requires a state to ensure that its territory is not used in ways harmful to other states.

[91] See *United States Diplomatic and Consular Staff in Tehran (US v Iran)*, Judgment (24 May 1980), [1980] ICJ Rep 3, ¶63.

best efforts to limit and reduce GHG emissions while pursuing various other objectives, including economic development and the protection of the human rights of individuals within its jurisdiction.[92] Its success in this endeavour is inevitably linked to the resources it commands and to the constraints it faces. Under the paradigm of a sustainable development,[93] states are not required to cease all adverse environmental impacts immediately but to strike a balance between economic development and the protection of the global environment. The UNFCCC thus recognizes that parties must implement their general obligation on climate change mitigation 'taking into account their common but differentiated responsibilities and their specific ... development priorities, objectives and circumstances',[94] while the Paris Agreement highlights more generally the relevance of 'different national circumstances'.[95] Mitigation obligations obviously do not trump other obligations, such as obligations to protect human rights or the environment, which justify some GHG emissions to ensure a minimal level of development.

In more practical terms, it is often difficult for a state to foresee what outcomes the mitigation action it is implementing will achieve. Time-specific commitments on climate change mitigation are typically made more than a decade in advance.[96] The evolution of a state's GHG emissions on a decadal scale depends not only on the successful implementation of appropriate mitigation action by the state, but also on economic, technological, and demographic circumstances that the state does not fully control and cannot always foresee.

Economic factors are perhaps the most obvious extraneous factor influencing a state's GHG emissions in unforeseeable ways. When the Kyoto Protocol was adopted, some careful observers could foresee that the collapse of emissions-intensive industries in Eastern Europe would bring quantities of cheap credits on international carbon markets ('hot air'),[97] but none could predict that the 2008 global economic crisis would lead to a significant (albeit transient) reduction in Annex I parties' emissions during the first commitment period.[98] GHG emissions data reported by Annex I country parties during the commitment period show significant year-by-year variation (especially in smaller countries), with a single-year

[92] See UNFCCC (n 2) art 3(4); Paris Agreement (n 4) Preamble ¶12.

[93] See UNFCCC (n 2) eg art 3(4); Rio Declaration (n 35); *Gabčíkovo-Nagymaros* (n 20) ¶141.

[94] UNFCCC (n 2) art 4(1) (chapeau).

[95] Paris Agreement (n 4) art 4(3).

[96] For instance, the Kyoto Protocol, adopted in 1997, defined QERLCs applicable to a commitment period 2008–12, and the NDCs communicated under the Paris Agreement in or around 2015 applied generally to 2025 or 2030. On the relevant ongoing negotiations under the Paris Agreement, see Yamide Dagnet and Nathan Cogswell, 'Setting a Common Time Frame for Nationally Determined Contributions', WRI Working Paper (2 December 2019) <https://perma.cc/EL6M-Z3H9>.

[97] Sebastian Oberthür and Hermann E Ott, *The Kyoto Protocol: International Climate Policy for the 21st Century* (Springer 1999) 197ff.

[98] Glen P Peters and others, 'Rapid Growth in CO2 Emissions after the 2008–2009 Global Financial Crisis' (2011) 2 Nature Climate Change 2, 4.

deviation up to 15 per cent around the five-year commitment-period average.[99] Again, a decade later, responses to the Covid-19 pandemic led to temporary emission reductions in many countries, thus facilitating compliance with the Doha Amendment and the Cancun pledges—and, for the Netherlands, with the judgment in *Urgenda*[100]—in ways that could not have been anticipated.

Economic factors can facilitate the achievement of a mitigation outcome, but they can also conceivably hinder it. A state's rapid economic development, for instance, could challenge its ability to achieve a predetermined target relating to territorial emissions.[101] Mitigation action can be vulnerable to sector-specific events as well as geopolitical circumstances which influence the production of relevant goods and services (eg copper, uranium, or electronic chips) or international trade in such goods and services (eg 2022 sanctions against Russia's energy exports).

Other important uncertainties are associated with the speed of innovation and deployment in relation to technologies that facilitate climate change mitigation (eg renewable energy production and storage) and with the success of policies aimed at promoting these new technologies.[102] For instance, the capacity of a state to reduce GHG emissions from road vehicles depends in part on the development and deployment of new technologies (eg electrical cars), which is influenced not just by its own national policies but also by the efforts of other states to promote such technologies.[103] Last but not least, a country's GHG emissions depend inevitably on its population—more individuals use more electricity and drive more cars—which may be affected in unexpected ways, for instance due to changes in fertility rates, life expectancy, or international migration. The combination of all these factors makes it virtually impossible for a state (especially a small one) to be confident of its ability to achieve a predetermined mitigation outcome a decade or more later, especially if this outcome must be achieved only by regulating emissions within its own territory.

[99] See the compilations of national reports on UNFCCC, 'True-Up Period Information Report by the Secretariat' (2015) <https://perma.cc/MZX4-3EAQ>, showing, for instance, that Estonia's 2009 emissions were 15 per cent lower than its 2008–12 average, while the 2008 emissions of Lithuania and Romania were 14 per cent higher than in the period average.

[100] See Zhu Liu and others, 'Near-Real-Time Monitoring of Global CO2 Emissions Reveals the Effects of the COVID-19 Pandemic' (2020) 11 Nature Communications 5172; John M Reilly, J-H Henry Chen, and Henry D Jacoby, 'The COVID-19 Effect on the Paris Agreement' (2021) 8 Humanities and Social Sciences Communications 16; Corinne Le Quéré and others, 'Fossil CO_2 Emissions in the Post-COVID-19 Era' (2021) 11 Nature Climate Change 197.

[101] See Andries F Hof and others, 'Global and Regional Abatement Costs of Nationally Determined Contributions (NDCs) and of Enhanced Action to Levels Well below 2°C and 1.5°C' (2017) 71 Environmental Science & Policy 30.

[102] See Howard Kunreuther and others, 'Integrated Risk and Uncertainty Assessment of Climate Change Response Risks' in Ottmar Edenhofer and others (eds), *Climate Change 2014: Mitigation of Climate Change: Working Group III Contribution to the Fifth Assessment Report of the Intergovernmental Panel on Climate Change* (CUP 2014) 158.

[103] Opinion of Mr Stéphane Hoynck, Advocate General of the Conseil d'Etat, on *Grande-Synthe v France* (1 July 2021), ECLI:FR:CECHR:2020:427301.20201119, No 427301, 10.

4. The Effectiveness of Obligations of Conduct

a) The perceived ineffectiveness of obligations of conduct

A frequent assumption in the literature on international climate law is that obligations of conduct are somehow less effective than obligations of result.[104] In particular, the fact that the Paris Agreement imposes an obligation of conduct with regard to the implementation of NDCs[105] has generally been viewed as a weakness of the treaty, based precisely on an assumption that obligations of conduct are something less than obligations of result.[106]

It needs repeating that, notwithstanding whether an obligation is an obligation of conduct or an obligation of result, it is a (binding) obligation. In this regard, the Tribunal in *Indus Waters Kishengenga* observed that a provision, albeit 'worded in "best endeavours" terms', could be 'obligatory and not merely aspirational in nature'.[107] And Dinah Shelton highlighted that, '[f]rom the perspective of international responsibility, it does not matter whether the obligation is one of conduct or one of result, because a breach of either duty can be considered a wrongful act'.[108]

The gist of the criticism of obligations of conduct is that they are less effective because they do not guarantee the realization of the outcome. Thus, Rajamani and Brunnée rightly observe that 'since Parties do not have an obligation of result in relation to the NDCs, a party could fall short of its NDC without the consequences that attach to breaches of a legal obligation under the law of state responsibility'.[109] Similarly, the ILC noted with regard to the protection of the atmosphere that, 'where significant adverse effects materialize, that does not automatically constitute a failure of due diligence'.[110] A state would not be in breach of its obligation of conduct, even if the objective is not achieved, as long as the party has taken appropriate measures.

[104] See eg Christine Bakker, 'The Paris Agreement on Climate Change: Balancing "Legal Force" and "Geographical Scope"' (2015) 15 Italian YB Intl L 299, 307; Daniel Bodansky, 'The Paris Climate Change Agreement: A New Hope?' (2016) 110 AJIL 288, 295; Harald Winkler, 'Mitigation' in Daniel Klein and others (eds), *The Paris Agreement on Climate Change: Analysis and Commentary* (OUP 2017) 146; Daniel Bodansky, Jutta Brunnée, and Lavanya Rajamani, *International Climate Change Law* (OUP 2017) 231; Meinhard Doelle, 'Assessment of Strengths and Weaknesses' in Daniel Klein and others (eds), *The Paris Agreement on Climate Change* 378; Peter Lawrence and Daryl Wong, 'Soft Law in the Paris Climate Agreement: Strength or Weakness?' (2017) 26 RECIEL 276; James Crawford, 'The Current Political Discourse Concerning International Law' (2018) 81 MLR 1, 21.

[105] Paris Agreement (n 4) art 4(2), second sentence.

[106] See Lavanya Rajamani, 'Ambition and Differentiation in the 2015 Paris Agreement: Interpretative Possibilities and Underlying Politics' (2016) 65 ICLQ 493, 497; Crawford, 'The Current Political Discourse' (n 104) 21; Jutta Brunnée, 'Procedure and Substance in International Environmental Law' (2019) 450 RdC 9, 194, characterizing the general commitments under the UNFCCC as 'non-binding', seemingly on the ground that they do not require states to 'achieve [an] emission goal'.

[107] *Indus Waters Kishenganga (Pakistan/India)*, Partial Award (18 February 2013), 31 RIAA 55, ¶372.

[108] Dinah Shelton, 'Equitable Utilization of the Atmosphere: A Rights-Based Approach to Climate Change?' in Stephen Humphreys (ed), *Human Rights and Climate Change* (CUP 2009) 122.

[109] Lavanya Rajamani and Jutta Brunnée, 'The Legality of Downgrading Nationally Determined Contributions under the Paris Agreement: Lessons from the US Disengagement' (2017) 29 JEL 537, 542.

[110] ILC, 'Atmosphere' (n 53) commentary on guideline 3, ¶6.

Yet, this scenario, while not impossible, is rather unlikely. The obligation to take appropriate measures towards the objective of the NDC, under Article 4(2) of the Paris Agreement, is a continuing obligation: these measures must be adjusted if unforeseeable circumstances so require. Economic growth can substantially affect the ability of a state to achieve its NDC without additional measures; yet, under the most likely scenarios, it would also enable the state to implement additional measures by making use of its increased revenues generated as a result of this growth. Crucially, the Paris Agreement does not require its parties to limit themselves to territorial measures. If the state is unable to implement such measures at home, it should also be able to make use of the international transfer of mitigation outcomes under the relevant procedures established by the Paris Agreement.[111] A rapid economic growth would normally enable a national government to spare additional financial resources, if not to achieve immediate emission reduction within its territory, then to purchase mitigation outcomes from other countries.

Thus, scenarios where unforeseeable extraneous factors would prevent a party from achieving its NDC despite its best endeavour and the availability of international transfers of mitigation outcomes would be rather exceptional. A plausible example would be Japan's situation in 2011, following the Tōhoku earthquake and tsunami, the Fukushima nuclear disaster, and the state's decision to shut down multiple nuclear power plants, which led to a sudden fallback on fossil fuels at a time where the state could certainly not spare many resources to finance mitigation action overseas.[112] A situation of warfare could be another plausible scenario. Such scenarios may (but would not necessarily) coincide with circumstances precluding wrongfulness, such as *force majeure*, which would excuse non-compliance even with an obligation of result.[113] All in all, Bodansky rightly notes that the difference between an obligation of conduct and an obligation of result under the Paris Agreement 'appears small, since the test of whether a state has implemented its NDC might be seen as whether it has achieved its NDC'.[114]

b) The relative strengths of obligations of conduct

As generally understood in the civil law tradition, obligations of conduct are not necessarily less effective than obligations of result.[115] Suggestions to the contrary, in the climate law literature, tell only one part of the story: while there are circumstances where an obligation of result requires more than an obligation of conduct does, there are also circumstances where the opposite is true. A state could be found in breach of its obligation of conduct based on its failure to take appropriate

[111] Paris Agreement (n 4) art 6(2), 6 (4).
[112] See generally David Cyranoski, 'Japan Considers Nuclear-Free Future' (2012) 486 Nature 15.
[113] See ILC, 'State Responsibility' (n 23) arts 23–25.
[114] Bodansky, 'A New Hope?' (n 104), 304.
[115] See André Tunc, 'La distinction des obligations de résultat et des obligations de diligence' (1945) 1 Juris-Classeur Périodique 449; Combacau (n 22) 194, 196.

measures even if, somehow, the objective had been met. To revert to a classic example, a medical doctor may have breached their obligation of conduct by failing to give an appropriate treatment to their patient even if the patient miraculously recovered on their own (eg by luck or thanks to the intervention of another doctor).[116] The breach of an obligation of conduct can be identified even when it has not caused any harm.[117]

This observation has two important implications. One is that it confirms the applicability of the principle of prevention to climate change mitigation by refuting a potential objection. The objection is that a state (or at least a small one), acting alone, cannot effectively prevent harm through climate change mitigation because the causes of climate change are largely beyond its control. Therefore, the objection goes, a state does not have an obligation to take measures aimed at harm prevention. Chapter III argued that this objection is invalid because a tiny contribution to a very large objective is not necessarily insignificant and, in any case, states have an obligation to cooperate to achieve together what they cannot achieve individually.[118] At any rate, it now appears that this objection must be rejected because the ability of the debtor to achieve the outcome is not an essential element to an obligation of conduct—it is sufficient for the debtor to have some influence on the likelihood of the outcome. Notwithstanding its ability to secure the avoidance of harm, the state must take measures within its power to try to avoid such harm, as far as there is a plausible theory that its efforts may not be vain. This plausible theory, in the case of climate change mitigation, is based perhaps most convincingly on international cooperation: if other states follow the same reasoning, harm will be significantly mitigated.

The notion that obligations of conduct are applicable notwithstanding the likelihood of success is supported by the ICJ's judgment in *Bosnian Genocide*. Serbia submitted that, even if it had adopted a different course of action, it may not have been able to prevent the genocide in Srebrenica. The Court, however, held that this objection was 'irrelevant to the breach of the obligation of conduct in question'.[119] This is because, as the Court highlighted, 'the possibility remain[ed] that the combined efforts of several States, each complying with its obligation to prevent, might have achieve the result—averting the commission of genocide—which the efforts of only one State were insufficient to produce'.[120] Likewise, even though a state is unable to prevent 'dangerous' anthropogenic climate change on its own, it must nevertheless try, hoping that other states will cooperate, as they must. On the other

[116] See Combacau (n 22) 194; Wolfrum (n 13) ¶92. For obvious reasons, such cases are rarely brought to courts in civil action.

[117] Yann Kerbrat, 'Obligations procédurales et obligations de fond en droit international des dommages transfrontieres' in Ioannis Prezas (ed), *Substance et procédure en droit international public: Dialectique et influences croisées* (Pedone 2019) 14.

[118] See 109–110.

[119] *Genocide (Bosnia v Serbia)* (n 30) ¶430.

[120] Ibid.

hand, a difference with the obligation to prevent a genocide is that the achievement of the objective of climate change mitigation is more gradual and linear: any state can be sure to achieve some mitigation outcome, and thus to contribute to the prevention of global environmental harm, notwithstanding what other states do.

Another, more practical implication of characterizing a mitigation obligation as an obligation of conduct is that the assessment of compliance with this obligation can take place much earlier than the assessment of compliance with an obligation of result. Finding a breach of an obligation of result normally requires a retrospective determination that the result has not been achieved. With regard to mitigation action, this finding would, in principle, only be made once information on GHG emissions have been reported and ascertained.[121] By contrast, noncompliance with an obligation of conduct can take place in vivo, based on evidence of what the state *is doing*—without awaiting the result of what the state *has done*.

A case in point is the ICJ's Advisory Opinion on the immunity from legal process of Param Cumaraswamy, a Special Rapporteur of the UN Commission on Human Rights. Several lawsuits had been filed in Malaysia against Mr Cumaraswamy and, at the time of the Opinion, Malaysian courts had not yet reached their final decisions on the admissibility of the case. Malaysia argued that its obligation under the Convention on the Privileges and Immunities of the United Nations was 'an obligation of result', thus suggesting that no breach could be ascertained before a decision of a domestic court on the admissibility of the lawsuits.[122] The Court, however, construed the Convention as the source of an obligation of conduct, requiring the state to take appropriate steps to secure Mr Cumaraswamy's immunity. As such, it found that Malaysia had breached this obligation because the national government had failed to inform judges of the Secretary-General's finding that Mr Cumaraswamy was entitled to immunity.[123]

c) Illustrations

This relative strength of an obligation of conduct is of particular relevance with regard to quantified mitigation commitments. This can be illustrated by contrasting the examples of Canada under the first commitment period of Kyoto Protocol and the United States in the first few years after the entry into force of the Paris Agreement.

QERLCs, under the Kyoto Protocol, were defined as obligations of result:[124] as such, no breach of a QERLC could be constituted before the end of the commitment

[121] But see Opinion of Mr Stéphane Hoynck, Advocate General of the Conseil d'Etat, on *Grande-Synthe v France* (19 November 2020), ECLI:FR:CECHR:2020:427301.20201119, No 427301, English translation <https://perma.cc/9Y88-VY5T> 18.

[122] *Immunity of a Special Rapporteur* (n 29) ¶58; Verbatim Record of Public Sitting on 8 December 1998 in *Immunity of a Special Rapporteur* (n 29), CR 98/16, 23, 27. See also Convention on the Privileges and Immunities of the United Nations (13 February 1946, in force 17 September 1946) 1 UNTS 15, art 22.

[123] *Immunity of a Special Rapporteur* (n 29) ¶¶62, 67(2)(a).

[124] See above at 192.

period or demonstrated before the completion of subsequent years-long reporting and review processes.[125] This deficiency benefitted Canada which, for years, had failed to take appropriate measures to achieve its QERLC, but was nevertheless able to avoid any breach of its substantive commitment. Canada's national communications made no mystery of its failure to implement measures aimed at limiting and reducing its emissions in order to achieve its target.[126] As such, if the Kyoto Protocol had created an obligation of conduct, a breach would have been constituted during the first years of the commitment period. In reality, however, Canada could avoid both a breach of its obligation of result and a finding of non-compliance under the Protocol's compliance mechanism—which would otherwise have been merely a matter of time[127]—by withdrawing from the Kyoto Protocol with effect two weeks before the end of the commitment period.[128]

Consider now the situation of the United States under the Trump administration. The United States decided to suspend the implementation of multiple national measures on climate change mitigation in 2017,[129] even though its withdrawal from the Paris Agreement would only become effective in 2020.[130] If the Paris Agreement had created an obligation of result for the United States to achieve its NDC, like the Kyoto Protocol did with regard to QELRCs, it would not have precluded the course of action taken by the United States. A breach of this hypothetical obligation of result would only have been constituted in 2025, the year in which the United States was to achieve the mitigation objective defined by its NDC—by then, however, the withdrawal would have become effective, which could have reduced both the prospects of a finding of non-compliance and its relevance. In other words, the United States would have benefited from exactly the same deficiency of an obligation of result as Canada did under the Kyoto Protocol: the fact that a breach of an obligation of result can only be demonstrated retrospectively,

[125] Following the end of CP1 at the end of 2012, the process of verification took place until mid-2017.

[126] Canada, Third National Communication under the UNFCCC (2001) 83; Canada, Fourth National Communication under the UNFCCC (2006) 148; Canada, Fifth National Communication under the UNFCCC (2010) 64–65, revealing a major gap between Canada's projected emissions and its commitment. See also UNFCCC Secretariat, Compliance Committee, Report on the Twelfth Meeting of the Facilitative Branch Held on 22–23 October 2012, CC/FB/12/2012/3 (2012).

[127] Canada could theoretically have achieved compliance in extremis by purchasing emission units under the Protocol's flexibility mechanism.

[128] UNFCCC Secretariat, 'Report of the In-depth Review of the Fifth National Communication of Canada', FCCC/IDR.5/CAN (10 November 2011) ¶126. See also UNFCCC Secretariat, Compliance Committee, Report on the Eleventh Meeting of the Facilitative Branch Held on 6–8 February 2012, CC/FB/11/2012/2 (2012) ¶¶13–14, concluding that the Branch 'was seized of an early warning issue relating to Canada' after an expert review team's report had raised concerns 'in connection with potential non-compliance by Canada'.

[129] See Executive Order 13783 of 28 March 2017, Promoting Energy Independence and Economic Growth, 82 Fed Reg 16093; Donald Trump, Remarks on Paris Climate Agreement (1 June 2017); Sabin Center for Climate Law, 'The Climate Deregulation Tracker' (no date) <https://perma.cc/4W4U-5E5Z>.

[130] Paris Agreement (n 4) art 28(1)–(2).

when the result should have been achieved, rather than prospectively, when efforts should be made.

Instead, the Paris Agreement created an obligation of conduct, and there is little doubt that the inaction of the US federal government between 2017 and 2020 constituted a breach of this obligation.[131] This breach was constituted as soon as President Trump announced that 'the United States will cease all implementation of the nonbinding Paris accord', including by 'ending the implementation of the nationally determined contribution'.[132] This assessment is unaffected by the possibility that the United States may nevertheless achieve its 2025 objective (an outcome that became more likely following the 2020 presidential elections). This assessment is also unaffected by the efforts implemented by a coalition of subnational authorities, civil society organizations, and citizens to achieve the 2025 mitigation target despite the inaction of the federal government,[133] as this coalition was not acting on behalf of the United States as a state.

In particular, the spontaneous efforts implemented by US subnational authorities from 2017 to 2020 would likely not be considered as fulfilling the state's obligation of conduct, notwithstanding the possible effectiveness of these measures. This is because obligations of conduct have generally been interpreted as requiring the initiation of a dedicated plan of action by the highest-ranking state organs or agents with relevant functions and responsibilities. Thus, in *LaGrand*, the obligations of conduct imposed on the United States by an order of the ICJ—the obligation to 'take all measures at its disposal to ensure that Walter LaGrand is not executed'[134]—was construed as being directed towards the federal government, the state's governor, and the Supreme Court.[135] The Court's finding that the United States had breached this obligation was not based on the execution of Mr LaGrand (even though it was presumably directed and carried out by state agents), but on the failure of 'the various competent United States authorities to take all the steps they could have taken to give effect to the Court's Order'.[136] This obligation would have been breached even If the executioner had refused to perform the execution, inasmuch as higher national authorities had failed to take the necessary measures to prevent the execution. Likewise, in its Advisory Opinion regarding the immunity from legal process of Mr Cumaraswamy, the ICJ interpreted Malaysia's obligation as requiring the national government to convey information about the

[131] See Catherine Amirfar and Ashika Singh, 'The Trump Administration and the Unmaking of International Agreements Essay' (2018) 59 Harv Intl LJ 443, 447–48; Mohit Khubchandani, 'The United States and the Paris Agreement on Climate Change' (2019) 22 Max Planck Yrbk UN L 70; Mario Gervasi, 'On the United States' Decision to Withdraw from and Cease Implementation of the Paris Agreement on Climate Change' (2019) 18 Chinese JIL 777, ¶28.

[132] Trump (n 129).

[133] See '"We Are Still In" Declaration' (5 June 2017) <https://perma.cc/J64W-C7CK>.

[134] See *LaGrand* (n 28) ¶29.

[135] Ibid ¶¶112–14.

[136] Ibid ¶115.

immunity of a UN agent to national courts.[137] These decisions suggest that there needs to be a chain of instructions from the highest-ranking relevant organs to the operational organs in charge of implementing relevant measures—one which was clearly missing under the Trump administration.[138]

5. From Obligations of Conduct to Obligations of Result

The real shortcoming of obligations of conduct, as compared to obligations of result, relates not to their legal force or their stringency, but to the practicality of assessing compliance with them. In the case of an obligation of result, compliance is assessed simply based on the realization of the intended outcome. For instance, the compliance of a party to the Kyoto Protocol with its QERLCs can be determined on the basis of emissions data, which the party must report.[139] Once the tedious technical work of monitoring, reporting, and verifying a party's GHG emissions has been completed, the numbers provide an incontrovertible basis for an assessment of compliance.

By contrast, assessing compliance with an obligation of conduct involves a more perilous appraisal, not only of what the state has done, but also of what precisely it could and should have done.[140] Consider, for instance, the obligation of a party to the Paris Agreement to take the necessary measures to achieve its NDC.[141] To assess compliance with this obligation implies the assessment of a level of diligence required from the state. One may find some indications of this standard of conduct in the context in which the obligation arises: the Paris Agreement surely conveys a general sense of urgency[142] and highlights some principles and criteria to determine parties' respective obligations.[143] National circumstances are also relevant: a state would be expected to take effective action, for instance, if its projected emission trajectory presents major inconsistencies with the objective contained in its NDC. Yet, these indications are overly abstract; they do not provide a precise definition that can be used to determine objectively whether a state has exercised due diligence.

This difficulty of assessing compliance in no way affects the legal force of obligations of conduct—judges must decide cases before them even when the law

[137] *Immunity of a Special Rapporteur* (n 29) ¶62.

[138] To the contrary, the Trump administration attempted to prevent mitigation action by subnational authorities, including through litigation. See eg *US v California* (DC ED California, 2020) 444 FSupp3d 1181.

[139] See Kyoto Protocol (n 59) art 7(1).

[140] See *Alabama* (n 27) 129; Combacau (n 22) 195; Knox, 'The Myth and Reality' (n 38) 294; Study Group on Due Diligence (n 24) 1081–82; Viñuales 'Due Diligence' (n 26) 112.

[141] Paris Agreement (n 4) art 4(2), second sentence.

[142] See ibid Preamble ¶5 ('urgent threat'), art 2(1)(a) (1.5/2°C targets), art 4(1) ('as soon as possible').

[143] See ibid (n 4) art 4(3).

contains no clear and specific rules.[144] In practice, however, the difficulty of assessing compliance with an obligation of conduct could hinder its implementation. From the viewpoint of national governments, compliance achieves few political gains, and non-compliance entails little risk of naming and shaming if the implementation of the obligation cannot be readily assessed.

Yet, a central argument of this book is that there are some practical ways to assess compliance with obligations of conduct in a relatively objective and predictable manner. At the most basic level, this relies on logical inference. An obligation of conduct can be interpreted as requiring the implementation of appropriate steps; the failure of a state to take such steps can demonstrate (in relation to necessary measures) or suggest (in relation to other appropriate measures) non-compliance with its obligation of conduct.

The relevance of this method can be illustrated with the classic example of an obligation of conduct: that of a medical doctor. The doctor would presumably have failed to comply with their obligation to treat their patient to the best of their abilities (an obligation of conduct) if they did not ask the patient what they were suffering from, conduct an examination, and communicate their diagnosis and prescription, as any of these steps are among the appropriate measures that follow logically from their obligation of conduct. There may at times be valid reasons for the doctor not to carry out all these measures, but the doctor should be able to give these reasons when prompted to justify their omissions.

Thus, when the ICJ was prompted to assess compliance with an obligation of conduct, it often interpreted it as implying the implementation of specified steps. For instance, the Court held that, in order to ensure Mr Cumaraswamy's immunity from legal process, the Malaysian government had to inform its courts of the letter it received from the UN Secretary-General according to which Mr Cumaraswamy was entitled to immunity.[145] It also found that, in order to ensure that Mr LaGrand would not be executed during the Court's proceedings, the US federal government had to plead with the Governor of Arizona for a temporary stay.[146] In these two cases, the breach of the obligations of conduct was evidenced by the fact that the governments had no valid explanation for their omission to take these simple steps that they would have been strongly expected to take.

In light of these observations, the remainder of this chapter aims to determine the circumstances under which the failure of a state to take a specific step could be considered as prima facie evidence of its breach of general mitigation obligations. While the distinction between procedural and substantive obligations could be thought to be helpful in this regard, closer scrutiny in section B shows that it is not. Instead, section C suggests and defines an alternative concept of corollary

[144] See above at 14.
[145] *Immunity of a Special Rapporteur* (n 29) ¶62.
[146] *LaGrand* (n 28) ¶112.

duties, the breach of which is prima facie evidence of the breach of general mitigation obligations.

B. Substance and Procedure

Legal scholarship and judicial decisions have often posited a distinction between substantive and procedural obligations. This distinction is familiar in any legal field, but particularly so in international environmental law[147] (having featured prominently in two recent ICJ judgments)[148] and in the literature on international climate law.[149]

This distinction can be applied at different levels of analysis. In relation to general international law, the distinction that is made between substance and procedure is often a distinction between the primary norms from which disputes arise and the secondary norms on the settlement of these disputes.[150] By contrast, in the literature on international environmental and climate law, the distinction between substance and procedure is more often used to refer to two different types of primary norms.[151] It is this latter distinction—among primary norms—on which this section focuses.

This section presents a sceptical perspective on the relevance of this distinction at least for what concerns climate change mitigation. It highlights issues regarding the practicality and, overall, the effectiveness of this distinction. With regard to practicality, Brunnée has already pointed out that 'it is exceedingly difficult, if not impossible, to provide a general definition of what counts as substantive and procedural'.[152] What makes this distinction not just impractical but also ineffective is that there does not seem to be any actual consequences entailed by the characterization of a mitigation obligation as either procedural or substantive. The distinction between substance and procedure does not help interpret or apply mitigation obligations. In particular, the violation of a procedural obligation relating to climate change mitigation does not necessarily indicate the breach of a general obligation of conduct on climate change mitigation.

[147] See Brunnée (n 106) 89, noting the 'uncontroversial nature of the distinction between procedural and substantive obligations in the field'.

[148] See *Pulp Mills* (n 20) ¶¶67—266; *Certain Activities* (n 47) ¶¶101—20, 146—223.

[149] See Kerryn Anne Brent, 'The Certain Activities Case: What Implications for the No-Harm Rule?' (2017) 20 APJEL 28; Lavanya Rajamani, 'Innovation and Experimentation in the International Climate Change Regime' (2020) 404 RdC 9, 114–22, 198–204.

[150] See Elihu Lauterpacht, 'Principles of Procedure in International Litigation' (2011) 345 RdC 387; Robert Kolb, 'General Principles of Procedural Law' in Andreas Zimmermann, Christian Tomuschat, and Karin Oellers-Frahm (eds), *The Statute of the International Court of Justice: A Commentary* (3rd edn, OUP 2019) 966–8 (paras 3–4). A procedural norm could become a substantive norm if it becomes the object of a dispute.

[151] Brunnée (n 106) 94.

[152] Ibid 95.

On the other hand, this sceptical perspective does not deny the possibility, even the usefulness, of describing an obligation as either substantive or procedural as a broad qualification which can, for instance, be used to organize a survey of legal norms or an assessment of their evolution.[153] In other words, this distinction may play a role in what Ronald Dworkin calls a 'strategy of exposition' of the law, when one seeks to determine 'the most illuminating way in which the legal system of a nation may be described',[154] even if it is not eventually useful when interpreting or applying the law. By analogy, when introducing a norm, it may be useful to highlight its 'centrality', 'importance', or 'precision', even though these qualifications say nothing about the legal force, nature, or scope of the norm at issue.

1. The Distinction

The distinction between procedure and substance has often been made in judicial decisions and the doctrine on international environmental law. It is central, for instance, to the ICJ judgments in *Pulp Mills* and *Certain Activities*, which discuss separately questions of compliance with procedural and substantive obligations.[155] The basic idea behind this differentiation seems to be that, while procedural obligations relate to technical and practical details, a substantive obligation is concerned with something more 'foundational'.[156] In this broad sense, scholars have noted the multiplication of procedural norms in international environmental law. As early as 1997, Phoebe Okowa observed 'the proliferation of treaty instruments requiring States not so much to prevent environmental harm as to observe a number of discrete procedures before permitting the conduct of activities which may cause such harm'.[157] Koskenniemi suggested that states prefer to assume procedural rather than substantive obligations in environmental law as procedural obligations 'do not prejudice any State's substantive policy or its view about the limits of its own freedom of action'.[158]

Closer investigation reveals the difficulty of a clear-cut distinction between procedure and substance. For instance, the ICJ considered EIA as the object of (mainly) a substantive obligation in *Pulp Mills*,[159] but merely as a procedural obligation in *Certain Activities*.[160] More fundamentally, Duvic-Paoli observed that

[153] See Kerbrat (n 117) 11. See also Martti Koskenniemi, 'Peaceful Settlement of Environmental Disputes' (1991) 60 Nordic J Intl L 73; Phoebe N Okowa, 'Procedural Obligations in International Environmental Agreements' (1997) 67 BYBIL 275; Lavanya Rajamani and Jacqueline Peel, 'Reflections on a Decade of Change in International Environmental Law' (2021) 10 Cambridge Intl LJ 6, 17.

[154] Ronald Dworkin, *Taking Rights Seriously* (Bloomsbury 2013) 87.

[155] *Pulp Mills* (n 20) ¶282(1)–(2); *Certain Activities* (n 47) ¶¶101–12, 146–73.

[156] Brunnée (n 106) 93.

[157] Okowa (n 153) 275.

[158] Koskenniemi (n 153) 74.

[159] *Pulp Mills* (n 20) ¶¶116–21, 203–19.

[160] *Certain Activities* (n 47) ¶¶146–62.

the ICJ had 'failed to clarify the criteria used to assess whether an obligation falls under the substantive or procedural obligation category'.[161] Like Marion Lemoine-Schonne,[162] Brunnée noted that 'it is difficult to draw a bright line between the two categories'.[163] It is noteworthy that the conceptual confusion between procedure and substance may not be limited to international environmental law—in a broader context, Thomas Main noted that the line between substance and procedure had often been described 'with unflattering adjectives such as "vague", "unpredictable", "amorphous", "unresolvable", "unclear", "chameleon-like", "murky", "blurry", "hazy", and "superbly fuzzy"'.[164]

The Oxford English Dictionary provides a broad and a narrow definition of procedure. The broad definition refers to 'the performance of particular actions'.[165] Any positive obligation, by definition, implies the performance of particular actions, and what is commonly referred to as substantive obligation certainly includes negative as well as positive obligations. One could read the dictionary's definition as suggesting that a procedural obligation is an obligation to *achieve* a specified action, as opposed to obligations to make an earnest endeavour. Yet, this would merely replicate the dichotomy between obligations of result and obligations of conduct and would not reflect the distinction commonly made between procedure and substance: substantive obligations are generally understood to include obligations of result as well as obligations of conduct.

Therefore, the relevant definition must be the narrower one compiled in the Dictionary, in which procedure refers to 'the fact or manner of proceeding with any action, or in any circumstance or situation'.[166] This definition better coincides with the prevailing use of the concept of procedural obligation in international environmental and climate law. Rajamani, for instance, suggests that procedural obligations are those that 'require Parties to follow discrete procedures', whereas substantive obligations 'set standards for State behaviour'.[167] Procedures are accordingly viewed as merely instrumental: procedural obligations indicate a step to be taken, which is expected to go in the right direction, whereas substantive

[161] Leslie-Anne Duvic-Paoli, *The Prevention Principle in International Environmental Law* (CUP 2018) 204.

[162] Marion Lemoine-Schonne, 'Substance et procédure en droit international du climat' in Prezas (n 117) 24.

[163] Brunnée (n 106) 92.

[164] Thomas O Main, 'The Procedural Foundation of Substantive Law' (2009) 87 Wash U L Rev 801, 815.

[165] 'Procedure' in Oxford English Dictionary (online edn, OUP 2021).

[166] Ibid.

[167] Rajamani, 'Innovation and Experimentation' (n 149) 114. See also *Pulp Mills* (n 20) ¶77; Okowa (n 153) 275, suggesting that procedural obligations are 'instrumental, in so far as they are designed to ensure that the substantive decisions reached take into account anticipated environmental harm and the interests of those States likely to be affected'; Brunnée (n 106) 94, noting that 'the notion of procedure tends to be associated with the rules governing processes and remedies that allow for substantive law to be determined and enforced in practice'.

obligations directly indicate the direction that must be followed or the destination that must be reached.

In this view, in order to determine whether an obligation is procedural or substantive, one needs to identify and compare its object (ie what the obligation requires) and its purpose (ie the most direct goal that this obligation seeks to achieve). If the object and the purpose of an obligation are identical, the obligation is substantive. For instance, the Kyoto Protocol's QERLCs require emission reduction as a goal in itself: the object of this obligation coincides with its purpose. By contrast, if the object and the purpose of the obligation differ, the obligation is procedural. Thus, the Kyoto Protocol's obligations to report information are mainly instrumental—they aim to promote compliance with QELRCs, for instance by raising the political costs of non-compliance.[168] This assessment, however, may face practical difficulties. In particular, this test relies on an assessment of the purpose of an obligation, a matter on which well-informed observers can have reasonable disagreements.[169]

Following this approach, one could tentatively identify procedural obligations relating to climate change mitigation from various sources. Climate treaties, for instance, create procedural obligations regarding the reporting of information on GHG emissions[170] and the communication of intended mitigation action (eg NDCs).[171] Customary law includes procedural obligations on the conduct of EIAs,[172] notification and consultation,[173] and negotiation.[174] And mitigation obligations implied from human rights treaties may involve procedural requirements created by express treaty obligation (eg to adopt 'legislative measures')[175] and by interpretation of treaty provisions (eg obligation to implement various procedures to identify and regulate activities alleged to affect the enjoyment of human rights).[176] On the other hand, general mitigation obligations are substantive in nature, notwithstanding whether they arise from customary international law or from the UNFCCC, since their object coincides with their purpose. Likewise,

[168] Kyoto Protocol (n 59) art 7(1).

[169] By analogy, on the identification of the purpose of a treaty, see Isabelle Buffard and Karl Zemanek, 'The "Object and Purpose" of a Treaty: An Enigma?' (1998) 3 Austrian Rev of Intl & Eur L 311, 319; David S Jonas and Thomas N Saunders, 'The Object and Purpose of a Treaty: Three Interpretive Methods' (2010) 43 Vand J Trasnatl L 565, 577–80.

[170] See UNFCCC (n 2) art 12; Kyoto Protocol (n 59) art 7; Paris Agreement (n 4) art 13.

[171] UNFCCC (n 2) art 4(1)(b), art 4(2)(a); Paris Agreement (n 4) art 4(2), first sentence. See generally Crawford, 'The Current Political Discourse' (n 104) 21; Brunnée (n 106) 199.

[172] See *Pulp Mills* (n 20) ¶204.

[173] See *Certain Activities* (n 47) ¶¶104, 168.

[174] See *North Sea Continental Shelf (Germany/Denmark, Germany/Netherlands)*, Judgment (20 February 1969), [1969] ICJ Rep 3, ¶86; *Fisheries Jurisdiction (UK v Iceland)*, Judgment on Merits (25 July 1974), [1974] ICJ Rep 3, ¶75; *Gabčíkovo-Nagymaros* (n 20) ¶141; *Pulp Mills* (n 20) ¶146.

[175] ICESCR (n 25) art 2(1). See also *Shrestha v Prime Minister*, Order 074-WO-0283, decision 10210, NKP 61(3) (SC Nepal, 25 December 2018) <https://perma.cc/YM27-HH73>.

[176] See HRC, General Comment No 31 (n 79) ¶8; ECHR (Grand Chamber), *Nachova v Bulgaria*, App No 43577/98, 2005-VII ECHR 1, ¶16; *McCann v UK* (ECtHR, 13 May 2008) 47 EHHR 40, ¶161.

quantified commitments under the Kyoto Protocol are also, probably, substantive in nature.[177] By contrast, it is less clear whether commitments requiring a state to take measures corresponding with the programme it has communicated under the UNFCCC,[178] or with the NDC it has communicated under the Paris Agreement,[179] should be considered as creating procedural or substantive obligations. However, as subsection 2 shows, the question is immaterial because no consequences are associated with the distinction between substantive and procedural obligations.

2. An Ineffective Distinction

While scholarship and judicial decisions often distinguish between procedure and substance, it is far from clear what effects, if any, are supposed to be associated with this distinction.[180] A common assumption seems to be that procedural obligations are less demanding, less effective, or otherwise less important than substantive obligations.[181] Another plausible thesis is that the distinction could be relevant in assessing the consequences of the breach of an obligation, in particular with regard to reparation, although it is not clear what precisely these consequences would be. The following shows that no such effects are automatically associated with the characterization of an obligation as either procedural or substantive in nature.

Like substantive obligations, procedural obligations can be important, effective, and demanding. Thus, Sandrine Maljean-Dubois suggests that the obligation to communicate an NDC—a procedural obligation—is '[t]he central obligation of the Paris Agreement',[182] although this may be underestimating the importance of the substantive obligation to take the necessary measures to achieve NDCs. On the other hand, one could argue that the most onerous commitment originally assumed by developing country parties under the UNFCCC was their procedural obligation to monitor and report GHG emissions within their territory,[183] rather than their substantive obligation to adopt and implement mitigation action,[184] as

[177] However, one could suggest that the purpose of QERLCs was not so much to achieve (limited) mitigation outcomes during the commitment periods but rather to facilitate further negotiations through an initial show of good will on the part of developed states. Arguably, it was both.

[178] UNFCCC (n 2) art 4(2)(a).

[179] Paris Agreement (n 4) art 4(2), second sentence.

[180] See generally Kerbrat (n 117) 14; Lemoine-Schonne (n 162); Brunnée (n 106) 106–14.

[181] See Main (n 164) 811; Sebastian Oberthür and Lisanne Groen, 'Hardening and Softening of Multilateral Climate Governance towards the Paris Agreement' (2020) 22 J Envtl Policy & Planning 801, 803.

[182] Sandrine Maljean-Dubois, 'The Paris Agreement: A New Step in the Gradual Evolution of Differential Treatment in the Climate Regime?' (2016) 25 RECIEL 151, 157. See also Lavanya Rajamani, 'Integrating Human Rights in the Paris Climate Architecture: Contest, Context, and Consequence' (2019) 9 Climate Law 180, 197.

[183] UNFCCC (n 2) art 4(1)(a).

[184] Ibid art 4(1)(b). But see Farhana Yamin and Joanna Depledge, *The International Climate Change Regime: A Guide to Rules, Institutions and Procedures* (CUP 2004) 175.

the latter, when interpreted in light of the state practice of the early 1990s, did not impose a high standard of conduct.[185] While the relative importance of procedural obligations in these climate treaties certainly has to do with the lack of substantive obligations, they may achieve far more than unambitious substantive obligations. In the broader context of international environmental law, Judge Christopher Greenwood rightly noted in a separate opinion in *Pulp Mills* that the characterization of international environmental law obligations as procedural 'should not be taken as in any way minimizing their importance ... a breach of these procedural obligations is a serious matter'.[186]

Likewise, there is no reason to believe that procedural and substantive obligations can be implemented through different mechanisms. Rosa Fernández Egea observed that compliance mechanisms established by environmental treaties tend to focus on procedural obligations rather than on substantive ones.[187] While this may often be true, nothing prevents the inclusion of substantive obligations within the scope of such mechanisms. In fact, the compliance mechanisms created under the Kyoto Protocol and the Paris Agreement may allow, under certain circumstances, a review of compliance with substantive obligations.[188] Likewise, the distinction between procedure and substance is not directly relevant to determining the rules that international courts and tribunals apply or the conditions in which the responsibility of a state can be invoked for an internationally wrongful act.[189] The law on international responsibility does not differentiate between substance and procedure when defining a breach of an international obligation as a constituent element of an internationally wrongful act.[190] Crawford noted unambiguously that 'substantive obligations and procedural obligations will be treated in the same manner for the purposes of establishing responsibility'.[191] Thus, in principle, the obligation of a state responsible for an internationally wrongful act 'to make full reparation for the injury caused by the internationally wrongful act'[192] applies in the same way to substantive and procedural obligations.

[185] See Vienna Convention on the Law of Treaties (23 May 1969, in force 27 January 1980) 1155 UNTS 331, art 31(3)(c).

[186] *Pulp Mills* (n 20) Separate Opinion of Judge Greenwood, ¶9.

[187] Rosa M Fernández Egea, 'State Responsibility for Environmental Harm, "Revisited" within the Climate Change Regime' in Sandrine Maljean-Dubois and Lavanya Rajamani (eds), *La mise en œuvre du droit international de l'environnement, Implementation of International Environmental Law* (Martinus Nijhoff 2011) 388.

[188] Decisions 27/CMP.1, 'Procedures and Mechanisms Relating to Compliance under the Kyoto Protocol' (9–10 December 2005) FCCC/KP/2005/8/Add.3, 92, Annex §V.4(a); 20/CMA.1, 'Modalities and Procedures for the Effective Operation of the Committee to Facilitate Implementation and Promote Compliance Referred to in Article 15, Paragraph 2, of the Paris Agreement' (15 December 2018) FCCC/PA/CMA2018/3/Add.2, 59, Annex ¶20 (on the basis of a submission by the party concerned).

[189] ILC, 'State Responsibility' (n 23) art 2.

[190] Ibid.

[191] James Crawford, *State Responsibility: The General Part* (CUP 2013) 232. See also above at 198.

[192] ILC, 'State Responsibility' (n 23) art 31.

Yet, a hypothesis worth considering is that the distinction between procedure and substance may be relevant when assessing the injury caused by an internationally wrongful act and, consequently, when determining the content of the obligation to make reparation. The obligation to provide full reparation must 'wipe out all the consequences of the illegal act and reestablish the situation which would, in all probability, have existed if that act had not been committed',[193] but it must not 'give the injured State more than it would have been entitled to if the obligation had been performed'.[194] If an injury is financially assessable, it must be repaired through restitution or compensation; if it is not, it can only consist in satisfaction (eg a declaratory relief).[195] One could suggest that the breach of a procedural obligation cannot cause a financially assessable injury and, as such, that reparation for the breach of a procedural obligation would necessarily be limited to satisfaction.

Some support to this hypothesis can be found in five ICJ judgments. The first three judgments relate to breaches of the procedural obligation of states parties to the Vienna Convention on Consular Relations, when arresting or detaining citizens of another state party, to inform them of their right to consular assistance.[196] In *LaGrand*, and again in *Avena*, the ICJ found the United States in breach of this obligation and consequently under a secondary obligation to make reparation. As to the form of reparation, however, the Court did not find it necessary for the United States to pay compensation or to annul the convictions or sentences;[197] instead, the United States was only required to 'allow review and reconsideration of the conviction[s] and sentence[s]'.[198] Subsequently, in *Jadhav*, the Court found Pakistan responsible for a similar breach of the Vienna Convention on Consular Relations and it rejected India's claim for the annulment of Mr Lagrand's conviction and sentence, considering that a procedure of review and reconsideration would be an appropriate remedy for the breach of Pakistan's procedural obligation.[199] The Court justified its findings on purely factual grounds: it saw no reason to presume that the deprivation of consular assistance had had any effect on the convictions or sentences.[200] Nevertheless, one could see these judgments as suggesting that the reparation for the breach of a procedural obligation would normally be limited to procedural remedies, rather than compensation.

In two other judgments on international environmental law, the ICJ came closer to making an explicit link between the procedural nature of the obligation that

[193] *Factory at Chorzów (Germany v Poland)*, Judgment on Merits (13 September 1928), PCIJ Rep Series A No 17, 47. See generally ILC, 'State Responsibility' (n 23) art 31.

[194] ILC, 'State Responsibility' (n 23) commentary on art 34, ¶3.

[195] Ibid arts 36(2); 37(1); commentary on art 37, ¶3.

[196] Vienna Convention on Consular Relations (24 April 1963, in force 19 March 1967) 596 UNTS 261, art 36(1)(b).

[197] *Avena and Other Mexican Nationals (Mexico v US)*, Judgment (31 March 2004), [2004] ICJ Rep 12, ¶117. In *LaGrand*, Germany had withdrawn its compensation claim. See *LaGrand* (n 28) ¶¶10, 125.

[198] *LaGrand* (n 28) ¶128(7); *Avena* (n 197) ¶153(9).

[199] *Jadhav (India v Pakistan)*, Judgment (17 July 2019) [2019] ICJ Rep 418, ¶138.

[200] *Avena* (n 197) ¶122; *Jadhav* (n 199) ¶136.

had been breached and the limitation of reparation to satisfaction. First, in *Pulp Mills*, the Court found that Uruguay had breached several procedural obligations under the Statute of the River Uruguay when approving the construction of industrial facilities without notifying Argentina.[201] Argentina submitted that Uruguay's obligation to repair should take the form of restitution—namely, through the dismantlement the facilities.[202] Uruguay protested that there would be a 'striking disproportion' between 'the purpose of the rule breached' and an order to dismantle the facilities.[203] The Court agreed with Uruguay that neither restitution nor compensation would be appropriate forms of reparation for the breach of these obligations,[204] asserting that a 'finding of wrongful conduct by Uruguay in respect of its *procedural obligations* per se constitutes a measure of satisfaction for Argentina'.[205] By contrast to *LaGrand* and *Avena*, the Court in *Pulp Mills* thus highlighted the procedural nature of the obligation in question, even though it did not expressly justify its conclusion on this basis. The Court employed a similar reasoning—and maintained a similar ambivalence—in *Certain Activities* where, after holding that Costa Rica had breached its procedural obligation to carry out an EIA prior to the construction of a road,[206] it rejected Nicaragua's request for restitution and compensation on this basis.[207]

In none of these cases did the Court exclude the possibility that the breach of a procedural obligation could cause financially assessable injury that would create obligations of restitution or compensation. In fact, even when the Court characterized obligations as procedural, it did not seem to attach any legal effect to this qualification. Thus, Judge Donoghue noted in a separate opinion in *Certain Activities* that she did not 'find it useful to draw distinctions between "procedural" and "substantive" obligations, as the Court has done'.[208] As will appear in section C, this distinction between procedure and substance has distracted from a more useful distinction, in relation to the application of an obligation of conduct, between discrete obligations and corollary duties.

C. Corollary Duties

This section outlines a method to test compliance with an obligation of conduct by identifying duties that are the corollaries of the obligation at issue. These corollary duties relate to the necessary or otherwise appropriate measures that a debtor

201 *Pulp Mills* (n 20) ¶¶111, 122.
202 Ibid ¶270.
203 Ibid ¶271.
204 Ibid ¶¶275–76.
205 Ibid ¶269 (emphasis added).
206 *Certain Activities* (n 47) ¶162.
207 Ibid ¶226.
208 Ibid Separate Opinion of Judge Donoghue, ¶9.

must take to comply with her obligation of conduct. Non-performance of a corollary duty demonstrates, or at least suggests, the breach of the obligation of conduct from which this duty derives. This method could be used to test a state's compliance with its obligations of conduct on climate change mitigation—including the general mitigation obligations arising from the UNFCCC and customary international law, the more specific obligation to implement NDCs under the Paris Agreement, or even the mitigation obligations that can be implied from human rights and environmental treaties.

The emphasis in this section is on the methodology and its reflections in judicial practice. Subsection 1 explains further how corollary duties can be identified and how they can be used to test compliance with obligations of conduct. Subsection 2 shows that the ICJ in *Pulp Mills* and *Certain Activities* first appeared to identify corollary duties but, in a bizarre logical twist, did not find that the breach of these corollary duties demonstrates the breach of the obligation of conduct from which they were derived. This inconsistency, it is argued, is closely linked to the Court's misguided attempt to rely on a distinction between procedural and substantive obligations instead of a distinction between discrete obligations and corollary duties. Subsection 3 contrasts these two judgments with the arbitral award in *South China Sea* and the practice of human rights institutions, which view the breach of corollary duties as evidence of non-compliance with the obligations from which these duties are derived. Subsection 4 discusses the applicability and significance of this test with regard to general mitigation obligations. This section preludes to a comprehensive survey of corollary duties on climate change mitigation in Chapter VII.

1. A Test of Compliance with Obligations of Conduct

A method to assess a state's compliance with its general mitigation obligations relies on the identification of corollary duties. Corollary duties are initially identified based on a descending reasoning—as a direct logical implication of an obligation of conduct—followed by a test of compatibility with general state practice (ie an element of ascending reasoning). By contrast, ascending reasoning plays a more central role in the identification of a discrete obligation.[209]

A corollary duty may—but does not have to—coincide with a discrete obligation. For instance, monitoring GHG emissions is a discrete commitment under a provision of the UNFCCC,[210] but it is also arguably a corollary of general mitigation obligations inasmuch as monitoring GHG emissions is an indispensable prerequisite for national mitigation action. The existence of a discrete obligation

[209] See 91.
[210] UNFCCC (n 2) arts 4(1)(a), 12(1).

provides some support to the inference of the corollary duty by confirming its likely compatibility with state practice.

The distinction between discrete obligations and corollary duties has important implications, in particular under the law of state responsibility, with regard to the scope of the obligation of a state responsible for a wrongful act 'to make full reparation for the injury caused by [that] act'.[211] If the discrete obligation is narrow and procedural in nature, its breach will probably not lead to a financially assessable injury; as such, the reparation will usually be limited to satisfaction.[212] By contrast, the breach of a corollary duty—even if narrow and procedural—suggests the breach of the obligation of conduct from which it originates, which would entail secondary obligations of restitution or compensation. For instance, the failure of a state to monitor GHG emissions could imply far greater remedies if it is construed as evidence of a breach of the state's general mitigation obligations than if it is viewed merely as the breach of a discrete procedural obligation.[213]

The distinction between discrete obligations and corollary duties does not overlap with any of the concepts introduced above—the differentiation between general and specific mitigation obligations,[214] the dichotomy between conduct and result,[215] or the distinction between procedure and substance.[216] For instance, climate treaties define *discrete* commitments that can be either general[217] or specific,[218] may require alternatively a conduct[219] or a result,[220] and could relate to substance[221] or procedure.[222] Corollary duties are more specific than the obligations from which they originate, but their specificity does not necessarily set them apart from discrete obligations. And neither are corollary duties necessarily procedural in nature,[223] nor are procedural obligations necessarily the corollary of other obligations.

The identification of corollary duties is instrumental to the judicial application of the obligations of conduct that form the backbone of international climate law. It is typically far easier to prove that a state has failed to take specific steps that

[211] ILC, 'State Responsibility' (n 23) art 31.

[212] See above at 212.

[213] This book does not discuss the nature of remedial obligations for the breach of a substantive obligation on climate change mitigation. On the possibility of reparation for breach of an obligation owed towards the international community as a whole, 'in the interest of the injured State or of the beneficiaries of the obligation breached', see generally ILC, 'State Responsibility' (n 23) art 48(2)(b). See also *Activities in the Area* (n 37) ¶180.

[214] See above at 183.

[215] See above at 185.

[216] See above at 206.

[217] UNFCCC (n 2) art 4(1)(b).

[218] Ibid art 5.

[219] Paris Agreement (n 4) art 4(2), second sentence.

[220] Kyoto Protocol (n 59) art 3(1).

[221] UNFCCC (n 2) art 4(1)(b).

[222] Paris Agreement (n 4) art 13(7).

[223] See generally *Certain Activities* (n 47) Separate Opinion of Judge Donoghue, ¶10.

are essential to complying with its obligation of conduct than it is to determine that, overall, the state has not implemented the requisite level of mitigation action. Assessing compliance with corollary duties may be the most convenient way, perhaps even the only realistic way, of testing a state's compliance with its general mitigation obligations.

On the other hand, this test only goes one way: it can demonstrate noncompliance with general mitigation obligations, but it cannot conclusively demonstrate compliance. One could question, from a theoretical perspective, whether an obligation of conduct can be entirely broken down into corollary duties that consist in obligations of result.[224] At any rate, it is practically impossible to make an exhaustive list of such corollary duties, many of which are highly context-specific. As such, one could not conclusively prove that a state has taken all the steps that are necessary or appropriate to implement its obligation of conduct. Yet, this limitation does not affect the relevance of this test, for instance in the context of litigation (whether before a national or international court), as the burden of proof would normally fall on the party claiming that the state has breached its obligation of conduct.[225]

2. Confusion in Two ICJ Judgments

In *Pulp Mills* and *Certain Activities*, the ICJ noted that some 'procedural' obligations were the logical implication of the obligation to prevent transboundary environmental harm. Yet, when finding a breach of these specific obligations, the Court did not conclude that the state had also violated its obligation of prevention. Thus, the Court failed to draw the logical consequences of a breach of what it had otherwise appeared to identify as corollary duties.

a) *Pulp Mills*

In *Pulp Mills*, Argentina claimed that Uruguay had breached its obligations under the Statute of the River Uruguay (a treaty) by authorizing the construction of industrial facilities. Argentina invoked a general 'obligation to take all necessary measures' to prevent transboundary environmental harm, along with more specific obligations requiring the conduct of an EIA, prior notification of the state likely to be affected, and consultation with that state.[226] The Court held that Uruguay

[224] See generally *Pulp Mills* (n 20) ¶78, rejecting the view that 'a party may fulfil its substantive obligations by complying solely with its procedural obligations'; Brunnée (n 106) 143, noting that 'due diligence imposes substantive … and procedural requirements … so that a State would not be acting diligently by meeting only the latter but not the former'.

[225] See *Maritime Delimitation in the Black Sea (Romania v Ukraine)*, Judgment (3 February 2009), [2009] ICJ Rep 61, ¶68.

[226] *Pulp Mills* (n 20) ¶22.

had failed to implement its specific obligations to inform and notify Argentina about its plans.[227] Nevertheless, the Court did not find any 'conclusive evidence' that Uruguay had failed to comply with its general obligation on the prevention of transboundary environmental harm.[228]

The Court heard Argentina's view that, within the Statute of the River Uruguay, 'the procedural obligations were intrinsically linked to the substantive obligations', so that 'a breach of the former entailed a breach of the latter'.[229] The Court appeared to agree with the premises of Argentina's submission. It acknowledged that the treaty reflected the substantive obligation of prevention by requiring states 'to act with due diligence' by adopting 'appropriate rules and measures' and exercising 'a certain level of vigilance in their enforcement'.[230] It also recognized that several provisions of the treaty, creating procedural obligations, were in fact identifying some of the measures 'necessary in order to fulfil the obligation of prevention'.[231] Yet, the Court did not recognize the logical implication of these observations—namely, that a breach of a procedural obligation would entail the breach of the obligation of which it is the corollary.[232]

This inconsistency was immediately brought to light by a joint dissenting opinion of Judges Awn Al-Khasawneh and Bruno Simma. As these two judges noted, 'the conclusion whereby noncompliance with the pertinent procedural obligations has eventually had no effect on compliance with the substantive obligations is a proposition that cannot be easily accepted'.[233] Indeed, a state cannot be thought to have complied with its general obligation to prevent transboundary environmental harm if it has not taken the necessary steps to prevent harm. But, like Argentina, Al-Khasawneh and Simma did not frame their comment on the basis of the right concepts. The judgment was inconsistent, not because it ignored the procedural nature of the obligations breached, but because it eluded their logical relation with the state's general obligation of prevention.

Thus, both the majority and the dissenting judges were misled by their reliance of an unhelpful distinction between procedure and substance.[234] Not all procedural obligations are corollary to an obligation of conduct: a procedural obligation may favour the realization of an objective which is not the object of a separate obligation. Using the confusion to its advantage, Uruguay rightly denounced 'the

[227] Ibid ¶¶111, 122.
[228] Ibid ¶265.
[229] Ibid ¶68.
[230] Ibid ¶197.
[231] Ibid ¶102. See also ¶¶115, 204.
[232] Ibid ¶78.
[233] Ibid, Dissenting Opinion of Judges Al-Khasawneh and Simma, ¶26. See also Yann Kerbrat and Sandrine Maljean-Dubois, 'La Cour internationale de Justice face aux enjeux de protection de l'environnement: Réflexions critiques sur l'arrêt du 20 avril 2010, Usines de pâte à papier sur le fleuve Uruguay (Argentine c. Uruguay)' (2011) 115 RDGIP 39.
[234] The only relation that the Court could find between procedural and substantive obligations was an enigmatic 'functional link'. See *Pulp Mills* (n 20) ¶79.

belief that the breach of procedural obligations *necessarily* entails the breach of substantive ones'.[235] In fact, Al-Khasawneh and Simma's view was fully compatible with Uruguay's contentions since the dissenting judges only referred to '*pertinent* procedural obligations'[236]—but they did not identify the condition under which (procedural) obligations should be considered as 'pertinent'. By focusing on the artificial distinction between procedural and substantive obligations, the Court and its members missed the important difference that had to be made between discrete obligations and corollary duties. If the procedural obligations which had been breached were the corollaries of the obligation of prevention, the Court should also have found a breach of the latter.

b) *Certain Activities*

Five years after *Pulp Mills*, the ICJ's judgment in *Certain Activities* decided on claims brought by Costa Rica against Nicaragua and by Nicaragua against Costa Rica, where each state argued (among other things) that the other had breached customary international law obligations relating to the protection of the environment. On the one hand, the Court dismissed Costa Rica's claim that Nicaragua had breached either its procedural or substantive obligations when dredging a river.[237] On the other hand, the Court accepted Nicaragua's claim that Costa Rica had breached some of its obligations when authorizing the construction of a road. More specifically, the Court found that Costa Rica had 'failed to comply with its obligation [under general international law] to evaluate the environmental impact of the construction of [a] road' before authorizing this project[238]—an obligation that the Court characterized as procedural. However, the Court rejected Nicaragua's claims, on this basis, that Costa Rica had breached its substantive obligation to prevent transboundary environmental harm.[239]

Thus, this decision is affected by the same logical inconsistency as *Pulp Mills*—but this inconsistency became only more obvious in relation to customary, rather than treaty, obligations. When reading a treaty, it is tempting (rightly or wrongly) to elude the problem of individuation of norms by merely assuming that to each provision corresponds a separate and independent norm. By contrast, when identifying customary norms, one is naturally led to consider the logical relations that bind the norms in a coherent legal system.[240]

The Court in *Certain Activities* relied on its prior finding, in *Pulp Mills*, of the existence of an obligation to conduct an EIA under customary international law. But

[235] Ibid ¶74 (emphasis added). See also ¶78.

[236] Ibid, Dissenting Opinion of Judges Al-Khasawneh and Simma, ¶26 (emphasis added).

[237] *Certain Activities* (n 47) ¶¶112, 120.

[238] Ibid ¶173.

[239] Ibid ¶217.

[240] See Orfeas Chasapis-Tassinis, 'Customary International Law: Interpretation from Beginning to End' (2020) 31 EJIL 235, 247–49.

while quoting its conclusion in *Pulp Mills*,[241] the Court did not retrace its own reasoning leading to the identification of this obligation. In *Pulp Mills*, the Court had identified an EIA obligation from both ascending and descending reasoning. With regard to descending reasoning, the Court had noted that 'due diligence, and the duty of vigilance and prevention which it implies, would not be considered to have been exercised' if a party planning a project likely to cause transboundary environmental harm did not undertake an EIA.[242] This statement strongly suggests that the obligation to conduct an EIA is a corollary of the obligation of prevention so that a breach of the former would constitute a breach of the latter. Reliance on this reasoning should have precluded the Court in *Certain Activities* from identifying a breach of the EIA duty without also suspecting a violation of the obligation of prevention from which the EIA duty is an integral part.

The Court came to a different conclusion because it confused obligations of conduct and of result. The Court cited its judgment in *Pulp Mills* to characterize the obligation of prevention as, essentially, an obligation of conduct.[243] Accordingly, to determine whether Costa Rica has complied with this obligation, the Court should have determined whether the state had taken appropriate steps; its failure to implement an EIA suggested that it had not. Instead, the Court's assessment of compliance with the obligation of prevention focused on the result—the Court questioned whether Costa Rica was 'responsible for any transboundary harm',[244] that is, whether any such harm had occurred as the result of Costa Rica's conduct. Thus, the Court dismissed Nicaragua's claim that Costa Rica had breached this obligation on the ground that 'Nicaragua ha[d] not proved that the construction of the road caused it significant transboundary harm'.[245] As such, while the Court rightly identified the obligation of prevention as an obligation of conduct, it wrongly applied it as if it was an obligation of result.

This inconsistency did not go unnoticed. In her separate opinion, Judge Donoghue observed that '[t]he requirement to exercise due diligence, as the governing primary norm, is an obligation of conduct that applies to all phases of a project'.[246] She insisted that the question whether a state had complied with its obligation of prevention 'must be answered in light of the particular facts and circumstances', including 'specific procedural or substantive rules that give effect to this due diligence obligation'.[247] Thus, she suggested that the conduct of an EIA ought to be construed essentially as a corollary to the obligation of prevention.[248] Likewise,

[241] *Certain Activities* (n 47) ¶104. See also ¶153.

[242] *Pulp Mills* (n 20) ¶204.

[243] *Certain Activities* (n 47) ¶104, citing *Pulp Mills* (n 20) ¶101. See also *Pulp Mills* (n 20) ¶187; *Activities in the Area* (n 37) ¶111; *South China Sea* (n 26) ¶944.

[244] *Certain Activities* (n 47) ¶113. See also ¶174.

[245] Ibid ¶217. See also ¶¶196, 207, 211, 213, 216.

[246] Ibid Separate Opinion of Judge Donoghue, ¶9.

[247] Ibid (Donoghue) ¶10.

[248] Ibid (Donoghue) ¶¶13–15.

Judge John Dugard highlighted that '[t]he principle of prevention is ... implemented through a number of specific obligations, which include the obligation to carry out an environmental impact assessment'.[249] And Judge Hisashi Owada emphasized that conducting an EIA 'is one important constituent element of the process that emanates from the international obligation of States to act in due diligence to avoid or mitigate significant transboundary harm, rather than a separate and independent obligation standing on its own under general international law'.[250]

By and large, scholars have also been critical of the Court's reasoning. Brunnée noted the paradox that, 'although the very point of the [harm prevention] rule is to require appropriate steps to prevent significant transboundary harm, the ICJ has not treated a failure to take the requisite steps ... as sufficient to give rise to a violation of the substantive duty'.[251] Kerryn Anne Brent, likewise, highlighted the conflict between the general understanding of the obligation of prevention as a due diligence obligation and its result-oriented interpretation by the Court.[252] Duvic-Paoli remarked that, 'if prevention, as an obligation of due diligence, can only be fulfilled when a number of other procedural obligations are met, it is difficult to understand how a breach of a procedural obligation does not automatically lead to a breach of prevention'.[253]

3. The Identification of Corollary Duties in Other Judicial Decisions

Other judicial and quasi-judicial bodies have interpreted and applied obligations of conduct more consistently by identifying their corollary duties. In particular, the arbitral award in *South China Sea* construed provisions on environmental protection in UNCLOS as defining a general obligation and some of its corollaries. Thus, when it found breaches of the corollary duties, the Tribunal rightly concluded that the general obligation had also been breached. An analogy can also be drawn with judicial practice in international human rights law, where regional courts and international treaty bodies have long relied on the identification and assessment of compliance with corollary duties to interpret and apply obligations of conduct.

a) *South China Sea*

The arbitral tribunal in *South China Sea* had to decide on fifteen submissions brought by the Philippines against China on the application of various aspects of UNCLOS, including its provisions on the protection of the marine environment.

[249] *Certain Activities* (n 47) Separate Opinion of Judge *Ad hoc* Dugard, ¶8.
[250] *Certain Activities* (n 47) Separate Opinion of Judge Owada, ¶18.
[251] Brunnée (n 106) 102 (emphasis removed).
[252] Brent (n 149) 54–55.
[253] Duvic-Paoli (n 161) 337.

In this regard, the final award clearly distinguishes between general and specific obligations on environmental protection.

On the one hand, the Tribunal characterized the obligation of states 'to protect and preserve the marine environment'[254] under Article 192 of UNCLOS as a 'general obligation ... the content of which is informed by other provisions of Part XII and other applicable rules of international law'.[255] Among these other norms, the Tribunal emphasized that the interpretation of this general obligation was to be informed by the customary obligation on the prevention of transboundary environmental harm.[256] Consistently with the ICJ's judgments in *Pulp Mills* and *Certain Activities*, the tribunal characterized this general obligation of prevention as an 'obligation of conduct' requiring states to exercise 'due diligence', including by 'adopting appropriate rules and measures' and by exercising 'a certain level of vigilance in their enforcement and the exercise of administrative control'.[257]

On the other hand, the tribunal highlighted that other treaty provisions on the protection of 'rare or fragile ecosystems' (Article 194(5) of UNCLOS), on cooperation (Articles 123 and 197), and on EIA (Article 206), among others, provide additional details to the general obligation under Article 192.[258] The Tribunal found that these specific obligations existed both as discrete obligations and as an integral part of the general obligation under Article 192—as part of the 'appropriate rules and measures' that states must take to comply with their due diligence obligation.[259]

The Tribunal decided the case consistently with its finding that these specific obligations were corollaries of the general obligation of prevention. With regard to contentious fishing activities in the Scarborough Shoal and the Second Thomas Shoal, the Tribunal found that China had failed 'to take necessary measures to protect and preserve the marine environment with respect to the harvesting of endangered species from [a] fragile ecosystems'.[260] It characterized this omission not only as a breach of the (relatively) specific obligation under Article 194(5), but also as a breach of the general obligation of prevention under Article 192.[261] Similarly, with regard to construction activities in the Spratly Islands, the Tribunal found that China had failed to cooperate and to communicate an EIA, in breach of specific obligations under Articles 123, 197, and 206 of UNCLOS and, at the same time, of the general obligation under Article 192.[262] The Tribunal thus found that China had

[254] United Nations Convention on the Law of the Sea (10 December 1982, in force 16 November 1994) 1833 UNTS 3, art 192.
[255] *South China Sea* (n 26) ¶941.
[256] Ibid.
[257] Ibid ¶944. See also *Sub-Regional Fisheries Commission* (n 51) ¶131.
[258] *South China Sea* (n 26) ¶¶946–47.
[259] Ibid ¶¶941, 944–45.
[260] Ibid ¶964.
[261] Ibid.
[262] Ibid ¶993.

breached its general obligation of prevention, not on grounds of the existence of environmental harm per se, but because the state had failed to take the steps it was required to take to prevent this harm, as established by other, more specific treaty provisions.[263]

b) Interpretation of positive human rights obligations

The *South China Sea* award contributed to clearing up the confusion that *Pulp Mills* and *Certain Activities* had created in the legal doctrine on international environmental law about the possibility of testing compliance with an obligation of conduct based on its corollary duties. By contrast, no such confusion seems to exist in contemporary international human rights law, where it is common judicial practice to rely on corollary duties in order to assess compliance with obligation of conduct. Thus, the obligation of states to protect human rights—an obligation of conduct[264]—has routinely been applied through its corollary duties.

Like environmental treaties, human rights treaties contain some provisions that define some corollaries of the general obligation of conduct they create. For instance, the ICCPR requires each state party to 'take the necessary steps … to adopt such legislative or other measures as may be necessary to give effect to' civil and political rights.[265] Most corollary duties, however, were inferred through interpretation. Thus, the Human Rights Committee interpreted the 'general legal obligation imposed on States Parties' to the ICCPR as including the obligation to 'adopt legislative, judicial, administrative, educative and other appropriate measures'.[266] More specific corollary duties were identified in relation to each right. For instance, the Human Rights Committee interpreted the general obligation to protect the right to life as implying, among other things, that states parties must 'disband irregular armed groups … and reduce the proliferation of potentially lethal weapons to unauthorized individuals', while also taking measures 'to prevent, investigate, punish and remedy' crime.[267]

Likewise, the ECtHR interpreted a general obligation of conduct to 'secure … rights and freedoms'[268] as implying more specific steps. For instance, with regard to the right to life, the Court held that states must 'put … in place effective criminal-law provisions to deter the commission of offences against the person backed up by law-enforcement machinery for the prevention, suppression and

[263] Ibid ¶1203(B)12–13.

[264] See above at 194.

[265] International Covenant on Civil and Political Rights (16 December 1966, in force 23 March 1976) 999 UNTS 171, art 2(2). See also ICESCR (n 25) art 2(1); American Convention on Human Rights (22 November 1969, in force 18 July 1978) 1144 UNTS 123 ('Pact of San José') art 2; African Charter on Human and Peoples' Rights (27 June 1981, in force 21 October 1986) 1520 UNTS 217, art 1.

[266] HRC, General Comment No 31 (n 79) ¶7.

[267] HRC, General Comment No 36, 'Article 6: Right to Life', CCPR/C/GC/36 (3 September 2019) ¶21.

[268] Convention for the Protection of Human Rights and Fundamental Freedoms (4 November 1950, in force 3 September 1953) 213 UNTS 221, art 1.

sanctioning of breaches of such provisions'.[269] More specifically, when a crime has been committed, the Court found that states must conduct effective official investigations[270] and, when criminals can be identified, prosecute them, if only to demonstrate the state's 'capacity to enforce criminal law against those who unlawfully took the life of another'.[271] A state's failure to implement any of these corollary duties is characterized as a breach of the general obligation of conduct.[272]

Thus, judicial and quasi-judicial practice in human rights law exemplifies how corollary duties help to test compliance with obligations of conduct. Whether a state has complied with the requisite standard of conduct is a question that can hardly be answered in abstract terms. It is far more practical to test a state's compliance with its obligation of conduct by assessing whether it has breached such corollary duties. As such, the process of adjudication in human rights law orbits around the identification of corollary duties. Many of these duties are highly contextual: for instance, a state's obligation to investigate only arises when a crime has been committed, and prosecution cannot be an obligation unless investigations were successful. This method holds great promise for the application of general mitigation obligations.

4. Identifying Corollary Duties on Climate Change Mitigation

Like the obligation to prevent transboundary environmental harm and the obligation to protect human rights, general obligations on climate change mitigation are obligations of conduct that can be interpreted as implying corollary duties. The failure of a state to implement any of these corollary duties suggests that the state is in breach of its general mitigation obligations. The following provides some preliminary thoughts on the way this concept could help interpret general mitigation obligations.

Corollary duties are identified mainly through a descending reasoning—as a direct logical implication from the obligation of mitigation—whose conclusions must be broadly compatible with general state practice. For instance, the ICJ in *Pulp Mills* identified transboundary EIA as a logical implication of the obligation of prevention.[273] The award in *South China Sea* illustrates the possibility of interpreting a specific treaty obligation (eg Article 206 of UNCLOS, defining an EIA obligation) as confirming a corollary duty derived from another, more general

[269] *Osman v UK*, App No 23452/94, 1998-VIII ECHR, ¶115.

[270] See *McCann* (n 176) ¶161.

[271] *Nachova* (n 176) ¶160.

[272] See eg *Ireland v UK*, Application No 5310/71, Series A No 25 (1978) 2 EHRR 25, ¶238. See generally Nina Le Bonniec, *La procéduralisation des droits substantiels par la Cour européenne des droits de l'homme: Réflexion sur le contrôle juridictionnel du respect des droits garantis par la Convention européenne des droits de l'homme* (Pedone 2017).

[273] *Pulp Mills* (n 20) ¶204.

treaty obligation (Article 192, defining the obligation of prevention).[274] The interpretation of human rights law highlights the relevance of any consensus among the state parties as to the corollary duties that can be inferred from a general obligation.[275]

In a similar manner, climate treaties and separate customary norms may reflect corollaries to general mitigation obligations, although not every treaty or customary obligation relevant to climate change mitigation is necessarily a corollary duty.[276] For instance, states may accept obligations relating to the way they implement mitigation action—such as obligations to promote public participation or gender equality in climate action—which are not instrumental to the mitigation of climate change and, as such, cannot constitute corollary duties of general mitigation obligations. Moreover, even when a corollary duty coincides with a discrete obligation, it is not necessarily the case that the two norms have the same nature and scope. By analogy, while the ICJ found that the Espoo Convention provided some evidence of a customary EIA requirement, it declined to defer entirely to the provisions of the Espoo convention when interpreting the scope or content of this customary requirement.[277] The nature and scope of a corollary duty are limited to what states have generally accepted as the corollary of the general obligation, even when states have also agreed to discrete obligations that are more demanding.

Chapter VII shows that corollary duties require relatively far-reaching action on climate change mitigation. As part of its duty of vigilance,[278] each state must assess its contribution to global GHG emissions. Having identified climate change as a cause of concern and having recognized each state's common but differentiated responsibility, every state must also develop a strategy on climate change mitigation and it must cooperate in good faith with other states, most obviously by refraining from any attempt to free-ride on their efforts. The UNFCCC commitment for all parties to 'formulate [and] implement ... programmes containing measures to mitigate climate change'[279] thus highlights the requirement that states complete successive steps: a state is in breach of the obligation expressly defined by this provision if it does not formulate a programme or if, having formulated a programme, it does not implement it.

Subsequent international negotiations have prompted states to accept more specific commitments which provide benchmarks to assess their compliance with

[274] See n 262.

[275] See *Stübing v Germany*, App No 43547/08 (ECtHR, 12 April 2012) <http://hudoc.echr.coe.int/eng?i=001-110314> ¶¶61, 66.

[276] For instance, obligations relating to climate change adaptation are obviously not corollary of general mitigation obligations.

[277] *Pulp Mills* (n 20) ¶205; *Certain Activities* (n 47) ¶104. See also *Activities in the Area* (n 37) ¶149. See generally Convention on Environmental Impact Assessment in a Transboundary Context (25 February 1991, in force 10 September 1997) 1989 UNTS 309 ('Espoo Convention').

[278] *Gabčíkovo-Nagymaros* (n 20) ¶140; *Pulp Mills* (n 20) ¶¶197, 204.

[279] UNFCCC (n 2) art 4(1)(b). See also ibid art 4(2)(a).

general mitigation obligations. Under the Kyoto Protocol, Annex I parties consented to an obligation of result 'amenable to objective performance assessment, irrespective of whether or not a party acted diligently in attempting to meet its target'.[280] By contrast, the Paris Agreement requires each party to communicate NDCs and to take appropriate measures to achieve their objectives.[281] Under the Paris Agreement, the mandatory adoption of NDCs and the voluntary communication of long-term strategies lead each party to develop its narrative about what it plans to do and aims to achieve.[282] Notwithstanding the legal force of these communications, any inconsistencies between this narrative and the party's actual conduct should raise doubts about its compliance with its general mitigation obligations. The failure of a state to fulfil its own targets may not provide definitive evidence of a breach of general mitigation obligations, but it could nevertheless create a presumption and, thus, reverse the burden of proof on the state to justify that it has taken appropriate measures.

Conclusion

States have a variety of obligations relating to the mitigation of climate change. A distinction is often drawn between procedural and substantive obligations. While this distinction may be a useful way to describe obligations and account for the evolution of the law, it does not provide an effective tool for their interpretation. The dichotomy between obligations of result and of conduct is more helpful. General mitigation obligations are obligations of conduct: states must make an endeavour to mitigate climate change, but they are not directly bound to achieve any specific outcome.

Assessing compliance with such obligations is difficult because it requires a detailed and rather subjective appraisal of the state's requisite level of mitigation action. In practice, assessing compliance with obligations of conduct often relies on the identification of corollary duties and on an assessment of compliance with these corollary duties. For instance, a state breaches its general mitigation obligation if it fails to formulate a strategy on climate change mitigation or if, having formulated a strategy, it fails to act consistently with it. Corollary duties are not purely procedural: a state would be in breach of its general mitigation obligation if the steps it is implementing were not commensurate to its target or if the target itself were not in line with the state's understanding of its requisite level of mitigation action.

280 Brunnée (n 106) 196.
281 Paris Agreement (n 4) art 4(2).
282 Ibid art 4(19).

Chapters VI and VII explore two alternative ways of applying general mitigation obligations. Chapter VI looks in more detail at the possibility of addressing the issue frontally by quantifying a state's requisite level of mitigation action; it shows that this approach, while perhaps not entirely impossible, would involve an extraordinary degree of judicial discretion. Chapter VII builds more directly on the method outlined in this chapter: it seeks to identify some of the main duties that are the corollary to general mitigation obligations so that non-performance of these duties indicates a breach of general mitigation obligations.

VI

The Requisite Level of Mitigation Action

Introduction

The contents of states' obligations on climate change mitigation have frequently been described in hyperbolic terms. For instance, decisions of the Conference of the Parties to the UNFCCC (COP) have called on each state to implement its '*highest possible* mitigation efforts',[1] while Boyd suggested that states 'must . . . dedicate *the maximum available financial and material resources*' to climate change mitigation.[2] By analogy, the International Court of Justice (ICJ) in *Pulp Mills* described the obligation of prevention as a state's obligation 'to use *all the means at its disposal* in order to avoid activities' causing transboundary environmental harm.[3] The African Commission on Human and Peoples' Rights even suggested that states ought to take 'reasonable *and other* measures' to prevent environmental harm affecting human rights.[4]

In truth, states are certainly not required to take unreasonable measures, nor can they be expected to invest 'all' the resources they command on the sole objective of preventing transboundary environmental harm or mitigating climate change. Rather than climate change mitigation at all costs, general mitigation obligations are to be interpreted as obligations of due diligence, requiring states to exercise

[1] Decisions 1/CP.17, 'Establishment of an Ad Hoc Working Group on the Durban Platform for Enhanced Action' (11 December 2011) FCCC/CP/2011/9/Add.1, 2, ¶7; 2/CP.18, 'Advancing the Durban Platform' (8 December 2012) FCCC/CP/2012/8/Add.1, 19, ¶5; 1/CP.20, 'Lima Call for Climate Action' (14 December 2014) FCCC/CP/2014/10/Add.1, 2, ¶18; 1/CP.21, 'Adoption of the Paris Agreement' (12 December 2015) FCCC/CP/2015/10/Add.1, 2, ¶105 (emphasis added). See also Paris Agreement (12 December 2015, in force 4 November 2016) (2016) 55 ILM 740, art 4(3); Decisions 1/CP.24, 'Preparations for the Implementation of the Paris Agreement and the First Session of the Conference of the Parties Serving as the Meeting of the Parties to the Paris Agreement' (15 December 2018) FCCC/CP/2018/10/Add.1, 2, ¶14; 1/CP.25, 'Chile Madrid Time for Action' (25 December 2019) FCCC/CP/2019/13/Add.1, 2, ¶10.

[2] David R Boyd, Report of the Special Rapporteur on the Issue of Human Rights Obligations Relating to the Enjoyment of a Safe, Clean, Healthy and Sustainable Environment, A/74/161 (2019) ¶70 (emphasis added). See also International Covenant on Economic, Social and Cultural Rights (16 December 1966, in force 3 January 1976) 993 UNTS 3, art 2(1).

[3] *Pulp Mills on the River Uruguay (Argentina v Uruguay)*, Judgment (20 April 2010), [2010] ICJ Rep 14, ¶101 (emphasis added). See also *Certain Activities Carried Out by Nicaragua in the Border Area (Costa Rica v Nicaragua) and Construction of a Road in Costa Rica along the San Juan River (Nicaragua v Costa Rica)*, Judgment on Merit (16 December 2015), [2015] ICJ Rep 665, ¶104; ILC, 'Draft Articles on Prevention of Transboundary Harm from Hazardous Activities' [2001] II(2) YBILC 146, art 3.

[4] Social and Economic Rights Action Center/Nigeria, Communication No 155/96 (African Commission of Human and Peoples' Rights, October 2001) ¶52 (emphasis added).

International Law Obligations on Climate Change Mitigation. Benoit Mayer, Oxford University Press. © Benoit Mayer 2022.
DOI: 10.1093/oso/9780192843661.003.0006

'reasonable care'[5] and to take the measures that are 'reasonably appropriate'.[6] The paradigm of a sustainable development reflects the idea that states must seek to strike a balance between climate change mitigation and other priorities relating for instance to other aspects of the protection of human rights, economic development, and environmental protection.[7] It is also broadly understood that the content of a state's mitigation obligation depends, among other things, on its national circumstances, in particular its responsibilities and capabilities.[8]

This chapter and Chapter VII explore two alternative methods to determine whether a state has complied with its mitigation obligations. This chapter confronts the problem head on: it explores the possibility of interpreting a state's mitigation obligation as requiring the state to implement a requisite level of mitigation action, which could be expressed, for instance, as a percentage of emission reduction that the state must achieve by a given time. More specifically, this chapter discusses the possibility of inferring a state's requisite level of mitigation action from international objectives, in particular the temperature targets of the Paris Agreement. Yet, this chapter shows that this approach runs into multiple legal and practical difficulties, making its adoption difficult, if not impossible. By contrast, Chapter VII approaches the question less directly but more effectively by identifying some of the steps that a state could be expected to take when complying with its general mitigation action—namely, the corollary duties of cooperation, vigilance, and consistency.

As obligations of conduct, general mitigation obligations require states to invest a certain *level of effort* with the view to regulating greenhouse gas (GHG) emissions. An obvious difficulty when applying these obligations, however, is that there is no simple and convenient way of measuring the level of effort put forth by a state. In principle, emission pricing (eg a carbon tax) would be a neat reflection of the intensity of a state's mitigation action, but emission pricing measures only apply to some emissions in some sectors and some countries,[9] and then often in conjunction with other regulations and incentives,[10] so that the explicit 'price' that may be

[5] Study Group on Due Diligence in International Law, 'Second Report on Due Diligence' (2016) 77 ILA Rep Conferences 1062, 1063.

[6] *Responsibilities and Obligations of States Sponsoring Persons and Entities with Respect to Activities in the Area*, Advisory Opinion (1 February 2011), [2011] ITLOS Rep 10, ¶120. See also Samantha Besson, 'La *due diligence* en droit international' (2020) 409 RdC 153, 269.

[7] See United Nations Framework Convention on Climate Change (9 May 1992, in force 21 March 1994) 1771 UNTS 107, art 3(4)–(5); Rio Declaration on Environment and Development (14 June 1992) A/CONF.151/26 (vol I) (1992) 31 ILM 874, Principles 1, 4.

[8] UNFCCC (n 7) art 3(1); Rio Declaration (n 7) principle 7. See also René Lefeber, 'Climate Change and State Responsibility' in Rosemary Rayfuse and Shirley V Scott (eds), *International Law in the Era of Climate Change* (EE 2012) 335; Lavanya Rajamani, 'Due Diligence in International Climate Change Law' in Heike Krieger, Anne Peters, and Leonhard Kreuzer (eds), *Due Diligence in the International Legal Order* (OUP 2020) 172.

[9] See World Bank, State and Trends of Carbon Pricing (2019).

[10] For instance, in addition to an emission trading scheme that covers energy production, the EU imposes energy efficiency standards that increase the effort that its citizens must make to reduce these GHG emissions. See Directive 2012/27 of 25 October 2012, OJ 2012 L315/1.

imposed on GHG emissions is neither a comprehensive nor a reliable indication of mitigation efforts. Another difficulty is that an instrument that puts a price on emissions may not have the exclusive objective of mitigating climate change—fuel taxes, for instance, may aim to reduce local air pollution or traffic congestion—so that a carbon price may not reliably reflect the efforts that a state puts forth specifically on climate change mitigation.

Some economic studies seek to assess carbon prices that are implicit in a state's policies, but such implicit prices can only be determined through complex economic analysis, which inevitably relies on debatable attribution of intent—for instance, the assumption that a technical regulation on the thermal insulation of buildings aims to mitigate climate change rather than, for instance, reducing local air pollution or ensuring energy security.[11] Thus, implicit carbon price analyses do not provide a practicable way to assess whether a state is applying a level of diligence consistent with that of other states.

As such, the assessment of a state's requisite level of mitigation action typically consists not in an assessment of the level of effort that the state must make, but in an assessment of the result that the state is expected to achieve. Thus, the assessment of a state's mitigation action, whether in the context of litigation or as independent reviews by civil society associations, usually refers to the percentage of emission limitation or reduction that the state ought to achieve by a given time. Although this analysis focuses on results, rather than on conduct, it is not necessarily inconsistent with the nature of general mitigation obligations as obligations of conduct as long as all relevant national circumstances are duly taken into account to determine what the level of effort that the state is required to implement can be expected to achieve. In other words, the analysis typically consists in inferring a corollary duty of result from a state's general mitigation obligation in light of relevant circumstances. As these circumstances may change over time, a judicial assessment of a state's requisite level of mitigation action may need to be revisited, especially when the analysis is applied to determining a target to be achieved many years later.

One of the most prominent examples of such an analysis is to be found in the judgment of the Supreme Court of the Netherlands in *Urgenda*. Having interpreted the state's human rights obligation as requiring it to comply with its customary obligation on climate change mitigation,[12] the Court upheld the interpretation of this customary obligation as requiring the state to achieve at least 25 per cent emission reduction by 2020 compared with 1990 levels.[13] Civil society organizations have been seeking similar decisions in other cases which they brought to domestic courts, regional human rights courts, and international treaty bodies[14] but

[11] See Claudio Marcantonini and A Denny Ellerman, 'The Implicit Carbon Price of Renewable Energy Incentives in Germany' (2015) 36 Energy J 205, 206–07.

[12] Issues with this part of the judgment are discussed above at 161.

[13] *Urgenda v Netherlands*, ECLI:NL:HR:2019:2007 (SC, 20 December 2019), English translation in (2020) 59 ILM 811.

[14] See generally 131.

so far with little success.[15] Beyond human rights law, the decision in *Urgenda* has inspired similar arguments based on domestic legal norms such as constitutional doctrines[16] or tort law.[17] All these cases, as Kim Bouwer noted, pursue the 'holy grail' of climate litigation: 'a high-stakes, high-profile and high-ambition action that seeks to solve many problems in one sexy, heroic action'.[18] In concrete terms, these cases are typically based on a claim that states must implement mitigation action beyond what they have expressly committed to through their nationally determined contributions (NDCs). Thus, notwithstanding their different legal bases or even whether they are brought to domestic or international jurisdictions (or quasi-jurisdictions), these cases raise similar questions inasmuch as they invite a judge to determine the level of mitigation action that a state must implement.

The judgment in *Urgenda* and the submissions in other cases follow a similar structure. First, a collective objective on climate change mitigation is identified—typically by reference to the temperature targets (1.5/2°C) that states have agreed upon in the Paris Agreement.[19] Second, burden-sharing criteria are used to determine what this collective objective means for a specific state at a particular time. However, the two steps of this reasoning are plagued by serious flaws. For one, states have neither expressly nor impliedly agreed to an obligation to adopt or implement mitigation action that is consistent with a specific interpretation of the temperature targets. Overall, it is doubtful whether the temperature targets and the burden-sharing criteria that states have agreed upon are sufficiently specific to enable a meaningful and objective judicial determination of a state's requisite level of mitigation action. If this judicial determination is possible at all in the current

[15] The applicants in *Grande-Synthe*, *Neubauer*, and *Klimaatzaak* have achieved some success on similar submissions, but the Courts' emphasis has been on the internal consistency of the states' mitigation strategies rather than on the consistency of these strategies with the courts' assessment of the states' requisite level of mitigation action. See *Grande-Synthe v France* (Conseil d'Etat, 19 November 2020), ECLI:FR:CECHR:2020:427301.20201119; *Oxfam v France*, Application 1904967, Decision 44-008.60-01-02-02.R (Administrative Tribunal, Paris, 2 February 2021); *Neubauer v Germany*, 1 BvR 2656/18 (Federal Constitutional Court, 24 March 2021) <https://perma.cc/UJM6-QCCY>; *Klimaatzaak v Belgium*, case 2015/4585/A (French-Speaking Tribunal of First Instance of Brussels, 17 June 2021), English translation <https://perma.cc/68ZJ-2F96>; *Grande-Synthe v France* (Conseil d'Etat, 1 July 2021), ECLI:FR:CECHR:2021:427301.20210701.

[16] See eg *Environnement Jeunesse v Attorney General* [2021] QCCA 1871, 2021 CarswellQue 18893 (Quebec); *Juliana v US* (9th Cir, 2020) 947 F3d 1159; *La Rose v The Queen* [2020] FC 1008; *Misdzi Yikh v Canada* [2020] FC 1059; *Neubauer* (n 15); C-565/19 P, *Carvalho v Parliament*, ECLI:EU:C:2021:252 (CJEU, 25 March 2021); *Reynolds v State* (Circuit Court of Florida, 2020) No 2018-CA-819, 2020 WL 3410846; *Aji P v State* (Court of Appeal of Washington, 2021) 16 Wash. App. 2d 177, 480 P.3d 438; *Sagoonick v State* (Supreme Court of Alaska, 2022) 503 P.3d 777. *Neubauer* was the only one among these cases to be decided (partly) in favour of the plaintiffs.

[17] See eg *Milieudefensie v Royal Dutch Shell*, ECLI:NL:RBDHA:2021:5337 (DC The Hague, 26 May 2021), English translation <https://perma.cc/VKG6-TZ4A>; *Klimaatzaak* (n 15). But see also eg *American Electric Power Co v Connecticut* (2011) 564 US 410; *Smith v Fonterra* [2021] NZCA 552, [2022] NZRMA 65; *Minister for the Environment v Sharma* [2022] FCAFC 35. BC202201738.

[18] Kim Bouwer, 'The Unsexy Future of Climate Change Litigation' (2018) 30 JEL 483, 489. See also Kim Bouwer, 'Lessons from a Distorted Metaphor: The Holy Grail of Climate Litigation' (2020) 9 TEL 347.

[19] See Paris Agreement (n 1) art 2(1)(a).

state of climate law, it inevitably implies an unusual degree of judicial discretion on matters of major consequences for states' interests.

Section A shows that it would be difficult to determine whether a state acts consistently with collective objectives on climate change mitigation as both these objectives and related burden-sharing criteria remain ill defined. Moreover, section B argues that, under their most likely interpretation, mitigation obligations do not require states to adopt or implement mitigation action objectively consistent with these temperature targets, even though these targets are undeniably part of the context in which mitigation obligations are to be interpreted. In any case, section C explores the dilemma that a judge faces when tasked with determining a state's requisite level of mitigation action in the absence of a predetermined benchmark.

A. The Difficulty of Assessing the Consistency of National Action with Collective Objectives

It is often assumed that collective objectives on climate change mitigation—in particular, the temperature targets adopted in the Paris Agreement—could be used as a touchstone to determine each state's requisite level of mitigation action, for instance in the form of an emission budget.[20] However, this section shows that such analysis is hindered by the lack of specificity of mitigation objectives and the lack of agreement among states on burden-sharing criteria. On each of these two aspects, subsections 1 and 2 include reflections on the Court's reasoning in *Urgenda* and on pleadings in other, ongoing cases.

1. The Lack of Agreement on Collective Objectives

a) The gradual definition of a collective objective

States have sought to define a global objective on climate change mitigation, first with the adoption of the UN Framework Convention on Climate Change (UNFCCC) and later with the progressive definition of temperature targets. The 'ultimate objective' of the UNFCCC 'and any related legal instruments that the [COP] may adopt', as defined in its Article 2, 'is to achieve ... stabilization of [GHG] concentrations in the atmosphere at a level that would prevent dangerous

[20] The common reference to a 'carbon budget' ignores the non-negligible contribution of other GHGs to climate change. Another limitation of the budget approach (even when applied to all emissions) is that it eludes the importance of the timing of emission limitation—delaying emissions would allow more time for various physical, ecological, and social systems to adapt to climate change. See Joeri Rogelj and others, 'Estimating and Tracking the Remaining Carbon Budget for Stringent Climate Targets' (2019) 571 Nature 335; Bård Lahn, 'A History of the Global Carbon Budget' (2020) 11 WIREs Climate Change e636.

anthropogenic interference with the climate system'.[21] Thus, as Philippe Sands noted, the UNFCCC 'implicitly recognizes that some climate change is inevitable'.[22] In other words, climate change is construed as a crisis that must be mitigated, not as one that can be avoided entirely. The objective is to avoid an interference with the climate system that would be 'dangerous'.

Yet, the UNFCCC does not define what would constitute such 'dangerous' interference, and a broad range of interpretations is possible.[23] Is a 'dangerous' interference one that creates a risk for at least one individual, for a state, or for humankind as a whole? For a specimen, a species, or the global ecosystem? And what level of risk should be considered dangerous anyway? One could argue, for instance, that any interference with the climate system is dangerous by nature, all the more as not everything is known about the reaction of the climate system to such interference.[24] Surely, even an infinitesimal impact on the climate system is bound to affect at least some individuals and some animals and plants in some ways.

Following the adoption of the UNFCCC, the EU promoted the adoption of a more specific objective: holding the increase in global average temperature below 2°C.[25] In 2009, the Copenhagen Accord 'recognized the scientific view that the increase in global temperature should be below 2 degrees Celsius'.[26] Rather than merely a scientific finding, however, this target was inevitably the result of an inherently political decision, as it involved weighing the costs and benefits of mitigation action in light of values.[27] The Copenhagen Accord also introduced the idea that states should 'cooperate in achieving the peaking of global and national emissions as soon as possible'.[28] Finally, it called for 'consideration of strengthening the

[21] UNFCCC (n 7) art 2.

[22] Philippe Sands, 'The United Nations Framework Convention on Climate Change' (1992) 1 RECIEL 270, 272.

[23] David G Victor, *Global Warming Gridlock: Creating More Effective Strategies for Protecting the Planet* (CUP 2011) 5, noting that '"safety" is a product of circumstances and interests not just geophysics'.

[24] Ottmar Edenhofer and others, 'Summary for Policymakers' in Ottmar Edenhofer and others (eds), *Climate Change 2014: Mitigation of Climate Change: Working Group III Contribution to the Fifth Assessment Report of the Intergovernmental Panel on Climate Change* (CUP 2014) 5.

[25] See Samuel Randalls, 'History of the 2°C Climate Target' (2010) 1 WIREs Climate Change 598; Piero Morseletto, Frank Biermann, and Philipp Pattberg, 'Governing by Targets: Reductio Ad Unum and Evolution of the Two-Degree Climate Target' (2017) 17 Intl Envtl Agreements: Politics, Law & Economics 655.

[26] Copenhagen Accord of 18 December 2009, appended to Decision 2/CP.15, 'Copenhagen Accord' (18–19 December 2009) FCCC/CP/2009/11/Add.1, ¶1.

[27] See Reto Knutti and others, 'A Scientific Critique of the Two-Degree Climate Change Target' (2016) 9 Nature Geoscience 13, 13, noting that 'no scientific assessment has clearly justified or defended the 2°C target as a safe level of warming, and indeed, this is not a problem that science alone can address'. See also below at 269.

[28] Copenhagen Accord (n 26) ¶2. See also Decisions 1/CP.16, 'The Cancun Agreements: Outcome of the work of the Ad Hoc Working Group on Long-Term Cooperative Action under the Convention' (10–11 December 2010) FCCC/CP/2010/7/Add.1, 2, ¶6; 1/CP.18, 'Agreed Outcome Pursuant to the Bali Action Plan' (8 December 2012) FCCC/CP2012/8/Add.1, 3, ¶1; UNGA Res 68/212 'Protection of Global Climate for Present and Future Generations of Humankind (20 December 2013) ¶9.

long-term goal referencing various matters presented by science, including in relation to temperature rises of 1.5 degrees Celsius'.[29]

In 2010, the Cancun Agreements formally endorsed the 2°C target, noting that 'Parties should take urgent action to meet this long-term goal'.[30] It also highlighted 'the need to consider ... strengthening the long-term global goal ... in relation to a global average temperature rise of 1.5°C'.[31] Accordingly, the COP decided 'to periodically review the adequacy of [this] long-term global goal ... in the light of the ultimate objective of the Convention'.[32] The following year, COP17 used both targets as benchmarks for global mitigation action when '[n]oting with grave concern the significant gap between' what states had pledged to achieve by 2020 and 'aggregate emission pathways consistent with having a likely chance of holding the increase in global average temperature below 2°C or 1.5°C above pre-industrial levels'.[33] COP18 reaffirmed that parties would 'urgently work towards the deep reduction in global [GHG] emissions required to hold the increase in global average temperature below 2°C above pre-industrial levels and to attain a global peaking of global [GHG] emissions as soon as possible'.[34]

The first periodic review of the adequacy of the long-term global goal concluded at COP21 with the adoption of a new goal: 'to hold the increase in the global average temperature to well below 2°C above pre-industrial levels and to pursue efforts to limit the temperature increase to 1.5°C above pre-industrial levels'.[35] The Paris Agreement affirmed this objective[36] and further suggested that, to achieve it, parties should collectively 'reach global peaking of [GHG] emissions as soon as possible ... and ... undertake rapid reduction thereafter ... so as to achieve a balance between anthropogenic emissions by sources and removals by sinks of [GHGs] in the second half of this century'.[37] COP21 also noted that the national targets defined in intended NDCs did 'not fall within least-cost 2°C scenarios'.[38] A second periodic review of the adequacy of the long-term global goal should be concluded in 2022, but it is understood that its outcome 'will not result in an alteration or

[29] Copenhagen Accord (n 26) ¶12.

[30] Decision 1/CP.16 (n 28) ¶4.

[31] Ibid. See also ¶139; Decisions 2/CP.17, 'Outcome of the Work of the Ad Hoc Working Group on Long-Term Cooperative Action under the Convention' (11 December 2011) FCCC/CP/2011/9/Add.1, 4, third recital before ¶5, second recital before ¶32; 1/CP.18 (n 28) second recital before ¶79.

[32] Decision 1/CP.16 (n 28) ¶138. See also Decisions 1/CP.17 (n 1) ¶6; 2/CP.17 (n 31) ¶¶157–67; 1/CP.18 (n 28) ¶¶79–91.

[33] Decision 1/CP.17 (n 1) Preamble ¶3 (emphasis removed). See also Decisions 1/CP.18 (n 28) second recital before ¶4, third recital before ¶14; 2/CP.18 (n 1) Preamble ¶4; 1/CP.19, 'Further Advancing the Durban Platform' (23 November 2013) FCCC/CP/2013/10/Add.1, 3, Preamble ¶4; 1/CP.20 (n 1) Preamble ¶7; 1/CP.21 (n 1) Preamble ¶10; 1/CP.25 (n 1) ¶8.

[34] Decision 1/CP.18 (n 28) ¶1.

[35] Decision 10/CP.21, 'The 2013–2015 Review' (13 December 2015) FCCC/CP/2015/10/Add.2, 23, ¶4.

[36] Paris Agreement (n 1) art 2(1)(a).

[37] Ibid art 4(1).

[38] Decision 1/CP.21 (n 1) ¶17.

redefinition of the long-term global goal' agreed at COP21.[39] It will be followed by the first 'global stocktake' under the Paris Agreement, where the parties will 'assess the collective progress towards achieving the purpose of this Agreement and its long-term goals'.[40]

States have emphatically reaffirmed temperature targets in various other forums beyond the UNFCCC regime. The UN General Assembly first took note of the 2°C target adopted by the COP,[41] expressing 'great concern' for the lack of ambition in individual pledges towards 2020,[42] before acknowledging the enhanced objective defined by the Paris Agreement,[43] echoing the COP's assessment that initial NDCs 'are not sufficient' to achieve this objective.[44] Likewise, the Human Rights Council stressed the importance of achieving the temperature targets mentioned in the Paris Agreement on the ground that 'this would significantly reduce the risks and impacts of climate change'.[45] The temperature targets of the Paris Agreement have also been acknowledged or affirmed by the Conferences of the Parties to the Convention on Biological Diversity,[46] to the Ramsar Convention on Wetlands,[47] and to the World Heritage Convention.[48]

b) An incomplete political agreement

The temperature targets of the Paris Agreement are less evasive than the ultimate objective of the UNFCCC, but they remain extremely vague. Legal scholars have often affirmed that these temperature targets 'provide the basis for [the]

[39] Decision 5/CP.25, 'Scope of the Second Periodic Review of the Long-Term Global Goal under the Convention and of Overall Progress towards Achieving It' (15 December 2019) FCCC/CP/2019/13/Add.1, 26, ¶¶5, 7. See also Carl-Friedrich Schleussner and Claire L Fyson, 'Scenarios Science Needed in UNFCCC Periodic Review' (2020) 10 Nature Climate Change 272.

[40] Paris Agreement (n 1) art 14(1). See also Decision 19/CMA.1, 'Matters Relating to Article 14 of the Paris Agreement and Paragraphs 99–101 of Decision 1/CP.21' (15 December 2018) FCCC/PA/CMA/2018/3/Add.2, 53.

[41] See Res 68/212 (n 28) ¶9.

[42] See UNGA Res 70/205 (22 December 2015) Preamble ¶5.

[43] See UNGA Resolutions 71/228 (21 December 2016) A RES/71/228, ¶4; 72/219 (20 December 2017) ¶4; 73/232 (20 December 2018) ¶4; 74/219 (19 December 2019) ¶3; 75/217 (21 December 2020) ¶6.

[44] See Res 74/219 (n 43) ¶5.

[45] Human Rights Council Resolutions 38/4 (5 July 2018) A/HRC/RES/38/4, Preamble ¶9; 41/21 (12 July 2019) A/HRC/RES/41/21, Preamble ¶10; 44/7 (16 July 2020) A/HRC/RES/44/7, Preamble ¶10; 47/24 (14 July 2021) A/HRC/RES/47/24, Preamble ¶10.

[46] COP/CBD decision 14/5, 'Biodiversity and Climate Change' (Sharm El-Sheikh, 17–29 November 2018) Preamble ¶¶4, 7.

[47] See Convention on Wetlands of International Importance Especially as Waterfowl Habitat (2 February 1971, in force 21 December 1975) 996 UNTS 245 ('Ramsar Convention'); Conference of the Contracting Parties to the Ramsar Convention on Wetlands Res XIII.13, 'Restoration of Degraded Peatlands to Mitigate and Adapt to Climate Change and Enhance Biodiversity and Disaster Risk Reduction' (21–29 October 2018) ¶12.

[48] WHC Decision 41 COM 7, 'State of Conservation of the Properties Inscribed on the World Heritage List' (2017) WHC/17/41.COM/18, 8, ¶22; WHC Decision 42 COM 7 (2018) WHC/18/42.COM/18, 8, ¶29.

calculation'[49] of a global emission budget and emissions pathways, acknowledging only certain 'ranges of uncertainty'.[50] However, for the four reasons presented below, these targets are not accompanied with sufficient detail to define a valuable benchmark for global mitigation action. If a global emission budget is to be inferred from these temperature targets, the level of uncertainty associated with it will be such as to render it essentially meaningless.[51] Temperature targets indicate a direction of travel—they clearly imply that more mitigation action is needed—but not a destination point for international action on climate change mitigation.

First, there is no obvious way to make sense of a mitigation objective that is made up of not one but two different targets—and, as the global average temperature has already increased by an estimated 1.09°C above pre-industrial levels,[52] the difference between 1.5 and 2°C is substantial.[53] It is a tenet of treaty interpretation that treaty provisions are to be read 'in a way that gives meaning to all of them, harmoniously'[54]—a principle often referred to as the doctrine of effectiveness (*effet utile*) or by reference to the maxim *Ut res magis valeat quam pereat*.[55] Yet, it is unclear how an interpretation of the Paris Agreement's mitigation objective could make sense of both targets at the same time. Rajamani and Jacob Werksman have suggested that the objective is to achieve both targets,[56] but this would deprive the 2°C target of its meaning as its achievement is necessarily implied by the achievement of the 1.5°C target. An interpretation discarding the 1.5°C target is no more convincing as it would discard terms of the treaty. The nuanced phrasing of the Paris Agreement seems to suggest a distinction between an endeavour ('pursuing efforts' towards 1.5°C) and a result (2°C), but while such distinction between conduct and result can be made with regard to obligations, it does not readily make sense when applied to a collective objective that states, at any rate, will only endeavour to

[49] Jutta Brunnée, 'Procedure and Substance in International Environmental Law' (2019) 450 RdC 9, 198.

[50] Lavanya Rajamani and Jacob Werksman, 'The Legal Character and Operational Relevance of the Paris Agreement's Temperature Goal' (2018) 376 Philos Trans R Soc A 2016.0458, 5.

[51] See Glen P Peters, 'Beyond Carbon Budgets' (2018) 11 Nature Geoscience 378.

[52] Richard P Allan and others, 'Summary for Policymakers' in Valérie Masson-Delmotte and others (eds), *Climate Change 2021: The Physical Science Basis. Contribution of the Working Group I to the Sixth Assessment Report of the Intergovernmental Panel on Climate Change* (accepted version subject to final editing, IPCC 2021) §A.1.2.

[53] Myles Allen and others, 'Summary for Policymakers' in Valérie Masson-Delmotte and others (eds), *Global Warming of 1.5°C: An IPCC Special Report* (IPCC 2019) 12, noting that 'model pathways' consistent with the 2°C target would require a 25 per cent emission reduction by 2030, while those consistent with the 1.5°C target (with no or limited overshoot) would require a 45 per cent emission reduction.

[54] Appellate Body Report, *Argentina—Safeguard Measures on Imports of Footwear*, WT/DS121/AB/R (12 January 2000) ¶81 (emphasis removed).

[55] Richard Gardiner, *Treaty Interpretation* (2nd edn, OUP 2015) 66. See also Appellate Body Report, *Korea—Definitive Safeguard Measures on Imports of Certain Dairy Products*, WT/DS98/AB/R (12 January 2000) ¶¶81–81; *Territorial Dispute (Libya /Chad)*, Judgment (3 February 1994), [1994] ICJ Rep 6, ¶47; ILC, 'Draft Articles on the Law of Treaties' [1966] II(2) YBILC 219, ¶6.

[56] Rajamani and Werksman (n 50) 11.

achieve—inasmuch as no legal consequences are attached to the non-achievement of this objective.

Second, states have not agreed on the definition of certain technical modalities that are essential for making sense of either temperature target. For instance, states have not specified the time horizon to which these targets apply: they discussed a 2100 horizon when negotiating the Paris Agreement[57] (in no small part because of the paucity of, and uncertainties associated with, multi-centennial climate models),[58] but they never formally agreed on this or any other horizon.[59] Nor have states decided whether the objective is that global temperatures should constantly remain below 1.5/2°C, or whether a temporary overshoot is permissible as long as temperatures then stabilize to meet the target(s) by the time horizon. Significant implications also follow from necessary choices between alternative definitions of 'global average temperature'[60] and (in light of natural climatic variability) 'pre-industrial levels'.[61]

Third, there remains significant scientific uncertainty regarding both the current level of warming and its future evolution. On the one hand, the above-mentioned estimate that the global average temperature has already increased by 1.09°C is associated with an uncertainty range from 0.95–1.20°C for a 90 per cent likelihood[62]—a considerable range, given the proximity of the 1.5°C target. The further increase in global average temperature consistent with the Paris Agreement could thus be situated anywhere between 0.3°C (assuming a current warming of 1.2°C and a target of 1.5°C) and 1.05°C (for a current warming of 0.95°C and a target of 2°C).

On the other hand, scientists do not know everything about how the climate system will react to increased atmospheric concentrations in GHGs (eg given possible non-linear feedbacks such as 'tipping points')[63] and how it will be influenced by natural factors (eg volcanic activities and variation in solar activity)[64] in the coming decades. As such, an emission budget could only be associated with

[57] Decision 1/CP.20 (n 1) Annex.

[58] June-Yi Lee and others, 'Future Global Climate: Scenario-Based Projections and Near-Term Information' in Masson-Delmotte and others (eds), *Climate Change 2021* (n 52) §4.7.

[59] An alternative hypothesis is that the temperature targets apply to the level at which global warming will stabilize in the long term.

[60] Widely used definitions include near-surface air temperature as well as land and sea surface temperature, which evolve differently. See Myles R Allen and others, 'Framing and Context' in Masson-Delmotte and others (eds), *Global Warming of 1.5°C* (n 53) 56, noting that '[f]or ambitious mitigation goals, and under conditions of rapid warming or declining sea ice ... the difference can be significant'; Katarzyna B Tokarska and others, 'Recommended Temperature Metrics for Carbon Budget Estimates, Model Evaluation and Climate Policy' (2019) 12 Nature Geoscience 964.

[61] See Allen and others, 'Framing and Context' (n 60) 57–59.

[62] Allan and others (n 52) §A.1.2.

[63] Joeri Rogelj and others, 'Mitigation Pathways Compatible with 1.5°C in the Context of Sustainable Development' in Masson-Delmotte and others (eds), *Global Warming of 1.5°C* (n 53) 104–08.

[64] See Allen and others, 'Framing and Context' (n 60) 59; Katarzyna B Tokarska and others, 'Uncertainty in Carbon Budget Estimates Due to Internal Climate Variability' (2020) 15 Environmental Research Letters 104064.

an estimated probability of achieving a temperature target. Using the terminology of the Intergovernmental Panel on Climate Change (IPCC), it is unclear whether the mitigation objective of the Paris Agreement implies that states should adopt a course of conduct estimated to be 'as likely as not' to achieve a temperature target (ie an estimated 50 per cent chance of achieving it), one 'likely' to achieve this target (66 per cent chance), or one 'very' or even 'extremely' likely" to achieve it (90 or 95 per cent chance).[65] While the COP[66] and the General Assembly[67] once suggested that the emission pathway ought to have 'a likely chance' (ie an estimated 66 per cent chance) of achieving both targets, states have decided not to include this indication in the Paris Agreement.[68]

Fourth, a long-term mitigation objective does not easily translate into a year-specific target against which global emission pathway can be compared. Even if a temperature target could determine an emission budget, there are many ways that this budget could be spent over time and as many mitigation pathways that are consistent with this budget. Thus, Detlef van Vuuren and Keywan Riahi noted that 'there is no clear, single "law" that would directly determine the required emissions levels' in the medium-term that are necessary to achieve a long-term mitigation objective.[69] The IPCC acknowledges that '[t]here is no simple relationship between the next few decades and long-term stabilization', if only because present emissions could be balanced by future deployment of GHG removal technologies.[70] The IPCC's mitigation scenarios seek 'to find the least-cost pathway to meet a long-term goal',[71] but assessing the costs of long-term mitigation pathways involves consideration of the present value of future costs—a policy question, rather than a scientific one, inasmuch as it involves values rather than merely technical expertise.[72] Overall, while cost-effectiveness is obviously an important consideration, it does not necessarily set aside all other relevant policy considerations which may plead for accelerated or delayed mitigation action, including questions of social justice, intergenerational justice, and aversion to risk.

These four difficulties combine in ways that make it particularly challenging to translate temperature targets into an emission budget with any degree of precision.

[65] Allen and others, 'Framing and Context' (n 60) 77. See also Mike Hulme, 'On the "Two Degrees" Climate Policy Target' in Ottmar Edenhofer and others (eds), *Climate Change, Justice and Sustainability: Linking Climate Change and Development Policy* (Springer 2012) 123–24.

[66] See n 33.

[67] Res 70/205 (n 42) Preamble ¶5.

[68] On proposals to include this phrase in the Agreement, see Decision 1/CP.20 (n 1) Annex.

[69] Detlef P van Vuuren and Keywan Riahi, 'The Relationship between Short-Term Emissions and Long-Term Concentration Targets' (2011) 104 Climatic Change 793, 793.

[70] David G Victor and others, 'Introductory Chapter' in Edenhofer and others (eds), *Climate Change 2014* (n 24) 134.

[71] Leon Clarke and others, 'Assessing Transformation Pathways' in Edenhofer and others (eds), *Climate Change 2014* (n 24) 433.

[72] Ibid 449, noting that '[d]ifferent methods can be used to sum costs over time' and that the IPCC uses a discount rate 5 per cent per year. See also William D Nordhaus, 'A Review of the Stern Review on the Economics of Climate Change' (2007) 45 J Econ Literature 686.

The IPCC's Special Report on Global Warming of 1.5°C (SR1.5) estimates that a 66 per cent probability of holding global warming below 1.5°C by the end of the century implies a remaining budget (as of 2018) of 420 gigatonnes of carbon dioxide (Gt CO_2), whereas a 50 per cent chance of holding it below 2°C allows up to 1,500 Gt CO_2 emissions.[73] Not only do these estimates differ substantially, but each of them is also associated with extremely high levels of uncertainty. These uncertainties are 'increasingly relevant as a specific temperature limit is approached',[74] with geophysical uncertainties alone suggesting 'at least a ±50% possible variation for remaining carbon budgets for 1.5°C-consistent pathways'.[75] Moreover, these carbon budgets do not take into account emissions in other GHGs, which are associated with additional uncertainties.[76] Overall, these estimates vary significantly from those published by the IPCC just four years earlier in the Fifth Assessment Report (AR5) due to varying methodologies and assumptions.[77] A particularly controversial question in any such projection regards the assumption that negative emission technologies such as bioenergy with carbon capture and storage could be deployed on a large scale in the second half of the century in order to make up for some carbon dioxide emissions in previous decades[78] and that relying on such future GHG removal is reasonable.[79]

The drafters of the Paris Agreement would have been particularly ill advised to adopt a temperature target without any of the necessary clarifications if they had in sight that it could be used in a judicial assessment of a state's requisite level of mitigation action. Such, however, was not their intention, and it is not the effect of the Paris Agreement to impose an obligation on states to implement mitigation action consistent with these targets.[80] Rather, the temperature target contained in the Paris Agreement should be understood as a vague indication of what the Agreement means by 'strengthen[ing] the global response to the threat of climate change'[81]—an indication of the direction of travel rather than a clear determination of the endpoint.

[73] Rogelj and others, 'Mitigation Pathways' (n 63) 108.

[74] Ibid 96.

[75] Ibid 107.

[76] Ibid 101.

[77] Ibid.

[78] See T Gasser and others, 'Negative Emissions Physically Needed to Keep Global Warming below 2°C' (2015) 6 Nature Communications 1; Henry Shue, 'Climate Dreaming: Negative Emissions, Risk Transfer, and Irreversibility' (2017) 8 JHRE 203; JCM Pires, 'Negative Emissions Technologies: A Complementary Solution for Climate Change Mitigation' (2019) 672 Science of the Total Environment 502.

[79] See Gareth Davies, 'An Emission-Reduction Commitment Is a Plan for the Future: Developing and Using New NETs Should Be at the Heart of That Plan' in Benoit Mayer and Alexander Zahar (eds), *Debating Climate Law* (CUP 2021); Duncan McLaren and Wil Burns, 'It Would Be Irresponsible, Unethical, and Unlawful to Rely on NETs at Large Scale Instead of Mitigation' in Mayer and Zahar, *Debating Climate Law*.

[80] See below at 250.

[81] Paris Agreement (n 1) art 2(1) (chapeau). See generally Daniel Bodansky, 'The Paris Climate Change Agreement: A New Hope?' (2016) 110 AJIL 288, 303.

Thus, while the temperature targets do not define a specific destination, they do point to the need to enhance global mitigation action. The IPCC noted a 'medium agreement' among scientists that the current trajectory of global GHG emissions 'is inconsistent with' the 1.5 and 2°C targets.[82] Projections based on current NDCs suggest that states would use most or all of their remaining emission budgets consistent with either temperature target in the 2020s alone.[83] States themselves have repeatedly acknowledged that the aggregate effect of their current commitments falls short of what is needed to achieve the mitigation goal defined by the Paris Agreement.[84] When the targets are construed merely as a broad indication of the direction of travel, the difference between 1.5 and 2°C or the technical modalities and assumptions associated with these targets are of limited relevance. As Reto Knutti and colleagues noted, 'the decisions that need to be taken now to limit warning to 1.5 or 2°C are very similar'.[85]

c) Applications in judicial settings

These difficulties result in great confusion when a judge seeks to determine a state's requisite level of mitigation action by inference from temperature targets, or when a claimant suggests such a judicial analysis. Reading relevant judicial decisions and party submissions, one is under the impression that conclusions are reached in the most haphazard ways.[86]

In particular, the judicial decisions in *Urgenda*—from the District Court of the Hague, to the Court of Appeal, all the way to the Supreme Court of the Netherlands—are a cautionary tale. First decided a few months before the adoption of the Paris Agreement, this case was based only on the 2°C target as approved in previous COP decisions. This conveniently eluded the first difficulty described above—making sense of a mitigation objective composed of two temperature targets. The Court of Appeal of the Hague upheld the interpretation of this target by the District Court as requiring an emission pathway as likely as not (ie a 50 per cent chance) to hold the increase in the global average temperature below 2°C above its pre-industrial level.[87] The Court of Appeal then turned to the work of the IPCC to determine what this interpretation of the 2°C target implied.

[82] Victor and others (n 70) 113.

[83] UNFCCC Secretariat, 'Aggregate Effect of the Intended Nationally Determined Contributions: An Update', FCCC/CP/2015/7 (30 October 2015) ¶222.

[84] See n 205.

[85] Knutti and others (n 27) 13.

[86] See Benoit Mayer, 'Interpreting States' General Obligations on Climate Change Mitigation: A Methodological Review' (2019) 28 RECIEL 107. See also Benoit Mayer, 'The Duty of Care of Fossil-Fuel Producers for Climate Change Mitigation: Milieudefensie v. Royal Dutch Shell' (2022) 11(2) TEL (forthcoming), highlighting similar logical flaws in a judicial decision imposing a mitigation target to an oil and gas company.

[87] *Urgenda v Netherlands*, ECLI:NL:RBDHA:2015:7145 (DC The Hague, 24 June 2015), ILDC 2456 (NL 2015) ¶2.19; *Urgenda v Netherlands*, ECLI:NL:GHDHA:2018:2591 (CA The Hague, 9 October 2018), English translation in (2020) 67 NILR 342, ¶12. See also Benoit Mayer, 'The State of the Netherlands v. Urgenda Foundation: Ruling of the CA The Hague (9 October 2018)' (2019) 8 TEL 167.

At that time, the latest available IPCC report was AR5 (published in 2014). AR5 suggested that a 50 per cent chance of limiting global warming below 2°C would be achieved with a scenario whereby GHG concentrations in the atmosphere would be limited to 500 parts per million of carbon dioxide equivalent (ppm CO_2 eq) ('500 ppm scenario').[88] However, the Court of Appeal decided to disregard AR5 scenarios entirely, on the ground that AR5 had not categorically excluded the possibility of a large-scale deployment of negative emissions technologies in the second half of the century.[89] The Court thus brushed away, in a few strokes of a pen, the IPCC's careful weighing of years of scientific debates.[90] Instead, the Court relied on mitigation scenarios presented in the IPCC's Fourth Assessment Report (AR4, published in 2007),[91] which suggested that a 50 per cent chance of limiting global warming to 2°C implied a 450 ppm scenario.[92] With atmospheric concentrations slightly above 450 ppm CO_2 eq in 2017,[93] the difference between the 450 ppm scenario suggested by AR4 and the 500 ppm scenario suggested by AR5 can hardly be overstated.

Following another appeal by the state, the Supreme Court upheld the judgment of the Court of Appeal. Like the Court of Appeal, the Supreme Court disregarded AR5 scenarios, asserting that 'no technology' existed to remove carbon dioxide on a large scale,[94] and relied instead on AR4 scenarios.[95] Backing the Court of Appeal and seeking to minimize the implications of this decision, the Supreme Court claimed that, like AR4, AR5 indicated a 450 ppm scenario 'as part of the objective that global warming not exceed 2°C'.[96] Thus, the Supreme Court failed to appreciate the critical question of the likelihood of achieving a certain temperature target: AR5 indicates a 450 ppm scenario for a 66 per cent chance of achieving a 2°C target, whereas AR4 indicates this scenario for a 50 per cent chance of achieving this target.[97]

Overall, neither the Court of Appeal nor the Supreme Court appeared to realize the time-sensitivity of these scenarios.[98] What could reasonably have been

[88] Edenhofer and others, 'Summary for Policymakers' (n 24) 10.

[89] *Urgenda* (CA) (n 87) ¶49.

[90] See Ottmar Edenhofer and others, 'Technical Summary' in Edenhofer and others (eds), *Climate Change 2014* (n 24) 70–72.

[91] *Urgenda* (CA) (n 87) ¶¶12, 49.

[92] Brian Fisher and others, 'Issues Related to Mitigation in the Long-Term Context' in Bert Metz and others (eds), *Climate Change 2007: Contribution of the Working Group III to the Fourth Assessment Report of the Intergovernmental Panel on Climate Change* (CUP 2007) 227.

[93] European Environment Agency, 'Atmospheric Greenhouse Gas Concentrations' (2019) (454 CO_2 eq in 2017). See also Edenhofer and others, 'Summary for Policymakers' (n 24) 8.

[94] *Urgenda* (SC) (n 13) ¶7.2.5.

[95] Ibid 7.2.1.

[96] Ibid 7.2.4.

[97] Edenhofer and others, 'Summary for Policymakers' (n 24) 10.

[98] The same flaw can be found in many party submissions in climate litigation. See eg Applicants Memorandum (24 May 2018) in T-330/18, *Carvalho v Parliament*, ECLI:EU:T:2019:324 (CJEU, 8 May 2019) <https://perma.cc/8JB4-DMZB> ¶261.

achieved by 2020 if measures had been implemented when AR4 was published (in 2007) could not necessarily be achieved by the time the case was brought to court (in 2015) and was decided (in 2018 before the Court of Appeal and in 2019 before the Supreme Court). Mitigation scenarios are essentially an estimate of the policies and measures that could realistically be implemented and the mitigation outcomes that they could achieve over time.[99] As time passes, the choices that are made necessarily narrow down what can be achieved, especially in the short-term. As of 2007, the most likely scenario for a 50 per cent chance of achieving a 2°C target relied on the rapid implementation of mitigation action by developed states, which would have achieved 25–40 per cent emission reduction by 2020 compared with 1990.[100] A decade later, as developed states had largely failed to act consistently with this objective,[101] achieving even the lowest end of that spectrum had become far more difficult, and it may have made more sense for developed states to focus on mitigation strategies relying more heavily on policies and measures resulting in faster emission reductions in the following decade.

Other judicial procedures are facing similar questions with regard to the interpretation of the temperature targets. They often point to different answers. While the Court of Appeal in *Urgenda* was satisfied with a 50 per cent chance of achieving the 2°C target, the applicants in various other cases and scholars reviewing their submissions suggested that states ought to pursue mitigation pathways with a 66 per cent[102] or higher[103] chance of achieving the 2°C or, alternatively, the 1.5°C target.[104] For instance, an individual complaint before the Committee on the Rights of the Child suggested a stringent carbon budget drawn from SR1.5's projection for a 50 per cent chance of achieving a 1.5°C target with no, or limited, temperature overshoot.[105]

In addition, applicants often seem to struggle to provide courts with a consistent interpretation of these temperature targets. Thus, applicants in *Environnement Jeunesse v Canada* suggested that the 2°C target should be interpreted as requiring the achievement of a 450 ppm scenario as the scenario that AR5 associated with a

[99] See Julian M Allwood and others, 'Glossary, Acronyms and Chemical Symbols' in Edenhofer and others (eds), *Climate Change 2014* (n 24) 1267 (definition of 'mitigation scenario').

[100] Terry Barker and others, 'Technical Summary' in Metz and others (eds) (n 92) 90; Fisher and others (n 92) 198, noting that 'a given stabilization target can be consistent with a range of interim targets'.

[101] Edenhofer and others, 'Summary for Policymakers' (n 24) 14.

[102] See Applicants Memorandum (*Carvalho*) (n 98) ¶218; Applicants Memorandum in *Environnement Jeunesse v Attorney General* [2019] QCCS 2885, 2019 CarswellQue 6311 (26 November 2018) <https://perma.cc/4BCS-CYQW> ¶2.38.

[103] See Jesse Lambrecht and Claudia Ituarte-Lima, 'Legal Innovation in National Courts for Planetary Challenges: Urgenda v State of the Netherlands' (2016) 18 Envtl L Review 57, 62, suggesting that even a 66 per cent chance of achieving the 2°C target may be insufficient.

[104] See Applicants Memorandum in *Neubauer* (n 15) (6 February 2020) English translation <https://perma.cc/94AZ-UZHM> 44 (66 per cent chance of achieving the 1.5°C target).

[105] Petition to the CRC, 'Sacchi/Argentina' (filed 23 September 2019) <https://perma.cc/G44B-6EAP> ¶69. See generally Allen and others, 'Summary for Policymakers' (n 53) 12.

66 per cent chance of achieving this target[106] (the same concentration scenario as the Courts in *Urgenda* had used, but on different grounds).[107] However, the applicants interpreted the 450 ppm scenario as a scenario where atmospheric concentrations in GHGs would never exceed 450 ppm,[108] thus misrepresenting the IPCC AR5's mitigation scenarios, which admits the near unavoidability of a temporary overshoot[109]—and apparently without realizing that this threshold had already been exceeded.[110]

Likewise, the applicants' memorandum in *Notre Affaire à tous v France* built on SR1.5's projection for a 50 per cent chance of achieving a 1.5°C target to suggest that global GHG emissions should be reduced by 45 per cent from 2010 to 2030[111]—which would imply that global emissions should be limited to around 33 Gt CO_2 eq per year by 2030.[112] Yet, another section of the same memorandum refers to a target of limiting global GHG emissions to 40 Gt CO_2 eq per year by 2030,[113] citing a UN Environment Programme (UNEP) report based (like Environnement Jeunesse's submissions) on the IPCC's AR5 projection for a 66 per cent chance of achieving a 2°C target.[114]

Some other applicants did not seem interested in such scientific subtleties—even though their case relied entirely on them. The claimants in *Mataatua District Māori Council v New Zealand* simply asserted that, to keep warming within 2°C, 'it is scientifically considered that greenhouse gas concentrations need to stay below the level of 450 ppm'.[115] By contrast, according to the applicants in *Ali v Pakistan*, 'the best available scientific knowledge … dictates that to restore a stable climate system, the dangerous levels of CO_2 currently in our atmosphere must be reduced to below … 350 ppm atmospheric CO_2 by the year 2100'[116]—a target that would require not only the immediate cessation of all CO_2 emissions but also the deployment of massive efforts to remove large quantities of CO_2 from the atmosphere.

106 Applicants Memorandum (*Environnement Jeunesse*) (n 102) ¶2.38.

107 See n 95.

108 Applicants Memorandum (*Environnement Jeunesse*) (n 102) ¶¶2.39, 2.46.

109 See Edenhofer and others, 'Technical Summary' (n 90) 52.

110 See n 93. The application was dismissed on procedural grounds; the decision was upheld in appeal. See *Environnement Jeunesse* (QCCS) (n 102); *Environnement Jeunesse* (CCA) (n 16). The case is currently under appear before the Supreme Court of Canada. See *Environnement Jeunesse v Canada (Attorney General)*, 2022 CarswellQue 2830, notice of appeal (11 February 2022).

111 Applicants Complementary Memorandum in *Oxfam* (n 15) (14 March 2019) <https://perma.cc/4QRM-CSGD> 9.

112 Myles Allen and others, 'Technical Summary' in Masson-Delmotte and others (eds), *Global Warming of 1.5°C* (n 53) 33.

113 Applicants Complementary Memorandum (*Oxfam*) (n 111) 57.

114 UNEP, 'Emissions Gap Report 2018' (UNEP 2018) xix.

115 Applicants Memorandum in Support of Urgency Application in *Re Mataatua District Māori Council v NZ*, Wai 2607 (Waitangi Tribunal, pending) (4 July 2017) <https://perma.cc/GJL4-G9J5> ¶13.

116 Applicants Memorandum in *Ali v Pakistan* (Supreme Court of Pakistan, pending) (April 2016) <https://perma.cc/28B4-PSNP> 29. Carbon dioxide concentrations in the atmosphere were at 408 ppm in 2018. European Environment Agency, 'Atmospheric Greenhouse Gas Concentrations' (European Environment Agency 2019).

2. The Lack of Agreement on Burden Sharing

Even if collective objectives were clear and specific, it remains that they do not readily translate into individual targets. States have accepted that their mitigation obligations depend on various differentiation principles, but they have not agreed on a comprehensive burden-sharing formula.

a) Differentiation principles

The principle of sovereign equality[117] does not necessarily imply that every state always has the same rights and obligations—some rights and obligations apply differently as a function of the circumstances. Thus, positive human rights obligations are resource-dependent: states are required to invest more resources in protecting human rights when they have more resources available.[118] Likewise, states have long discussed, and sometimes agreed upon, a different treatment of developing countries in international trade law.[119]

Climate change mitigation is a strong case for differentiation. In fact, it would hardly be possible to imagine how mitigation obligations could apply uniformly to every state. For instance, an equal level of emissions (other than zero) would be far more constraining on countries with a large population than on smaller states. Equal per capita emissions may have a greater moral traction, but it would ignore states' varying capacities to transit away from existing emission-intensive economic systems or to avoid building such systems in the first place. Mitigation action has generally been understood as an effort to depart from current GHG emissions pathways rather than to immediately achieve a predetermined level of GHG emissions. An equal rate of emission reduction from a base year, on the other hand, would be more constraining to states that already have a low emission level in that base year. A state's capacity to limit and reduce its GHG emissions depends on various national circumstances, including its financial and technological capacity (eg ability to invest in clean energy), geographical situation (eg availability of sources of renewable energy), economy (eg export-oriented industry), and climate (eg the need for heating and air-conditioning).

Accordingly, while states have widely accepted the need for differentiation from the outset of international negotiations on climate change, they have also recognized that more than one criterion had to be taken into account.[120] The UNFCCC

[117] Charter of the United Nations (26 June 1945, in force 24 October 1945) art 2(1).

[118] See ICESCR (n 2) art 2(1); HRC, General Comment No 3, 'Article 2 (Implementation at the National Level)', HRI/GEN/1/Rev.6 (29 July 1981) ¶10; Lavanya Rajamani, *Differential Treatment in International Environmental Law* (OUP 2006) 20–24.

[119] See WTO Committee on Trade and Development, Note by the Secretariat, 'Implementation of Special and Differential Treatment Provisions in WTO Agreements and Decisions', WT/COMTD/W/77 (25 October 2000); Rajamani, *Differential Treatment* (n 118) 24–29.

[120] See UNGA Resolutions 44/229 (22 December 1989) Preamble ¶7; 45/212 (21 December 1990) Preamble ¶9.

affirmed that its parties would be guided, in particular, by a principle of common but differentiated responsibilities and respective capabilities (CBDRRC)[121] and that, '[a]ccordingly', developed states 'should take the lead in combating climate change and the adverse effects thereof'.[122] States have reaffirmed this principle within the UNFCCC regime[123] and beyond, including at the UN General Assembly[124] and the Human Rights Council.[125] CBDRRC has also been recognized as a relevant principle in other aspects of global environmental protection,[126] including on the protection of the ozone layer[127] and the regulation of mercury pollution.[128]

However, the CBDRRC principle is not the only ground for differentiation that states have agreed upon. Beside CBDRRC, the UNFCCC mentions the relevance of 'equity'[129] and states' 'social and economic conditions',[130] as well as their 'specific national and regional development priorities, objectives and circumstances'.[131] The Bali Action Plan adds a mention of 'other relevant factors'.[132] The Cancun Agreements highlights the need to 'tak[e] into full consideration the different circumstances of Parties'.[133] The Paris Agreement consolidates these various elements by suggesting that the implementation of the treaty ought to be guided by 'equity and the principle of [CBDRRC], in the light of different national circumstances'[134] (CBDRRC+).

Differentiation has been implemented in various ways. The UNFCCC requires every party to take their CBDRRC 'into account' when implementing their obligations.[135] More specifically, the Convention imposes general obligations on every

[121] UNFCCC (n 7) art 3(1); art 4(1).

[122] Ibid art 3(1). See also art 4(2)(a).

[123] See Kyoto Protocol to the United Nations Framework Convention on Climate Change (11 December 1997, in force 16 February 2005) 2303 UNTS 162, art 10; Paris Agreement (n 1) art 2(2).

[124] See Res 75/217 (n 43) ¶2.

[125] See Res 47/24 (n 45) Preamble ¶11.

[126] See Rio Declaration (n 7) principle 7. See also UNFCCC (n 7) Preamble ¶7.

[127] Meeting of the Parties to the Montreal Protocol, 16th session, 'Prague Declaration on Enhancing Cooperation among Chemicals-Related Multilateral Environmental Agreements' (2004) ¶1; 19th session, Montreal Declaration (2007) Preamble ¶3.

[128] Minamata Convention on Mercury (10 October 2013, in force 16 August 2017) (2016) 55 ILM 582, Preamble ¶5.

[129] UNFCCC (n 7) art 3(1).

[130] Ibid Preamble ¶7.

[131] Ibid art 4(1). See also Kyoto Protocol (n 123) art 10.

[132] Decision 1/CP.13, 'Bali Action Plan' (14–15 December 2007) FCCC/CP/2007/6/Add.1, 3, ¶1(a).

[133] Decision 1/CP.16 (n 28) ¶1. See also Decision 1/CP.20 (n 1) ¶3 ('in light of different national circumstances').

[134] Paris Agreement (n 1) art 2(2). See also ibid Preamble ¶4, arts 4(3), 4(19); Decisions 3/CMA.1, 'Matters Relating to the Implementation of the Paris Agreement' (15 December 2018) FCCC/PA/CMA/2018/3/Add.1, 3, Preamble ¶4; 1/CMA.2, 'Chile Madrid Time for Action' (15 December 2019) FCCC/PA/CMA/2019/6/Add.1, 2, ¶6. See generally eg Christina Voigt and Felipe Ferreira, 'Dynamic Differentiation: The Principles of CBDR-RC, Progression and Highest Possible Ambition in the Paris Agreement' (2016) 5 TEL 285; Lavanya Rajamani, 'The Principle of Common but Differentiated Responsibilities and Respective Capabilities in the International Climate Change Regime' in Rosemary Lyster and Robert RM Verchick (eds), *Research Handbook on Climate Disaster Law* (EE 2018) 46.

[135] UNFCCC (n 7) art 4(1), chapeau.

state, but in a slightly stronger language on the parties listed in Annex I,[136] with additional obligations relating to support applicable only to the parties listed in Annex II.[137] The Kyoto Protocol upholds a bifurcation between Annex I parties and other parties by imposing substantive mitigation commitments only on the former.[138] In subsequent negotiations, states have gradually agreed to a more nuanced approach to differentiation, reflecting concerns with the rapid increase of GHG emissions in some developing countries. Unlike the UNFCCC and the Kyoto Protocol, the Paris Agreement merely refers to undefined classes of 'developed' and 'developing' states,[139] and it requires every party to communicate NDCs that 'reflect' CBDRRC+.[140] More specifically, the Agreement suggests that developed country parties will undertake economy-wide absolute emission reduction targets, whereas developing country parties will 'move over time towards economy-wide emission reduction or limitation targets'.[141]

As the CBDRRC+ principle is widely accepted and reflected in state practice, it ought to be taken into account when interpreting states' general mitigation obligations, including under customary international law. Yet, it is far from clear what precisely this principle implies.

b) The indeterminacy of differentiation principles

While states agree that CBDRRC+ ought to guide the interpretation of general mitigation obligations, they do not fully agree on what, precisely, CBDRRC+ means. States representatives have long aligned their interpretation of CBDRRC+ to what best fits their national interests.[142] Thus, from the outset of international negotiations, a sharp disagreement appeared about the relevance of historical emissions and, more generally, causal responsibility.[143] On the one hand, developing states insisted that developed states were responsible for climate change as GHG emissions resulted from activities that were mostly caused by, or otherwise benefited to,

[136] Cf ibid art 4(1)(b), 4(2)(a).

[137] See ibid art 4(3)–(5).

[138] See Decision 1/CP.1, 'The Berlin Mandate: Review of the Adequacy of Article 4, paragraph 2 (a)–(b), of the Convention, Including Proposals Related to a Protocol and Decisions on Follow-Up' (7 April 1995) FCCC/CP/1995/7/Add.1, 4, ¶¶1(a), 2(b); Kyoto Protocol (n 123) arts 3(1), 10.

[139] See Lavanya Rajamani, 'Ambition and Differentiation in the 2015 Paris Agreement: Interpretative Possibilities and Underlying Politics' (2016) 65 ICLQ 493, 509.

[140] See Paris Agreement (n 1) art 4(3).

[141] Ibid art 4(4).

[142] See Andreas Lange and others, 'On the Self-Interested Use of Equity in International Climate Negotiations' (2010) 54 Europ Econ Rev 359; Mattias Hjerpe and others, 'Common Ground for Effort Sharing? Preferred Principles for Distributing Climate Mitigation Efforts' (Working Papers in Economics No 491, 2011).

[143] See Duncan French, 'Developing States and International Environmental Law: The Importance of Differentiated Responsibilities' (2000) 49 ICLQ 35; Mario Prost and Alejandra Torres Camprubi, 'Against Fairness: International Environmental Law, Disciplinary Bias, and Pareto Justice International Law and Practice' (2012) 25 LJIL 379, 387–88. While some states have softened their position over time, the two diametrically opposed arguments remain influential to date.

developed states.[144] On the other hand, developed states accepted differentiation merely on the basis of their capacity.[145] These alternative approaches to differentiation have substantial implications for the interpretation of the relevant obligations. Responsibility-based arguments suggest a strong obligation of developed states to mitigate climate change and perhaps even to repair the harm they have caused to others. Capacity-based differentiation, by contrast, would more likely be left to a larger extent to the goodwill of developed states in ways similar to international aid.[146] While state representatives have moderated their original position and showed a willingness to compromise, and the distinction between developed and developing states has complexified with the rapid economic development of emerging economies, substantial differences remain to date between the position adopted by most developed countries and that of most developing countries.[147]

The CBDRRC principle does not solve this disagreement as much as it eludes it. As Susan Biniaz observed, the UNFCCC drafters could not agree 'on whether developed countries were to take the lead because of their "responsibilities", "capabilities", or both';[148] they ensured that the treaty adopted 'a formulation that admits of two different interpretations.'[149] The additional references to 'equity' and various 'circumstances' and 'factors,'[150] and later on 'national circumstances,'[151] likewise, opens the door to various possible interpretations.

States have agreed on some elements of a burden-sharing formula. Beside the ambiguous notion that developed states are to 'take the lead in combatting climate change,'[152] a broad consensus exists regarding the relevance of capacity-related circumstances such as the availability of financial and technical resources. Thus, the UNFCCC highlights 'the need for equitable and appropriate contributions' by developed country parties, taking into account their 'economic structures and resource bases' among other 'individual circumstances.'[153] Both the Rio

[144] Ministers of Foreign Affairs of the Group of 77, 'Caracas' Declaration made on the Occasion of the 25th Anniversary of the Group (21–23 June 1989) A/44/361, ¶II–34. See also Beijing Ministerial Declaration on Environment and Development (14–19 June 1991) in (1992) 1 Chinese J of Population Resources & Envt 54, ¶12.

[145] See Written statement of the United States on Principle 7 of the Rio Declaration, in Report of the United Nations Conference on Environment and Development, A/CONF.151/26 (vol IV) (28 September 1992) ¶16.

[146] See Benoit Mayer, 'Conceiving the Rationale for International Climate Law' (2015) 130 Climatic Change 371, 373–74.

[147] See Martin Kesternich, Andreas Löschel, and Andreas Ziegler, 'Negotiating Weights for Burden Sharing Rules in International Climate Negotiations: An Empirical Analysis' (2021) 23 Envtl Econ & Policy Studies 309.

[148] Susan Biniaz, 'Comma but Differentiated Responsibilities: Punctuation and 30 Other Ways Negotiators Have Resolved Issues in the International Climate Change Regime' (2016) 6 Mich J Envlt & Admin L 37, 40.

[149] Ibid 39.

[150] See nn 129–31.

[151] See Paris Agreement (n 1) art 2(2).

[152] UNFCCC (n 7) art 3(1).

[153] Ibid art 4(2)(a).

Declaration[154] and the UNFCCC[155] recognize the need to balance environmental protection with economic development through the concept of sustainable development, which the Paris Agreement mentions no fewer than twelve times.[156]

In contrast, some other potential burden-sharing criteria remain controversial. In particular, developed states have remained reluctant to acknowledge the relevance of responsibility-related circumstances such as historical emissions, financial benefits from GHG-intensive activities, and consumption of GHG-intensive commodities and services. Only one COP decision attributes developed states' obligation to take the lead in combatting climate change to their 'historical responsibility'.[157] Another circumstance that may be increasingly invoked by developing states is the country's exposure and vulnerability to the impacts of climate change, including in terms of costs of adaptation and other types of loss and damage. While climate treaties recognize the need to 'give full consideration'[158] to the unique situation of developing states, in particular those most affected by the impacts of climate change,[159] it is unclear whether and how far this justifies differentiation with regard to their mitigation obligation.

Consistently, capacity-related factors have played a dominant role in negotiations on burden sharing, at least among developed states. During the negotiation of the Kyoto Protocol, the COP discarded proposals by some developing states that emphasized the relevance of historical responsibility;[160] instead, it considered that differentiation among Annex I parties should be decided based on 'the differences in starting points and approaches, economic structures and resource bases, the need to maintain strong and sustainable growth, available technologies and other individual circumstances, as well as the need for equitable and appropriate contributions by each of these Parties to the global effort'.[161] In turn, the EU's effort-sharing decisions aimed at 'balancing considerations of fairness and solidarity',[162] taking into account 'the need for sustainable economic growth across the

[154] See Rio Declaration (n 7) principles 3, 4.

[155] See UNFCCC (n 7) Preamble ¶¶4, 22, 23, arts 3(4), 4(1).

[156] See Paris Agreement (n 1) Preamble ¶9, arts 2(1), 4(1), 6(1), 6(2), 6(4), 6(4)(a), 6(8), 6(9), 7(1), 8(1), 10(5).

[157] See Decision 1/CP.16 (n 28) second recital before paragraph 36.

[158] UNFCCC (n 7) art 4(8). See also ibid arts 4(9)–(10); Paris Agreement (n 1) arts 4(6), 7.

[159] UNFCCC (n 7) art 4(8)(a)–(e), (g).

[160] See Venezuela and others, 'Main Elements for Inclusion in a Protocol or Another Legal Instruments', FCCC/AGBM/1997/Misc.1/Add.1, 30 (1997); Brazil, 'Proposed Elements of a Protocol to the United Nations Framework Convention on Climate Change', FCCC/AGBM/1997/Misc.1/Add.3, 7 (1997). See also Lasse Ringius, Asbjørn Torvanger, and Arild Underdal, 'Burden Sharing and Fairness Principles in International Climate Policy' (2002) 2 Intl Envtl Agreements 1.

[161] UNFCCC COP3, Note by Secretariat: Revised Text under Negotiation, FCCC/CP/1997/2 (12 November 1997) 31.

[162] European Council, Conclusions (24 October 2014) EUCO169/14, ¶2.2. See also Regulation (EU) 2018/842 of the European Parliament and of the Council of 30 May 2018 on binding annual greenhouse gas emission reductions by Member States from 2021 to 2030 contributing to climate action to meet commitments under the Paris Agreement and amending Regulation (EU) No 525/2013 [2018] OJ L156/26, Preamble ¶2.

Community' and 'the relative per capita GDP of Member States'[163] but without any mention of differences in historical emissions among these states.

Disagreements among parties persist to date, as reflected by the variety of approaches at play in NDCs. A synthesis report by the UNFCCC Secretariat notes that parties identified the following criteria as relevant for evaluating fairness and ambition: 'responsibility and capability; share of emissions; development and/or technological capacity; mitigation potential; cost of mitigation actions; the degree of progression or stretching beyond the current level of effort; and the link to objectives and global goals'.[164] These criteria are not mutually exclusive—on the contrary, parties largely agree that 'no single indicator can accurately reflect fairness or a globally equitable distribution of [their] efforts'.[165] Yet, there are innumerable ways of weighing these criteria and, thus, nearly infinite room for states to disagree on what represents their 'fair share' in global mitigation action.

c) Applications in judicial settings

The lack of agreed-upon burden-sharing formula hinders any attempt at a judicial determination of a state's requisite level of mitigation action. To elude the issue, applicants and the judges that accepted their arguments have constantly sought to downplay the relevance of differentiation. Admittedly, references have been made to some burden-sharing criteria such as the state's historical and current emissions,[166] population,[167] profits drawn from the GHG-emitting industries,[168] or its 'technical and economic capacity'[169] and emissions profile.[170] However, applicants and judges have not generally gone to any length in explaining how these various criteria ought to be weighed. In practice, the working assumption in the context of climate litigation has been that the mitigation objective applicable to developed states as a group is also applicable to any state taken in isolation: a fallacy of division.[171]

[163] Decision No 406/2009/EC of the European Parliament and of the Council of 23 April 2009 on the effort of Member States to reduce their greenhouse gas emissions to meet the Community's greenhouse gas emission reduction commitments up to 2020 [2009] OJ L140/136, Preamble ¶8.

[164] UNFCCC Secretariat, 'Aggregate Effect' (n 83) ¶172. See also discussion in Nicholas Chan, 'Climate Contributions and the Paris Agreement: Fairness and Equity in a Bottom-Up Architecture' (2016) 30 Ethics & Intl Affairs 291, 295–96; Megan Mills-Novoa and Diana M Liverman, 'Nationally Determined Contributions: Material Climate Commitments and Discursive Positioning in the NDCs' (2019) 10 WIREs Climate Change e589; Claire Swingle, 'Climate Justice after the Paris Agreement: Understanding Equity through Nationally Determined Contributions' in Paul G Harris (ed), *A Research Agenda for Climate Justice* (EE 2019); Lavanya Rajamani and others, 'National "Fair Shares" in Reducing Greenhouse Gas Emissions within the Principled Framework of International Environmental Law' (2021) 21 Climate Policy 983

[165] UNFCCC Secretariat, 'Aggregate Effect' (n 83) ¶170.

[166] Applicants Memorandum (*Environnement Jeunesse*) (n 102) ¶¶2.48–2.49.

[167] Ibid ¶2.50.

[168] *Urgenda* (CA) (n 87) ¶66.

[169] Applicants Memorandum (*Carvalho*) (n 98) ¶154(a).

[170] *Thomson v Minister for Climate Change Issues* [2017] NZHC 733, [2018] 2 NZLR 160, ¶¶59, 160.

[171] Patrick J Hurley and Lori Watson, *A Concise Introduction to Logic* (13th edn, Cengage 2018) 178.

Thus, the Supreme Court in *Urgenda* asserted that, '*in principle*, the target from AR4 [of 25 to 40 percent emissions reduction by 2020 compared with 1990 for Annex I Parties as a group] also applies to the individual States within the group of Annex I countries'.[172] The Court then noted that there was no 'obvious' ground for a lower reduction rate to apply to the Netherlands than to other developed states.[173] In place of a detailed analysis of the Netherlands' capability and responsibility, the Court stated that the Netherlands was 'one of the countries with very high per capita emissions'.[174] The Court took note of the fact that the Netherlands had agreed upon 'one of the highest reduction percentages applicable to the EU Member States', before merely asserting that that 'this high percentage corresponds to the possibilities and responsibilities of the Netherlands'.[175]

Yet, there is no evidence of a 'principle' of international law according to which every individual (developed) state must achieve an identical mitigation target. To the contrary, negotiations have systematically led to the adoption of national targets that vary substantially in order to reflect national circumstances. Under the Kyoto Protocol's first commitment period, quantified emission limitation and reduction commitments ranged from 92 to 110 per cent of the state's 1990 baseline;[176] those applicable to the second commitment period ranged from 76 to 99.5 per cent of the same baseline.[177] NDCs include targets ranging from 9.8 to 75 per cent emission reduction.[178] The EU member states agreed among themselves to successive national targets (for emissions not covered by the EU-wide emission trading scheme) that vary within a range representing 53 per cent of the states' 2005 baselines.[179] Thus, substantial variations in national targets, even among developed states, is the principle rather than the exception. And yet this principle is tremendously difficult for a court to apply.

172 *Urgenda* (SC) (n 13) ¶7.3.2 (emphasis added). See also Statement of Claim in *Mataatua* (n 115) (30 May 2016) <https://perma.cc/VE94-KPQU> ¶83(a), implying the same assumption.

173 *Urgenda* (SC) (n 13) ¶7.3.4.

174 Ibid ¶7.3.4.

175 Ibid ¶7.3.4.

176 Kyoto Protocol (n 123) Annex B.

177 Doha Amendment to the Kyoto Protocol (8 December 2012, in force 31 December 2020) C.N.718.2012.TREATIES-XXVII.7.c art 1.A.

178 UNFCCC Secretariat, 'Aggregate Effect' (n 83) ¶9. These percentages are not directly comparable as they build on different types of commitments, baselines, timeframes, scopes, and assumptions, but they provide a crude reflection of the range of ambition.

179 See Council Decision 2002/358/CE of 25 April 2002 concerning the approval, on behalf of the European Community, of the Kyoto Protocol to the United Nations Framework Convention on Climate Change and the joint fulfilment of commitments thereunder [2002] OJ L130/1, Annex II, displaying 53 per cent variation between the +25 per cent emission limitation target applicable to Greece and the −28 per cent emission reduction target applicable to Luxemburg under the first commitment period of the Kyoto Protocol; Decision 406/2009 (n 163) Annex II, displaying a 40 per cent variation between the 20 per cent emission limitation target applicable to Bulgaria and the −20 per cent emission reduction target applicable to Denmark, Ireland, and Luxemburg, to be achieved by 2020, compared with 2005 levels; Regulation 2018/842 (n 162) Annex I (40 per cent variation).

Other pleadings have relied on simplistic arguments. For instance, the applicants in *Carvalho* relied on the premise that carbon budgets ought to be distributed between states on an equal per capita basis.[180] This assertion finds no support in either climate treaties or state practice and, while equal per capita carbon budget has some moral traction, so do a number of other equity criteria relating to responsibility and capability.[181] From a policy perspective, equal per capita carbon budgets would patently fail to exploit opportunities for more effective mitigation action where they lie, such as the ability of developing countries to 'leap-frog' a high-emission development stage directly into an advanced low-emission economy: by delaying mitigation action in the name of equality, this theory would further harm those already affected by the impacts of climate change.

B. The Limited Legal Force of Temperature Targets

Even if a party was able to overcome all the difficulties presented in section A and to demonstrate that a state has failed to act consistently with the temperature targets, questions remain about the legal force of these temperature targets. In this regard, two apex national courts have recently expressed views that are difficult to reconcile. In *Urgenda*, the Supreme Court of the Netherlands found that the state's obligation to protect the right to life and to family life under the European Convention on Human Rights (ECHR), interpreted in light of customary international law, implied an obligation for the state to do its fair share in achieving a 2°C target, which, in the Court's assessment, required a minimum 25 per cent reduction in GHG emissions by 2020 compared with 1990.[182] Just about a year later, the UK Supreme Court in *Friends of the Earth* found that the Airport National Policy Statement had validly been adopted following consultations on the basis of documents that had made no mention of the temperature targets of the Paris Agreement. In the Court's assessment, 'the Paris Agreement did not impose an obligation on any state to adopt a binding domestic target to ensure that [its mitigation] objectives were met'.[183] As mentioned in section A, party submissions in several other cases currently pending before national courts and supranational human rights institutions refer to temperature targets as a touchstone to assess states' alleged lack of ambition on climate change mitigation.[184]

[180] Applicants Memorandum (*Carvalho*) (n 98) ¶266.

[181] See Marc Fleurbaey and others, 'Sustainable Development and Equity' in Edenhofer and others (eds), *Climate Change 2014* (n 24) 317–21. See also Paul Baer and others, 'Greenhouse Development Rights: A Framework for Climate Protection that is "More Fair" than Equal per Capita Emissions Rights' in Stephen M Gardiner and others (eds), *Climate Ethics: Essential Readings* (OUP 2010) 215.

[182] *Urgenda* (SC) (n 13). See also *Neubauer* (n 15) ¶3.

[183] *R (Friends of the Earth) v Heathrow* [2020] UKSC 52, [2021] 2 All ER 967, ¶71.

[184] See Sacchi/Argentina (n 105) ¶¶174–75 et passim; Complaint in *Do-Hyun Kim v South Korea* (Constitutional Court of South Korea, pending) 2020 Heonma 389 (13 March 2020), English

This section assesses the legal force and normative implications of the 1.5 and 2°C targets. It refutes the frequent assumption, instrumental in *Urgenda* and the claims it inspired, that states have accepted an obligation to adopt and implement mitigation action consistent with the temperature targets. The lack of express treaty provision or consistent state practice, it is argued, prevents the identification of an obligation on states to adopt or implement mitigation action consistent with this objective. Nevertheless, the section suggests, the objective is relevant to the interpretation of the standard of due diligence applicable in relation to existing treaty and customary obligations on climate change mitigation so far as this interpretation is in line with state practice. At present, these targets essentially reflect an agreement among states about the direction of travel—the need for more mitigation action—and about the urgency of travelling in this direction. Going forward, agreement by states on this mitigation objective could facilitate new normative developments, in particular the emergence of benchmarks to assess states' mitigation action based either on states' shared understanding of particular implications of temperature targets (eg time-specific milestones) or on each state's own understanding of such implications.

1. The Dubious Obligation of Consistency with the Temperature Targets

It is often assumed that the adoption of temperature targets implies an obligation for each state to adopt and implement mitigation action that represent its fair share of the global efforts required to meet these targets.[185] Yet, acceptance of an objective does not necessarily indicate acceptance of an obligation to act consistently with this objective. The following shows that, under the most likely legal interpretations, no such obligation can currently be found under climate treaties, customary law, or human rights treaties. The opposite conclusion could only be based on an exclusively descending reasoning—one which would fail to acknowledge that, in practice, most states do not act consistently with the mitigation objectives they have agreed upon.

translation <https://perma.cc/Y57D-5P45>; *Duarte Agostinho v Portugal*, Communicated Case No 39371/20 (ECtHR, 13 November 2020) <http://hudoc.echr.coe.int/eng?i=001-206535> 2; *Verein Klimaseniorinnen Schweiz v Switzerland*, Communicated Case No 53600/20 (ECtHR, 17 March 2021) <http://hudoc.echr.coe.int/eng?i=001-209313> 1–2.

[185] See *Gloucester Resources v Minister for Planning* [2019] NSWLEC 7, ¶440 ('Under the Paris Agreement, each party commits to make its contribution to keeping the global average temperature rise to the 1.5–2°C range by reducing their GHG emissions through their Nationally Determined Contributions'); *Urgenda* (SC) (n 13) ¶5.7.1; *Sharma v Minister for the Environment* [2021] FCA 560, ¶86. But see *Minister for the Environment v Sharma* (n 17).

a) Climate treaties

Legal scholarship on the Paris Agreement has repeatedly characterized the temperature targets as the source of a 'collective obligation',[186] an unusual concept in international law.[187] Both Rajamani and Voigt, for instance, have suggested a dichotomy between the obligations that apply to states individually and those that they hold collectively, contrasting such individual or collective obligations with non-binding 'goals, values and expectations'.[188] If 'collective obligation' is to be understood as an obligation held single-handedly by a collective, it is arguably a contradiction in terms: a collective cannot hold an obligation and be held responsible if it breaches this obligation unless it has a legal personality,[189] in which case it is in fact holding the obligation 'individually'. Neither Rajamani nor Voigt appears to claim that the Paris Agreement created an international organization or any other type of international legal person. What Rajamani, Voigt, and other scholars refer to as a 'collective obligation' is, in fact, merely an objective.[190]

Admittedly, this objective could have certain implications for state obligations. In particular, states could have consented to an individual obligation to adopt or implement mitigation action consistent with these temperature targets. Yet, no evidence of any such obligation can be found in any climate treaty. The general commitment of the parties to the UNFCCC to implement 'programmes containing measures to mitigate climate change'[191] does not mention any objective, nor do subsequent COP decisions relate this obligation to the long-term goal they have

[186] Rajamani, 'Ambition and Differentiation' (n 139) 503; Daniel Bodansky, 'The Legal Character of the Paris Agreement' (2016) 25 RECIEL 142, 145–47; Jacqueline Peel, 'Climate Change' in André Nollkaemper and Ilias Plakokefalos (eds), *The Practice of Shared Responsibility in International Law* (CUP 2017) 1024; Anna Huggins, 'The Evolution of Differential Treatment in International Climate Law: Innovation, Experimentation, and "Hot" Law' (2018) 8 Climate Law 195, 204. The same concept has been used in relation to the Kyoto Protocol: see Cinnamon P Carlarne and Mohamed S Helal, 'A Conversation about Climate Change Law and the "International Community"' (2018) 8 Climate Law 229, 240; Lavanya Rajamani, 'Innovation and Experimentation in the International Climate Change Regime' (2020) 404 RdC 9, 35.

[187] The concept is mostly unheard of in the public international law literature, except as a synonym for obligations *erga omnes* (ie obligations owed to each member of a collective): see Malgosia A Fitzmaurice, 'International Protection of the Environment' (2001) 293 RdC 9, 218–19; James R Crawford, 'State Responsibility' in *Max Planck Encyclopedia of Public International Law* (online edn, OUP 2006) ¶49. Any obligation on climate change mitigation is, by nature, owed to the international community as a whole rather than to any individual beneficiary.

[188] Christina Voigt, 'The Paris Agreement: What Is the Standard of Conduct for Parties?' (2016) 18 QIL 17, 17. See also Lavanya Rajamani, 'The 2015 Paris Agreement: Interplay between Hard, Soft and Non-Obligations' (2016) 28 JEL 337, 343; Gu Zihua, Christina Voigt, and Jacob Werksman, 'Facilitating Implementation and Promoting Compliance with the Paris Agreement under Article 15: Conceptual Challenges and Pragmatic Choices' (2019) 9 Climate Law 65, 86 (fn 68); Rajamani, 'Innovation and Experimentation' (n 186) 108.

[189] *Reparation for Injuries Suffered in the Service of the United Nations*, Advisory Opinion (11 April 1949), [1949] ICJ Rep 174, 179.

[190] See also Maiko Meguro, 'Litigating Climate Change through International Law: Obligations Strategy and Rights Strategy' (2020) 33 LJIL 933, 949. See discussion, in the context of human rights treaties, above at 153.

[191] UNFCCC (n 7) art 4(1)(b). See also art 4(2)(a).

adopted. And the Paris Agreement—as the UK Supreme Court pointed out—does indeed not 'impose an obligation on any state to adopt a binding domestic target to ensure that those objectives were met'.[192] While two COP decisions have recommended that 'Parties should take urgent action to meet'[193] the 2°C target, this does not create a legal obligation: the word 'should' does not suggest an obligation, which, in any case, the COP does not have the authority to create.

Each party to the Paris Agreement must adopt and seek to achieve NDCs[194] that reflect its 'highest possible ambition',[195] but the treaty abstains from making any link between individual ambition and collective objective. A provision of the Paris Agreement notes that, with their NDCs, parties 'are to undertake and communicate ambitious efforts … with the view to achieving the purpose'[196] of the treaty, but the phrasing of this provision—the aggregative plural and the use of the phrase 'are to' rather than 'shall'—does not indicate the creation of a new obligation.[197] The Paris Agreement further establishes a global stocktake mechanism to assess 'the collective progress towards achieving' the temperature targets and notes that '[t]he outcome of the global stocktake shall inform Parties in updating and enhancing' their mitigation action.[198] This betrays at most an expectation that parties would be interested in achieving the targets, but it does not impose on them a legal obligation to do so. Another provision of the Paris Agreement establishes an 'enhanced transparency framework',[199] but neither this treaty provision nor the related decision of the Meeting of the Parties to the Paris Agreement (CMA) contains any direct mention of the temperature targets defined in the Paris Agreement, let alone anything to suggest that the parties must act consistently with this objective.

Rather than setting the scope of any obligation, the mention of temperature targets in the Paris Agreement can only help to identify the object and purpose of the treaty.[200] A treaty must be interpreted 'in light of' its object and purpose,[201] but the object and purpose of a treaty cannot make up for the absence of specific provisions.[202] As such, while a party's commitment to communicate NDCs that

[192] *Friends of the Earth* (n 183) ¶71. See also *Bushfire Survivors for Climate Action Inc v Environment Protection Authority* [2021] NSWLEC 92, paras. 96–97, finding that the federated state's implied statutory duty to take measures against climate change does not imply an obligation to implement mitigation action consistent with the 1.5°C target of the Paris Agreement.

[193] Decisions 1/CP.16 (n 28) ¶4; 2/CP.17 (n 31) recital 3 before ¶5, recital 2 before ¶32.

[194] Paris Agreement (n 1) art 4(2). See also Benoit Mayer, 'Article 4: Mitigation' in Geert van Calster and Leonie Reins (eds), *The Paris Agreement on Climate Change: A Commentary* (EE 2021).

[195] Paris Agreement (n 1) art 4(3).

[196] Ibid art 3.

[197] See above 52.

[198] Paris Agreement (n 1) art 14(1), (3).

[199] Ibid art 13(1).

[200] Rajamani and Werksman (n 50) 3.

[201] Vienna Convention on the Law of Treaties (23 May 1969, in force 27 January 1980) 1155 UNTS 331, art 31(1).

[202] See *Arbitral Award of 31 July 1989 (Guinea-Bissau v Senegal)*, Judgment (12 November 1991), [1991] ICJ Rep 53, ¶56; *Land, Island and Maritime Frontier Dispute (El Salvador/Honduras, Nicaragua intervening)*, Judgment (11 September 1992), [1992] ICJ Rep 351, ¶¶375–76; *Federal Reserve Bank of New York v Bank Markazi*, Case A28, Decision DEC 130-A28-FT (19 December 2000) (2000) 36

'reflect its highest possible ambition' could be interpreted in light of the mitigation objective of the Paris Agreement, this does not necessarily create an immediate obligation for the party to implement mitigation action consistent with the temperature targets. In fact, if the parties had been willing to define an objective that could be used as a benchmark for each party's NDC, they would have been particularly misguided to adopt an objective as vague as the temperature targets and not to accompany it with more specific burden-sharing criteria.[203] Nor would they have created a normative system relying on the national determination of each state's mitigation action if they had in mind that each state had to achieve a 'fair share' that was predetermined or, otherwise, could be calculated and imposed on states.

Beside their object and purpose, treaties must be interpreted in light of '[a]ny subsequent practice in the application of the treaty'.[204] Yet, subsequent state practice does not suggest that climate treaties are to be interpreted as requiring states to act consistently with temperature targets. Suggesting the contrary, the parties to the UNFCCC and to the Paris Agreement have repeatedly recognized the existence of a significant gap between the aggregate effect of their mitigation efforts and what the temperature targets would imply.[205] UNEP estimates that the full implementation of NDCs would most likely lead to a global warming of 2.6–2.7°C, whereas the full implementation of long-term pledges could lower this warming to approximately 2.2°C.[206] Climate Action Tracker, a tool developed by a consortium of research agencies to assess whether national mitigation action is in line with temperature targets, suggests that only eight of the thirty-three parties it assessed (among the largest GHG emitters) have communicated NDCs that are '2°C compatible', of which only two are also '1.5°C compatible'.[207] In other words, states do not generally act in a way that is commensurate with an understanding that their pledges must be consistent with achieving either temperature target.

b) Customary law

Chapter III notes that customary law can be identified in two ways: through an ascending reasoning based on empirical evidence of general state practice accepted as law and through a descending reasoning relying on deductions from the

Iran–US Claims Tribunal Reports 5, ¶58; Mark E Villiger, *Commentary on the 1969 Vienna Convention on the Law of Treaties* (Martinus Nijhoff 2008) 428 (para 14); Richard Gardiner (n 55) 211, 219; Oliver Dörr, 'Article 31' in Olivier Dörr and Kirsten Schmalenbach (eds), *Vienna Convention on the Law of Treaties: A Commentary* (2nd edn, Springer 2018) 586–87 (para 57); Paul Gragl and Malgosia Fitzmaurice, 'The Legal Character of Article 18 of the Vienna Convention on the Law of Treaties' (2019) 68 ICLQ 699, 710.

[203] See above at 238.

[204] VCLT (n 201) art 31(3)(b).

[205] See references in n 33.

[206] UNEP DTU Partnership, 'Emissions Gap Report 2021' (UNEP 2021) xxiv. See also Victor and others (n 70) 113.

[207] Climate Action Tracker, 'Countries' (no date) <https://climateactiontracker.org/countries/>.

premises of the international legal order.[208] The ascending method enjoys greater recognition in both judicial practice and legal doctrine. Yet, this does not 'preclude a measure of deduction as an aid, to be employed with caution',[209] while taking 'care ... to avoid abstract reasoning that does not take into account the overall political context'.[210] The deductive approach may be able to play a complementary role when state practice is indecisive or otherwise ill-established, but it does not permit the identification of a rule that is clearly at odds with the general practice of states.

Further, Chapter III identified a customary obligation on climate change mitigation from both an ascending method and a descending method.[211] Descending and ascending reasoning may suggest different contents for this obligation. When the Supreme Court of the Netherlands in *Urgenda* interpreted this customary norm as implying that each state must do its fair share in global efforts to achieve collective objectives on climate change mitigation such as the 2°C target, it relied exclusively on a descending reasoning. The Court did not demonstrate (or even assert) any element of state practice consistent with this obligation for a state to act in line with the 2°C target.[212] The Court's interpretation was based on the 'assumption' that the 2°C target 'is probably the critical limit above which there is risk of dangerous climate change'.[213] The Court attributes this assumption to the IPCC,[214] thus considering it as a scientific fact when, in fact, this target was (and could not have been anything other than) the result of a political decision.[215]

An ascending reasoning, however, inevitably disproves the Court's conclusion in *Urgenda*. As noted above, states—on their own admission and as assessed by scientific studies, international organizations, and civil society organizations alike[216]—have not generally been adopting and implementing a level of mitigation action consistent with either temperature target.[217] Under the prevailing doctrine on the identification of customary international law, the existence of inconsistent state practice precludes the identification of a customary obligation requiring states to act consistently with temperature targets.

[208] See above at 91.

[209] ILC, 'Draft Conclusions on Identification of Customary International Law' in ILC Report, 70th session, A/73/10 (2018) 119, commentary on conclusion 2, ¶5. See also *Corfu Channel (UK v Albania)*, Judgment on Merits (9 April 1949), [1949] ICJ Rep 4, 22; *Pulp Mills* (n 3) ¶204.

[210] Christian Tomuschat, 'Obligations Arising for States without or against Their Will' (1993) 241 RdC 195, 294.

[211] See above at 106.

[212] The Court highlighted the acceptance of the target, but acceptance as law is not sufficient to identify a norm of customary international law under the ascending approach: it must be complemented by evidence of general state practice. See ILC, 'Customary International Law' (n 209) conclusions 2, 3.

[213] *Urgenda* (SC) (n 13) ¶¶7.2.1.

[214] Ibid ¶¶7.2.1.

[215] See above at 232, and below at 269.

[216] See nn 33, 205–07.

[217] The decision in *Urgenda* could itself be considered as an element of state practice. See ILC, 'Customary International Law' (n 209) conclusion 5. Yet, it remains an exception.

c) Human rights treaties

Human rights treaties may require states to implement some mitigation action.[218] If so, human rights treaties would have to be interpreted in light of 'relevant rules of international law applicable in the relations between the parties',[219] including rules arising from climate treaties and customary international law, as the Court did in *Urgenda*.[220] Yet, as discussed above, neither of these sources require states to act consistently with the temperature targets.

At times, human rights institutions have followed an extensive approach to systemic integration. The European Court of Human Rights (ECtHR), in particular, has referred to rules contained in poorly ratified treaties[221] or in texts without any binding force,[222] provided that these documents reflect what the Court calls 'common ground in modern societies'. Here again, however, consistency with the 1.5 or 2°C targets cannot be considered as 'common ground' when state practice does not generally (or, at least, not in aggregate) reflect a requirement for such consistency. The paradox is perhaps most evident in the application filed in *Duarte Agostinho*, a case pending before the ECtHR, where it is argued that thirty-three of the forty-seven members of the Council of Europe—all of the high-income countries—are acting in breach of an obligation to act consistently with the temperature targets.[223] It is doubtful that a norm could be considered as 'common ground' when it is allegedly so widely discarded in state practice.

Thus, human rights treaties do not provide a more convincing legal basis for requiring states to adopt or implement mitigation action consistent with the temperature targets than climate treaties or customary law. In whichever way one looks at the question, the interpretation of states' mitigation obligations is limited to what states have accepted, and, absent a clear treaty provision, current state practice inevitably dismisses any suggestion that states may have already accepted an obligation to adopt or implement mitigation action consistent with the 1.5 or 2°C targets.

2. Implications of the Temperature Targets for the Interpretation of States' Obligations

Although states have accepted no obligation to adopt and implement mitigation action consistent with the 1.5 or 2°C target, their emphatic attachment to these targets may not be entirely inconsequential. At the very least, as noted above,

[218] See above at 129–179.
[219] VCLT (n 201) art 31(3)(c).
[220] But, on the existence of narrow 'windows of applicability', see above at 171.
[221] See *Marckx v Belgium*, App No 6833/74, 31 ECHR (Ser A), ¶41; *Mazurek v France*, App No 34406/97, 2000-II ECHR 1, ¶49; *Demír v Turkey*, App No 34503/97, 2008-V ECHR 333, ¶86.
[222] See *Goodwin v UK*, App No 28957/95, 2002-VI ECHR 1, ¶100; *Sørensen v Denmark*, App No 52562/99, 2006-I ECHR 1, ¶74.
[223] *Duarte Agostinho* (n 184).

these targets are a component of the object and purpose in light of which the Paris Agreement is to be interpreted.[224] Moreover, states' agreement on temperature targets suggests an anticipatory acceptance as law of any pertinent state practice that may emerge subsequently. Collective objectives have implications for the determination of the standard of conduct applicable under general mitigation obligations and, more specifically, for the corollary duties that can be derived from these general obligations.

States' general obligations on climate change mitigation under the UNFCCC and customary international law are obligations of conduct or due diligence.[225] As the International Tribunal on the Law of the Sea has observed, due diligence is a 'variable concept' that 'may change over time' and 'in relation to the risks involved in the activity'.[226] The requirement applicable to a state under its general mitigation obligations depends on the state's circumstances (eg its economic situation),[227] but also on the importance of the interest requiring protection.[228] Temperature targets are relevant in understanding the level of urgency that states attach to climate change mitigation and, thus, in determining the standard applicable to general mitigation obligations.

The 2°C and a fortiori 1.5°C targets signal that states need to enhance their mitigation action, highlighting the need for states to take 'urgent action' towards achieving 'deep cuts in global … emissions'[229] and to 'strengthen national policies'.[230] Had the Paris Agreement only indicated a 2°C target, it would have suggested a less demanding standard of due diligence than it did with the addition of a reference to 1.5°C; more urgency would have been conveyed if the treaty had only mentioned 1.5°C. Although states are not required to adopt or implement mitigation action consistent with the temperature targets, the adoption of these targets reveals the seriousness of the issue and the need for every state to consider enhancing its ambition.

More concretely, state practice confirms the existence of at least five obligations that can be logically derived from states' general mitigation obligations in light of the acceptance of the temperature targets. Though mostly procedural in nature, these implications are not devoid of practical significance. And while some of these obligations are partly reflected in climate treaties, their content, scope, and nature may be better understood when these duties are identified as an implication of states' general mitigation obligations.

224 See above at 253.

225 See above at 185.

226 *Activities in the Area* (n 6) ¶117. See also Neil McDonald, 'The Role of Due Diligence in International Law' (2019) 69 ICLQ 1041.

227 See UNFCCC (n 7) art 3(1); ILC, 'Prevention of Transboundary Harm' (n 3) commentary on art 3, ¶13.

228 Study Group on Due Diligence in International Law (n 5) 1082.

229 Decisions 1/CP.16 (n 28) ¶4; 2/CP.17 (n 31) third recital before ¶5, second recital before ¶32.

230 Presidents of COP23 and COP24, Talanoa Call for Action (2018) 2.

First, states must take reasonable steps to monitor the achievement of temperature targets as it constitutes the collective objective they agreed upon. By analogy, the customary obligation to prevent transboundary environmental harm has been interpreted as requiring the exchange of relevant information to monitor environmental protection.[231] More specifically, the parties to the UNFCCC and the Paris Agreement have committed to report on their emissions and their action on climate change mitigation.[232] In line with this, states can be expected to share relevant information to assess collective progress towards achieving the temperature targets, including information on their emissions as well as scientific knowledge on the evolution of the climate system.

Second, states must negotiate in good faith additional commitments with a view to achieving the temperature targets.[233] By analogy, as the ICJ noted with regard to maritime delimitation, states must 'not merely go through a formal process of negotiation ... they are under an obligation so to conduct themselves that the negotiations are meaningful'.[234] Most states have long been striving to agree on commitments that show an increasing level of ambition,[235] thus making the achievement of temperature targets more likely. A state would be acting in breach of this obligation to negotiate in good faith, in particular, if it sought to free-ride on the mitigation action of other states.[236]

Third, states must take the temperature targets into account in conducting regular reviews of their mitigation action. The Paris Agreement requires each party to communicate an NDC every five years,[237] noting that each Party's successive NDCs 'will represent a progression beyond the Party's then current [NDC]'.[238] The parties to the Paris Agreement decided that, when communicating new NDCs or updating their existing NDCs, they should 'consider' the gap between national targets and collective objectives.[239] By 2020, most of the parties to the Paris Agreement, including most major GHG emitters, had either updated their first NDC or communicated a second one, often in ways that enhanced their ambition on climate change mitigation.[240] Such policy reviews may also become necessary as a consequence of new insights into the implications of the temperature targets

[231] See *MOX Plant (Ireland v UK)*, Order on Provisional Measures (3 December 2001), [2001] ITLOS Rep 95, ¶89(1)(a); ILC, 'Prevention of Transboundary Harm' (n 3) art 8.

[232] See UNFCCC (n 7) art 12; Paris Agreement (n 1) art 13.

[233] Evan J Criddle and Evan Fox-Decent, 'Mandatory Multilateralism' (2019) 113 AJIL 272, 319.

[234] *North Sea Continental Shelf (Germany/Denmark, Germany/Netherlands)*, Judgment (20 February 1969), [1969] ICJ Rep 3, ¶85.

[235] Paris Agreement (n 1) art 4(3).

[236] See Eric A Posner and David Weisbach, *Climate Change Justice* (Princeton UP 2010) 181–83; Criddle and Fox-Decent (n 233) 320–21.

[237] Paris Agreement (n 1) art 4(9).

[238] Ibid art 4(3).

[239] Decision 1/CMA.2 (n 134) ¶8. See also Decision 1/CP.21 (n 1) ¶¶23–24; Paris Agreement (n 1) art 14(3).

[240] Climate Action Tracker, 'Climate Target Update Tracker' (no date) <https://climateactiontracker.org/climate-target-update-tracker/>.

for global mitigation action. In this sense, the High Court of New Zealand held that the publication of an IPCC report taking stock of new scientific insights into the global mitigation action necessary to achieve the 2°C target required the government to consider reviewing its long-term national mitigation objective.[241]

Fourth, states must consistently justify how their individual mitigation action contributes to the achievement of the temperature targets. The parties to the Paris Agreement are specifically obligated to provide information on how they consider their NDC to be 'fair and ambitious in the light of its national circumstances' and how their NDC 'contributes towards' achieving the objective of the UNFCCC and the mitigation objective of the Paris Agreement.[242] Nothing really prevents parties from fulfilling this requirement in a formalistic fashion, and some have precisely done so, for instance with a mere assertion that their NDC 'is an ambitious, fair and responsible contribution to global efforts',[243] 'is in line with the objectives of the Paris Agreement',[244] or 'represents [their] fair share of the efforts to achieve the global long-term goal of the Paris Agreement'.[245] However, some parties have gone further in justifying their NDC, for instance, by listing the factors and criteria that they considered as relevant in assessing what constitutes their fair share.[246]

Fifth, states must take temperature targets into account when deciding whether to authorize activities that will result in substantial amounts of GHG emissions. Almost every state has established a mandatory procedure to assess the likely environmental impacts of certain activities before authorizing them, and many states have integrated an assessment of GHG emissions as part of this process.[247] The significance of the activity's GHG emissions can be evaluated on the basis of the state's specific commitments, in particular its NDC's mitigation objectives, but it should also arguably be appraised in light of global temperature targets, given NDCs' lack of ambition and their limited temporal, geographical, and material scope. States are not generally under any obligation to prohibit projects that are inconsistent with global temperature targets (and such a finding of inconsistency is, in any case, nearly impossible), but decision-makers and various stakeholders who are typically consulted in the process should be informed about the implications of the proposed activity in light of global mitigation pathways likely to realize these temperature targets. Thus, various jurisdictions already require global environmental

[241] *Thomson* (n 170) ¶94.

[242] Decision 4/CMA.1, 'Further Guidance in Relation to the Mitigation Section of Decision 1/CP.21' (15 December 2018) FCCC/PA/CMA/2018/3/Add.1, 6, Annex I ¶¶6–7. The obligation to comply with this provision arises from Paris Agreement (n 1) art 4(8). See also Decisions 1/CP.20 (n 1) ¶14; 1/CP.21 (n 1) ¶27.

[243] Australia, First NDC, Updated (2020) 6. All NDCs are available on the UNFCCC's interim registry at <https://www4.unfccc.int/sites/NDCStaging>.

[244] Brunei, First NDC (2020) 9.

[245] Zambia, First NDC, Updated (2020) 18.

[246] Switzerland, First NDC, Updated (2020) 13–15; Brazil, First NDC, Updated (2020) 7–9.

[247] Benoit Mayer, 'Climate Assessment as an Emerging Obligation under Customary International Law' (2019) 68 ICLQ 271.

objectives to be considered as part of the assessment of the likely environmental impacts of a proposed activity, in particular in the context of a strategic environmental assessment.[248]

3. The Broader Normative Potential of the Temperature Targets

States have accepted temperature targets as a collective mitigation objective, but as shown above, they are yet to accept an obligation to adopt and implement consistent mitigation action. At present, two main obstacles prevent the identification of this obligation. First, it is unclear what precisely temperature targets imply in terms of global efforts and, a fortiori, as to the action needed for a particular state at a given time.[249] Second, general state practice is not generally consistent with an obligation to adopt and implement action to realize the temperature targets.[250] Yet, the law in this regard is rapidly evolving, and it cannot be excluded that temperature targets could achieve greater normative relevance in the years to come.

This last subsection envisages two near- to medium-term scenarios in which states would assume new obligations in relation to temperature targets. In the first scenario, states gradually accept an obligation to act consistently with a shared understanding of the temperature targets or of their implications. In the second scenario, each state accepts an obligation to act consistently with its own understanding of the temperature targets. These two scenarios are not mutually exclusive. To some extent, there are already signs of both scenarios—but especially the second one—starting to unfold.

a) First scenario: towards shared understandings of the implications of temperature targets

In one scenario, state practice would develop in a way that indicates and follows a common understanding of what the temperature targets mean or imply. The COP or the CMA would likely play an instrumental role in defining this common understanding, which states would confirm by adopting and implementing consistent policies and measures. This common understanding would become legally binding, if not through amendments to climate treaties, then as part of general commitments on climate change mitigation under the UNFCCC,[251] interpreted

[248] Directive 2001/42/EC of the European Parliament and of the Council of 27 June 2001 on the assessment of the effects of certain plans and programmes on the environment [2001] 197/30, Annex I [(e)]; Protocol on Strategic Environmental Assessment to the Convention on Environmental Impact Assessment in a Transboundary Context (21 May 2003, in force 11 July 2010) 2785 UNTS 140 ('Kiev Protocol'), Annex IV ¶5. But see *Friends of the Earth* (n 183) ¶143, holding that the EU law obligation for decision-makers to take international environmental objectives into account does 'not impose a standard of perfection'.

[249] See above at 231.

[250] See above at 251.

[251] UNFCCC (n 7) arts 4(1)(b), 4(2)(a).

in light of subsequent agreements or subsequent practice between the parties.[252] It would also become legally binding under customary international law as an application of states' general obligation of conduct, interpreted in light of an emerging state practice.

This scenario would more likely be realized in relation to purported implications of temperature targets—with which the consistency of state practice could more realistically be assessed—than with the temperature targets themselves. For instance, states could accept that temperature targets imply a particular global mitigation pathway characterized by certain milestones.[253] So far, states have shown some interest in defining three such time-specific milestones,[254] although none has been accepted as law and one has already become obsolete.

First, just as the 2°C target was gaining traction, states suggested a range of emission reductions that developed country parties should achieve by 2020. The 2007 Bali Action Plan highlighted the need for 'deep cuts in global emissions',[255] referring to a page of AR4 according to which, '[u]nder most equity interpretations, developed countries as a group would need to reduce their emissions significantly by 2020 (10–40% below 1990 levels)' in order to achieve mitigation outcomes that the report associated with cost-effective scenarios for holding global warming around or below 2°C.[256] Negotiations on a 2020 target then moved gradually from the COP to the Meeting of the Parties to the Kyoto Protocol (CMP), presumably as a way to bypass US opposition. In 2010, both COP16 and CMP6 called upon Annex I parties to raise the level of ambition of their mitigation pledges 'in accordance with the range indicated' by AR4.[257] In the CMP decision, this provision was an allusion to the range consistent with the 'lowest [stabilization] levels assessed by the [IPCC]', which, according to the Decision's Preamble, required Annex I parties 'to reduce emissions in a range of 25–40 per cent below 1990 levels by 2020'.[258] CMP7 affirmed more directly the aim of ensuring that Annex I parties' aggregate emissions

[252] VCLT (n 201) art 31(3)(a)–(b). See also ILC, 'Draft Conclusions on Subsequent Agreement and Subsequent Practice in Relation to the Interpretation of Treaties' in ILC Report, 70th session, A/73/10 (2018) 12, conclusion 11.

[253] The periodic review of the adequacy of the long-term global goal under the UNFCCC provides an opportunity for negotiations aimed at defining such implications of the long-term targets. See n 39.

[254] In addition to the targets presented in the following, states have considered the adoption of a common 2050 target. See Decisions 1/CP.13 (n 132) ¶1(a); 1/CP.16 (n 28) ¶5; 2/CP.17 (n 31) Preamble ¶2, ¶¶1–3. See also Paris Agreement (n 1) art 4(1), defining only a global emission reduction pathway rather than a target applicable to each state taken individually. The communication of long-term low GHG emission development strategies may help to build a consensus on common mid-century targets. See Paris Agreement (n 1) art 4(19). For an early assessment of long-term mitigation strategies, see Climate Action Tracker, 'Paris Agreement Turning Point' (2020) <https://perma.cc/JUZ4-C9PL>.

[255] Decision 1/CP.13 (n 132) Preamble ¶5 (fn 1).

[256] Barker and others (n 100) 90.

[257] Decisions 1/CP.16 (n 28) ¶37; 1/CMP.6, 'The Cancun Agreements: Outcome of the Work of the Ad Hoc Working Group on Further Commitments for Annex I Parties under the Kyoto Protocol at its Fifteenth Session' (10–11 December 2010) FCCC/KP/CMP/2010/12/Add.1, 3, ¶4.

[258] Decision 1/CMP.6 (n 257) Preamble ¶6. See generally Lavanya Rajamani, 'The Cancun Climate Agreements: Reading the Text, Subtext and Tea Leaves' (2011) 60 ICLQ 499, 508.

'are reduced at least 25–40 per cent' by 2020.[259] The 2012 Doha Amendment to the Kyoto Protocol defined quantified commitments for some developed country parties that were anticipated to achieve an aggregate 18 per cent emission reduction by 2020,[260] but CMP8 also decided that each developed country party would revisit its commitment by 2014 'in line with an aggregate reduction of [GHG emissions] of at least 25 to 40 per cent below 1990 levels by 2020'.[261]

However, this potential milestone did not attract sufficient support in state practice to emerge as a legal rule. The COP started expressing concern in 2011 about a 'significant gap' between parties' pledges towards 2020 and the COP's interpretation of the 1.5 and 2°C targets.[262] This gap between intended mitigation action and collective targets only widened during the following years.[263] The CMP8 decision, in 2012, was the last to mention the 25–40 per cent emission reduction target. Subsequent COP and then CMA decisions have alluded to the need for states to implement mitigation action by 2020 that would be in line with 'aggregate emission pathways consistent with' agreed temperature targets, but they did not specify the emission reduction that these pathways implied.[264] States' agreement to the 25–40 per cent emission reduction target was always limited and tentative, even within the CMP, which could not agree on its inclusion within the Doha Amendment. Despite the process adopted at CMP8, no party ended up revisiting its commitment by 2014 or thereafter.[265] Thus, for lack of consistent state practice, any agreement relating to this target that may have started to emerge among the parties to the Kyoto Protocol between 2010 and 2012 had become obsolete by 2014.[266] This conclusion would not be affected if it appeared that the 25 per cent emission reduction target had been achieved as a result of measures aimed at managing the Covid-19 pandemic[267] as these measures do not evidence acceptance of an obligation to

[259] Decision 1/CMP.7, 'Outcome of the Work of the Ad Hoc Working Group on Further Commitments for Annex I Parties under the Kyoto Protocol at its Sixteenth Session' (11 December 2011) FCCC/KP/CMP/2011/10/Add.1, 2, Preamble ¶10.

[260] See Doha Amendment to the Kyoto Protocol (8 December 2012, in force 31 December 2020) C.N.718.2012.TREATIES-XXVII.7.c, art 1(C) (inserting article 3(1*bis*) in the Kyoto Protocol).

[261] Decision 1/CMP.8, 'Amendment to the Kyoto Protocol Pursuant to its Article 3, Paragraph 9 (the Doha Amendment)' (8 December 2012) FCCC/KP/CMP/2012/13/Add.1, 2, ¶7.

[262] Decision 1/CP.17 (n 1) Preamble ¶3.

[263] See Michel GJ den Elzen, Andries F Hof, and Mark Roelfsema, 'Analysing the Greenhouse Gas Emission Reductions of the Mitigation Action Plans by Non-Annex I Countries by 2020' (2013) 56 Energy Policy 633.

[264] See n 33.

[265] UNFCCC CMP10, 'Report on the High-Level Ministerial Round Table on Increased Ambition of Kyoto Protocol Commitments', FCCC/KP/CMP/2014/3 (2014).

[266] But see *Urgenda* (SC) (n 13) ¶7.2.11, suggesting 'a high degree of international consensus' on this objective by the mid-to-late 2010s.

[267] Some preliminary data suggest that the GHG emissions of Annex I country parties might have decreased by roughly 25 per cent in 2020 compared with 1990 as the result of measures taken to counter the pandemic. See Zhu Liu and others, 'Near-Real-Time Monitoring of Global CO2 Emissions Reveals the Effects of the COVID-19 Pandemic' (2020) 11 Nature Communications 5172; Corinne Le Quéré and others, 'Fossil CO_2 Emissions in the Post-COVID-19 Era' (2021) 11 Nature Climate Change 197.

mitigate climate change and, in any case, the resulting emission reductions are transient in nature.

Second, states have sought to define and agree on a 2030 mitigation target as an implication of the 1.5 and 2°C targets. In 2015, the COP21 decision on the adoption of the Paris Agreement noted that the parties' intended NDCs were projected to lead to 55 Gt CO_2 eq emissions per year in 2030 and stated that 'much greater emissions reduction efforts [would] be required than those associated with' NDCs in order to achieve the temperature targets of the Agreement.[268] More specifically, the decision suggested that achieving the 2°C target implied reducing global GHG emissions to 40 Gt CO_2 eq emissions per year by 2030 and it referred to the forthcoming SR1.5 to identify the emission level consistent with the 1.5°C target.[269] SR1.5's mitigation scenarios with no or limited overshoot typically showed a further decline in global GHG emissions in the 2020s, reaching a level of between 25 and 30 Gt CO_2 eq per year by 2030.[270] In 2021, COP26 and CMP3 interpreted the 1.5°C target as 'requir[ing] rapid, deep and sustained reductions in global [GHG] emissions', including a 45 per cent reduction in CO_2 emissions by 2030 compared with 2010 and 'deep reductions in other' GHGs.[271]

Although some states have enhanced their commitments, states have not generally been adopting the measures necessary to achieve either of these 2030 targets.[272] The emergence of state practice consistent with the achievement of a time-specific target is highly time sensitive: states may have been able to adopt relatively cost-effective measures in 2015 in order to reduce their emissions to 40 Gt CO_2 eq per year by 2030 but, if they did not immediately adopt these measures, achieving the target will require faster emission reduction, hence more stringent measures, which makes the emergence of consistent state practice increasingly improbable.[273] Despite some progress at COP26, the 2030 target remains at risk of becoming obsolete, in much the same way as the 2020 target did somewhere between 2012 and 2014 as states realize that this target has, for any practical purpose, become out of reach. And even if this target does not become obsolete, for instance if states adopt measures whose aggregate effect is projected to achieve something close to the target, it will remain difficult, in the absence of any agreed-upon burden-sharing formula, to determine which state is failing to make its requisite contribution to collective efforts.

[268] Decision 1/CP.21 (n 1) ¶17.

[269] Ibid.

[270] Allen and others, 'Summary for Policymakers' (n 53) 18.

[271] Decisions 1/CP.26, 'Glasgow Climate Pact' (13 November 2021) FCCC/CP/2021/12/Add.1 (advance version), 2, ¶17; 1/CMA.3, 'Glasgow Climate Pact' (13 November 2021) FCCC/PA/CMA/2021/10/Add.1 (advance version), 2, ¶22.

[272] Decision 1/CP.21 (n 1) ¶17; UNEP DTU Partnership (n 206).

[273] By analogy, see above at 240.

Third, states have considered defining the implications of temperature targets with regard to 'peaking' in GHG emissions.[274] A report by the World Resources Institute suggests that, except for Turkey, every Annex I country party's emissions have peaked and started to decrease.[275] This establishes a general practice as far as developed country parties are concerned. Yet, there is little evidence that states have accepted this practice as a legal norm. The Copenhagen Accord and the Cancun Agreements appeared to move towards reflecting an acceptance of national peaking for developed states as a legal requirement by highlighting the need for cooperation in reaching the peak in '*global* and *national*' GHG emissions 'as soon as possible', 'recognizing that the time frame for peaking will be longer in developing countries'.[276] However, subsequent COP decisions and the Paris Agreement only mentioned the aim of *global* peaking,[277] presumably because asserting an obligation to achieve national peaking only for developed country parties was discordant with the more flexible approach to differentiation championed by the Paris Agreement, and perhaps also because it would have directly pointed a finger at Turkey. The developed country parties that have peaked have not generally presented peaking as compliance with a legal requirement. However, as many developing states are expected to peak in the coming decades, states could one day recognize national peaking as a necessary milestone that every state—or, at least, every industrialized state—must reach in order to achieve the temperature targets.

Standards that avoid a precise quantification of states' requisite level of mitigation action could become more relevant over time. In particular, as they further reduce their GHG emissions, states could identify certain activities as inherently inconsistent with ambitious collective targets and as incompatible with general mitigation obligations. Many states, for instance, have already taken, announced, or considered steps to prohibit the routine flaring in oil and gas extraction and processing,[278] the use of coal for power generation,[279] or even the use of fossil fuel for road transportation.[280] As these standards gain recognition, a presumption could arise that a state that does not take similar steps is failing to contribute its fair share in global efforts towards achieving the temperature targets.

[274] UNFCCC (n 7) art 4(2)(a)–(b), implying that Annex I parties would reach individually or jointly a peak in their GHG emissions by 2000.

[275] Kelly Levin and David Rich, 'Turning Points: Trends in Countries' Reaching Peak Greenhouse Gas Emissions over Time' (WRI 2017). By contrast, only eleven developing country parties had peaked or were expected to have peaked by 2020.

[276] Copenhagen Accord (n 26) ¶2; Decision 1/CP.16 (n 28) ¶6 (emphasis added).

[277] Decisions 2/CP.17 (n 31) Preamble ¶2, ¶2; 1/CP.18 (n 28) ¶1; Paris Agreement (n 1) art 4(1).

[278] World Bank, 'Zero Routine Flaring by 2030' (no date) <https://perma.cc/V34J-29HZ>, endorsed by thirty-one national governments.

[279] Powering Past Coal Alliance, 'Declaration' (no date) <https://perma.cc/5SFA-X93V>, signed by forty-eight national governments (as of May 2022).

[280] Framework Law No 21428 of 24 December 2019 on Mobility, 24 December 2019, JORF 299 (France), art 73(II)(2), setting the objective of ending sales in new fossil fuel-powered road vehicles by 2040.

b) Second scenario: towards a requirement of internal consistency in each state's interpretation of temperature targets

A second potential scenario would see the emergence of an obligation for each state to adopt and implement mitigation action consistent with *its own interpretation of* the temperature targets and burden-sharing criteria—a theory that can be referred to as 'subjective consistency'. By contrast to the focus of the first scenario on a shared understanding of temperature targets ('objective consistency'), this second scenario involves a decentralized process of interpretation, taking account of the different meanings that states may attach to temperature targets and their different approaches to burden sharing. Two types of constraints would be imposed upon states. First, a state's interpretation of the temperature targets would need to be plausible. For instance, it would have to be informed by science and to build on some of the differentiation criteria that numerous states consider as relevant.[281] Second, a state would be required to act consistently with its interpretation of these temperature targets over time. As such, a state would not be permitted to revise its interpretation of the temperature targets for the sole purpose of justifying its failure to implement the level of mitigation action implied by this interpretation.

State practice already provides some evidence suggesting that this scenario is starting to unfold. Two independent scientific studies suggest that NDCs are generally consistent with at least one of just a few alternative interpretations of states' requisite mitigation action in line with temperature targets.[282] The problem is that states do not choose between these alternative interpretations randomly: whether this is for strategic reasons or out of sincere belief, each national government tends to select one of the plausible equity interpretations that implies the least demanding mitigation action on its part.[283] Thus, Yann Robiou du Pont and Malte Meinshausen showed that the aggregate effect of NDCs 'matches that of a world where each country follows the least-stringent vision of effort-sharing for their circumstance'.[284] This scenario may not ensure the achievement of the temperature targets, but it may nevertheless require states to implement substantial efforts to depart from baseline emission pathways.

Various rules and processes under the Paris Agreement could facilitate the realization of this scenario, in particular by requiring states to justify their mitigation action on the basis of their interpretation of the temperature targets. As noted

[281] See above at 246.

[282] See Xunzhang Pan and others, 'Exploring Fair and Ambitious Mitigation Contributions under the Paris Agreement Goals' (2017) 74 Environmental Science & Policy 49; Yann Robiou du Pont and Malte Meinshausen, 'Warming Assessment of the Bottom-Up Paris Agreement Emissions Pledges' (2018) 9 Nature Communications 4810.

[283] See Vegard Tørstad and Håkon Sælen, 'Fairness in the Climate Negotiations: What Explains Variation in Parties' Expressed Conceptions?' (2018) 18 Climate Policy 642; Kesternich, Löschel, and Ziegler (n 147).

[284] Robiou du Pont and Meinshausen (n 282) 3. A similar modelling of climate action was developed in Malte Meinshausen and others, 'National Post-2020 Greenhouse Gas Targets and Diversity-Aware Leadership' (2015) 5 Nature Climate Change 1098.

above, the parties to the Agreement must not only communicate NDCs,[285] but also justify how the party considers these NDCs to be fair and ambitious and to contribute to the achievement of the temperature targets.[286] The Agreement further suggests that parties' NDCs should be informed by the outcome of a global stocktake on the collective progress towards achieving these temperature targets.[287] Thus, states are already expected to provide consistent justification for their mitigation action on the basis of a plausible interpretation of the temperature targets. While neither the Paris Agreement nor any implementation decision expressly requires parties to act consistently with their interpretation of the temperature targets, internal inconsistencies could spark protests and this, over time, could contribute to the identification of a legal requirement that a state's mitigation action should be in line with its own interpretation of the temperature targets.[288]

In addition to NDCs, the Paris Agreement invited parties to communicate long-term low-GHG emissions development strategies.[289] These documents will further contribute to defining each party's interpretation of the temperature targets, creating at least an expectation that states will implement mitigation action consistent with their long-term strategy over time. It is unclear whether parties are authorized to revise their long-term strategy, in particular in ways that reduce the ambition of their mitigation action, given the general notion, affirmed by the Paris Agreement, that '[t]he efforts of all Parties will represent a progression over time'.[290] When a party reiterates its long-term goal in its NDC, at least it would appear to be bound not to downgrade it without a legitimate reason to do so.[291] The realization of this scenario would confirm that parties are precluded from revising their interpretation of the temperature targets, whether embodied in NDCs, long-term strategy, or any other declaration or statement, if this is for the sole purpose of evading international responsibilities as doing so would be inconsistent with a general obligation of cooperation in good faith.[292]

It remains, however, that, as parties generally select interpretations of temperature targets that are favourable to them, overall mitigation action under this scenario may not be sufficient to achieve the temperature targets. The limitation of this scenario could be corrected if each state were to commit to doing more than

[285] Paris Agreement (n 1) art 4(2) first sentence.

[286] See n 242.

[287] Paris Agreement (n 1) art 14(3).

[288] ILC, 'Customary International Law' (n 209) commentary on conclusion 10, ¶2.

[289] Paris Agreement (n 1) art 4(19).

[290] Ibid art 3.

[291] Ibid art 4(3); Lavanya Rajamani and Jutta Brunnée, 'The Legality of Downgrading Nationally Determined Contributions under the Paris Agreement: Lessons from the US Disengagement' (2017) 29 JEL 537. See also discussion above at 55–56.

[292] VCLT (n 201) art 26. See also, on the concept of estoppel, *Frontier Case (Argentine/Chile)*, Award (9 December 1966), 16 RIAA 109, 164; *Temple of Preah Vihear (Cambodia v Thailand)*, Judgment on Merits (15 June 1962), [1962] ICJ Rep 6, Separate Opinion of Vice-President Alfaro, 39; *Delimitation of the Border (Eritrea/Ethiopia)*, Award (13 April 2002), 25 RIAA 83, ¶3.9.

it considered to be its fair share. For instance, states could agree to pursue a more stringent target merely as a way of ensuring the achievement of existing targets.[293] This is perhaps one way of explaining states' agreement on two distinct temperature targets: while 2°C might be the 'real' objective, states could have realized that achieving it is only possible if each of them implements the level of mitigation action that *it* sees as consistent with a 1.5°C target. Another way this scenario could be made more effective would be if states were to narrow down the range of what they consider as plausible, hence permissible, interpretations of temperature targets. They could do so both by agreeing on time-specific milestones that they consider to be implied by the temperature targets and by clarifying their common understanding of differentiation principles through developments similar to those considered under the first scenario.

All in all, these two scenarios are complementary. National interpretations of equity may help to determine a state's fair share in achieving temperature targets, in particular, in relation to a specific milestone collectively agreed upon. In practical terms, it is the combination of these two scenarios that presents the best prospect of realizing the full normative potential of the temperature targets.

C. Judicial Methodologies

Section A has demonstrated that states are yet to agree on sufficiently specific objectives and burden-sharing criteria to allow an objective assessment of a state's requisite level of mitigation action. Moreover, section B has shown that, in the current state of the law, states have no obligation to act consistently with collective mitigation objectives. On the other hand, previous chapters have identified general mitigation obligations, requiring states to exercise due diligence with regard to climate change mitigation. To assess whether a state has complied with these general mitigation objectives, a judge could be called upon to determine this requisite level of mitigation action, but the absence of predetermined benchmark to make this determination would put them in an often inextricable position.

This section considers what judges have done, or could do, in this position. As the question is one relating to the interpretation and application of international law, not of judicial procedure, it should in principle apply similarly to judges working within domestic or international courts—international law ought, presumably, to be interpreted the same way by any judge who applies it.[294] The section

[293] Robiou du Pont and Meinshausen (n 282).

[294] When applying international law, a domestic judge acts in principle as an international judge. See Georges Scelle, 'Règles générales du droit de la paix' (1933) 46 RdC 327. But see Helmut Philipp Aust and George Nolte (eds), *The Interpretation of International Law by Domestic Courts: Uniformity, Diversity, Convergence* (OUP 2016), showing that, in reality, national courts tend to add some national 'colour' to their interpretation of international law, reflecting for instance their own legal tradition.

involves a review of judicial decisions and party submissions in relation to climate change mitigation, mainly at the domestic level. It also discusses some judicial decisions (often before international courts and tribunals) in other circumstances where judges faced similar challenges but identified plausible solutions that could be relevant in the context of climate litigation.

On these bases, the section shows that, in the context of domestic litigation on climate change, judges have constantly sought to rely on predetermined benchmarks—even when these benchmarks were highly artificial—and that this resulted in inconsistent decisions. Rather, it is argued, judges should embrace the role that equity (in its broad international law meaning, distinct from the more specific meaning attached to the word in English law) will inevitably play in determining a state's requisite level of mitigation action, thus striving for a fair rather than an (elusive) 'true' answer.

1. The Vain Quest for Predetermined Benchmarks

Applicants and judges have often approached the determination of a state's requisite level of mitigation action with the assumption that there had to be one simple, objective, and almost mechanical way to determine a state's requisite level of mitigation action. To elude the difficulties shown above (the indeterminacy of collective objectives and the lack of a comprehensive burden-sharing formula),[295] they tried to find this answer in elusive authorities: non-binding documents, scientific reports, and civil society assessments.

a) Illusory legal benchmarks

At times, applicants and judges have sought to determine a state's requisite level of mitigation action on the basis of documents with no, limited, or untested legal value. Here again, the judgment of the Supreme Court of the Netherlands in *Urgenda* provides a handy illustration of the challenges facing climate litigation.

The Court attached significant weight to the fact that the Netherlands and some EU institutions had once considered the possibility of adopting an EU-wide target of 30 per cent emission reduction by 2020 (compared with 1990 levels) before agreeing, in 2011, to a 20 per cent emission reduction target. The Court observed that, by 2007, the Netherlands was 'working from the premise of a 30% reduction target in 2020 compared to 1990' and that, two years later, the state contemplated a similar goal as its 'negotiating objective in the context of the climate conference in Copenhagen in 2009'.[296] The Court finally noted that, in the course of international

[295] See above at 231.
[296] *Urgenda* (SC) (n 13) ¶2.1(27).

negotiations in 2010, the EU 'offered to commit itself to' a 30 per cent emission reduction target[297] and 'expressed the need' for such level of mitigation action.[298]

Yet, none of these supports the Court's assertion, later in the same judgment, that it had been a state's 'policy' to achieve a 30 per cent emission reduction target, until 2011, when the state 'adjusted its target ... downwards'.[299] The 30 per cent emission reduction target had never been the state's official target or policy, let alone its commitment; it had only ever been a negotiating position. This negotiating position might be relevant in assessing the state's requisite level of mitigation action (eg it reflects the state's own understanding that this target was fair and realistic), but surely not as directly as if it had been a firm legal commitment.

In a similar turn, the applicants in *Klimaatzaak v Belgium* referred to ongoing discussions within EU institutions in support of their claim that the EU's 2030 target of 40 per cent emission reduction compared with 1990 is sufficient. In addition to a non-binding resolution of the European Parliament (which, on its own, does not have the legal authority to impose such a target on Member States), they alluded to the intention of the European Commission to propose to the Council an enhancement of this target to 55 per cent emission reduction.[300] Yet, the Court of First Instance duly noted that mere policy proposals did not impose any legal obligation on Belgium.[301]

b) Illusory scientific benchmarks

Alternatively, judges and applicants have sought to defer to scientific expertise to determine a state's requisite level of mitigation action. Thus, the Committee on Economic, Social and Cultural Rights asserted that a report by the IPCC had shown that achieving a 1.5°C target 'is imperative'.[302] The High Court of New Zealand attributed the 2°C target to the IPCC,[303] while the applicants in *Mataatua District Māori Council* related the 1.5°C target to a 'scientific consensus'.[304] The Supreme Court of the Netherlands in *Urgenda* claimed that '[c]limate science had ... arrived at the insight that a safe warming of the earth must not exceed 1.5°C'.[305] The Court also suggested the existence of a '*scientifically supported necessity* of reducing emissions by 30% in 2020' in the EU.[306] Likewise, the District Court of the Hague had

[297] Ibid ¶7.2.6.
[298] Ibid ¶7.3.3.
[299] Ibid ¶7.4.2. See also Chris W Backes and Gerrit A van der Veen, 'Urgenda: The Final Judgment of the Dutch Supreme Court' (2020) 17 Journal for European Envt & Planning L 307, 311.
[300] Applicants Memorandum ('Conclusions Principales') in *Klimaatzaak* (n 15) (1 February 2019) <https://perma.cc/93TQ-ZQ7G> ¶555.
[301] *Klimaatzaak* (n 15) 81.
[302] CESCR, Statement: 'Climate Change and the International Covenant on Economic, Social and Cultural Rights', E/C.12/2018/1 (31 October 2018) ¶2.
[303] *Thomson* (n 170) ¶11(a).
[304] Applicants Memorandum in Support of Urgency Application (*Mataatua*) (n 115) ¶12.
[305] *Urgenda* (SC) (n 13) ¶4.3.
[306] Ibid ¶7.2.6 (emphasis added).

suggested that the need for Annex I parties to reduce their emissions by 25–40 per cent by 2020 compared with 1990 was 'scientifically proven'.[307]

In fact, states themselves are not immune to the same confusion, as internationally agreed documents have repeatedly attributed temperature targets to science, despite their political origin. Thus, the Copenhagen Accord asserted the existence of a 'scientific view that the increase in global temperature should be below 2 degrees Celsius';[308] and the COP suggested that deep cuts in GHG emissions consistent with the 2°C target were 'required according to science'.[309] Similarly, the Paris Agreement stated that, after a global peak in GHG emissions, 'rapid reductions' should be undertaken 'in accordance with best available science',[310] thus suggesting that scientific expertise would be able to define precisely how rapid emission reductions would need to be. It is noteworthy that none of these invocations of 'science' indicates which particular scientific discipline could prove the need for a specific level of global or national mitigation action.

Such reliance on scientific expertise is untenable. While there is no question that knowledge acquired from research in various scientific fields (ranging from physical geography to economics and political science) can, and should, inform the interpretation of collective mitigation objectives and burden-sharing criteria, science cannot single-handedly determine either of these.[311] Science is essentially a method to assess what *is*, and by implication to predict what *will* or *would be* in some hypothetical cases (eg what would happen if emissions reach a certain level), but it is not a method to determine what *ought to be* (eg how much effort ought to be implemented to prevent further global environmental harm, and at what cost).[312] The determination of states' requisite level of mitigation action is not merely a scientific problem, but it is essentially a normative one: states have not agreed on the precise rules to determine what each of them must do, and neither law nor moral philosophy provide any definitive answer.[313] Economists, building on climate models, can develop estimates of the most cost-effective way of achieving specified global emission reduction pathways, but these projections are only as good as the assumptions on which they build—such as the assumption that cost-effectiveness should be the only principle guiding mitigation action to

[307] *Urgenda* (DC) (n 87) ¶4.85. See also Backes and van der Veen (n 299) 312–15.

[308] Copenhagen Accord (n 26) ¶1. See also Decisions 1/CP.16 (n 28) ¶4; 2/CP.17 (n 31) third recital before ¶5, second recital before ¶32.

[309] Decision 1/CP.16 (n 28) ¶4.

[310] Paris Agreement (n 1) art 4(1). See also art 14(1), suggesting that 'the best available science' should also inform the global stocktake.

[311] See *Neubauer* (n 15) ¶35, noting that limits set to CO_2 concentration and global warming are questions of policy that natural sciences cannot answer.

[312] David Hume famously demonstrated that factual statements about what 'is' cannot lead to conclusions about what 'ought to be' without the intervention of normative premises (values). See David Hume, *A Treatise of Human Nature* (Clarendon Press 1896)book III, pt I, §I.

[313] See generally Stephen M Gardiner, *A Perfect Moral Storm: The Ethical Tragedy of Climate Change* (OUP 2011).

the exclusion of distributive and intergenerational justice, among other relevant principles.

Some scientists may, of course, have expressed their take on the desirable level of global or national mitigation action, but those are inevitably scientists' personal views rather than *the* scientific view. Thus, David Victor denounced the 'scientist's myth' according to which 'scientific research can determine the safe level of global warming'.[314] As Victor noted, the 2°C target 'isn't based on much science',[315] but, rather, on 'policy processes ... that elicit what governments are willing and able to do'.[316] Likewise, Knutti and colleagues pointed out that 'no scientific assessment has clearly justified or defended the 2°C target as a safe level of warming, and indeed, this is not a problem that science alone can address'.[317]

As to the IPCC, it is bound to be 'neutral with respect to policy',[318] and—despite the frequent assertions to the contrary—its reports have never recommended any temperature target or mitigation pathway.[319] The IPCC's mitigation scenarios, from which came the 25 per cent emission reduction that the judgment in *Urgenda* singled out, aim to provide '[a] plausible description of how the future may develop',[320] not to promote any course of action. These scenarios involve a range of 'equity interpretations'[321] about the location and timing of mitigation action; such assumptions do not necessarily reflect the law or values accepted by states. The IPCC expressly recognized that 'a considerable range of 2020 and 2030 emissions can be consistent with specific long-term goals' under various normative assumptions.[322]

c) Illusory objectivity of civil society assessments

As a last resort, applicants have sometimes turned to civil society assessments as a touchstone to determine whether a state's mitigation action is sufficient. The demand for such assessments has mainly been met by Climate Action Tracker.[323] For instance, the applicants in *Duarte Agostinho*, having acknowledged that states have not agreed on any comprehensive burden-sharing formula, contended 'that the Court ought to adopt/rely upon the approach taken by the Climate Action

[314] Victor (n 23) 5.

[315] Ibid 6.

[316] Ibid 49. See also references n 25.

[317] Knutti and others (n 27) 13. See also Andy Stirling, 'Keep it Complex' (2010) 468 Nature 1030; Yun Gao, Xiang Gao, and Xiaohua Zhang, 'The 2°C Global Temperature Target and the Evolution of the Long-Term Goal of Addressing Climate Change: From the United Nations Framework Convention on Climate Change to the Paris Agreement' (2017) 3 Engineering 272.

[318] IPCC, 'Principles Governing IPCC Work' (1–3 October 1998, last revised 14–18 October 2013) ¶2.

[319] See Edenhofer and others, 'Technical Summary' (n 90) 37 (box TS.1), 51–64. See generally Knutti and others (n 27) 16.

[320] Aviel Verbruggen (ed), 'Glossary' in Metz and others (eds) (n 92) 820.

[321] Barker and others (n 100) 90.

[322] Clarke and others (n 71) 433.

[323] See n 207.

Tracker'.[324] Likewise, the petition in *Sacchi* relied on the '"fair share" model' developed by Climate Action Tracker to estimate whether the five respondent states were pursuing a sufficient level of mitigation action.[325]

The most obvious flaw in these submissions relates to the applicants' assumption that states have an obligation to communicate and implement NDCs that are consistent with (at least) a 2°C target. However, Climate Action Tracker finds that less than one-quarter of the NDCs it assesses are compatible with the 2°C target.[326] Accordingly, Climate Action Tracker shows that the legal argument of the applicants is inconsistent with the state practice in light of which the relevant norms of international law are to be interpreted. In the absence of an express treaty basis, a norm of international law cannot emerge when most states act contrary to it.

Yet, a more fundamental flaw of arguments relying on assessments by civil society organizations is that such organizations have no legal authority to determine a state's requisite level of mitigation action. The methodology developed by Climate Action Tracker inevitably involves an interpretation of collective mitigation objectives and burden-sharing criteria, based on multiple questionable assumptions.[327] As such, it is unsurprising that Climate Action Tracker's assessment often differs from the assessment arrived at by other organizations engaging in similar endeavours. For instance, Paris Equity Check found that the first NDCs of India and Indonesia were consistent with two of the five 'equity approaches' to a 2°C that it defines, whereas Climate Action Tracker suggested that India's NDC is '2°C compatible' but that Indonesia's is 'highly insufficient'.[328] Yet another tool, Climate Equity Reference, provides widely different assessments depending on the assumptions that the viewer is invited to select.[329]

Civil society assessments could be said to offer some interesting insights when all of them provide similar conclusions (as they do regarding some states)[330] but even a consensus among civil society organizations does not necessarily reflect a consensus among states. If a court was to rely on assessments by civil society organizations, it would, in effect, be outsourcing the exclusively judicial function of interpreting the law to these organizations.[331] As such, no more than non-binding

[324] Application Form (*Duarte Agostinho*) (n 184) (2 September 2020) <https://perma.cc/8DW2-LTCB> Annex ¶31.

[325] Sacchi/Argentina (n 105) ¶214.

[326] See n 184.

[327] A summary presentation of this methodology is available at Climate Action Tracker, 'Methodology' (no date) <https://climateactiontracker.org/methodology/>.

[328] Climate Action Tracker, 'Countries' (n 207); Paris Equity Check, 'Pledge Warming Check' (no date) <http://paris-equity-check.org/warming-check.html>. Both websites were accessed on 23 March 2022.

[329] Climate Equity Reference, 'Calculator' (no date) <https://calculator.climateequityreference.org/>.

[330] Climate Action Tracker and Paris Equity Check agree that the NDCs of Argentina, Russia, Saudi Arabia, Turkey, and Vietnam are 'critically insufficient' or inconsistent with any equity approaches to a 2°C target.

[331] On the concept of 'exclusively judicial functions', see *Pulp Mills* (n 3) Joint Dissenting Opinion of Judges Al-Khasawneh and Simma, ¶12.

documents or scientific expertise do civil society assessments define benchmarks for the judicial determination of a state's requisite level of mitigation action.

2. Falling Back on Equity

States have accepted general mitigation obligations, but they have not agreed on a benchmark to determine a state's requisite level of mitigation action. Rather than searching for a 'true' solution on bases that are inevitably questionable, a judge (whether domestic or international) accepting the task of interpreting a state's general mitigation obligation would inevitably have to fall back on equity (in its broad international law meaning, ie equity *infra legem*).

a) The equity embedded within the law

Judges are often expected to be 'no more than the mouth that pronounces the words of the law'[332]—'to apply the law as [they] find ... it, not to make it'.[333] In reality, however, applying the law—any law—in any case worth litigating requires more than the mechanical application of legal rules. A judge's duty to adjudicate[334] implies that, in the absence of clear rules, they must resort to subsidiary sources of law, whether analogy, God's judgment, the local custom, Roman law, their own conscience, or the law recognized by 'civilized' nations—that is, on equity.[335] Thus, as Vaughan Lowe points out, 'the application of abstract norms to concrete cases necessarily involves recourse to principles and techniques often brought under the heading of "equity"'.[336] Two equally trained and intelligent judges hearing the same case may come to different conclusions. It is not necessary here to enter into the theoretical debate on whether this difference results from the exercise of judicial discretion[337] or merely from the limited capacity of judges to understand the law:[338] suffice it to note that, at least in practical terms, a judge needs to rely on equity to apply the law.[339] Equity (in its general sense) plays a subsidiary but

[332] Montesquieu, The Spirit of Laws (1748, Thomas Nugent tr, Nourse and Vaillant pub 1752) 180.

[333] *South West Africa (Ethiopia and Liberia v South Africa)*, Second Phase Judgment (18 July 1966), [1966] ICJ Rep 6, ¶89.

[334] On the prohibition of *non liquet* in contentious cases, see discussion above at 15.

[335] Alfredo Mordechai Rabello, 'Non Liquet: From Modern Law to Roman Law' (1974) 9 Israel L Rev 63, 64–66.

[336] Vaughan Lowe, 'The Role of Equity in International Law' (1992) 12 Aust YBIL 54, 55.

[337] See HLA Hart, *The Concept of Law* (3rd edn, OUP 2012) 132; Joseph Raz, The Authority of Law: Essays on Law and Morality (OUP 1979) 194.

[338] Dworkin argued for the latter theory, suggesting that 'Hercules'—'a lawyer of superhuman skill, learning, patience and acumen'—would be able to find the 'right' interpretation of the law in all circumstances. See Ronald Dworkin, *Taking Rights Seriously* (Bloomsbury 2013) 132–59.

[339] See Ronald Dworkin, *A Matter of Principle* (OUP 1985) 4, conceding that 'there is little point in either asserting *or* denying an "objective" truth for legal claims'.

ubiquitous role in the process of applying the law in any legal system, and international law is no exception.[340]

The equity that judges apply is unmistakably embedded within the law (*infra legem*).[341] A judge would commit a denial of justice if they were to set aside the applicable law on equitable grounds (ie applying equity *contra legem*)—unless a superior rule requires them to set aside primary rules on equitable grounds, in which case they would really be applying equity *infra legem*. Likewise, a judge does not ordinarily have the power to apply equity outside of the law (*praeter legem*):[342] if a judge 'falls back' on equity in the absence of clear primary rule, this either is in application of a secondary rule (albeit often implicit) commanding the court to do so (hence *infra legem*) or else it is an abuse of power. As the ICJ noted in *Fisheries Jurisdiction (UK v Iceland)*, relying on equity is 'not a matter of finding simply an equitable solution, but an equitable solution derived from the applicable law'.[343]

Domestic legal systems have gradually reduced the role of equity through the accretion of detailed statutory rules, binding precedents, and persuasive authorities. By contrast, equity continues to play a prominent role in many aspects of international law due to the paucity of specific legal rules, the ambiguity of many hard-fought treaty provisions, and the fuzzy nature of customary international law; and because the limited practice of litigation means that many cases are *primae impressionis* in at least some respects. Judge Manley Hudson once noted that 'principles of equity have long been considered to constitute a part of international law',[344] an opinion that remains widely shared in both judicial practice[345] and the doctrine.[346] The role of equity within international law must be identified and interpreted by any judge interpreting international law, notwithstanding whether this is within an international or a domestic court.[347]

Equity is bound to be central to a judicial assessment of what a state is required to do to comply with its general obligations on climate change mitigation under international law. Equity has long been recognized as playing an instrumental

[340] See *Affaire des biens britanniques au Maroc espagnol (Spain v UK)*, Award (1 May 1925), 2 RIAA 615, 640; Institut de Droit International, 'La compétence du juge international en équité' (1937) 40 Ann Inst Droit Intl 271, 271; Michael Akehurst, 'Equity and General Principles of Law' (1976) 25 ICLQ 801, 808.

[341] See eg *Continental Shelf (Tunisia/Libya)*, Judgment (24 February 1982), [1982] ICJ Rep 18, ¶71.

[342] This article is interested in cases decided on the basis of the law, to the exclusion of cases decided *ex aequo et bono*.

[343] *Fisheries Jurisdiction (UK v Iceland)*, Judgment on Merits (25 July 1974), [1974] ICJ Rep 3, ¶78.

[344] *Diversion of Water from the Meuse (Netherlands v Belgium)*, Judgment (28 June 1937), PCIJ Rep Series A/B No 73, Individual Opinion by Mr Hudson, 76. See also *Pinson (France) v United Mexican States*, Decision No 1 (19 October 1928), 5 RIAA 327, 355.

[345] Support has been expressed, for instance in *North Sea Continental Shelf* (n 234) Separate Opinion of Judge Jessup, 84; *Fisheries Jurisdiction (UK v Iceland)* (n 343) Separate Opinion of Judge Dillard, 64 (fn 1); *Maritime Delimitation in the Area between Greenland and Jan Mayen (Denmark v Norway)*, Judgment (14 June 1993), [1993] ICJ Rep 38, Separate Opinion of Judge Weeramantry, ¶79.

[346] See eg Wolfgang Friedmann, *The Changing Structure of International Law* (Colum UP 1964) 197; James Crawford, *Brownlie's Principles of Public International Law* (8th edn, OUP 2012) 44.

[347] See n 294.

role in the interpretation of states' obligation to cooperate on the protection of global environmental resources 'in a spirit of global partnership',[348] and climate treaties recognize explicitly that states must cooperate 'on the basis of equity'.[349] Thus, the Supreme Court in *Urgenda* could not have reached its conclusion that the Netherlands had to achieve a 25 per cent emission reduction by 2020, compared with 1990, based solely on the mechanical application of legal rules informed by science. The judgment inevitably relied on various equity assumptions when interpreting the 2°C target as a long-term global mitigation objective, estimating what mitigation action had to be implemented by 2020, and assessing the share of global mitigation action that the Netherlands had to carry out. Yet, the Court did not acknowledge, let alone justify, its use of equity. Absent a careful appraisal of equity, the judgment was poorly reasoned and weakly justified; if the court arrived at a conclusion that was not manifestly absurd, it was—as far as one could see by reading the judgment—by luck rather than by reason.

Domestic judges may not feel comfortable engaging in lengthy, detailed discussions of equity as, in most legal systems, this is no longer part of usual judicial practice. But no judicial assessment of a state's requisite level of mitigation action can be conducted in a convincing fashion in the absence of an explicit appraisal of equity.

b) Equity in the judicial interpretation of international law

Equity plays a manifest role in many aspects of international law, such as the determination of equitable compensation in circumstances where an accurate assessment of the damage is impossible,[350] the delimitation of land or maritime territories,[351] or the apportionment of natural resources,[352] but no field of litigation better illustrates the usefulness of a consistent appraisal of equity than judicial

[348] Rio Declaration (n 7) principle 7. See also United Nations Convention on the Law of the Sea (10 December 1982, in force 16 November 1994) 1833 UNTS 3, art 140(2); Convention on Biological Diversity (5 June 1992, in force 29 December 1993) 1760 UNTS 79, art 1.

[349] UNFCCC (n 7) art 3(1). See also Paris Agreement (n 1) art 2(2).

[350] See *Responsabilité de l'Allemagne à Raison des Dommages Causés dans les Colonies Portugaises du Sud de l'Afrique (Portugal/Germany)*, Award (31 July 1928), 2 RIAA 1013, 1031; *Judgment of the Administrative Tribunal of the ILO upon Complaints Made against the UNESCO*, Advisory Opinion (23 October 1956), [1956] ICJ Rep 77, 100; *Loan Agreement between Italy and Costa Rica (Italy/Costa Rica)*, Award (26 June 1988), 25 RIAA 21, 72–73; *Ahmadou Sadio Diallo (Guinea v DRC)*, Judgment on Compensation (19 June 2012), [2012] ICJ Rep 324, ¶36.

[351] See *Grisbådarna (Norway/Sweden)*, Award (14 March 1908), 11 RIAA 147, 160; *Frontier Dispute (Burkina Faso/Mali)*, Judgment (22 December 1986), [1986] ICJ Rep 573, ¶¶27–28, 149–50; *Land, Island and Maritime Frontier Dispute* (n 202) ¶¶262–63, 418.

[352] See *Fisheries Jurisdiction (UK v Iceland)* (n 343) ¶78. See also *Indus Waters Kishenganga (Pakistan/India)*, Final Award (20 December 2013), 31 RIAA 309, ¶¶78–116. While the Tribunal does not expressly refer to equity or any equivalent notion, its determination of the 'minimal flow' of water that India must ensure is highly similar to the approach deployed in other courts and tribunals with regard to maritime delimitation, and it has been interpreted as an application of the principle of equitable utilization. See Jasmine Moussa, 'Implication of the Indus Water Kishenganga Arbitration for the International Law of Watercourses and the Environment' (2015) 64 ICLQ 697, 711; Kishor Uprety, 'The Kishenganga Arbitration: Reviving the Indus Treaty and Managing Transboundary Hydropolitics' (2015) 14 Chinese JIL 497, ¶¶69–70.

decisions on maritime delimitation. Exclusive economic zones and continental shelves are maritime areas in which states have exclusive rights over the exploitation of natural resources.[353] No general rule determines maritime boundaries when two or more states have overlapping claims over the same areas.[354] Since the *North Sea Continental Shelf* judgment in 1969, the ICJ, the International Tribunal for the Law of the Sea, and arbitral tribunals have settled several dozens of disputes on maritime delimitation based, largely, on equity *infra legem*.[355] This judicial practice outlines the type of reasoning that a judge (whether in a domestic or international court) could follow when interpreting states' general mitigation obligations on the basis of equity *infra legem*.

These successive decisions on maritime delimitation have sought to balance predictability and fairness in legal interpretation. The analysis has generally consisted in two main stages.[356] The first stage applies a clear and objective rule to define a provisional delimitation. Whenever possible, this rule is that of equidistance: each point of the disputed maritime area is attributed to the closest coastal state.[357] Equidistance has generally been preferred to alternative methods, such as the bisector method, because of its 'combination of practical convenience and certainty of application'.[358] Yet, judges have also acknowledged the need to add some nuance to equidistance, which can attach major consequences to the slightest geographical features (eg the shape of the coast near the border or the presence of an island of a state near the coast of another).[359]

In the second stage of their analysis, judges have adjusted the provisional delimitation to reflect the national circumstances they considered relevant. Unlike equidistance, national circumstances are 'case-specific'.[360] While judicial findings are not entirely predictable, they have nevertheless been relatively consistent. In particular, judges have mostly focused on circumstances relating to the geography of the coasts, thus reflecting the origin of maritime entitlement as reflected in the adage that 'the land dominates the sea'.[361] They have considered departing from

[353] See UNCLOS (n 348) arts 56, 77.

[354] See *Continental Shelf (Libya/Malta)*, Judgment (3 June 1985), [1985] ICJ Rep 13, ¶¶39–40; Prosper Weil, *The Law of Maritime Delimitation: Reflections* (CUP 1989) 29.

[355] See generally Yoshifumi Tanaka, *Predictability and Flexibility in the Law of Maritime Delimitation* (Hart 2006).

[356] See Stephen Fietta and Robin Cleverly, *A Practitioner's Guide to Maritime Boundary Delimitation* (OUP 2016) 55–95.

[357] See Massimo Lando, *Maritime Delimitation as a Judicial Process* (CUP 2019) 102.

[358] *North Sea Continental Shelf* (n 234) ¶23. The bisector method has been used when geographical circumstances precluded the use of equidistance. See *Territorial and Maritime Dispute between Nicaragua and Honduras in the Caribbean Sea (Nicaragua v Honduras)*, Judgment (8 October 2007), [2007] ICJ Rep 659, ¶280; *Delimitation of the Maritime Boundary in the Atlantic Ocean (Ghana/Côte d'Ivoire)*, Judgment (23 September 2017), [2017] ITLOS Rep 4, ¶289.

[359] *North Sea Continental Shelf* (n 234) ¶89(a).

[360] *Delimitation of the Exclusive Economic Zone and the Continental Shelf (Barbados v Trinidad and Tobago)*, Award (11 April 2006), 27 RIAA 147, 242. See also *Continental Shelf (Libya/Malta)* (n 354) ¶48.

[361] See *North Sea Continental Shelf* (n 234) ¶96. See generally Bing Binb Jia, 'The Principle of the Domination of the Land over the Sea: A Historical Perspective on the Adaptability of the Law of the Sea to New Challenges' (2014) 57 GYIL 53; Fietta and Cleverly (n 356) 67.

the provisional delimitation when the shape of the coast or the presence of islands would have a significant and unjustifiable impact on states' entitlements[362] or otherwise in order to avoid an excessive disparity between a state's coastal length and its maritime entitlements.[363] On the other hand, judges have persistently refused to take into account any circumstances unrelated to the origin of maritime entitlements, such as navigation patterns,[364] states' relative prosperity[365] or populations,[366] the geology or geomorphology of the seabed,[367] or even the foreseeable evolution of coastline resulting from the impacts of climate change.[368] Judges have accepted to consider access to natural resources as a relevant circumstance but only to avoid 'catastrophic repercussions for the livelihood and economic well-being of the population of the countries concerned'.[369]

At times, the reliance of these decisions on equity has attracted criticism. In a dissenting opinion in *North Sea Continental Shelf*, Vice-President Vladimir Koretsky voiced concerns over the risk of 'subjective and therefore at times arbitrary evaluations'.[370] Michael Akehurst reacted to this and a few other early decisions by speculating that 'the number of cases submitted to international tribunals will vary in inverse proportion to the reliance on equity by judges and arbitrators'.[371] This latter prediction, however, has not come true. States' approval of this judicial methodology is evidenced by the sheer number of cases, a high proportion of which were introduced by special agreements between the parties.[372] The

362 See *Continental Shelf (UK/France)*, Decision (30 June 1977), 18 RIAA 3, ¶202.

363 See *North Sea Continental Shelf* (n 234) ¶101(D)(3); *Maritime Delimitation in the Black Sea (Romania v Ukraine)*, Judgment (3 February 2009), [2009] ICJ Rep 61, ¶¶210–16; *Bay of Bengal Maritime Boundary (Bangladesh v India)*, Award (7 July 2014), 32 RIAA 1, ¶397.

364 *Territorial and Maritime Dispute (Nicaragua v Colombia)*, Judgment (19 November 2012), [2012] ICJ Rep 624, ¶222. See also UNCLOS (n 348) art 58. By contrast, navigation patterns may be relevant to the delimitation of territorial sea: see *Beagle Channel (Argentina/Chile)*, Award (18 February 1977), 21 RIAA 53, ¶110.

365 *Continental Shelf (Tunisia/Libya)* (n 341) ¶107; *Delimitation of the Maritime Boundary (Guinea/Guinea-Bissau)*, Award (14 February 1985), 19 RIAA 149, ¶123; *Continental Shelf (Libya/Malta)* (n 354) ¶50 ('such considerations are totally unrelated to the underlying intention of the applicable rules of international law'); *Delimitation (Barbados v Trinidad and Tobago)* (n 360) ¶241; *Black Sea* (n 363) ¶198; *Territorial and Maritime Dispute (Nicaragua v Colombia)* (n 364) ¶223.

366 *Jan Mayen* (n 345) ¶80.

367 See *Continental Shelf (Libya/Malta)* (n 354) ¶¶39–40; *Delimitation of the Maritime Boundary in the Bay of Bengal (Bangladesh/Myanmar)*, Judgment (14 March 2012), [2012] ITLOS Rep 4, ¶322.

368 *Bay of Bengal Maritime Boundary (Bangladesh v India)* (n 363) ¶399.

369 *Jan Mayen* (n 345) ¶75. See also *Delimitation of the Maritime Boundary in the Gulf of Maine Area (Canada/US)*, Judgment (12 October 1984), [1984] ICJ Rep 246, ¶237; *Maritime Delimitation (Eritrea/Yemen)*, Award in the Second Stage (17 December 1999), 22 RIAA 335, ¶72.

370 *North Sea Continental Shelf* (n 234) Dissenting opinion of Vice-President Koretsky, 166. See also Wolfgang Friedmann, 'The North Sea Continental Shelf Cases: A Critique' (1970) 64 AJIL 229, 229, noting that the ICJ's decision is 'surely one of the most ... debatable decisions in the history of the Court'.

371 Akehurst (n 340) 811. See also DM McRae, 'Delimitation of the Continental Shelf between the United Kingdom and France: The Channel Arbitration' (1978) 15 Can YB Intl L 173, 195–96; Emmanuel Decaux, 'L'arrêt de la Cour internationale de Justice dans l'affaire du plateau continental (Tunisie c. Jamahiriya arabe libyenne)' (1982) 28 AFDI 357.

372 See Alex G Oude Elferink, Tore Henriksen, and Signe Veierud Busch, 'The Judiciary and the Law of Maritime Delimitation: Setting the Stage' in Alex G Oude Elferink, Tore Henriksen, and Signe Veierud Busch (eds), *Maritime Boundary Delimitation: The Case Law: Is It Consistent and Predictable?*

success of dispute settlement with regard to maritime dispute settlement stems from the ability of judges to achieve 'a degree of predictability'[373] while also allowing a measure of flexibility—recognizing that maritime delimitation is not a matter that can be settled through the automatic application of a simple rule or through the operation of a mathematical equation.[374]

A loose analogy can be drawn between cases on maritime delimitations and those involving the assessment of a state's requisite level of mitigation action. In both cases, the judge is asked to 'draw a line'—a physical delimitation or an abstract benchmark—in application of the law but in the absence of a determinate legal rule. However, these cases have, so far, been approached in sharply different ways for understandable, albeit questionable, reasons. A key lesson of the judicial experience on maritime delimitation is that decisions relying heavily on equity are far more convincing if they feature a careful, nuanced, and detailed analysis of equity. This conclusion holds for climate litigation, despite the obvious limitations of the analogy. The determination of a state's requisite mitigation action is certainly an even more complex issue than maritime delimitation as it involves burden sharing among all states rather than the delimitation of an area between only two (or a few) states—but this only seems to highlight the need for a more careful, nuanced, and detailed analysis of equity. And, while mitigation obligations have so far mostly been interpreted by domestic judges in cases concerning a single state, rather than in contentious cases before international courts and tribunals, this distinction could explain, but does not appear to justify, the judges' reluctance to justify their equity assumptions.

c) The equitable assessment of a state's requisite level of mitigation action

An equitable judicial assessment of a state's requisite level of mitigation action cannot merely follow a predetermined, 'mechanical' process.[375] Rather, the judge is to make an overall assessment of all relevant norms in light of national circumstances. By analogy, the ICJ in *North Sea Continental Shelf* noted that 'it is the balancing-up of all [relevant] considerations that will produce [an equitable] result rather than reliance on one to the exclusion of all others'.[376] International

(CUP 2018) 29–32, listing twenty-nine relevant cases, fifteen of which are based on advanced consent. See generally Christian Tomuschat, 'Competence of the Court: Article 36' in Andreas Zimmermann, Christian Tomuschat, and Karin Oellers-Frahm (eds), *The Statute of the International Court of Justice: A Commentary* (3rd edn, OUP 2019) 744–45 (para 43).

[373] Alex G Oude Elferink, Tore Henriksen, and Signe Veierud Busch, 'Conclusions' in Elferink, Henriksen, and Busch (n 372) 396. See also Lando (n 357) xvii.

[374] See *Delimitation (Barbados v Trinidad and Tobago)* (n 360) ¶373; Jonathan I Charney, 'Progress in International Maritime Boundary Delimitation Law' (1994) 88 AJIL 227, 227.

[375] See generally Benoit Mayer, 'The Judicial Assessment of States' Action on Climate Change Mitigation' (2022) 35 LJIL (forthcoming).

[376] *North Sea Continental Shelf* (n 234) ¶93.

courts and tribunals, in maritime delimitation cases, have repeatedly noted that maritime delimitation cannot be determined by any 'magic formulas'[377] and can only be 'approximate'.[378] Two judges would likely not arrive at precisely the same conclusion when assessing a state's requisite level of mitigation action, but a balanced equitable assessment should ensure that their conclusions do not differ too substantially.

The collective mitigation objectives accepted by states are relevant in this overall assessment, but only in a very general manner. These objectives reflect the degree of urgency that states associate with climate change mitigation.[379] Whether the target is 1.5 or 2°C, states have accepted not only that they need to keep implementing a level of mitigation action consistent with the current general practice but also that they will have to enhance this action over time. On the other hand, neither climate treaties nor general state practice provide any support to the idea that states are under an immediate obligation to implement mitigation action consistent with these temperature targets.[380]

Burden-sharing principles must also be taken into account in determining a state's requisite level of mitigation action. When the state has presented a coherent and plausible interpretation of these principles, this interpretation should be taken into account by the judge.[381] In any case, the judge's interpretation of burden sharing should properly reflect the diversity of national emissions profiles, especially for countries with highly specialized economies—the potential for mitigation action in sheep-farming New Zealand are not the same as in coal-burning Poland. The judge should consider the state's ability to reduce emissions from the main sectors, for instance in light of possible renewable energy developments or economic diversification policies, considering also the financial and technical capacities available to the state. Responsibility-related factors should be taken into account at this point, along with other factors such as the demographic evolution, in particular from international migration, among other things. These factors cannot be integrated within a mathematical formula, but judges should be able to arrive at some level of agreement as to what, in light of these various relevant elements, appears to be fair and equitable.

[377] *Delimitation (Barbados v Trinidad and Tobago)* (n 360) ¶373. See also *Maritime Boundary in the Bay of Bengal (Bangladesh/Myanmar)* (n 367) ¶317 ('There is no general rule in this respect. Each case is unique and requires specific treatment, the ultimate goal being to reach a solution that is equitable'); *Jan Mayen* (n 345) Separate Opinion of Judge Weeramantry, ¶157; ILC, 'Draft Articles on the Law of Treaties' (n 55), joint commentary on arts 27–28, ¶4, noting that 'the interpretation of documents is to some extent an art, not an exact science'.

[378] *Territorial and Maritime Dispute (Nicaragua v Colombia)* (n 364) ¶158; *Black Sea* (n 363) ¶111.

[379] See above at 257.

[380] See above at 251.

[381] See above at 265.

Conclusion

Assessing a state's requisite level of mitigation action represents a daunting task for any court. The collective objectives that states have (vaguely) agreed to pursue and the burden-sharing principles that they have outlined provide limited assistance in determining what precisely a state must achieve at a given time to comply with its general mitigation obligations. This indeterminacy of the content of general mitigation obligations does not affect their existence as legal obligations,[382] but it complicates considerably their application and could impede their implementation.[383]

To determine a state's requisite mitigation action, a judge would need to exercise a considerable level of discretion. Many judges could feel uncomfortable with this stretch of judicial functions and reject claims before them—perhaps most easily so in national courts, where such decisions would raise important questions relating to the separation of powers[384] and where a court may lack the time and resources to conduct the detailed appraisal of facts and legal principles that an equitable decision would require. Nevertheless, some judges will likely follow the approach first followed by the Supreme Court of the Netherlands in *Urgenda*. If so, the judges would be well advised to recognize the absence of a predetermined benchmark and, instead, engage in an explicit, careful, nuanced, and detailed appraisal of equity in light of national circumstances.

[382] See *North Sea Continental Shelf* (n 234) ¶46; Sandra Fredman, *Human Rights Transformed: Positive Rights and Positive Duties* (OUP 2008) 72.

[383] Frank Biermann, '"Common Concern of Humankind": The Emergence of a New Concept of International Environmental Law' (1996) 34 Archiv des Völkerrechts 426, 432–33.

[384] See *Juliana* (n 16) 1174; *Reynolds* (n 16) ¶3; *Aji P* (n 16) 458; *Sagoonick* (n 16) 782.

VII
Appropriate Measures

Introduction

Chapter VI has revealed the considerable challenges that a judge faces when trying to assess the requisite level of action implied by states' general mitigation obligations. With the exception of the decisions in *Urgenda*, courts generally prefer not to second-guess a state's requisite level of mitigation action, instead granting a broad margin of appreciation to the political branches of government. This, however, does not mean that courts are unable to identify any breaches of general mitigation obligations.

This chapter shows an alternative—often more effective—method to test a state's compliance with its general mitigation obligations, namely, by assessing whether the state is taking the sort of measures that it would be expected to be taking while exercising due diligence. For instance, the International Law Commission (ILC) once observed that a state's due diligence obligation to prevent transboundary environmental harm requires that state to formulate relevant policies; to reflect them, when needed, in 'legislative and administrative regulations'; and to implement them 'through various enforcement mechanisms'.[1] As such, a state would appear to be in breach of its general mitigation obligations if it was not adopting relevant policies or if, having adopted such policies, it was failing to take essential steps to implement them.[2]

A state, in principle, is free to select the specific measures it will implement to mitigate climate change, provided that, in aggregate, these measures reach the requisite level of mitigation action.[3] For instance, despite a growing expectation

[1] ILC, 'Draft Articles on Prevention of Transboundary Harm from Hazardous Activities' (2001) II(2) YBILC 146, commentary on art 3, ¶10.

[2] See above at 213. See also *Pulp Mills on the River Uruguay (Argentina v Uruguay)*, Judgment (20 April 2010), [2010] ICJ Rep 14, Joint dissenting opinion of Judges Al-Khasawneh and Simma, ¶26, noting that 'respect for procedural obligations assumes considerable importance and comes to the forefront as being an essential indicator of whether, in a concrete case, substantive obligations were or were not breached'; Jutta Brunnée, 'Procedure and Substance in International Environmental Law: Confused at a Higher Level?' (2016) 5 ESIL Reflection 6.

[3] See United Nations Framework Convention on Climate Change (9 May 1992, in force 21 March 1994) 1771 UNTS 107, Preamble ¶10; Jorge E Viñuales, 'Due Diligence in International Environmental Law: A Fine-Grained Cartography' in Heike Krieger, Anne Peters, and Leonhard Kreuzer (eds), *Due Diligence in the International Legal Order* (OUP 2020) 120, noting two exceptions with regard to 'obligations that have been jurisprudentially considered to be technical expressions of the prevention principle'.

International Law Obligations on Climate Change Mitigation. Benoit Mayer, Oxford University Press. © Benoit Mayer 2022.
DOI: 10.1093/oso/9780192843661.003.0007

that states (especially developed ones) will seek to reduce their reliance on thermal coal,[4] a state may decide to keep some coal plants running—or even open new ones—as long as it can rely on other mitigation policies and measures to produce the equivalent mitigation outcomes. This flexibility allows national governments to decide how best to reconcile the need to contribute to climate change mitigation with other national priorities such as economic development and social welfare. On the other hand, the measures that the state takes must reflect its due diligence. As such, a state would most obviously be in breach of its general mitigation obligations if it 'knowingly refused to take any measures whatsoever'.[5] In addition, this chapter suggests that a state would also be in breach of its general mitigation obligations if it systematically failed to take appropriate measures.

Some measures are a necessary component of any state's attempt to mitigate climate change. Thus, a state would not be exercising due diligence if it did not monitor the main sources of greenhouse gas (GHG) emissions within its territory or, having identified significant sources of emissions, if it did not establish a process to explore potential ways of regulating them. Many more measures are not strictly necessary to ensure compliance with general mitigation obligations but their implementation is nevertheless to be expected from a state that exercises due diligence. While the non-performance of such appropriate measures leads to no definitive conclusion, it suggests that the state might not be exercising its best endeavour. When a state's failure to take appropriate measures constitutes a systematic pattern, it justifies a presumption that the state is not exercising due diligence. For instance, a developed state does not necessarily breach its general mitigation obligations merely because it continues to rely on thermal coal, but the state should be able to explain this decision, for instance by showing that it has taken alternative measures of a similar effect.

This chapter builds on a distinction between discrete obligations and corollary duties that was introduced in Chapter V.[6] General mitigation obligations can be interpreted as implying corollary duties. These duties can be identified from a mostly descending reasoning, but they must not be incompatible with state practice;[7] and they can be used to determine a state's compliance with its general mitigation obligations. Corollary duties and discrete obligations may have similar contents,[8] and one could constitute part of the relevant context to interpret the other. However, a judge needs to resist the simplistic assumption that any breach of a

[4] See below at 318.

[5] Study Group on Due Diligence in International Law, 'Second Report on Due Diligence' (2016) 77 ILA Rep Conferences 1062, 1073.

[6] See above at 213.

[7] See above at 223.

[8] For instance, transboundary environmental impact assessment is both a corollary of the obligation of prevention and a discrete treaty obligation. See *Pulp Mills* (n 2) ¶101; *South China Sea (Philippines v China)*, Award (12 July 2016), 31 RIAA 153, ¶993.

discrete obligation relating to climate change mitigation automatically implies a breach of the state's general mitigation obligation. For instance, a slight delay in the submission of a national communication under the UN Framework Convention on Climate Change (UNFCCC) could constitute a breach of a discrete treaty commitment,[9] but it hardly constitutes a breach of general mitigation obligations, given that such delays are very common[10] and, overall, that they do not represent a major impediment to the state's mitigation action. More systemic patterns of non-compliance with discrete obligations, however, can constitute important indicia, or even conclusive evidence, of a breach of general mitigation obligations.

Thus, the method of applying general mitigation obligations proposed in this chapter relies in most cases on the holistic assessment of a set of indicia, rather than on a single action or omission, to flag potential cases of non-compliance. A state's systematic failure to take measures that other states largely accept as appropriate would constitute prima facie evidence (ie a rebuttable presumption) that the state is in breach of its general mitigation obligations, with the effect, in contentious proceedings, of shifting the burden of proof onto the state to demonstrate its compliance with these obligations.[11]

The following sections identify a number of appropriate measures and show how a state's failure to take these measures could evidence a breach of its general mitigation obligations. Each section identifies a broad corollary duty, which itself can be broken down in more specific duties, pointing to more concrete measures. The first corollary duty is the duty of cooperation: a state seeking to mitigate climate change would inevitably attempt to cooperate with other states, in particular by negotiating in good faith, seeking to participate in relevant multilateral agreements, and not trying to free-ride on the efforts of other states. The second corollary duty is the duty of vigilance: a duly diligent state would seek a better understanding of climate change, including its causes and potential ways to address them, in particular when authorizing relevant activities. The third corollary duty is the duty of consistency: a diligent state would seek to act in line with its assessment of the goals and principles that guide international action and consistently with its understanding about the causes of climate change and ways to address them.

Each of these three main duties is a necessary component of a state's mitigation action. As such, the failure of a state to implement any of these three duties would be conclusive evidence of its breach of its general mitigation obligations. A holistic assessment of a set of indicia can be used to determine whether the state has implemented any of these three main duties in light of the more specific measures that

[9] See UNFCCC (n 3) art 12(5).

[10] See n 126.

[11] See generally Rüdiger Wolfrum and Mirka Möldner, 'International Courts and Tribunals, Evidence' in *Max Planck Encyclopedia of Public International Law* (online edn, OUP 2006) ¶79.

it entails. A holistic assessment can also take into account a nuanced (non-binary) assessment of the implementation of the three main duties to determine, overall, whether the state appears to be taking climate change mitigation seriously enough. Either way, the assessment is to be conducted by comparing the state's conduct with what could be expected from an average state in the same circumstances, as evidenced by general state practice. A presumption that the state is not complying with its general mitigation obligations arises if this comparison reveals systematic shortcomings.

The three corollary duties identified in this chapter are interrelated and complementary. While the duties of cooperation and vigilance may appear rather formalistic or 'procedural', they provide the benchmarks that can be used, in application of the duty of consistency, to assess whether the state appears to be implementing adequate mitigation action. At the risk of oversimplifying, it could be said that the duty of cooperation helps define the state's understanding of general mitigation obligations, the duty of vigilance helps shed light on the state's ability to implement concrete measures, and the duty of consistency requires the state to implement these concrete measures—that is, to put words into action. A state is most likely complying with its general mitigation obligations if it complies with the three corollary duties—if it negotiates the modalities of international cooperation in good faith, monitors its GHG emissions with a view of understanding how it can reduce them, and implements the measures that are needed according to its own assessment. This method is thus able to identify most of (but not necessarily all) the breaches of general mitigation obligations.

A. Duty of Cooperation

General mitigation obligations imply perhaps most obviously a duty of cooperation. States have emphatically recognized that the mitigation of climate change requires international cooperation. The duty of cooperation implies that the state should negotiate international agreements in good faith, seek to participate in these agreements, and not attempt to free-ride on other states' mitigation action.

1. Foundations

A distinction can be made between a discrete obligation and a corollary duty of cooperation. The obligation of cooperation arises under customary international law and the UN Charter;[12] it has been interpreted by numerous General Assembly

[12] Charter of the United Nations (26 June 1945, in force 24 October 1945) arts 1(3), 55–56.

resolutions[13] and issue-specific treaties.[14] This obligation applies to various environmental issues, in particular those of a global nature, including climate change.[15] Thus, the UNFCCC and multiple subsequent documents acknowledge that 'the global nature of climate change calls for the widest possible cooperation by all countries'.[16] However, the contents of this obligation of cooperation is poorly understood. International courts and tribunals suggest that this obligation requires states, at least, to consult and negotiate in good faith when an agreement is needed.[17] Some have also suggested that states may have 'to take other-regarding interests into account'[18] or even to demonstrate something akin to solidarity,[19] although there is limited evidence of such solidarity in state practice.

By contrast, the duty of cooperation is merely a corollary of general mitigation obligations. Various authorities confirm the possibility of identifying a duty of cooperation as an implication of a due diligence obligation. For instance, the order of the International Tribunal for the Law of the Sea (ITLOS) in *MOX Plant* inferred a duty of cooperation as a 'fundamental principle in the prevention of pollution of the marine environment under ... general international law'.[20] Likewise, the Human Rights Committee interpreted the obligation to protect human rights as implying, when relevant, an obligation to cooperate—for instance to ensure that every child has a nationality[21] and to facilitate family unity or reunification.[22] And the German Federal Constitutional Court interpreted a constitutional provision on the right to life as requiring the state to seek a solution to climate change on the international plane.[23]

[13] See Declaration on Principles of International Law Concerning Friendly Relations and Cooperation among States in Accordance with the Charter of the United Nations, UNGA Resolutions 625 (XXV) (24 October 1970) 123; Declaration on the Establishment of the New International Economic Order, 3201(S-VI) (1 May 1974) ¶3; Charter of Economic Rights and Duties of States, 3281 (XXIX) (12 December 1974); World Summit Outcome, 60/1 (16 September 2005) ¶71.

[14] See Pierre-Marie Dupuy, 'The Place and Role of Unilateralism in Contemporary International Law' (2000) 11 EJIL 19, 22–23. See above at 104.

[15] See Declaration of the United Nations Conference on the Human Environment (16 June 1972) A/Conf.48/14/Rev.1 (1972) 11 ILM 1416 ('Stockholm Declaration'), principle 24; Charter of Economic Rights and Duties (n 13) art 3; Rio Declaration on Environment and Development (14 June 1992) A/CONF.151/26 (vol I) (1992) 31 ILM 874, principle 7.

[16] UNFCCC (n 3) Preamble ¶7. See also references at 111.

[17] See *Railway Traffic between Lithuania and Poland*, Advisory Opinion (15 October 1931), PCIJ Rep Series A/B No 42, 116; *Lac Lanoux*, Award (16 November 1957), 12 RIAA 281, ¶11.

[18] Eyal Benvenisti, 'Sovereigns as Trustees of Humanity: On the Accountability of States to Foreign Stakeholders' (2013) 107 AJIL 295, 296.

[19] For a critical discussion, see Rüdiger Wolfrum, 'Cooperation, International Law of' in *Max Planck Encyclopedia of Public International Law* (online edn, OUP 2010) ¶3.

[20] *MOX Plant (Ireland v UK)*, Order on Provisional Measures (3 December 2001), [2001] ITLOS Rep 95, ¶82. See also *Land Reclamation by Singapore in and around the Straits of Johor (Malaysia v Singapore)*, Order on Provisional Measures (8 October 2003), [2003] ITLOS Rep 10, ¶92.

[21] HRC, General Comment No 17, 'Article 24 (Rights of the Child)', HRI/GEN/1/Rev.1 (7 April 1989), ¶8.

[22] HRC, General Comment No 19, 'Article 23 (The Family)', HRI/GEN/1/Rev.1 (27 July 1990), ¶5.

[23] *Neubauer v Germany*, 1 BvR 2656/18 (Federal Constitutional Court, 24 March 2021) <https://perma.cc/UJM6-QCCY> ¶149. See also above at 158.

By contrast to the discrete obligation of cooperation, the corollary duty applies only if and insofar as cooperation is an appropriate step to comply with general mitigation obligations. Yet, climate change certainly falls within the 'growing class of environmental problems' that are 'global in extent' and, according to the Stockholm Declaration, 'require extensive cooperation among nations'.[24] Thus, states have emphatically acknowledged cooperation as an essential component of effective mitigation action.[25] As such, a state's failure to cooperate on climate change mitigation would constitute a breach of its *obligation* of cooperation, but it would also, in most instances, evidence a breach of the state's general mitigation obligations and the *duty* of cooperation that they entail.

This distinction between the duty and the obligation of cooperation is also apparent when ascertaining questions of jurisdiction and admissibility in international dispute settlement. An international court with jurisdiction to apply the UNFCCC could find a breach of the general mitigation obligations it contains,[26] and the duty of cooperation that these commitments entail, but it may not have jurisdiction to apply the general obligation of cooperation arising from customary international law. Similarly, a human rights treaty body could make its decision based on the duty of cooperation implied by a state's obligation to protect human rights, but not based on the obligation of cooperation that arises from general international law.[27] A domestic court that admits standing on the basis of human rights law, likewise, could apply a corollary duty of cooperation, even if it cannot apply the discrete obligation of cooperation. As such, while the *obligation* of cooperation will mainly be applied in state-to-state adjudication processes allowing a court to apply general international law, there could be more opportunities for the application of the *duty* of cooperation.

The contents of the duty and obligation of cooperation may differ. As noted above, there remains considerable uncertainty about what precisely the obligation of cooperation entails.[28] The interpretation of the duty of cooperation, by contrast, could build not only on state practice and judicial decisions (from an ascending reasoning) but also more heavily on the purpose of the obligations from which this duty is derived (descending reasoning). The cooperation that is required under the duty of cooperation is that which, in light of state practice, could reasonably be expected from a state exercising due diligence in relation to climate change

[24] Stockholm Declaration (n 15) ¶7. For a similar interpretation of human rights law as requiring cooperation on environmental protection, see *Environment and Human Rights*, Advisory Opinion OC-23/17 (15 November 2017) IACtHR Series A No 2.

[25] See n 16. See also John Knox, Report of the Special Rapporteur on the issue of human rights obligations relating to the enjoyment of a safe, clean, healthy and sustainable environment, A/HRC/31/52 (2016) ¶42, noting that 'States have consistently treated climate change as a global problem that requires a global response'.

[26] UNFCCC (n 3) art 4(1)(b), 2(4)(a).

[27] See also above at 155. But see Knox, 2016 Report (n 25) ¶¶42–44.

[28] See above at 284.

mitigation. As the following shows, this duty of cooperation can be interpreted as requiring a state to negotiate climate agreements in good faith, to seek to participate in these agreements, and not to attempt to free-ride on the mitigation action of other states.

2. Negotiation

A first application of the duty of cooperation is that a state must negotiate with other states in good faith with the objective of promoting effective mitigation action. A state, having emphatically recognized that effective responses to climate change require international cooperation,[29] would be negligent if it did not promote such cooperation by playing an active and constructive role in international negotiations.

The duty to negotiate the modalities of international cooperation is a logical implication of the obligation of cooperation. Further, to the extent that there exists a dispute with regard to states' obligations on climate change mitigation,[30] negotiation is also a requirement under Article 33 of the UN Charter, which requires states to find a way to settle international disputes peacefully.[31] Judicial decisions have recognized various aspects of the duty of negotiation in situations involving a comparable need for international cooperation. In particular, the International Court of Justice (ICJ) in *North Sea Continental Shelf* noted that maritime delimitation could not be determined fully through the mechanical application of abstract rules but that it 'must be the object of agreement between the States concerned'.[32] Accordingly, it found that the parties were 'under an obligation to enter into negotiations with a view to arriving at an agreement' on this matter.[33] In *Fisheries Jurisdiction (UK v Iceland)*, the Court held that the parties were 'under mutual obligations to undertake negotiations in good faith for the equitable solution of their differences concerning their respective fishery rights'.[34] In a multilateral context, the ICJ's Advisory Opinion on *Nuclear Weapons* noted that nuclear disarmament

[29] See n 16.

[30] See *Obligations Concerning Negotiations Relating to Cessation of the Nuclear Arms Race and to Nuclear Disarmament (Marshall Islands v India)*, Judgment on Jurisdiction and Admissibility (5 October 2016), [2016] ICJ Rep 255, ¶¶34–37; *Application of the Convention on the Prevention and Punishment of the Crime of Genocide (Gambia v Myanmar)*, Order on Provisional Measures (23 January 2020), [2020] ICJ Rep 3, ¶¶20–31.

[31] See UN Charter (n 12) art 33(1). See also UNFCCC (n 3) art 14(1); *Mavrommatis Palestine Concessions (Greece v UK)*, Jurisdiction (30 August 1924), PCIJ Rep Series A/B No 2, 11–15; Lucius Caflisch, 'Cent ans de règlement pacifique des différends interétatiques' (2001) 288 RdC 9, 245, 275–77.

[32] *North Sea Continental Shelf (Germany/Denmark, Germany/Netherlands)*, Judgment (20 February 1969), [1969] ICJ Rep 3, ¶85.

[33] Ibid ¶85(a).

[34] *Fisheries Jurisdiction (UK v Iceland)*, Judgment on Merits (25 July 1974), [1974] ICJ Rep 3, ¶79(3).

'necessitates the co-operation of all States'[35] before concluding that there exists 'an obligation to pursue in good faith and bring to a conclusion negotiations leading to nuclear disarmament'.[36]

This duty to negotiate is particularly relevant in relation to the protection of shared natural resources.[37] The tribunal in *Lake Lanoux* had already emphasized the duty of states sharing a watercourse to negotiate an agreement on the utilization of the watercourse.[38] The ICJ in *Pulp Mills* highlighted that negotiation is 'all the more vital when a shared resource is at issue, ... which can only be protected through close and continuous co-operation'.[39] In this judgment and the subsequent one in *Certain Activities*, the Court situated the duty to negotiate as an aspect of the general obligation of prevention.[40] These judicial interpretations are buttressed by treaty practice: numerous multilateral environmental agreements require states to carry out negotiations when one of them expresses concern with the potential impacts of activities carried out by another.[41] Such negotiations can be bilateral or multilateral, depending on whether the subject matter concerns the management of transboundary or global environmental resources.[42]

Consistently, states have acknowledged their duty to negotiate agreements on climate change mitigation. The very recognition of climate change as a 'common concern of humankind' points to the need for cooperation and, thus, for such negotiations.[43] The parties to each successive climate treaty have committed to 'make every effort to reach agreement on any proposed amendment'.[44] The parties to the UNFCCC further recognized their own need, acting through the Conference of the Parties, to 'review the adequacy' of the commitments made by Annex I parties[45] as

[35] *Legality of the Threat or Use of Nuclear Weapons*, Advisory Opinion (8 July 1996), [1996] ICJ Rep 226, ¶100.

[36] Ibid ¶105(2)(F). See generally ibid, Declaration of President Bedjaoui, ¶23; Kai Ambos and Matthais Lippold, 'The ICJ and Nuclear Disarmament: Towards a Universal Obligation?' *EJIL:Talk!* (8 July 2020) <https://perma.cc/8C7G-WSCG>.

[37] See ILC, 'Prevention of Transboundary Harm' (n 1) art 9.

[38] *Lac Lanoux* (n 17) ¶11.

[39] *Pulp Mills* (n 2) ¶81.

[40] Ibid ¶115; *Certain Activities Carried Out by Nicaragua in the Border Area (Costa Rica v Nicaragua) and Construction of a Road in Costa Rica along the San Juan River (Nicaragua v Costa Rica)*, Judgment on Merit (16 December 2015), [2015] ICJ Rep 665, ¶104.

[41] See United Nations Convention on the Law of the Sea (10 December 1982, in force 16 November 1994) 1833 UNTS 3, art 198; Convention on Environmental Impact Assessment in a Transboundary Context (25 February 1991, in force 10 September 1997) 1989 UNTS 309 ('Espoo Convention'), art 5; Convention on the Law of the Non-Navigational Uses of International Watercourses (21 May 1997, in force 17 August 2014) (1997) 36 ILM 700, art 17.

[42] See UNCLOS (n 41) art 118; Protocol on Environmental Protection to the Antarctic Treaty (4 October 1991, in force 14 January 1998) 2941 UNTS 3 ('Madrid Protocol'), art 18; *Fisheries Jurisdiction (UK v Iceland)* (n 34) ¶72; John Collier and Vaughan Lowe, *The Settlement of Disputes in International Law: Institutions and Procedures* (OUP 2000) 22.

[43] See UNFCCC (n 3) Preamble ¶2; Paris Agreement (12 December 2015, in force 4 November 2016) (2016) 55 ILM 740, Preamble ¶12; UNGA Res 45/212 (21 December 1990) Preamble ¶2.

[44] UNFCCC (n 3) art 15(3). See also Kyoto Protocol to the United Nations Framework Convention on Climate Change (11 December 1997, in force 16 February 2005) 2303 UNTS 162, art 20(3). See also Paris Agreement (n 43) art 22.

[45] UNFCCC (n 3) art 4(2)(d).

well as to '[p]eriodically examine [their] obligation ... in the light of the objective of the Convention'[46] and to make corresponding recommendations.[47] And the Paris Agreement established a formal stocktaking process 'to assess the collective progress towards achieving the purpose of this Agreement'[48]—a process that could structure continuing negotiations on ambition in national commitments.[49]

Judicial decisions help understand the content of the duty to negotiate. Thus, it is well established that 'an obligation to negotiate does not imply an obligation to reach an agreement',[50] and a state's duty to consult with another state does not provide a right of veto to the other.[51] On the other hand, international courts and tribunals have insisted that this duty is more than a mere formality. The tribunal in *Lake Lanoux* found that a negotiating state is 'to take into consideration the various interests involved, to seek to give them every satisfaction compatible with the pursuit of its own interests, and to show that in this regard it is genuinely concerned to reconcile the interests of' the other states.[52] Another tribunal, in *German External Debts*, pointed out that a duty to negotiate requires a state to be willing 'to abandon earlier positions and to meet the other side part way'.[53] As the ICJ noted in *North Sea Continental Shelf*, states must conduct themselves so 'that the negotiations are meaningful, which will not be the case when either of them insists upon its own position without contemplating any modification of it'.[54] In *Fisheries Jurisdiction*, the Court added that each party 'must in good faith pay reasonable regard to the legal rights of the other'.[55] And, as the Court recalled in *Gabčíkovo-Nagymaros*, the parties are 'to find an agreed solution that takes account of' relevant norms of international law,[56] which thus implies a duty to ensure respect of the rights of third parties.[57]

[46] Ibid art 7(2)(a).
[47] Ibid art 7(2)(g).
[48] Paris Agreement (n 43) art 14(1).
[49] See generally Alexander Zahar, 'Collective Progress in the Light of Equity under the Global Stocktake' (2019) 9 Climate Law 101.
[50] *Railway Traffic between Lithuania and Poland* (n 17) 116. See also *Tacna-Arica Arbitration (Chile/Peru)*, Award (20 July 1922), 2 RIAA 921, 929; *North Sea Continental Shelf* (n 32) ¶87; *Pulp Mills* (n 2) ¶150; *Application of the International Convention on the Elimination of All Forms of Racial Discrimination (Georgia v Russia)*, Judgment on Preliminary Objections (11 April 2011), [2011] ICJ Rep 70, ¶150. But see *Nuclear Weapons* (n 35) ¶¶99–100, 105(2)(F), suggesting an obligation of result.
[51] See *Lac Lanoux* (n 17) ¶11; ILC, 'Prevention of Transboundary Harm' (n 1) commentary on art 9, ¶2.
[52] *Lac Lanoux* (n 17) ¶11. See generally Manilla Declaration on the Peaceful Settlement of International Disputes, UNGA Res 37/10 (15 November 1982).
[53] *Decisions of the Mixed Graeco-German Arbitral Tribunal Set Up under Article 304 in Part X of the Treaty of Versailles (Greece/Germany)*, Award (26 January 1972), 19 RIAA 27, ¶62. See also *North Sea Continental Shelf* (n 32) ¶85(a); *Kuwait v Aminoil*, Final Award (24 March 1982) (1982) 21 ILM 976, ¶70(i).
[54] *North Sea Continental Shelf* (n 32) ¶85(a). See also *Railway Traffic between Lithuania and Poland* (n 17) 116; *Pulp Mills* (n 2) ¶146; *Racial Discrimination (Georgia v Russia)* (n 50) ¶¶157–159.
[55] *Fisheries Jurisdiction (UK v Iceland)* (n 34) ¶78. See also UNGA Res 53/101 (8 December 1998) ¶2(a).
[56] *Gabčíkovo-Nagymaros Project (Hungary/Slovakia)*, Judgment (25 September 1997), [1997] ICJ Rep 7, ¶141.
[57] *Fisheries Jurisdiction (UK v Iceland)* (n 34) ¶72. See generally *North Sea Continental Shelf* (n 32) ¶85(b); Res 53/101 (n 55) Preamble ¶6, ¶2(c). On good faith, see generally UN Charter (n 12) art

On this basis, it is possible to imagine various concrete circumstances where the state would fail to comply with its duty to negotiate—which would create a strong presumption that the state is in breach of its general mitigation obligations. An obvious case would be that of a state displaying no 'genuine attempt to negotiate'[58]—for instance, a state unjustifiably failing to send adequate representations to multilateral climate negotiations. Evan Criddle and Evan Fox-Decent suggested that a breach of a duty to negotiate in good faith could also be established 'if a state arbitrarily breaks off or delays negotiations, declines to follow established procedures for negotiation, or refuses to consider counter-proposals or relevant equitable considerations.'[59] In a broader context, the UN General Assembly pointed out that negotiating states must 'endeavour to maintain a constructive atmosphere during the negotiations' and 'facilitate the pursuit or conclusions of negotiations by remaining focused throughout on the main objectives of the negotiations.'[60] As such, obstructive strategies in the course of climate negotiations could raise doubts about the state's compliance with its duty of cooperation.[61]

3. Treaty Participation

A second application of the duty of cooperation concerns participation in climate treaties. Although a state is free to decide whether to participate in a treaty, its decision not to ratify a climate treaty, or subsequently to withdraw from it, could be an indication that it is not complying with its general mitigation obligations. The state could conceivably rebut this presumption by demonstrating that its decision not to participate is consistent with its duty of cooperation, although, in most circumstances, the state would still be expected to comply with the gist of the treaty in which it is unable or unwilling to participate.

The argument here does not question the positivist tenet that international law emanates from states' 'free will.'[62] As states are equal,[63] no state can impose its will

2(2); Vienna Convention on the Law of Treaties (23 May 1969, in force 27 January 1980) 1155 UNTS 331, Preamble ¶4, art 26.

[58] *Racial Discrimination (Georgia v Russia)* (n 50) ¶159.

[59] Evan J Criddle and Evan Fox-Decent, 'Mandatory Multilateralism' (2019) 113 AJIL 272, 309. See also *Lac Lanoux* (n 17) ¶11; *Application of the Interim Accord of 13 September 1995 (Macedonia v Greece)*, Judgment (5 December 2011), [2011] ICJ Rep 644, ¶¶132–38.

[60] Res 53/101 (n 55) ¶2(e)–(f).

[61] On accusation of obstructionism in climate negotiations, see Joanna Depledge, 'Striving for No: Saudi Arabia in the Climate Change Regime' (2008) 8(4) Global Envtl Politics 9; Ben Doherty, 'US Accused of Obstructing Talks at UN Climate Change Summit', *The Guardian* (11 December 2018).

[62] *SS Lotus (France/Turkey)*, Judgment (7 September 1927), PCIJ Rep Series A No 10, 18. See above at 22.

[63] See UN Charter (n 12) art 2(1).

onto another state.[64] States can arguably limit this sovereign right by accepting an obligation to ratify a treaty,[65] but no such limitation exists in relation to climate treaties: even though participation in climate treaties is general state practice, there is no evidence that states have accepted it as the object of a legal obligation. To the contrary, the fact that states included withdrawal procedures in climate treaties dispels any possible doubts about the voluntary nature of participation in these treaties.[66]

On the other hand, participation in climate treaties can be expected from a diligent state, in light of general mitigation obligations and states' repeated acknowledgement that climate change mitigation involves international cooperation.[67] Thus, multilateral decisions and resolutions have constantly called upon states to ratify climate treaties,[68] and many states protested, or expressed disappointment, in the rare instances where one of them decided not to participate in, or to withdraw from, a climate treaty.[69]

There could conceivably be circumstances where a state would be unable, or even unwilling for justifiable reasons, to participate in a climate treaty; but these circumstances would not necessarily preclude that state from cooperating in other ways. The most obvious circumstance relates to the inability of certain self-governing entities whose status is unclear or contested to sign or ratify climate treaties.[70] Notwithstanding their unresolved status under international law and to the extent that they are subjects of international law, these entities would be expected to seek

[64] Robert Jennings and Arthur Watts (eds), *Oppenheim's International Law: Volume 1 Peace* (9th edn, OUP 2008)§108 (341).

[65] See eg Association Agreement between the European Union and its Member States, of the one part, and Ukraine, of the other part [2014] OJ 161/3, art 8. With regard to the obligation of a state to ratify the ECHR and its Protocols after accession to the Council of Europe, see Council of Europe Parliamentary Assembly Res 1031, 'Honouring of Commitments Entered into by Member States when Joining the Council of Europe' (14 April 1994) <https://perma.cc/YJ84-5ADH> ¶9; Jean-Francois Flauss, 'Les conditions d'admission des pays d'Europe Centrale et Orientale au sein du conseil de l'Europe' (1994) 5 EJIL 401, 409; Eckart Klein, 'Membership and Observer Status' in Stefanie Schmahl and Marten Breuer (eds), *The Council of Europe: Its Law and Policies* (OUP 2017) 46.

[66] See UNFCCC (n 3) art 25; Kyoto Protocol (n 44) art 27; Paris Agreement (n 43) art 28. No state appears to have opposed these provisions in the course of treaty negotiations or following their adoption.

[67] See, by analogy, John Knox, Report of the Special Rapporteur on the issue of human rights obligations relating to the enjoyment of a safe, clean, healthy and sustainable environment, A/HRC/37/59 (2018) ¶38, positing that '[n]o State should ever seek to withdraw from any of its international obligations to protect against transboundary or global environmental harm'.

[68] See UNGA Resolutions 49/120 (19 December 1994) ¶1; 57/257 (20 December 2002) ¶2; 58/243 (23 December 2003) ¶2; 59/234 (22 December 2004) ¶2; 60/197 (22 December 2005) ¶2; 61/201 (20 December 2006) ¶3; 62/86 (10 December 2007) ¶2; 62/86 (10 December 2007) ¶2; 63/32 (26 November 2008) ¶3; 64/73 (7 December 2009) ¶2; 65/159 (20 December 2010) ¶2; 71/228 (21 December 2016) ¶3; 72/219 (20 December 2017) ¶¶3, 12; 73/232 (20 December 2018) ¶3; 74/219 (9 December 2019) ¶2; 75/217 (21 December 2020) ¶3.

[69] See Jonathan Watts and Kate Connolly, 'World Leaders React after Trump Rejects Paris Climate Deal', The Guardian (2 June 2017).

[70] See in particular UNFCCC (n 3) art 20, allowing signature 'by States Members of the United Nations or of any of its specialized agencies or that are Parties to the Statute of the International Court of Justice and by regional economic integration organizations'. It is unclear whether accession (art 22) is subject to the same condition.

relevant ways to cooperate on the mitigation of climate change.[71] Another possible circumstance, albeit less likely, would concern a state which, while able to ratify a climate treaty, is unwilling to do so because of some concerns with specific provisions of the treaty.[72] A case in point is Turkey's early reluctance to ratify the Paris Agreement on the ground that its status as a developing country was not expressly recognized by other states.[73] But notwithstanding whether Turkey had reasonable grounds not to participate in the Paris Agreement, this would not prevent it from taking similar measures, including by publishing a nationally determined contribution (NDC) and taking the necessary measures to achieve it.

Even if a state had good reasons not to participate in a climate treaty, this does not alter the general mitigation obligations applicable under customary international law. As Criddle and Fox-Decent point out, a state that has withdrawn from a climate treaty remains precluded 'from ignoring the global impacts of its climate policies and withdrawing entirely from multilateral engagement'—it 'must continue to cooperate with other states to pursue an equitable, global plan of action'.[74] The customary mitigation obligation applicable to the state or entity independently from its participation in any climate treaty may be interpreted in light of the provisions of a climate treaty to which this state or entity is not participating (unless the state has persistently objected to these provisions) as the state or entity would be expected to follow the international rules and standards that are generally accepted.[75] Thus, states that have been unwilling to participate in the Paris Agreement, as well as self-governing entities unable to do so, have generally implemented rules and procedures similar to those defined by the Paris Agreement, for instance with the publication of their contribution to global mitigation action.[76] And, while the US decision to withdraw from the Paris Agreement reflected a general disengagement with international cooperation on climate change mitigation on the part of the federal government, it led many subnational governments to reaffirm what they envisioned as the *duty* of the United States—independent from its treaty commitment—to implement its NDC.[77]

[71] Thus Taiwan participates in deliberations on climate change mitigation conducted under the aegis of APEC.

[72] Climate treaties do not permit reservations. See UNFCCC (n 3) art 24.

[73] Lavanya Rajamani, 'Ambition and Differentiation in the 2015 Paris Agreement: Interpretative Possibilities and Underlying Politics' (2016) 65 ICLQ 493, 513. Turkey eventually ratified the Agreement in 2021.

[74] Criddle and Fox-Decent (n 59) 277.

[75] By analogy, see UNCLOS (n 41) arts 211, 226; Yoshifumi Tanaka, *The International Law of the Sea* (CUP 2019) 333–35. See generally RR Baxter, 'Multilateral Treaties as Evidence of Customary International Law' (1965) 41 BYBIL 275.

[76] See Kosovo, 'Strategy on Climate Change 2014–2024' (2014); Taiwan, 'Intended Nationally Determined Contribution' (2015); Turkey, INDC (2015); Hong Kong, 'Climate Action Plan 2030+' (2017). See also Benoit Mayer, 'Climate Change Mitigation in the Hong Kong Special Administrative Region' (2017) 7 Climate Law 65.

[77] See '"We Are Still In" Declaration' (5 June 2017) <https://perma.cc/J64W-C7CK>.

4. Prohibition of Free-riding

Climate change mitigation raises a well-known collective action problem.[78] As Eric Posner and David Weisbach pointed out, 'even if a nation is better off with a treaty [on climate change mitigation] than without, it will be better off still if everyone else signs the treaty and it does not'.[79] Each state could seek to maximize its interests by attempting to free-ride on mitigation action implemented by others but, as other states follow the same reasoning, climate change would remain largely unabated. As such, any international cooperation on climate change mitigation must build on the premise that states have a duty not to attempt to free-ride on the action of others.[80]

The duty not to free-ride can be construed as an application of a principle of non-discrimination in environmental protection. This principle suggests that, in implementing measures relating to harmful activities under its control, a state ought not to distinguish between the environmental resources situated within its territory and those situated beyond its territory. This principle is relatively well recognized, in international environmental law, inasmuch as individuals' procedural rights are concerned: states have frequently accepted that they must not make any distinctions on the basis of an individual's domicile in granting access to information, opportunities to participate in decision-making, and rights to remedies and compensation, for what concerns environmental protection.[81] Beyond this, several authors have argued that the principle of non-discrimination also applies to more substantive matters, including substantive standards of protection.[82] Knox, in particular, contended that, when implementing environmental impact assesments (EIAs), 'countries should apply the same environmental protections to potential harm in other countries that they apply to such harm in their own'.[83] Boyle suggested more broadly that 'the non-discrimination principle requires the polluting

[78] See above at 3.

[79] Eric A Posner and David Weisbach, *Climate Change Justice* (Princeton UP 2010) 181.

[80] See Thomas W Merrill, 'Golden Rules for Transboundary Pollution' (1996) 46 Duke LJ 931, 936; Posner and Weisbach (n 79) 182–83.

[81] See International Watercourses Convention (n 41) art 32; ILC, 'Prevention of Transboundary Harm' (n 1) art 15; ILC, 'Draft Principles on the Allocation of Loss in the Case of Transboundary Harm Arising out of Hazardous Activities' [2006] II(2) YBILC 58, principle 8(2). See also Espoo Convention (n 41) art 2(6); Convention on the Transboundary Effects of Industrial Accidents (17 March 1992, in force 19 April 2000) 2105 UNTS 457, art 9; Convention on Access to Information, Public Participation in Decision-Making and Access to Justice in Environmental Matters (25 June 1998, in force 30 October 2001) 2161 UNTS 447 ('Aarhus Convention'), art 3(9); Regional Agreement on Access to Information, Public Participation and Justice in Environmental Matters in Latin America and the Caribbean (4 March 2018, in force 22 April 2021) ('Escazú Agreement'), art 3(a); John Knox, 2018 Report (n 67) ¶¶7–9 ('Framework principle 3').

[82] Henri Smets, 'Le principe de non-discrimination en matière de protection de l'environnement' (2000) 4 Revue Européenne de Droit de l'Environnement 3; John H Knox, 'The Myth and Reality of Transboundary Environmental Impact Assessment' (2002) 96 AJIL 291; Alan Boyle, 'Human Rights and the Environment: Where Next?' (2012) 23 EJIL 613, 639–40.

[83] Knox, 'Myth and Reality' (n 82) 292.

state to treat extra-territorial nuisances no differently from domestic nuisances'.[84] In other words, states would be required to implement the same level of due diligence in preventing transboundary (or global) environmental harm as they do with regard to domestic environmental harm.

However, a substantive principle of non-discrimination finds sparse support in state practice and little evidence of acceptance as law.[85] Besides several recommendations adopted by the Council of the Organization for Economic Co-operation and Development (OECD) in the 1970s and 1980s,[86] the main 'example' invoked by the proponents of a substantive non-discrimination principle is a regional environmental protection treaty ratified by four Scandinavian states.[87] More specific empirical evidence of state practice or acceptance as law is difficult to come by: as Knox pointed out, 'the adverse effects of pollution tend to decrease with distance', which implies that '[i]n most cases, … the domestic environmental standard of the state of origin … will necessarily provide at least as much protection extraterritorially as it does domestically'.[88] In addition, there is no common metric to compare the substantive standards that a state implements in order to prevent local and transboundary or global environmental harm—which makes it more difficult to test the validity of this theory.

Despite this limited empirical validation, at least a core non-discrimination principle can be justified as an indispensable implication of the duty of states to cooperate in good faith. This core principle only requires that a state does not *deliberately* discount transboundary or global environmental harm when devising its policies and measures on environmental protection. By contrast to a fully fledged non-discrimination principle, this core principle does not require a delicate assessment and comparison of the level of diligence evidenced in the state's efforts to protect local and global environment. What this core principle suggests largely overlaps with a standard interpretation of the duty to cooperate in good faith as requiring a state to act in a 'spirit of honesty'[89] and 'to refrain from taking unfair advantage'[90] of others.

A state could be found in breach of this core principle of non-discrimination based on evidence that decisions were made *with the intent* to evade the state's

[84] Boyle (n 82) 639–40.

[85] Alan Boyle and Catherine Redgwell, *International Law and the Environment* (4th edn, OUP 2021) 169–70. See also Merrill (n 80) 954.

[86] OECD Council Recommendation C(74)224 (21 November 1974) (1975) 14 ILM 242, Annex ¶4; OECD Council Recommendation C(77)28 (17 May 1977) (1977) 16 ILM 977; OECD Council Recommendation C(78)77 (21 September 1978) (1978) 17 ILM 1530.

[87] Convention on the Protection of the Environment between Denmark, Finland, Norway and Sweden (19 February 1974, in force 5 October 1976) 1092 UNTS 279, art 2.

[88] Knox, 'Myth and Reality' (n 82) 313.

[89] *Interpretation of the Algerian Declarations of 19 January 1981 (Claims against US Nationals)* (1982) 62 ILR 595, 605.

[90] Mark E Villiger, *Commentary on the 1969 Vienna Convention on the Law of Treaties* (Martinus Nijhoff 2008) 425.

international responsibilities and to free-ride on the mitigation efforts of other states. For instance, the United States once justified its withdrawal from the Paris Agreement merely as a way to promote US interests, without any consideration for the state's international obligations,[91] and the Trump administration further directed federal agencies *not* to take into account extraterritorial or global environmental impacts when assessing proposed activities.[92] In other, more subtle cases, the intention to discount global environmental harm may be inferred from a pattern of domestic environmental regulation systematically discounting or discarding global environmental harm, for instance when the law of a country provides detailed and effective measures to reduce local air pollution, but not to limit GHG emissions.

B. Duty of Vigilance

Beside cooperation, general mitigation obligations also imply a duty of vigilance. This duty has three main applications: states must promote knowledge of climate change through research and education, they must gather and share country-specific information, and they must assess the impacts of activities implemented under their control.

1. Foundations

A state would not be complying with its general mitigation obligations if it was not at least trying to gain awareness of the problem of climate change, its causes, its impacts, and potential solutions. Thus, a duty of vigilance has often been inferred as a corollary of due diligence obligations under international law. Neil McDonald, for instance, defined a state's due diligence obligation as entailing, among other things, that the state 'undertak[e] fact-finding, to properly understand a set of circumstances before it takes a particular course of action'.[93] Likewise, the Study Group on Due Diligence of the International Law Association noted that a state's due diligence obligation may require it 'to use best efforts to gain knowledge of activity within its territory or jurisdiction'.[94] It has even been suggested that the duty of

[91] Donald Trump, Remarks on Paris Climate Agreement (1 June 2017), justifying the US withdrawal from the Paris Agreement as a way to promote US interests, without taking foreign interests into consideration.

[92] Executive Order 13783 of 28 March 2017, Promoting Energy Independence and Economic Growth, 82 Fed Reg 16093 (US), s 5(c).

[93] Neil McDonald, 'The Role of Due Diligence in International Law' (2019) 68 ICLQ 1041, 1042. See also Boyle and Redgwell (n 85) 159.

[94] Study Group on Due Diligence in International Law, 'Second Report on Due Diligence' (n 5), 1073.

vigilance 'in practice is essentially the same' as the duty of due diligence[95]—but this overlooks the existence of other corollaries of due diligence, in particular the requirement that states are to act upon the knowledge gained through exercising vigilance.

International courts and tribunals have recognized this corollary duty of vigilance in various circumstances. As early as 1923, Huber noted in an arbitral award that a state is required to exercise 'a certain vigilance' in ensuring domestic peace and social order as part of its due diligence obligation to protect foreign nationals.[96] Likewise, the ICJ in *Armed Activities on the Territory of the Congo* held that an occupying power's responsibility 'is engaged ... for any lack of vigilance in preventing violations of human rights and international humanitarian law by other actors present in the occupied territory'.[97]

This duty of vigilance is particularly well recognized in relation to states' due diligence obligations on environmental protection. The ICJ in *Fisheries Jurisdiction (UK v Iceland)* interpreted a state's obligation to manage shared environmental resources as involving 'the obligation to keep [these resources] under review'.[98] In *Gabčíkovo-Nagymaros*, the Court acknowledged more broadly that, 'in the field of environmental protection, vigilance and prevention are required'.[99] In *Pulp Mills*, the Court reaffirmed the requirement of vigilance as a corollary of a state's due diligence obligation in relation to the prevention of environmental harm[100] and highlighted its implication that states must monitor activities undertaken by non-state actors,[101] including by undertaking 'an environmental impact assessment on the potential effects' of such activities[102] and through a 'continuous monitoring' of the effects of the activity on the environment.[103]

This position is also reflected in the work of the ILC. The Draft Articles on the Prevention of Transboundary Harm suggest that states' due diligence obligation 'extends to taking appropriate measures to identify activities which involve [the] risk [of such harm]'.[104] The ILC further interpreted the precautionary approach as implying 'the need for States to review their obligations of prevention in a continuous manner to keep abreast of the advances in scientific knowledge'.[105] The

[95] Study Group on Due Diligence in International Law, 'First Report' (2014) 76 ILA Rep Conferences 947, 954.

[96] *Affaire des biens britanniques au Maroc espagnol (Spain v UK)*, Award (1 May 1925), 2 RIAA 615, 642.

[97] *Armed Activities on the Territory of the Congo (DRC v Uganda)*, Judgment (19 December 2005), [2005] ICJ Rep 168, ¶179.

[98] *Fisheries Jurisdiction (UK v Iceland)* (n 34) ¶72.

[99] *Gabčíkovo-Nagymaros* (n 56) ¶140.

[100] *Pulp Mills* (n 2) ¶¶185, 188.

[101] Ibid ¶197.

[102] Ibid ¶204. See also *Certain Activities* (n 40) ¶104.

[103] *Pulp Mills* (n 2) ¶205. See also *Certain Activities* (n 40) ¶¶161, 228.

[104] ILC, 'Prevention of Transboundary Harm' (n 1) commentary on art 3, ¶5.

[105] Ibid commentary on art 10, ¶7.

Draft Guidelines on the Protection of the Atmosphere also construe the due diligence obligation of states to protect the atmosphere as requiring 'a certain level of vigilance in ... the exercise of administrative control applicable to public and private operators, such as the monitoring of activities undertaken by such operators'.[106]

A state must not only find out about activities taking place in its territory, but it must also share information it has which may be relevant to other states. Thus, the ICJ in *Corfu Channel*, having concluded that 'the laying of the minefield ... could not have been accomplished without the knowledge of the Albanian Government', held that Albania's obligation 'consisted in notifying ... the existence of a minefield in Albanian territorial waters and in warning the approaching British warships of the imminent danger to which the minefield exposed them'.[107] Treaty practice and Security Council resolutions confirm the duty of states to exchange information as part of their due diligence obligation, for instance to prevent terrorist attacks on one another's territory.[108]

This, too, has been well recognized in relation to environmental protection. The Rio Declaration highlights states' duty to 'provide prior and timely notification and relevant information to potentially affected States on activities that may have a significant adverse transboundary environmental effect',[109] as well as the duty to 'immediately notify other States of any natural disasters or other emergencies that are likely to produce sudden harmful effects on the environment of those States'.[110] In *Certain Activities*, the ICJ concluded that, if an EIA affirms a risk of significant transboundary harm, 'the State planning to undertake the activity is required, in conformity with its due diligence obligation, to notify the potentially affected State ... where that is necessary to determine the appropriate measures to prevent or mitigate that risk'.[111] Many multilateral environmental agreements require their parties to exchange information on the state of the environment, on the activities likely to cause further environmental impacts, and on the measures that they are taking to protect the environment.[112] Treaties requiring states to conduct an EIA

[106] ILC, 'Draft Guidelines on the Protection of the Atmosphere' in ILC Report, 72nd session, A/76/10 (2021) 13, commentary on guideline 3, ¶6.

[107] *Corfu Channel (UK v Albania)*, Judgment on Merits (9 April 1949), [1949] ICJ Rep 4, 22.

[108] See International Convention for the Suppression of the Financing of Terrorism (9 December 1999, in force 10 April 2002) 2178 UNTS 197, art 18(3); UNSC Res 1373 (28 September 2001) S/RES/1373, ¶2(b).

[109] Rio Declaration (n 15) principle 19. See also ILC, 'Prevention of Transboundary Harm' (n 1) arts 8, 12.

[110] Rio Declaration (n 15) principle 18. See also ILC, 'Prevention of Transboundary Harm' (n 1) art 17.

[111] *Certain Activities* (n 40) ¶104. See also ibid, Separate Opinion of Judge Donoghue, ¶20.

[112] UNCLOS (n 41) arts 198, 200; Vienna Convention for the Protection of the Ozone Layer (22 March 1985, in force 22 September 1988) 1513 UNTS 293, arts 2(2)(a), 4(1); Convention on Biological Diversity (5 June 1992, in force 29 December 1993) 1760 UNTS 79, arts 14, 17, 26; International Watercourses Convention (n 41) arts 9, 11–12. See also Philippe Sands and Jacqueline Peel, *Principles of International Environmental Law* (4th edn, CUP 2018) 685–94.

also require them to share their findings with other states concerned or—with regard to global commons—with all states, either through direct notification[113] or with the intermediary of international institutions.[114]

2. Climate Science

A first application of the duty of vigilance points to a duty to promote knowledge about climate change, its impacts, and potential response measures. A state would not be exercising due diligence if, having acknowledged that 'change in the Earth's climate and its adverse effects are a common concern of humankind',[115] it was not seeking to have a good understanding of such change. This understanding may be acquired by national research, but also through the free flow of information among scientists and within societies. As such, this first application of the duty of vigilance consists both in a negative duty requiring a state to refrain from impeding the circulation of information on climate change and in a resource-dependent positive duty to take appropriate measures to promote a better knowledge of climate change.

Climate treaties reflect these duties in two ways. First, the UNFCCC requires its parties to promote 'scientific, technological, technical, socio-economic and other research'[116] and to 'cooperate in the full, open and prompt exchange of relevant … information'.[117] Many states have directed public research funding towards acquiring a better understanding of climate change,[118] and the Intergovernmental Panel on Climate Change (IPCC) epitomizes the cooperation of scientists from various nations. Second, states have committed to promote education and raise awareness on climate change and its effects.[119] As such, many states have taken measures to include climate science in school curricula.[120]

In practical terms, it is difficult to assess compliance with the open-ended, positive duty to promote a better knowledge of climate change. At any rate, while they certainly constitute appropriate measures, neither research nor education policies are strictly necessary conditions for a state to take effective measures on climate

[113] Espoo Convention (n 41) art 3; International Watercourses Convention (n 41) art 12.

[114] UNCLOS (n 41) art 204; Madrid Protocol (n 42) Annex I arts 3.3–3.4.

[115] UNFCCC (n 3) Preamble ¶2. See also UNGA Res 43/53 (6 December 1988) ¶1.

[116] UNFCCC (n 3) art 4(1)(g).

[117] Ibid art 4(1)(h). See also art 5; Kyoto Protocol (n 44) art 10(d).

[118] See eg Climate Change and Energy Transition Law, No 7 (20 May 2021), 121 BOE 62009 (Spain) arts 35–36; Law No 2021-1104 of 22 August 2021, JORF 196 (France), art 2.

[119] UNFCCC (n 3) art 6. See also Kyoto Protocol (n 44) art 10(e); Paris Agreement (n 43) art 12. See also Decisions 11/CP.8, 'New Delhi Work Programme on Article 6 of the Convention' (1 November 2002) FCCC/CP/2002/7/Add.1, 23; 15/CP.18, 'Doha Work Programme on Article 6 of the Convention' (7 December 2012) FCCC/CP/2012/8/Add.2, 17; 17/CP.22, 'Improving the effectiveness of the Doha Work Programme on Article 6 of the Convention' (17 November 2016) FCCC/CP/2016/10/Add.2, 10.

[120] See Sara Reardon, 'Climate Change Sparks Battles in Classroom' (2011) 333 Science 688.

change mitigation. As such, the failure of a state to take sufficient measures to promote research or education on climate change would not generally constitute definitive evidence, but only an indicium, that the state is not complying with its general mitigation obligations. Things could be different when a state is acting in breach of its negative duty, for instance by engaging in a systematic attempt to deny or undermine the general knowledge and understanding of climate change.[121] Such conduct would more likely suffice to constitute prima facie evidence of a breach of general mitigation obligations.

3. Monitoring and Reporting

Another application of the duty of vigilance is that a state must gather and share country-specific information, including information on both its GHG emissions and the policies and measures that it is implementing, or planning to implement, to regulate these emissions. A state would not be exercising due diligence with regard to climate change if it was not seeking to understand its contribution to causing the problem and the effect of the action it is taking to address it. Sharing country-specific information, in turn, enables other countries to have a better understanding of current and foreseeable GHG emissions and to plan accordingly.

This duty to gather and share country-specific information is well reflected in climate treaties. The UNFCCC and the Paris Agreement require that each party regularly produce an inventory of its GHG emissions and communicate 'a general description of steps taken or envisaged' in application of their general obligations.[122] These treaty commitments must be implemented in light of modalities adopted by decisions of the Conference of the Parties,[123] for instance with regard to the timing and the content of these reports.[124]

Treaty commitments on monitoring and reporting have not always been consistently reflected in state practice. Although many states have developed mechanisms to gather and report relevant information,[125] developing states in particular

[121] By analogy, see William C Tucker, 'Deceitful Tongues: Is Climate Change Denial a Crime' (2012) 39 Ecology Law Quarterly 831; Lisa Benjamin, 'The Road to Paris Runs through Delaware: Climate Litigation and Directors' Duties' [2020] Utah L Rev 313.

[122] UNFCCC (n 3) arts 12(1)(b). See also art 12(1)(a); Paris Agreement (n 43) art 13(7). See also above at 45 and 62 respectively.

[123] See UNFCCC (n 3) arts 2(1)(a), 12(1)(a); Paris Agreement (n 43) art 13(7)(a).

[124] For an overview, see Benoit Mayer, 'Transparency under the Paris Rulebook: Is the Transparency Framework Truly Enhanced?' (2019) 9 Climate Law 40.

[125] See Ley general de cambio climático (General Law on Climate Change), DOF 6 January 2012, translation, amended by decree, DOF 13 July 2018 (Mexico) arts 74–75, 87–88; Commission Implementing Regulation (EU) 2018/2066 of 19 December 2018 on the monitoring and reporting of greenhouse gas emissions pursuant to Directive 2003/87/EC of the European Parliament and of the Council and amending Commission Regulation (EU) No 601/2012 [2018] OJ L334/1; Commission Implementing Regulation (EU) 2018/2067 of 19 December 2018 on the verification of data and on the accreditation of verifiers pursuant to Directive 2003/87/EC of the European Parliament and of the Council [2018] 334/94; Федеральный Закон Об Ограничении Выбросов Парниковых Газов

have often accumulated substantial delays in communicating their reports,[126] and not infrequently they have missed some of the required information. Yet, a state's failure to comply with specific treaty commitments does not automatically entail a breach of its general mitigation obligation. The latter would occur only in situations involving a state's persistent, structural, or intentional failure to gather and report relevant country-specific information.

4. Activity Assessment

A last aspect of the duty of vigilance is the duty of a state not to authorize without due consideration any proposed activities likely to make the situation worse. The following retraces the identification of environmental assessment as a corollary of the general obligation of prevention before documenting its progressive recognition as a way to mitigate climate change. The use of environmental assessment as a tool for climate change mitigation—in short, climate assessment—is not fully recognized as a discrete international law obligation, but it is a measure that states are widely expected to take as part of their due diligence. As such, whether a state conducts climate assessments is a strong indicium of its compliance with its general mitigation obligations.

a) Environmental assessment as an international law obligation

Environmental assessment is a procedure aimed, first, at understanding and, second, at either avoiding or reducing the environmental impacts of a proposed activity; it involves a scientific study of these impacts and a process of public deliberation aimed at advising the decision taken by public authorities. Following its adoption in US law in 1969,[127] environmental assessment procedures have become mandatory in almost every jurisdiction.[128] A distinction is often drawn between

(Federal Law on Limiting Greenhouse Gas Emissions), No 296-ФЗ (2 July 2021) art 8; Alexander Zahar and Hao Zhang, 'Monitoring, Reporting, and Verification of Greenhouse Gas Emissions in China' in Xiangbai He, Hao Zhang, and Alexander Zahar (ed), *Climate Change Law in China in Global Context* (Routledge 2020).

[126] For instance, numerous non-Annex I parties (including some parties that are neither least-developed countries nor small island developing states) have failed to publish a national communication every four years, as per their commitment. See generally UNFCCC Secretariat, 'National Communication Submissions from Non-Annex I Parties' (no date) <https://unfccc.int/non-annex-I-NCs>; Decision 1/CP.16, 'The Cancun Agreements: Outcome of the Work of the Ad Hoc Working Group on Long-Term Cooperative Action under the Convention' (10–11 December 2010) FCCC/CP/2010/7/Add.1, 2, ¶60(b).

[127] National Environmental Protection Act of 1969 s 102, 42 USC 4332.

[128] See Tseming Yang, 'The Emergence of the Environmental Impact Assessment Duty as a Global Legal Norm and General Principle of Law' (2018) 70 Hastings LJ 525, 545; UNEP, *Assessing Environmental Impacts: A Global Review of Legislation* (2018); Richard Morgan, 'Environmental Impact Assessment: The State of the Art' (2012) 30 Impact Assessment & Project Appraisal 5; Neil Craik, 'The

the 'EIA' of projects, which is almost universally adopted, and the 'strategic environmental assessment' (SEA) of plans, programmes, or policies, which is mainly implemented in developed countries.[129] The Rio Declaration affirms that EIAs 'shall be undertaken for proposed activities that are likely to have a significant adverse impact on the environment'.[130] Yet, as Boyle and Redgwell observed, determining whether the activity is 'likely to have a significant adverse impact on the environment' is one of the main reasons for doing an environmental assessment.[131] As such, a state could be expected to conduct an environmental assessment any time it has 'reasonable grounds for believing that planning activities ... may cause' such impact.[132]

Environmental assessment procedures have been used not only to protect national environmental resources, but also to prevent transboundary environmental harm.[133] The parties to the Espoo Convention and its Kiev Protocol, adopted by the UN Economic Commission for Europe, have committed to carrying out EIAs and SEAs for proposed activities likely to affect the environment of other parties.[134] Other multilateral[135] and bilateral[136] treaties require states to carry out EIAs as a way of protecting resources situated beyond their territory.

As noted above,[137] the ICJ in *Pulp Mills* identified EIAs as a requirement under customary international law when a project is liable to create significant transboundary environmental impacts.[138] In doing so, the Court relied concurrently on ascending and descending approaches to the identification of customary international law.[139] Relying on an ascending reasoning, it suggested that the EIA

Assessment of Environmental Impact' in Emma Lees and Jorge E Viñuales (eds), *Oxford Handbook of Comparative Environmental Law* (OUP 2019).

[129] See eg Directive 2001/42/EC of the European Parliament and of the Council of 27 June 2001 on the assessment of the effects of certain plans and programmes on the environment [2001] 197/30; Directive 2011/92/EU of the European Parliament and of the Council of 13 December 2011 on the assessment of the effects of certain public and private projects on the environment Text with EEA relevance [2012] OJ L26/1.

[130] Rio Declaration (n 15) principle 17.

[131] Boyle and Redgwell (n 85) 191.

[132] Ibid (emphasis in the original), quoting UNCLOS (n 41) art 206.

[133] The opposite would constitute a discrimination and be inconsistent with states' obligation to co-operate in good faith on environmental protection. See above at 293.

[134] Espoo Convention (n 41); Protocol on Strategic Environmental Assessment to the Convention on Environmental Impact Assessment in a Transboundary Context (21 May 2003, in force 11 July 2010) 2785 UNTS 140 ('Kiev Protocol').

[135] UNCLOS (n 41) art 206; Madrid Protocol (n 42) art 8; Convention on Biological Diversity (n 112) art 14(1)(a).

[136] Agreement Concerning Frontier Rivers (16 September 1971, in force 1 January 1972) 825 UNTS 191 art 3(2).

[137] See above at 296.

[138] *Pulp Mills* (n 2) ¶204. See also *Responsibilities and Obligations of States Sponsoring Persons and Entities with Respect to Activities in the Area*, Advisory Opinion (1 February 2011), [2011] ITLOS Rep 10, ¶147 (citing *Pulp Mills*); *Certain Activities* (n 40), ¶104; ILC, 'Prevention of Transboundary Harm' (n 1) art 7; Pierre-Marie Dupuy and Jorge E Viñuales, International Environmental Law (2nd edn, CUP 2018) 78–79.

[139] See above at 93.

requirement could be identified by induction from 'a practice' and its 'acceptance among States'.[140] In addition, from a descending reasoning, the Court added that 'due diligence, and the duty of vigilance and prevention which it implies, would not be considered to have been exercised' if a state did not conduct an environmental assessment before approving the implementation of the project.[141] The Court's judgment in *Certain Activities* maintained the same ambivalence as to the approach used to identify EIA as a norm in customary law.[142] Separate opinions in the two judgments reveal the Court's internal division between judges convinced by an ascending reasoning[143] and those with a predilection for a descending reasoning.[144]

This dissension implies two different conceptions of the relation between EIAs and due diligence. If the EIA requirement is a corollary of the general obligation of prevention (as a descending reasoning suggests), the failure of a state to carry out an EIA automatically constitutes a breach of this general obligation. Yet, while the conduct of an EIA may certainly be an appropriate and useful measure to prevent environmental harm, it is not strictly a necessary measure—a state could conceivably achieve a high level of environmental protection without implementing a fully fledged EIA. Thus, the ICJ's majority found it necessary to buttress its conclusion by alluding to empirical evidence of state practice and acceptance as law.[145] Following the ICJ's reliance on both the descending and ascending approaches, the failure of a state to conduct an EIA should not necessarily be considered as conclusive evidence of a breach of the state's general obligation of prevention, even though it constitutes at least an indicium of such a breach.

In further analysis, one's assessment of the relation between EIAs and the prevention obligation depends in large part on one's definition of an EIA. Despite the nearly universal nature of EIAs broadly speaking, the scope and content of these procedures vary significantly between jurisdictions. On the one hand, a state would almost necessarily have to be found in breach of its obligation of prevention if it failed to impose even a simple scientific assessment before approving a project likely to have major, long-term, and irreversible transboundary environmental

[140] *Pulp Mills* (n 2) ¶204.

[141] Ibid. See also *Certain Activities* (n 40) ¶104; *Activities in the Area* (n 138) ¶147.

[142] See *Certain Activities* (n 40) ¶104.

[143] See *Pulp Mills* (n 2) Separate Opinion of Judge Cançado Trindade, ¶¶71, 96; *Certain Activities* (n 40) Separate Opinion of Judge Donoghue, ¶9; Separate Opinion of Judge Owada, ¶¶13–22; Separate Opinion of Judge Cançado Trindade, ¶¶54–57. See also *Request for an Examination of the Situation in Accordance with Paragraph 63 of the Court's Judgment of 20 December 1974 in the Nuclear Tests (New Zealand v France) Case (NZ v France)*, Order (22 September 1995), [1995] ICJ Rep 288, Dissenting Opinion of Judge Weeramantry, 344–46; *Gabčíkovo-Nagymaros* (n 56) Separate Opinion of Judge Weeramantry, 113.

[144] See *Certain Activities* (n 40) Separate Opinion of Judge Dugard, ¶¶9, 17; Separate Opinion of Judge Bhandari, ¶31. See also *Activities in the Area* (n 138) ¶145; Neil Craik, 'The Duty to Cooperate in the Customary Law of Environmental Impact Assessment' (2020) 69 ICLQ 239, 245.

[145] The Court only asserted the existence of such empirical evidence. But see Neil Craik, *The International Law of Environmental Impact Assessment: Process, Substance and Integration* (CUP 2008) 23–53.

impacts. It is arguably a necessary implication of due diligence that this assessment should be conducted prior to the approval of the project[146] and, more generally, that the study should be conducted in a manner that permits a genuine assessment of its impacts.[147] On the other hand, states should be allowed to assess the need for an EIA for projects of lesser consequences, to determine the specific content of the assessment in each case,[148] and (as far as compliance with their obligation of prevention is concerned) to decide whether and, if so, how to conduct public consultations.[149] Thus, as Judge Donoghue noted, there is 'scope for variation in the way that States of origin conduct the assessment, so long as the State meets its obligation to exercise due diligence in preventing transboundary environmental harm'.[150]

b) Environmental assessment as a tool for climate change mitigation

Environmental assessment has been recognized as an appropriate tool for environmental protection beyond the circumstances of the *Pulp Mills* case, where the project was threatening to cause harm to the territory of another state.[151] As ITLOS noted in its advisory opinion on *Activities in the Area*, this procedure 'may also apply to activities with an impact on the environment in an area beyond the limits of national jurisdiction'.[152] Several treaty regimes define EIA procedures to protect the environment beyond national jurisdiction.[153] Yet, climate treaties do not create a clear obligation for states to use environmental assessment systematically as a tool for climate change mitigation. The UNFCCC only requires its parties to '[t]ake climate change considerations into account, to the extent feasible, in their relevant social, economic and environmental policies and actions'.[154]

The Draft Guidelines on the Protection of the Atmosphere adopted by the ILC observe that 'States have the obligation to ensure that an environmental impact assessment is undertaken of proposed activities under their jurisdiction or control which are likely to cause significant adverse impact on the atmosphere in terms

[146] *Pulp Mills* (n 2) ¶205.

[147] *South China Sea* (n 8) ¶990.

[148] *Pulp Mills* (n 2) ¶205.

[149] States may have other obligations requiring them to ensure public consultations in such processes. See eg Aarhus Convention (n 81) art 6.

[150] *Certain Activities* (n 40) Separate Opinion of Judge Donoghue, ¶13.

[151] EIA has also been construed as a tool to protect the environment within the state's territory as a corollary of an obligation to protect human rights in circumstances where environmental harm would affect the enjoyment of these rights. See *Hatton v UK*, App No 36022/97, 2003-VIII ECHR 189, ¶128; Social and Economic Rights Action Center/Nigeria, Communication No 155/96 (African Commission of Human and Peoples' Rights, October 2001) ¶53; *Taşkın v Turkey*, App No 46117/99, 2004-X ECHR 179, ¶119.

[152] *Activities in the Area* (n 138) ¶148. See also *South China Sea* (n 8) ¶¶987–93.

[153] See n 135. On ongoing negotiations on the protection of biodiversity beyond national jurisdiction, see Myron H Nordquist and Ronán Long (eds), *Marine Biodiversity of Areas beyond National Jurisdiction* (Brill 2021).

[154] UNFCCC (n 3) art 4(1)(f). This provision then mentions impact assessments but only as a way to minimize the adverse impact of climate action, that is, as a tool for adaptation.

of … atmospheric degradation'.[155] The Commentary suggests that the precedents developed in a transboundary context 'should be applied a fortiori to those activities potentially causing global atmospheric degradation'.[156] Yet, while the Draft Guidelines mention 'activities involving intentional large-scale modification of the atmosphere' (ie geo-engineering activities) as an example,[157] the ILC did not take a clear position on the application of this obligation in relation to activities that involve unintentional and typically smaller atmospheric impacts through GHG emissions. The a fortiori argument to justify the use of EIAs as a tool for climate change mitigation is compelling only insofar as the EIA is—and, overall, is recognized by states as being—as effective in mitigating climate change as it is in preventing transboundary environmental harm.

In recent years, many states have adapted environmental assessment procedures as a tool for the mitigation of climate change.[158] These climate assessment procedures have variously been applied through the judicial interpretation of pre-existing statutes,[159] the adoption of new statutes,[160] or evolving administrative practices.[161] Some jurisdictions are yet to see any development,[162] whereas two countries—Kazakhstan[163] and New Zealand[164]—have deliberately excluded GHG emissions from the scope of their environmental assessment procedures based on a (dubious)

[155] ILC, 'Atmosphere' (n 106) guideline 4.

[156] Ibid commentary guideline 4, ¶6.

[157] Ibid.

[158] See Benoit Mayer, 'Climate Assessment as an Emerging Obligation under Customary International Law' (2019) 68 ICLQ 271.

[159] See *Greenpeace Australia Ltd v Redbank Power Co* [1994] NSWLEC 178, ILDC 985 (AU 1994); *Mid States Coalition for Progress v Surface Transportation Board* (8th Cir, 2003) 345 F3d 520; *Earthlife Africa Johannesburg v Minister of Environmental Affairs*, [2017] ZAGPPHC 58, [2017] 2 All SA 519; *Save Lamu v National Environmental Management Authority*, NET 196/2016 (26 June 2019) (Kenya) ¶138.

[160] See Directive 2014/52/EU of the European Parliament and of the Council of 16 April 2014 amending Directive 2011/92/EU on the assessment of the effects of certain public and private projects on the environment Text [2014] OJ L124/1, Preamble ¶13, Annex IV ¶¶4–5; Impact Assessment Act, SC 2019, c28 (Canada), s 22; The Environment Protection Act, No 9 of 2019 (2076.06.24) (Nepal) ss 3–14.

[161] See Ministry of Ecology and Environment, 建设项目环境影响技术评估导则 (Guideline for technical review of environment impact assessment), HJ616-2011 (1 January 2011) <https://perma.cc/NME8-LHEY> (China) ¶6.3.2.8; Ministry of Ecology and Environment, 规划环境影响评价技术导则总纲 (Technical Guidelines for Strategic Environmental Assessment: General principles), HJ130-2019 (1 March 2019) English translation <https://perma.cc/HBS6-KTF5> pt A6.

[162] For instance, Hong Kong has never modified the list of types of environmental impacts that are to be assessed under its 1997 Environmental Impact Assessment Ordinance. See Technical Memorandum on Environmental Impact Assessment Process, Special Supplement No 5 of Gazette No 20, Vol 139 (16 May 1997) (Hong Kong); Benoit Mayer and Wu Lan, 'The Environmental Impact Assessment Ordinance: Two Decades, No Change' (June 2019) Hong Kong Lawyer 44.

[163] О внесении изменений и дополнений в некоторые законодательные акты Республики Казахстан по экологическим вопросам (On Amendments and additions to some legislative acts of the Republic of Kazakhstan on environmental issues), Law of 3 December 2011, No 505-IV, art 1 (modifying art 39(2) of the Environmental Code); Қазақстан Республикасының Экология Кодексі (Environmental Code of the Republic of Kazakhstan), Law of 2 January 2021, No 400-VI, English translation <https://perma.cc/KUX8-LN8Q> arts 66(6), 106(6).

[164] Resource Management (Energy and Climate Change) Amendment Act 2004, Public Act 2004 No 2 (NZ).

belief that the creation of a national market-based mechanism would be sufficient to keep GHG emissions in check.[165]

Beside this emerging state practice, climate assessment has achieved growing international recognition. Multilateral development banks and other development institutions have extended their EIA procedures as a tool for climate change mitigation in recognition of a 'good industrial practice'.[166] The parties to the Espoo Convention agreed that 'activities with linkages to climate change' are among those that can have 'long-range transboundary impacts', thus falling within the scope of the Convention.[167] In 2017, the Joint Meeting of the Parties to the Espoo Convention and to its Kiev Protocol on Strategic Environmental Assessment recognized SEA as 'a key tool for the development of national climate change action and planning, and for the incorporation of specific climate change mitigation and adaptation measures into regional development and sectoral plans, programmes and policies'.[168]

When used as a tool for climate change mitigation, environmental assessment procedures may need some refining. Like many other environmental issues, climate change occurs not as the result of a single activity but because of the cumulative effect of multiple activities over time. This certainly does not preclude the application to climate change of a procedure that, in some views, aims 'precisely' to require this kind of cumulative impact analysis.[169] While no affected population can be identified or consulted in the assessment of a given project liable to contribute only a tiny fraction to global GHG emissions, it remains possible for the state to consult with any interested member of the public.[170] There is no obvious

[165] Market-based mechanisms typically address less than half of a jurisdiction's current GHG emissions, thus leaving much room for EIA effectiveness. Moreover, by avoiding situations of carbon lock-in, climate assessment facilitates the adoption of more stringent emission caps under subsequent periods of implementation of market-based mechanisms.

[166] World Bank, Review and Update of the World Bank's Safeguard Policies: Environmental and Social Framework (Proposed Third Draft) (4 August 2016) <https://perma.cc/344W-NAEN> ¶59. See also Asian Development Bank, Safeguard Policy Statement (2009) 16; UN Development Programme, 'Social and Environmental Standards' (2014) 20; Asian Infrastructure Investment Bank, 'Environmental and Social Framework' (2016) 28; World Bank, 'Environmental and Social Framework' (2017) <https://perma.cc/EA7H-CXE3> 4 et passim; 'The Equator Principles' (4th edn, 2020) <https://perma.cc/QGG7-L2NK>.

[167] UNECE, 'Guidance on the Practical Application of the Espoo Convention', ECE/MP.EIA/8 (2006) ¶26. See also Espoo Convention (n 41).

[168] Minsk Declaration by the Representatives of the UNECE Member States and the European Union, ECE/MP.EIA/23.Add.1–ECE/MP.EIA/SEA/7.Add.1 (13–16 June 2017) ¶9.

[169] *Center for Biological Diversity v National Highway Traffic Safety Administration* (9th Cir, 2008) 538 F3d 1172, 1217. See also *Environmental Defence Society v Taranaki Regional Council*, A184/2002, [2002] NZ Envt C 441, ¶22; Jill Gunn and Bram F Noble, 'Conceptual and Methodological Challenges to Integrating Sea and Cumulative Effects Assessment' (2011) 31 Environmental Impact Assessment Review 154; A John Sinclair, Meinhard Doelle, and Peter N Duinker, 'Looking Up, Down, and Sideways: Reconceiving Cumulative Effects Assessment as a Mindset' (2017) 62 Environmental Impact Assessment Review 183.

[170] By analogy, no population is directly affected by purely ecological values, which are nevertheless often considered in environmental assessment procedures.

benchmark to assess the significance of the GHG emissions resulting from a single activity, but state practice already shows possible solutions ranging from predetermined standards and economic valuation[171] to a comparison of the activity's emissions with the relevant targets.[172] Thus, despite some difficulties, state practice demonstrates the possible use of environmental assessment as a tool for climate change mitigation.[173]

Thus, states have largely accepted climate assessment as a logical implication of their general mitigation obligations. In some rare cases, climate assessment—or, at least, a scientific assessment that informs the decision, whether or not it involves public participation—could be construed as an indispensable component of due diligence. For instance, a state would arguably be acting in breach of its general mitigation obligation if it approved the construction of many coal power plants without any consideration for their climate impact. In many more instances where climate assessment is not strictly necessary, it may nevertheless be considered as an appropriate measure, the implementation of which would generally be expected from a diligent state, so that the failure of a state to implement a climate assessment could form part of a set of indicia justifying a presumption that the state is not complying with its general mitigation obligations.

C. Duty of Consistency

Beside cooperation and vigilance, general mitigation obligations imply a duty of consistency. A state must take and implement measures and policies to mitigate climate change based on the information available to the state and to its understanding of its obligations. A state would be in breach of its duty of consistency, hence also of its general mitigation obligations, if its actions were routinely at odds with its own words.

[171] See eg Environment and Climate Change Canada, 'Technical Update to Environment and Climate Change Canada's Social Cost of Greenhouse Gas Estimates' (March 2016) <https://perma.cc/C8WH-EMEC>; Interagency Working Group on Social Cost of Greenhouse Gases, Technical Support Document: Social Cost of Carbon, Methane, and Nitrous Oxide Interim Estimates under Executive Order 13990 (February 2021) <https://perma.cc/M988-KH32> 3, 14–16.

[172] See *Center for Biological Diversity v California Department of Fish and Wildlife* (SC Cal, 2015) 62 Cal4th 204, 220–21; *Earthlife Africa Johannesburg* (n 159) ¶90; Constitutional Court Case E875/2017 (29 June 2017) VfSlg No 17339/2004, ECLI:AT:VFGH:2017:E875.2017 (Austria); *R (Friends of the Earth) v Heathrow* [2020] UKSC 52, [2021] 2 All ER 967.

[173] See Mayer, 'Climate Assessment' (n 158); Benoit Mayer, 'The Emergence of Climate Assessment as a Customary Law Obligation' in Benoit Mayer and Alexander Zahar (eds), *Debating Climate Law* (CUP 2021). But see Alexander Zahar, 'Environmental Impact Assessment for Greenhouse Gas Emissions Is Pie in the Sky' in Mayer and Zahar, *Debating Climate Law*.

1. Foundations

An obligation of due diligence requires a state not only to maintain vigilance, but also to take concrete measures when the exercise of vigilance sheds light on issues that need addressing.[174] In principle, the standard of conduct applicable in relation to general mitigation obligations can be assessed by taking into account the nature of the environmental concern and relevant national circumstances.[175] Yet, as Chapter VI has shown, it would be extremely challenging to determine a state's requisite level of mitigation action. In contentious proceedings, whether before a domestic or an international court, the burden of proof would initially be for the applicant to demonstrate that the state at issue has failed to take appropriate measures[176] or, at least, to refute the presumption that the state acted in good faith[177]—but an applicant would seldom be able to provide such prima facie evidence through a quantitative analysis of the state's requisite level of mitigation action.[178] Instead, a more probable line of argument would assess the consistency of a state's conduct with its own understanding of its obligations. Evidence that the state was not implementing the measures that it had itself identified as appropriate may not directly prove a breach of its due diligence obligation, but it could be enough to reverse the burden of proof: it would then be for the state to demonstrate the adequacy of its climate mitigation strategy.

One should presume that a state is not complying with its general mitigation obligations, and the duty of consistency that they entail, if this state is not acting consistently with its own findings about the need for mitigation action. At least three types of inconsistencies could be relevant. First, inconsistencies can appear between a state's understanding of collective objectives and burden-sharing criteria, on the one hand, and its mitigation action, on the other hand—that is, the state may fail to implement the level of mitigation action that it recognized as its fair share. Second, inconsistencies can also appear between a state's mitigation strategy and the more concrete policies and measures that it implements—that is, the state may fail to take measures consistent with its own mitigation strategy. Third, inconsistencies could be found between a state's mitigation action and emerging standards of good practice that the state has accepted or to which it has not persistently objected.

[174] See *Corfu Channel (UK v Albania)* (n 107) 22; *Gabčíkovo-Nagymaros* (n 56) ¶140; *Pulp Mills* (n 2) ¶¶185, 188, 205. See also *Activities in the Area* (n 138) ¶147.

[175] See generally Study Group on Due Diligence, 'Second Report' (n 5) 1081–82; Samantha Besson, 'La *due diligence* en droit international' (2020) 409 RdC 153, 269–79.

[176] On the burden of proof for a state which asserts a breach of the state's obligation to prove it, see eg *Pulp Mills* (n 2) ¶162.

[177] See Michel Virally, 'Review Essay: Good Faith in Public International Law' (1983) 77 AJIL 130, 132.

[178] See above at 231.

Some support for this duty of consistency can be found in the literature and jurisprudence on good faith or on estoppel (using this term in a broader sense than in common law),[179] which submit that a state cannot freely change its interpretation of the law or of the facts for its own benefit. As Arnold McNair famously put it, a state 'cannot blow hot and cold'.[180] More specifically, Judge Ricardo Alfaro's separate opinion in *Temple of Preah Vihear* notes the general acceptance of a principle according to which 'a State party to an international litigation is bound by its previous acts or attitude when they are in contradiction with its claims in the litigation'.[181] This principle, encompassed in the precept *Allegans contraria non audiendus est*, has been presented as a general principle of law recognized in many national legal systems,[182] and it has repeatedly been applied in international judicial decisions.[183] Human rights bodies have extensively (and perhaps excessively) drawn on this idea when interpreting a state's due diligence obligation to protect human rights in light of the standards that the state had accepted, for instance through the adoption of national laws,[184] its consent to international norms,[185] or even its acquiescence to the emergence of a common ground in the application of human rights standards.[186]

International law provides states with considerable latitude in determining its mitigation strategy,[187] and a state may have good reasons for adjusting this strategy, even perhaps in ways that end up decreasing its overall ambition on climate change mitigation.[188] It remains, however, that questions could be asked when a state's conduct evidences a sudden, self-serving change in its assessment of its ability to mitigate climate change or in its interpretation of burden-sharing criteria. In many

[179] See discussion in *Temple of Preah Vihear (Cambodia v Thailand)*, Judgment on Merits (15 June 1962), [1962] ICJ Rep 6, Separate Opinion of Vice-President Alfaro, 39–40; Thomas Cottier and Jörg Paul Müller, 'Estoppel' in *Max Planck Encyclopedia of Public International Law* (online edn, OUP 2007) ¶2.

[180] Arnold D McNair, 'The Legality of the Occupation of the Ruhr' (1924) 5 BYBIL 17, 35.

[181] *Temple of Preah Vihear* (n 179) Separate Opinion of Vice-President Alfaro, 39.

[182] Robert Kolb, *La bonne foi en droit international public: Contribution à l'étude des principles généraux de droit* (PUF 2000) 357–58.

[183] See *Jurisdiction of the European Commission of the Danube*, Advisory Opinion (8 December 1927), PCIJ Rep Ser B No 14, 23; *Legal Status of Eastern Greenland (Denmark v Norway)*, Judgment (5 April 1933), [1933] 1933 PCIJ Ser A/B No 53, 68–69; *Arbitral Award made by the King of Spain on 23 December 1906*, Judgment (18 November 1960), [1960] ICJ Rep 19, 213; *Frontier Case (Argentine/Chile)*, Award (9 December 1966), 16 RIAA 109, 164; *Filleting within the Gulf of St Lawrence (Canada/France)*, Award (17 July 1986), 19 RIAA 225, ¶99; *Delimitation of the Border (Eritrea/Ethiopia)*, Award (13 April 2002), 25 RIAA 83, ¶3.9. See also ILC, 'Draft Articles on the Law of Treaties' [1966] II YBILC 219, commentary on art 42, ¶1. But see Cottier and Müller, (n 179) ¶3, suggesting that 'restrictive and more precise notions of estoppel prevail', without justifying why this would preclude the applicability of broader notions.

[184] See *López Ostra v Spain*, App No 16798/90 (1994) 303-C ECHR Series A, ¶¶16–22; *Fadeyeva v Russia*, App No 55723/00, 2005-IV ECHR 255, ¶¶97–98.

[185] See generally Adamantia Rachovitsa, 'The Principle of Systemic Integration in Human Rights Law' (2017) 66 ICLQ 557.

[186] See eg *Demír v Turkey*, App No 34503/97, 2008-V ECHR 333, ¶85.

[187] UNFCCC (n 3) Preamble ¶10.

[188] On progression and non-regression under the Paris Agreement, see above at 55–57.

cases, such inconsistencies would constitute prima facie evidence of a breach of general mitigation obligations or otherwise be part of a set of indicia to the same effect.

2. Consistency with Collective Objectives

A first application of the duty of consistency concerns the relation of national mitigation strategies with collective objectives. On the one hand, national mitigation strategies are reflected in commitments, pledges, or in various domestic documents (eg statutes and policies); some of the most obvious examples include NDCs and long-term strategies communicated under the Paris Agreement. On the other hand, collective objectives are generally adopted through climate treaties or decisions of the Conference of the Parties to the UNFCCC (COP)—the 1.5/2°C targets of the Paris Agreement being the most prominent example.[189]

The adoption of a collective objective does not necessarily imply an obligation of consistency. Thus, as discussed in Chapter VI, states have not accepted any obligation to adopt mitigation strategies consistent with the collective objective of the Paris Agreement. The commitment that each party communicate NDCs that 'reflect its highest possible ambition'[190] does not require NDCs to be consistent with this collective objective; in fact, current NDCs, in aggregate, are not consistent with this objective.[191] At any rate, assessing the consistency of an NDC with this collective objective would be particularly challenging, given the lack of specificity of the objective and the absence of an agreed-upon burden-sharing formula.[192]

Yet, Chapter VI has also noted the possible emergence of a requirement of 'subjective consistency', requiring a state to act consistently with its own interpretation of collective objectives and burden-sharing criteria.[193] Subjective consistency is an indication of a state's compliance with its general mitigation obligations: it could legitimately be expected that a state, exercising due diligence with regard to the mitigation of climate change, would be acting in line with its own, plausible interpretation of collective mitigation objectives and burden-sharing criteria.

This duty of subjective consistency has at least four implications. First, a diligent state should be able to present a plausible explanation of the consistency of its mitigation strategy with the collective objectives and burden-sharing criteria to which it has agreed. This expectation is partly reflected in a procedural commitment: each party to the Paris Agreement is required to justify, within its NDC, how it considers

[189] See Paris Agreement (n 43) art 2(1)(a). See also Decision 10/CP.21, 'The 2013–2015 Review' (13 December 2015) FCCC/CP/2015/10/Add.2, 23, ¶4.

[190] Paris Agreement (n 43) art 4(3).

[191] See above at 253.

[192] See above at 231.

[193] See above at 265.

that this contribution 'is fair and ambitious in the light of its national circumstances' and how it 'contributes towards achieving the objective of the Convention' as specified by the Paris Agreement.[194] By contrast to objective consistency, this expectation of subjective consistency is not precluded by state practice: while the aggregate effect of NDCs is inconsistent with any unique interpretation of the temperature targets, scientific studies suggest that, when taken in isolation, almost every NDC is consistent with at least one of a few plausible interpretations of these targets.[195] There is also a growing expectation that a state would have a long-term plan towards carbon neutrality—including not just a long-term carbon neutrality target, but also a defined pathway towards this target, the implementation of which could be monitored.[196]

Second, a diligent state should review its mitigation strategy on a regular basis and in response to relevant developments. This expectation is fuelled by provisions of the Paris Agreement that require the communication of new NDCs every five years[197] and allow for additional adjustments.[198] Reviews are needed not just to extend mitigation strategies in time, but also to ensure that a mitigation strategy remains consistent with the state's understanding of collective mitigation objectives and burden-sharing principles in light of evolving national and international circumstances. Thus, an EU Regulation requires that the Commission 'review relevant Union legislation in order to enable the achievement of [its 2030] target', determine a 2040 target '[w]ith the view to achieving the [EU's] climate-neutrality objective', review this target following the global stocktake, and keep the regulations of these provisions 'under review in light of international developments and efforts undertaken to achieve the long-term objectives of the Paris Agreement'.[199] Likewise, the High Court of New Zealand in *Sarah Thomson* suggested that the scientific findings reflected in the publication of a new IPCC assessment report should have led the state to consider the need to review its mitigation strategy.[200] In application of this notion of consistency, one could expect that the states which had

[194] Decisions 4/CMA.1, 'Further Guidance in Relation to the Mitigation Section of Decision 1/CP.21' (15 December 2018) FCCC/PA/CMA/2018/3/Add.1, 6, Annex I ¶¶6–7. See also Paris Agreement (n 43) art 4(8); 1/CP.20, 'Lima Call for Climate Action' (14 December 2014) FCCC/CP/2014/10/Add.1, 2, ¶14; 1/CP.21, 'Adoption of the Paris Agreement' (12 December 2015) FCCC/CP/2015/10/Add.1, 2, ¶27.

[195] Xunzhang Pan and others, 'Exploring Fair and Ambitious Mitigation Contributions under the Paris Agreement Goals' (2017) 74 Environmental Science & Policy 49; Yann Robiou du Pont and Malte Meinshausen, 'Warming Assessment of the Bottom-Up Paris Agreement Emissions Pledges' (2018) 9 Nature Communications 4810.

[196] See Paris Agreement (n 43) art 4(19); UNFCCC Secretariat, 'Communication of Long-Term Strategies' (no date) <https://unfccc.int/process/the-paris-agreement/long-term-strategies>.

[197] Paris Agreement (n 43) art 4(9).

[198] Ibid art 4(11).

[199] Regulation (EU) 2021/1119 of the European Parliament and of the Council of 30 June 2021 establishing the framework for achieving climate neutrality and amending Regulations (EC) No 401/2009 and (EU) 2018/1999 [2021] 243/1, art 4(2)–(3), (6)–(7).

[200] *Thomson v Minister for Climate Change Issues* [2017] NZHC 733, [2018] 2 NZLR 160, ¶94. See also Climate Action and Low Carbon Development Act 2015 (Act No 46/2015) amended 2021 (Act No 32/2021) (Ireland) s 6D(2)(b).

based their mitigation strategy on the 2°C target adopted at COP16[201] would adjust these strategies following the adoption of the (apparently) more demanding 1.5/2°C targets at COP21.[202] Likewise, one would think that the recognition of an 'ambition gap' would lead each state to question the adequacy of its mitigation strategy. This latter observation is partly supported by provisions of the Paris Agreement requiring that each new NDC 'be informed by the outcomes of the global stocktake',[203] a process aimed at assessing 'the collective progress towards achieving the purpose of this Agreement and its long-term goals'.[204]

Third, a diligent state should not ordinarily make abrupt changes in its interpretation of collective objectives and burden-sharing criteria. In this sense, the Supreme Court of the Netherlands in *Urgenda* was suspicious of the state's change of mind with regard to its potential 2020 target: the state had first suggested a possibility of achieving a 30 per cent emission reduction by 2020, compared with 1990, before finding that a less ambitious EU-wide target was sufficient to ensure consistency with the 2°C target.[205] There is no question that a state may change its policy (and a fortiori, in the case at issue, its negotiating position), but such changes could suggest that the state is not exercising due diligence if they are purely opportunistic or imply bad faith. To take a clearer, hypothetical example, a developing country that has long asserted the relevant of historical emissions as a burden-sharing criterion will appear in bad faith if it abruptly changes its mind as its own share of historical emissions increases as a consequence of its industrial development.

Fourth, a diligent state should not ordinarily downgrade the ambition displayed in its national mitigation strategy—at least, not until it is confident that the collective mitigation objectives it has agreed upon will be achieved. This is largely an implication of the first and third observations above: a state would not generally be able to downgrade its mitigation strategy without altering its interpretation of collective objectives and burden-sharing criteria, or without losing the ability to make a plausible argument that its strategy is consistent with these objectives. This expectation is partly reflected in the Paris Agreement, which suggests that '[t]he efforts of all Parties will represent a progression over time'[206] and that each

[201] Decision 1/CP.16 (n 126) ¶4. See also UNFCCC Secretariat, 'Aggregate Effect of the Intended Nationally Determined Contributions: An Update', FCCC/CP/2015/7 (30 October 2015) ¶178.

[202] Paris Agreement (n 43) art 2(1)(a); Decision 10/CP.21 (n 189) ¶4. See EU, First NDC, Updated (2020), referring for the first time to the 1.5°C target and containing a more demanding target than the EU's intended NDC, although the two changes are not explicitly linked. But see *Neubauer* (n 23) ¶¶166–68, considering that a national mitigation objective adopted based on a 2°C target remained sufficient to comply with the state's obligation to protect human rights (although it is unclear whether the Court would have come to the same conclusion if it had been applying a more general obligation of due diligence).

[203] Paris Agreement (n 43) art 4(9). See also ibid art 14(3).

[204] Ibid art 14(1).

[205] *Urgenda v Netherlands*, ECLI:NL:HR:2019:2007 (SC, 20 December 2019), English translation in (2020) 59 ILM 811, ¶7.4.1–7.4.2. See also *Do-Hyun Kim v South Korea* (Constitutional Court of South Korea, pending) 2020 Heonma 389 <https://perma.cc/Y57D-5P45>, regarding a downward adjustment of national mitigation action.

[206] See Paris Agreement (n 43) art 3.

successive NDC will 'represent a progression beyond the Party's then current' NDC.[207] Overall, the Paris Agreement expressly recognizes the possibility for a party to 'adjust its existing [NDC] with a view to enhancing its level of ambition',[208] thus implying that a downward adjustment is not ordinarily permissible.[209] Some national laws reflect a notion of progression (or non-regression),[210] albeit often in rather vague terms—without defining how progression is to be determined (eg in terms of absolute or per capita emission, annual rate of emission reduction, or implicit carbon price). It remains, however, that a state could plausibly justify a downward adjustment of its mitigation strategy on the basis of an unexpected change in national circumstances, for instance as the result of a sudden demographic growth induced by unforeseeable mass migration or an armed conflict, even if such circumstances do not amount to circumstances precluding wrongfulness. Therefore, here again, inconsistencies would only constitute an indicium of non-compliance, which the state may be able to refute.

3. Consistency with National Mitigation Strategy

Another application of the duty of consistency is that a state can be expected generally to act consistently with its mitigation strategy—notwithstanding whether this strategy is expressed through commitments, pledges, or domestic laws and policies. The failure of a state to implement its national mitigation strategy can be demonstrated by analysing the policies and measures it is adopts and implements or by assessing the mitigation outcomes it achieves while accounting for extraneous circumstances.

A state's fulfilment of its commitments is perhaps the most obvious touchstone to determine its compliance with its general mitigation obligations.[211] A state would presumably not be exercising due diligence if, for instance, it failed to achieve its quantified emission limitation or reduction commitment under the Kyoto Protocol, to implement its NDC under the Paris Agreement,[212] or to ensure compliance with sector-specific commitments relating to climate change mitigation, thus falling short of what the state had itself recognized as its obligation. The expectation that states will comply with their mitigation commitments is reinforced by the practice of adopting statutory provisions requiring national governments to

207 Ibid art 4(3).
208 Ibid art 4(11).
209 See above at 56.
210 Bundes-Klimaschutzgesetz (Federal Climate Change Act), 12 December 2019, BGBl I 2513, amended 2021 (Germany), s 3(3); Canada Net-Zero Emissions Accountability Act, SC 2021, c22, s 3; Climate Change and Energy Transition Law (Spain) (n 118) art 2(l).
211 See *Neubauer* (n 23) ¶¶169–70.
212 See Lavanya Rajamani, 'Due Diligence in International Climate Change Law' in Krieger, Peters, and Kreuzer (eds) (n 3) 163, 169, described NDCs as 'regime-specific markers of due diligence'.

take measures towards achieving national mitigation objectives (eg NDCs) and to periodically review the adequacy of these measures.[213] A German law, for instance, obligates the federal government to take 'immediate' corrective action if emission data reveal that statutory carbon budget is being exceeded.[214]

The presumption that a state would be in breach of its general mitigation obligations if it does not fulfil its commitments, though strong, could conceivably be rebutted: a state could well be able to demonstrate that, in spite of the breach of a commitment it had made, it had nevertheless implemented measures that were overall in line with the due diligence implied from its general mitigation obligations. For instance, a state could show that, while it was unable to regulate its territorial GHG emissions in line with its NDC, it managed to reduce global GHG emissions substantially by decreasing its exportation of fossil fuels, thus—when all factors are considered—contributing significantly, in other ways, to global mitigation action. The presumption created by the breach of a commitment, however, would shift the burden of proof onto the state.

Beyond its commitments, a state exercising due diligence would also be expected to act consistently with its national mitigation strategy reflected in non-binding pledges or in domestic law and policies. For instance, the Paris Agreement invites parties to communicate 'long-term low greenhouse gas emission development strategies',[215] although it does not require its parties to implement measures consistent with these strategies, and these strategies do not necessarily constitute unilateral declarations capable of creating legal obligations.[216] Moreover, many states have been adopting framework legislation or other policy instruments that define a national strategy on climate change mitigation.[217] And some countries have established processes and institutions—often as administrative agencies with a certain degree of independence from political powers—to assess national mitigation action and make recommendations, including by assessing the state's capacity to enhance its mitigation action.[218] These various strategic documents and

[213] See Climate Change Act 2008, c 27, amended (UK) s 4(1); Bundesgesetz über die Reduktion der CO_2-Emissionen (Federal Act on the Reduction of CO_2 Emissions) of 23 December 2011, AS 6989 (2012), amended 2021 <https://perma.cc/8HKC-FANS> art 40; Climate Action and Low Carbon Development Act (n 200) s 4; Klimatlag (Climate Act) (SFS 2017:720) (Sweden) ss 4–5; Environmental Code (Kazakhstan) (n 163) art 283(4) ('State bodies and officials ... are obligated, within their remit, to take actions to ensure the implementation' of the NDCs); EU Regulation 2021/1119 (n 199) arts 2(2), 4(2)–(3), 4(6)–(7), 6(3); Ley general de cambio climático (Mexico) (n 125) ss 98–105.

[214] Bundes-Klimaschutzgesetz (Germany) (n 210) s 8. See also Lov om klima (Climate Act) No 865 (26 June 2020) <https://perma.cc/RKM7-76MT> (Denmark) s 7(4).

[215] Paris Agreement (n 43) art 4(19).

[216] See discussion above at 63.

[217] See Gabriela Iacobuta and others, 'National Climate Change Mitigation Legislation, Strategy and Targets: A Global Update' (2018) 18 Climate Policy 1114; Eloise Scotford and Stephen Minas, 'Probing the Hidden Depths of Climate Law: Analysing National Climate Change Legislation' (2019) 28 RECIEL 67.

[218] See Climate Change Act (UK) (n 213) ss 32–43; Environment Protection Act (Nepal) (n 160) ss 32–34; Ley general de cambio climático (Mexico) (n 125) arts 51–57; Climate Change Act, No 11 (2016) Kenya Gazette Supplement No 68, ss 5–7; Decree No 2019-439 of 14 May 2019, Haut Conseil pour le climat (High Council on Climate), JORF 112 (France); Lov om klima (Denmark) (n 214) ss 3–5, 10–12;

assessment processes do not create discrete international law obligations, but they ought at least to inform the party's own assessment of the policies and measures that it should implement—and a state cooperating in good faith would be expected to act consistently with its own understanding of its responsibilities.

National courts have already been called upon to check that states were taking measures consistent with their mitigation strategies. The judgment of the Irish Supreme Court in *Friends of the Irish Environment* confirms the expectation that, when adopting a long-term strategy, the state should devise specific measures to implement it. In that case, the Court quashed the National Mitigation Plan on the ground that the government had failed to give sufficient details for an observer to understand how the state was planning to achieve its mid-century target.[219] French administrative courts in *Grande-Synthe*[220] and *Notre Affaire à tous*[221] imposed on the national government the adoption of additional mitigation action to ensure the achievement of its national strategy. In *Grande-Synthe*, in particular, the State Council relied on recommendations by two independent national institutions to determine that the state was yet to adopt measures in line with the ambition it had expressed.[222] Similarly, in *Klimaatzaak*, a tribunal of first instance found that Belgium had breached its duty of care by failing to take sufficient mitigation action, in particular, on the ground that the state's own projections indicated that the measures it was implementing, or was considering implementing, fell short of its national 2030 target.[223] By contrast, the UK Supreme Court in *Friends of the Earth* upheld the approval of the extension of the Heathrow Airport, in part because this decision was 'consistent with the advice' the government had received from an independent statutory body in charge of advising on the design and implementation of the national mitigation strategy.[224]

Thus, the legal nature of a national mitigation strategy (whether under domestic or international law) has only limited weight when assessing whether the state has taken appropriate measures in light of its duty of consistency. A state's failure to fulfil a binding commitment or a statutory goal may create a stronger presumption that the state has breached its due diligence obligation than if the strategy was

Executive Order 14008 of 27 January 2021, Tackling the Climate Crisis at Home and Abroad, 86 Fed Reg 7619 ss 202–03; EU Regulation 2021/1119 (n 199) art 3.

[219] *Friends of the Irish Environment v Ireland* [2020] IESC 49, [2020] 2 ILRM 233, ¶¶6.46, 9.2.

[220] *Grande-Synthe v France* (Conseil d'Etat, 19 November 2020), ECLI:FR:CECHR:2020:427301.20201119, ¶¶15–16, noting that France's decision to delay emission reduction lacks proper justification; *Grande-Synthe v France* (Conseil d'Etat, 1 July 2021), ECLI:FR:CECHR:2021:427301.20210701, ¶¶5–7, ordering the state to adopt new, appropriate measures within nine months.

[221] *Oxfam v France*, Application 1904967, Decision 44-008.60-01-02-02.R (Administrative Tribunal, Paris, 2 February 2021) ¶¶30–31.

[222] *Grande-Synthe* (2021) (n 220) ¶5.

[223] *Klimaatzaak v Belgium*, case 2015/4585/A (French-Speaking Tribunal of First Instance of Brussels, 17 June 2021), English translation <https://perma.cc/68ZJ-2F96> ¶¶72–73.

[224] *Friends of the Earth* (n 172) ¶166. See also Climate Change Act (UK) (n 213) s 32.

merely a pledge or a policy, but this is only a question of degree—a mere policy may indicate the state's own understanding of what constitutes appropriate mitigation action on its part, and even a recommendation by an independent national institution could have some evidential value. This observation nuances, in particular, the importance of the legal force (or lack thereof) of NDCs.[225] Even if the Paris Agreement did not create an obligation for parties to implement their NDCs, and leaving aside the possibility that NDCs may constitute unilateral declarations capable of creating legal obligations on their own, it remains that NDCs express states' own interpretations of their general mitigation obligations, so that a state's failure to implement its NDCs would be an indication of its breach of these general mitigation obligations.

The duty of consistency may also be applied to the relations between different components of a state's mitigation strategy. In particular, as many states are adopting long-term mitigation targets, questions will increasingly be asked about the consistency of their short- and medium-term commitments, pledges, and policies with these long-term targets. A difficulty in this regard relates to uncertainties about the shape of national emission reduction pathways—that is, the timing of emission reduction. While some national strategies define the pathway to achieve a medium- or long-term target,[226] others do not. In the absence of such defined strategy, one surely cannot assume that a state's long-term emission reduction pathway will be linear (ie that it will consist in a fixed, absolute amount of emission reduction each year),[227] nor is a state legally required to follow the most cost-effective pathway possible.[228] Nevertheless, a diligent state would likely define a clear long-term emissions pathway against which the action of successive national governments can be assessed in order to discourage unreasonably delay mitigation action.[229] Canada, for instance, adopted statutory provisions requiring a Minister to set adequate targets for milestone years,[230] to

[225] See above at 57 and 71.

[226] See Regulation (EU) 2018/842 of the European Parliament and of the Council of 30 May 2018 on binding annual greenhouse gas emission reductions by Member States from 2021 to 2030 contributing to climate action to meet commitments under the Paris Agreement and amending Regulation (EU) No 525/2013 [2018] OJ L156/26, art 4(2), imposing 'a linear trajectory'.

[227] The difficulty of developing and deploying new technologies, the rapid rate of diffusion once a technology's deployment has reached a tipping point, and the challenge of addressing emissions from all sources would rather suggest that mitigation outcomes (expressed as deviation from business-as-usual scenarios) in each sector of the global economy would follow a sigmoid-shaped curve, characterized initially by a slow rate of emission limitation or reduction followed by a sharp decrease in emissions, that eventually slows down to a horizontal asymptote. See generally Danny Cullenward and David G Victor, *Making Climate Policy Work* (Polity 2020) 4; Anders Bjørn, Shannon Lloyd, and Damon Matthews, 'From the Paris Agreement to Corporate Climate Commitments: Evaluation of Seven Methods for Setting "Science-Based" Emission Targets' (2021) 16 Environmental Research Letters 054019.

[228] *Thomson* (n 200) ¶176.

[229] See eg Climate Action and Low Carbon Development Act (n 200) ss 3, 6A; Klimatlag (Sweden) (n 213) s 3; EU Regulation 2021/1119 (n 199) arts 2.

[230] Canada Net-Zero Emissions Accountability Act (n 210) ss 7–8.

establish and implement a plan to reach these targets,[231] to assess progress,[232] and to take adequate corrective measures if necessary.[233] When a government adopts milestone targets, whether out of a statutory obligation or by choice, compliance with general mitigation obligations can be tested by assessing the reasonableness of the state's assumptions about the shape of its emission reduction pathway. Thus, the German constitutional court in *Neubauer* interpreted Germany's constitutional law as prohibiting excessive reliance on future efforts to achieve a long-term mitigation target.[234]

Finally, a state may be expected to ensure the implementation of its mitigation strategy by embodying it in national law and establishing processes to ensure the consistency of its national policies and measures. The Preamble to the UNFCCC recalls that 'States should enact effective environmental legislation',[235] and various states have recently been adopting framework legislations.[236] One may question the conclusions of the Supreme Court of Nepal that the national government has a discrete obligation to adopt a legislation on climate change[237] (or the possibility for a national court to apply this obligation against the political branches of government),[238] but there is certainly a growing expectation that a diligent state would ordinarily adopt a legislation or take equivalent steps (eg an executive order). As such, the absence of legislation or equivalent measures to ensure the implementation of a state's mitigation strategy could constitute an indicium that the state is not complying with its general mitigation obligations.

[231] Ibid ss 9–10.

[232] Ibid ss 14–15.

[233] Ibid s 15.

[234] *Neubauer* (n 23) ¶182.

[235] UNFCCC (n 3) Preamble ¶11. See also Rio Declaration (n 15) principle 11. By analogy, human rights treaties often emphasize that states' due diligence obligation implies the adoption of legislative measures. See International Covenant on Civil and Political Rights (16 December 1966, in force 23 March 1976) 999 UNTS 171, art 2(1); International Covenant on Economic, Social and Cultural Rights (16 December 1966, in force 3 January 1976) 993 UNTS 3, art 2(2).

[236] See eg Climate Change Act (UK) (n 213); Ley general de cambio climático (Mexico) (n 125); Climate Change Act (Kenya) (n 218); Law No 2019-1147 of 8 November 2019 on Energy and Climate, JORF 261 (France); The Environment Protection Act (Nepal) (n 160); Bundes-Klimaschutzgesetz (Germany) (n 210); Lov om klima (Denmark) (n 214); EU Regulation 2021/1119 (n 199); Climate Action and Low Carbon Development Act (n 200); Federal Law on Limiting Greenhouse Gas Emissions (Russia) (n 125); Climate Change and Energy Transition Law (Spain) (n 118); Canada Net-Zero Emissions Accountability Act (n 210). See generally Sarah Louise Nash and Reinhard Steurer, 'Taking Stock of Climate Change Acts in Europe: Living Policy Processes or Symbolic Gestures?' (2019) 19 Climate Policy 1052.

[237] *Shrestha v Prime Minister*, Order 074-WO-0283, Decision 10210, NKP 61(3) (SC, 25 December 2018) <https://perma.cc/YM27-HH73> ¶5.

[238] See *Grande-Synthe* (2020) (n 220) ¶2; Constitutional Council, Decision 2021-825 DC, Loi portant lutte contre le dérèglement climatique et renforcement de la résilience face à ses effets (13 August 2021) ¶3, each interpreting the doctrine of the separation of power as precluding the Court from ordering the drafting of a bill or the passing of a law.

4. Consistency with Emerging Standards

A last aspect of the duty of consistency is that a state exercising due diligence can be expected to take measures that are consistent with international good practices. States may not have accepted these good practices as law, but they have increasingly recognized them as standards that they should aspire to achieve. These good practices involve, for instance, the gradual abandonment of the use of coal for power generation, the phasing out of fossil-fuel subsidies, or even steps towards the prohibition of internal combustion engines on vehicles. In rare cases, a state's compliance with some of these standards—for instance a reduced reliance on coal as a source of energy—may be the only realistic way for a state to achieve its overall mitigation objective. But even when following these standards is neither mandatory nor necessary, it could be part of a set of indicia reflecting a state's diligence on climate change mitigation: a state's failure to take some of the most obvious measures that would achieve mitigation outcomes would constitute a strong indication that the state is not complying with its general mitigation obligations.[239]

One of the most widely recognized standards regards the progressive elimination of fossil-fuel subsidies. The Kyoto Protocol requires Annex I parties to adopt and implement policies and measures such as the '[p]rogressive reduction or phasing out of market imperfections, fiscal incentives, tax and duty exemptions and subsidies that run counter to the objective of the Convention'.[240] The G20 has repeatedly called upon states to '[r]ationalize and phase out over the medium term inefficient fossil fuel subsidies that encourage wasteful consumption'[241] and it has set up a process through which states report and peer-review existing subsidies.[242] The 2009 Leader's Declaration of the Asia-Pacific Economic Cooperation expressed a commitment 'to rationalise and phase out over the medium term fossil

[239] See also Naomi Roht-Arriaza, 'Private Voluntary Standard-Setting, the International Organization for Standardization, and International Environmental Lawmaking' (1995) 6 YB Intl Envtl L 107, 151, observing that '[t]ort litigants may well turn to compliance with [voluntary] environmental management systems as benchmarks for what was possible, or even customary, in establishing compliance or non-compliance with the standard of care'; Boyle and Redgwell (n 85) 165, noting that a 'way of identifying what due diligence requires is to look at standards established by international regulatory bodies', or even 'industry standards . . . in the absence of anything else'.

[240] Kyoto Protocol (n 44) art 2(1)(a)(v). See also UNFCCC (n 3) art 4(2)(a).

[241] G20 (Pittsburgh Summit), 'Leaders' Statement' (2009) ¶29; G20 (Seoul Summit), 'Leaders' Statement' (2010) ¶13; G20 (Cannes Summit), 'Leaders' Statement' (2011) ¶20; G20 (Los Cabos Summit), 'Leaders' Statement' (2012) ¶74; G20 (St Petersburg Summit), 'Leaders' Statement' (2013) ¶94; G20 (Brisbane Summit), 'Leaders' Communiqué' (2014) ¶18; G20 (Antalya Summit), 'Leaders' Communiqué' (2015) ¶23; G20 (Hangzhou Summit), 'Leaders' Communiqué' (2016) ¶24; G20 (Hamburg Summit), 'Action Plan' (2017) s 6; G20 (Bariloch Summit), 'Energy Ministers Communiqué' (2018); G20 (Osaka Summit), 'Leaders' Declaration' (2019) ¶37; G20 (Rome Summit), 'Leaders' Declaration' (2021) ¶27.

[242] G20 (St Petersburg Summit) (n 241) ¶94. While the peer-review system was generally qualified as 'voluntary', this qualificative was dropped once in G20 (Hamburg Summit) (n 241) s 6. See also G7 Climate and Environment Ministers' Communiqué (21 May 2021).

fuel subsidies that encourage wasteful consumption',[243] and the UN Secretary-General has also been advocating for fossil-fuel subsidies to end.[244] Finally, COP26 adopted a decision calling upon parties to 'accelerate efforts towards the ... phase-out of inefficient fossil fuel subsidies'.[245] While none of these initiatives impose a discrete obligation to eliminate fossil-fuel subsidies, they do raise an expectation that a state would consider phasing out subsidies with an increasing sense of urgency, while, at the very least, seeking not to introduce new ones.[246]

The reduction of reliance on coal for power generation is the object of another emerging standard of good practice, especially among developed countries. Here again, states have not agreed on a discrete obligation. Thus, the Kenya Environment Tribunal rightly noted that, '[a]s long as coal power plant projects meet the required standards of the law and abide by conditions imposed to mitigate potential impacts then they remain a viable and an acceptable mode of power generation'.[247] Yet, the Tribunal also reflected the gradual emergence of a good practice standard when noting that 'coal fired power plants remain, for the time being, a lawful option'.[248] On the other hand, the Advocate General in *Grande-Synthe* justly characterized the closing of coal plants as 'a priority' that had emerged within a 'global conversation' about climate change mitigation.[249] The 'Powering Past Coal Alliance', a transnational initiative, has advocated the phasing out the use of coal for power generation by 2030 in OECD member countries and by 2050 in the rest of the world.[250] The UN Secretary-General[251] and some human rights institutions[252] have also called for the phasing out of coal. COP26 agreed to call

[243] APEC (Singapore Summit), 'Leaders' Declaration' (2009). See also APEC (Vladivostok Summit), 'Leaders' Declaration' (2012) Annex B, Strengthening APEC Energy Security; APEC (Bali Summit), 'Leaders' Declaration' (2013) ¶18(f); APEC, Leaders' Declaration (Beijing Summit) (2014) ¶36; APEC, Leaders' Declaration (Manila Summit) (2015) ¶4(g); APEC, Leaders' Declaration (Lima Summit) (2016).

[244] See UN Meetings Coverage and Press Releases, '"Climate Emergency Is the Fight of Our Lives, for Our Lives", Secretary-General Tells Summit, Urging That No More New Coal Power Plants Be Built after 2020', SG/SM/19759-ENV/DEV/1997 (2019).

[245] Decision 1/CP.26, 'Glasgow Climate Pact' (13 November 2021) FCCC/CP/2021/12/Add.1 (advance version), 2, ¶20. See also Decision 1/CMA.3, 'Glasgow Climate Pact' (13 November 2021) FCCC/PA/CMA/2021/10/Add.1 (advance version), 2, ¶36.

[246] See David R Boyd, Report of the Special Rapporteur on the Issue of Human Rights Obligations Relating to the Enjoyment of a Safe, Clean, Healthy and Sustainable Environment, A/74/161 (2019) ¶77(a).

[247] *Save Lamu* (n 159) ¶17.

[248] Ibid ¶18.

[249] Opinion of Mr Stéphane Hoynck, Advocate General of the Conseil d'Etat, on *Grande-Synthe v France* (1 July 2021), ECLI:FR:CECHR:2020:427301.20201119, No 427301, 11.

[250] Powering Past Coal Alliance, 'Declaration' (no date) <https://perma.cc/5SFA-X93V>, signed by forty-eight national governments (as of May 2022).

[251] See UN News, 'Secretary-General urges countries to end "deadly addiction" to coal' (2 March 2021) <https://perma.cc/E2UE-DMHA>.

[252] Concluding Observations of CEDAW on the Eighth Periodic Report of Korea, CEDAW/C/KOR/CO/8 (2018) ¶¶14–15; of the CRC on the Combined Fifth and Sixth Periodic Reports of Australia, CRC/C/AUS/CO/5-6 (2019) ¶41; on the Combined Fourth and Fifth Periodic Reports of Japan, CRC/C/JPN/CO/4-5 (2019) ¶37. See also Boyd (n 246) ¶¶77–78.

for accelerated efforts towards 'the phasedown of unabated coal power',[253] with the G20 concurrently committing to stop funding unabated coal power generation projects.[254] On the other hand, many states are still approving the construction of new coal plants, including a few OECD member states.[255] As such policies become increasingly unusual in the years to come, more questions will be raised about their consistency with general mitigation obligations.

Various initiatives seek to address other large sources of GHG emissions. For instance, states have shown an interest in regulating the production and supply of fossil fuels,[256] advocated for the protection of rainforests,[257] floated the idea of prohibiting new road vehicles equipped with an internal combustion engine,[258] and sought to prevent routine flaring during the extraction and processing of oil and gas.[259] Questions are also increasingly asked about the right of a state to produce large quantities of fossil fuels (especially coal) for export, thus facilitating emissions in other countries.[260] These emerging standards are not the object of discrete obligations, nor are they generally a necessary component of states' mitigation action, and yet, a state's mitigation action is increasingly assessed in light of these standards.[261] A state that is actively engaging with all or most of these standards is probably exercising due diligence; one that is engaging with few or none of them is probably not.

[253] Decision 1/CP.26 (n 245) ¶20. See also Decision 1/CMA.3 (n 245) ¶36.

[254] See e.g. G20 (Rome Summit) (n 241) ¶28.

[255] Ryna Yiyun Cui and others, 'Quantifying Operational Lifetimes for Coal Power Plants under the Paris Goals' (2019) 10 Nature Communications 4759, 3.

[256] See Michael Lazarus and Harro van Asselt, 'Fossil Fuel Supply and Climate Policy: Exploring the Road Less Taken' (2018) 150 Climatic Change 1.

[257] See UNFCCC (n 3) art 4(1)(d); Kyoto Protocol (n 44) art 2(1)(a)(ii); Paris Agreement (n 43) art 5; SGD 14.4; Glasgow Leaders' Declaration on Forests and Land Use (2 November 2021) <https://perma.cc/LU68-VKS4>.

[258] See IEA, 'Global EV Outlook 2020: Entering the Decade of Electric Drive?' (2020) 86–90; UK Secretary of State for Business, Energy and Industrial Strategy, 'Energy White Paper: Powering our Net Zero Future' (2020) 13; France, Ministry for the Ecological and Solidary Transition, 'National Low Carbon Strategy: The Ecological and Inclusive Transition towards Carbon Neutrality' (2020) 107.

[259] See World Bank, 'Zero Routine Flaring by 2030' (no date) <https://perma.cc/V34J-29HZ>, endorsed by thirty-one national governments.

[260] See eg *Montana Environmental Information Center v US Office of Surface Mining* (DC Montana, 2017) 274 FSupp3d 1074, 1099; *Gloucester Resources v Minister for Planning* [2019] NSWLEC 7; *Center for Biological Diversity v Bernhardt* (9th Cir, 2020) 982 F3d 723, 740; *Sovereign Iñupiat for a Living Arctic v Bureau of Land Management* (DC Alaska, 2021) 555 FSupp3d 739. But see eg *Natur og Ungdom v Norway*, Case No 20-051052SIV-HRET (SC, 22 December 2020), English translation <https://perma.cc/5PCS-A8YH>.

[261] See eg the Concluding Observations of CEDAW on the Ninth Periodic Report of Norway, CEDAW/C/NOR/CO/9 (2017) ¶14; on the Eighth Periodic Report of South Korea, CEDAW/C/KOR/CO/8 (2018) ¶¶14–15; of CESCR on the Fourth Periodic Report of Argentina, E/C.12/ARG/CO/4 (2018) ¶¶13–14; on the Fourth Periodic Report of Ecuador, E/C.12/ECU/CO/4 (2019), ¶37.

Conclusion

Identifying a breach of a general mitigation obligation requires an overall assessment of the state's conduct. This assessment is not easy, but it is not impossible. As an alternative to a judicial determination of a state's requisite level of mitigation action discussed in Chapter VI, this chapter has shown the possibility of breaking down general mitigation obligations into more concrete corollary duties, which enables a holistic assessment of a state's mitigation action on the basis of a set of indicia. The duties of cooperation, vigilance, and consistency that general mitigation obligations entail point to multiple concrete indicia that, taken as a whole, give a relatively comprehensive picture of a state's conduct.

VIII
General Conclusion

This study has attempted to develop a comprehensive account of the international law obligations regarding climate change mitigation. The first task has been to identify these obligations. Much of the contemporary climate law literature focuses on climate treaties and nationally determined contributions (NDCs), often characterizing the latter as 'voluntary', hence 'non-binding'. One of the purposes of this book has been to challenge this account, showing that the parties to the Paris Agreement have at least an obligation of conduct to take the necessary measures to achieve their NDC—this, in effect, requires seldom less, and often more, than an obligation of result. Beyond the Paris Agreement and notwithstanding whether it constitutes a unilateral declaration capable of creating legal obligations, an NDC is likely to be used as a benchmark to assess the state's compliance with its general mitigation obligations.

Overall, this book has shown that specific commitments under the UN Framework Convention on Climate Change (UNFCCC) regime are not the most important mitigation obligations—in fact, they are rarely invoked in climate litigation. The general mitigation commitments arising under the UNFCCC and other general mitigation obligations under customary international law are more difficult to interpret, but they are often more demanding than specific commitments. These general obligations have frequently been discarded in the climate law scholarship, seemingly on account of a narrow positivism assuming that, in the absence of clear and specific rules providing otherwise, states are free to emit greenhouse gasses (GHGs). However, there is no reason to assume that states have an inherent right to emit GHGs (to be restricted only based on state consent) that comes at the expense of the right not to be harmed by other states' GHG emissions. Rather than one right at the expense of the other, the default position in international law must involve a balance of opposing rights, a mid-point to be determined in light of state practice and acceptance as law. Thus, despite the adoption of several climate treaties, customary law will continue to apply until states agree on acceptable levels of GHG emissions and, overall, on their allocation.

On the other hand, this book has challenged the interpretation of human rights treaties as the source of fully fledged mitigation obligation, as best illustrated by the judgment of the Supreme Court of the Netherlands in *Urgenda*. Climate change certainly affects the enjoyment of human rights, and the obligation to protect a human right within the state's territory may justify some cooperation on climate

International Law Obligations on Climate Change Mitigation. Benoit Mayer, Oxford University Press. © Benoit Mayer 2022.
DOI: 10.1093/oso/9780192843661.003.0008

change mitigation. However, human rights treaties open only a narrow window on the applicability of general mitigation obligations. The size of this window depends on the scope of the treaty, the importance of the right, the benefits of mitigation action for the protection of the right within the scope of the treaty, and the potential unintended consequences.

The book has also shown the possibility of applying general mitigation obligations in meaningful ways, including through litigation. General mitigation obligations, as obligations of conduct, imply a standard of care that is particularly difficult to pinpoint. In principle, general mitigation obligations indicate a level of effort that the state must implement, which implies the likely achievement of a certain level of mitigation action. Here again, the judgment in *Urgenda* is a cautionary tale, being based not only on a misreading of climate science but also on a range of questionable premises, not least the presumption that states have an obligation to act consistently with an objective interpretation of the 2°C target. Overall, while the judicial assessment of a state's requisite level of mitigation action is perhaps not entirely impossible, it would involve an extraordinary degree of judicial discretion, which most judges would likely seek to avoid.

A more likely way of applying general mitigation obligations consists in comparing the measures that the state has implemented with those that it could reasonably have been expected to implement. These necessary or otherwise appropriate measures can be characterized as the corollary 'duties' of general mitigation obligations; these corollary duties do not necessarily correspond to discrete obligations. The distinction between discrete obligations and corollary duties is analytically more helpful than the differentiation of substantive and procedural obligations with which the International Court of Justice has struggled in its last two judgments on international environmental law: corollary duties are not necessarily procedural, and a procedural requirement is not necessarily the corollary of a general norm. A state that fails to cooperate in good faith, to exercise vigilance, or to act consistently with its own findings would likely be in breach of its general mitigation obligations if the failure to fulfil these duties shows that it is not implementing as much effort on climate change mitigation as an average state. Climate litigation is progressively exploring the vast potential of corollary duties as an effective way to challenge a state's compliance with its general mitigation obligations.

The international law on climate change mitigation is in constant evolution. As this manuscript was finalized in the last days of 2021, dozens of cases were pending before national and regional courts that directly engage with many of the questions discussed at length in this book, while international litigation is becoming increasingly likely. State practice is also developing at a fast pace with the adoption of new laws and the communication of new or updated NDCs and long-term strategies, while international negotiations continue both within the UNFCCC and beyond, including through a burgeoning of transnational initiatives. While the book will soon lack important references, the structure of international law obligations on climate change mitigation will remain as it is for many years; until, that is, a comprehensive international agreement is reached that would consolidate international law obligations by defining acceptable levels of GHG emissions and their allocation among states.

Selected Bibliography

Books

Alston, P, and Goodman, R, *International Human Rights* (2nd edn, OUP 2012)

Alvarez, A, *Unstable Ground: Climate Change, Conflict, and Genocide* (Rowman & Littlefield 2017)

Atapattu, S, *Human Rights Approaches to Climate Change* (Routledge 2016)

Aust, A, *Modern Treaty Law and Practice* (3rd edn, CUP 2014)

Aust, HP, and Nolte, G (eds), *The Interpretation of International Law by Domestic Courts*: Uniformity, Diversity, Convergence (OUP 2016)

Bantekas, I, Stein, MA, and Anastasiou, D (eds), *The UN Convention on the Rights of Persons with Disabilities: A Commentary* (OUP 218)

Bellissent, J, *Contribution à l'analyse de la distinction des obligations de moyens et des obligations de résultat* (LGDJ 2001)

Bodansky, D, Brunnée, J, and Hey, E (eds), *The Oxford Handbook of International Environmental Law* (OUP 2008)

Bodansky, D, Brunnée, J, and Rajamani, L, *International Climate Change Law* (OUP 2017)

Boyle, A, and Redgwell, C, *International Law and the Environment* (4th edn, OUP 2021)

Bradley, CA (ed), *Custom's Future: International Law in a Changing World* (CUP 2016)

Bradlow, D, and Hunter, D (eds), *Advocating Social Change through International Law* (Brill 2020)

Buendia, C, and others (eds), *2019 Refinement to the 2006 IPCC Guidelines for National Greenhouse Gas Inventories* (IPCC 2019)

Carlarnet, CP, Gray, KR, and Tarasofksy, R (eds), *The Oxford Handbook of International Climate Change Law* (OUP 2016)

Collier, J, and Lowe, V, *The Settlement of Disputes in International Law: Institutions and Procedures* (OUP 2000)

Core Writing Team and others (eds), *Climate Change 2014: Synthesis Report: Contribution of Working Groups I, II and III to the Fifth Assessment Report of the Intergovernmental Panel on Climate Change* (IPCC 2015)

Corten, O, and Klein, P, *The Vienna Conventions on the Law of Treaties: A Commentary* (OUP 2011)

Cournil, Christel (ed), *La fabrique d'un droit climatique* (Pedone 2021)

Craik, N, *The International Law of Environmental Impact Assessment: Process, Substance and Integration* (CUP 2008)

Crawford, J, *Brownlie's Principles of Public International Law* (8th edn, OUP 2012)

Crawford, J, *State Responsibility: The General Part* (CUP 2013)

Cullenward, D, and Victor, DG, *Making Climate Policy Work* (Polity 2020)

Depledge, J, *The Organization of Global Negotiations: Constructing the Climate Change Regime* (Earthscan 2005)

De Guchteneire, P, Pécoud, A, and Cholewinski, R (eds), *Migration and Human Rights: The United Nations Convention on Migrant Workers' Rights* (CUP 2009)

Dörr, O, and Schmalenbach, K (eds), *Vienna Convention on the Law of Treaties: A Commentary* (2nd edn, Springer 2018)

Dupuy, PM, and Viñuales, JE, *International Environmental Law* (2nd edn, CUP 2018)
Duvic-Paoli, LA, *The Prevention Principle in International Environmental Law* (CUP 2018)
Dworkin, R, *A Matter of Principle* (OUP 1985)
Dworkin, R, *Taking Rights Seriously* (Bloomsbury 2013)
Edenhofer, O, and others (eds), *Climate Change, Justice and Sustainability: Linking Climate Change and Development Policy* (Springer 2012)
Edenhofer, O, and others (eds), *Climate Change 2014: Mitigation of Climate Change: Working Group III Contribution to the Fifth Assessment Report of the Intergovernmental Panel on Climate Change* (CUP 2014)
Elferink, AGO, Henriksen, T, and Busch, SV (eds), *Maritime Boundary Delimitation: The Case Law: Is It Consistent and Predictable?* (CUP 2018)
Fastenrath U, and others (eds), *From Bilateralism to Community Interest: Essays in Honour of Bruno Simma* (OUP 2011)
Faure, M (ed), *Elgar Encyclopedia of Environmental Law* (Edward Elgar 2015)
Field, CB, and others (eds), *Climate Change 2014: Impacts, Adaptation, and Vulnerability: Part A: Global and Sectoral Aspects: Working Group II Contribution to the Fifth Assessment Report of the Intergovernmental Panel on Climate Change* (CUP 2014)
Fietta, S, and Cleverly, R, *A Practitioner's Guide to Maritime Boundary Delimitation* (OUP 2016)
Fitzmaurice, M, and Tamada, D, (eds), *Whaling in the Antarctic: Significance and Implications of the ICJ Judgment* (Brill Nijhoff 2016)
Føllesdal, A, Peters, B and Ulfstein, G (eds), *Constituting Europe* (OUP 2013)
Fredman, S, *Human Rights Transformed: Positive Rights and Positive Duties* (OUP 2008)
Freestone, D (ed), *The 1982 Law of the Sea Convention at 30: Successes, Challenges and New Agenda* (Martinus Nijhoff 2013)
Freestone, D, and Streck, C (eds), *Legal Aspects of Carbon Trading: Kyoto, Copenhagen, and Beyond* (OUP 2009)
Friedmann, W, *The Changing Structure of International Law* (Colum UP 1964)
Gardiner, RK, *Treaty Interpretation* (2nd edn, OUP 2015)
Gardiner, SM, *A Perfect Moral Storm: The Ethical Tragedy of Climate Change* (OUP 2011)
Gardiner, SM, and others (eds), *Climate Ethics: Essential Readings* (OUP 2010)
Grotius, H, *The Rights of War and Peace* (1625, Liberty Fund 2012)
Harris, D, and others, *Law of the European Convention on Human Rights* (4th edn, OUP 2018)
Harris, JW, *Law and Legal Science: An Inquiry into the Concepts: Legal Rule and Legal System* (Clarendon Press 1979)
Harris, PG (ed), *A Research Agenda for Climate Justice* (Edward Elgar 2019)
Harrison, J, *Saving the Oceans through Law: The International Legal Framework for the Protection of the Marine Environment* (OUP 2017)
Hart, HLA, and Honoré, T, *Causation in the Law* (OUP 1985)
Hart, HLA, *The Concept of Law* (3rd edn, OUP 2012)
Havel, BF, and Sanchez, GS, *The Principles and Practice of International Aviation Law* (CUP 2014)
He, X, Zhang, H, and Zahar, A (ed), *Climate Change Law in China in Global Context* (Routledge 2020)
Hollo, EJ, Kulovesi, K, and Mehling, M (eds), *Climate Change and the Law* (Springer 2013)
Hume, D, *A Treatise of Human Nature* (Clarendon Press 1896)
Humphreys, S (ed), *Human Rights and Climate Change* (CUP 2009)

Jamieson, D, *Reason in a Dark Time: Why the Struggle against Climate Change Failed—and What It Means for Our Future* (OUP 2014)

Jenks, CW, *The Prospects of International Adjudication* (Stevens & Sons 1964)

Jennings, R, and Watts, A (eds), *Oppenheim's International Law: Volume 1 Peace* (9th edn, OUP 2008)

Jodoin, S, *Forest Preservation in a Changing Climate: REDD+ and Indigenous and Community Rights in Indonesia and Tanzania* (CUP 2017)

Kälin, W, and Künzli, J, *The Law of International Human Rights Protection* (2nd edn, OUP 2019)

Karim, MS, *Prevention of Pollution of the Marine Environment from Vessels: The Potential and Limits of the International Maritime Organisation* (Springer 2015)

Kavanagh, A (ed), *Arguing about Law* (Routledge 2013)

Kelsen, H, *Principles of International Law* (Rinehart 1952)

Klein, D, and others (eds), *The Paris Agreement on Climate Change: Analysis and Commentary* (OUP 2017)

Knox, JH, and Pejan, R (eds), *The Human Right to a Healthy Environment* (CUP 2018)

Kolb, R, *La bonne foi en droit international public: Contribution à l'étude des principles généraux de droit* (PUF 2000)

Koskenniemi, M, *From Apology to Utopia: The Structure of International Legal Argument* (CUP 2006)

Kosolopova, E, *Interstate Liability for Climate Change-Related Damage* (Eleven 2013)

Krieger, H, Nolte, G, and Zimmermann, A (eds), *The International Rule of Law: Rise or Decline?* (OUP 2019)

Lando, M, *Maritime Delimitation as a Judicial Process* (CUP 2019)

Lauterpacht, H, *Function of Law in the International Community* (Clarendon 1933)

Lees, E, and Viñuales, JE (eds), *Oxford Handbook of Comparative Environmental Law* (OUP 2019)

Lepard, BD (ed), *Reexamining Customary International Law* (CUP 2017)

Liivoja, R, and Petman, J (eds), *International Law-Making: Essays in Honour of Jan Klabbers* (Routledge 2014)

Lin, J, *Governing Climate Change: Global Cities and Transnational Lawmaking* (CUP 2018)

Linderfalk, U, *On the Interpretation of Treaties: The Modern International Law as Expressed in the 1969 Vienna Convention on the Law of Treaties* (Springer 2007)

Lomborg, B, *False Alarm: How Climate Change Panic Costs Us Trillions, Hurts the Poor, and Fails to Fix the Planet* (Basic Books 2020)

Lyster, R, and Verchick, RRM (eds), *Research Handbook on Climate Disaster Law* (Edward Elgar 2018)

Maljean-Dubois, S, and Rajamani, L (eds), *La mise en œuvre du droit international de l'environnement, Implementation of International Environmental Law* (Martinus Nijhoff 2011)

Masson-Delmotte, V, and others (eds), *Global Warming of 1.5°C: An IPCC Special Report* (IPCC 2019)

Masson-Delmotte, V, and others (eds), *Climate Change 2021: The Physical Science Basis. Contribution of the Working Group I to the Sixth Assessment Report of the Intergovernmental Panel on Climate Change* (accepted version subject to final editing, IPCC 2021)

Mayer, B, and Zahar, A (eds), *Debating Climate Law* (CUP 2021)

Mayer, B, *The Concept of Climate Migration* (Edward Elgar 2016)

Mayer, B, *The International Law on Climate Change* (CUP 2018)

McDonald, J, McGee, J, and Barnes, R (eds), *Research Handbook on Climate Change, Oceans and Coasts* (Edward Elgar 2020)

Milanović, M, *Extraterritorial Application of Human Rights Treaties* (OUP 2011)

Miller, D, *Solved: How the World's Great Cities Are Fixing the Climate Crisis* (Buffalo 2020)

Moeckli, D, Shah, S, and Sivakumaran, S (eds), *International Human Rights Law* (OUP 2018)

Nollkaemper, A, and others, *International Law in Domestic Courts* (OUP 2019)

Nollkaemper, A, and Plakokefalos, I (eds), *The Practice of Shared Responsibility in International Law* (CUP 2017)

Nordhaus, WD, *The Climate Casino: Risk, Uncertainty and Economics for a Warming World* (Yale UP 2013)

Nordquist, MH, and Long, R (eds), *Marine Biodiversity of Areas beyond National Jurisdiction* (Brill 2021)

Oberthür, S, and Ott, HE, *The Kyoto Protocol: International Climate Policy for the 21st Century* (Springer 1999)

Pauwelyn, J, *Conflict of Norms in Public International Law: How WTO Law Relates to Other Rules of International Law* (CUP 2003)

Penner, JE, *The Idea of Property in Law* (OUP 2000)

Posner, EA, and Weisbach, D, *Climate Change Justice* (Princeton UP 2010)

Prezas, I (ed), *Substance et procédure en droit international public: Dialectique et influences croisées* (Pedone 2019)

Proelss, A (ed), *United Nations Convention on the Law of the Sea: A Commentary* (Beck 2017)

Ragazzi, M (ed), *International Responsibility Today: Essays in Memory of Oscar Schachter* (Brill 2005)

Rajamani, L, *Differential Treatment in International Environmental Law* (OUP 2006)

Rayfuse, R, and Scott, SV (eds), *International Law in the Era of Climate Change* (Edward Elgar 2012)

Raz, J, *The Concept of a Legal System: An Introduction to the Theory of Legal System* (Clarendon Press 1980)

Rothwell, D, and others (eds), *The Oxford Handbook of the Law of the Sea* (OUP 2015)

Saganek, P, *Unilateral Acts of States in Public International Law* (Brill 2015)

Sands, P, and Peel, J, *Principles of International Environmental Law* (4th edn, CUP 2018)

Saul, B, Kinley, D, and Mowbray, J, *The International Covenant on Economic, Social and Cultural Rights* (OUP 2014)

Schwarzenberger, G, *Inductive Approach to International Law* (Stevens & Sons 1965)

Shahabuddeen, M, *Precedent in the World Court* (CUP 1996)

Shelton, D (ed), *The Oxford Handbook of International Human Rights Law* (OUP 2013)

Simma, B, and others (eds), *The Charter of the United Nations* (vol 2, OUP 212)

Siorat, L, *Le problème des lacunes en droit international* (LGDJ 1959)

Suy, E, *Les actes juridiques unilatéraux en droit international public* (LGDJ 1962)

Tanaka, Y, *Predictability and Flexibility in the Law of Maritime Delimitation* (Hart 2006)

Tanaka, Y, *The International Law of the Sea* (CUP 2019)

Tobin, J (ed), *The UN Convention on the Rights of the Child: A Commentary* (OUP 2019)

Ulfstein, G, and Keller, H (eds), *UN Human Rights Treaty Bodies: Law and Legitimacy* (CUP 2012)

Van Calster, G, and Reins, L (eds), *The Paris Agreement on Climate Change: A Commentary* (Edward Elgar 2021).

Verheyen, R, *Climate Change Damage and International Law: Prevention Duties and State Responsibility* (Brill 2005)

Victor, DG, *Global Warming Gridlock: Creating More Effective Strategies for Protecting the Planet* (CUP 2011)

Villiger, ME, *Commentary on the 1969 Vienna Convention on the Law of Treaties* (Martinus Nijhoff 2008)
Viñuales, JE (ed), *The Rio Declaration on Environment and Development: A Commentary* (OUP 2015)
Vranes, E, *Trade and the Environment: Fundamental Issues in International Law, WTO Law, and Legal Theory* (OUP 2009)
Weeramantry, CG, *Universalising International Law* (Brill 2004)
Weil, P, *The Law of Maritime Delimitation: Reflections* (CUP 1989)
Wewerinke-Singh, M, *State Responsibility, Climate Change and Human Rights under International Law* (Hart 2019)
Yamin, F, and Depledge, J, *The International Climate Change Regime: A Guide to Rules, Institutions and Procedures* (CUP 2004)
Zahar, A, *Climate Change Finance and International Law* (Routledge 2016)
Zimmermann, A, Tomuschat, C, and Oellers-Frahm, K (eds), *The Statute of the International Court of Justice: A Commentary* (3rd edn, OUP 2019)
Zweigert, K, and Drobnig, U (eds), *International Encyclopedia of Comparative Law* (Springer 1983)

Articles

Abeyratne, R, 'The Legal Status of the Chicago Convention and its Annexes' (1994) 19 Air & Space L 113
Abeyratne, R, 'Carbon Offsetting as a Trade Related Market Based Measure for Aircraft Engine Emissions' (2017) 51 JWT 425
Aceves, WJ, 'Cost–Benefit Analysis and Human Rights' (2018) 95 St John's L Rev 431
Acosta Alvarado, PA, and Rivas-Ramírez, D, 'A Milestone in Environmental and Future Generations' Rights Protection: Recent Legal Developments before the Colombian Supreme Court' (2018) 30 JEL 519
Akehurst, M, 'Custom as a Source of International Law' (1976) 47 BYBIL 1
Akehurst, M, 'Equity and General Principles of Law' (1976) 25 ICLQ 801
Alston, P, and Quinn, G, 'The Nature and Scope of States Parties' Obligations under the International Covenant on Economic, Social and Cultural Rights' (1987) 9 H Rts Q 156
Amirfar, C, and Singh, A, 'The Trump Administration and the Unmaking of International Agreements Essay' (2018) 59 Harv Intl LJ 443
Backes, CW, and van der Veen, GA, 'Urgenda: The Final Judgment of the Dutch Supreme Court' (2020) 17 Journal for European Envt & Planning L 307
Bakker, C, 'The Paris Agreement on Climate Change: Balancing "Legal Force" and "Geographical Scope"' (2015) 15 Italian YB Intl L 299
Baxter, RR, 'Multilateral Treaties as Evidence of Customary International Law' (1965) 41 BYBIL 275
Baxter, RR, 'Treaties and Customs' (1970) 129 RdC 25
Baxter, RR, 'International Law in "Her Infinite Variety"' (1980) 29 ICLQ 549
Benjamin, L, 'The Road to Paris Runs through Delaware: Climate Litigation and Directors' Duties' [2020] Utah L Rev 313
Benvenisti, E, 'Sovereigns as Trustees of Humanity: On the Accountability of States to Foreign Stakeholders' (2013) 107 AJIL 295
Besson, S, 'La *due diligence* en droit international' (2020) 409 RdC 153
Biermann, F, '"Common Concern of Humankind": The Emergence of a New Concept of International Environmental Law' (1996) 34 Archiv des Völkerrechts 4

Biniaz, S, 'Comma but Differentiated Responsibilities: Punctuation and 30 Other Ways Negotiators Have Resolved Issues in the International Climate Change Regime' (2016) 6 Mich J Envlt & Admin L 37

Bjørn, A, Shannon Lloyd and Damon Matthews, 'From the Paris Agreement to Corporate Climate Commitments: Evaluation of Seven Methods for Setting "Science-Based" Emission Targets' (2021) 16 Environmental Research Letters 054019

Blutman, L, 'Conceptual Confusion and Methodological Deficiencies: Some Ways That Theories on Customary International Law Fail' (2014) 25 EJIL 529

Bodansky, D, 'The United Nations Framework Convention on Climate Change: A Commentary' (1993) 18 Yale J Intl L 451

Bodansky, D, 'Customary (and Not So Customary) International Environmental Law' (1995) 3 Indiana J Global Legal Studies 105

Bodansky, D, 'Introduction: Climate Change and Human Rights: Unpacking the Issues' (2010) 38 Georgia J Intl & Comp L 511

Bodansky, D, 'The Copenhagen Climate Change Conference: A Post-Mortem' (2010) 104 AJIL 230

Bodansky, D, 'The Legal Character of the Paris Agreement' (2016) 25 RECIEL 142

Bodansky, D, 'The Paris Climate Change Agreement: A New Hope?' (2016) 110 AJIL 288

Bordin, FL, 'Reflections of Customary International Law: The Authority of Codification Conventions and ILC Draft Articles in International Law' (2014) 63 ICLQ 535

Bouwer, K, 'The Unsexy Future of Climate Change Litigation' (2018) 30 JEL 483

Bouwer, K, 'Lessons from a Distorted Metaphor: The Holy Grail of Climate Litigation' (2020) 9 TEL 347

Boyle, A, 'Developments in the International Law of Environmental Impact Assessments and their Relation to the Espoo Convention' (2011) 20 RECIEL 227

Boyle, A, 'Human Rights and the Environment: Where Next?' (2012) 23 EJIL 613

Boyle, A, 'Climate Change, the Paris Agreement and Human Rights' (2018) 67 ICLQ 759

Brent, KA, 'The Certain Activities Case: What Implications for the No-Harm Rule?' (2017) 20 APJEL 28

Brown, Chester, 'International, Mixed, and Private Disputes Arising under the Kyoto Protocol' (2010) 1 JIDS 447

Brownlie, I, 'Politics and Law in International Adjudication' (2003) 97 ASIL Proc 282

Brunnée, J, 'COPing with Consent: Law-Making Under Multilateral Environmental Agreements' (2002) 15 LJIL 1

Brunnée, J, 'Procedure and Substance in International Environmental Law' (2019) 450 RdC 75

Brunnée, J, 'International Environmental Law and Climate Change: Reflections on Structural Challenges in a "Kaleidoscopic" World' (2020) 33 Georgetown Envtl L Rev 113

Buffard, I, and Zemanek, K, 'The "Object and Purpose" of a Treaty: An Enigma?' (1998) 3 Austrian Rev of Intl & Eur L 311

Caflisch, L, 'Cent ans de règlement pacifique des différends interétatiques' (2001) 288 RdC 9

Campbell-Duruflé, C, and Atapattu, SA, 'The Inter-American Court's Environment and Human Rights Advisory Opinion: Implications for International Climate Law' (2018) 8 Climate Law 321

Carlarne, CP, and Helal, MS, 'A Conversation about Climate Change Law and the "International Community"' (2018) 8 Climate Law 229

Chan, N, 'Climate Contributions and the Paris Agreement: Fairness and Equity in a Bottom-Up Architecture' (2016) 30 Ethics & Intl Affairs 291

Charney, JI, 'The Persistent Objector Rule and the Development of Customary International Law' (1986) 56 BYBIL 1

Charney, JI, 'Progress in International Maritime Boundary Delimitation Law' (1994) 88 AJIL 227

Chasapis-Tassinis, O, 'Customary International Law: Interpretation from Beginning to End' (2020) 31 EJIL 235

Chimni, BS, 'Customary International Law: A Third World Perspective' (2018) 112 AJIL 1

Craik, N, 'The Duty to Cooperate in the Customary Law of Environmental Impact Assessment' (2020) 69 ICLQ 239

Crawford, J, 'Chance, Order, Change: The Course of International Law' (2013) 365 RdC 9, 90–112

Crawford, J, 'The Current Political Discourse Concerning International Law' (2018) 81 MLR 1

Criddle, EV, and Fox-Decent, E, 'Mandatory Multilateralism' (2019) 113 AJIL 272

Cui, RY, and others, 'Quantifying Operational Lifetimes for Coal Power Plants under the Paris Goals' (2019) 10 Nature Communications 4759

D'Amato, A, 'Do We Owe a Duty to Future Generations to Preserve the Global Environment?' (1990) 84 AJIL 190

Daugirdas, K, 'How and Why International Law Binds International Organizations' (2016) 57 Harv Intl LJ 325

Decaux, E, 'L'arrêt de la Cour internationale de Justice dans l'affaire du plateau continental (Tunisie c. Jamahiriya arabe libyenne)' (1982) 28 AFDI 357

Den Elzen, MGJ, Hof, AF, and Roelfsema, M, 'Analysing the Greenhouse Gas Emission Reductions of the Mitigation Action Plans by Non-Annex I Countries by 2020' (2013) 56 Energy Policy 633

Depledge, J, 'Striving for No: Saudi Arabia in the Climate Change Regime' (2008) 8(4) Global Envtl Politics 9

Desgagné, R, 'Integrating Environmental Values into the European Convention on Human Rights' (1995) 89 AJIL 263

Doelle, M, 'Climate Change and the Use of the Dispute Settlement Regime of the Law of the Sea Convention' (2006) 37 Ocean Development & Intl Law 319

Doelle, M 'The Heart of the Paris Rulebook: Communicating NDCs and Accounting for Their Implementation' (2019) 9 Climate Law 3

Dupuy, PM, 'Soft Law and the International Law of the Environment' (1990) 12 Mich J Intl L 420, 343

Dupuy, PM, 'Reviewing the Difficulties of Codification: On Ago's Classification of Obligations of Means and Obligations of Result in Relation to State Responsibility' (1999) 10 EJIL 371

Dupuy, PM, 'The Place and Role of Unilateralism in Contemporary International Law' (2000) 11 EJIL 19

Erling, UW, 'How to Reconcile the European Union Emissions Trading System (EU ETS) for Aviation with the Carbon Offsetting and Reduction Scheme for International Aviation (CORSIA)?' (2018) 43 Air & Space L 371

Farer, T, 'The Hierarchy of Human Rights' (1992) 8 Am U J Intl L & Policy 115

Feria-Tinta, M, and Milnes, SM, 'The Rise of Environmental Law in International Dispute Resolution: The Inter-American Court of Human Rights Issues, a Landmark Advisory Opinion on the Environment and Human Rights' (2016) 27 YB Intl Envtl L 64

Fitzmaurice, G, 'The Law and Procedure of the International Court of Justice 1951–4: Treaty Interpretation and Other Treaty Points' (1957) 33 BYBIL 203

Fitzmaurice, MA, 'International Protection of the Environment' (2019) 293 RdC 9
Freeman, AV, 'Responsibility of States for Unlawful Acts of their Armed Forces' (1955) 88 RdC 263
French, D, 'Developing States and International Environmental Law: The Importance of Differentiated Responsibilities' (2000) 49 ICLQ 35
Friedmann, W, 'The North Sea Continental Shelf Cases: A Critique' (1970) 64 AJIL 229
Gasser, T, and others, 'Negative Emissions Physically Needed to Keep Global Warming below 2°C' (2015) 6 Nature Communications 1
Gearty, C, 'Do Human Rights Help or Hinder Environmental Protection? (2010) 1 JHRE 7
Gervasi, M, 'On the United States' Decision to Withdraw from and Cease Implementation of the Paris Agreement on Climate Change' (2019) 18 Chinese JIL 98
Gragl, P, and Fitzmaurice, M, 'The Legal Character of Article 18 of the Vienna Convention on the Law of Treaties' (2019) 68 ICLQ 699
Gravotta, N, 'A Great Nation Keeping Its Word: The Role of Tribal Treaty Rights in Climate Change Litigation Note' (2021) 29 NYU Envtl LJ 118
Grubb, M, 'Full Legal Compliance with the Kyoto Protocol's First Commitment Period: Some Lessons' (2016) 16 Climate Policy 673
Gunn, J, and Noble, BF, 'Conceptual and Methodological Challenges to Integrating Sea and Cumulative Effects Assessment' (2011) 31 Environmental Impact Assessment Review 154
Guzman, AT, 'Against Consent' (2011) 52 Va JIL 747
Happold, M, 'The Relationship between the United Nations Framework Convention on Climate Change and Other Rules of Public International Law, in Particular on States' Responsibility for the Adverse Effects of Climate Change' (Legal Response Initiative, 2013)
Hardin, G, 'The Tragedy of the Commons' (1968) 162 Science 1243
Helfer, LR, and Wuerth, IB, 'Customary International Law: An Instrument Choice Perspective' (2015) 37 Mich J Intl L 563
Hertogen, A, 'Letting Lotus Bloom' (2015) 26 EJIL 901
Higgins, R, 'A Babel of Judicial Voices: Ruminations from the Bench' (2006) 55 ICLQ 791
Hjerpe, M, and others, 'Common Ground for Effort Sharing? Preferred Principles for Distributing Climate Mitigation Efforts' (Working Papers in Economics No 491, 2011)
Hof, AF, and others, 'Global and Regional Abatement Costs of Nationally Determined Contributions (NDCs) and of Enhanced Action to Levels Well below 2°C and 1.5°C' (2017) 71 Environmental Science & Policy 30
Hook, M, and others, 'Tort to the Environment: A Stretch Too Far or a Simple Step Forward?' (2021) 33 JEL 195
Huggins, A, 'The Evolution of Differential Treatment in International Climate Law: Innovation, Experimentation, and "Hot" Law' (2018) 8 Climate Law 195
Hulme, M, 'Attributing Weather Extremes to "Climate Change": A Review' (2014) 38 Progress in Physical Geography 499
Iacobuta, G, and others, 'National Climate Change Mitigation Legislation, Strategy and Targets: A Global Update' (2018) 18 Climate Policy 1114
Jaśkowski, M, 'External Aspects of the EU ETS in Aviation in Light of CORSIA' (2021) 23 ICLR 271
Jegede, AO, 'Arguing the Right to a Safe Climate under the UN Human Rights System' (2020) 9 Intl HRL Rev 184
Jenks, CW, 'The Conflict of Law-Making Treaties' (1953) 30 BYBIL 401
Jia, BB, 'The Principle of the Domination of the Land over the Sea: A Historical Perspective on the Adaptability of the Law of the Sea to New Challenges' (2014) 57 GYIL 53

Jonas, DS, and Saunders, TN, 'The Object and Purpose of a Treaty: Three Interpretive Methods' (2010) 43 Vand J Trasnatl L 565
Joyner, DH, 'Why I Stopped Believing in Customary International Law' (2019) 9 Asian JIL 31
Karlsson-Vinkhuyzen, SI, and others, 'Entry into Force and Then? The Paris Agreement and State Accountability' (2018) 18 Climate Policy 593
Kelly, JP, 'The Twilight of Customary International Law' (1999) 40 Va JIL 449
Kerbrat, Y, and Maljean-Dubois, S, 'La Cour internationale de Justice face aux enjeux de protection de l'environnement: Réflexions critiques sur l'arrêt du 20 avril 2010, Usines de pâte à papier sur le fleuve Uruguay (Argentine c. Uruguay)' (2011) 115 RDGIP 39
Kerr, BP, 'Clear Skies or Turbulence Ahead? The International Civil Aviation Organization's Obligation to Mitigate Climate Change' (2020) 16 Utrecht LR 101
Kesternich, M, Löschel, A, and Ziegler, A, 'Negotiating Weights for Burden Sharing Rules in International Climate Negotiations: An Empirical Analysis' (2021) 23 Envtl Econ & Policy Studies 309
Khubchandani, M, 'The United States and the Paris Agreement on Climate Change' (2019) 22 Max Planck Yrbk UN L 70
Klabbers, J, 'The Redundancy of Soft Law' (1996) 65 Nordic J Intl L 167
Klabbers, J, 'The Undesirability of Soft Law' (1998) 67 Nordic J Intl L 381
Knox, JH, 'Climate Change and Human Rights Law' (2009) 50 Va JIL 163
Knox, JH, 'The Myth and Reality of Transboundary Environmental Impact Assessment' (2002) 96 AJIL 291
Knutti, R, and others, 'A Scientific Critique of the Two-Degree Change Target' (2016) 9 Nature Geoscience 13
Koji, T, 'Emerging Hierarchy in International Human Rights and Beyond: From the Perspective of Non-derogable Rights' (2001) 12 EJIL 917
Koskenniemi, M, 'Peaceful Settlement of Environmental Disputes' (1991) 60 Nordic J Intl L 73
Krisch, N, 'The Decay of Consent: International Law in an Age of Global Public Goods' (2014) 108 AJIL 1
Lahn, B, 'A History of the Global Carbon Budget' (2020) 11 WIREs Climate Change e636
Lambrecht, J, and Ituarte-Lima, C, 'Legal Innovation in National Courts for Planetary Challenges: Urgenda v State of the Netherlands' (2016) 18 Envtl L Review 57
Lange, A, and others, 'On the Self-Interested Use of Equity in International Climate Negotiations' (2010) 54 Europ Econ Rev 359
Lauterpacht, E, 'Principles of Procedure in International Litigation' (2011) 345 RdC 387
Lawrence, P, and Wong, D, 'Soft Law in the Paris Climate Agreement: Strength or Weakness?' (2017) 26 RECIEL 276
Lazarus, M, and van Asselt, H, 'Fossil Fuel Supply and Climate Policy: Exploring the Road Less Taken' (2018) 150 Climatic Change 1
Levin, K, and Rich, D, 'Turning Points: Trends in Countries' Reaching Peak Greenhouse Gas Emissions over Time' (WRI 2017)
Liston, G, 'Enhancing the Efficacy of Climate Change Litigation: How to Resolve the "Fair Share Question" in the Context of International Human Rights Law' (2020) 9 Cambridge Intl LJ 241
Loucaides, L, 'Environmental Protection through the Jurisprudence of the European Convention on Human Rights' (2004) 75 BYBIL 249
Lowe, V, 'The Role of Equity in International Law' (1992) 12 Aust YBIL 54
Lusk, G, 'The Social Utility of Event Attribution: Liability, Adaptation, and Justice-Based Loss and Damage' (2017) 143 Climatic Change 201
Main, TO, 'The Procedural Foundation of Substantive Law' (2009) 87 Wash U L Rev 801

Maljean-Dubois, S, 'The Paris Agreement: A New Step in the Gradual Evolution of Differential Treatment in the Climate Regime?' (2016) 25 RECIEL 151
Maljean-Dubois, S, and Rajamani, L, 'L'Accord de Paris sur les changements climatiques du 12 décembre 2015' (2015) 61 AFDI 615
Maljean-Dubois, S, Spencer, T, and Wemaere, M, 'The Legal Form of the Paris Climate Agreement: A Comprehensive Assessment of Options' (2015) 9 CCLR 68
Marcantonini, C, and Ellerman, AD, 'The Implicit Carbon Price of Renewable Energy Incentives in Germany' (2015) 36 Energy J 205
Marjanac, S, and Patton, L, 'Extreme Weather Event Attribution Science and Climate Change Litigation: An Essential Step in the Causal Chain?' (2018) 36 J Energy & Natural Resources L 265
Mason-Case, S, 'On Being Companions and Strangers: Lawyers and the Production of International Climate Law' (2019) 32 LJIL 625
Mayer, B, 'Conceiving the Rationale for International Climate Law' (2015) 130 Climatic Change 371
Mayer, B, 'Human Rights in the Paris Agreement' (2016) 6 Climate Law 109
Mayer, B, 'Construing International Climate Change Law as a Compliance Regime' (2018) 7 TEL 115
Mayer, B, 'International Law Obligations Arising in Relation to Nationally Determined Contributions' (2018) 7 TEL 251
Mayer, B, 'Obligations of Conduct in the International Law on Climate Change: A Defence' (2018) 27 RECIEL 130
Mayer, B, 'The Place of Customary Norms in Climate Law: A Reply to Zahar' (2018) 8 Climate Law 261
Mayer, B, 'The State of the Netherlands v. Urgenda Foundation: Ruling of the Court of Appeal of The Hague (9 October 2018)' (2019) 8 TEL 167
Mayer, B, 'A Review of the International Law Commission's Guidelines on the Protection of the Atmosphere' (2019) 20 Melbourne JIL 453
Mayer, B, 'Climate Assessment as an Emerging Obligation under Customary International Law' (2019) 68 ICLQ 271
Mayer, B, 'Interpreting States' General Obligations on Climate Change Mitigation: A Methodological Review' (2019) 28 RECIEL 107
Mayer, B, 'Climate Change Mitigation as an Obligation under Human Rights Treaties?' (2021) 115 AJIL 3
Mayer, B, 'Temperature Targets and State Obligations on the Mitigation of Climate Change' (2021) 33 JEL 585
Mayer, B, 'International Advisory Proceedings on Climate Change' (2023) 44 Mich J Intl L (forthcoming)
McAdam, J, 'Protecting People Displaced by the Impacts of Climate Change: The UN Human Rights Committee and the Principle of Non-refoulement' (2020) 114 AJIL 708
McDonald, N, 'The Role of Due Diligence in International Law' (2019) 69 ICLQ 1041
McLachlan, C, 'The Principle of Systemic Integration and Article 31(3)(C) of the Vienna Convention' (2005) 54 ICLQ 279
McNair, AD, 'The Legality of the Occupation of the Ruhr' (1924) 5 BYBIL 17
McRae, DM, 'Delimitation of the Continental Shelf between the United Kingdom and France: The Channel Arbitration' (1978) 15 Can YB Intl L 173
McRae, DM, 'The Legal Effect of Interpretative Declarations' (1979) 49 BYBIL 155
Meguro, M, 'Litigating Climate Change through International Law: Obligations Strategy and Rights Strategy' (2020) 33 LJIL 933

Meguro, M, 'State of the Netherlands v. Urgenda Foundation' (2020) 114 AJIL 729
Mehling, MA, 'The Comparative Law of Climate Change: A Research Agenda' (2015) 24 RECIEL 341
Meinshausen, M, and others, 'National Post-2020 Greenhouse Gas Targets and Diversity-Aware Leadership' (2015) 5 Nature Climate Change 1098
Merrill, TW, 'Golden Rules for Transboundary Pollution' (1996) 46 Duke LJ 931
Mills-Novoa, M, and Liverman, DM, 'Nationally Determined Contributions: Material Climate Commitments and Discursive Positioning in the NDCs' (2019) 10 WIREs Climate Change e589
Minnerop, P, 'Integrating the "Duty of Care" under the European Convention on Human Rights and the Science and Law of Climate Change: The Decision of The Hague Court of Appeal in the Urgenda Case' (2019) 37 J Energy & Natural Resources L 149
Minnerop, P, and Otto, F, 'Climate Change and Causation: Joining Law and Climate Science on the Basis of Formal Logic' (2020) 27 Buff Envtl LJ 49
Minnerop, P, and Røstgaard, I, 'In Search of a Fair Share: Article 112 Norwegian Constitution, International Law and an Emerging Inter-jurisdictional Discourse in Climate Litigation' (2021) 44 Fordham Intl LJ 847
Mintz-Woo, K, and Leroux, J, 'What Do Climate Change Winners Owe, and to Whom?' (2021) 37 Econ. & Phil. 462
Mitchell, RB, 'Climate Law: Accomplishments and Areas for Growth' (2018) 8 Climate Law 135
Morgan, R, 'Environmental Impact Assessment: The State of the Art' (2012) 30 Impact Assessment & Project Appraisal 5
Morseletto, P, Biermann, F, and Pattberg, P, 'Governing by Targets: Reductio Ad Unum and Evolution of the Two-Degree Climate Target' (2017) 17 Intl Envtl Agreements: Politics, Law & Economics 655
Moussa, J, 'Implication of the Indus Water Kishenganga Arbitration for the International Law of Watercourses and the Environment' (2015) 64 ICLQ 697
Nash, SL, and Steurer, R, 'Taking Stock of Climate Change Acts in Europe: Living Policy Processes or Symbolic Gestures?' (2019) 19 Climate Policy 1052
Nasiritousi, N, and Linnér, BO, 'Open or Closed Meetings? Explaining Nonstate Actor Involvement in the International Climate Change Negotiations' (2016) 16 Intl Envtl Agreements: Politics, Law and Economics 127
Newcomb Hohfeld, W, 'Some Fundamental Legal Conceptions as Applied in Judicial Reasoning' (1913) 23 Yale LJ 16
Nicholson, CTM, 'Climate Change and the Politics of Causal Reasoning: The Case of Climate Change and Migration' (2014) 180 Geographical J 151
Nollkaemper, A, and others, 'Guiding Principles on Shared Responsibility in International Law' (2020) 31 EJIL 15
Nordhaus, WD, 'A Review of the Stern Review on the Economics of Climate Change' (2007) 45 J Econ Literature 686
Oberthür, S, and Groen, L, 'Hardening and Softening of Multilateral Climate Governance towards the Paris Agreement' (2020) 22 J Envtl Policy & Planning 801
Okowa, PN, 'Procedural Obligations in International Environmental Agreements' (1997) 67 BYBIL 275
Orakhelashvili, A, 'Restrictive Interpretation of Human Rights Treaties in the Recent Jurisprudence of the European Court of Human Rights' (2003) 14 EJIL 529
Pan, Xunzhang, and others, 'Exploring Fair and Ambitious Mitigation Contributions under the Paris Agreement Goals' (2017) 74 Environmental Science & Policy 49

Peel, J, and Lin, J, 'Transnational Climate Litigation: The Contribution of the Global South' (2019) 113 AJIL 679

Peel, J, and Osofsky, HM, 'A Rights Turn in Climate Change Litigation?' (2018) 7 TEL 37

Pellet, A, 'The Normative Dilemma: Will and Consent in International Law-Making' (1988) 12 Aust YBIL 22

Pellet, A, 'Le droit international à la lumière de la pratique: L'introuvable théorie de la réalité' (2021) 414 RdC 9

Peters, B, 'Zur Anwendbarkeit der Europäischen Menschenrechtskonvention in Umwelt- und Klimaschutzfragen' (2021) 59 AdV 164

Peters, GP, 'Beyond Carbon Budgets' (2018) 11 Nature Geoscience 378

Pickering, J, and others, 'Global Climate Governance Between Hard and Soft Law: Can the Paris Agreement's "Crème Brûlée" Approach Enhance Ecological Reflexivity?' (2019) 31 JEL 1

Pires, JCM, 'Negative Emissions Technologies: A Complementary Solution for Climate Change Mitigation' (2019) 672 Science of the Total Environment 502

Pisillo-Mazzeschi, R, 'The Due Diligence Rule and the Nature of the International Responsibility of States' (1992) 35 GYIL 9

Plakokefalos, I, 'Prevention Obligations in International Environmental Law' (2012) 23 YB Intl Envtl L 3

Posner, EA, 'Climate Change and International Human Rights Litigation' (2006) 155 U Pa L Rev 1925

Posner, EA, 'Human Welfare, Not Human Rights' (2008) 108 Colum L Rev 1758

Preston, BJ, 'The Influence of the Paris Agreement on Climate Litigation: Legal Obligations and Norms (Part I)' (2021) 33 JEL 1

Prost, M, and Camprubi, AT, 'Against Fairness: International Environmental Law, Disciplinary Bias, and Pareto Justice International Law and Practice' (2012) 25 LJIL 379

Pyć, D, 'Ship Energy Efficiency Measures and Climate Protection' (2021) 23 Int C L Rev 241

Quane, H, 'Silence in International Law' (2014) 84 BYIL 241

Rabello, AM, 'Non Liquet: From Modern Law to Roman Law' (1974) 9 Israel L Rev 63

Rachovitsa, A, 'The Principle of Systemic Integration in Human Rights Law' (2017) 66 ICLQ 557

Rajamani, L, 'The Increasing Currency and Relevance of Rights-Based Perspectives in the International Negotiations on Climate Change' (2010) 22 JEL 391

Rajamani, L, 'The Making and Unmaking of the Copenhagen Accord' (2010) 59 ICLQ 824

Rajamani, L, 'The Cancun Climate Agreements: Reading the Text, Subtext and Tea Leaves' (2011) 60 ICLQ 499

Rajamani, L, 'Ambition and Differentiation in the 2015 Paris Agreement: Interpretative Possibilities and Underlying Politics' (2016) 65 ICLQ 493

Rajamani, L, 'The 2015 Paris Agreement: Interplay between Hard, Soft and Non-Obligations' (2016) 28 JEL 337, 343

Rajamani, L, 'Integrating Human Rights in the Paris Climate Architecture: Contest, Context, and Consequence' (2019) 9 Climate Law 180

Rajamani, L, 'Innovation and Experimentation in the International Climate Change Regime' (2020) 404 RdC 9

Rajamani, L, and Brunnée, J, 'The Legality of Downgrading Nationally Determined Contributions under the Paris Agreement: Lessons from the US Disengagement' (2017) 29 JEL 537

Rajamani, L, and others, 'National "Fair Shares" in Reducing Greenhouse Gas Emissions within the Principled Framework of International Environmental Law' (2021) 21 Climate Policy 983

Rajamani, L, and Werksman, J, 'The Legal Character and Operational Relevance of the Paris Agreement's Temperature Goal' (2018) 376 Philos Trans R Soc A 2016.0458
Randalls, S, 'History of the 2°C Climate Target' (2010) 1 WIREs Climate Change 598
Raustiala, K, 'Form and Substance in International Agreements' (2005) 99 AJIL 581
Raz, J, 'Dworkin: A New Link in the Chain Review' (1986) 74 Cal L Rev 1103
Reilly, JM, Chen, JHH, and Jacoby, HD, 'The COVID-19 Effect on the Paris Agreement' (2021) 8 Humanities and Social Sciences Communications 16
Riley, S, 'Architectures of Intergenerational Justice: Human Dignity, International Law, and Duties to Future Generations' (2016) 15 J Hum R 272
Ringius, L, Torvanger, A, and Underdal, A, 'Burden Sharing and Fairness Principles in International Climate Policy' (2002) 2 Intl Envtl Agreements 1
Roberts, AE, 'Traditional and Modern Approaches to Customary International Law: A Reconciliation' (2001) 95 AJIL 757
Robinson, M, 'Social and Legal Aspects of Climate Change' (2014) 5 JHRE 15
Robiou du Pont, Y, and Meinshausen, M, 'Warming Assessment of the Bottom-up Paris Agreement Emissions Pledges' (2018) 9 Nature Communications 4810
Robiou du Pont, Y, and others, 'Equitable Mitigation to Achieve the Paris Agreement Goals' (2017) 7 Nature Climate Change 38
Rogelj, J, and others, 'Scenarios towards Limiting Global Mean Temperature Increase below 1.5°C' (2018) 8 Nature Climate Change 325
Rogelj, J, and others, 'Estimating and Tracking the Remaining Carbon Budget for Stringent Climate Targets' (2019) 571 Nature 335
Roht-Arriaza, N, 'Private Voluntary Standard-Setting, the International Organization for Standardization, and International Environmental Lawmaking' (1995) 6 YB Intl Envtl L 107
Rouxel, M, 'The Paris Rulebook's Rules on Transparency: A Compliance Pull?' (2020) 14 CCLR 18
Sands, P, 'The United Nations Framework Convention on Climate Change' (1992) 1 RECIEL 270
Sands, P, 'Climate Change and the Rule of Law: Adjudicating the Future in International Law' (2016) 28 JEL 19
Savaresi, A, 'The Paris Agreement: A New Beginning?' (2016) 34 JERL 16
Savaresi, A, and Auz, J, 'Climate Change Litigation and Human Rights: Pushing the Boundaries' (2019) 9 Climate Law 244
Schachter, O, 'International Law in Theory and Practice' (1982) 178 RdC 9
Schachter, O, 'The Emergence of International Environmental Law' (1991) 44 J Intl Affairs 457
Scheffran, J, Ide, T, and Schilling, J, 'Violent Climate or Climate of Violence? Concepts and Relations with Focus on Kenya and Sudan' (2014) 18 IJHR 369
Schleussner, CF, and Fyson, CL, 'Scenarios Science Needed in UNFCCC Periodic Review' (2020) 10 Nature Climate Change 272
Schlosberg, D, 'Further Uses for the Luxury/Subsistence Distinction' (2019) 21 British J Politics & Intl Rel 295 (2019)
Schneider, L, and Kollmuss, A, 'Perverse Effects of Carbon Markets on HFC-23 and SF6 Abatement Projects in Russia' (2015) 5 Nature Climate Change 1061
Schwarzenberger, G, 'The Inductive Approach to International Law' (1947) 60 Harv LR 539
Scotford, E, and Minas, S, 'Probing the Hidden Depths of Climate Law: Analysing National Climate Change Legislation' (2019) 28 RECIEL 67
Scott, SV, and Ambler, O, 'Does Legality Really Matter? Accounting for the Decline in US Foreign Policy Legitimacy Following the 2003 Invasion of Iraq' (2007) 13 EJIR 67

Setzer, J, and Higham, C, 'Global Trends in Climate Litigation' (Grantham Research Institute on Climate Change and the Environment 2021)

Shany, Y, 'The Extraterritorial Application of International Human Rights Law' (2019) 409 RdC 9

Shue, H, 'Subsistence Emissions and Luxury Emissions' (1993) 15 L & Policy 39

Shue, H, 'Climate Dreaming: Negative Emissions, Risk Transfer, and Irreversibility' (2017) 8 JHRE 203

Sinclair, AJ, Doelle, M, and Duinker, PN, 'Looking Up, Down, and Sideways: Reconceiving Cumulative Effects Assessment as a Mindset' (2017) 62 Environmental Impact Assessment Review 183

Skogly, S, 'The Requirement of Using the "Maximum of Available Resources" for Human Rights Realisation: A Question of Quality as Well as Quantity?' (2012) 12 HRL Rev 393

Smets, H, 'Le principe de non-discrimination en matière de protection de l'environnement' (2000) 4 Revue Européenne de Droit de l'Environnement 3

Stirling, A, 'Keep it Complex' (2010) 468 Nature 1030

Streck, C, Keenlyside, P, and Unger, M, 'The Paris Agreement: A New Beginning' (2016) 13 JEEPL 3

Sun, Z, 'International Legal Personality of the Hong Kong Special Administrative Region' (2008) 7 Chinese JIL 339

Talmon, S, 'Determining Customary International Law: The ICJ's Methodology between Induction, Deduction and Assertion' (2015) 26 EJIL 417

Thirlway, H, 'The Law and Procedure of the International Court of Justice 1960-1989: Part Seven' (1996) 66 BYBIL 1

Thomas, C, 'La distinction des obligations de moyens et des obligations de résultat' (1937) 57 Revue Critique de Législation et de Jurisprudence 636

Thorp, T, 'Climate Justice: A Constitutional Approach to Unify the Lex Specialis Principles of International Climate Law' (2012) 8 Utrecht LR 7

Tokarska, KB, and others, 'Recommended Temperature Metrics for Carbon Budget Estimates, Model Evaluation and Climate Policy' (2019) 12 Nature Geoscience 964

Tokarska, KB, and others, 'Uncertainty in Carbon Budget Estimates Due to Internal Climate Variability' (2020) 15 Environmental Research Letters 104064

Tomuschat, C, 'Obligations Arising for States without or against their Will' (1993) 241 RdC 195

Tørstad, V, and Sælen, H, 'Fairness in the Climate Negotiations: What Explains Variation in Parties' Expressed Conceptions?' (2018) 18 Climate Policy 642

Tucker, WC, 'Deceitful Tongues: Is Climate Change Denial a Crime' (2012) 39 Ecology Law Quarterly 831

Tunc, A, 'La distinction des obligations de résultat et des obligations de diligence' (1945) 1 Juris-Classeur Périodique 449

Uprety, K, 'The Kishenganga Arbitration: Reviving the Indus Treaty and Managing Transboundary Hydropolitics' (2015) 14 Chinese JIL 497

Velders, GJM, and others, 'The Importance of the Montreal Protocol in Protecting Climate' (2007) 104 PNAS 4814

Velders, GJM, and others, 'Preserving Montreal Protocol Climate Benefits by Limiting HFCs' (2012) 335 Science 922

Vihma, A, 'Climate of Consensus: Managing Decision Making in the UN Climate Change Negotiations' (2015) 24 RECIEL 58

Voigt, C, 'The Paris Agreement: What Is the Standard of Conduct for Parties?' (2016) 18 QIL 17

Voigt, C, and Ferreira, F, 'Dynamic Differentiation: The Principles of CBDR-RC, Progression and Highest Possible Ambition in the Paris Agreement' (2016) 5 TEL 285
Weil, P, 'Towards Relative Normativity in International Law?' (1983) 77 AJIL 413
Weil, P, 'The Court Cannot Conclude Definitively... Non Liquet Revisited' (1998) 36 Colum J Transnatl L 109
Weiss, DB, 'Our Rights and Obligations to Future Generations for the Environment' (1990) 84 AJIL 198
Werksman, J, 'Remarks on the International Legal Character of the Paris Agreement' (2019) 34 Maryland JIL 343
Wewerinke-Singh, M, and McCoach, A, 'The State of the Netherlands v. Urgenda Foundation: Distilling Best Practice and Lessons Learnt for Future Rights-Based Climate Litigation' (2021) 30 RECIEL 275
Wewerinke-Singh, N, and Salili, DH, 'Between Negotiations and Litigation: Vanuatu's Perspective on Loss and Damage from Climate Change' (2019) 20 Climate Policy 681
Worster, WT, 'The Inductive and Deductive Methods in Customary International Law Analysis: Traditional and Modern Approaches' (2013) 45 Georgetown JIL 445
Wright, Q, 'Conflicts between International Law and Treaties' (1917) 11 AJIL 566
Yang, T, 'The Emergence of the Environmental Impact Assessment Duty as a Global Legal Norm and General Principle of Law' (2018) 70 Hastings LJ 525
Zahar, A, 'The Contested Core of Climate Law' (2018) 8 Climate Law 244
Zahar, A, 'Collective Progress in the Light of Equity under the Global Stocktake' (2019) 9 Climate Law 101
Zahar, A, 'Collective Obligation and Individual Ambition in the Paris Agreement' (2020) 9 TEL 165
Zaman, ST, 'Exploring the Legal Nature of Nationally Determined Contributions (NDCs) under International Law' (2015) 26 YB Intl Envtl L 98
Zhang, H, 'Implementing Provisions on Climate Finance Under the Paris Agreement' (2019) 9 Climate Law 21
Zihua, G, Voigt, C, and Werksman, J, 'Facilitating Implementation and Promoting Compliance with the Paris Agreement Under Article 15: Conceptual Challenges and Pragmatic Choices' (2019) 9 Climate Law 65

Index

For the benefit of digital users, indexed terms that span two pages (e.g., 52–53) may, on occasion, appear on only one of those pages.

9 780192 843661

Made in the USA
Las Vegas, NV
19 September 2026

7bcd22ab-5cbc-492d-b41a-e5d2e70048ffR02